Computing Fundamentals

DATE DUE

			PRINTED IN U.S.A.

Computing Fundamentals
INTRODUCTION TO COMPUTERS

Faithe Wempen
Rosie Hattersley
Richard Millett
Kate Shoup

WILEY

Computing Fundamentals: Introduction to Computers

Published by
John Wiley & Sons, Inc.
10475 Crosspoint Boulevard
Indianapolis, IN 46256
www.wiley.com

Copyright © 2015 by Faithe Wempen

Published by John Wiley & Sons, Inc., Indianapolis, Indiana

Published simultaneously in Canada

ISBN: 978-1-119-03971-6
ISBN: 978-1-119-03962-4 (ebk)
ISBN: 978-1-119-03978-5 (ebk)

Manufactured in the United States of America

10 9 8 7 6 5 4 3 2 1

For general information on our other products and services please contact our Customer Care Department within the United States at (877) 762-2974, outside the United States at (317) 572-3993 or fax (317) 572-4002.

Wiley publishes in a variety of print and electronic formats and by print-on-demand. Some material included with standard print versions of this book may not be included in e-books or in print-on-demand. If this book refers to media such as a CD or DVD that is not included in the version you purchased, you may download this material at http://booksupport.wiley.com. For more information about Wiley products, visit www.wiley.com.

Library of Congress Control Number: 2014954670

To Margaret

About the Author

Faithe Wempen, M.A., is a Microsoft Office Master Instructor, an A+ Certified PC technician, and an adjunct instructor of Computer Information Technology at Indiana University/Purdue University at Indianapolis. She is the author of more than 140 books on computer hardware and software, and her online courses have educated more than a quarter of a million students for corporate clients, including Hewlett Packard and Sony.

About the Contributors

Rosemary Hattersley is a U.K.-based tech journalist with extensive experience writing for PC Advisor, Computeractive, and Macworld as well as a number of other technology and business websites and publications. She is the author of Hudl For Dummies and co-author of Wiley's iPad For the Older and Wiser, 3rd Edition, both from Wiley.

Richard Millet is a lead instructor working for Firebrand Training. He has over 30 years of experience in the computer industry and has worked with all versions of Windows since its inception. He is responsible for producing training material for companies, specializing in computer security. He also delivers technical training on a wide variety of subjects to all age groups from college students upwards. He currently lives in Berkshire, England, with his wife Shelagh and Merlin the cat.

Kate Shoup has authored more than 30 books and has edited scores more. Kate has also co-written a feature-length screenplay (and starred in the ensuing film) and worked as the sports editor for NUVO Newsweekly. When not writing, Kate, an Indy Car fanatic, loves to ski, read, and ride her motorcycle. She lives in Indianapolis, Indiana, with her fiancé, her daughter, and their dog.

Credits

Acquisitions Editor
Stephanie McComb

Project Editor
Sara Shlaer
Tom Dinse

Technical Editor
Nick Vandome
Richard Millett

Copy Editor
Debbye Butler

Manager of Content Development and Assembly
Mary Beth Wakefield

Marketing Director
David Mayhew

Professional Technology & Strategy Director
Barry Pruett

Business Manager
Amy Knies

Associate Publisher
Jim Minatel

Executive Editor
Jody Lefevere

Project Coordinator
Erin Zeltner

Compositor
TCS/SPS

Proofreader
Wordsmith Editorial

Indexer
Potomac Indexing, LLC

Cover Designer
Mike E. Trent

Cover Image
©iStock.com/Adriana3d

Acknowledgments

Thank you to my wonderful editing team at Wiley, including Stephanie McComb, Sara Shlaer, Tom Dinse, Nick Vandome, Richard Millett, and Debbye Butler, for keeping me on track and making my writing as good as it can be. Your professionalism and good humor made this a pleasant project, and your editing skills made it a quality product.

Contents at a Glance

Contents

Part II: Software 105

Chapter 4: Operating System Basics 107

Chapter 9: Word Processing with Microsoft Word 277

Chapter 16: Network and Internet Privacy and Security 545

Introduction

Welcome to *Computing Fundamentals: Introduction to Computers!* This book is designed to prepare you for success in a modern world full of computers—not only the traditional computers such as desktop and notebook PCs, but also computers that you interact with in other places too, like your bank's ATM or your employer's computerized cash register. In this book, you will learn about the technologies that drive our computerized society, including the Internet and local area networks (LANs).

What You Will Learn

This book will help you become a digitally literate person — that is, someone who understands how computer technology fits into our modern society and knows how to navigate a variety of computing environments. The topics covered include the following:

- *Operating systems:* You'll compare major operating systems and learn what types of devices each operating system is designed to run on. You'll learn how to navigate in Windows 8.1 too, including how to run applications and manage files.

- *Computer hardware and concepts:* You'll learn about the physical parts of computers, including input, processing, output, and storage.

- *Computer software and concepts:* You will find out about the main types of application software and what each type is useful for. You'll learn how to choose, install, update, use, and remove applications in Windows 8.1.

- *Troubleshooting:* You'll find out what the most common problems are when working with computers and how to solve them.

- *Common application features:* You'll find out what all the Office applications have in common, such as commands for saving, printing, and using the Clipboard.

- *Word processing:* You'll learn how to create documents with Microsoft Word.

- *Spreadsheets:* You'll learn how to create spreadsheets with Microsoft Excel.

- *Presentations:* You'll learn how to create presentation graphics with Microsoft Power-Point.

- *Databases:* You'll learn how to create basic databases with Microsoft Access.

- *Collaboration:* You will learn about the collaboration features in Office applications, such as comments and markup.

- *Browsers:* You will learn how to use a web browser to find information on the Internet.

- *Networking concepts:* You will find out how computer networks work, including the hardware and software required for them.

- *Digital communication:* You will learn how to communicate online in a variety of ways, including email, instant messaging, video chat, and web conferencing.

- *Digital citizenship:* You will learn the etiquette standards and customs of the online world, the legal and ethical issues involved in worldwide online computing.

- *Safe computing:* You'll find out what the dangers are in using the Internet and other networks and learn methods of protecting your privacy and safeguarding your computer and its data.

Chapter Features

Each chapter provides many different ways of helping you learn, not only in the printed book, but also in the online resource supplements. Here is a quick summary of the aids you will find in this book:

- **Learning Objectives:** Each chapter starts out with a list of learning objectives, giving you a practical look at what you will learn.

> Learning objectives
>
> ☐ Identify the basic parts of an Office application's interface
> ☐ Use common features that all Office applications share
> ☐ Save, open, and create data files
> ☐ Print your work and email it to others
> ☐ Adjust the options of an Office application

- **Definitions:** Key terms appear in color in the text, and their definitions appear in the margin for easy lookup. The key terms are also compiled into a glossary in the back of the book.

> Scrolling the display does not move the insertion point. To move the insertion point , click where you want it to go, or use the directional arrow keys on your keyboard to move it. In Excel, there is no insertion point, but a thick outline around the active cell shows the cell in which content will be entered.
>
> **insertion point** The flashing vertical line that indicates where typed text will appear.

- **Notes, Tips, and Cautions:** These special-purpose notes appear in the text whenever there is extra information you should know.

> Ctrl+S is the keyboard shortcut for the Save command; Ctrl+N is the shortcut for the New command (to start a new file); and Ctrl+O is the shortcut for the Open command to open an existing file.
>
> **TIP**

- **Careers in IT:** In these features, you will learn about some careers that relate to the topics you are studying.

> **Careers in IT**
>
> **Programmer**
>
> A programmer writes the instructions that become computer programs. Whether it's an operating system, a utility, or a game, a programmer takes a general concept like "open a dialog box with user controls for adjusting the graphics quality" and makes it a reality by writing the exact instructions needed, line by line. The programmer then compiles those instructions into a usable program, or combines them with the instructions written by another programmer or group of programmers to make a larger program. More experienced programmers may also participate in developing the requirements for a program. A programmer should have at least an Associate Degree in Computer Technology, Computer Science, or Information Technology, and should be familiar with at least two or three different programming languages.
>
> © iStockphoto.com/nullplus

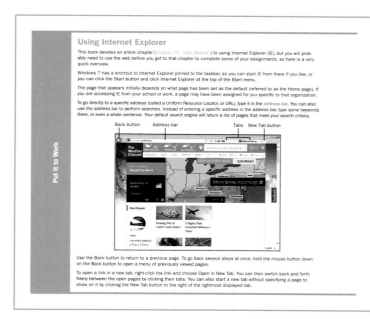

Put It to Work: These features explain practical uses for the topics you are learning about, and in some cases suggest activities you can try to put the information to immediate use.

Privacy and Security: These features spotlight information that may be useful in keeping you safe from privacy and security violations, such as security features in an application or a type of hardware or software that enhances security.

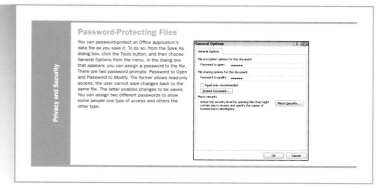

Troubleshooting: These features provide information about solving common problems with the technology you are learning about.

New Technology: In these features, you will learn about up-and-coming tools and technologies to watch for in the next few years, or recently developed innovations that are improving people's lives right now.

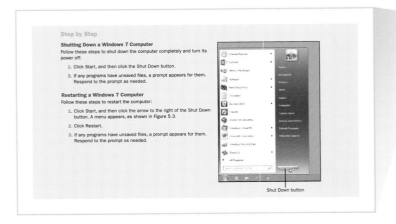

■ **Step by Step:** Where it is useful to have exact step-by-step instructions for performing a task, a special Step by Step box appears listing the steps to follow.

■ **Quick Review:** At the end of each major section of a chapter are several review questions that you can use to test your understanding of the material. If you can't easily answer these questions, you should re-read the section.

End-of-Chapter Features

At the end of each chapter, you will find special features that will help you review the key points of the chapter and test and demonstrate your learning.

■ **Summary:** A section-by-section summary briefly reviews the main points of the chapter, with the key terms you should know highlighted.

Summary

Understanding System Software

System software includes the BIOS, the operating system, and utility programs that perform system maintenance and protection.

A computer's **platform** is its type of hardware. Only certain operating systems can run on certain platforms. The **Intel platform**, also called IBM-compatible, is the most popular platform; this platform's most popular operating system is Windows. The 32-bit Intel version is called **x86**, and the 64-bit version is called **x64**.

Most operating systems use a **graphical user interface (GUI)**, but some operating systems, especially those designed for use on servers, use a **command-line interface**. UNIX is an example.

There are many types of **utility software** for performing various system maintenance tasks. **Antivirus**, **firewall**, and **anti-spyware** programs protect from outside attacks and malicious software (**malware**). **Anti-spam** programs cut down on the amount of junk email you receive. A **disk checking program** can find and fix file system errors, and a **registry cleanup program** can find and fix inconsistent or unneeded entries in the **registry**. **Backup software** can automate the process of backing up important files.

Comparing the Major Operating Systems

Mac OS X is the operating system on most Apple desktop and notebook computers. Its latest version is OS X 10.9, code named **Mavericks**. Its main competitor is **Microsoft Windows**, which is the most popular operating system in the world, used on more than 90% of all desktop and notebook PCs.

Linux is an open-source operating system based on UNIX. The basic version is free, but you can purchase a packaged collection of add-ons and utility programs with it called a distribution (**distro**). A distro typically includes a GUI, as an alternative to Linux's native command-line interface.

You can run multiple operating systems on a single computer by setting it up to **multi-boot**, or to use a **virtual machine** to run the secondary operating system within the first one.

A **thin client** operating system such as Chrome OS is designed for small portable notebook computers that are used primarily for going online.

A **server** is a computer that serves an entire network rather than an individual user. The most popular server operating systems are **Linux**, **UNIX**, and **Windows Server**.

Tablets and smartphones have an operating system that is preinstalled on a chip (**system-on-chip**, or **SoC**). Users can download **apps**, which are add-on applications that extend the device's capabilities. The popular SoC operating systems are **iOS**, **Android**, **Windows RT**, and **Windows Phone**.

Understanding Device Drivers

A **device driver** translates between the operating system and a hardware device. You can update a device driver to solve some performance problems you may have with the device, and **roll back** the driver if the new driver doesn't work as well as the previous one.

When you install a new piece of hardware, Windows uses a technology called Plug and Play to identify the device and locate a driver for it if possible.

■ **Key Terms:** A list of the vocabulary words from the chapter appears, so you can make sure you know each one. If a word on this list doesn't sound familiar, page back through the chapter to review its definition.

Key Terms

AutoCorrect	Ribbon
AutoRecover	ScreenTip
Backstage view	scroll
cell cursor	scroll bar
color palette	scroll box
default file location	selection handle
dialog box launcher	shortcut menu
embed fonts	standard colors
group	status bar
insertion point	tab
keyboard shortcut	template
object	theme
Office Clipboard	theme colors
Quick Access Toolbar (QAT)	Zoom controls

Test Yourself

Fact Check

1. Which of these is NOT a type of system software?
   a. word processing software
   b. backup software
   c. BIOS
   d. operating system
2. Which operating system has a command-line interface by default?
   a. iOS
   b. UNIX
   c. Android
   d. Windows RT
3. Which of these is a thin client OS?
   a. Windows Server
   b. Chrome OS
   c. Mac OS X
   d. UNIX
4. In a _____, users employ a keyboard to type commands at a prompt.
   a. command-line interface
   b. graphical user interface
   c. utility interface
   d. compressed interface
5. What file system is the default for Windows 7 system volumes?
   a. NTFS
   b. FAT32
   c. HFS+
   d. UDF
6. A volume letter is followed by what symbol?
   a. ; (semi-colon)
   b. % (percent sign)
   c. : (colon)
   d. & (ampersand)
7. Where in Windows Explorer does a file's path appear?
   a. address bar
   b. ribbon
   c. title bar
   d. navigation pane

● **Test Yourself:** A variety of exercises help you demonstrate your knowledge, including:

● Fact Check: A short multiple-choice quiz.

Fact Check

1. Which of these is NOT a type of system software?
   a. word processing software
   b. backup software
   c. BIOS
   d. operating system
2. Which operating system has a command-line interface by default?
   a. iOS
   b. UNIX
   c. Android
   d. Windows RT

● Matching: An exercise in which you match terms to their meanings.

Matching

Match the term to its description.

a. x86
b. GUI
c. Linux
d. shell
e. SoC
f. UDF
g. root directory

1. _____The 32-bit version of the Intel platform
2. _____A user interface that uses pictures and a pointing device to issue commands
3. _____An open-source operating system used on a variety of platforms
4. _____An operating system's user interface
5. _____The file system used on DVDs
6. _____An operating system that comes preinstalled on a chip on a portable device
7. _____The top-level folder on a volume

- Sum It Up: A variety of open-ended questions that guide you to put your newly acquired knowledge into your own words.

Sum It Up

1. List three types of system software.
2. What is the difference between an OS and a platform?
3. List five types of utility programs.
4. List three operating systems that would run on an IBM-compatible desktop PC.
5. Name three operating systems used on smartphones.
6. Explain the purpose of Plug and Play technology.
7. Explain the purpose of partitioning a drive.
8. Give an example of a complete path to a file, and explain the parts of the path.

Explore More

Linux Distros

Suppose you want to put Linux on an older desktop PC and give it to a relative who wants to use the Internet. But that person doesn't know much about computers, so you must find a Linux distro that is very easy to use, even for a beginner. Do a web search on the terms *Linux distro beginner*. Based on the information you find, choose two Linux distros you think would meet your needs, and explain why you chose the ones you did.

Examining File Associations

Windows 7 has default extension associations for various file types. For example, when you double-click on a file with a txt extension, Windows 7 opens it in Notepad because Notepad is the default application for the txt extension.

When you have more than one application that is capable of opening a certain type of file, you may want to change Windows's default setting for that extension. For example, if you have both Microsoft Word and WordPad, you might prefer one over the other for opening files with an rtf extension.

- Explore More: These activity suggestions provide ideas for going further with several of the topics you learned about in the chapter.

- Think It Over: These philosophical and practical discussion questions can be springboards to personal writing assignments or used as in-class or small-group discussion starters.

Think It Over

NTFS Compression and Encryption

NTFS compression and encryption both make files slightly slower to access. In addition, using encryption introduces another level of responsibility into file management because you must back up the encryption key so you can get your files back in the event of a system disaster that causes the hard drive to be inaccessible via the operating system. Given those drawbacks, do you think either of those features would be worth it to you, personally?

Backup Scheduling

Suppose you were designing your own backup schedule for your computer. Which folders or files would you back up? Regarding the files you did not choose to back up, why did you exclude them? How often would you perform a full backup? How often would you perform a differential or incremental backup—and which would it be? Think about your answers, and give a reason for each one.

Online Features

You can enhance your understanding of the material by exploring the book's companion website at www.wiley.com/go/computingfundamentalsintro. On the website, you'll find

- Additional Fact Check questions and answers for each chapter.
- Practice labs for the chapters in Part III, "Microsoft Office 2013."

Part I
Computer Basics and Hardware

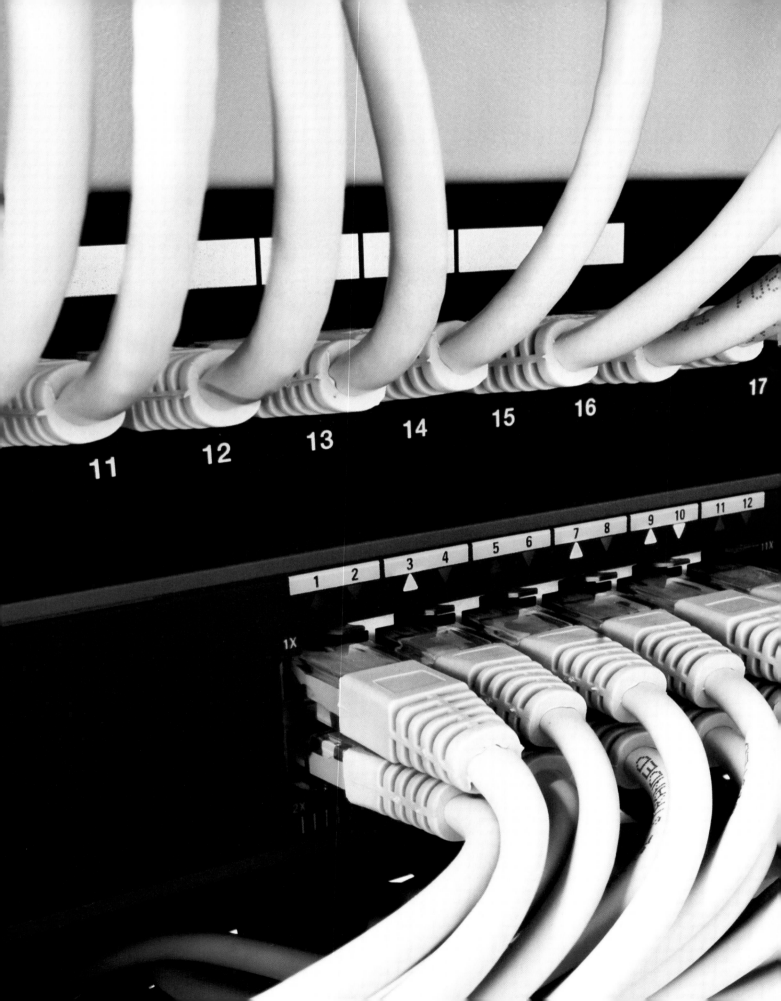

Chapter 1

Computer Basics

Learning objectives

- ☐ Understand the purpose and elements of information systems
- ☐ Recognize the different types of computers
- ☐ Distinguish the main software types
- ☐ Identify the components of a computer system
- ☐ Understand how computers communicate

Understanding Information Systems

Identifying Computer Types

Understanding Software Types

Computer System Components

How Computers Communicate

Welcome to *Computing Fundamentals!* This book helps prepare you for success in a world that is filled with computers. At work, at school, at home, in stores, and as you travel, computers help make things run more smoothly.

Think about the average day in your life, all the places you go and all the things you do. How many of those involve a computer of some type? Probably quite a few. For example, you might wake up in the morning to the sound of a digital alarm clock. As you eat breakfast, you might browse the day's news on your home computer or a tablet PC. The vehicle you ride in to work or school probably has at least one computerized component in it, and perhaps as you travel you talk to a friend on your cell phone. When you get to work or school, your supervisor or teacher might use a computer to assign work to you or to teach a lesson. On the way home, you might stop at a restaurant where a cashier inputs your order into a computer-based ordering system that then relays your order to the kitchen staff in the back. Before you go to bed, you might watch a DVD movie using a DVD player and a digital TV, both with computers in them.

In this chapter, you will learn the basics that most computer systems have in common, whether it's a desktop PC, a smartphone, or the software in your car that tells you it's time for an oil change. You'll find out how computers represent, encode, and process data, and how they communicate with one another. Many of the topics that this chapter covers in overview form are explored in greater detail later in the book.

Understanding Information Systems

information system An interconnected environment for managing and processing data using a computer.

An information system is a complete interconnected environment in which raw data—quantifiable facts and figures—is turned into useful information. An information system includes the following parts: people, hardware, software, procedures, and data (see Figure 1.1).

- **People:** If you think about it, the only reason computers exist is to help people accomplish their goals. Therefore when planning an information system, it's critical to understand what the people hope to get out of it. Do they need certain information? Do they need the computer to activate a device that performs a task? Are they looking to be entertained or educated? The first step in planning an information system is to analyze the requirements of the people.

- **Hardware:** When most people think of computers, they immediately think of hardware, the physical parts of the computer system. The hardware includes circuit boards with silicon chips and transistors mounted on them, input devices like keyboard and mouse, and output devices like printers and monitors.

- **Software:** Computer hardware just sits there idle unless it has software, which is a program that tells the hardware what to do. There are many different levels of software, including the operating system (like Windows or Mac OS) and applications (like a word processing or accounting programs).

- **Procedures:** The software doesn't run itself (usually). People must interact with the computer to tell it what software to run. For example, before you can write checks with your accounting software, you must start up the software, open the file that stores the data for the business, and issue the command that opens the checking account register. You can learn procedures from the online Help system in the application, from a printed user manual, from a training class, or by trial and error.

- **Data:** Computer programs operate upon the data they receive. For example, in your accounting software, you enter data about the checks you are writing—the date, the amount, the recipient—and the program stores that data so you can recall it later.

People

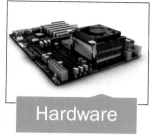
Hardware

Software

1. Power on the computer.

2. Open Microsoft Word.

3. Type the current date.

Procedures

	A	B	C	D
1	**Division**	**Current**	**Previous**	**Change**
2	East	47,552	42,522	(5,030)
3	West	19,581	22,541	2,960
4	North	33,110	35,918	2,808
5	South	42,855	38,481	(4,374)
6				
7				

Data

Figure 1.1 An information system involves these five components.

Information Systems Manager

An Information Systems (IS) manager looks at the "big picture" of a company's computer systems. As you discover in this chapter, an information system consists of people, procedures, software, hardware, and data The IS manager is the person who brings them all together to get results. An IS manager might oversee an initiative to satisfy an information need, such as for production managers to receive daily reports. This initiative might include assembling a team of programmers, identifying the required hardware and software, developing procedures for handling the information request, and delivering the data to the managers in an easy-to-use format.

Careers in IT

Quick Review

1. What are the five parts of an information system?

2. What is the difference between hardware and software?

3. What is the difference between software and data?

Identifying Computer Types

As you learned in the preceding section, hardware is the physical part of the computer system. Hardware consists of components inside a computer as well as the external devices that interact with it, such as printers, cables, and monitors.

hardware The physical parts of the computer system.

Personal Computers

When most people think about computers, they picture a personal computer, or PC. This type of computer is called *personal* because it is designed for only one person to use at a time. Personal computers fall into several categories that are differentiated from one another by their sizes. The most common sizes are:

personal computer A computer designed to be used by only one person at a time.

desktop PC A computer designed to be set up at a desk and not often moved, with input and output devices separate from the system unit.

system unit The main part of the computer, containing the essential components.

notebook PC A portable PC where the screen and keyboard fold up against one another for storage and transport; also known as a laptop.

pointing device An input device such as a mouse or touchpad that enables users to move an onscreen pointer to select content and issue commands.

netbook A small notebook PC designed primarily for accessing the Internet.

tablet PC A lightweight slate-style computer with a touch screen, designed for easy portability.

- **Desktop PC:** A computer designed to be used at a desk, and seldom moved. This type of computer consists of a large metal box called a system unit that contains most of the essential components, with a separate monitor, keyboard, and mouse that all plug into the system unit (see Figure 1.2).

- **Notebook PC:** A portable computer designed to fold up like a notebook for carrying, as shown in Figure 1.3. The cover opens up to reveal a built-in screen, keyboard, and pointing device, which substitutes for a mouse. This type of computer is sometimes called a laptop. A smaller version of a notebook PC is sometimes referred to as a netbook (which is short for *Internet book*, implying that this type of computer is primarily for accessing the Internet rather than running applications).

- **Tablet PC:** A portable computer that consists of a touch-sensitive display screen mounted on a plastic frame with a small computer inside, as in Figure 1.4. There is no built-in keyboard or pointing device; a software-based keyboard pops up onscreen when needed, and your finger sliding on the screen serves as a pointing device.

© iStockphoto.com/Viktorus

Figure 1.2 A desktop PC contains a separate system unit, monitor, keyboard, and mouse.

© iStockphoto.com/daboost

Figure 1.3 A notebook PC has a built-in monitor, keyboard, and pointing device, such as a touchpad.

© iStockphoto.com/UmbertoPantalone

Figure 1.4 A tablet computer is a touch-sensitive slate.

- **Smartphone**: A mobile phone that can run computer applications and has Internet access capability (see Figure 1.5). Smartphones usually have a touch-sensitive screen, provide voice calls, text messaging, and Internet access. Many have a variety of location-aware applications, such as a global positioning system (GPS) and mapping program and a local business guide.

© iStockphoto.com/scanrail

Figure 1.5 A smartphone combines the capabilities of a cell phone with a small touch-sensitive tablet screen.

smartphone A cellular phone that includes computer applications and Internet access capability.

global positioning system (GPS) A device that determines your current position by communicating with an orbiting satellite and provides maps and driving directions.

Multi-User Computers

Multi-user computers are designed to serve groups of people, from a small office to a huge international enterprise. Here are some common types of multi-user computers:

- **Server**: A computer dedicated to serving and supporting a network, a group of network users, and/or their information needs. Many networks employ servers to provide a centrally accessible storage space for data, and share common devices like printers and scanners. A small network server may look similar to a desktop PC, but may have a different operating system, such as Windows Server or Linux. A large server that manages a wide-ranging network may look similar to a mainframe. A group of servers located together in a single room or facility is called a server farm, or server cluster. Large Internet service provider (ISP) companies maintain extensive server farms.

- **Mainframe**: A large and powerful computer capable of processing and storing large amounts of business data. For example, a mainframe might collect all the sales data from hundreds of digital cash registers in a large department store and make it available to executives. The modern mainframe unit itself is a large cabinet, or a series of cabinets, each about the size of a refrigerator (see Figure 1.6). A mainframe may be stored in its own air-conditioned room in a business or school, and may have multiple employees monitoring and maintaining it. In earlier decades, smaller and less-expensive multi-user computers called minicomputers were employed in many businesses, but minicomputers are no longer widely used.

server A computer that is dedicated to performing network tasks such as managing files, printers, or email for multiple users.

server farm A group of servers located in the same physical area.

mainframe A large and powerful computer capable of serving many users and processing large amounts of data at once.

Figure 1.6 A mainframe is a powerful business computer system that can receive and process data from many sources at once.

supercomputer The largest and most powerful type of computer, surpassing the capability of a mainframe, typically used in research and academics.

■ **Supercomputer**: A supercomputer is the largest and most powerful type of computer available, occupying large rooms and even entire floors of a building. Supercomputers are often employed in fields such as cryptanalysis (code breaking), molecular modeling, weather forecasting, and climate mapping. Supercomputers typically are used in high-tech academic, governmental, and scientific research facilities. Figure 1.7 shows a supercomputer.

Figure 1.7 This IBM Blue Gene/P supercomputer is located at the Argonne National Laboratory in Lemont, Illinois, USA.

Mapping the Human Genome

Supercomputers played a critical role in the Human Genome Project (HGP), a multi-national research project that sought to define the unique genetic sequences that comprise the 23 chromosome pairs of human DNA. The project began in the 1980s, and by April 2003, 99% of the human genome had been mapped with 99.99% accuracy. Work continues on genomes today, with thousands of human genomes completely sequenced and many more mapped at a more basic level. The power of a supercomputer was essential for processing the enormous amount of data. The data that this project collected may help researchers develop cures for diseases like cancer, as well as promote advances in biotechnology and molecular medicine.

© iStockphoto.com/cosmin4000

Quick Review

1. What is a brief definition of "personal computer"?

2. What key characteristics of a desktop PC distinguish it from a notebook PC?

3. What are the differences between a server, a mainframe, and a supercomputer?

Understanding Software Types

Software tells the hardware what to do, but different kinds of software accomplish that at different levels. The following sections provide an overview of the types of software a computer might include.

software The programs that tell the computer what to do.

BIOS

The most basic software is the Basic Input Output System (BIOS). This software is stored on a read-only chip on the motherboard so that it doesn't accidentally get changed or corrupted. This important software helps the computer start up and performs some basic testing on the hardware.

BIOS The software that initializes and tests the system at startup.

Operating Systems

The operating system (OS) manages all the computer's activities after startup. The operating system serves several purposes:

operating system Software that maintains the computer's interface, manages files, runs applications, and communicates with hardware.

- **It provides the user interface** that humans use to communicate commands and receive feedback.

- **It runs applications,** and enables humans to interact with them.

- **It controls and manages the file storage system.**

- **It communicates with the hardware,** instructing it to take action to accomplish tasks. For example, the OS tells the printer to print a document, and tells the monitor what image to display.

Microsoft Windows is the most popular operating system; Figure 1.8 shows the Windows 8.1 interface. Other operating systems include Mac OS and Linux for desktop and notebook PCs, UNIX for mainframes and servers, and Android for tablets and smartphones. Versions of Windows and Apple iOS also power tablets and smartphones. Each operating system has its own unique set of features, benefits, and drawbacks, so it pays to learn as much as you can about the operating systems available and choose a computer that will run the operating system that best fits your needs. You will learn much more about operating systems in general in Chapter 4, "Operating System Basics," and more about the Windows 8.1 interface in Chapter 5, "Introduction to Windows 8.1," and Chapter 6, "Windows 8.1 Administration and Maintenance."

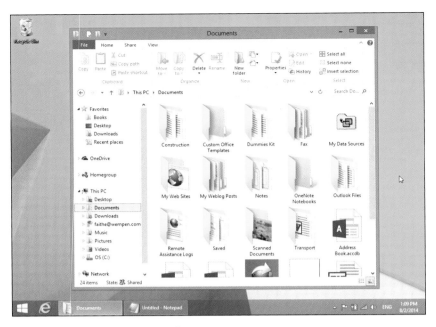

Figure 1.8 The Windows 8.1 interface.

Step by Step

Identifying Your Windows Version

Each version of Microsoft Windows is available in multiple editions; some editions have more features than others. Windows 8.1 comes in two editions: Windows 8.1 and Windows 8.1 Pro. Use this procedure to determine what version and edition of Windows you have on your computer:

1. Right-click the Start button on the desktop (the Windows logo icon in the lower left corner of the desktop) and choose System. An information page appears.

2. Look under the Windows edition heading. The version and edition of your Windows operating system appear there. If a service pack is installed, that information also appears.

This book uses Windows 8.1 for all its examples.

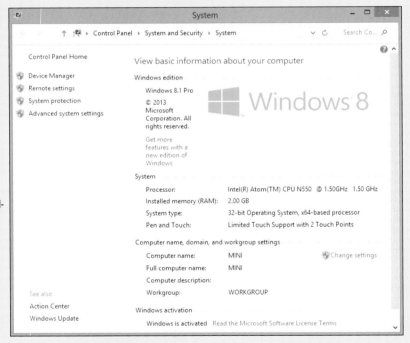

Utilities

In addition to the main components of an operating system, utility software may also be available, either provided free with the OS or added on. Utility programs assist with a wide range of system maintenance and security functions, such as checking storage disks for errors, blocking security and privacy threats, and backing up important files.

utility software Software that performs some useful service to the operating system, such as optimizing or correcting the file storage system, backing up files, or ensuring security or privacy.

Application Software

Application software is software that is designed to do something productive or fun, something of interest to a human user. The OS keeps the computer running, but the applications give people a reason to use the computer.

application software Software that helps a human perform a useful task for work or play.

Most computers come with some application software already installed. You can purchase additional software, and many applications are available for free. The software may be provided on a CD or DVD, or may be downloaded and installed over the Internet.

Productivity software helps you accomplish practical tasks such as managing your money, charting numeric data, writing documents, storing data, and sending email. Perhaps the best known example in this software category is Microsoft Office, a suite of applications that includes a word processor, a spreadsheet application, a database application, an application for creating business presentations, and an email and contact management system. A suite is a group of applications that are designed to work well together and which share some common interface characteristics. Notice in Figure 1.9 that each of the three applications has a similar toolbar across the top.

productivity software Software that helps a human perform one or more business or personal enrichment tasks.

Microsoft Office A productivity suite of applications commonly used in businesses for word processing, spreadsheets, databases, presentation, and email.

suite A group of applications designed to complement each other's capabilities and work together closely, often with a consistent interface between the applications.

Figure 1.9 These Microsoft Office applications—Word, Excel, and PowerPoint—share a common interface.

In addition to general suites like Office, dozens of other types of productivity software perform functions specific to certain professions, like accounting, customer relationship management (CRM), and appointment scheduling. On the technical side, software is available to help engineers and technicians create technical drawings and blueprints, develop new computer software, operate manufacturing and testing machinery, and much more.

Software as a Service (SaaS) A model of software sales that leases access to the software rather than selling a copy outright to the user.

Using Online Apps

Did you know that you can also use some software without installing it on your computer? Software as a Service (SaaS) is a new way of thinking about accessing and paying for software. Rather than buying a software product once, installing it on your computer and "owning" it forever, with the SaaS model you pay a usage fee for the software, which remains the property of the company. The software and any associated data are stored online. The company provides free updates for as long as you keep renewing your usage. Microsoft Office can optionally be rented this way through the Office 365 program, and many other applications are also being offered as services. SaaS has many benefits. The cost is typically lower than for buying the software outright, and updates and new versions are free and automatically provided.

Applications can also assist in education and training. For example, applications can train employees to perform new tasks or to use new productivity software, and can test their understanding of the training by administering and auto-scoring quizzes. In schools, applications can be used to simulate laboratory experiments and experiences, to assist with note-taking and review, and to help instructors create multimedia learning materials that students can use at their own pace. Some classes are even delivered entirely online through web-based software.

Applications can also entertain. You can find a wide variety of applications related to virtually any interest—cooking, sports and fitness, photography, science, and thousands more topics. There are thousands of games designed for every age group and interest, from simple matching and memory games to epic fantasy adventures to realistic first-person shooting games. In Chapter 6 you'll learn about the Entertainment Software Ratings Board (ESRB) and the rating system it assigns to games to help make sure that children have age-appropriate games.

Quick Review

1. What are the four key functions of an operating system?

2. How is application software different from an operating system?

3. What is productivity software? Name the widely used productivity suite available from Microsoft.

Computer System Components

Every computer system is made up of multiple electronic components. These components fall into four broad categories that serve different purposes in the information processing cycle, shown in Figure 1.10. You will learn more about the information processing cycle in Chapter 2, "The System Unit."

information processing cycle The four-step process that data moves through as it is processed by a computer. Consists of input, processing, output, and storage.

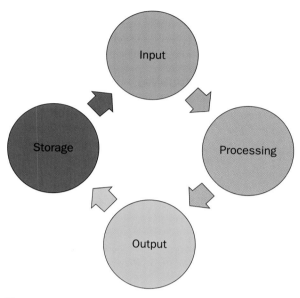

Figure 1.10   The information processing cycle.

- **Input:** Components that help humans put data into the computer. Examples include a keyboard, mouse, and touch screen.

- **Processing:** Components that move and process the data inside the computer. The motherboard and its processor and memory chips fall into this category.

- **Output:** Components that provide the results of the processing to humans. The monitor is the primary output device; other examples include printers and speakers.

- **Storage:** Components that store software and data until it is needed. Storage components include hard drives, USB flash drives, and DVDs.

As you learned earlier in this chapter, the system unit is the main box that constitutes the computer. Some devices are external—that is, they are outside the system unit—and some are internal. On a desktop PC, most input and output devices are external; on a notebook, tablet, or smartphone, they are an integral part of the device but external devices can be added. Figure 1.11 shows the computer's main components and their roles in information processing.

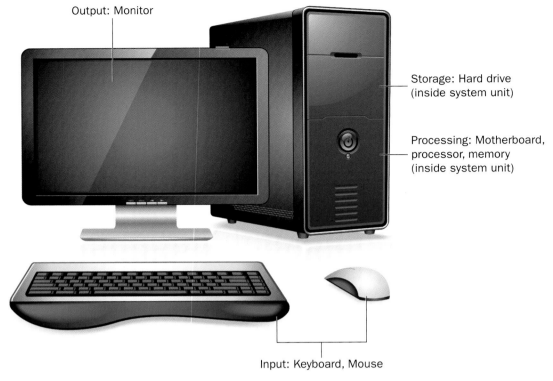

Output: Monitor

Storage: Hard drive (inside system unit)

Processing: Motherboard, processor, memory (inside system unit)

Input: Keyboard, Mouse

Figure 1.11   Components of a typical desktop computer system.

How Data Is Represented on a Computer

bit A single binary digit, with a value of either 1 (on) or 0 (off).

byte An 8-digit binary number, composed of eight bits.

The smallest unit of data in a computer is a bit. A bit is a single binary digit, with either a 1 (on) or 0 (off) value. Eight bits can combine to make a byte, which is an 8-digit binary number, as shown in Figure 1.12

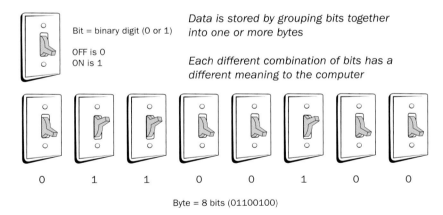

Bit = binary digit (0 or 1)

OFF is 0
ON is 1

Data is stored by grouping bits together into one or more bytes

Each different combination of bits has a different meaning to the computer

0   1   1   0   0   1   0   0

Byte = 8 bits (01100100)

Figure 1.12   Computers combine eight binary digits (bits) to make a byte.

Modern systems work with thousands, millions, and even billions of bytes at a time. Table 1.1 lists the names for certain multiples of bytes.

Table 1.1: Common Quantities of Bytes

Term	Number of Bytes
Kilobyte (KB)	1024 (approximately one thousand)
Megabyte (MB)	1,048,576 (approximately one million)
Gigabyte (GB)	1,073,741,824 (approximately one billion)
Terabyte (TB)	1,099,411,627,776 (approximately one trillion)
Petabyte (PB)	1,125,899,906,842,624 (approximately one quadrillion)

Both memory and storage capacities are measured in bytes. For example, a computer might have 8GB RAM (memory) and a 500GB hard drive.

NOTE

Input Devices

An input device provides a way to get data into the computer. The oldest and most common input device is a keyboard. A desktop PC has an external keyboard, while a notebook PC has a built-in keyboard. Tablets and smartphones have a software-based keyboard that pops up onscreen when needed.

keyboard An input device that allows users to type data into a computer using a standard set of typing keys.

Computers that use a graphical interface usually employ a pointing device. The pointing device moves an on-screen pointer (usually an arrow) to align with objects onscreen, and then the user presses a button on the pointing device to do something to the pointed-at object. A mouse is the most common pointing device, but there are many other types too, such as trackballs, touchpads, and touch-sensitive screens. You will learn more about input devices in Chapter 3, "Input, Output, and Storage."

Processing Devices

The motherboard is the large circuit board inside the computer that everything else plugs into. The key components located on the motherboard are the processor (also called the Central Processing Unit, or CPU) and the memory (also called Random Access Memory, or RAM). To support these components, the motherboard has electrically conductive pathways called buses that carry the data from place to place, and a chipset, which is a controller that directs the bus traffic. Figure 1.13 shows a motherboard removed from the computer case so you can see it more clearly.

motherboard A large circuit board inside a computer that controls the operations of all other components.

processor The chip in the computer that performs math calculations, processing data. Also called the Central Processing Unit (CPU).

memory Temporary electronic storage that holds the values of data bits using transistors.

bus A conductive pathway built into a circuit board, used to move data.

chipset The controller chip on a circuit board.

Chapter 2, "The System Unit," covers these components in more detail and explains how they work together.

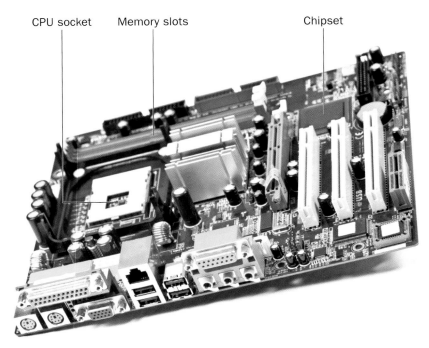

CPU socket   Memory slots   Chipset

© iStockphoto.com/kirstypargeter

Figure 1.13   A motherboard.

Output Devices

Information comes out of a computer through an output device such as a monitor. When you move the mouse or type a character on a keyboard, you see the results instantly on the monitor. The monitor helps you communicate with the operating system; without the monitor, you wouldn't know if the OS had received and understood your instructions or if the application had accepted the data you input. Besides monitors, other output devices include printers (for producing hard-copy output) and speakers (for providing audio feedback).

Storage Devices

Storage devices enable software and data to be preserved and reused. Storage can be either removable or non-removable. (Non-removable storage is actually removable too if you have the right tools and knowledge, but in this case the distinction refers to being *easily* removable or not.)

The most common type of storage is an internal hard drive, which is a sealed metal box inside the system unit. Hard drives are usually internal, making them non-removable. Some hard drives are removable, though; external hard drives easily connect to and disconnect from a port on the outside of the system unit. Other removable storage devices include USB flash drives and optical discs (CDs and DVDs). Chapter 3 covers storage devices in more detail and explains the technologies behind them.

Quick Review

1. Name at least two devices from each of these categories: input, processing, output, and storage.

2. What is the purpose of the motherboard?

How Computers Communicate

Early computers did not communicate easily with one another. Data was typically carried between computers on floppy disks and other low-capacity removable disks, or sent using slow dial-up modems. Network connections were difficult to set up and transferred data very slowly. Nowadays, however, communication technology has advanced greatly, and there are many choices for making computers connect to one another.

Ethernet Networking

Most computers today are part of one or more networks. A network is a group of computers that share resources (such as printers or Internet service) and/or data (such as files). The most common network standard is Ethernet. Ethernet networks can be either wired or wireless (or a combination of the two), but the term Ethernet is most often applied to the wired kind of connection. Figure 1.14 shows an Ethernet port on the side of a notebook PC. Most PCs have a network adapter, which provides network connectivity services and a port into which you can plug an Ethernet cable. The most common kind of Ethernet cable uses twisted pairs of copper wiring and an RJ-45 connector, which is like a telephone connector except slightly wider.

network Two or more computers connected to share data and resources.

Ethernet The current dominant standard for local area networking devices.

network adapter A hardware component that enables a computer to connect to a network.

© iStockphoto.com/fotoscape

Figure 1.14   Ethernet is the most common type of network connection. Most computers have an Ethernet port.

Wireless Ethernet is more often called Wi-Fi, or 802.11. That number refers to the standard number assigned to it by the Institute of Electrical and Electronics Engineers (IEEE, pronounced "eye-triple-ee"). Different Wi-Fi sub-types have different letter designations, such as 802.11g or 802.11n. Most portable devices such as tablets and smartphones use wireless connections and do not have the capability for wired networking. Chapter 13, "Networking and Internet Basics," explains networking technology in more detail.

Wi-Fi Wireless Ethernet. Another name for it is IEEE 802.11, its technical standard.

router A gathering point for the computers in a LAN to connect with to participate in the network.

broadband A fast, always-on network connection.

switch A connection box for Ethernet networks that physically connects the devices in the network. Unlike a router, a switch does not have the complex capabilities that allow it to communicate outside its own network.

fiber optic cable Cable that carries data using light pulses through a bundle of glass fibers.

backbone The central connection pathways of a network, where connection speeds are high and the data pathway is wide.

In a small network, such as in a home or small business, one end of an Ethernet cable plugs into the computer, and the other end plugs into a controller box called a router that manages the network traffic between the connected devices. If you have broadband (always on) Internet access, the device that brings that service into your home or business is frequently called the router, and then the router shares the Internet connection among all the computers.

If you have a Wi-Fi wireless router and a wireless network adapter in the computer, the computer can connect to the router via radio frequency (RF) waves, so no cables are required.

In large-scale networks, Ethernet is still the standard, but some different hardware is employed. Large panels of switches can connect hundreds of computers into a central network system, as shown in Figure 1.15. Cables with fiber optic technology are used in the network's backbone to carry large amounts of network traffic faster and more efficiently.

© iStockphoto.com/mishooo

Figure 1.15 Business networks can contain hundreds of computers, each connected with a separate cable to a port on a switch.

peer-to-peer A network where all computers can both share with and access resources from other computers on the same network; a decentralized network.

client/server network A network that contains one or more servers.

Some networks, such as small home and business networks with fewer than a dozen or so computers, are peer-to-peer. That means there is no one computer that controls the network; all the computers can cooperate to share data with each other. Networks that are larger than that typically have one or more servers dedicated to network data sharing, and such networks are called client/server networks.

Bluetooth Networking

Bluetooth An inexpensive short-range networking technology used for computer-to-device connections such as computer-to-printer or phone-to-headset.

Bluetooth is a short-range wireless alternative to wireless Ethernet (Wi-Fi), used primarily to connect wireless devices directly to specific computers. For example, you might have a Bluetooth wireless headset for your cell phone, or a Bluetooth speaker for your MP3 player. Bluetooth's limited range (10 meters) makes it impractical as a replacement for Wi-Fi, but it provides an easy and economical way for one device to connect with another within a limited space without Ethernet hardware.

The Internet

The Internet is the world's largest computer network. When you use the Internet, your computer becomes a member of this giant network, and you can communicate with any other computer on the Internet, to the extent that its owner has chosen to make it available. For example, you can exchange email messages, download files, and view web pages stored anywhere in the world.

Internet A global packet-switched network created cooperatively by multiple companies, governments, and standards organizations.

Individual computers don't connect directly to the Internet, however; they go through an Internet service provider (ISP), a company that provides a connection to the Internet for a fee. Your ISP may be your local phone or cable TV company, or at work it may be a service that your school or employer partners with. An ISP provides a device (a modem or terminal adapter) that translates your computer's requests into Internet-compatible data.

Internet service provider (ISP) A company that maintains a direct connection to the Internet and leases access to it to individuals and companies.

Wireless Router Security

A wired router is fairly secure by nature because you have to have physical access to it to plug a cable into it. A wireless router, however, is not secure because anyone within transmission range can connect to it. Wireless routers come with optional security features you can enable that will assign a code (like a password) that is required for a computer to connect to it. The first time that computer connects to the router, a prompt appears for the code; after the first successful connection, the code is stored and the computer can connect to the router automatically.

If you do not enable security on your wireless router, you should make sure that you do not have file sharing enabled on any of your computers. Otherwise an unknown person could not only use your Internet connection without permission, but could also view, change, copy, and even delete your important data files. An intruder might also be able to gather enough information about you from your data files to steal your identity.

To enable security on a wireless router, check the documentation that came with the router. You will find instructions there to open a web browser and go to an IP address for the router to display a web page on which you can change router settings and set up security.

Privacy and Security

The Internet functions using a set of standards called Transmission Control Protocol/Internet Protocol (TCP/IP). It is this shared communication language that makes global communication possible. TCP/IP defines how data will be treated as it is broken up into packets for transmission, sent through a series of routers across the world, and reassembled into its original form at the receiving end.

Transmission Control Protocol/Internet Protocol (TCP/IP) The protocol suite (set of rules) that defines how data will move on the Internet and on most other modern networks.

Quick Review

1. What is the most common standard for wired networking?

2. How many servers does a peer-to-peer network need?

3. What types of connections are most suitable for Bluetooth networking?

Summary

Understanding Information Systems

An **information system** is a complete interconnected environment in which raw data—quantifiable facts and figures—is turned into useful information. An information system includes the following parts: people, hardware, software, procedures, and data.

Identifying Computer Types

A **personal computer (PC)** is a computer designed for only one person to use at a time. Examples include **desktop PCs**, **notebook PCs**, **tablet PCs**, and **smartphones**. Other computers support multiple users at once, including **servers**, **mainframes**, and **supercomputers**.

Understanding Software Types

Software tells the hardware what to do. The **operating system** (**OS**) manages the computer's activities. An operating system provides a user interface, runs applications, manages files, and communicates with hardware.

Application software is software that is designed to do something productive or fun. **Productivity software** helps you accomplish practical tasks; one example is the **Microsoft Office** suite. A **suite** is a group of applications designed to work together. Software may be bought on CD or DVD, downloaded and installed, or may be leased as **Software as a Service** (**SaaS**).

Computer System Components

The **information processing cycle** consists of these four parts: input, processing, output, and storage. Each component in a computer contributes to one or more parts of that cycle.

Input devices move data into a computer. Examples include a **keyboard** and **mouse**. A mouse is a type of **pointing device**; pointing devices move the onscreen pointer and select objects onscreen.

Processing components manipulate the data inside the PC, and include the **motherboard** and its **processor**, **memory**, **chipset**, and **buses**.

Output devices deliver the results of the processing to the user. The **monitor** (display screen) is the most common output device; others include speakers and printers.

How Computers Communicate

Most computers are part of one or more **networks.** The most common network standard is **Ethernet**, which can be wired or wireless. Wireless Ethernet is called **Wi-Fi**. To connect to a network, the computer needs a network adapter (wired or wireless). A home network uses a **router** to connect the computers to one another and to connect to a shared **broadband** Internet connection if available.

Large networks use multiple banks of **switches** to connect the computers together, and may use **fiber optic cable** for the **backbone** portions of the network that need high data throughput.

Small networks (fewer than a dozen computers) may operate in **peer-to-peer** mode, where all computers share with each other. Larger networks use a **client/server** management method where one or more dedicated computers function as servers.

Bluetooth is a short-range wireless alternative to Wi-Fi, used primarily to connect wireless devices directly to specific computers.

The **Internet** is a huge worldwide computer network based on **Transmission Control Protocol/ Internet Protocol (TCP/IP)**. To participate in the Internet, individuals and companies must contract with an **Internet service provider (ISP)** for access.

Key Terms

application software
backbone
BIOS
bit
Bluetooth
broadband
buses
byte
chipset
client/server
desktop PC
Ethernet
fiber optic cable
global positioning system (GPS)
hard drive
hardware
information processing cycle
information system
Internet
Internet service provider (ISP)
keyboard
mainframe
memory
Microsoft Office
monitor

motherboard
netbook
network
network adapter
notebook PC
operating system (OS)
peer-to-peer
pointing device
processor
productivity software
router
server
server farm
smartphone
software
Software as a Service
suite
supercomputer
switch
system unit
tablet PC
Transmission Control Protocol/Internet Protocol (TCP/IP)
utility software
Wi-Fi

Test Yourself

Fact Check

1. Which of these is NOT one of the five parts of an information system?

    a. data

    b. procedures

    c. people

    d. networks

2. Which of these would be most appropriate for managing and storing patient records in a large hospital?

    a. peer-to-peer network

    b. mainframe

    c. personal computer

    d. supercomputer

3. Windows 8.1 and UNIX are examples of a(n) _____ _____ (two words).

4. True or false: Computer games are a type of application software.

    a. True

    b. False

5. The information processing cycle consists of four phases: input, _____, output, and storage.

    a. productivity

    b. preparation

    c. processing

    d. promotion

6. True or false: A trackball is a type of output device.

    a. True

    b. False

7. A _____ is a pathway on a circuit board through which data moves.

    a. router

    b. chipset

    c. bus

    d. motherboard

8. True or false: Wi-Fi is a synonym for Bluetooth.

    a. True

    b. False

9. A _____/server network contains at least one server.

    a. chipset

    b. suite

    c. system

    d. client

10. The Internet is based on what protocol suite?

    a. TCP/IP

    b. Ethernet

    c. ISP

    d. BIOS

Matching

Match the computer type to its description.

    a. desktop

    b. mainframe

    c. notebook

    d. server

e. supercomputer

f. tablet

1. _____Personal computer with input and output devices separate from the system unit

2. _____Touchscreen computer with no separate keyboard and mouse

3. _____Portable PC that folds for transport, containing a built-in keyboard and built-in display screen

4. _____A computer dedicated to serving the network to which it is connected

5. _____A large, powerful, cabinet-sized computer designed to process large amounts of input and output

6. _____A powerful, room-sized computer for scientific research

Sum It Up

1. What are the five parts of an information system?

2. What is the difference between a server and a mainframe?

3. What distinguishes an operating system from an application?

4. What are the four parts of the information processing cycle?

5. What is Wi-Fi, and what equipment does it require?

Think It Over

Software as a Service

Suppose you had the chance to buy a productivity suite like Microsoft Office for a certain price and keep that version indefinitely, or to subscribe to a service that enabled you to use Office for as long as you continued paying the subscription fee. Suppose that the subscription cost was 1/20th per month of the cost to buy it outright. Which would be a better value for you, and why?

What if it were a game that you could either buy or subscribe to? Would you rather buy it outright and be able to play it forever, or would you rather subscribe to it?

Shopping for Tablet PCs

Suppose you are shopping for a tablet PC for use in your classes. Using the Internet, research at least one model of iPad, one tablet that has the Windows 8 OS, and one model that uses the Android OS. Then answer the following questions:

- Which tablet has the fastest processor and the most memory?

- Which tablet OS has the most apps available for it?

- Which model has the longest battery life?

- Which tablets have the capability of attaching external keyboards?

- Which tablet has the largest screen size and the highest resolution?

- What features do you personally find most important, and which model would serve those needs best?

Suppose your family pays for broadband Internet service, and you have a wireless router that allows everyone in the family to share the Internet connection. The wireless router has security on it, so that a code is required to connect to it. This prevents your neighbors from using your Internet connection without permission. A neighbor asks for the code so he and his family can use your Internet connection. What do you say? Explain how you came to your decision.

- No, it would be unfair to the ISP for you to use the Internet without paying for it. You must pay for your own separate connection.

- Yes, you can use it, but you must pay me for part of the expense of the service.

- Yes, you can use it for free. Here is the code.

- Some other answer (explain).

Chapter 2

The System Unit

Learning objectives

- ☐ Recognize how data is processed
- ☐ Understand processors
- ☐ Understand memory types and functions
- ☐ Identify and use ports and buses
- ☐ Troubleshoot common system unit problems

The heart of any computer is its system unit. As you learned in Chapter 1, "Computer Basics," the system unit is the main body of the computer, containing the essential components it needs to function.

If you have ever shopped for a computer, you probably noticed that some models cost much more than others—many times more. The quality and features of the components inside the system unit are the primary reason why cost varies so widely. Two computers can look identical from the outside but be very different in their capabilities and performance levels.

In this chapter, you will learn what happens inside the system unit, and what role each key component plays in making the computer fast and efficient at performing the tasks you ask of it. When you understand these things, you will be able to decipher a computer's technical specifications with confidence and select the models that have the best balance of cost and features for your situation.

Bench Repair Technician

A bench repair technician is like a mechanic for computers. As the word **bench** implies, this technician works primarily at a workbench in a repair shop, although mobile repair technician positions are also available. Bench repair technicians can diagnose system problems with computers that customers bring in for repairs, including both hardware problems like defective parts and software problems like virus infections. This position requires either a two-year degree in Computer Technology or a professional certification such as CompTIA's A+ certification. It is a good job for someone who prefers working mostly with the computers themselves rather than with their users.

Understanding CPUs

central processing unit (CPU) The main processor in a computer.

Every computer has at least one processor, also called a central processing unit (CPU). The CPU contains millions of tiny transistors and pathways that take in data and instructions, process (calculate) the data according to the instructions, and output the results of the calculations. A computer may also have smaller processors used in specific subsystems, such as a graphics processor.

Every CPU includes the following components:

- The **control unit** manages the flow of data through the CPU. It directs data to and from the other components within the CPU.

- The **arithmetic logic unit (ALU)** component does the actual processing. It receives data and instructions and delivers a result. For example, if it received the numbers 3 and 5, and the instruction *Sum*, it would return 8.

- **Registers** are holding areas for both data and instructions. There are many different registers, each with its own special purpose. For example, there are registers that hold data, registers that hold instructions, registers that store logical states (yes/no), temporary values that serve as increment counters, and so on.

Figure 2.1 walks through a very simple example that takes two numbers, divides one by the other, and outputs the result. Numbers are shown in decimal form in this diagram, but in actuality all numbers and instructions would be represented as binary codes (that is, codes consisting of only 1s and 0s).

CPU Data Processing Example

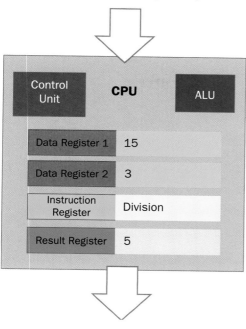

A. Control unit fetches the data and places it in data registers.

B. Control unit fetches the instruction and places in an instruction register.

C. Control unit decodes the instruction to determine what needs to happen, and tells the ALU.

D. ALU executes the instruction and places the result in a result register.

E. Control unit orders the data in the result register to exit the CPU, where it is stored in memory.

Figure 2.1 Data and instructions enter the CPU and are processed, producing output.

The Machine Cycle

The process of accepting input, processing it, and ejecting output is sometimes referred to as a machine cycle. A machine cycle consist of these steps:

machine cycle One complete cycle of the CPU's activities of fetching, decoding, executing, and storing.

1. **Fetch:** The control unit requests that the data and instructions it needs be fetched from memory and moved into the CPU.

2. **Decode:** The control unit translates the instructions into a form the ALU understands.

3. **Execute:** The ALU processes the instructions.

4. **Store:** The control unit releases the result from the CPU, and it is stored in memory.

Figure 2.2 illustrates this cycle. You can also trace the same basic procedure in Figure 2.1 to understand how the parts of the CPU relate to the activities. The CPU performs billions of machine cycles per second, with the exact timing being determined by the system clock (also called the system timer), a chip on the motherboard that provides the timing for all the system components to operate, as a metronome might do.

system clock A crystal on the motherboard that sets the timing for data moving through the system, such as between memory and the CPU. This chip contains a crystal that oscillates at a certain frequency to produce the timing pulses.

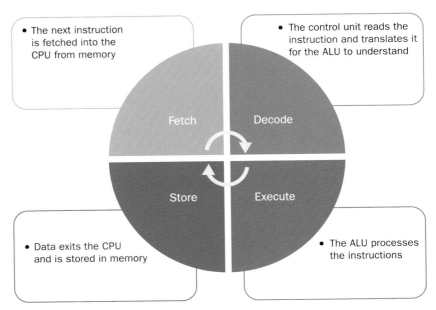

- The next instruction is fetched into the CPU from memory
- The control unit reads the instruction and translates it for the ALU to understand

Fetch | Decode

Store | Execute

- Data exits the CPU and is stored in memory
- The ALU processes the instructions

Figure 2.2 A machine cycle consists of these four steps.

Physical Composition of a CPU

semiconductor Material that is electricity-neutral, neither a good conductor nor a flow preventer.

Physically, a CPU is a very small and thin sheet of semiconductor material (usually silicon) with a complex array of tiny transistors and pathways stamped into it with a die. Semiconductor material is used for CPUs because it does not affect the flow of electricity one way or another: it neither conducts it nor impedes it. The components inside the CPU are so small that you need a microscope to see them.

The CPU is fragile, so it is protected by a sturdy ceramic and metal casing; some models are mounted on miniature square circuit boards. The underside of this casing contains either tiny pins or tiny metal dots, precisely spaced, that align with connectors on the CPU socket on the motherboard. Each pin or each dot is a separate communication line, carrying a different piece of data. Figure 2.3 shows both sides of a CPU designed for a desktop PC, for example. CPUs come in different sizes and have to match the socket type on the corresponding motherboard.

Cores

core A set of the essential processor components that work together (control unit, ALU, and registers). A CPU may have multiple cores.

Most modern CPUs have multiple cores, so they can complete multiple tasks simultaneously, as if they physically were more than one CPU. A core consists of a separate set of the essential processor components (control unit, ALU, and registers). Most models of the Intel i7 processor have four cores, for example. All of the CPU's cores are located on the same chip.

© iStockphoto.com/scanrail

Figure 2.3   A typical CPU, back and front.

Caches

In theory, the CPU is capable of executing a function with every tick of the system clock (called a clock cycle). However, in practice, the CPU sometimes is idle because there is a delay between the request for data to be retrieved from memory and its delivery. The bus (pathway) between memory and the CPU is not as fast as the CPU's internal speed, so several clock cycles may pass when the CPU is idle. A delay caused by waiting for another component to deliver data is called latency.

To help minimize latency, CPUs have caches. A cache is a small amount of very fast memory located near (or within) the CPU. Data that the CPU has recently used, or is predicted to need soon, is placed in the cache for temporary holding. That way, if the CPU calls for the data, it's more readily available and there is less delay.

CPUs have a multi-level cache system. Whenever the CPU needs some data, it first checks the Level 1 (L1) cache to see if it's there. If the CPU does not find what it needs in the L1 cache, it checks the L2 cache. This cache is also on the CPU itself. Finally, if the L2 cache does not have it, the CPU checks the L3 cache.

How much of a difference can the caches make? A big difference: Fetching data from an L3 cache takes 10 times as long as from an L1 cache. See Table 2.1.

clock cycle One tick of the system clock.

latency A period of waiting for another component to deliver data needed to proceed.

cache A small amount of fast memory located near or within the CPU.

Table 2.1: How Caches Help Minimize Latency

Location	Average number of clock cycles required to retrieve data
L1 cache	2 to 3 clock cycles
L2 cache	10 clock cycles
L3 cache	20 to 30 clock cycles
Main memory	100 or more clock cycles

All of these caches are located on the CPU itself on modern CPUs. Older CPUs have only two cache levels, with the L3 being on the motherboard. On CPUs with multiple cores, each core has its own L1 cache. The L2 cache might also be individual to each core, or two cores might share an L2 cache. The L3 cache is shared among all cores.

A smaller cache is quicker to check because there's less data to go through, so the Level 1 (L1) cache is fairly small, and each of the other two caches is progressively larger. The cache sizes vary by CPU model. The Intel Core i7 CPU, for example, has an L1 cache of 64KB per core, an L2 cache of 256KB per core, and a shared L3 cache of between 4 MB and 8 MB.

CPU Performance Factors

hertz One cycle per second, a measurement of activity speed.

gigahertz (GHz) One billion hertz.

The most obvious performance factor for a CPU is its maximum speed, measured in billions of hertz, or gigahertz (GHz). Although the actual speed is dictated by the motherboard's system clock, each CPU has an advertised maximum speed, which is the highest speed at which the CPU's manufacturer assures that it will reliably function. If a CPU is pushed to run faster than its rating (for example, by putting it in a motherboard that runs the CPU faster), it is said to be overclocked. An overclocked CPU is more prone to overheating, processing errors, and reliability issues.

overclock To push a CPU to run faster than the speed for which it is rated.

word size The number of bits that the CPU can accept as input simultaneously.

A CPU's word size also makes a difference. The word size is the number of bits that the CPU (or a single core of the CPU, if multi-core) can accept as input simultaneously. Most desktop and notebook PCs have 64-bit CPUs, but some tablets, netbooks, and smartphones have 32-bit CPUs; see Figure 2.4.

TIP Windows comes in both 32-bit (x86) and 64-bit (x64) versions. When selecting a copy of Windows for a device, keep in mind that 32-bit CPUs can only run the 32-bit version of Windows. 64-bit CPUs can run either 64-bit or 32-bit versions of Windows, but run better with the 64-bit.

benchmark A consistent measurement of performance.

instructions per second A measurement of a CPU's throughput capability, taking into consideration factors such as number of cores and latency.

Because modern CPUs have many technology improvements in them, speed and word size alone do not form a reliable benchmark of a CPU's capability. Another way to look at performance is how many instructions per second the CPU can process. For example, suppose you have two CPUs that both have a speed rating of 3.4 GHz. If each one processed one operation per clock cycle, with no delays and with a single core, each one might be able to output 3.4 billion operations per second (usually expressed as Giga instructions per second, or GIPS). However, one of them might have multiple cores, multiplying that theoretical maximum. And, realistically, there is always going to be latency, no matter how efficient the processing technology becomes. Each CPU will also have some advanced data handling technologies that reduce the average latency (the idle time waiting for data) by differing amounts.

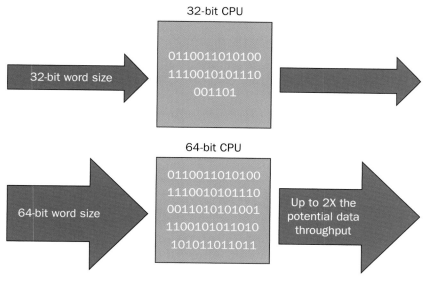

Figure 2.4   64-bit CPU has twice the word size of a 32-bit CPU, so the 64-bit CPU can theoretically input and output date at twice the rate. In actual use, many other factors also play a part, so the performance boost is less than 2x.

Benchmarking

It can be difficult to fairly compare one CPU to another in terms of performance. Benchmark software is available that runs a series of processing tests on a system and creates a report and a numeric score based on those tests. Such software also test other subsystems, such as graphics processing, because other hardware besides the CPU makes a difference in how an application performs as well. One popular benchmark program is SiSoftware SANDRA. Its Lite version is free for personal and educational use. See www.sisoftware.net for the latest version.

Put It to Work

The two largest manufacturers of CPUs are the companies Intel and Advanced Micro Devices (AMD). Their CPUs are roughly equivalent in performance level, but the internal architectures of the CPUs are different. A motherboard will support one or the other, but not both. Some people prefer one brand over the other and claim that one brand or model is superior for using a certain kind of software. Such claims are a moving target, though, as each company continues to develop new and better CPUs.

Quick Review

1. What are the three main components inside a CPU?

2. What are the four steps in a machine cycle?

3. What is the purpose of a cache?

4. What is a multi-core CPU?

Understanding Memory

The word *memory* has a biological origin, of course, referring to the way human brains store memories and learned facts. In computer terms, memory is an electronic chip with integrated circuits that store on/off values, as you learned in Chapter 1, "Computer Basics." Like the human brain, memory stores and retrieves data. Also like human memory, there is both short-term (temporary) and long-term (permanent) memory storage. Some memory is dynamic, in that it stores data only until the computer is turned off. Dynamic memory (also called volatile memory) must be constantly refreshed. Static memory (also called non-volatile memory) retains whatever you put in it indefinitely; the transistors do not require constant electrical power to retain their contents.

Another way to classify memory is whether it can be overwritten with new data or not. Random Access Memory (RAM) can be rewritten freely; Read-Only Memory (ROM) cannot (at least not in the same way that RAM can; see the following Note). All ROM is static, but RAM can be either dynamic (more common) or static.

dynamic memory Memory that does not retain its data unless it is constantly electrically refreshed.

static memory Memory that retains its data without electricity being constantly applied.

Random Access Memory (RAM) Memory that can have its values changed freely, an unlimited number of times.

Read-Only Memory (ROM) In general, memory that cannot be rewritten. However, there are exceptions to that in newer types of ROM.

Electrically Erasable Programmable ROM (EEPROM) ROM that can be erased and reprogrammed with electricity.

NOTE When is ROM not *really* read-only? Actually plenty of times. Over the years, as technology has advanced, companies have figured out ways to make certain types of ROM chips rewritable. The first generation used a special machine that reprogrammed the chips; this type of ROM was called Erasable Programmable ROM (EPROM). Later ROM chips were erasable with strong electrical pulses; this was called Electrically Erasable Programmable ROM (EEPROM); this technology was used to allow the BIOS chip on a motherboard to be updated without having to remove it.

The early versions of EEPROM could only erase and rewrite the entire chip at once, but newer versions allow specific blocks to be rewritten while preserving the data in other blocks. This advanced ROM-rewriting technology is used in USB flash drives and solid-state hard drives. Unlike RAM, which can be rewritten unlimited times, there is a limit to how many times an EEPROM can be rewritten, but the limit is very high (up to 100,000), so it is seldom an issue.

How Computers Use Memory

Computers use different types of memory in various ways. Here are some of the most common memory uses:

- **System memory:** The main memory in a computer system, such as the RAM installed on the PC's motherboard, is dynamic RAM (DRAM). System memory is installed in slots on the motherboard, perpendicular to the motherboard itself.

- **Component memory:** Many components have a small amount of memory built in for their own use. For example, a printer might have RAM that holds the information about the page it is printing, and a display adapter might have memory to hold the data about the image it is displaying on the monitor. Component memory is typically DRAM unless the component's function requires it to be otherwise because that's the least expensive kind.

- **ROM-BIOS:** A motherboard has an EEPROM chip that contains the low-level startup instructions for the hardware. To prevent corruption that would prevent the system from starting up, this chip is not rewritable except with a special utility program.

- **Caches:** The L1, L2, and L3 caches in a CPU are a type of static RAM (SRAM).

- **USB flash drives, memory cards, and solid-state hard drives:** As mentioned in the earlier note, these devices use a type of EEPROM to store data. This type of EEPROM is also called flash memory; its enhanced technology allows data to be written and rewritten to it multiple times.

© iStockphoto.com/algre

Memory

© iStockphoto.com/MauMyHaT

Understanding System Memory

Each computer has a certain amount of system memory, also called RAM or main memory. It is dynamic RAM (DRAM), so it loses its contents if it is not constantly being electrically refreshed.

System memory forms a workspace that the operating system uses. When you open an application, that application is placed in system memory, and when you open a data file, it is placed there too. When you make changes to a data file, those changes wait in memory until you write them to a more permanent storage area by saving your work. The more system memory you have, the more applications and files you can have open at once.

© iStockphoto.com/BrianAJackson

system memory The main pool of dynamic RAM (DRAM) on the motherboard.

virtual memory Memory that is simulated by swapping data out of memory and storing it temporarily on the hard drive.

paging file The area of the hard drive set aside for use as virtual memory. Also called a **swap file**.

Windows also uses virtual memory to help prevent a computer from running out of memory. Virtual memory is a file on the hard drive used as an extension to main memory. This file is called the paging file or swap file. When the physical memory gets full (or nearly full), Windows moves some data to the paging file on the hard drive. It then makes a note of where the data came from and where it is now, and then frees up that space in memory to hold something else. When a program requests that data, Windows moves something else out of memory, swaps the old data back in again, and then responds to the request. Virtual memory is much slower than regular memory because the hard drive is a relatively slow device, so it's not desirable to use—but it's better than running out of memory entirely and not being able to do more work without closing some programs. The more physical memory a PC has, the less it needs to rely on virtual memory. That is why adding more physical memory to a computer improves its performance.

Step by Step

Checking Out Virtual Memory

Use this procedure to determine the size of your Windows 8.1 system's swap file and find out which drive it is stored on.

1. Right-click the Start button on the desktop and then click System.

2. In the panel at the left, click Advanced System Settings.

4. On the Advanced tab, in the Performance area, click Settings.

5. In the Performance Options dialog box, click the Advanced tab.

6. In the Virtual memory section, click the Change button.

7. Clear the Automatically Manage Paging File Size for All Drives check box.

8. Check to see which drive the paging file is on. It is on C: in the figure shown here.

9. In the Total Paging File Size for All Drives section, take note of the Currently Allocated amount. This is the size of the paging file.

10. Click Cancel to close the dialog box without saving changes; then close all open windows.

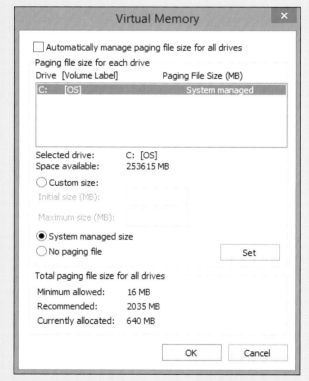

memory address The numeric address of a particular addressable area in memory.

The data in RAM is assigned a specific location, known as a memory address, and the operating system maintains a database of what data is stored where. Any data can go into any area of the RAM, depending on what's free at the moment. That's why it's called *random access memory*—because the system can access any area in RAM as easily as any other area.

Physically, system memory comes mounted on small rectangular circuit boards called dual inline memory modules (DIMMs). These circuit boards fit into memory slots on the motherboard. There are different types and speeds of DIMMs, so you must match the memory to the motherboard's requirements. Figure 2.5 shows two different types of DIMMs. As you can see, some DIMMs are bare circuit boards, while others have a metal plate covering most of the DIMM. Each ceramic chip mounted on the DIMM contains a silicon wafer, the memory itself. For notebook computers, **small outline DIMMs (SO-DIMMs)** are used instead; they do the same thing as DIMMs but are a different size and shape. Figure 2.6 shows a SO-DIMM.

© iStockphoto.com/aguirre_mar, © iStockphoto.com/mkos83

Figure 2.5   Some DIMMs have a metal plate covering the chips for better heat dissipation.

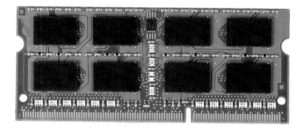

© iStockphoto.com/GeniusKp

Figure 2.6   A small outline DIMM (SO-DIMM) is used in notebook computers.

System memory actions are synchronized with the system clock in modern PCs, just as the actions of the CPU are. Therefore, the system memory used in today's systems is often referred to as synchronous dynamic RAM (SDRAM).

The slowest and most basic type of SDRAM is single data rate (SDR). This RAM moves one word of data per tick of the system clock. SDR SDRAM is found only in older systems.

Double data rate (DDR) SDRAM performs two actions per clock tick. DDR2 SDRAM doubles that even further, and can perform four actions per clock tick, and DDR3 SDRAM doubles it again, to eight actions. You might guess that DDR4 doubles it again, but it doesn't; DDR4 contains some technical improvements over DDR3 but keeps the same data rate. Each type of DIMM has a different number of pins, so these DIMMs aren't physically interchangeable. A motherboard typically supports only one type of DIMM.

Memory capacity is described in bytes (usually megabytes or gigabytes). SDRAM DIMMs come in different capacities, such as 2GB or 4GB. An average desktop PC might have 4GB to 8GB of system memory, which might be installed in either two or four DIMM slots.

Upgrading Memory

Don't assume that you can add more memory to your computer. Some computers may already have the maximum memory installed that their motherboard will accept. And in other systems, upgrading the memory means replacing the currently installed memory with higher-capacity DIMMs. Suppose you have a desktop PC with two RAM slots in the motherboard, and each slot currently contains a 2GB DIMM. If you want to upgrade to more RAM, you would need to remove the 2GB DIMMs and replace them with 4GB DIMMs—assuming, of course, that the motherboard supported 4GB DIMMs, which isn't a given. You would need to check the PC's documentation, or look up the motherboard's specs online. You might be able to trade in the 2GB DIMMs at a computer shop for a discount on the 4GB DIMMs, or you might be able to sell them to some other computer user.

TIP The 32-bit version of Windows can support only 4GB of RAM. If your computer has more than that, make sure you have the 64-bit version of Windows or some of your RAM will be unused. Sometimes the motherboard has a limit on the amount of RAM that can be recognized, so check your computer's documentation before you rush out and buy more RAM.

Quick Review

1. What is the difference between static and dynamic memory?

2. What is a DIMM?

3. In SDRAM, what does the "S" stand for, and what does it mean about the speed at which the RAM operates?

Understanding Motherboards

motherboard A large circuit board inside a computer that controls the operations of all other components.

Both the CPU and the memory plug into the motherboard. Motherboards vary in many ways, including the CPUs and memory they support, the technology used in their chipset, the expansion slots they have, and the external ports they support.

chipset The controller chip on a circuit board.

The motherboard's capabilities are determined by its chipset. The chipset contains the controllers that direct the traffic along the motherboard's buses, specify which memory and CPUs the motherboard can accept, and route data to expansion slots and ports as needed.

A motherboard typically supports only one brand of CPU, and only a limited array of specific CPU models (usually one or two models with allowances made for various speeds). It also usually supports only one kind of RAM, in a few different capacities. Table 2.2 lists the specifications for an Intel motherboard, for example. Figure 2.7 shows a motherboard that is similar to the specs shown.

Table 2.2: Example Motherboard Specifications

Form factor	ATX (12" x 9.6")
CPUs supported	i7-990X, i7-908X, i7-980, i7-975, i7-970, i7-965, i7-960, i7-950, i7-940, i7-930, i7-920
Built-in audio support	Intel High Definition Audio subsystem
	Three analog audio ports (3.5mm ports)
Memory	Two 240-pin DDR3 SDRAM sockets
	Support for DDR3 1600 MHz, 1333 MHz, or 1066 MHz RAM
	Support for up to 8 GB of system memory
Built-in video support	ATI CrossFire display adapter built into motherboard
	VGA and DVI ports
Built-in Ethernet support	Gigabit LAN subsystem
	RJ-45 port
Expansion slots	Two PCI slots One PCI Express x16 slot One PCI Express x4 slot
External ports	Four USB 2.0 ports Two PS/2 ports (keyboard and mouse) RCA audio ports
Disk drive connectors	Four internal Serial ATA connectors One 40-pin Parallel ATA connector

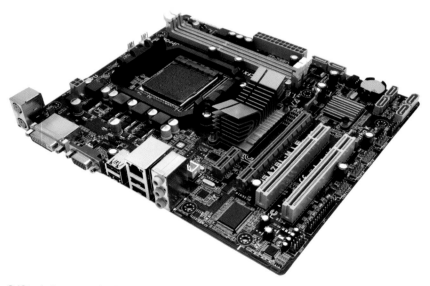

Figure 2.7   A typical motherboard.

Form Factor

The form factor of the motherboard is its physical size and shape. It is significant because the motherboard must be able to physically fit into the system unit case. The motherboard described in Table 2.2 supports several different CPUs, but most of them are the same basic CPU at different speeds: the Intel i7.

form factor The size and shape of a circuit board, such as a motherboard.

Expansion Slots

expansion slot A slot in the motherboard into which an expansion card (a small circuit board) can be installed.

expansion card A small circuit board that fits into a slot on the motherboard to add functionality.

Peripheral Component Interface (PCI) A motherboard slot that accepts PCI expansion boards. PCI is considered a legacy interface (mostly obsolete).

PCI Express (PCIe) A new and updated version of the PCI motherboard slot. Different numbers of channels are used in different sized PCIe slots, such as 16, 4, or 1.

Expansion slots are plastic slots on the motherboard. Inside the slots are metal contacts that connect with metal contacts on smaller circuit boards called expansion cards that fit into them. There are many expansion devices you can buy, adding capabilities that might not be built into the motherboard, or adding a more feature-rich version of a built-in device. For example, you might add a Wi-Fi adapter to a desktop PC with an expansion card, or a dial-up modem, or you might replace the on-board display adapter built into your motherboard with a model that has a faster graphics processor.

Different motherboards have different numbers and types of slots. Each slot type has its own separate bus, delivering its own combination of width and speed. Recall from Chapter 1 that a bus is a data pathway within a circuit board. Some buses are parallel, meaning they can carry multiple bits simultaneously. For example, the system bus is usually 64-bit. Other buses are serial, meaning they are only one lane, and carry only one bit at a time.

The motherboard described in Table 2.2 has three expansion slots: one conventional Peripheral Component Interface (PCI) slot (an older type of slot, for backward compatibility with older devices) and two of a newer type, PCI Express (PCIe). PCIe slots come in different widths, such as x16 (16 channels, used mostly for display adapters) and x4 and x1 (used mostly for non-display components). Those numbers refer to the number of channels of data that can be carried simultaneously. Figure 2.8 shows some slots in a different motherboard; this one has one x1, one x4, and two x16 slots, as well as one regular PCI slot.

Photo by Snickerdo; licensed under Creative Commons.

Figure 2.8   PCI and PCIe slots in a motherboard.

Notebook PCs are more likely than desktops to have a wide variety of built-in components, so there is less need for expansion slots. That's good, because there's not much room for them.

On a notebook PC, there might be an externally accessible expansion slot called an ExpressCard slot. ExpressCards are small circuit boards encased in a metal cartridge. They add device capabilities to notebook PCs in much the same way that expansion slots do in desktop PCs. Over the last two decades, there have been other versions of this same basic technology, called PC Card and CardBus, which accepted slightly different-sized cards. ExpressCard slots are waning in popularity, and many new notebook computers do not have them.

There also might be a removable panel on a notebook PC with a PCI Express Mini Card socket, into which you can install a small expansion board that uses the motherboard's internal PCIe bus. One common use for this type of socket is to add a Wi-Fi adapter. Figure 2.9 shows a PCI Express Mini Card and its connector.

ExpressCard A metal cartridge inserted into an externally accessible slot in a notebook PC that adds a capability to the system, such as wireless networking.

PCI Express Mini Card A small circuit board that can be installed in a notebook PC's PCI Express Mini expansion bay to add a capability to the computer, such as wireless networking.

Photo by Bastiaan van den Berg; licensed under Creative Commons.
Figure 2.9 A PCI Express Mini Card.

Built-in Components

Notice that the motherboard described in Table 2.2 also has built-in components for video, audio, and networking. Having these components built in means that you don't need to buy separate circuit boards for those capabilities, and you don't need expansion slots for such cards. That is one reason the motherboards in Table 2.2 and Figure 2.7 don't have many expansion slots—they don't need many because the three most commonly added expansion features are already built in.

 Each of those three built-in components has its own external ports built into the motherboard. The display adapter may have a Digital Visual Interface (DVI) connector, a Video Graphics Adapter (VGA) connector, or both. DVI is the newer, digital type of monitor connector used with digital monitors (which include most flat-screen LCD monitors); VGA is the older, analog type used with the boxy older CRT style of monitor and with some older or inexpensive LCD monitors.

Digital Visual Interface (DVI) A digital port for connecting a monitor to a PC.

Video Graphics Adapter An analog port for connecting a monitor to a PC.

The audio component support results in several small (3.5mm) round external connectors for plugging in speakers, headphones, and microphones. They are usually color-coded: pink for microphone, green for speakers or headphones, and blue for line input.

The Ethernet support results in an RJ-45 jack as an external connector. An RJ-45 jack looks like a telephone connector but is slightly wider and has eight metal contacts in it, rather than the two or four of a telephone connector.

Other Common External Connectors

The motherboard described in Table 2.2 has only a few types of external ports, which is typical of newer systems. Universal Serial Bus (USB) is the most common multipurpose port type; many devices use USB ports, including keyboards, mice, and printers. The word *serial* in the name refers to the fact that the data travels through the cable one bit at a time. There are different generations of USB, with different speeds. This motherboard's USB ports are all version 2.0 (also called Hi-Speed USB). Table 2.3 notes the speed for each version.

Universal Serial Bus (USB) A general-purpose port for connecting external devices to a PC.

Table 2.3: USB Versions and Speeds

Version	Speed
USB 1.1	1.5 megabits per second
USB 2.0	48 megabits per second
USB 3.0	4 gigabits per second

NOTE Data transfer speed from a serial device is usually expressed in bits, rather than bytes, as in Mbit/sec, which stands for megabits per second.

This motherboard also supports one IEEE 1394A port, also called a FireWire port. FireWire is a competitor to USB. It has not caught on quite as widely, but it is used for some external hard drives and digital video equipment.

IEEE 1394A A connector used to connect certain types of devices to a computer that require high-speed connection, such as some external hard drives and video cameras. A competitor to USB. Also called FireWire.

Older systems may have a variety of other external ports, for backward compatibility with older devices. Motherboards with these older ports are still available today, but they are becoming less and less common. The most common legacy ports are:

PS/2 port: This is a small round port that used to be used for mice and keyboards before USB became popular. They are usually color-coded: purple for the keyboard and green for the mouse.

PS/2 port A connector used to connect some older keyboards and mice to a computer. PS stands for Personal System. This connector was first introduced with the IBM PS/2 computer in 1987.

Parallel (LPT) port: This is a 25-pin connector, with the holes arranged in two rows. It used to be used for printers before USB became the dominant interface for printers. The port on the computer is a female connector, meaning it has holes; the

parallel port A port used to connect some older printers to a computer. It is sometimes called an LPT port, which stands for Line Printer.

connector on the cable that plugs into it is a male connector, containing pins that fit in the holes. This type of connector is sometimes called a DB-25 connector.

Serial (COM) port: This is a 9-pin connector (DB-9), with the pins arranged in two rows. It is a male connector on the motherboard, and the cable that plugs into it is female. This type of port used to be an all-purpose port for a variety of external devices, much like USB is today.

Drive Connectors

Most motherboards have two types of drive connectors. The older type is Parallel ATA (PATA), and it is used with older hard drives and most CD and DVD drives. This type of connector has 40 pins arranged in two rows, and uses a ribbon cable to connect the device to the motherboard.

The newer type is Serial ATA (SATA), a more compact connector that uses a thin round cable. SATA is used with newer hard drives. You will learn more about drive connectors in Chapter 3, "Input, Output, and Storage."

serial port A port used to connect some very old external devices to a computer. It is sometimes called a COM port, which stands for Communications (although actually many types of ports operate serially, not just this one).

ATA Short for AT Attachment. The IBM PC AT was an early type of computer (1984) that was among the first to support modern hard drive technology.

Parallel ATA (PATA) A type of connector used for older disk drives and optical drives such as CD and DVD drives.

Serial ATA (SATA) A type of connector used for newer disk drives.

Step by Step

Exploring Your Motherboard

Use this procedure to see what components and connectors your motherboard has. Use a desktop computer for this exercise.

1. Shut down the computer, and open up the system unit. You may need a Phillips screwdriver. Ask your instructor for assistance if needed. **Do not touch anything inside the system unit.**

2. Locate the following components. Ask your instructor to confirm that you are correct:

   - CPU (may be under a fan)
   - System memory
   - Built-in USB ports
   - Other built-in ports (name them if you can)
   - Expansion slots (identify the type if you can)

3. Trace each cable from the motherboard to the components to see how components such as the hard drive and power supply attach to the motherboard.

4. Close the system unit's case and replace any screws you removed.

Quick Review

1. What does a motherboard's chipset do?

2. If you see a DVI port built into a motherboard, what type of capability can you assume is built into the motherboard?

3. What is PCI Express (PCIe)?

Understanding Power Supplies

The power from your wall outlet is alternating current (AC), and is either 110 volt (v) or 220v, depending on the country in which you live. Computer components require direct current (DC) and require much lower voltages. A power supply has two jobs:

power supply A component that converts AC power from a wall outlet to DC power and decreases the voltage to the level needed for the computer to operate.

- It converts AC to DC power.
- It decreases the voltage to the amount required for each component.

> **NOTE** Alternating current (AC) constantly switches the polarity between positive and negative through the wires. AC is able to travel great distances reliably and economically without losing its strength, which is why it is the type delivered to homes and businesses. Direct current (DC) does not alternate the polarity; the positive always sends power, and the neutral (ground) always receives it back. Batteries generate DC current, for example; DC power cannot travel very far without degrading.

In a desktop PC, a power supply is a large silver metal box mounted in one corner of the system unit, with many bundles of colored wires and connectors emerging from it (see Figure 2.10). The wire colors are significant; each wire color carries a different voltage. Each connector has the appropriate wires running to it to deliver the exact voltage required for each connected device. Table 2.4 summarizes the most common wire colors and their uses. Of these, the most common are the first three: red, yellow, and black. The connector shown in Figure 2.11, for example, uses one red wire, one yellow wire, and two black wires. The power comes in on the red and yellow wires, and the black wires are for grounding.

A desktop PC's power supply has a fan in it, and when you start up the PC, the fan starts up too. The fan pulls hot air out of the power supply, and has a side benefit of circulating air through the entire system unit too.

© iStockphoto.com/DonNichols

Figure 2.10   A desktop PC's power supply.

© iStockphoto.com/aarrows

Figure 2.11   A power connector for a Serial ATA (SATA) hard drive. The drive requires both +5 and +12 power, supplied on the red and yellow wires, respectively.

Table 2.4: Voltages for Common Power Supply Wire Colors

Wire Color	Voltage
Black	Ground/Neutral
Red	+5v
Yellow	+12v
White	-5v
Blue	-12v

In addition to the several types of connectors that go to internal devices such as drives, the power supply also has one big connector, containing 20 or more wires arranged in two rows. Figure 2.12 shows an example. This connector plugs directly into the motherboard, and powers all its components that do not have separate power connectors.

© iStockphoto.com/ebrink

Figure 2.12 This connector runs from the power supply to the motherboard, delivering all the different voltages that devices that connect directly into the motherboard might need.

On a notebook PC, the power supply is built in. The power cord typically contains a *transformer block* (sometimes called a brick) that steps down and converts the voltage. Figure 2.13 shows an example. When a notebook PC is plugged into AC power, its battery recharges. The battery automatically

© iStockphoto.com/Nickondr

Figure 2.13 A power cord for a notebook PC includes a transformer block that converts the power to the type and voltage needed.

transformer block A thick block built into a power cable for a device that handles the conversion of AC power to DC and steps down the voltage to the level needed.

provides DC power at the correct voltage, so no power conversion is needed when running on battery power.

Troubleshooting Common System Unit Problems

When your computer won't start up, it can be an annoying or even frightening experience. It is not always obvious what is wrong with it. By understanding some of the common symptoms of problems, however, you can make a more educated guess when problems occur, and you might even be able to fix the problem yourself.

No Response

If the computer doesn't show any signs of life when you press its Power button (no lights and no fan noises), it is most likely not receiving electricity. Check the outlet, the power cord, and the power strip (if you are using one) to make sure there is no break in the connection. Some power strips have on/off switches.

After you have confirmed that electricity is not the issue, try holding down the PC's Power button for 10 seconds and then releasing it. Then press the Power button again normally to try again to turn the computer on. If the PC has

© iStockphoto.com/BenThomasPhoto

placed itself into a low-power mode such as Sleep and gotten stuck there, holding down the Power button will turn off the computer completely, releasing it from that mode.

If you are working with a mobile device such as a smartphone or tablet, check online for instructions about how to do a system reset for your device. It may involve holding down multiple buttons at the same time, for example. Most devices have both a soft reset and a hard reset option. A soft reset restarts the device and preserves your data. A hard reset wipes out all the data and customization on your device, restoring it to its original factory settings. A hard reset is sometimes necessary if a device locks up and can't be revived; this can happen if a system update goes wrong, for example, or if you install an application that corrupts system settings.

soft reset A device reset that retains all the device's settings and data.

hard reset A device reset that wipes out all custom data and settings, returning the device's software to its factory-new condition.

A defective power supply, CPU, or motherboard can also cause a system to seem completely dead. If you have tried all the earlier suggestions, the next step is to consult a computer professional to help you determine the root cause of the problem.

Fan Noise but Nothing Onscreen

When you turn the computer on, if you see lights flas.h on its buttons or hear its fans spinning but you see nothing onscreen, check to make sure the monitor is connected properly and powered on. If the monitor is okay, then the device is receiving power but it is unable to complete its power-on self test (POST). The POST is a software procedure built into the BIOS; the device must pass this basic internal testing before the operating system can load.

If you have this problem after installing new hardware, the new hardware is probably at fault. Try removing it and then restarting to see if the system boots correctly without the device. Then try reinstalling the device. If the problem starts again, the device may be defective or incompatible with your computer.

As the computer starts up, it is normal for it to beep once. If you hear multiple beeps, you may have a problem with memory. You may have recently installed some memory that is incompatible with your motherboard, or you may have installed it incorrectly.

Because there is no error message, this is a difficult type of error to troubleshoot on your own. A computer professional may want to use a POST card, which is an expansion board that fits into one of the motherboard's empty expansion slots. The card monitors the start-up process and displays a two-digit code that describes the point at which the start-up process has stalled. The POST card comes with a manual that deciphers the codes. For example, the code may indicate that the memory is at fault, or the CPU, or the motherboard itself.

power-on self test (POST) A low-level hardware test that occurs at start-up, before the operating system loads.

POST card An expansion board that is placed in an empty expansion slot in a motherboard; it displays a numeric code that helps in troubleshooting errors where no text appears onscreen.

Error Message on a Black Screen

If you see some gray or white text on a black background, that's good—it means that your system passed its POST. If the start-up stalls in this mode, and displays an error message, it means that either your system is having a problem with a specific component or it can't find and start the operating system. You might see a *Keyboard Stuck* message, for example, if you have something sitting on your keyboard that is making one or more of the keys seem pressed. A *No Operating System* or *Non-System Disk Error* message could mean that your hard drive does not contain an operating system, or it could mean that the start-up process could not find your hard drive. Perhaps it is defective, or perhaps its connector has come loose. A common reason for the Non-System Disk error is that you may have left a USB flash drive or external drive connected and the system is trying to load the operating system from this device. Remove the device and then restart the system.

If you see an error message at start-up, research it online. You can usually find advice on the web that will help you troubleshoot.

Some of the solutions you may find online may suggest that you view or change settings in your CMOS Setup program (sometimes called BIOS Setup). This utility is built into your motherboard. You can access it at start-up by pressing the key that activates it. There should be a message onscreen at start-up telling you what key that is. (It might be F1, for example.) If you press this key quickly when you see that message, the BIOS Setup program starts.

CMOS Setup A built-in setup utility in the motherboard that enables users to adjust certain low-level configuration settings.

NOTE

Perhaps you are wondering why the motherboard's setup utility is called CMOS Setup. CMOS stands for Complementary Metal Oxide Semiconductor. It's a type of RAM chip that requires very little electricity to maintain. In the early days of PCs, the BIOS chip was completely unchangeable, so system designers needed a way to store the settings that users wanted to make to the low-level settings, such as the date, time, hard drive type, and so on. The motherboard had a CMOS chip that stored those settings, powered by a small battery on the motherboard. When the battery died, all your motherboard custom settings were erased and you had to reenter them. Motherboards no longer have CMOS chips today because the BIOS is on an EEPROM chip that can be updated, but the setup utility is still called CMOS Setup.

There are many different CMOS Setup versions, and they all work a little differently, so read the instructions onscreen for navigating the program. Figure 2.14 shows a generic example. You might be able to use the arrow keys on your keyboard to move a cursor around in the program, or you might be able to use your mouse to select options.

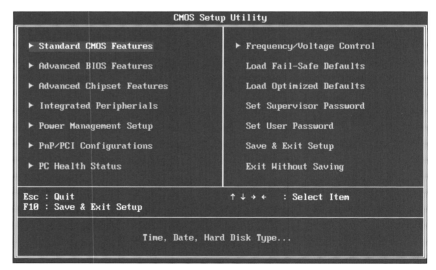

Figure 2.14 One example of a CMOS Setup utility; yours may look very different.

The BIOS Setup program enables you to adjust low-level system settings that control how your motherboard works and how it interacts with the hardware. For example, you can change the boot order of the system, specifying which drive it should try to boot from first at start-up. You can also enable or disable built-in components such as video, audio, and networking; turn certain ports on and off; and control how the motherboard reports the hardware to the operating system.

After making changes, exit the utility, saving your changes. It is usual for F10 to be the shortcut key for saving and exiting in CMOS Setup programs, but check for an onscreen message, as in Figure 2.14.

Instead of a traditional BIOS, some newer computers have Unified Extensible Firmware Interface (UEFI). UEFI is very similar to a BIOS, and configured in basically the same way. However, the process for entering the UEFI setup is different from entering BIOS/CMOS setup on a Windows 8.1 system. Instead of pressing a startup key, you go through Windows to boot into UEFI.

Step by Step

Exploring Your CMOS Setup

Use the following procedure to boot into CMOS setup and see what settings can be changed.

1. Restart your computer, and watch the screen carefully for a message that tells you what key to press to enter setup. It may be a function key (F1 through F12). When you see the message, press the key as quickly as possible. If Windows begins to start, you missed the opportunity; after Windows finishes loading, shut down and try again. If Windows starts up without showing you the key to press, use the following procedure "Accessing UEFI Setup from Windows 8.1."

2. In the CMOS Setup program, determine how to move between options. For example, you might use the arrow keys. There should be onscreen messages to instruct you.

3. Determine how to change an option. For example, you might press Enter after highlighting an option to open a menu of choices, and then use the arrow keys to select one of the menu choices.

4. Determine how to move between sections. Most CMOS Setup programs are organized into multiple sections or pages.

5. Determine how to exit CMOS Setup without saving your changes. There should be an onscreen message with this information.

6. Exit CMOS Setup without saving your changes.

Accessing UEFI Setup from Windows 8.1

Use this if Windows 8.1 doesn't show you a key to press at startup to enter CMOS setup.

1. Select the Settings charm.

2. Select Change PC Settings.

3. In the navigation pane at the left, select Update and Recovery.

4. In the navigation pane at the left, select Recovery.

5. Under the Advanced startup heading, select Restart Now. Wait for the PC to restart.

6. At the Choose an option screen, select Troubleshoot.

7. At the Troubleshoot screen, select Advanced Options.

8. At the Advanced Options screen, select UEFI Firmware Settings.

9. At the UEFI Firmware Settings screen, click Restart.

10. Return to Step 2 under "Exploring Your CMOS Setup."

Error Message on a Bright Blue Screen

If your operating system is Microsoft Windows, you might see a text error message with gray or white text on a bright blue background. This error usually reports a serious hardware or memory problem that prevents Windows from starting (or continuing, if you get this while Windows is already running). Some people call this type of message a "blue screen of death," or BSOD. Figure 2.15 shows an example. All you can do when this error occurs is turn your computer off at the Power button, and then restart it and hope that the error doesn't recur. If you see the same message multiple times, and you have recently installed new hardware, remove it; it is incompatible with your system or is malfunctioning. If you haven't done anything different recently, look up the error message's code online for troubleshooting help, or consult a computer professional.

```
A problem has been detected and Windows has been shut down to prevent damage
to your computer.

PFN_LIST_CORRUPT

If this is the first time you've seen this Stop error screen,
restart your computer. If this screen appears again, follow
these steps:

Check to make sure any new hardware or software is properly installed.
If this is a new installation, ask your hardware or software manufacturer
for any Windows updates you might need.

If problems continue, disable or remove any newly installed hardware
or software. Disable BIOS memory options such as caching or shadowing.
If you need to use Safe Mode to remove or disable components, restart
your computer, press F8 to select Advanced Startup Options, and then
select Safe Mode.

Technical information:
*** STOP: 0x0000004e (0x00000099, 0x00900009, 0x00000900, 0x00000900)


Beginning dump of physical memory
Physical memory dump complete.
Contact your system administrator or technical support group for further
assistance.
```

Figure 2.15   A "blue screen of death" error message.

Windows Hangs at Start-up

If you get past the black or blue text-based screens to the Starting Windows graphic, but then Windows doesn't start up correctly, the problem is likely a Windows setting. See the section "Troubleshooting Start-up and Performance Problems" in Chapter 6 for help starting the computer in Safe Mode and figuring out what driver or application may be causing the problem.

PC Shuts Down or Freezes

If your system frequently shuts down or locks up after it has been operating for about 10 to 15 minutes, overheating is the most common cause. Many of the components in the system unit get hot as they operate, especially the CPU, the graphics processor, and the larger chips involved in the motherboard's chipset. Some chips that get especially hot have aluminum or copper blocks on top of them with baffles (ridges or wings) to increase the amount of surface that air touches. These blocks

© iStockphoto.com/scanrail

are called heat sinks; they work by channeling heat away from the hot component; the air around the heat sink picks up the heat. In an active heat sink, a fan then blows that hot air away. In a passive heat sink, there is no fan; passive heat sinks rely on other fans nearby that are cooling the system unit in general to carry the heat away. If a component is overheating, you may have a defective fan in one of your active heat sinks. Try looking inside the system unit when the PC is running to see if you can identify a fan that isn't spinning. Another thing to check is to make sure the fan is not blocked with dust. The fans are designed to pull air in from the outside to cool the components. They also import dirt and dust, which can block the fans.

heat sink A copper or aluminum block that diverts heat away from a heat-generating component such as a CPU. When not paired with a fan, called a passive heat sink.

active heat sink A heat sink that is paired with a fan.

Quick Review

1. How do you determine what key to press at start-up to enter CMOS Setup?

2. What are the symptoms of overheating?

3. What is a BSOD?

Summary

Understanding CPUs

A **central processing unit (CPU)** contains a **control unit**, an **arithmetic logic unit (ALU)**, and **registers**. They work together in a process called a **machine cycle**, which consists of fetching, decoding, executing, and storing. The CPU operates at the pace dictated by the **system clock**, executing billions of operations per second. One tick of that clock is a **clock cycle**. When the CPU sits idle during a clock cycle because it is waiting for data it needs, that wait time is called **latency**. To minimize latency, CPUs have multiple **caches**, including L1, L2, and L3.

Physically, the CPU is a **semiconductor** wafer of silicon. Most modern CPUs have multiple **cores**; each core has its own control unit, ALU, and registers. A CPU has a maximum speed, measured in **gigahertz (GHz)**. When a CPU is run faster than it is rated for, it is being **overclocked**, and overheating and reliability problems can result. A CPU's **word size** is the number of bits it can accept as input simultaneously. Modern CPUs in personal computers are usually either 32-bit or 64-bit. Windows is available in both 32-bit and 64-bit versions. CPU performance can be described in the number of **instructions per second** it can process, but it is more reliably measured using **benchmarking** software.

Understanding Memory

Memory can be either **dynamic** (losing its data when it loses power) or **static** (retaining its data). **Random access memory (RAM)** can be freely rewritten, and can be either static or dynamic. **Read-only memory (ROM)** is always static. **Electrically Erasable Programmable ROM (EEPROM)** is a type of ROM that can be changed with electricity; flash memory and solid-state hard drives employ a type of EEPROM.

System memory resides on the motherboard and is used as a work area for the operating system. Some components also have their own memory. **Virtual memory** is hard drive space that simulates extra memory by allowing the operating system to swap data into and out of the real memory into a **swap file**.

Physically, system memory comes in **dual inline memory modules (DIMMs)**. They are synchronous with the system clock, making them **synchronous dynamic RAM (SDRAM)**. SDRAM can be **single data rate (SDR), double data rate (DDR)**, DDR2, DDR3, or DDR4. DDR RAM can perform two actions per clock tick.

Understanding Motherboards

The **motherboard**'s capabilities are determined by its **chipset**. A motherboard's **form factor** is its physical size.

Motherboards have **expansion slots**, each type of slot having its own **bus** on the motherboard. **Peripheral Component Interface (PCI)** is an older type of expansion slot; a newer type is **PCI Express (PCIe)**, which comes in a variety of sizes based on the number of channels, such as x1, x4, or x16. Some notebook computers have **ExpressCard** slots or **PCI Express Mini Card** slots.

Some of the ports that a motherboard may have built in include **Digital Visual Interface (DVI)** and **Video Graphics Adapter (VGA)** for video, 3.5mm analog plugs for audio, and **RJ-45** for Ethernet networking. Internally, a motherboard has connectors for disk drives, including **Parallel ATA (PATA)** and **Serial ATA (SATA)**.

A **Universal Serial Bus (USB)** port is a general-purpose expansion port. There are three variants: 1.1, 2.0, and 3.0. Each has different speed capabilities, with USB 3.0 being the fastest. **IEEE**

1394A, also called FireWire, is an alternative to USB, and is used on some external hard drives and digital video cameras. Older ports that a system might have include **PS/2**, **parallel (LPT)**, and **serial (COM)**.

Understanding Power Supplies

The computer's **power supply** converts AC to DC power and steps down the voltage to the amount required. The colors of the wires on the connectors on the power supply are significant, indicating different voltages. On a notebook PC, a **transformer block** built into the power cable provides the same functions as the power supply in a desktop PC.

Troubleshooting Common System Unit Problems

If the computer has no power, check for electrical connectivity. Try holding down the power button on the computer for 10 seconds to clear any low-power mode the computer may have gotten stuck in. Find instructions in your device's documentation to do a **soft reset** or **hard reset** as needed.

If you don't see anything onscreen, your computer has failed its **power-on self test (POST)**. A computer professional may be able to diagnose it with a **POST card**. Some fixes may require you to enter **CMOS Setup** to change or check a setting. A message at start-up will tell you what key to press to enter CMOS Setup. Overheating problems can occur when fans stop working, especially fans on **active heat sinks**.

Key Terms

active heat sink
benchmark
cache
Central Processing Unit (CPU)
chipset
CMOS setup
core
Digital Visual Interface (DVI)
double data rate (DDR)
dual inline memory module (DIMM)
dynamic memory
Electrically Erasable Programmable ROM (EEPROM)
expansion card
expansion slot
ExpressCard
form factor
gigahertz (GHz)
hard reset
heat sink
hertz
IEEE 1394A
instructions per second
latency
machine cycle
memory address
motherboard
overclock

paging file
Parallel ATA
parallel port
PCI Express (PCIe)
PCI Express Mini Card
Peripheral Component Interface (PCI)
POST card
power supply
power-on self test (POST)
PS/2 port
Random Access Memory (RAM)
Read-Only Memory (ROM)
semiconductor
Serial ATA
serial port
single data rate (SDR)
soft reset
static memory
swap file
synchronous dynamic RAM (SDRAM)
system clock
system memory
transformer block
Universal Serial Bus (USB)
Video Graphics Adapter (VGA)
virtual memory
word size

Test Yourself

Fact Check

1. _____ are data holding areas inside the CPU.

    a. Control units

    b. ALUs

    c. DVIs

    d. Registers

2. A(n) _____ consists of these steps: fetch, decode, execute, store.

    a. system unit

    b. information cycle

    c. machine cycle

    d. ALU

3. L1, L2, and L3 are all types of CPU _____.

    a. ALUs

    b. cores

    c. registers

    d. caches

4. The memory in a USB flash drive is a type of _____.

    a. DRAM

    b. EEPROM

    c. SRAM

    d. CPU

5. A(n) _____ is a circuit board containing memory chips.

    a. CPU

    b. DDR

    c. DIMM

    d. SDR

6. The motherboard's capabilities are determined by its chipset.

    a. True

    b. False

7. DVI and VGA are both types of _____ ports.

    a. sound

    b. network

    c. display

    d. printer

8. True or false: An active heat sink includes a cooling fan.

   a. True

   b. False

9. The two main functions of a _____ are to convert AC power to DC power and decrease the voltage of the electricity entering the computer.

10. When does the POST occur at start-up?

    a. Before any text appears onscreen.

    b. After text appears onscreen, but before Windows begins to load.

    c. After Windows begins to load, but before it finishes loading.

    d. After Windows finishes loading.

Matching

Match the memory-related term to its definition.

   a. DIMM

   b. L1 cache

   c. ROM-BIOS

   d. SDRAM

   e. system memory

   f. virtual memory

1. _____ The main memory in a computer, used as the RAM installed on the motherboard.

2. _____ The EEPROM chip that contains the low-level start-up instructions for the hardware.

3. _____ Static RAM inside the CPU that holds data that may be needed again shortly.

4. _____ A swap file on the hard drive for data temporarily removed from memory.

5. _____ A rectangular circuit board containing memory chips.

6. _____ RAM that operates synchronously with the system clock.

Sum It Up

1. What are the three basic components inside a CPU?

2. What are the four steps of the machine cycle, and how do the parts you named in #1 fit into it?

3. How do the L1, L2, and L3 caches improve CPU performance?

4. What is the difference between static and dynamic memory?

5. What are four ways in which one motherboard may differ from another?

6. Why does a power supply have different colored wires?

Explore More

Download the free 2014 version of SiSoftware SANDRA, a benchmarking utility, from www.sisoftware.net.

If you have time (at least 30 minutes), run the Overall Score test. If not, run only the Processor Arithmetic test and the Cache & Memory Latency tests. Examine the results, and compare them to the results of your classmates who are using different computers.

What is the Aggregated Score for processor arithmetic? This score is represented in GOPS (giga-operation per second).

What is the rated speed and type of the CPU? In Windows, click the Start button, and then right-click Computer and choose Properties. Note the processor information that appears on that screen. Does it match what the utility detected?

What is the memory latency score? Notice the L1, L2, and L3 cache scores are expressed in "clocks." This means that those caches, on average, take that many clock cycles to retrieve from. Compare the results to Table 2.1's averages. How did your CPU's caches do?

If time permits, run other benchmarks using this utility; your instructor may assign additional tests to complete.

Completing a System Inventory

Using the categories listed in Table 2.2 as a basis, create a description of your system's mother-board, as completely as you can describe it. If you can find its model number (usually stamped on the board itself), look it up online to see if its specs are available. If not, do your best to deduce its characteristics by looking at what ports are built in and by using the System Information utility in Windows.

Exploring Power Voltages

To do this exploration, you will need a desktop PC and a voltmeter (or a multimeter that measures DC volts). Your instructor may need to guide you through the process. Wear an anti-static wrist strap or take other anti-static precautions as directed by your instructor.

1. Turn on your meter and set it to DC volts. You should have a red probe and a black probe.

2. Open the system unit case, and locate the large connector that joins the power supply to the motherboard.

3. Turn on the PC.

4. Insert the black probe down into one of the sockets where a black wire connects, so that the probe touches the bare metal wire.

5. Insert the red probe down into one of the sockets where a red wire connects, so that the probe touches the bare metal wire.

6. Read the display on the meter. It should be approximately +5v.

7. Repeat Steps 4–6 with several other wire colors, and record the readings you get.

8. Turn off the meter and put it away.

9. Turn off the computer, and close the system unit case.

Think It Over

Is Faster Always Desirable?

Is it important to you, when buying a new computer, to have the fastest and best CPU available, even if it costs more? Does it make more financial sense to pay more now for a CPU that will become obsolete less quickly a few years in the future? Or is it better to buy a lesser CPU, even if you have to replace the computer sooner because it will no longer be powerful enough to run the latest programs in a few years?

Shopping with Expandability in Mind

If you were buying a computer today, what expansion slots and ports would be important for your new computer to have, and why? That is, what device would you plan to install later that might need those slots or ports?

Self-Troubleshoot or Call a Professional?

Suppose your computer did not start up normally. How much time and effort are you willing to put into troubleshooting it yourself before you give up and involve a computer professional? Are you willing to spend an hour working on it? Two hours? Five or more? At what point it is worth the money to pay to have it fixed? There is no right or wrong answer, but explain your decision.

Chapter 3

Input, Output, and Storage

Learning objectives

☐ Define input and describe the available types of keyboards and pointing devices

☐ Describe scanning and image-capturing device types and features

☐ Define output and explain the types of output devices available

☐ Differentiate between types of monitors and explain their features

☐ Differentiate between types of printers and identify the best printer for a task

☐ Classify storage devices according to their capacities, interface, and media

☐ Explain cloud and network storage, and identify online and network-based storage technologies

Selecting and Using Input Devices

Selecting and Using Output Devices

Choosing Appropriate Storage Devices

Chapter 2 explained the inner workings of a computer inside the mysterious box known as the system unit. In this chapter, you'll look at how data moves into and out of that system unit—via input and output devices.

Different kinds of computers accept input from different sources. For example, a desktop PC might have a keyboard and mouse, whereas a tablet PC or smartphone might have a touch screen and some built-in buttons. Output can include messages and data that appear on the monitor screen, a hard-copy printout, and audio cues or prompts the computer might generate, such as a warning beep or the playback of your favorite song. Storage devices hold information for later use; they vary by capacity, by interface, and by the medium used to store the files.

In this chapter, you will learn about the types of input, output, and storage devices available, and how to choose the right one for a particular computer system and task.

Database Administrator

Businesses store large amounts of data, and that data is often much more valuable than the hardware on which it is stored. Information about customers, orders, product inventory, suppliers, and market trends must be readily and reliably available for the business to thrive. A database administrator is an expert in managing, summarizing, and safeguarding large amounts of data. Database administrators also plan and create well-organized database systems for storing new and existing data. For this career, a Bachelor of Science or Associate of Science degree in an Information Technology-related field would be useful.

© iStockphoto.com/bjdlzx

Selecting and Using Input Devices

Whenever you type a letter in a word processor or issue the command to open or close the word processing program, you use an input device. Input devices allow the user to communicate with the operating system and applications. In this section, you will learn about several types of input devices.

input device Hardware that enables the computer to accept commands or data from a human user.

Keyboards

A keyboard enables you to enter typed data—letters, numbers, and symbols. A keyboard can be a separate device that plugs into the system unit (as with a desktop PC) or a built-in keyboard (as with a notebook PC).

There are many sizes and types of keyboards, but most English-language keyboards use the same key arrangement, called QWERTY. The name comes from the first six letter keys on the top row of letters, from left to right. Figure 3.1 shows a QWERTY keyboard.

QWERTY The standard layout for English-language keyboards.

This type of keyboard has a number of specialty keys as well as the numbers, letters, and symbols. Specialty keys include:

- **Function keys** (F1 through F12) perform special actions when pressed. The action assigned to each key depends on the operating system or application you are using.

© iStockphoto.com/Youst

Figure 3.1 The QWERTY keyboard layout.

- **Toggle keys** turn a feature on or off each time they are pressed. For example, the Caps Lock key toggles between upper- and lower-case letter typing mode, and the Num Lock key toggles between the numeric keypad on the keyboard (if it has one) providing number entry or functioning as a set of directional arrows.

- **Modifier keys** change the meaning of other keys when they are pressed in combination with them. For example, the Shift key, when pressed in combination with a letter, makes that letter uppercase. Other keys, such as Ctrl and Alt, can be used with other keys to issue special command shortcuts. For example, a common keyboard shortcut in Windows is Ctrl+C (press both keys simultaneously) for copying selected content.

On a notebook computer, an Fn key may be present; it's an extra modifier key that allows you to access special functions assigned to certain keys. For example, you might see a sun symbol and an up arrow on one of the function keys. You could hold down Fn and press that function key to increase the brightness of the display. Check the manual that came with your notebook computer to find out more about the actions you can take with the Fn key.

NOTE

- **Positional keys** such as the Home, End, Page Up, and Page Down keys, as well as the directional arrow keys, scroll the display or move the insertion point in applications.

insertion point The flashing vertical line that indicates where typed text will appear

In Appendix B, "Customizing Windows 8.1," you will learn how to set up the operating system to use alternative keyboard layouts for different languages.

NOTE

wireless keyboard A keyboard that connects to the computer wirelessly rather than with a cable.

ergonomic keyboard A keyboard that is designed with features that help reduce stress on the user's hands and wrists.

A wireless keyboard does not require a cable connection to the computer, allowing for greater ease of use. An ergonomic keyboard is a keyboard that is designed to minimize the stress on the user's body (see Figure 3.2). It may have a built-in palm or wrist support, for example. A bilingual keyboard has characters in more than one language on its keys, so when you switch to a different keyboard layout in the operating system, the characters on the keyboard match what you are typing.

virtual or onscreen keyboard A replica of a keyboard on the screen that users can tap or click to simulate typing.

© iStockphoto.com/pengpeng

Figure 3.2   An ergonomic keyboard.

Step by Step

Using a Virtual Keyboard

Devices that don't have physical keyboards, like tablets and smartphones, use a virtual keyboard, which is a software replica of a keyboard that pops up on the touch screen. Even if you have a regular keyboard, you can still try out a virtual keyboard in Windows if you like. Follow these steps to use the virtual keyboard in Windows 8.1:

1. From the Start screen, type **key** and then click On-Screen Keyboard. A window appears showing a virtual keyboard.

2. Open an application in which you can type text, such as Notepad. To open Notepad, from the Start screen, type **notepad**, and then click Notepad.

3. Experiment with the keyboard by clicking keys to type the letters.

4. When you are finished, click the Close (X) button in the upper-left corner of the On-Screen Keyboard window.

5. Close the application you opened in Step 2 without saving your changes.

Pointing Devices

A pointing device is a piece of hardware that enables you to move an onscreen pointer in a graphical user interface like Microsoft Windows. A mouse is the most common pointing device. It is a palm-sized object that you move across a flat surface to move the pointer on the display. A mouse has one or more buttons on it; you press the buttons to act upon whatever the pointer is pointing at.

mouse A pointing device that the user moves with his or her hand across a flat surface to move an onscreen pointer.

A mouse can be either mechanical or optical. A mechanical mouse has a chamber on its underside with a rubber ball in it. As you roll the mouse across a flat surface, the ball turns, activating sensors inside the chamber that translate the ball's movement to onscreen pointer activity. An optical mouse has a light-emitting diode (LED) and a sensor on its underside, as shown in Figure 3.3. The light bounces off the surface and the sensor measures it, and those measurements are reported back to the computer to tell the pointer how to move. Mechanical mice need frequent cleaning; optical mice are maintenance-free and have virtually replaced the mechanical type.

© iStockphoto.com/luismmolina

Figure 3.3 The underside of an optical mouse contains a red light and a sensor that measures its reflection from the surface the mouse is used on.

mechanical mouse A mouse that operates by rolling a rubber ball inside a chamber containing sensors.

optical mouse A mouse that operates by bouncing light off a flat surface and measuring the reflection.

Like a keyboard, a mouse can have a wire (cord) connecting it to the computer, or it can be wireless. A wireless mouse communicates with a transceiver connected to a USB port to exchange data with the computer, or uses a technology called Bluetooth to communicate via radio waves. A wireless mouse requires a battery, whereas a wired mouse draws the small amount of power it needs from the computer via its cord.

wireless mouse A mouse that communicates wirelessly with a transceiver connected to the computer, so it does not need a cord.

transceiver A unit that provides the wireless transmission for a cordless device like keyboard or mouse, usually plugged in to a USB port.

Other pointing devices are also available. For example, a trackball is a stationary device with a ball on top (or on the side) that you roll with your fingers. See Figure 3.4. A trackball requires less space on a desk to operate and some people find it more comfortable to use than a mouse. Many notebook computers have a built-in touchpad, which is a small rectangular touch-sensitive pad with buttons below it. See Figure 3.5. You can drag your finger on the pad to move the onscreen pointer, and press the buttons to click.

trackball A pointing device in which the user moves the pointer by rolling a ball with his or her fingers.

touchpad A pointing device consisting of a touch-sensitive pad on which the user drags a finger to move the pointer.

Table 3.1 summarizes the actions you can take with pointing devices.

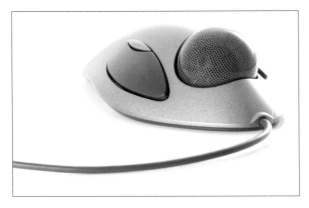

© iStockphoto.com/epixx

Figure 3.4 A trackball is stationary; the user moves the ball with his or her fingers.

© iStockphoto.com/vincomfoto

Figure 3.5 A touchpad is a touch-sensitive area that the user drags a finger across to move the pointer onscreen.

Table 3.1: Pointing Device Actions

Action	Description
Click	Press and release the left button once.
Double-click	Press and release the left button twice in quick succession.
Right-click	Press and release the right button once.
Drag	Press the left button and then move the pointer while the button remains held down.
Right-drag	Press the right-button and then move the pointer while the button remains held down.

touch screen A touch-sensitive display monitor that functions both as an input and an output device.

A touch screen can enable you to use your finger as a pointing device. Tap or drag your finger across a touch screen to perform mouse-equivalent operations. Table 3.2 summarizes the actions you can take using a touch screen.

Table 3.2: Touch Screen Actions

Action	Description
Tap	Tap the screen with your finger, quickly pressing and releasing on the same spot.
Double-tap	Tap the same spot twice in succession.
Drag	Touch one finger to the screen and then drag your finger to another spot. This action is used to move objects, usually described in instructions in relation to an object onscreen, such as "drag the folder icon."
Swipe	To drag, usually from one edge of the screen toward the center. This is usually described in instructions from a certain direction, as in "swipe in from the right side."
Tap and hold	Press a certain area and hold your finger on that spot. This is roughly equivalent to the mouse action of right-clicking.
Pinch	Touch two fingers in different spots and then move your fingers together. This action is often used to zoom out (make things appear smaller).
Stretch	Touch two fingers to the screen near each other and then drag your fingers apart. This action is often used to zoom in (make things appear larger).
Rotate	Touch two fingers on an object and then drag them in a circular motion. This action is used to rotate an object in certain apps.

A joystick, shown in Figure 3.6, is a specialized pointing device used primarily in gaming. It consists of a vertically mounted stick that can be tilted in any direction. A set of buttons on the base of the joystick enable you to perform actions, such as shooting or jumping in a game.

joystick A pointing device consisting of a vertically mounted stick that can be tilted in any direction.

Drawing Tablets

A drawing tablet, also called a digitizing tablet, is a specialized type of touchpad designed for drawing. The user draws on the tablet with a pen-shaped pointer called a stylus, and the drawing shows up onscreen. Professional graphic artists use drawing tablets to draw directly into a computer program to create both technical and artistic drawings. Figure 3.7 shows a drawing tablet.

© iStockphoto.com/chrisboy2004

Figure 3.6 A joystick.

drawing tablet A flat rectangular touch-sensitive surface on which a user can draw with a stylus to create onscreen artwork.

stylus A pen-shaped pointer used to drag across the surface of a touch-sensitive screen.

© iStockphoto.com/ppart

Figure 3.7 A drawing tablet.

Sensory Input

Many portable devices, such as smartphones and tablets, have new types of input technology that detect direction, motion, and/or location. For example, some devices have a **global positioning system (GPS)** to detect your location, an **accelerometer** to tell how fast you are moving, a **compass** to report what direction you are facing, and a **gyroscope** to report the orientation of the device. It is the gyroscope, for example, that tells a phone or tablet when you turn it on its side so it can change the orientation of the screen.

New Technologies

Scanning Devices

digitize To convert something from hard-copy to digital (computerized) form.

charge-coupled device (CCD) The light-sensitive sensor in a scanner that records the amount of light bounced back from the image.

A scanner digitizes hard-copy photos and documents and stores them electronically. Scanners work by shining a bright light on the surface of the page and measuring the amount of light that bounces back from it using a photosensitive charge-coupled device (CCD). Lighter areas bounce back more light than darker areas. For color scanning, multiple sensors are used, each one picking up a different color: red, green, and blue.

multi-function device (MFD) A device that combines the functions of a printer, a copier, and a scanner into one unit, and also a fax in some models.

flatbed scanner A scanner that has a large flat glass surface on which the page to be scanned is placed.

document feeder A mechanical feature of some scanners that enables multiple pages to be scanned consecutively without user intervention.

Most scanners are flatbed models, as in Figure 3.8, where you place the image on a flat piece of glass and then a sensor and light bar moves beneath it to capture the image. A flatbed scanner may optionally have a document feeder on it so multiple pages can be queued for scanning. There are also smaller portable scanners that either feed in one sheet at a time past a stationary sensor and light bar, or that you hold in your hand and manually move across the image to be scanned.

© iStockphoto.com/nicolas_
Figure 3.8   A flatbed scanner.

When you scan text, you can use optical character recognition (OCR) software to convert the scanned image to text that you can work with in a text editing program.

bar code reader A scanner that reads and interprets bar codes such as UPC symbols.

Universal Product Code (UPC) A bar code system used for identifying products for sale.

One very simple type of scanner is a bar code reader, shown in Figure 3.9. Bar codes are vertical stripes of varying widths and spaces that represent numeric values. The most common type of bar code is a Universal Product Code (UPC), the bar code that identifies a product that consumers buy at a store.

A bar code reader examines the bars and inputs their numeric values into the computer. A bar code reader can be hand-held, like a gun-type unit that a warehouse worker might use to look up an item, or stationary, like the scanner in a grocery store checkout kiosk. Bar codes are

© iStockphoto.com/UltraONEs

Figure 3.9 A bar code reader.

used everywhere that numeric accuracy is important for tracking physical items. For example, they are used in many manufacturing businesses to track parts, finished products, and orders. Shipping services use them to track the packages as they move from their origin to their destination, and retail stores use them at digital cash registers to scan purchased items and look up their prices.

QR code (which stands for Quick Response) is a new type of scanner-readable code that is replacing UPC codes in many places. It's a two-dimensional barcode. Whereas a standard bar code is read in only one direction (analyzing the width and spacing of the bars), a QR code is a square panel with encoded data in both dimensions. QR codes can store more data than bar codes, making them more useful for providing information about an item. Figure 3.10 shows an example of a QR code being scanned by a smartphone.

QR code A two-dimensional variant of a bar code, containing more information than a traditional bar code.

© iStockphoto.com/pinstock

Figure 3.10 QR codes can be scanned by smartphones (with an appropriate app installed) as well as by specialized scanners.

Scanning QR Codes

Many smartphones with cameras have QR readers built into them, so your phone can serve as a QR scanner. When you scan a QR code that you see on an advertisement, for example, you might be taken to the company's website or to a coupon for the product. If you have a smartphone, see if it has a code reader app. If it doesn't, download a free one. Then locate a QR code (look in magazines, on billboards, on subways, and anywhere else that companies advertise) and scan it with your phone to see what happens.

magnetic card reader A scanner that reads and deciphers the information on the magnetic strip on a credit card or other ID card.

radio frequency identification (RFID) chip A computer chip that communicates wirelessly with a device to authenticate a user.

Another type of scanner used in many businesses is a magnetic card reader, shown in Figure 3.11. You use one of these every time you swipe a credit card to pay for a purchase, for example. Magnetic card readers read the encoded data on the magnetic strip on the back of your credit card or ID card and transfer that data into a computer. Some credit cards have a radio frequency identification (RFID) chip in them that enables you to pass them in front of a radio frequency card reader to read the card's data without it physically touching a reader. RFID chips are also used in security systems to allow employees access to secure areas of a building if they are wearing an RFID-equipped ID badge.

© iStockphoto.com/ugurhan

Figure 3.11 A magnetic card reader.

Fingerprint Readers

A fingerprint reader is a type of biometric scanner—that is, a scanner that scans something about a human body that is used to identify that person. Many computer systems use fingerprint readers as a form of user authentication. The fingerprint of the person logging in is compared to a database of pictures of the fingerprints of authorized users. Other types of biometric scanners include facial recognition, voice recognition, and retina scanners.

© iStockphoto.com/LongHa2006

Certain industries use specialized scanners to simplify data entry. For example, companies that grade standardized testing use an optical mark recognition (OMR) system that detects the presence of a pencil or ink mark on certain spots on a standardized form. Banking institutions save time and cut down on entry errors by using a magnetic-ink

© iStockphoto.com/jimd_stock

Figure 3.12   The routing numbers on checks are written with magnetic ink so they can be read by MICR machines.

character recognition (MICR) system to read the routing and account numbers on checks and deposit slips, as in Figure 3.12.

optical mark recognition A scanner that detects the presence of a pencil or ink mark on certain areas of a standardized form.

magnetic-ink character recognition (MICR) The scanning system used in the banking industry to read routing and account numbers on checks and deposit slips.

Capture Devices

The scanners you have learned about so far read existing data and scan existing photographs and documents. Image capture devices, on the other hand, capture new content.

A capture device can capture either still images or motion video. Some devices do both, but most are designed primarily for one type or another. A digital camera is designed primarily for still photos, and looks much like a film camera; a digital video camera is designed primarily for motion video. See Figure 3.13. Both work using the same basic technology; the digital video camera captures many frames (individual still images) per second and stores them in a single file. When you play back the still images in chronological order, the image appears to be moving. Digital video cameras can also capture sound to accompany the video clips, which can be played back synchronously with the images. Many modern smartphones have built-in cameras that can take still photos and record video clips.

digital camera A camera that captures and stores still images in digital form.

digital video camera A video camera that captures and stores motion video in digital form.

frame A still image that makes up part of a digital video clip.

© iStockphoto.com/Chiyacat (left), © iStockphoto.com/arsenik (right)

Figure 3.13   A digital camera (left) and a digital video camera (right).

Some digital video cameras are stand-alone; you can take them out into the world and capture video, and then connect the video camera to a computer to transfer, edit, and save the video clips. Other cameras are webcams, as in Figure 3.14, which are simple video cameras that lack their own storage and capture controls. They remain permanently attached to the computer, and store their video clips or still images directly on the computer's storage drives. They rely on video capture software on the computer to start and stop the capture process. Webcams are often used for online video chatting through services such as Skype.

© iStockphoto.com/temniy

Figure 3.14   A webcam.

webcam A digital video camera that must remain connected to a computer as it operates.

Audio Input Devices

Most personal computers support audio input, either through a built-in audio adapter on the motherboard or through an add-on **sound card**. A computer's audio ports may support speakers, headphones, microphones, and both analog and digital external audio device input. An example of an external audio input device is a home stereo system; an external digital audio device might be a digital piano keyboard.

audio adapter Also called a **sound card**. A component of a computer system that accepts and processes audio input and delivers audio output.

If you have a microphone and voice input software, you can speak into the microphone to issue commands to the computer and to input text into a word processing program. Some people with disabilities use voice input to control the computer as a substitute for a keyboard or mouse, and some people who have a lot of text to enter but don't type very quickly may find voice input more efficient than trying to type all the text. People who use audio input frequently find that it is worthwhile to buy a high-quality microphone headset, as in Figure 3.15, because it provides more accurate voice pickup.

voice recognition software Software that recognizes spoken words that match words in its database to digitize spoken language.

There are two kinds of voice input software: voice recognition and speech recognition. Voice recognition software recognizes spoken words that match words in its database. It does not pay attention to the tone or inflection of the speaker's voice. People who speak with a heavy accent may have difficulty with such software. Voice recognition is included with Microsoft Windows and Microsoft Office. Speech recognition software is teachable software that learns an individual's pronunciation and vocal inflection. Each user trains the software by reading long passages of text into the microphone; the software records what each word sounds like when that person pronounces it, and can also learn new words.

speech recognition software Software that can learn an individual's pronunciation and vocal inflection and translate it into digitized text.

© iStockphoto.com/paylessimages

Figure 3.15 A headset microphone works well for voice input software use.

Quick Review

1. Name three kinds of pointing devices.

2. Besides numbers, letters, and symbols, what other kinds of keys are found on a keyboard and what do they do?

3. What hardware is required for audio input?

4. What is the difference between a digital video camera and a webcam?

Selecting and Using Output Devices

Output devices make the computer's processed information available to a human user. Without output devices, there would be little reason to have a computer, because it wouldn't produce anything you could use. The most common types of output devices are display screens, printers, and speakers.

Display Screens

A display screen is a video screen that the computer uses to provide information to a human user. A display screen can be built into a device, as it is with smartphones, tablets, and notebook PCs, or it can be a separate unit (a monitor), as it is with the majority of desktop PCs.

display screen A video screen that a computer uses to provide output to a human user.

Display screens create their images by filling in tiny dots called pixels with different colors. The pixels are so small and so close together that the human eye sees them as continuous color gradients rather than individual blocks. Monitors differ in the technology they use to illuminate those pixels.

pixel An individual colored dot in a graphic or on a display screen.

liquid crystal display (LCD) A flat-screen display technology that passes electricity through liquid crystals to create a display image.

organic light-emitting diode (OLED) A flat-screen technology that uses organic matter that lights up in response to electrical current to create a display image.

active matrix An LCD type in which each pixel is actively maintained by a separate transistor.

thin-film transistor An improved type of active matrix common in modern monitors and display screens.

passive matrix An LCD type in which each pixel maintains its state on its own until it decays or is refreshed.

high-definition TV (HDTV) A television that displays at least 1920 × 1080 resolution (also known as 1080p).

high-definition multimedia interface (HDMI) A type of connector used to connect an HDTV to another device, such as a computer or a home theater system.

Built-in display screens are thin and flat, and most of them use liquid crystal display (LCD) technology. Most modern stand-alone monitors are also LCD, like the one shown in Figure 3.16. This technology has two polarized filters, with a liquid crystal substance between them. One filter is at an angle, so light doesn't pass through it automatically. When electricity hits a crystal, it twists, refracting the light so that it passes through the second filter and lights up the display in a certain spot. Color displays have separate filters for red, green, and blue. Some new mobile devices use organic light-emitting diode (OLED) technology, which used organic matter that lights up in response to an electrical current.

© iStockphoto.com/dem10

Figure 3.16   An LCD monitor has a thin, flat screen.

Flat-screen displays vary in the number of transistors used to create the display image. In an active matrix, each individual pixel in the display is actively maintained by a separate transistor. Almost all LED screens today are an improved variant of an active matrix called thin-film transistor (TFT). In a passive matrix (which is cheaper to manufacture), each pixel maintains its state on its own until it decays or is refreshed. An OLED screen may be active matrix or passive matrix depending on the model.

NOTE A high-definition TV (HDTV) can also be used as a computer monitor by connecting the computer to one of its high-definition multimedia interface (HDMI) input ports.

cathode ray tube (CRT) An older type of monitor technology that uses a vacuum tube and electron guns to create a display image.

triad A cluster of three phosphors: one red, one green, and one blue.

Cathode ray tube (CRT) is an older monitor technology that uses a large vacuum tube and electron guns to create a display image on a phosphor-covered glass. See Figure 3.17. The electrons strike phosphors on the monitor glass and briefly light up. The display is refreshed many times per second to maintain the image. The phosphors are arranged in triads: red, green, and blue, as shown in Figure 3.18. Depending on what color a particular pixel should be, different phosphors illuminate within that triad. CRT monitors are heavy and bulky compared to LCDs, and have mostly been replaced by LCD monitors. You may still see one in use with an older computer, however.

Figure 3.17   A CRT monitor is housed in a large plastic boxlike case.

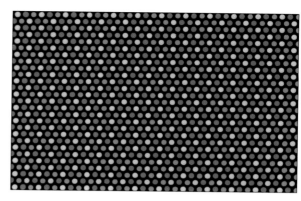

Figure 3.18   An extreme close-up of part of a CRT monitor's screen, showing how triads of red, green, and blue appear.

You also may encounter a few specialized monitor types. For example, some e-book readers have a special type of screen called electronic paper (e-paper). This type of screen retains its image but is unpowered except when the display changes, so it uses much less power than a device with an LCD screen. A digital or **smart whiteboard** is a large writing board in a conference room or other meeting area that is connected to a computer, so that whatever is written on the board is also saved on the computer. Digital tools and buttons also appear on the screen for interacting with the data collected, as shown in Figure 3.19. A digital projector (see Figure 3.20) accepts display data like a monitor does, but instead of showing the image on its own screen, it projects an image in large format on a nearby screen or wall.

e-paper A monitor technology used in book readers in which the screen retains its image but is unpowered except when the display changes.

digital whiteboard A whiteboard that is connected to a computer, so that whatever is written on the board is saved on the computer.

digital projector A projector that accepts input from a computer.

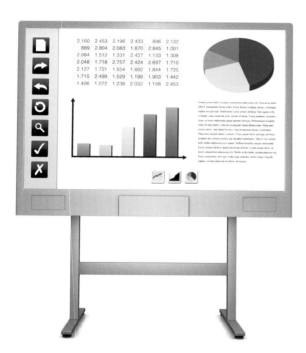

Figure 3.19   A digital whiteboard.

Figure 3.20   A digital projector.

Digital projectors differ from one another in their brightness, measured in lumens. The brighter the projector, the better it will display when the image is projected at a large size in a well-lit room. An inexpensive projector having 1,500 lumens would be okay for a small, dark room; a more expensive projector might have 4,000 lumens.

lumens The measurement of brightness of a digital projector's image.

resolution The number of pixels that comprise a display, horizontally and vertically.

maximum resolution The highest display mode (the greatest number of pixels) a display can support.

A display screen has a maximum resolution, which is the highest display mode it can support. Display modes are expressed as *horizontal number of pixels × vertical number of pixels*, such as 1600 × 900. On an LCD monitor, maximum resolution is sometimes called native resolution. See Figure 3.21.

Horizontal resolution: number of pixels horizontally. For example, 1600.

Vertical resolution: number of pixels vertically. For example, 900.

Aspect ratio: ratio of horizontal to vertical resolution. For example, 1600:900 is a 16:9 ratio.

Figure 3.21 A screen's resolution is described as horizontal × vertical pixels.

One quirk of LCD monitors is that if you use any resolution that is lower than the native one, the display may not appear as sharp and crisp. Therefore, you should run an LCD in its native resolution whenever possible. If the icons and text are too small to read, adjust the text and icon size in the operating system's settings.

aspect ratio The ratio of width to height on a display screen, such as 4:3 (standard) or 16:9 (wide).

When selecting a display mode in the operating system, you should choose one that matches the aspect ratio of the display screen. The aspect ratio is the ratio of width to height—in other words, the relative dimensions of the screen. Some monitors have a traditional 4:3 aspect ratio, but many LCD screens use a wide-screen 16:9 aspect ratio instead.

Resolutions and LCD Monitors

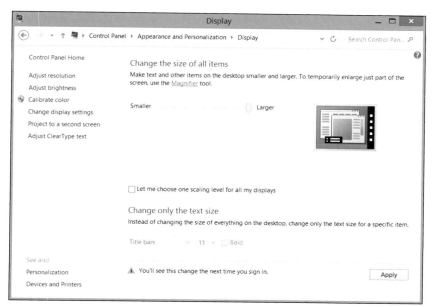

Most LCD displays look fuzzy at any resolution other than their highest one. However, the highest resolution display mode may make the text and icons so small that they are difficult to see and work with. As a work-around, you can change the text and icon size in Windows. After switching to the highest resolution for your display, right-click on the desktop and choose Screen Resolution. Click the Make Text and Other Items Larger or Smaller hyperlink. Then drag the Change the Size of All Items slider to adjust the size. If the slider is not available, mark the Let Me Choose One Scaling Level for All My Displays check box and then choose one of the presets (Small, Medium, etc.). You may have to restart your computer after making this change before the new setting will take effect.

All display screens have a maximum refresh rate, the number of times each pixel is refreshed per second. The operating system's display mode determines the actual refresh rate that is used. On a CRT, using a high refresh rate (greater than 80 Hz) makes the monitor flicker less, resulting in less eyestrain for the user. On an LCD monitor, the refresh rate is somewhere around 60 Hz but is not as important because an LCD monitor is not prone to flickering.

refresh rate The number of times each pixel in a display is refreshed per second.

A display mode specifies a color depth, which is the number of binary digits needed to uniquely describe the color of each pixel. For example, an 8-digit binary number has 256 possible combinations of 0 and 1 (2 to the 8th power), so 8-bit color would allow for 256 different colors. Windows defaults to 32-bit color that would allow for over four billion colors (also called True Color); an alternative is 16-bit color (also called High Color).

color depth The number of bits needed to describe the color of each pixel in a certain display mode, such as 16-bit or 32-bit.

A display screen relies on the computer's display adapter to tell it what to do. The display adapter, in turn, takes its orders from the operating system to specify the display mode (resolution, refresh rate, and color depth). The display adapter requires its own memory, which it uses to hold the color information for each pixel as it operates, and which it uses to render 3D objects and control special video effects in certain

display adapter The computer component that communicates instructions from the operating system to the display.

applications. If the display adapter is built into the motherboard, the display adapter may reserve some of the motherboard's memory for its own use. If the display adapter is a separate circuit board, it has its own memory mounted directly on the circuit board.

Step by Step

Exploring Display Modes in Windows 8.1

Follow these steps to see the current display settings in Windows 8.1:

1. Right-click on the desktop and choose Screen Resolution.

2. Make a note of the Resolution setting. Open the Resolution drop-down list and see what other settings are available. Are you currently using the highest setting?

3. Click the Advanced Settings hyperlink.

4. In the dialog box that appears, on the Adapter tab, click the List All Modes button.

5. In the List All Modes dialog box and scroll through the list to see what modes your display adapter supports. Notice that a display mode consists of three factors: resolution (for example, 1366 × 768), color depth (for example, True Color [32 bit]), and refresh rate (for example, 60 Hertz).

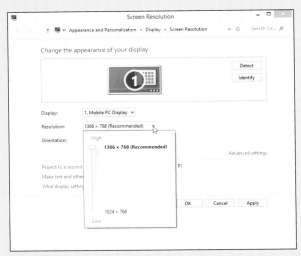

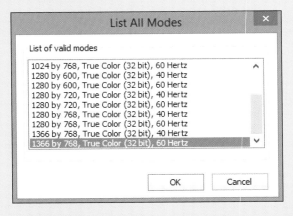

6. Click Cancel to close the dialog box without making a change.

7. Click the Monitor tab, and note the current Screen refresh rate setting.

8. Click Cancel to close the dialog box.

9. Click Cancel to close the Control Panel window.

Printers

Printers generate hard copy—that is, physical printed pages you can hold in your hands. Over the years there have been many different printer technologies, each with its own characteristics and benefits. In this section, you'll learn about several printer types and find out what differentiates one printer from another.

hard copy Physically printed pages of a document or a printed photo; the opposite of soft (electronic) copy.

Printer Features

When selecting a printer, there are a number of factors to consider:

- Initial cost: How much does the printer cost?

- Per-page cost: How much does it cost to print a page, taking into account the price of the consumables? How much does the ink, toner, or ribbon cost, and how many pages will it print before you have to replace it? Are there other parts in the printer that wear out and have to be replaced after a certain number of pages?

consumables Printing supplies that must be replaced with use, such as paper and ink.

- Resolution: How many individual dots per inch (dpi) does the printed image consist of? A higher resolution results in a sharper image, as shown in Figure 3.22. A low-resolution printer might output at 300 dpi, while a high-resolution printer might output at 1200 dpi.

dots per inch (dpi) A measurement of printed image quality, the number of individually colored dots in one row (or column) of one inch of the printed file. A printout can have a different horizontal and vertical dpi, although this is not common.

Figure 3.22 A high-resolution printout contains more dots per inch, resulting in smoother lines and finer details.

- Speed: How many pages per minute can the printer output? A typical printer might output at somewhere between 10 and 20 pages per minute for black-and-white, and slightly less than that for color.

Keep in mind when comparing speeds that a printer's advertised speed refers to its maximum output after it has started printing; this speed doesn't take into account the time it takes for the computer to send the job to the printer and for the printer to process that data internally and start the printing process. If you print one or two pages at a time, you will not achieve the advertised speeds; it will likely take the printer 30 seconds or so to eject the first page of a print job.

- Color: Does the printer print in color, or just in black-and-white? If it prints in color, can it print photos well? Some printers are designed specifically for photos, and have special inks for them and/or use special glossy paper for photos.

- Paper handling: Does it have multiple paper trays, so you can have two sizes of paper loaded at once? How much paper can it hold at once? How well does it print on heavy cardstock or envelopes without bending or creasing them? Does the printer have any special paper-handling features, such as the capability to print on both sides of the paper (duplexing) without the user manually flipping the paper over? What is the largest size paper it can accept?

- Interface: Most printers use the USB interface to connect directly to a computer. Can the printer also connect to a network? Does it require a cable to connect it to the network, or can it connect wirelessly?

- Multi-function: Is it just a printer, or can it perform other tasks too, like scanning, copying, and/or faxing? A multi-function device (MFD) can save you money and space if you would otherwise have to buy separate machines for those functions.

Table 3.3 at the end of this section compares the principal types of printers along these factors.

Impact versus Non-Impact Printers

A printer can be either impact or non-impact. An impact printer creates the image on the page by striking the page through an inked ribbon. A non-impact printer places the ink on the page in some other way (for example, using heat or electricity), without striking the paper.

The only type of impact printer still sold today is dot matrix. In a dot matrix printer, the print head consists of a block of movable pins (which is, as the technology name implies, a *matrix* of *dots*). Depending on what letter it needs to form, it pushes different pins forward to form that letter, and then the exposed pins strike the paper through the ribbon to form that letter. The pins then pull back and different pins are pushed forward to form the next letter. Impact printers are slow and noisy, print only in one color, and do not print graphics very realistically. However, they do have one important benefit that non-impact printers lack: Because they strike the paper with some force, they can print on multipart carbon copy forms. This capability, along with the low cost per page, has kept dot matrix printers from becoming completely obsolete. Figure 3.23 shows a close-up of the print head on a dot matrix printer.

duplexing To print on both sides of the paper.

impact printer A printer that makes the image on the page by striking it through an inked ribbon.

non-impact printer A printer that makes the image on the page using a method that does not physically strike the paper.

dot matrix A in impact printer that uses movable pins to form letters and then strikes the page through an inked ribbon with the pins.

cost per page The total cost of the consumable supplies required to print a page, calculated by dividing the cost of the paper and ink/toner/ribbon by the number of pages it produces before being depleted.

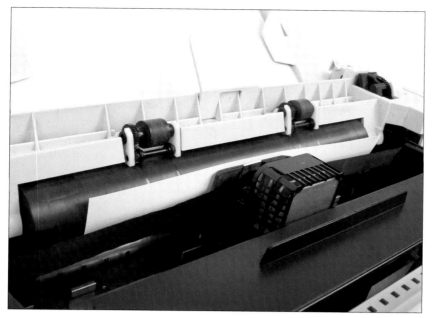

© iStockphoto.com /sewer11

Figure 3.23 A dot matrix printer's print head consists of a block containing movable pins that push forward to form letters. Note the inked ribbon between the head and the paper.

Inkjet Printers

An inkjet printer sprays liquid ink onto a page through a set of very small nozzles (ink jets). The depending on the model, an ink jet printer uses either heat or electricity to make the ink squirt out of the nozzles. Figure 3.24 shows an inkjet printer.

Most inkjet printers are color models, having four separate ink cartridges: black, cyan, magenta, and yellow. Some models designed for photo printing have even more cartridges for greater photo realism, and may also have a memory card slot so you can print photos directly from the card rather than having to go through a computer.

Inkjet printers are popular in homes and small businesses because the cost of the printer is very low, so it's economical to get started. However, the ink cartridges are expensive and don't last for very many pages, so high-volume printing on an inkjet printer can be very expensive. The special glossy paper needed for best-quality photo printing can also be expensive.

inkjet printer A printer that squirts ink onto paper with small nozzles (jets) to form the page image.

© iStockphoto.com/gmnicholas

Figure 3.24 An inkjet printer.

CAUTION

If an inkjet printer sits idle for weeks at a time, the ink in the nozzles dries out, and you may see quality problems with your printouts. Running the printer's self-cleaning cycle may restore the print quality, but doing so wastes some ink, driving up the cost per page even higher. Unfortunately there is not much you can do to prevent this; it's just something to be aware of when selecting a printer technology.

laser printer A printer that forms the page image by transferring toner to the paper via a rotating drum with electrical charges.

Laser printers are popular in business because they are fast, they handle high-volume printing well, and the cost per page is low. They also produce good-quality, high-resolution output, and both color and black-and-white models are available. The main drawback is the initial cost, which can be higher than for other printer types. Figure 3.25 shows a laser printer.

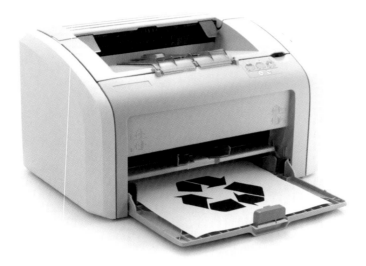

© iStockphoto.com/Draganr

Figure 3.25   A laser printer.

drum The rotating cylinder inside a laser printer, on which the page image is formed with electrical charges.

toner The powdered mixture of plastic and iron used to form the image on a laser printer.

fuser The heating element in a laser printer that melts the toner, fusing it to the paper.

A laser printer prints by creating an image of the page on a rotating drum using varying levels of electrical charges. The drum is negatively charged and then a laser neutralizes the charge in some spots. When the drum rotates past a reservoir of toner (a powdered mixture of colored plastic particles and iron), the toner is attracted to the neutralized areas and clings to the drum. Then the paper rotates past positively charged paper, and the toner is pulled off the drum and onto the paper. A fuser element heats the paper, melting the plastic particles in the toner so that the particles stick to the paper permanently.

Table 3.3: Comparing Types of Printers

	Dot Matrix Printers	*Inkjet Printers*	*Laser Printers*
Initial Cost	Medium	Inexpensive	Expensive
Per-Page Cost	Inexpensive	Expensive	Inexpensive
Resolution	Poor	Good	Good
Speed	Slow	Medium	High
Color	No	Yes	Yes
Paper Handling	Continuous feed	Single low-capacity paper tray	Single or multiple paper trays, some are high-capacity
Suitable For	Multi-part forms, text-only printouts	Photo printing, low-volume home or small-business use	High-volume printing, business printing

Specialty Printers

In addition to the printer types discussed so far, a variety of special-purpose printers exist. You may see some of these printers in businesses, schools, and government offices.

Thermal printers transfer images to paper using heat. For example, some cash registers use a special thermal-coated paper for receipts; the cash register contains a simple direct thermal printer that heats certain areas of the paper so that it turns black and forms the text for your receipt. A thermal wax transfer printer melts a wax-based ink onto paper in tiny dots, using dithering to create different colors. It's a high-cost, medium-quality printout that was popular before color laser printers became economically feasible for ordinary users, but is seldom seen today. A thermal dye transfer printer, sometimes called a dye sublimation printer, heats ribbons containing dye and then diffuses the dye into specially coated paper. The print quality is outstanding, but the paper and the dye are both expensive. Some small-format snapshot printers use this technology.

A plotter is a large-format printer that excels at creating high-precision drawings like blueprints, maps, and engineering drawings. Figure 3.26 shows a plotter. Plotters are available that use a variety of printing technologies, including variants of inkjet and laser. On the other end of the size spectrum, some small-format specialty printers work with their own software to accomplish specific tasks, such as printing labels, postage, or work orders.

thermal printer A printer that transfers images to paper using heat.

direct thermal printer A printer that heats certain areas of specially coated paper so that it turns black and forms the image.

thermal wax transfer printer A printer that melts a wax-based ink onto paper in tiny dots.

dithering Placing different colored dots side by side in an image so that from a distance they appear to be a third color.

thermal dye transfer printer A printer that heats ribbons containing dye and then diffuses the dye onto specially coated paper.

plotter A large-format printer that creates high-precision documents such as maps and engineering drawings.

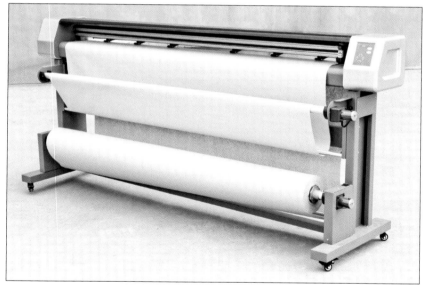

© iStockphoto.com/loonger

Figure 3.26 A plotter.

A 3D printer prints with plastic resin, rather than ink. It lays down layers of plastic on top of one another to produce a 3D object. 3D printing is a very new technology, and 3D printers are still out of the price range of most consumer hobbyists. However, the technology promises to revolutionize many industries. For example, 3D printing could be used to create prototypes of mechanical parts that would otherwise have to be custom-manufactured at a much higher cost, and workers in remote

3D printer A printer that prints layers of plastic resin that combine to create 3D objects.

locations such as Antarctica could use 3D printing to create tools and parts needed without waiting months for them to be delivered.

Audio Output Devices

The audio adapter in a computer handles both input and output. You learned earlier in this chapter how audio input comes in from microphones and digital musical instruments. The most common audio output devices are speakers and headphones.

Speaker systems designed for computers are somewhat different from speaker systems designed for home stereo and home theater systems. Typically, a single 3.5mm plug connects to an output port on the computer; you don't plug in the speakers separately to the computer. On a two-speaker system, one speaker connects to the computer and the other speaker connects to the first speaker. A system with more speakers than that usually has a central gathering point, such as a subwoofer into which all the speakers connect.

Step by Step

Adjusting Sound Output Volume in Windows

Windows provides a Volume control in the notification area that you can easily use to adjust the overall sound coming from your computer's speakers or headphone, and also mute or unmute the sound. You can also adjust the volume levels for individual components. Follow these steps to explore your computer's sound controls:

1. In the notification area, click the speaker icon. A slider appears.

2. Click the speaker graphic at the bottom of the slider. A red X appears on the button, indicating the sound is muted.

3. Click the Mixer hyperlink at the bottom of the slider. A dialog box opens showing individual sliders for each adjustable sound-producing item on your system. You may have more and different ones than shown here.

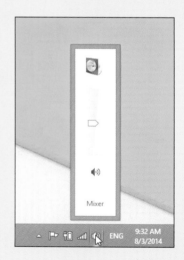

4. Adjust any of the sliders as needed, and then close the dialog box.

Another difference in computer speaker systems is that the speakers have magnetic shielding to protect nearby computer devices from electromagnetic interference (EMI). Most speakers are powered speakers, meaning they require an AC adapter or batteries to function. The power boosts the amplification of the sound, and is necessary because most computers don't have a built-in amplifier the way most home stereo systems do.

Depending on the computer, there may be a separate headphone jack, or you may need to unplug the speakers to plug in a headphone set.

electromagnetic interference (EMI) Distortion of electrical signals through a cable by a nearby magnetic field.

powered speakers Speakers that contain their own amplification, powered by either AC current or batteries.

Audio can also be output to a portable digital media player such as an iPod or iPhone, but that type of output is not the same as sending the audio to a speaker system. When you output music to a digital player, you are transferring files to the player, so the process is much more like copying files to an external drive than it is setting up sound output. The next section of this chapter discusses file storage and transfer.

NOTE

Quick Review

1. What is LCD technology?

2. Define monitor resolution and explain how it is measured.

3. Name three types of printers and give an example of an appropriate use for each.

Choosing Appropriate Storage Devices

As you learned in Chapter 2, "The System Unit," when a computer processes data, RAM (Random Access Memory) holds that data temporarily. RAM is known as primary storage because it's where the data must be in order to interact with the CPU. Data waits for the CPU's attention in memory, and then it waits again in memory when the CPU has finished processing it.

primary storage System RAM in a computer, where processed data is first stored after it exits the CPU.

For data to be safely and permanently stored, however, it must be placed in secondary storage. Secondary storage devices are nonvolatile, so they don't lose their contents when the computer's power is turned off. Secondary storage can include hard disk drives, solid state drives, CDs, DVDs, and network and cloud-based storage.

secondary storage Storage that retains data after the computer is turned off, such as a hard disk drive, DVD, or USB flash drive.

Storage devices are evaluated in these ways:

- Capacity: How much can it hold?

- Cost: How much does the storage cost per megabyte or gigabyte?

- Access speed: How quickly can the data be written and retrieved?

- Interface: How does it connect to the computer, and how fast is that connection?

- Media type: Is it magnetic, optical, or solid-state?

- Portability: Is the storage inside the system unit, or connected to it externally?

- Removability: Is the disc removable from the drive that reads and writes it, or are they one inseparable unit?

Table 3.5 at the end of this section compares the different types of storage devices along these factors.

In the following sections, you will learn about storage in general, and about several types of storage devices and their characteristics.

Data Storage Basics

file A group of related bits stored together under a single name.

folder A logical organizing unit for grouping related files together.

subfolder A folder within another folder.

volume A physical storage device, or a portion of one, that is assigned an identifying letter. Sometimes used interchangeably with *drive*, but a physical drive may actually contain multiple volumes.

A file is a named collection of bits that work together to represent a single object, such as an executable program, a spreadsheet, a picture, or a system file. Folders are logical organizing units for files. For example, a Windows-based computer has a Windows folder containing the system files needed to run Windows, a Users folder containing the data files and settings for each user account, and a Program Files folder containing the files needed for each installed application. A folder within a folder is called a subfolder; each of the aforementioned folders contains multiple subfolders. Files and folders are stored on volumes. Each volume has a letter followed by a colon, such as C: or D:. Figure 3.27 summarizes this structure.

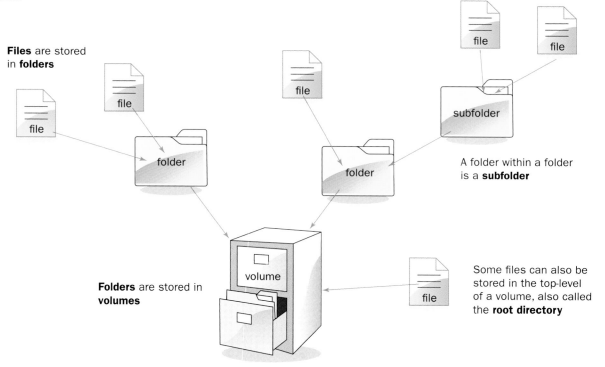

Figure 3.27 Files are stored in folders, which are stored in volumes.

disk One or more platters on which data is stored. Spelled *disc* when referring to the optical type (DVDs, CDs).

drive The mechanical components that read and write the data on a disk.

Some people use the terms disk (or disc), drive, and volume interchangeably, but they have different meanings. The term disk refers to a platter or set of platters on which data is stored. Examples include a hard disk drive (HDD) and a DVD. When referring to a CD, DVD, or Blu-ray, it is customary to spell the term *disc*. The term drive refers to the mechanical components that read and write the data on a disk. In some cases, such as with an HDD, the drive and its platters are physically inseparable, so the terms disk and drive have come to be synonymous; *hard disk* and *hard drive* refer to the same thing. When the disc is removable from the drive, however, as with a CD or DVD, the terms are separate. See Figure 3.28.

Solid-state storage devices such as USB flash drives are technically neither discs nor drives, because they have no platters and no moving parts. However, they are commonly referred to as drives anyway, as in the term *solid-state drive (SSD)*.

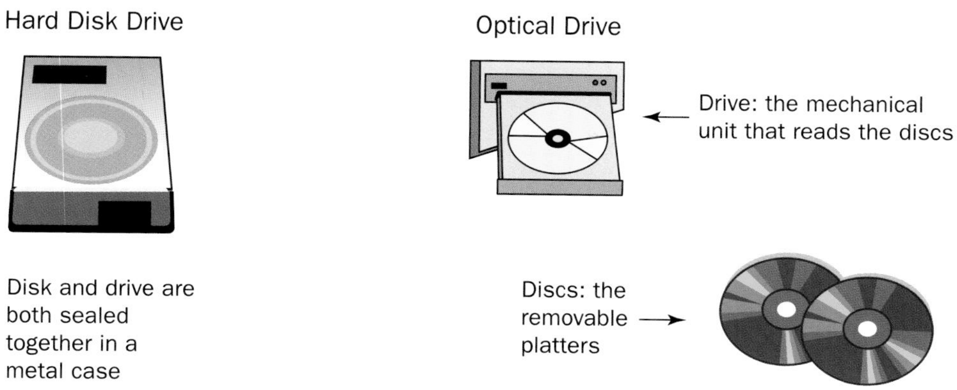

Hard Disk Drive

Optical Drive

Drive: the mechanical unit that reads the discs

Disk and drive are both sealed together in a metal case

Discs: the removable platters

Figure 3.28   In hard disk drives, the disk and drive are one unit; in optical drives, the disc and drive are separate.

Most commonly, each physical storage device acts as a single volume. For example, your DVD drive might have a volume letter of E: assigned to it. However, some high-capacity storage devices such as hard disk drives can be partitioned into multiple volumes, each of which appears in the operating system to be a separate storage device with its own letter.

Hard Disk Drives

A hard disk drive (HDD) is the most popular type of secondary storage for personal computers. Although newer technologies are emerging, HDDs remain the standard because of their high capacity and low cost.

An HDD consists of a stack of metal platters (usually 4 to 6) that are coated with iron dust. These platters spin on a common spindle inside a sealed metal casing. A set of read/write heads inside the HDD casing reads and writes data on the platters; there are heads on each side of each platter. The arms move in and out to reach different spots on the platters, and the disks move past the heads as they spin. The most common platter sizes are 3.5" in diameter on HDDs for desktop systems and 2.5" on HDDs for notebooks. Figure 3.29 shows the inside of a hard disk drive case.

The data is stored on the platters in patterns of magnetic polarity. The iron dust on the surface is very sensitive to magnetic polarity and can be easily magnetized. As the disk surface moves past a read/write head, the write head switches its polarity between positive and negative to change the polarity on the surface, creating a pattern of polarity changes. Each polarity change represents a 1 bit, and each area where there could have been a polarity change but there isn't one represents a 0 bit. An HDD has an internal controller that manages the physical reading and writing operations.

hard disk drive (HDD) A mechanical drive with an integrated set of disk platters that store data in patterns of magnetic polarity.

read/write head A component in a disk drive that reads and writes to the disk(s).

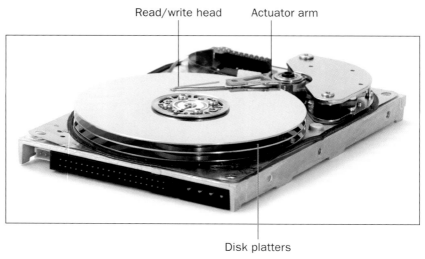

Read/write head   Actuator arm

Disk platters

© iStockphoto.com/rhambley

Figure 3.29   The inside of a hard disk drive.

track One of the concentric rings in a disk's organizational system.

A precise system exists for describing the physical locations on an HDD. The platters are divided into concentric circles, like the rings on a tree trunk cross-section, called tracks. Each platter's first track is track 0, the next one track 1, and so on. The track number tells the drive where to position the actuator arm that controls the position of the read/write heads. All the heads move together, so if one head is reading track 1 on one side of one platter, all the other heads are also reading track 1 on their side of their platter too. For this reason, tracks are not referred to individually, but as cylinders. A cylinder is the group of all the tracks at a single arm position. Figure 3.30 illustrates the relationship between these parts.

cylinder All the tracks at a single position of the read/write heads' actuator arm.

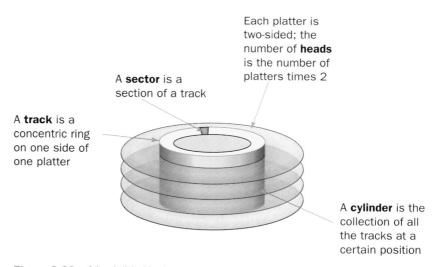

Each platter is two-sided; the number of **heads** is the number of platters times 2

A **sector** is a section of a track

A **track** is a concentric ring on one side of one platter

A **cylinder** is the collection of all the tracks at a certain position

Figure 3.30   A hard disk drive is organized into tracks, cylinders, heads, and sectors.

sector The smallest addressable unit of storage on a disk drive, at 512 bytes.

cluster A grouping of sectors. The number of sectors in a cluster depends on the file system and the disk size.

Each track is divided into segments called sectors. A sector holds exactly 512 bytes. Because there are so many sectors, and because almost every file is much larger than 512 bytes, sectors are grouped together into clusters, and the drive's controller addresses clusters rather than individual sectors. The number of sectors per cluster is determined by the drive's size and formatting, but most modern HDDs have 32 sectors per cluster.

An HDD can be internal or external, but most are internal, installed inside the system unit. An internal HDD connects to the motherboard using either a parallel ATA (PATA) or serial ATA (SATA) cable. An external HDD connects to a port on the outside of the system unit, and depending on the model may use a USB port, a FireWire (IEEE 1394a) port, or an external SATA (eSATA) port. You can buy enclosures that will convert an internal HDD to an external one.

See "Drive Connectors" in Chapter 2, "The System Unit," for more information about PATA and SATA. See the section "Other Common External Connectors" in Chapter 2 to learn more about USB and FireWire.

Optical Drives

An optical drive uses a light beam and sensor to read the data. The surface of a blank optical disc is shiny and reflects light strongly. When data is written to an optical disc, certain areas are burned with a laser so they are less reflective. The shiny areas are called *land*, and the less-shiny areas are called *pits*. Recall from the preceding section that on an HDD, transitions between positive and negative magnetic polarity indicate a 1 bit, and lack of transition indicates a 0 bit. On an optical disc, transitions between areas of greater and lesser reflectivity indicate a 1, and a consistent level of reflectivity indicates a 0. See Figure 3.31.

optical drive A drive that reads discs that are stored in patterns of greater and lesser reflectivity, such as a DVD or CD.

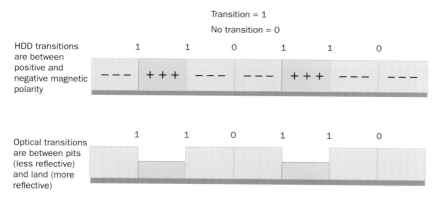

Figure 3.31   Magnetic and optical storage both look for transitions in the state of the disc surface.

There are several types of optical drives and discs. The oldest and most basic type is a compact disc (CD), which holds up to 900MB of data. CDs are used for small amounts of data and also for audio recordings. A digital versatile disc (DVD) can store up to 4.7GB per disc (single-sided, single layer). DVDs can also be double-sided, with recordings on both sides rather than recording on one and a label on the other. DVDs can also be dual-layer, where the top layer is semitransparent and read using a laser and sensor at a different angle than the lower layer. A double-sided, dual-layer DVD can hold up to 17GB of data. DVDs are used to distribute large applications, large amounts of data, and standard-definition movies. Blu-ray discs (BD) can store up to 128GB in up to four layers. They are used to distribute even larger amounts of data, or high-definition movies.

compact disc (CD) An optical disc used for storing music and data, holding up to 900 MB.

digital versatile disc (DVD) An optical disc used for storing standard-definition movies and data, holding up to 4.17 GB per side per layer.

Blu-ray disc (BD) An optical disc used for storing high-definition movies and data, holding up to 128GB.

All three types of discs can be read-only (ROM), recordable once (R), or rewriteable (RW). To record or rewrite a disc, you must have a drive with that capability that supports the type of disc you are using.

DVDs come in two competing recordable and rewriteable standards, abbreviated as plus and minus signs, like this: DVD+R and DVD-R. Some older home stereo systems do not support reading from +R and +RW discs, but otherwise the differences are unnoticeable to most consumers.

Table 3.4 lists the types of blank optical discs you can buy and their capacities.

Table 3.4: Optical Disc Types

Disc	Capacity	Notes
CD-ROM	650 to 900 MB	Read-only, used to distribute commercial music and software
CD-R	650 to 900 MB	Recordable once, used to burn CDs that will not change
CD-RW	650 to 900 MB	Rewriteable, used to burn CDs that might need to be changed later
DVD-ROM	4.7 GB per side and per layer	Read-only, used to distribute standard-definition music and software
DVD+R	4.7 GB per side and per layer	Recordable once, used to burn DVDs that will not change
DVD-R		Two competing standards; most optical drives in computers support both
		DVD drives also support CDs
DVD+RW	4.7 GB per side and per layer	Rewriteable, used to burn DVDs that might need to be changed later
DVD-RW		Two competing standards; most optical drives in computers support both
Blu-ray (BD)-ROM	25 to 128 GB, depending on number of layers	Read-only, used to distribute commercial high-definition movies
BD-R	25 to 128 GB depending on number of layers	Recordable once, used to burn BDs that will not change
		BD drives also support CDs and DVDs
BD-RW	25 to 128 GB, depending on number of layers	Rewriteable, used to burn BDs that might need to be changed later

CAUTION Optical discs are sturdy, but scratches, dirt, and fingerprints can prevent them from being read accurately. Store discs in a protective sleeve or case when you are not using them, and hold discs only by their edges. Don't let anything touch the shiny side of the disc, especially anything sharp or abrasive. If you need to write on a disc, write only on the label side, and use only a suitable soft marking pen.

Solid-State Drives

A solid-state drive (SSD) uses a type of EEPROM to store data in tiny transistors. As you learned in Chapter 2, electrically erasable programmable read-only memory (EEPROM) is a type of memory that stores its contents permanently; it is nonvolatile. Because it is electrically erasable, the computer can erase what's written there and rewrite it. The type of EEPROM used in solid-state drives can be erased and rewritten in small blocks, making it suitable for use as a storage device.

solid-state hard drive (SSHD) A high-capacity solid state storage device that substitutes for an HDD as the main storage drive in a computer.

When a solid-state drive is a large-capacity replacement for an HDD, it's sometimes called a solid-state hard drive (SSHD) to distinguish it from lower-capacity portable solid-state storage such as USB flash drives. Figure 3.32 shows a solid-state hard drive.

© iStockphoto.com/scanrail

Figure 3.32 A solid-state hard drive looks much like an HDD from the outside.

Solid-state drives are silent because they don't have any moving parts, and the access time is very fast because there are no read/write heads that have to move anywhere to get to the data. SSDs are more expensive than HDDs, though; you get much less capacity for the money. For this reason, SSHDs are found mostly in high-end desktop and notebook computers. Solid-state storage is common in tablets and smartphones, where high-capacity storage is not needed and being lightweight is a primary concern.

To balance between performance and cost, some systems have both a small SSD and a larger HDD. The SSD contains the start-up files and the operating system, and the HDD holds everything else. Hybrid drives are also available that combine the two technologies in a single physical unit.

Table 3.5 compares the principal types of storage devices.

Table 3.5: Comparing Storage Devices

	Hard Disk Drives	Optical Discs and Drives	Solid-State Hard Drives (SSDD)	USB Flash Drives
Capacity	Up to 4 TB	CD: 900MB DVD: 4.7 GB per side per layer, up to 15.9 GB in total BD: 25GB to 128GB	Up to 4 TB	Up to 1TB
Cost per GB	Inexpensive (5 to 7 cents per gigabyte)	Moderate (about 20 cents per gigabyte)	Expensive (about 75 cents per gigabyte)	Expensive (about 85 cents per gigabyte)
Access Speed	Medium to Fast	Slow	Very Fast	Medium (due to interface)
Interface	Internal: PATA, SATA External: USB, FireWire, eSATA	Internal: PATA, SATA External: USB, FireWire, eSATA	SATA	USB
Media Type	Magnetic	Optical	Solid-state memory	Solid-state memory
Easy Portability	Internal: No External: Yes	Yes	No	Yes
Suitable For	Main storage device for desktop and notebook computers	Backups, movies, music, transferring data between computers	Main storage for a desktop or notebook PC, tablet PC, or smartphone	Transporting data between computers

Network Volumes

As you've seen so far in this chapter, most computer storage is directly attached to the individual computer. This is known as local storage, or direct-attached storage (DAS). However, computers can also use a network to access storage that's not physically nearby.

Network storage can enable multiple users to access the same up-to-the-minute information simultaneously. For example, in a retail business with multiple checkout areas, all the checkout computers access a common database containing the item prices so that when the price of an item changes, all cashiers immediately have that information available. On a smaller scale, a family could store its movie and music collection on one computer, which then can share the collection with all the other computers in the household via the family's wireless network. Storage that is available via a network is called network-attached storage (NAS).

Generically speaking, network-attached storage can be a volume on a file server in a business network or a shared folder on an individual's personal computer. However, the term is most often applied to a NAS appliance, which is a specialized computing device built specifically for network file sharing. The appliance connects directly into the network and can be remotely configured from any computer, so it doesn't need its own input or output devices. NAS appliances are available for consumers as well as businesses; for example, you could connect an inexpensive NAS appliance to your home network to provide everyone in your family with always-on access to shared files.

Some large companies employ storage-area networks (SANs) to make central access to large amounts of data simple. A SAN logically combines the contents of multiple remote storage devices so that each individual computer connected to the SAN sees that storage pool as a single local drive.

When it is essential that data be kept safe and readily available, some companies store that data on a redundant array of independent disks (RAID). There are several types of RAID systems, and each type offers improvements over a single disk drive in performance, in data safety, or in both. Usually, when you store data on a disk, you write to one disk at a time. RAID systems have the ability to spread the data across multiple drives so each physical disk contains part of the data; this is called striping. For example, RAID0 stripes data across multiple physical disks to improve the speed at which data is accessed, and RAID1 mirrors the contents of a physical disk on another identical disk so that the data is always available even if the original disk fails. RAID5 combines the striping from RAID0 with a data storage method that enables the RAID unit to reconstruct lost data on any of the physical disks in the event of a disk failure.

Cloud-Based Storage

A cloud is a secure computing environment consisting of a set of remote servers that users access via the Internet. A cloud can include applications, communication with other users, and storage space (cloud storage).

One of the most popular individual cloud storage systems is Microsoft OneDrive. If you have a Microsoft account (which is free), you automatically get several gigabytes of OneDrive storage online. It is a secure

---

direct-attached storage (DAS) Storage that is directly connected to the computer that accesses it.

network-attached storage (NAS) Storage that is accessed via a network.

NAS appliance A specialized device that provides storage space to network users.

storage-area network (SAN) A distributed storage system that appears to each individual computer as a local volume on that computer.

redundant array of independent disks (RAID) A multi-disk storage system that optimizes performance, data safety, or both, depending on the type.

striping Spreading the data across multiple drives to improve performance or protect the data.

cloud A secure computing environment accessed via the Internet.

cloud storage Storage that is accessed from a cloud environment.

storage environment, and you can optionally choose to share certain folders or files with specific other people or with the public. Google also offers free cloud-based storage to users, as do many other online companies.

Businesses of all sizes also employ cloud storage. For example, a business with many locations might create a cloud-based information system for all employees to access, regardless of where they are. This information system might include customer and product information, order information, access to human resources data such as vacation schedules, and company-wide announcements and memos. A large company might maintain its own online server for implementing its cloud environment, or might contract with a third-party company to host its cloud.

Quick Review

1. Explain the difference between primary and secondary storage.

2. How does an HDD store data?

3. Differentiate between CDs, DVDs, and BDs in terms of capacity.

4. What is a solid-state hard drive (SSHD)?

Troubleshooting Common Input, Output, and Storage Problems

Table 3.6 provides some tips for troubleshooting problems you might encounter with the input, output, and storage devices you learned about in this chapter.

Table 3.6: Troubleshooting Input, Output, and Storage Problems

Problem	Probable Cause	Solution
Keyboard		
Keyboard not responsive	Connector not firmly plugged in, or keyboard has failed	Check connectors; try a different keyboard.
One key is not working	Key is stuck, or debris under key	Turn keyboard upside down and shake it, or use compressed air to blow out the debris under the keys.
Mouse		
No response from mouse	Connector not firmly plugged inDead batteries	Check connectors.If wireless, check batteries.
Mouse doesn't move in one direction	Contacts inside mouse are dirty or debris is covering a sensor	Clean the mouse.
Pointer jumps around erratically on screen	Display adapter is malfunctioning	Restart the computer. If the problem is not resolved, update the display adapter driver.
Display		
No display, no lights on monitor	Monitor is not powered on	Check power cord, press the Power button.
Monitor has amber light on front, and no display	Monitor is not getting a signal from the computer	Check connector, and make sure computer is on.
Display shows a green, blue, or red overall tint	Monitor cable connector is loose	Check connector.

continued

Table 3.6 continued

Problem	Probable Cause	Solution
Display is garbled or distorted	Display adapter driver is corrupted	Download a new copy of the driver and reinstall.
Some graphics don't appear correctly in certain games	Display adapter driver's current version is not compatible with the game	Download an updated version of the driver and reinstall.
Printer		
Vertical stripes, missing or wrong colors on inkjet printout	Inkjets are clogged	Run printer's cleaning utility (check printer documentation to find out how).
One edge of printout from a laser printer appears dirty, or stray toner overall on page	Loose toner inside printer	Clean printer thoroughly, following procedures in printer documentation.
Printing appears light or faded	Low toner	Shake toner cartridge from side to side to distribute remaining toner. Replace cartridge when possible.
Smudged ink on inkjet printout	Page is still wet	Let page dry before handling it.
Loose toner on laser printout	Fuser isn't working	Have printer serviced.
Blank pages from laser printer	Out of toner, or printer is malfunctioning	Replace toner cartridge; if that doesn't work, have printer serviced.
Sound		
No sound from speakers	Speakers are not plugged in, or volume is muted or turned down	Check volume control in the operating system, check connection to speakers.
Inadequate volume level	Speakers are not being powered, or main volume is turned down too low in operating system	Check speaker power source. Check volume control in operating system; there may be a mixer utility with separate controls for main (overall) volume and individual types of sounds, such as system sounds and music playback.
Operating system does not show any audio adapter installed (for example, no volume controls available)	Audio adapter driver is corrupted or audio adapter is failed	Restart the computer. If problem persists, reinstall audio adapter driver (download if needed from company's website). If problem persists, have computer serviced.
Sound is garbled or crackles	Audio adapter is malfunctioning, or speakers are damaged	Restart the computer. If problem persists, try replacing speakers, or have computer serviced.
Hard disk drive		
Hard disk drive not recognized by computer	Drive has failed, or connector has come loose	Check cable connectors between computer and drive. Check BIOS Setup program to see if BIOS recognizes the drive. Have computer serviced to replace drive and recover data if possible.
Read or write errors reported by operating system	Physical bad spots on the disk surface	Run a disk scanning program such as Error Checking in Windows 8.1.
Hard disk makes read/write noises almost continuously, even when you are not working with any files	There is not enough RAM in the computer, so the hard disk is being used for virtual memory	Install more RAM in the computer if possible.

Problem	Probable Cause	Solution
Optical discs		
Read errors	The disc is dirty or scratched	Clean the disc with a soft cloth. Use a scratch repair kit or service if the disc contains important data that needs to be recovered.
Disk won't eject using Eject button on computer or drive	Button may be malfunctioning	Open a file management window in the OS, right-click the drive, and choose Eject.
		Restart the computer.
		On some desktop optical drives that use a tray, there is a small hole in the front panel; straighten a paperclip wire and stick it in the hole to manually eject the tray.
Errors when writing to a disk	The recording speed is too high for the drive to handle, or other operations may be interfering with the CPU's attention to the writing process	Try recording at a slower speed; do not use the computer for anything else while the recording is taking place.

Summary

Selecting and Using Input Devices

Input devices allow the user to communicate with the computer. The most common input devices are a **keyboard** and **mouse**, both of which can be either wired or wireless. A keyboard can have an **ergonomic** design to prevent hand and wrist strain. Devices that lack a real keyboard use a **virtual keyboard** (software-based) to enable user input.

A pointing device controls the onscreen pointer in the user interface. A mouse can be **mechanical** or **optical**. Other pointing devices include **trackball** and **touchpad**. Some computers have a **touch screen** on which your finger can serve as a pointing device. A **drawing tablet** enables you to input drawings using a **stylus**.

A scanner **digitizes** a hard-copy photo using a **charge-coupled device (CCD)**. A scanner can be part of a **multi-function device (MFD)** that also includes a printer and copier. A **bar code reader** is a specialized type of scanner used for reading **Universal Product Code (UPC)** symbols. **Magnetic bar code readers** and **radio frequency identification (RFID) chips** are other types of scanning devices, as are **optical mark recognition (OMR)** systems and **magnetic-ink character recognition (MICR)** systems.

A capture device captures new content, rather than scanning existing content. Examples include **digital cameras** and **digital video cameras**. A **webcam** is a digital video camera that must remain connected to a computer in order to function.

Audio input can be used to control a computer with commands and to input music and sounds. Audio input requires an **audio adapter** (sound card). When using a microphone for audio input, **voice-recognition software** interprets speech by matching words in a database; **speech recognition software** is teachable software that learns an individual's pronunciation.

Selecting and Using Output Devices

A **display screen** is a video screen the computer uses for outputting information to the user. A stand-alone display screen is called a **monitor**. **Liquid crystal display (LCD)** is a popular type of flat-screen monitor technology. A newer alternative is **organic light-emitting diode (OLED)**. An LCD screen can be either **active matrix** (a version of which is **thin-film transistor**) or **passive matrix**. In active matrix, each **pixel** has its own transistor. A **high-definition TV (HDTV)** can also be used as a computer monitor via a **high-definition multimedia interface (HDMI)**.

Cathode ray tube (CRT) is an older monitor technology that uses a vacuum tube and electron guns to light up colored phosphors on a glass screen. Phosphors are arranged in **triads** of red, green, and blue.

Some specialized display types include **e-paper** (for book readers), **digital whiteboards**, and **digital projectors**. Projector brightness is measured in lumens.

A display screen has a **maximum resolution**, expressed as a number of pixels horizontally and vertically. The ratio of horizontal to vertical is its **aspect ratio**. The **refresh rate** is the number of times per second the display is refreshed. The number of bits needed to describe the color of a pixel is the **color depth**. A **display adapter** tells the display screen what to do.

The key factors in selecting a printer include initial cost, cost per page for **consumables**, print resolution (expressed in **dots per inch**), speed, color, interface, and paper handling. Printers can be **impact** (dot matrix printer) or **non-impact** (almost all other printer types), depending on whether or not they strike the page to make the image.

A **dot matrix printer** uses pins to strike an inked ribbon. They are inexpensive to operate and can print multi-part forms, but do not handle graphics well. An **ink jet printer** squirts liquid ink onto paper. The printer is inexpensive to buy and produces good quality color graphics, but the cost per page is high because of the cost of the ink cartridges. A **laser printer** transfers **toner** to a **drum** and then to paper, and then **fuses** the toner to the paper. It is economical per page and produces good quality output, but is expensive to buy initially. Specialty printers include **direct thermal**, **thermal wax transfer**, **thermal dye transfer**, and **plotters**.

Audio output comes through speakers and headphones. Speakers designed for computer use are **powered** and have shielding to prevent **electromagnetic interference (EMI)**.

Choosing Appropriate Storage Devices

Primary storage is RAM; **secondary storage** is permanent storage, such as a disk. **Files** are stored in **folders** or **subfolders**, on **volumes**. A **disk** is a platter (or multiple platters) that store data; a **drive** is the mechanical component that reads and writes the data. In some storage types, the disk and drive are inseparable.

A **hard disk drive (HDD)** is the most popular type of secondary storage for personal computers. It is magnetic and mechanical and usually internal to the system unit. Read/write heads magnetize different spots on the disk platters to store the data in **sectors** on **tracks**. A group of sectors is a **cluster**. A group of tracks at a specific read/write head position is a **cylinder**. HDDs can use either PATA or SATA connectors internally, or USB, FireWire, or eSATA externally.

An **optical drive** uses a light beam and sensor to read data on **compact discs (CD)**, **digital versatile discs (DVD)**, and/or **Blu-ray discs (BD)**.

A **solid-state drive (SSD)** uses EEPROM to store data in tiny transistors. **Solid-state hard drives (SSHD)** are a substitute for traditional HDDs as the main secondary storage in a computer.

Local drives are **direct-attached storage (DAS)**. Network-accessible storage is **network-attached storage (NAS)**. **NAS appliances** are simple computers designed to be used as network storage. A **storage-area network (SAN)** makes remote storage appear as a local volume on each individual computer.

A **redundant array of independent disks (RAID)** is a system that uses multiple physical HDDs to increase performance and reliability by spreading the data out across all the disks and implementing schemes for reconstructing the data in the event of one disk's failure.

Cloud storage is storage that the user accesses online via a **cloud**, which is a secure computing environment online.

Troubleshooting Common Input, Output and Storage Problems

If a device isn't working, check its connectors to make sure they are snug, and check to make sure the device is receiving power if it requires it.

If a keyboard key is stuck, shake the keyboard upside-down or use compressed air to blow debris out from under the keys. If a mouse doesn't move the pointer in one direction, clean the sensors on it. If wireless, check the batteries.

An amber light on the monitor means it is not getting a signal from the computer. Updating the display adapter's driver can solve various problems with the display quality.

For printer quality problems, clean the printer (including ink jets), and make sure there is enough ink or toner installed correctly.

For sound problems, check the volume control in the operating system to make sure it is not muted, and make sure the audio adapter's driver is installed correctly.

Key Terms

active matrix
aspect ratio
audio adapter
bar code reader
Blu-ray disc (BD)
cathode ray tube (CRT)
charge-coupled device (CCD)
cloud
cloud storage
cluster
color depth
compact disc (CD)
consumables
cost per page
cylinder
digital camera
digital projector
digital versatile disc (DVD)
digital video camera
digital whiteboard
digitize
direct thermal printer
direct-attached storage (DAS)
disk
display adapter
display screen
dithering
document feeder
dot matrix
dots per inch (dpi)
drawing tablet
drive
drum
duplexing
electromagnetic interference (EMI)
e-paper
ergonomic keyboard
file
flatbed scanner
folder
frame
fuser
hard copy
hard disk drive (HDD)
high-definition multimedia interface (HDMI)
high-definition TV (HDTV)

impact printer
inkjet printer
input device
insertion point
joystick
laser printer
liquid crystal display (LCD)
lumens
magnetic card reader
magnetic-ink character recognition (MICR)
maximum resolution
mechanical mouse
mouse
multi-function device
NAS appliance
network-attached storage (NAS)
non-impact printer
optical drive
optical mark recognition (OMR)
optical mouse
organic light-emitting diode (OLED)
passive matrix
pixel
plotter
powered speakers
primary storage
QR code
QWERTY
radio frequency identification (RFID) chip
read/write head
redundant array of independent disks (RAID)
refresh rate
resolution
secondary storage
sector
solid-state hard drive (SSHD)
speech recognition software
storage-area network (SAN)
striping
stylus
subfolder
thermal dye transfer printer
thermal printer
thermal wax transfer printer
thin-film transistor (TFT)
toner

touch screen
touchpad
track
trackball
transceiver
triad
Universal Product Code (UPC)

virtual keyboard
voice recognition software
volume
webcam
wireless keyboard
wireless mouse

Test Yourself

Fact Check

1. Tablets and smartphones use _____ keyboards.

   a. virtual

   b. ergonomic

   c. pointing

   d. numeric

2. Which of these is NOT one of the typical functions of a multi-function device (MFD)?

   a. printer

   b. scanner

   c. monitor

   d. copier

3. Thin-film transistor (TFT) is one type of what type of display?

   a. OLED

   b. active-matrix LCD

   c. passive-matrix LCD

   d. CRT

4. Which of these is an example of a printer consumable?

   a. read/write head

   b. dpi

   c. initial cost

   d. toner

5. The main drawback to an inkjet printer is:

   a. high cost per page

   b. high initial cost

   c. does not print in color

   d. does not print graphics

6. Which of these is primary storage?

   a. HDD

   b. SSHD

   c. RAM

   d. DVD

7. On an HDD, data is stored in

    a. sectors

    b. transistors

    c. pits

    d. optical tracks

8. What kind of storage is remote but appears to each individual computer as a local volume?

    a. DAS

    b. SAN

    c. NAS

    d. RAID

9. If a file is stored in a cloud, where is it located?

    a. Local area network

    b. Internet

    c. Local HDD

    d. USB flash drive

10. What should you do if there are stripes of missing or wrong colors on an inkjet printout?

    a. Reinstall the printer driver

    b. Replace the print head

    c. Run the printer's self-cleaning utility

    d. Buy higher quality paper

Matching

Match the term to its description.

    a. CRT

    b. HDD

    c. LCD

    d. OLED

    e. NAS

    f. SSD

1. _____A type of flat-screen monitor that twists liquid crystals using electricity to form the display image

2. _____A type of flat-screen monitor that applies electricity to organic matter to form the display image

3. _____A type of monitor that uses electron guns to illuminate phosphors to form the display image

4. _____A type of storage that uses rigid metal platters to store data magnetically

5. _____A type of storage that uses solid-state memory to store data

6. _____A type of storage that is accessed via a network

Sum It Up

1. List three input devices and three output devices.

2. How do wireless input devices communicate with the computer?

3. Explain briefly how LCD and CRT technologies form screen images.

4. List three types of printers and give an example of an appropriate use for each one.

5. Explain how HDD and SSHD differ internally.

6. Differentiate among DAS, NAS, SAN, and cloud storage.

Explore More

Input and Output Devices in Your World

For the next 24 hours, notice what computer input and output devices you see in use at school, at work, in your community, and at home. For example, at your local grocery store, you might see a digital cash register with a bar code scanner and a thermal receipt printer, and you might see a magnetic card reader for credit card processing. See how many devices from this chapter you can identify, and submit a list to your instructor of what you saw and where you saw it.

Speech Recognition in Windows 8.1

In Windows 8.1 you can turn on speech recognition whenever you want to use the feature. To do so, open the Control Panel and type **speech** in the search box. Next, click Speech Recognition and work through the wizard to configure the feature. Then start Speech Recognition by saying **Start Listening**.

Next, open Microsoft Word, start a new blank document, and speak the following text into your microphone:

I am learning to use a microphone as an input device in Windows. I am dictating this text aloud, and Microsoft Word is typing it for me. Speech recognition is part of Windows 8.1's Ease of Access features.

When you are finished speaking, correct any errors. Then either save or discard the Word document, as your instructor directs you to do.

Think It Over

How Much Does Printing Really Cost?

Suppose your employer needs to print about 3,000 invoices a month. He asks you to recommend a printer type and to prepare a cost estimate for the purchase of a printer. Weigh the options available, and do some Internet research to find suitable models and their prices. Research the cost of the consumables for the printers as well.

Prepare a report that summarizes the initial cost to buy the printer as well as the cost of consumables. Check the printer's documentation online to find out if there are any other parts that periodically need to be replaced (for example, the drum in a laser printer may need replacing at some point) and the number of pages the printer can produce before that replacement is necessary. Present the consumable cost per page, as well as an estimate of the monthly and yearly consumable cost.

Optional: Find a printer that has a lower cost per page than the printer you initially chose, and prepare the same report as before with the new cost data.

Solid-state hard drives (SSHD) are more expensive than HDDs, as you learned in this chapter. Nevertheless, some businesses are adopting them as the main storage devices for new personal computers that the companies buy. What might be the reasoning behind this? Brainstorm a list of the benefits you get with an SSHD compared to an HDD.

Optional: Use the Internet to research what other consumers who have purchased solid-state hard drives have said.

Backing Up Your Files

Suppose you want to back up your entire MP3 and home video collection, which currently occupies 100 GB on your computer's main HDD. Would it be better to buy an external HDD to do the backup or to back the files up onto optical discs? Consider not only cost, but also convenience, reliability, and ease of retrieving the files later. If you chose optical discs, which type would you use, and how many of them would you need? If you chose an external HDD, what size would you buy—one that the files barely fit on, or one with room for more files you might acquire later?

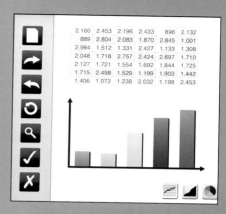

Part II
Software

2.160	2.453	2.196	2.433	896	2.132
889	2.804	2.083	1.870	2.845	1.001
2.984	1.512	1.331	2.427	1.133	1.308
2.048	1.718	2.757	2.424	2.697	1.710
2.127	1.721	1.554	1.692	1.844	1.725
1.715	2.498	1.529	1.199	1.903	1.442
1.406	1.072	1.238	2.032	1.198	2.453

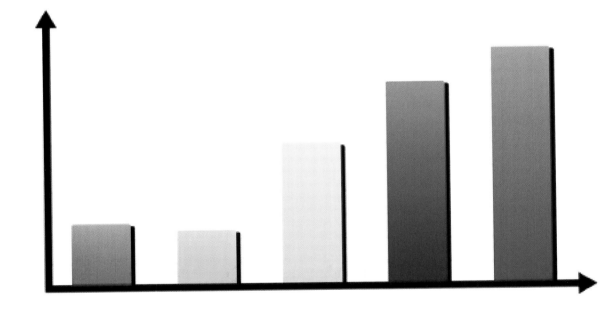

Chapter 4

Operating System Basics

Learning objectives

☐ Understand the types of operating systems available

☐ Differentiate among the major desktop operating systems

☐ Explain how device drivers work

☐ Explain computer file storage concepts

When you think about using a computer, you probably think about performing some useful task with it, or playing a game. Behind the scenes, though, is the software that keeps the computer running and responding to commands: the operating system (OS).

The operating system you use can make a big difference in how the computer behaves, how it respond to commands, what applications it can run, and what add-on hardware you can attach. By understanding the available operating systems and their benefits, you can make the right choice in selecting an operating system—or you can choose to purchase a device with the right operating system already built in.

In this chapter, you will learn about system software in general, and how operating systems work. You'll survey several popular operating systems and learn how they communicate with hardware, with the Internet, and with the user. You will also find out how computers store and manage files.

Programmer

A programmer writes the instructions that become computer programs. Whether it's an operating system, a utility, or a game, a programmer takes a general concept like "open a dialog box with user controls for adjusting the graphics quality" and makes it a reality by writing the exact instructions needed, line by line. The programmer then compiles those instructions into a usable program or combines them with the instructions written by another programmer or group of programmers to make a larger program. More experienced programmers may also participate in developing the requirements for a program. A programmer should have at least an Associate Degree in Computer Technology, Computer Science, or Information Technology, and should be familiar with at least two or three different programming languages.

© iStockphoto.com/nullplus

Understanding System Software

system software Software that starts the computer and keeps it running, performing basic system tasks such as running applications, managing files, and correcting errors.

System software includes BIOS, the operating system, and utility programs that perform system maintenance and protection tasks such as error correction and backup. Let's look at each category in more detail.

The System BIOS

As you learned in Chapter 2, "The System Unit," the Basic Input/Output System (BIOS) is the built-in software on the motherboard that starts the computer. It performs a power-on self-test (POST) at start-up, which ensures that all the critical hardware devices are functioning properly, including the CPU, the RAM, and the motherboard. If the hardware passes the tests, the BIOS looks for an operating system on one of the available drives, and then passes off control to the operating system to complete the boot process. The BIOS has a list of default settings it uses for managing memory and devices, but those settings can be overridden by user settings that you specify. You can change those settings through a setup program, as you learned in Chapter 2 in the section "Error Message on a Black Screen."

See the Step by Step exercise "Exploring Your CMOS Setup" in Chapter 2 to practice modifying BIOS settings.

The Operating System

The BIOS starts the computer at a basic level, but the operating system does the bulk of work to keep it running and to help the user accomplish tasks. Remember from Chapter 1, "Computer Basics," that the operating system performs these important functions (see Figure 4.1):

- It provides the user interface that humans use to communicate commands and receive feedback.

- It communicates with the hardware, instructing it to take action to accomplish tasks. For example, it communicates with the keyboard and mouse to accept input, and it communicates with the display screen to show output.

- It runs applications, and enables humans to interact with them.
- It controls and manages the file storage system.

An Operating System...

Figure 4.1 The functions performed by an operating system.

There are many kinds of operating systems, suited for a wide range of devices, from supercomputers to smartphones. Each operating system is optimized for the hardware it runs on and the tasks the user is likely to want to perform. For example, the operating system on a tablet computer is designed to be compact (because there is limited storage space in the tablet), easy to operate (because most users are not computer professionals), and fast to respond to simple commands, whereas the operating system in a server is designed to give computer professionals many options for managing and configuring the server and supporting users and databases.

Some operating systems are designed to run on just one specific plat-form. A platform is a type of hardware. For example, the type of hardware used in most Windows-based computers is called the Intel platform or the IBM-compatible platform. Those names originate from the makers of the early CPUs (Intel) and personal desktop computers (IBM). Several different operating systems run on the Intel platform, including Microsoft Windows, UNIX, and Linux. Most tablets and smartphones, on the other hand, support only one operating system. For example, devices built on the Macintosh platform such as the Apple iPad and iPhone support only the Apple iOS operating system.

platform A type of computer hardware that is compatible with certain operating systems.

Intel platform A platform that was originally based on CPUs made by Intel. The Intel platform can run Windows, UNIX, and Linux.

x86 The 32-bit version of the Intel platform.

x64 The 64-bit version of the Intel platform.

The 32-bit Intel platform is sometimes called x86. That name is a nod to the old Intel line of CPUs where the model numbers all ended in 86, such as 286, 386, and 486. The 64-bit Intel platform is sometimes called x64. Windows comes in both 32-bit and 64-bit versions, and when purchasing a copy of Windows, you must match the Windows version to the hardware platform you have.

NOTE

Modern Macs use Intel brand CPUs, but are still considered the Mac platform, not the Intel platform. There are major differences in the hardware between a Mac platform and an Intel platform system, including different motherboard designs and different ports.

graphical user interface (GUI) A user interface based on a graphical environment, in which users interact with it using a pointing device or touch screen as the primary input device.

command-line interface A user interface based on typing text at a command prompt.

An operating system can have either a graphical user interface (GUI) or a command-line interface. GUI interfaces are the norm in operating systems designed for most personal computing devices, such as desktops, notebooks, tablets, and smartphones. Users interact with the graphics they see onscreen by using a keyboard or mouse, or using a finger or stylus on a touch screen. In a command-line interface, users employ a keyboard to type commands at a prompt; the interface is text-only. Command-line operating systems were common in the early days of computing, but nowadays they are confined mostly to server operating systems. Figure 4.2 compares a GUI to a command-line interface.

Figure 4.2 A GUI (left) and a command-line interface (right).

An operating system can be single-user or multi-user. The operating systems on most personal devices are single-user. For example, only one person at a time typically uses a desktop PC with Windows installed. Server operating systems like UNIX, on the other hand, are designed to support multiple users accessing them simultaneously—for example, a dozen different digital cash registers in a retail store all simultaneously sending transactions to a central database.

Utility Software

utility software Software that performs some useful service to the operating system, such as optimizing or correcting the file storage system, backing up files, or ensuring security or privacy.

Utility software performs a task (or set of tasks) that optimizes, repairs, or safeguards the computer or its data. The difference between utility software and the operating system is sometimes not clear-cut, because most operating systems come with many utility programs built-in. For example, Microsoft Windows comes with utilities for checking a disk for errors and optimizing the way files are stored on an HDD (hard disk drive). Third-party utility software is also available, and may do a more thorough job at the task, combine multiple functions in a single interface, or have more advanced options for configuring how the tasks will run. For example, Figure 4.3 shows the Symantec Endpoint Protection, a security suite for business computers that can be remotely managed by IT professionals on each computer on the company network.

Figure 4.3   A third-party utility such as Symantec Endpoint Protection has more features and configuration options than the built-in utilities in Windows.

There are many types of utilities that protect the computer from attack by malware (harmful or maliciously created software). Antivirus programs find and remove viruses, for example, anti-spyware software finds and removes spyware and adware, firewall software blocks hackers from invading your system, and anti-spam software detects and segregates junk email. Some all-in-one protection suites such as Norton Security Suite protect against many types of threats at once. You will learn more about the different types of malware and their detection and removal in Chapter 16, "Network and Internet Privacy and Security."

Other utilities detect problems with the computer's operation. For example, a disk checking program can find and fix errors in the file system on a volume, and a registry cleanup program can find and fix inconsistent or unneeded entries in the registry, which is the system configuration database that Microsoft Windows uses. An uninstaller utility removes installed software along with any associated files and registry entries.

Backup software makes backup copies of your important files on a separate drive, for safekeeping. You can automate and schedule the backup process so it occurs without your intervention at whatever interval you specify.

malware Harmful or maliciously created software, such as a virus or spyware.

virus A type of malware that attaches itself to an executable file and spreads to other files when the program is run.

spyware A type of malware that spies on the user's activities and reports them back to the spyware's developer.

adware A type of malware that pops up unwanted ads on the screen.

firewall software Software that blocks hackers from accessing a computer by closing unnecessary services and ports.

anti-spam software Software that rejects junk email messages.

disk checking program Software that finds and fixes errors in the disk storage system.

registry cleanup program Software that analyzes the Windows registry and deletes unneeded entries.

registry The main system configuration database for Microsoft Windows.

uninstaller utility Software that removes installed software along with its associated files and registry entries.

Comparing the Major Operating Systems

When you think about operating systems, you probably think first of Microsoft Windows, which is the operating system used on more than 90 percent of all desktop and notebook PCs. You will learn a lot about Microsoft Windows in upcoming chapters. However, there are many other operating systems designed for a variety of computers and computer-related devices.

Desktop and Notebook Operating Systems

Mac OS X The graphical operating system designed for Apple's desktop and notebook computers.

Yosemite The code name for Mac OS X 10.10.

There are two main hardware platforms for desktop and notebook computers: Apple and Intel (IBM-compatible). The Apple Macintosh platform supports only the Apple operating system: Mac OS X (pronounced *Mac O-S-X*, although the X technically is the Roman numeral 10). This operating system has an attractive GUI and is easy to understand and use. Apple assigns the versions of Mac OS X code names as well as version numbers. The most recent version at this writing is called Yosemite (version 10.10). Figure 4.4 shows the Yosemite version of Mac OS X.

Copyright MacSources © 2014.

Figure 4.4 Mac OS X 10.10 (Yosemite).

The Macintosh platform has been popular with graphics professionals for decades, and much of the best page layout and graphics editing software was originally developed for the Mac. However, in recent years, similar software has become available for both Windows and Mac, so there is no reason to choose a Mac based on software compatibility anymore. You can run Windows on a Mac with the Mac program Boot Camp. There is also a Mac version of Microsoft Office.

Most Intel-based systems use Microsoft Windows. Like Mac OS X, Windows also has an attractive GUI and is easy to learn and use. Windows has the advantage of being the most popular OS, and therefore the one that more applications are written to run on.

Microsoft Windows The graphical Microsoft operating system designed for Intel-platform desktop and notebook computers.

The most recent version at this writing is Windows 8.1. Chapter 5 ("Introduction to Windows 8.1"), Chapter 6 ("Windows 8.1 Administration and Maintenance"), and Appendix B ("Customizing Windows 8.1") cover Windows 8.1 in detail; you will learn there how to run programs, manage files, and change configuration settings. Windows 8.1 has two user interface styles. Figure 4.2 showed the desktop interface, and Figure 4.5 shows the Start screen interface.

Figure 4.5   The Windows 8.1 Start screen.

Linux (pronounced *LIN-ucks*) is an operating system that looks and feels very similar to UNIX. It can run on a variety of platforms, including Intel-based desktops and notebooks, servers, and handheld devices. (Android, a popular OS for smartphones and tablets, is a variant of Linux.)

Linux An open-source, cross-platform operating system that runs on desktops, notebooks, tablets, and smartphones.

Linux was developed by Linus Torvalds. The name *Linux* is a combination of the words Linus and UNIX. Linux is open-source, which means that Mr. Torvalds retains ownership of his original code, but it is free to the public to use in any way they see fit. Users are free to modify the code, improve it, and redistribute it. Developers are not allowed to charge money for the Linux kernel itself (the main part of the operating system), but they can charge money for distributions (distros for short), which are packaged collections of add-ons and utility programs for Linux. Some of the most popular distros include SUSE Linux, Ubuntu Linux, and Red Hat Linux.

distribution or **distro**, a packaged collection of an open-source kernel such as Linux along with helpful add-ons and utilities.

Running More than One OS

If you want to run multiple operating systems on a single PC, one way is to set it up to **multi-boot**. Each time you start the computer, a menu appears asking which operating system you want to start up. Each operating system must be on a separate volume in order to multi-boot. Windows supports multi-booting; install the non-Windows OS first, and then when you install Windows, its Setup program will ask whether you want to set up multi-booting. The drawback to multi-booting is that each time you want to switch operating systems, you have to restart the computer.

Another way to experience multiple operating systems on the same PC is to use a virtualization program. **Virtualization** enables you to create an entire **virtual machine** inside an application, and install a different operating system on it. The main operating system of the PC is the host OS, and the one inside the virtual machine is the guest OS. You can easily switch back and forth between the host and guest operating systems. VMWare (`www.vmware.com/products`) is the most popular virtualization software; versions are available for individual PCs as well as for large-scale commercial use, such as running several server OS versions on the same server.

shell The user interface for an operating system. Some operating systems, like Windows, do not separate the shell from the kernel; others, like Linux, give you a choice of shells.

Linux is, at its core, a command-line operating system, as is UNIX. However, nearly all the distros contain multiple shells—utilities that allows a user to interact with the operating system. Most distros have a GUI sitting on top of the shell. These are highly graphical, and as attractive and easy to use as Windows and Mac OS X. Figure 4.6 shows the Ubuntu Linux shell, for example. Although most Windows and Mac OS X applications will not run in Linux, plenty of free, open-source equivalents for most software types are designed specifically for Linux, or have Linux versions.

Figure 4.6   The Ubuntu Linux GUI.

thin client A computer with minimal hardware, designed for a specific task. For example, a thin web client is designed for using the Internet.

Some portable computers, such as netbooks, don't require a powerful operating system like Windows for the simple tasks they are designed to perform, like checking email and surfing the web. On such computers, performance is better, and more storage space remains when a thin client operating system is used. A thin client is an operating system that is "thinner" (that is, smaller and more agile) than a regular desktop operating system. It doesn't have a lot of utilities or features, but it has the right ones for the system on which it is installed.

One popular thin client operating system is Chrome OS. Chrome is the name of both an operating system and a web browser, both produced by Google. Chrome OS is a variant of Linux and was developed through an open-source project called Chromium OS. This simple operating system comes preinstalled on some thin clients. It contains a simple file manager, the Google Chrome web browser, and a media player. It doesn't run most applications designed for other operating systems. Figure 4.7 shows a Chrome OS screen.

Chrome OS A thin client operating system created by Google for small notebook computers (netbooks).

Figure 4.7   Google Chrome OS.

New Thin Client Operating Systems

Chrome OS is far from the only operating system for thin web clients. Several other open-source operating systems have recently been released, such as Haiku (www.haiku-os.org), openThinClient (openthinclient.org), and ThinStation (www.thinstation.org) These operating systems require less powerful computers than Windows or Mac OS X because they are leaner and have fewer features. Using a thin client operating system on an older computer can make it perform better when doing activities like browsing the web or managing email. The downside of using a non-standard operating system is that few applications are available for it, so you may be limited to the applications that come with it (usually a text editor, a web browser, an email program, and a music player, at the minimum).

New Technologies

Operating Systems for Servers

Servers are computers that share resources so they are available over a network for multiple users to access. For example, a network might have a mail server that handles the company's internal email delivery, and a file server for storing and sharing files that everyone needs 24/7 access to. A company might also have a web server that makes the company's website available to the public on the Internet.

server A computer that is dedicated to performing network tasks such as managing files, printers, or email for multiple users.

Most servers use the Intel hardware platform (although some very large computers have proprietary operating systems, such as IBM's z-OS, on their mainframes instead). The three most popular server operating systems are UNIX, Windows Server, and Linux.

You learned about Linux in the preceding section; it's a very flexible open-source OS that can be used in many ways. Just as there are Linux distributions that include utilities and shells suitable for desktop use, there are also distros that package Linux for use as a server.

UNIX A multi-user, command-line operating system for servers.

UNIX (pronounced *YOU-nix*) is an older operating system, first developed in the 1970s for servers, and still popular today for that purpose. It's a command-line operating system, as you can see in Figure 4.8. Graphical shells are available, but server administrators often find it easier to work at the command prompt to accomplish the tasks they need to do. UNIX, like Linux, is cross-platform, so it runs on many different types of computer hardware.

Figure 4.8 UNIX is a command-line operating system.

Windows Server The server-optimized version of Microsoft Windows.

Windows Server is a version of Microsoft Windows that is optimized for use on servers. Its GUI is similar to that of the client version of Windows (that is, the version designed for individual PCs), but it has different features and utilities designed to help IT professionals control server activities. Windows Server versions don't match the client versions; they are released on a different schedule. The current version of Windows Server at this writing is 2012 R2, which resembles Windows 8.1, as shown in Figure 4.9.

Figure 4.9 Windows Server 2012 resembles Windows 8.1 in appearance but has different applications.

Operating Systems for Tablets and Smartphones

Tablets and smartphones have special operating system needs. They use solid state storage, which is expensive, so the amount of storage space is limited. Therefore, a large operating system is impractical; the operating system must be simple, easy to use, and above all, compact in size. The operating system comes preinstalled on a static memory chip on tablets and smartphones, so these platforms are often referred to as system-on-chip (SoC). A separate memory chip (or set of chips) is used to hold the data you create and the extra applications you install.

system-on-chip (SoC) An operating system that comes preinstalled on a chip on a portable device such as a smartphone.

For most of their capabilities, tablet and phone operating systems rely on third-party applications (apps) purchased or downloaded for free from an online store. Because users can freely select their own apps, there is no need to provide lots of preinstalled apps with the operating system, and each person's device can be customized for his or her preferred activities.

app An application, such as for a personal computer, tablet, or smartphone.

Portable Apple devices (such as iPhone and iPad) use an operating system called iOS. Its main advantage is its popularity—because it is so popular, thousands of apps are available for it via the Apple App Store. Figure 4.10 shows an iPad screen with iOS as the operating system.

iOS The Apple-created operating system for Apple tablets and phones.

The main competitor to iOS is Android, an open-source OS provided by Google. Android is popular on low-end tablets because it is free, and because many apps are available for it and many of them are free. Many smartphones also use a version of Android.

Android An open-source operating system used on a variety of portable devices, including tablets and smartphones.

Figure 4.10   The iPad runs the iOS operating system.

Microsoft has two different versions of Windows for portable devices. For tablets, there is Windows RT, which looks and works much like the Windows 8.1 Start screen but is designed for SoC devices. Most desktop applications won't run on a Windows RT system. Some Windows convertible tablets such as Surface Pro 3 use the full version of Windows 8.1 Pro, and not Windows RT. For smartphones, there is Windows Phone, an operating system designed specifically for phone use. Figure 4.11 shows a Windows Phone display.

Figure 4.11   The Windows Phone operating system.

Quick Review

1. Name the Windows version designed for each of these platforms: desktop computer, tablet, smartphone, and server.

2. Name three operating systems for servers.

3. Name three operating systems for smartphones.

Understanding Device Drivers

As you learned earlier in the chapter, one of the operating system's jobs is to communicate with the hardware. The problem with that, though, is that each piece of hardware speaks a different language, and they are all different from the language the operating system speaks. Device drivers help them communicate. Device drivers are files that translate the operating system's requests into the language of a particular device, and then translate back again when the device sends a message in return. Each device driver is designed for one specific device and one specific operating system, although it may work, fully or partially, with other similar devices or operating systems.

A device driver can be essential to a device's performance, and often when a device appears to be malfunctioning, it is really the driver's fault. For example, if you are playing a game and there are big white patches on the display in certain parts of the game, the display adapter's driver is probably at fault. It might be corrupted, but more likely it is just out-of-date or incompatible with the game. Downloading and installing an update for that driver might correct the problem.

Different operating systems have different means of keeping drivers up to date. In Mac OS X, for example, driver updates are downloaded automatically along with OS updates. In Windows 8.1, you can view driver versions and install new drivers via the Device Manager utility. You can also roll back an updated driver to the previous version if system problems occur after you install an update.

When you install a new piece of hardware, Windows uses a technology called Plug and Play to identify the device and locate a driver for it if possible. Thanks to Plug and Play, users can set up most devices by simply connecting them, and perhaps running a software utility on a CD that comes with the device.

device driver A file that translates instructions and messages between the operating system and a hardware device.

Device Manager A Windows utility that provides detailed information about the hardware devices installed on the PC.

roll back To return to a previous version, as in rolling back a device driver.

Plug and Play A standard that enables the BIOS and operating system to identify a hardware device and install a driver for it automatically if one is available.

Step by Step

Checking a Device Driver Version

If you are not sure if you have the latest version of a driver, check the driver version number and date, and compare it to the version available for download online.

1. Right-click the Start button and then click Device Manager.

2. Double-click the category of device to expand the category.

3. Double-click the device for which you want to check the driver version.

4. Click the Driver tab, and examine the driver date and version information that appears.

5. Click OK to close the dialog box when you are finished.

NOTE: Some device manufacturers do not update device drivers frequently for older operating systems, so even if your current device driver is a few years old, it may still be the most recent version available for Windows 8.1.

Updating a Device Driver

Follow these steps to update a driver:

1. In Device Manager, double-click the category of device to expand the category if it is not already expanded.

2. Double-click the device for which you want to update the driver.

3. Click the Driver tab and then click Update Driver.

4. Click Search Automatically for Updated Driver Software. The utility checks the Internet for an available update. If a driver is found, it is automatically downloaded and installed.

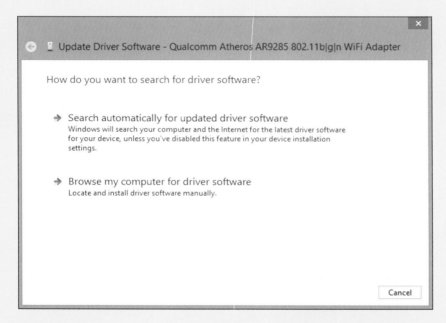

OR

If you have already downloaded an updated driver but haven't installed it yet, click Browse My Computer for Driver Software, and follow the prompts to locate and install it.

Rolling Back a Device Driver

If problems occur with your computer after you update a driver, follow these steps to return to the previous driver version:

1. In Device Manager, double-click the category of device to expand the category if it is not already expanded.

2. Double-click the device for which you want to roll back the driver.

3. Click the Driver tab and then click Roll Back Driver.

4. A confirmation box appears; click Yes.

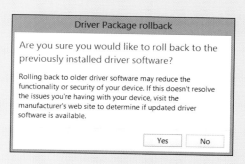

What If There's a Device Problem?

In Device Manager, you might occasionally see a yellow circle with an exclamation point in it superimposed on one of the device's icons, indicating there is a problem with the device. Usually the problem is that a usable driver has not yet been installed. Download a driver from the device manufacturer's website and install it (most come with a Setup program) to solve the problem. Another similar problem is that a device appears with a question mark icon and appears in an Other Devices category. Installing a driver for the device should also correct that problem too.

Quick Review

1. What is the purpose of a device driver?

2. What Windows utility is used to manage device drivers?

3. What does Plug and Play do?

Understanding Digital Storage

Most operating systems save and store files using the same basic principles, although the individual file formats may differ between platforms and operating systems. The following sections describe the logical organization of computer file systems.

Drives, Volumes, and File Systems

A drive is a physical storage unit, such as an HDD, a SSD, or a DVD drive. As you learned in Chapter 3, "Input, Output, and Storage," some drives are separate from their discs, as a DVD drive is. Other drives have the discs built-in, like in an HDD. And some drives are not technically "drives" at all, in that they have no moving parts, but are called drives for consistency; solid-state drives are an example of that. The term hard drive generically refers to both HDD and SSHD storage in popular usage.

Each drive has one or more volumes, which are logical divisions of storage areas. Volumes are represented by letters, such as C:. A small-capacity, removable storage device like a DVD or a USB flash drive has a single volume letter. A large-capacity storage device like an HDD or SSHD may be divided into multiple volumes.

partition To create logical divisions of the available space on a storage medium such as an HDD; or, a logical division of space on a storage medium.

format To create the file system on a volume.

file system A set of rules for storing and managing the files on a volume, such as NTFS or FAT32.

To prepare a hard drive for use, it must first be partitioned. Partitioning creates the logical divisions of the available space. A physical drive can logically be a single volume (one big partition with one volume letter assigned), or it can be split up into many pieces, each with its own volume letter. Each volume must then be formatted. Formatting organizes the available space by creating a file system on it. The file system determines how the files will be stored and retrieved logically.

New Technology File System (NTFS) The proprietary Microsoft file system used in modern versions of Windows.

system volume The volume on which the operating system files are stored.

FAT32 A file system used in Windows 95, Windows 98, and Windows Millennium Edition. FAT stands for File Allocation Table.

Hierarchical File System Plus (HFS+) The file system used with Mac OS X.

ISO 9660 A file system used on optical media such as CDs; also called CD File System, or CDFS.

Universal Disc Format (UDF) An extension of the ISO 9660 file system, a file system used on optical media such as CDs and DVDs.

Depending on the operating system and the utility you are using to partition and format the drive, different file systems may be available. Modern versions of Windows prefer the New Technology File System (NTFS) for the system volume (that is, the volume on which Windows itself is installed), but can also support FAT32, a file system used in earlier Windows versions. Mac OS X uses a file system called Hierarchical File System Plus (HFS+). Linux supports several different file systems, and the default file system installed depends on the distro. CDs and DVDs commonly use the ISO 9660 (also called CD File System, or CDFS) or the Universal Disc Format (UDF) file system. Table 4.1 outlines the most popular file systems.

Different file systems offer different features and benefits. NTFS, for example, provides features like file encryption, file compression, support for long filenames (up to 255 characters), and support for large-capacity volumes (up to 16 TB). You will learn about file encryption and compression later in this chapter.

Table 4.1: Popular File Systems

File System	Type of Disc	Operating System	Notes
NTFS	HDD, SSHD	Windows 2000 and higher	
FAT32	HDD, SSHD	Windows 95 and higher	Obsolete because it can't support volumes over 4GB in size
FAT16	HDD, SSHD	MS-DOS, all Windows versions	Obsolete, replaced by FAT32
FAT12	Floppy disks	MS-DOS, all Windows versions	Obsolete because floppy disks are obsolete
HFS+	HDD, SSHD	Mac OS X	
ISO 9660	Optical	Various	
UDF	Optical	Various	

Windows uses a Disk Management utility to provide information about the system's disks and drives and to allow users to perform disk-based maintenance operations.

CAUTION In the following Step by Step exercise, follow the steps provided only, and **do not make any other changes.** It is possible using Disk Management to render volumes inaccessible and wipe out their data.

Examining the Partitions and Volumes in Windows 8.1

Follow these steps to use the Disk Management tool to find out about your system's drives and their partitions and volumes:

1. Right-click the Start button and choose Disk Management. The Disk Management window opens.

2. Look in the lower section of the window. Each physical drive is listed here. In the example shown, Disk 0 is the physical HDD and CD-ROM 0 is the DVD drive, which is currently assigned the letter D: and has a disc in it with a volume name of Jul 28 2014 that uses the UDF file system.

Each volume appears on a separate line

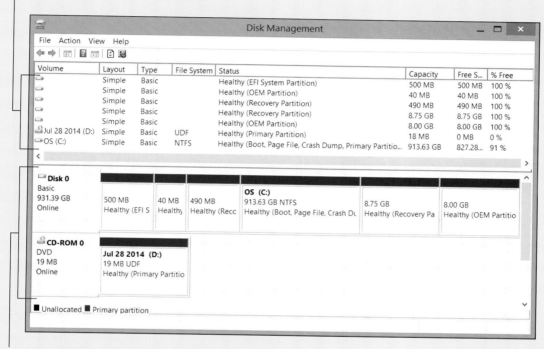

Each physical drive appears on a separate line

3. Note the designations next to each drive letter in the lower section. For example, Disk 0 is a Basic disk; that means it is not set up with Windows' Dynamic Disks feature. Its capacity is listed as 931.39 GB, and it is online (available). CD-ROM 0 is a DVD drive that is currently holding a disc with a 19 MB capacity.

4. Look in the upper section of the window. Each volume is separately listed, along with the file system, the status, the capacity, and the free space. In the example shown, Disk 0 has six partitions, with various designations. Having many partitions is common for a computer on which the operating system was preinstalled, because the PC manufacturer typically places recovery utilities on hidden partitions to help with the process of fixing the computer remotely when problems occur.

   - Healthy: This partition is functioning normally.

   - EFI System Partition: You'll see this partition on a system that uses UEFI instead of a traditional BIOS, as explained in Chapter 2. It contains files needed for the UEFI to function.

   - OEM Partition: OEM partitions are partitions that are placed on the hard drive by the computer manufacturer. OEM stands for Original Equipment Manufacturer.

   - Recovery Partition: Recovery partitions contain data you will need if you want to restore your computer to its original state using the recovery discs that you create (usually with an OEM-supplied utility and blank DVDs).

- Primary Partition: A primary partition is a bootable partition. There's always at least one primary partition per disk. Notice that there are two volumes listed as primary partitions, but they are on separate drives (the hard drive and the DVD drive).

- Boot: The boot partition is the partition that the system actually boots from. (Don't confuse this with the primary partition, which is simply bootable, not actually assigned the job of booting.)

- Page File: The page file is the file that virtual memory uses.

- Crash Dump: Any error logs generated from crashes will be placed on whatever partition is designated the crash dump partition.

5. Look in the upper section of the window. Each volume is separately listed, along with the file system, the status, the capacity, and the free space.

6. Open the File menu and click Exit.

How Files Are Organized in Folders

root directory The top level folder on a storage volume.

The top level of storage for a volume is its root directory. The root directory is like the lobby of a building. All other locations within the volume are accessed by going through it. The term *root directory* is a carryover from an earlier time when folders were called directories. Another name for the root directory is *top-level folder.*

path The complete descriptor of a file's location, including the volume and folders.

A file's path is the complete descriptor of its location. A file named Budget.txt located in the root directory of the C: drive, for example, would have a path like this:

```
C:\Budget.xlsx
```

The colon (:) in the preceding example path indicates that the letter preceding it is a volume letter. The \ follows a folder (directory) name. The example has no name before the \ because the root directory has no name.

Now suppose that file were in a folder called Personal. Its path would look like this:

```
C:\Personal\Budget.xlsx
```

As you learned in Chapter 3, a folder within a folder is called a subfolder. Suppose that the Personal folder had a subfolder called Financial, and our example file was in that folder. The path would look like this:

```
C:\Personal\Financial\Budget.xlsx
```

A volume's folder hierarchy can be complicated. There can be hundreds of folders in the root directory, and each of them can contain many levels of subfolders. A file management utility, such as File Explorer in Windows 8.1, provides a visual picture of the structure that you can browse. For example, in Figure 4.12, the example file appears in the Financial folder. The folder tree in the navigation pane at the left shows the complete path taken to get to that file.

folder tree A graphical representation of a volume's storage hierarchy, with subordinate branches for folders and subfolders.

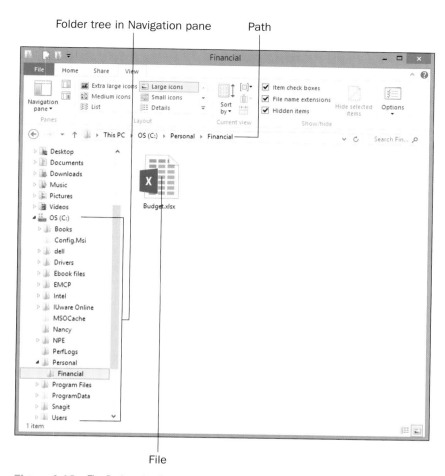

Figure 4.12   The Budget.xlsx file's complete path is illustrated in the navigation pane.

You can jump directly to any location by clicking its name in the navigation pane. You can expand and collapse folders there by double-clicking their names. You can also navigate by using the path that appears in the Address bar at the top of the Windows Explorer window. In Figure 4.12, the path appears like this:

OS (C:) ▶ Personal ▶ Financial

That's simply an alternative way of writing the path. If you click in the Address bar, you see the traditional version of the path instead, like this:

```
C:\Personal\Financial
```

Step by Step

Examining the Folder Structure in Windows 8.1

Follow these steps to use the File Explorer tool to browse the contents of the volumes folders on your computer:

1. Click the File Explorer shortcut on the taskbar, or right-click the Start button and choose File Explorer. File Explorer opens to the This PC location, showing all the volumes that it recognizes on your computer. Some volumes may not appear, so this may not be an exact one-to-one match with the volumes you saw in Disk Management earlier in the chapter. In this example, you see only a hard disk drive (C:), plus shortcuts to some user-specific folders.

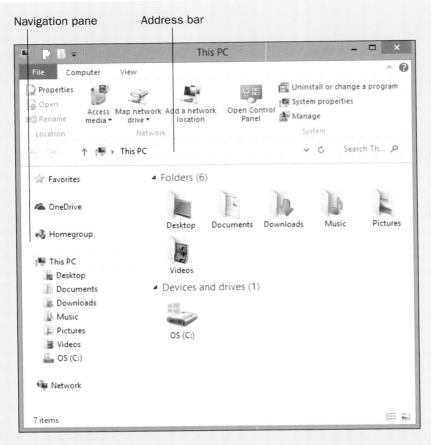

Navigation pane   Address bar

2. Double-click the C: drive in the main window. Its content appears. The folders appear first, followed by any files that are stored in the root directory.

3. Double-click the Windows folder. Its content appears, which includes many subfolders and many files.

4. In the Address bar at the top, click This PC to return to that screen.

5. In the navigation pane at the left, under the This PC heading, double-click the C: drive.

6. Scroll down in the navigation pane, and locate the Users folder and double-click it.

7. In the navigation pane, double-click the Public folder. Then double-click the Public Documents folder.

8. In the Address bar, click the right-pointing arrow to the left of This PC and then click Libraries.

9. Click the Close (X) button in the upper-right corner of the window to close it.

File Extensions and File Types

file extension A code at the end of a filename that indicates the file's type.

Each application has a specific format in which it saves the files you create in it. To help identify the file format, some operating systems (including Microsoft Windows) use file extensions. A file extension is a code following the name of the file that indicates its type. Extensions are separated from the filename by a period, like this: Myfile.docx. In this example, docx is the extension, and it indicates the Microsoft Word format.

Almost all files have file extensions in Windows, not just data files. For example, the executable files that run applications also have extensions, as do the Windows system files and their helper files. Table 4-2 lists some of the most common file extensions and their applications.

Table 4-2 shows some common default application assignments, but the actual application assigned to a particular extension depends on the settings in your operating system. You can configure the OS to associate a file type with any of the applications you have installed on your computer. When an extension is assigned to an application, and you double-click a data file with that extension, the data file automatically opens in the associated application (provided, of course, that the application is capable of handling that file type).

Table 4.2: Common File Extensions

Extension	File Type	Associated Application
txt	Text	Notepad, WordPad, Microsoft Word
gif, png, jpg, tif	Photo or graphic	Paint, Photoshop, or almost any other photo editing program
doc, docx, docm	Word processing document	Microsoft Word, some other word processing programs also support
rtf	Rich Text Format, a word processing document	WordPad, Microsoft Word, or almost any word processing program
xls, xlsx, slxm	Spreadsheet	Microsoft Excel
ppt, pptx, pptm	Presentation	Microsoft PowerPoint
mdb, accdb	Database	Microsoft Access
pdf	Portable document format (platform-independent formatted document)	Adobe Reader, Adobe Acrobat, limited support in Microsoft Word
xps	XML document format (Microsoft-specific platform-independent formatted document)	XPS Viewer, Windows 7 and higher, limited support in Microsoft Word
exe, com, bat	Executable program files	n/a
dll, ini, dat	Helper files for programs and for Windows itself	n/a
zip	Compressed archive file	Windows Explorer, or a third-party program such as WinZip

File Compression

Files can be made to take up less space by compressing them. Compressing a file applies an algorithm to it that makes the file smaller by storing it using more efficient notation. For example, suppose a file contains 36 zeroes in a row. Each character occupies one byte of space, so that's 36 bytes. But a compression algorithm could rewrite that as 0x36, resulting in code that occupies only 4 bytes. When the file is needed, it is decompressed into its original form again, but when it is stored on disk, it is in the smaller form. JPEG is a common graphic file format that uses compression, for example.

algorithm A step-by-step procedure for performing a calculation.

NTFS has an optional compression feature built in. You can enable or disable it for individual files and folders. The trade-off is that when a file or folder is compressed, it takes slightly longer to access it, because the internal compression algorithm must run before the decompressed file can be presented to you.

compressed archive A compressed file that contains one or more other files.

Another type of compression creates a compressed archive, which is a package file containing one or more files within a single compressed file. For example, files with a zip extension are compressed archives. Windows supports the zip archive format and treats zip files like folders. You can also use third-party utility programs such as WinZip to manage zipped archive files.

Step by Step

Enabling NTFS Compression

Follow these steps to see how to enable NTFS compression for a folder in Windows 8.1:

1. Right-click the Start button and choose File Explorer, or click the File Explorer shortcut on the taskbar.

2. Navigate to the desired folder, right-click it, and choose Properties.

3. On the General tab of the folder's Properties dialog box, click Advanced. The Advanced Attributes dialog box opens.

4. Mark the Compress Contents to Save Disk Space check box.

5. Click OK.

6. Click OK to close the Properties box. confirmation dialog box appears.

7. Choose Apply Changes to This Folder Only, or choose Apply Changes to This folder, Subfolders and Files.

   If you apply the change to the folder only, files and subfolders will be compressed only when they remain within this folder. If you apply the changes to all, files and subfolders will remain compressed when you move them to another location on an NTFS volume that is not compressed.

8. Click OK.

   Compressed folders and files appear in file listings with their names in bright blue, to help you remember that they are compressed.

Creating and Browsing a Compressed Archive File

Follow these steps to see how to create a compressed archive file in Windows 8.1:

1. Right-click the Start button and choose File Explorer, or click the File Explorer shortcut on the taskbar.

2. Navigate to the location that contains the files you want to compress and archive together into a single file.

3. Select the desired files and/or folders; then right-click the selection and choose Send To, and then click Compressed (zipped) folder.

The compressed archive file appears in the listing, named the same as the first (alphabetically) of the files or folders. The name is selected so you can type a different name to change it.

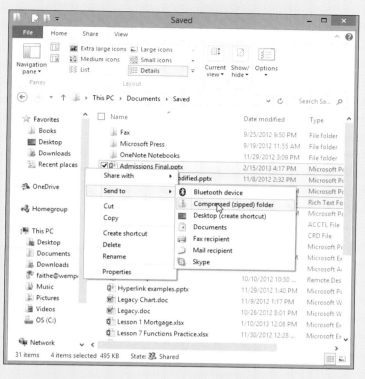

4. Type a new name for the compressed archive file, replacing the default one, and press Enter.

Backups

Because storage media sometimes fail, it's important to back up important files frequently. Businesses spend thousands of dollars on robust, automated systems that back up their servers nightly, as well as key files on individual computers in some cases. Home and small-business users can use smaller backup systems designed for individual PCs.

Backup software can save your backup files to external media, such as a writeable DVD or an external hard drive, or to a network or Internet location. To save space on the backup media, backup software creates its own compressed archive files in its own proprietary format. To restore from the backup, you must use the same backup software that was employed to create the backup. A backup can span multiple discs or volumes, and can include multiple archive files. The collection of archive files created for a single backup instance is called a backup set.

Each time backup software runs, only a small portion of the files will have changed since the last backup was created. In order to reduce the amount of time the backup takes, not all storage is fully backed up every time. Instead, the backup software reads each file's archive attribute (sometimes called an archive flag). When a file is backed up, its archive attribute is turned off. When the file changes, its archive attribute turns

backup software Software that enables and automates the process of backing up files to external media.

backup set A set of backup files created during a single backup operation.

archive attribute A file attribute that indicates whether or not a file has changed since its last backup.

on again. The operating system manages the archive attribute for each file automatically. The backup software can be configured to skip any files where the archive attribute is off, which omits any unchanged files from the backup set.

full backup A backup operation that backs up all files and sets their archive attribute to Off.

differential backup A backup operation that backs up all files that have the archive attribute set to On but does not change that attribute.

You can do a full backup or a partial one. A full backup backs up every file in the specified list, and clears each one's archive attribute (that is, sets it to Off). There are two types of partial backups. A differential backup backs up only files that have changed since the last full backup. Backing up the files does not change their archive attributes, so that the next time you do a backup, they are still marked to be backed up again. If you need to restore the files, you would need the last full backup set and then the most recent differential backup set. This method saves on media because you only have to keep two backup sets, and you can reuse the same media each time you perform a differential backup. However, the differential backup set gets larger every time you run it because more files will have changed, and over time the differential backup set can get fairly large. Therefore, a full backup should be done periodically (for example, every week or two) to keep the size of the differential backup set small.

incremental backup A backup operation that backs up all files that have the archive attribute set to On and then sets the attribute to Off.

An incremental backup, on the other hand, turns off the archive attribute for each file as it backs it up. Therefore, each time you run an incremental backup, it backs up only the files that have changed since the last incremental backup. If you need to restore the files, you would need the last full backup set and every incremental backup set that has been done since then. The backup runs quickly each time, because only the most recently changed files are backed up. However, the user has to maintain many backup sets to have a complete and current backup. Running a full backup creates another full set, and all the previous incremental backups can be discarded or overwritten.

> **TIP** Users who have just a few important files to back up may prefer to manually copy them to an external drive periodically rather than using backup software, especially if the files do not frequently change. Store your backups in a different physical location you're your computer if possible, so that you won't lose your data in the event of a fire or other disaster.

In addition to backing up data to an external hard drive or network location, you can also back it up to "the cloud"—that is, to a data storage site on the Internet. When you back up your files to the Internet, you can access them from anywhere that has an Internet connection. Microsoft OneDrive (formerly SkyDrive) is an example of one such site. After you set it up, it appears as a local folder on your computer. (Chapter 3, "Input, Output, and Storage," provides more information about Microsoft OneDrive.) Other examples of data storage sites in the cloud are Google Drive, iCloud, and Dropbox. All these storage providers offer users a certain amount of free storage with the option to buy additional capacity as needed. You could even be extra cautious and back up to both a hard drive and to a storage site in the cloud. That way, if something happens to one of your backups, you still have another copy of the data.

Businesses have robust backup systems that automatically back up files from each computer on the network as needed, to a safe location (usually off-site). They use backup utility programs designed for large-scale use, often with their own special backup hardware (called a backup appliance). A backup appliance is a special computer that controls a large pool of storage and uses it to store backup copies of the specified data. IT administrators manage these backup appliances; end-users do not have to worry about performing their own backups when a company-wide system is in place.

Because of the large amount of data stored, and the large amount of duplication in that data (for example, each Windows computer has the same Windows system files), many backup appliances employ deduplication techniques that seek to reduce the duplication in the backup sets by creating pointers to data that is already stored rather than storing additional copies of it.

In addition to having a backup plan, companies must also have a disaster recovery plan for their computers. Such a plan outlines how the company's IT department will proceed in the event that a disaster occurs that causes data or hardware loss. For example, a disaster recovery plan may specify which executives should be contacted, the vendor from whom to buy replacement hardware, and the order in which servers should be restored after the hardware becomes available.

backup appliance A specialized computer that performs backups and stores and retrieves backed up information.

deduplication The process of reducing or eliminating duplication in data backup sets.

disaster recovery plan A written plan that explains how a company will recover its IT operations after a natural or man-made disaster that causes data or hardware loss.

Quick Review

1. Define the terms volume, root directory, and folder, and explain how they work together.

2. Explain how a single physical drive can have multiple volumes with different file systems on them.

3. Explain NTFS encryption and compression and the purpose of each.

4. Describe the difference between full, incremental, and differential backups.

Summary

Understanding System Software

System software includes the BIOS, the operating system, and utility programs that perform system maintenance and protection.

A computer's **platform** is its type of hardware. Only certain operating systems can run on certain platforms. The **Intel platform**, also called IBM-compatible, is the most popular platform; this platform's most popular operating system is Windows. The 32-bit Intel platform is called **x86**, and the 64-bit version is called **x64**.

Most operating systems use a **graphical user interface (GUI)**, but some operating systems, especially those designed for use on servers, use a **command-line interface**. UNIX is an example.

There are many types of **utility software** for performing various system maintenance tasks. **Antivirus**, **firewall**, and **anti-spyware** programs protect from outside attacks and malicious software (**malware**). **Anti-spam** programs cut down on the amount of junk email you receive. A **disk checking program** can find and fix file system errors, and a **registry cleanup program** can find and fix inconsistent or unneeded entries in the **registry**. **Backup software** can automate the process of backing up important files.

Comparing the Major Operating Systems

Mac OS X is the operating system on most Apple desktop and notebook computers. Its latest version is OS X 10.10, code named **Yosemite**. Its main competitor is **Microsoft Windows**, which is the most popular operating system in the world, used on more than 90% of all desktop and notebook PCs.

Linux is an open-source operating system based on UNIX. The basic version is free, but you can purchase a packaged collection of add-ons and utility programs with it called a distribution (**distro**). A distro typically includes a GUI as an alternative to Linux's native command-line interface.

You can run multiple operating systems on a single computer by setting it up to **multi-boot** or to use a **virtual machine** to run the secondary operating system within the first one.

A **thin client** operating system such as Chrome OS is designed for small portable notebook computers that are used primarily for going online.

A **server** is a computer that serves an entire network rather than an individual user. The most popular server operating systems are **Linux**, **UNIX**, and **Windows Server**.

Tablets and smartphones have an operating system that is preinstalled on a chip (**system-on-chip**, or **SoC**). Users can download **apps**, which are add-on applications that extend the device's capabilities. The popular SoC operating systems are **iOS**, **Android**, **Windows RT**, and **Windows Phone**.

Understanding Device Drivers

A **device driver** translates between the operating system and a hardware device. You can update a device driver to solve some performance problems you may have with the device, and **roll back** the driver if the new driver doesn't work as well as the previous one.

When you install a new piece of hardware, Windows uses a technology called Plug and Play to identify the device and locate a driver for it if possible.

Understanding Digital Storage

A **drive** is a physical storage unit. It can be **partitioned** into one or more logical **volumes**. **Formatting** a volume places a **file system** on it, which it will use to store its files. **NTFS** is the most popular file system for modern versions of Windows; **FAT32** is an older file system used in earlier versions of Windows. **HFS+** is the Mac OS X file system, and **ISO 9660** (CD File System, or CDFS) and **Universal Disc Format (UDF)** are used for optical discs.

The top level of a storage volume is its **root directory**. A file's **path** is the complete descriptor of its location, including the volume and any folders you pass through to get to it. A **folder tree** is a graphic representation of a volume's folder structure. A **file extension** is a code following the filename that indicates its type.

File compression uses an **algorithm** to make the file smaller by storing it using more efficient notation. A **compressed archive** is a package file containing one or more other files. **Encrypting** a file stores it in a scrambled format so it cannot be snooped from outside of the operating system interface. Some editions of Windows come with a whole-drive encryption feature called **BitLocker**.

Backup software helps keep your data safe by backing it up to external media. The collection of files created for a single backup instance is a **backup set**. A backup can be **full**, **differential**, or **incremental**. You can use a **backup appliance** to back up more efficiently and automatically, and to reduce backup file size with **deduplication**.

Key Terms

adware
algorithm
Android
anti-spam software
app
archive attribute
backup appliance
backup set
backup software
Chrome OS
command-line interface
compressed archive
deduplication
Device Manager
device driver
differential backup
disaster recovery plan
disk checking program
distribution (distro)
FAT32
file extension
file system
firewall software
folder tree
format
full backup
graphical user interface (GUI)

Hierarchical File System Plus (HFS+)
incremental backup
Intel platform
iOS
ISO 9660
Linux
Mac OS X
malware
Yosemite
Microsoft Windows
New Technology File System (NTFS)
partition
path
platform
Plug and Play
registry
registry cleanup program
roll back
root directory
server
shell
spyware
system-on-chip (SoC)
system software
system volume
thin client
uninstaller utility

Universal Disc Format (UDF)
UNIX
utility software
virus
Windows Phone

Windows RT
Windows Server
x64
x86

Test Yourself

Fact Check

1. Which of these is NOT a type of system software?

    a. word processing software

    b. backup software

    c. BIOS

    d. operating system

2. Which operating system has a command-line interface by default?

    a. iOS

    b. UNIX

    c. Android

    d. Windows RT

3. Which of these is a thin client OS?

    a. Windows Server

    b. Chrome OS

    c. Mac OS X

    d. UNIX

4. In a _____, users employ a keyboard to type commands at a prompt.

    a. command-line interface

    b. graphical user interface

    c. utility interface

    d. compressed interface

5. What file system is the default for Windows system volumes?

    a. NTFS

    b. FAT32

    c. HFS+

    d. UDF

6. A volume letter is followed by what symbol?

    a. ; (semi-colon)

    b. % (percent sign)

    c. : (colon)

    d. & (ampersand)

7. Where in File Explorer does a file's path appear?

   a. address bar

   b. ribbon

   c. title bar

   d. navigation pane

8. What would you expect the extension of a compressed archive file to be?

   a. pdf

   b. xps

   c. zip

   d. docx

9. A virtual machine allows you to:

   a. run one operating system inside of another

   b. run more applications than you have memory to run normally

   c. speed up the CPU

   d. run a 64-bit operating system on a 32-bit platform

10. Which type of backup backs up every file in the specified list and clears each one's archive attribute?

   a. full

   b. differential

   c. incremental

   d. None of the above

Matching

Match the term to its description.

   a. x86

   b. GUI

   c. Linux

   d. shell

   e. SoC

   f. UDF

   g. root directory

1. _____The 32-bit version of the Intel platform

2. _____A user interface that uses pictures and a pointing device to issue commands

3. _____An open-source operating system used on a variety of platforms

4. _____An operating system's user interface

5. _____The file system used on DVDs

6. _____An operating system that comes preinstalled on a chip on a portable device

7. _____The top-level folder on a volume

Sum It Up

1. List three types of system software.

2. What is the difference between an OS and a platform?

3. List five types of utility programs.

4. List three operating systems that would run on an IBM-compatible desktop PC.

5. Name three operating systems used on smartphones.

6. Explain the purpose of Plug and Play technology.

7. Explain the purpose of partitioning a drive.

8. Give an example of a complete path to a file, and explain the parts of the path.

Explore More

Linux Distros

Suppose you want to put Linux on an older desktop PC and give it to a relative who wants to use the Internet. But that person doesn't know much about computers, so you must find a Linux distro that is very easy to use, even for a beginner. Do a web search on the terms *Linux distro beginner*. Based on the information you find, choose two Linux distros you think would meet your needs, and explain why you chose the ones you did.

Examining File Associations

Windows has default extension associations for various file types. For example, when you double-click on a file with a txt extension, Windows opens it in Notepad because Notepad is the default application for the txt extension.

When you have more than one application that is capable of opening a certain type of file, you may want to change Windows's default setting for that extension. For example, if you have both Microsoft Word and WordPad, you might prefer one over the other for opening files with an rtf extension.

You can work with file associations in either of two ways. You can browse a list of applications and see what extensions are associated with each one, or you can browse a list of extensions and see what applications are associated with each one. Open the Control Panel in Windows, click Programs, and click Default Programs. Then examine the settings and options available there. To browse by program, choose Set Your Default Programs. To browse by extension, choose Associate a File Type or Protocol with a Program.

Think It Over

NTFS Compression and Encryption

NTFS compression and encryption both make files slightly slower to access. In addition, using encryption introduces another level of responsibility into file management because you must back up the encryption key so you can get your files back in the event of a system disaster that causes the hard drive to be inaccessible via the operating system. Given those drawbacks, do you think either of those features would be worth it to you, personally? Explain your answer.

Backup Scheduling

Suppose you were designing your own backup schedule for your computer. Which folders or files would you back up? Regarding the files you did not choose to back up, why did you exclude them? How often would you perform a full backup? How often would you perform a differential or incremental backup—and which would it be? Think about your answers, and give a reason for each one.

Chapter 5

Introduction to Windows 8.1

Learning objectives

☐ Understand the Windows 8.1 interface

☐ Be able to start up and shut down Windows

☐ Know how to run applications

☐ Perform common file management tasks

Touring Windows 8.1

Starting Up and Shutting Down

Running Applications

Managing Files

In Chapter 4, "Operating System Basics," you learned about operating systems in general—what they do, how they work, how they differ from one another. In this chapter, you will turn your full attention toward one operating system in particular: Windows 8.1.

Windows 8.1 is a popular operating system, installed on millions of personal computers worldwide. This chapter starts with a tour of the Windows desktop and Start screen. You'll learn how to start up and shut down a Windows computer, and how to use special power-saving and security modes. You'll see how to run programs in Windows 8.1. Finally, you'll learn how to manage files using File Explorer, and perform common operations like copying, moving, renaming, and deleting files.

Health IT Specialist

In many countries, governments have recently enacted laws that require health-care providers to computerize certain parts of their practices. For example, patient health records, medical billing, supply and drug inventories, and medical equipment maintenance records will soon need to be in electronic form if they are not already. This requirement opens up many job opportunities for health IT specialists. A health IT specialist plans and sets up health-care recordkeeping systems that meet all government requirements, and keep such systems up to date and in good repair. This job requires at least an associate's degree in a computer-related field, with a bachelor's or master's degree preferred for supervisory positions.

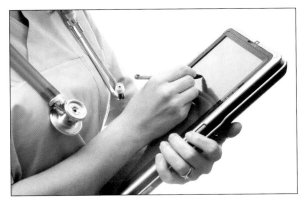
© iStockphoto.com/mkurtbas

Careers in IT

Start screen The tile-based interface from which you can start applications

desktop The Windows 8.1 interface, on which windows open containing applications. Can also refer specifically to the background image.

A Tour of Windows 8.1

Windows 8.1 has two main interfaces: the Start screen and the desktop. The Start screen provides shortcuts for applications you can run, and the desktop serves as your main work environment. When you start your Windows-based PC and sign in, either the desktop or the Start screen appears, depending on your computer's settings. Figures 5.1 and 5.2 show the Start screen and the desktop, respectively.

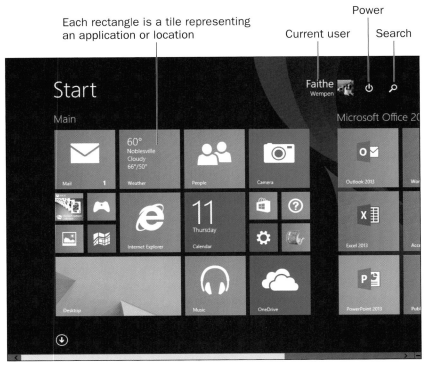

Figure 5.1   The Windows 8.1 Start screen.

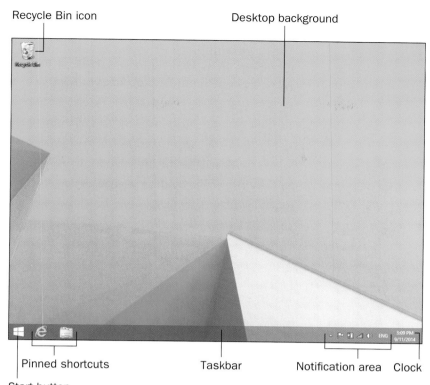

Recycle Bin icon   Desktop background

Pinned shortcuts   Taskbar   Notification area   Clock

Start button

Figure 5.2   The Windows 8.1 desktop.

You can switch back and forth between them easily:

- To switch from the desktop to the Start screen, click the Start button in the lower-left corner of the desktop, or press the Windows key on the keyboard. You can also display the Charms bar (covered Chapter 6, "Windows 78.1 Administration and Maintenance") and then click or tap the Start icon.

- To switch from the Start screen to the desktop, click the Desktop tile on the Start screen, or press the Esc key. (Esc doesn't always work; it only works if you have already displayed the desktop at least once since you signed in.) You can also point the mouse at the upper-left corner of the screen, so that a thumbnail image of the desktop appears, and then click that thumbnail image.

Perhaps you are wondering why Microsoft provides two such different interfaces in Windows 8.1. It is primarily due to Windows 8.1's support for mobile touchscreen devices. The Start screen interface is easy to navigate on a touchscreen, and the new Windows 8 apps (also called Windows Store apps) are optimized for touchscreen use. When Windows 8 was first released, desktop users complained that it was actually harder for them to accomplish their daily tasks in Windows 8 than it had been in Windows 7 because of the interface changes. Windows 8.1 includes updates to some of the features that make it easier for people on desktop and notebook PCs to use the operating system.

Windows 8 app An application that is native to the Windows 8 environment, and runs only under Windows 8. Also called *Windows Store app*.

The Start Screen

The Start screen is like a bulletin board; each of the rectangles on it, called tiles, are items that are pinned to it for quick access. This is *your* bulletin board, and you can customize it any way you like, including

tiles A square or rectangular block on the Start screen that represents an application or file.

unpinning items you don't use, pinning new items that you do use, resizing tiles, and rearranging tiles. All these skills are covered in Appendix A. For now, though, you will work with the Start screen as you find it, which may be somewhat different from what you saw in Figure 5.1. You may have different tiles, arranged differently, and at different sizes.

Modifying the Start Screen

If you can't wait for Appendix A to get started customizing your Start screen, here are a few tips:

- Right-click a tile for a menu from which you can pin or unpin an item on the Start screen and on the taskbar.

- Right-click a tile and then point to Reize to change its size.

- To move a file, click and hold down the mouse button on the tile for a few seconds and then drag it to a new location.

If there is more content on the Start screen than you can see at once, you can scroll to the right to see more. Use the scroll bar at the bottom of the screen, or if you are using a touch screen, swipe from right to left.

Apps list The list accessed from the Start screen of all installed applications

It's important to understand that the Start screen does not contain a complete list of all installed applications. To see that complete Apps list, click the down arrow at the bottom of the Start screen. The Apps list, shown in Figure 5.3, contains shortcuts for all installed apps, of all types.

Scroll to see more

Figure 5.3 The Apps list shows all the installed applications. Scroll to the right to see additional applications.

The Desktop

Your Windows desktop is like a physical workspace in some ways. You can have multiple files and projects open at the same time, spread out on the desktop so you can see each one of them. The desktop can be changed to suit your personal style. The desktop background can be a solid color, or it can be a picture of your choice. Figure 5.2 shows the default picture that comes with Windows 8.1. You will learn how to customize your desktop in Appendix A, "Customizing Windows 8.1."

The taskbar is the thin bar across the bottom of the screen. It is used to start programs and to manage the programs that are already running. At the far-left end is the Start button.

The small graphics you see on the desktop are called icons. An icon can sit on the desktop, as the Recycle Bin icon does in Figure 5.2, or it can be pinned to the taskbar for easy access. For example, in Figure 5.2, two pinned icons appear to the right of the Start button. The center of the taskbar is blank in Figure 5.2, but if any programs were running or windows open, buttons for those programs or windows would appear there. Some other icons are at the right end of the taskbar, but these aren't pinned there. That area is called the notification area (or system tray), and the icons there represent information from programs or system components that are running in the background, such as the Volume Control and the Battery Meter. At the far-right end of the taskbar is a clock.

When you click the Start button, the Start screen opens, as shown in Figure 5.1. When you right-click the Start button, you see a menu of shortcuts to some of the most popular administrative tools for Windows, such as Control Panel, Command Prompt, and File Explorer, as shown in Figure 5.4.

taskbar The bar along the bottom of the Windows desktop, from which you can start programs and manage running programs.

Start button The button that opens the Start screen.

icon A small picture representing a file, folder, application, or other object.

pinned Attached to a fixed feature onscreen, such as to the taskbar or the Start menu.

notification area The area to the left of the clock on the taskbar, containing icons for programs running in the background. Also called the **system tray**.

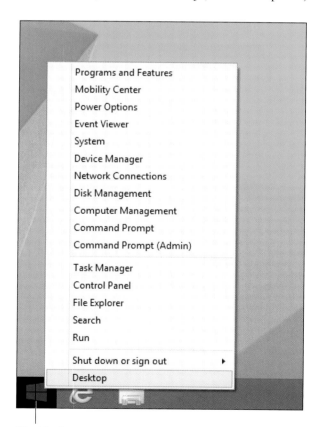

Start button

Figure 5.4 Right-clicking the Start button opens a menu of shortcuts to common tools.

Starting Up and Shutting Down

When you turn on the computer's power, Windows takes a minute or so to load, and then a Welcome screen appears showing a graphic and the current date and time. (You can change what graphic appears; see Appendix A.) From the Welcome screen, press any key (or swipe upward on a touchscreen) to access a sign-in prompt.

You might see thumbnail images representing all the user accounts on your computer; if you see that, click the one that represents your account. If you were previously signed in, you might see your own sign-in prompt immediately, and not have to select your account. (If you see someone else's account, click the Back arrow to return to the list of accounts.)

Type your password and press Enter, and Windows finishes starting up by loading the user settings for your account. These settings include your preferred display settings, as well as your keyboard, mouse, and sound settings.

NOTE To control which interface appears at startup, right-click an empty spot on the desktop's task-bar and choose Properties. On the Navigation tab of the Taskbar and Navigation Properties dialog box, mark or clear the When I Sign In or Close All Apps on a Screen, Go to the Desktop Instead of Start check box. There are several other check boxes in this same dialog box that you can mark or clear to further modify the behavior of the Start screen in relation to the desktop.

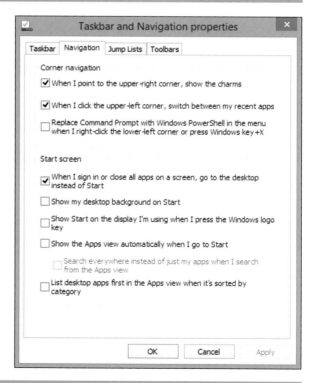

See "Managing User Accounts" in Chapter 6, "Windows 8.1 Administration and Maintenance," to learn how to add new accounts, change their passwords, and change the picture assigned to each account.

Shutting Down or Restarting the PC

When you shut down the PC, Windows shuts down and the computer stops using power. The next time you start the computer, Windows must reload itself into memory, which takes a minute or two. You should shut down a computer completely before moving it, storing it, or servicing it. You should also shut down the computer when prompted to do so by Windows itself. (A complete shutdown and restart is sometimes required to complete the installation of certain updates.) When you shut down the computer and then turn it back on again later, that's called a cold boot because the computer's circuitry has been off (and is therefore cold).

When you restart the PC, Windows shuts down, but the computer's power remains on, and Windows immediately restarts. Restarting is also called a warm boot because the computer stays on (warm) as it reboots. You should restart when Windows prompts you to do so (for example, after updates have been installed), and also as a troubleshooting technique if you begin to experience problems with Windows. To restart Windows, click the Power icon at the top of the Start screen and choose Restart from the menu, as shown in Figure 5.5.

shut down To quit Windows and turn the computer's power off.

cold boot To start up a computer from a power-off state.

warm boot To restart a computer that is already powered on.

Power

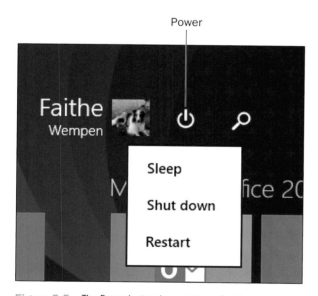

Figure 5.5 The Power button has a menu of options for shutting down and restarting.

Restarting Helps!

If you talk to any computer professional about a problem you are having with your computer, the first thing he or she will probably ask you is: *Have you tried restarting?* That's because restarting Windows can cure a variety of one-time or occasional problems that may occur. For example, suppose your mouse pointer starts jumping around wildly as you move the mouse. That's a problem with the display adapter, and it can almost always be cured by restarting the PC. Another common problem that restarting usually fixes is a keyboard that suddenly starts sending the wrong characters to the PC as you type.

Troubleshooting

Besides shutting down, there are several other ways to make the computer use less (or no) power. You will learn about them in the section "Placing the PC in a Low-Power Mode," later in this chapter.

Step by Step

Shutting Down a Windows 8.1 Computer

Follow these steps to shut down the computer completely and turn its power off:

1. Display the Start screen and then click the Power button. See Figure 5.5.
2. Click Shut Down.
3. If any programs have unsaved files, a prompt appears for them. Respond to the prompt as needed.

Restarting a Windows 8.1 Computer

Follow these steps to restart the computer:

1. Display the Start screen and then click the Power button. See Figure 5.5.
2. Click Restart.
3. If any programs have unsaved files, a prompt appears for them. Respond to the prompt as needed.

Placing the PC in a Low-Power Mode

Windows supports two special modes that you can place the computer in as an alternative to shutting down completely. In each of these modes, when the computer resumes operation, the desktop is just as you left it, including any open programs, windows, and files. This saves you time because you don't have to wait as long for Windows to start up as you normally would, and when it does start up, you don't have to reopen the applications and windows you want to continue working with.

sleep To place the computer in a low power consumption mode without shutting down running programs.

Sleep mode A power-saving mode that keeps RAM powered but turns off everything else to save power.

Sleep mode is a low-power state. It keeps the RAM powered, but shuts down all other components. RAM doesn't use much memory, so the computer consumes very little power. On a desktop computer, that means it uses less electricity. On a battery-powered computer, that means the battery lasts much longer. Waking up from Sleep mode is very quick—only a few seconds. Hibernate mode is a no-power-needed state. It copies the contents of RAM to a reserved area on the hard drive, and then shuts the power down completely. When the computer starts back up again, instead of booting normally, it reads the stored data back into memory, so you can pick up where you left off. Hibernate mode takes more time to wake up from than Sleep mode does (about 30 seconds, on the average), but that's less time than it would take to start the computer from being completely shut down.

Hibernate mode A power-saving mode that saves the contents of RAM to the hard drive and then shuts down all power. When the computer wakes up, it reads the saved data back into RAM so the computer does not have to restart completely.

To place the computer in one of these modes, select it from the Power button's menu on the Start screen, as shown in Figure 5.5. Closing the lid on a notebook computer usually puts the system into sleep mode automatically; you may see the power light flashing intermittently as an indication the computer is sleeping.

To wake up from Sleep mode, press any key on the keyboard, or, if that doesn't work, press the computer's Power button. To wake up from Hibernate mode, press the computer's Power button.

Stuck?

If your computer appears completely dead when you try to wake it up from Sleep or Hibernate mode, try holding down the computer's Power button for 10 seconds. Doing so will shut the PC down completely, resetting any special power mode it was previously in. You may see an error message when you restart the computer about Windows not shutting down correctly, and offering to start Windows in a special mode. Don't use a special mode; choose Start Windows Normally.

Troubleshooting

Signing Out and Switching Users

Windows 8.1 supports multiple user accounts. When one user is finished, he or she can sign out, which shuts down any running programs, closes any open data files, unloads all personal settings for that user, and returns to the sign in screen, with all the available users listed. From that point another user can sign in. Signing out closes the user's personal activities down, but it does not completely restart Windows. Therefore, it takes less time than a full restart. To sign out, click your username at the top of the Start screen and then click Sign Out. See Figure 5.6.

sign out To close a user account's session, closing all open programs and data files and unloading all of that user's personal settings.

Figure 5.6 Click your username at the top of the Start screen for a menu from which you can sign out, change users, or lock the PC.

If another user wants to use the computer for a short time, the first user may not want to take the time to shut down all applications and data files that he or she is working on. The Switch User command suspends the current user's session but does not end it, and returns to the sign in screen. Another user can then sign in. The users can switch back and forth freely between the open accounts, and other users can even sign in too. To switch users, click your username at the top of the Start screen and then click one of the other users listed on the menu that appears, as shown in Figure 5.6.

Switch User A Windows feature that enables another user to log in without the original user signing out first.

Why not just let another person sit down and use the computer for a few minutes, without switching? That's fine to do, as long as the first user doesn't mind the lack of privacy. Each logged-in user has his or her own separate personal files and settings, and anyone who uses the computer while you are logged in can see your files. Switching users also enables each user to have his or her own preferred settings, such as display resolution and color scheme.

Locking the PC

lock To prevent unauthorized users from using a computer by displaying a password prompt.

If you are going to be away from your computer for a while, you might not want other people to be able to see what you were working on or snoop on your computer while you are gone. To prevent such intrusion, you can use the Lock command. Locking preserves the current state of the computer but redisplays the Lock screen and then the sign in screen for your account. You must retype your password when you return to the computer to continue your session. Locking is similar to switching users except the sign in screen that appears shows the prompt only for the user who locked the PC, and not the full list of users that you see when you use Switch User.

To lock the PC, click your user name at the top of the Start screen, as shown in Figure 5.6, and click Lock. Alternatively, the PC can be locked by pressing the Windows key on the bottom left of the keyboard and the L key simultaneously.

Quick Review

1. What is the difference between Sign Out and Restart?
2. What is the difference between Sleep and Hibernate?
3. What is the difference between Lock and Switch User?

Running Applications

As you learned in Chapter 1, "Computer Basics," programs that perform some useful task (other than keeping the computer itself running) are known as *applications*. Running applications is the main reason Windows exists. Windows comes with a variety of small applications that it calls Accessories; these include a calculator, a text editor, a simple word processor, and a drawing program. You can also buy and install other applications on your own, and some computers come with some third-party applications already installed, such as a DVD movie player or a productivity suite such as Microsoft Office.

There are two kinds of applications you can run in Windows 8.1. One is the traditional type that also ran in earlier Windows versions, called **desktop applications**. These applications run in bordered windows on the desktop. The other kind, known as **Windows 8 apps** (or *Windows Store apps*), run full-screen, separate from the desktop. They have their own special controls, rather than the usual menus and toolbars. You will learn more about running each of these application types later in this chapter.

Starting an Application

To start an application, do any of the following:

- Click its shortcut on the taskbar, if it's pinned there

- Double-click its shortcut on the desktop, if there is a shortcut for it there

- Click its tile on the Start screen , if it has a tile there

- From the Start screen, click the down arrow to display the Apps list, and then click the application on that list

- From the Start screen, begin typing the application's name, and then click its name in the search results, as shown in Figure 5.7.

Figure 5.7   Begin typing the name of an application and then click it in the search results.

Put It to Work

Pinning Shortcuts

An easy way to re-find an application is to pin it, either to the Start screen or to the taskbar. If you pin it to the Start screen, it appears as a tile there. If you pin it to the taskbar, it appears to the right of the Start button. After locating the desired item on the Apps list, but before clicking it to select it, right-click it. On the menu that appears, choose Pin to Start or Pin to Taskbar.

Manipulating a Window

As the name implies, Microsoft Windows is based on windows—movable rectangular blocks in which different types of content appear. When you run a desktop application, it appears in its own window, and when you browse a file listing, that listing appears in its own window too. Figure 5.8 illustrates some basic parts of a window.

window A movable rectangular block in which content appears.

The title bar is the bar across the top of the window. If the window holds an application, it shows the application's name. If the application has a file open, it also shows the file's name. You can move a window around onscreen by dragging its title bar.

title bar The bar across the top of a window that shows the window's name; click the title bar and drag the window to move it.

Figure 5.8 Each window has these features in common.

The buttons at the far-right end of the title bar control the window's size.

minimize To shrink the window to a button on the taskbar.

Minimize: Hides the window by shrinking it down to a button on the taskbar. Use this button to get a window out of the way temporarily without closing it.

maximize To enlarge the window to fill the entire screen.

restore To shrink a window from its maximized state to the size it was before it was maximized.

Maximize: Enlarges the window to fill the entire screen. When a window is already maximized, this button changes to a **Restore** button, which returns the window to the size it was before you maximized it.

Close: Closes the window, exiting the application that was open in it (if applicable).

Step by Step

Move a Window

Follow these steps to move a window:

1. Position the mouse pointer over the window's title bar.

2. Hold down the left mouse button and drag the window to a new location.

Resize a Window

Follow these steps to resize a window:

1. Position the mouse pointer over the window's border. The pointer will turn into a double-headed arrow.

2. Hold down the left mouse button, and drag the border to change the window's size.

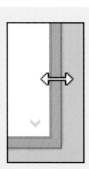

Each window has a border around its edges. You can position the mouse pointer over any part of the border and then drag to change the size of the window. If you drag a corner of the border, you can resize in both dimensions at once.

Navigating in a Desktop Application

Most desktop applications have one of two interfaces: a menu interface or a ribbon interface. A menu interface is typical of older applications and applications not developed by Microsoft; the ribbon interface is common in newer Microsoft applications.

A menu-based interface has a menu bar across the top of the screen, immediately below the title bar. You can click a menu name to open the menu, as shown in Figure 5.9. Notice in Figure 5.9 that some commands have keyboard shortcuts listed next to them. You can press those keys instead of using the menu system if you prefer.

menu bar A horizontal bar near the top of a window containing the names of menus that can be opened by clicking on the names.

keyboard shortcut Two or more keys that, when pressed in combination, issue a command.

If a program does not appear to have a menu bar, try pressing the Alt key. A menu bar may appear. **TIP**

Ellipsis indicates a dialog box will appear

Menu bar   Keyboard shortcut

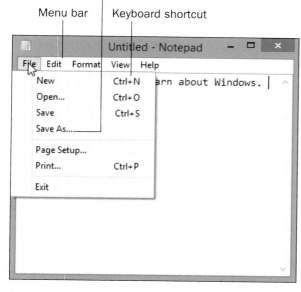

Figure 5.9 Menu-based application windows have these features.

Notice also that some commands have ellipses after them (. . .). These commands open dialog boxes, which are windows that prompt you for additional information. For example, if you click the Print command, the Print dialog box opens, prompting you to enter print settings, as shown in Figure 5.10.

dialog box A window that appears in response to selecting a command, prompting for more information about how the user wants the command to be executed.

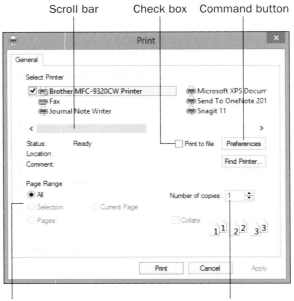

Scroll bar   Check box   Command button

Figure 5.10   Some menu commands open dialog boxes.

Option buttons   Text box with increment buttons

Dialog boxes have various ways of asking you for information. For example, the dialog box in Figure 5.10 has the following features:

- **Scrollable list:** The list of printers at the top of the dialog box has a scroll bar beneath it. You can drag the scroll box from side to side to scroll the listing, or click the arrow at one end of the scroll bar to scroll in that direction.

- **Check box:** A check box toggles a feature on or off. Click it to change its state.

- **Text box:** A text box enables you to enter text or a number directly into it.

- **Increment buttons:** Text boxes that only accept numeric values sometimes have increment buttons, which appear as small up and down arrows. You can click an arrow to increment (increase) or decrement (decrease) the number shown in the text box as an alternative to manually typing a number.

- **Option buttons:** Option buttons present a group of mutually exclusive values. When one option button in a group is selected, the previous selection is cleared.

- **Command buttons:** Command buttons are large rectangular buttons with text labels on them. Clicking a command button performs an action, such as the Print, Cancel, or Apply buttons in Figure 5.10, or opens another dialog box, as with the Preferences and Find Printer buttons.

toolbar A group of graphical buttons representing commands.

Some menu-based applications contain one or more toolbars, which are groups of graphical buttons that serve as shortcuts for issuing certain commands. Figure 5.11 shows an application that uses a toolbar. In most cases, you can point at a button on a toolbar to see a pop-up ScreenTip that tells the button's name or purpose.

Figure 5.11   Some menu-based applications contain toolbars.

Ribbon-based applications do not have a menu bar or toolbar. Instead, they have a tabbed ribbon, which is somewhat like a large multi-page toolbar. Each tab represents a different page of tools. Click a tab to access the buttons and other tools on that tab. Figure 5.12 shows an app called WordPad. It has two ordinary tabs, Home and View, containing commands you can select. It also contains a File tab, which is the blue tab to the left of the other two. The File tab opens a File menu, which contains commands for saving, opening, closing, and printing files. Microsoft Office programs use this same type of interface, so you will become very familiar with it in upcoming chapters.

ribbon The main toolbar in Office applications and some other Windows applications, consisting of multiple tabbed pages of commands.

In most ribbon-based applications, there is also a small toolbar above the tabs called the Quick Access toolbar. You can add a copy of any button to this toolbar to keep it handy. To add a button to it, right-click the button on the ribbon and choose Add to Quick Access Toolbar.

Quick Access toolbar   Tabs

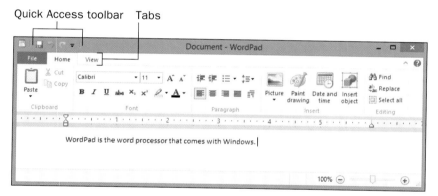

Figure 5.12   A ribbon-based interface.

In most applications, both menu-based and ribbon-based, you can right-click to open a shortcut menu (also called a context menu) and select commands from there. The shortcut menu's content changes depending on what you right-click and what you are doing. For example, if you right-click some text that you've selected, the shortcut menu contains commands to cut and copy it, as shown in Figure 5.13.

shortcut menu A context-sensitive menu that appears when you right-click an object onscreen.

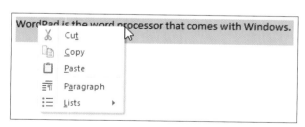

Figure 5.13   Right-clicking in an application opens a context-sensitive shortcut menu.

Exiting a Desktop Application

To close an application, close its window by clicking the Close (X) button in the upper-right corner, or open its File menu and choose Exit, or press Alt+F4 when the application window is active.

Using a Windows 8 App

After starting a Windows 8 app, you might wonder what to do next. Most Windows 8 apps do not have menus, toolbars, or ribbons visible. The key thing to remember in a Windows 8 app is *right-click*. Right-clicking opens a command bar at either the top or bottom of the application screen, and from there you can click a command on the command bar. Different commands appear on the command bar depending both on the application and on what area you right-clicked on. For example, if you right-click on a picture in the Photos app, commands appear for handling that individual photo, as shown in Figure 5.14.

Back button

Command bar

Figure 5.14   Right-clicking in a Windows 8 app displays a command bar from which you can select commands.

The other key thing to remember in a Windows 8 app is to look for a Back button (a left-pointing arrow button) near the upper-left corner; this button takes you back to the previous screen in the application. For example, in the Photos app, when you view a specific photo, you can click Back to return to the list of photos.

Exiting a Windows 8 App

To exit a Windows 8 app, you can do any of the following with the app displayed onscreen:

- On a touchscreen, drag down from the top of the screen to the bottom.

- Using the mouse, drag from the top of the screen to the bottom.

- Move the mouse pointer to the top of the screen, so that a black title bar appears for the app, and then click the Close (X) button at the far right end of that title bar.

- Press Alt+F4.

Switching Between Open Applications

You can have as many applications open as you like at once (subject to your computer's memory limitations), and switch among them freely. The easiest way to switch applications is to click the desired application's button on the taskbar. Each running desktop application appears on the taskbar, and you can also configure Windows to show Windows 8 apps on the taskbar too.

There are several methods of switching applications, outlined in the following steps.

Step by Step

Setting Up the Taskbar to Show Windows 8 Apps

Follow these steps to make sure that the taskbar is configured so that running Windows 8 apps appear there.

1. From the desktop, right-click the taskbar and choose Properties. The Taskbar and Navigation Properties dialog box opens.

2. On the Taskbar tab, mark the Show Windows Store Apps on the Taskbar check box.

3. Click OK.

Switch Between Running Apps Using the Taskbar

Follow these steps to switch apps using the taskbar.

1. From a Windows 8 app, press Alt+Esc to return to the desktop.

2. Click the app on the taskbar that you want to use.

Switch Between Running Apps with Alt+Tab

Follow these steps to switch apps using the Alt+Tab method.

1. Hold down the Alt key and tap the Tab key. A horizontal bar appears in the center of the screen with a thumbnail image of each running application.

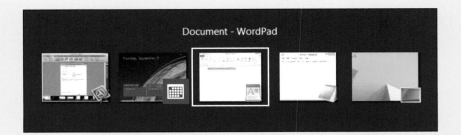

Document - WordPad

2. Press Tab repeatedly until the desired application's thumbnail is selected.

3. Release the Alt key.

Switch Between Running Windows 8 Apps

Follow these steps to switch among the Windows 8 apps that are open.

1. Point the mouse pointer to the upper-left corner of the screen. A thumbnail image appears of one of the open Windows 8 apps, or of the desktop. (This method considers the desktop to be a single application, regardless of how many desktop applications are running.)

2. Slide the mouse pointer downward slightly. An App Switcher bar appears at the side of the screen showing thumbnails of all running Windows 8 apps.

3. Click the thumbnail for the desired app.

Displaying Two Windows 8 Apps At Once

By default, each Windows 8 app fills the entire screen. Sometimes, however, you might want to see two Windows 8 apps side by side, or a Windows 8 app and a desktop app.

Step by Step

Displaying Two Windows 8 Apps at Once

Follow these steps to split the screen so that you can see two apps at once.

1. Open the first Windows 8 app to display.

2. Drag from the top of the screen downward until the full-screen app becomes a thumbnail image.

3. Drag to the left or right and then release the mouse button to drop the app into half of the screen.

4. Return to the Start screen, and start another Windows 8 app, or switch to the desktop. The second app appears in the other half of the screen.

5. If desired, drag the divider line between the panes to adjust the split percentage. To hide one of the applications so that the other is full-screen, drag the divider all the way in one direction.

Quick Review

1. How can you search the Start menu for the application you want to run?

2. In a menu-based interface, what does an ellipsis (. . .) indicate about a command?

3. In a ribbon-based interface, what happens when you click the File tab (the leftmost tab)?

Using Internet Explorer

This book devotes an entire chapter (Chapter 15, "Web Basics") to using Internet Explorer (IE), but you will probably need to use the web before you get to that chapter to complete some of your assignments, so here is a very quick overview.

Windows 8.1 has a shortcut to Internet Explorer pinned to the taskbar, so you can start the desktop version of IE from there.

The page that appears initially depends on what page has been set as the default (referred to as the Home page). If you are accessing IE from your school or work, a page may have been assigned for you specific to that organization.

To go directly to a specific address (called a Uniform Resource Locator, or URL), type it in the address bar. You can also use the address bar to perform searches. Instead of entering a specific address in the address bar, type some keywords there, or even a whole sentence. Your default search engine will return a list of pages that meet your search criteria.

Back button   Address bar   Tabs   New Tab button

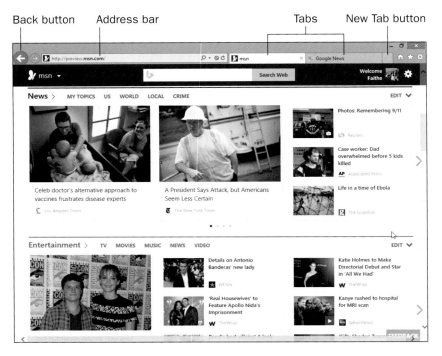

Use the Back button to return to a previous page. To go back several steps at once, hold the mouse button down on the Back button to open a menu of previously viewed pages.

To open a link in a new tab, right-click the link and choose Open in New Tab. You can then switch back and forth freely between the open pages by clicking their tabs. You can also start a new tab without specifying a page to show on it by clicking the New Tab button to the right of the rightmost displayed tab.

address bar The field above the menu bar in File Explorer that shows the current path.

Managing Files

As you learned in Chapter 4, a computer's file system consists of physical drives that contain volumes that have letters (with colons) assigned to them, like C: and D:. Each volume can contain folders, and each folder can contain files. Files can also exist at the top level of a volume's organization (its root directory).

In Windows 8.1, File Explorer is the tool for managing files. "Managing" is a pretty broad term, encompassing all the various operations you might perform on a file, including moving, copying, renaming, deleting, and viewing its properties. The rest of this chapter is devoted to teaching you those skills.

Understanding the File Explorer Interface

In many ways, File Explorer resembles any other desktop application window. It has a title bar, a menu bar, and window controls, all of which you learned about earlier in this chapter. It also has some extra features, though, that not every window has, shown in Figure 5.15.

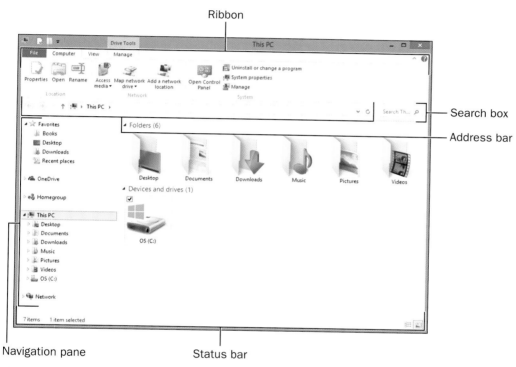

Figure 5.15 File Explorer has some tools and features that most application windows don't have.

- **Navigation pane:** The pane on the left side of the File Explorer window contains links for displaying various locations, both on your local computer and on any networks you may be connected to.

- **Ribbon:** As in many other applications, the ribbon in File Explorer is a multi-tabbed toolbar from which you select commands.

- **Address bar:** The address bar, which appears below the ribbon, shows the current path. You learned about paths in the "How Files Are Organized in Folders" section in Chapter 4.

- **Status bar:** This bar appears at the bottom of the window, and reports information about the currently displayed location.

- **Search box:** To find a particular file or folder in File Explorer, you can type a part of its name in the Search box and press Enter. The Search feature looks in files, folders, and objects in your Outlook data file (if you have one) and looks at both the filenames and their contents.

Navigating to Different Locations

When you open File Explorer, the location shown is This PC. This location is a starting point for accessing the drives and user folders on your system. It contains icons for each hard disk drive and each removable disc drive (such as a DVD drive), as well as shortcuts to your user folders. See Figure 5.15.

NOTE The Libraries feature was an important part of Windows 7 file storage, but it has been deemphasized in Windows 8.1, and shortcuts to libraries do not appear in the navigation bar by default in File Explorer. If you turn on the display of libraries (by right-clicking in the navigation pane and choosing Show Libraries), File Explorer opens by default to the Libraries location rather than to This PC. You will learn more about libraries later in this chapter.

One way to navigate to a different location is to click one of the links in the navigation pane (the left pane). The navigation pane contains these expandable sections, as shown in Figure 5.16:

- **Favorites:** Contains shortcuts for a few common locations, such as the desktop and Recent Places. You can also add your own location shortcuts here, for easy access to the locations you use the most.

- **OneDrive:** Contains shortcuts for the locally cached copies of your OneDrive folders, if you use that feature. OneDrive is the free cloud storage that comes with Windows 8.1 and Office 2013; it is free to anyone with a Microsoft account, which is also free.

homegroup A small group of mutually trusted computers on a peer-to-peer network such as in a home or small office.

- **Homegroup:** If your computer is part of a homegroup, a link to it appears. A homegroup is a type of networking used in home and small-business workgroup environments. You learn more about networking in Chapter 13, "Networking and Internet Basics."

- **This PC:** Contains a list of all the local volumes in an expandable folder tree.

- **Network:** Contains shortcuts for browsing a network if you are connected to one.

To expand a section, double-click its name, or point to it (so that a white triangle appears to its left) and then click the triangle to expand it. When a section is expanded in the folder tree, the triangle next to it appears black; click the black triangle to collapse the section again.

You can also navigate by double-clicking a folder in the main pane. For example, you could start out by clicking This PC in the navigation pane to display a list of volumes, and then double-clicking the C: volume, and then double-clicking a folder in the listing that appears, and keep double-clicking folders until you arrive at the file you are seeking.

If you want to go back one step in your navigation, click the Back button left-pointing arrow) in the upper left corner of the window. The Forward button (right-pointing arrow) takes you one step forward again after you have used Back.

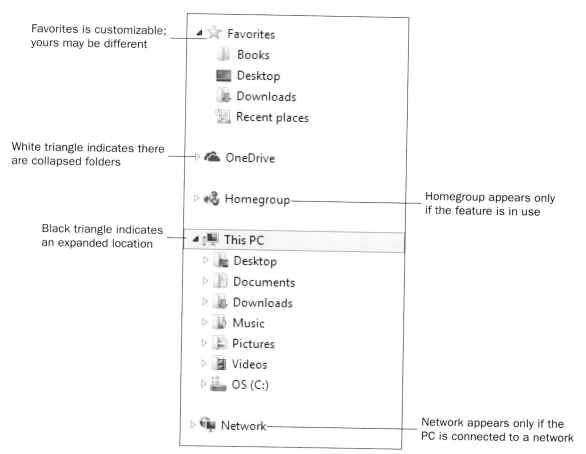

Favorites is customizable; yours may be different

White triangle indicates there are collapsed folders

Black triangle indicates an expanded location

Homegroup appears only if the feature is in use

Network appears only if the PC is connected to a network

Figure 5.16 Locations in the navigation pane.

If you want to go up one or more levels in the hierarchy, you can expand the folder tree in the navigation pane and click the folder location to jump to, or you can click the folder name in the address bar. You can also click any of the triangles between the folder names in the address bar to open a menu of locations at that same level and then click any location from the menu to jump to it.

Changing the View of a Location

Use the View tab on the ribbon to change to a different view. As shown in Figure 5.17, the Layout group on the View tab contains buttons for each of the available views. If you want Details or Large Icons view, you can alternatively use their shortcut icons on the status bar.

Select a view

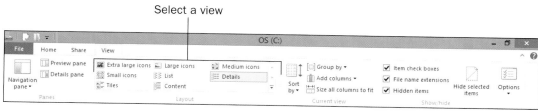

Figure 5.17 Choose a view from the View tab.

There are several other interesting viewing options on the View tab. For example, in the Panes group, you can toggle a Preview pane and a Details pane on and off, for previewing or getting information about selected files or folders. You can also sort and group the files using the commands in the Current View group. You'll learn more about customizing the File Explorer interface in Appendix A.

Understanding Libraries

library A virtual folder that combines the contents of one or more specified folders into a single view.

virtual folder A view that resembles a folder but has no direct equivalent in the computer's file system.

A library is not a folder, although it looks like one. It is a virtual folder created by combining the contents of several different folders in one pane. The Libraries feature enables you to work with the contents of many different locations at once, without worrying about where a particular file is actually stored. Libraries were enabled by default in Windows 7, but in Windows 8.1 they are not, and you must turn on their display in File Explorer in order to easily access them.

Step by Step

Enabling Library Display in File Explorer

Follow these steps to add the Libraries group to the navigation pane in File Explorer.

1. In File Explorer, in the navigation pane, right-click an empty area.

2. Click Show Libraries. A shortcut to each of your libraries now appears in the navigation pane. You can repeat these steps to turn the library display back off again.

NOTE As noted earlier, if you turn on the Libraries feature as in the previous steps, the default location shown each time File Explorer opens is Libraries, rather than This PC. After you complete this section of the chapter on libraries, you may wish to turn their display back off again. Future exercises in this book assume that the default File Explorer location is This PC.

Windows 8.1 comes with four libraries already set up for you: Documents, Music, Pictures, and Videos. Your libraries are unique to your user account; if someone else logs into the same PC, he will see his own libraries instead of yours. This provides for some privacy when multiple people share a computer. You can also create other libraries if you like.

NOTE Although the default library names reflect the types of files that Windows suggests you store in them, libraries are not limited to certain file types. You can store any files in any libraries.

Each library monitors the contents of one or more locations. For example, the Documents library might monitor three folders: the signed-in user's personal Documents folder (C:\Users*username*\Documents), a Public Documents folder (C:\Users\Public\Public Documents), and the signed-in user's Documents folder in his or her OneDrive cloud storage. You have complete control over which folders each library monitors, so you can add and remove folders from the list as desired.

When you save a file to your Documents library, where is that file actually saved, if the library represents multiple locations? That depends on which folder is set up to be the save location. In the Documents library, for example, the default save location is C:\Users\username\Documents.

save location The location where files are saved when a user saves them to a library.

Step by Step

Setting a Library to Monitor Additional Folders

Follow these steps to add another folder to a library's Locations list:

1. In File Explorer, in the navigation pane, right-click the desired library and choose Properties. The Properties dialog box opens for that library.

2. Click Add.

3. Navigate to the desired folder, select it, and then click the Include folder button.

4. Click OK.

Changing the Save Location for a Library

Follow these steps to change which folder a library stores files in when you save to that library:

1. In File Explorer, in the navigation pane, right-click the desired library and choose Properties. The Properties dialog box opens for that library.

2. In the Library Locations list, click the folder you want to use as the save location.

3. Click Set Save Location.

4. Click OK.

Creating a New Library

Follow these steps to create a new library:

1. In File Explorer, in the navigation pane, right-click Libraries, and on the menu that appears, point to New, and then click Library. A new library appears in the list, named New Library. The name is selected, so you can rename it.

2. Type a new name for the library and press Enter.

3. Right-click the new library and choose Properties. The Properties dialog box for the new library opens.

4. Add folders to the new library using the steps from "Setting a Library to Monitor Additional Folders."

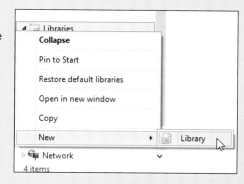

5. Choose the save location using the steps from the preceding instructions for "Changing the Save Location for a Library."

6. Open the Optimize This Library For: drop-down list and choose the file type that is most appropriate for this library, or leave it set to General Items if the library will contain a variety of content.

7. (Optional) If you do not want this library to appear in the navigation pane under Libraries, clear the Shown in Navigation Pane check box.

8. Click OK.

Perhaps you are wondering what the relationship is between the default libraries and the default user folders that appear under the This PC heading in the navigation pane, as well as in the This PC location in File Explorer. The answer is somewhat confusing. The shortcuts in the This PC location refer to individual folders named Documents, Pictures, Music, and Videos. These are four individual folders unique to the logged-in user. The shortcuts under Libraries refer not to actual folders, but to logical groupings of folders that include the folders under This PC but may also include other locations as well. For example, the Documents library may include the currently signed-in user's Documents folder plus the Documents folder for the Public user account, and also the documents in the current user's Documents folder in his OneDrive cloud.

Selecting Files and Folders

Before you can issue a command that affects a file or folder (for example, to move or copy it), you must first select that file or folder. If you are selecting only one file or folder, it's easy—just click it. It becomes highlighted. (The highlighting color varies depending on the color scheme you are using in Windows.) If, however, you want to act upon multiple files or folders at once, you must select them all before issuing the command.

contiguous Physically adjacent to one another.

non-contiguous Not adjacent.

When two or more files or folders are contiguous (adjacent) in the file listing, you can select them by clicking the first one and then holding down the Shift key while you click the last one. All the files between the two are also selected. When the files you want are non-contiguous (not adjacent), hold down the Ctrl key and then click individually on each one. See Figure 5.18. When you are finished making your selections, release the Ctrl key. To cancel a selection, click anywhere away from the selection.

TIP To select all the files and folders in the current location, press Ctrl+A.

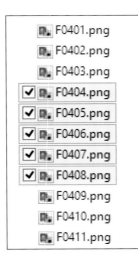
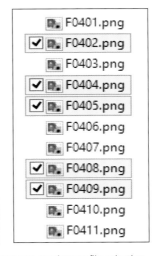

Figure 5.18   Contiguous versus non-contiguous file selection.

Creating New Folders

As you work in Windows, you may want to create new folders to organize your data. For example, you might create a separate folder for each project you work on. You could create them in your Documents folder, or in another other location on any volume to which you have access.

To create a new folder, navigate to the location within which you want to place the new folder, and then do any of the following:

- On the Home tab of the ribbon, click New Folder.

- Click the New Folder icon in the Quick Access Toolbar.

- Right-click an empty area of the file listing, point to New, and click Folder.

- Press Ctrl+Shift+N

A new folder appears with a generic name, with the name highlighted so you can easily change it. See Figure 5.19. Type the new name and press Enter.

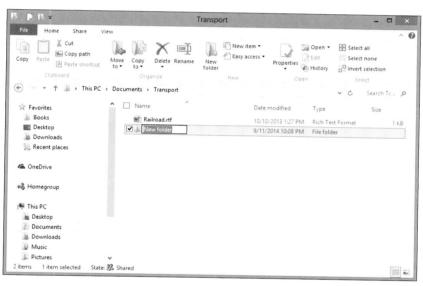

Figure 5.19   Creating a new folder.

Renaming and Deleting Files and Folders

There are many different ways to rename a file or folder. You can do any of the following:

- Select the file or folder and press F2 to make the name editable. Type the new name and press Enter.

- Click the file or folder to select it and then click it again to move the insertion point into the name. Edit the name and press Enter.

- Right-click the file or folder and click Rename. Edit the name and press Enter.

- Select the file or folder and then open the File menu and choose Rename. Edit the name and press Enter.

To delete a file or folder, select it and then do any of the following:

- Press the Delete key on the keyboard.
- Right-click the file and folder and click Delete.
- Open the File menu and click Delete.

Recycle Bin A temporary holding area for deleted content.

Deleting a file sends it to the Recycle Bin, which is a temporary holding area for deleted content. You can retrieve a deleted file or folder from the Recycle Bin.

Step by Step

Restoring a Deleted Item from the Recycle Bin

Follow these steps to retrieve a file or folder that you have deleted:

1. Double-click the Recycle Bin icon on the desktop to open the Recycle Bin window.

2. Select the deleted item to restore.

3. Click the Restore the Selected Items button on the ribbon's Recycle Bin Tools Manage tab.

Moving and Copying Files and Folders

You can move and copy files and folders from and to any location. This enables you to transfer your data files from your hard drive to a removable drive such as a USB flash drive, for example.

There are many ways to move and copy items. You can use the Windows Clipboard, or drag and drop files from one location to another, or you can use the Move to Folder or Copy to Folder command in File Explorer.

The Windows Clipboard is a temporary storage area in memory. When you use the Cut operation on an object (or group of objects), it is removed from its current location and placed on the Clipboard. Or, when you use the Copy operation on an object, the object remains in the current location but a copy of it is placed on the Clipboard. Then when you use the Paste operation, it is copied from the Clipboard to a new location. The object remains on the Clipboard until something else is placed there with either another Cut or another Copy operation. In this chapter, you use the Clipboard to copy and move files, but it can also be used to move or copy snippets of data from applications into other applications. For example, you can use it to copy certain cells from an Excel spreadsheet into a Microsoft Word document or into an email message you are composing.

Clipboard A reserved area in memory for temporarily holding content that has been cut or copied from an application or from File Explorer.

Table 5.1 lists the various ways of activating the Cut, Copy, and Paste commands in Windows 8.1.

Table 5.1: Using the Clipboard in Windows 8.1

Operation	Keyboard Method	Right-Click Method	Menu Method	Command Bar Method
Cut	Ctrl+X	Right-click and choose Cut	Open the Edit menu and click Cut	Click Organize and click Cut
Copy	Ctrl+C	Right-click and choose Copy	Open the Edit menu and click Copy	Click Organize and click Copy
Paste	Ctrl+V	Right-click and choose Paste	Open the Edit menu and click Paste	Click Organize and click Paste

Drag-and-drop is a technique for moving items from place to place. You can open the source and the destination locations in separate File Explorer windows onscreen and then drag items between them. When you drag between two locations on the same volume, the drag operation moves by default; if you want it to copy, hold down the Ctrl key as you drag. When you drag between two locations on different volumes, the drag operation copies by default; if you want it to move, hold down Shift as you drag.

If you are not sure whether the two locations are on the same volume, you can be sure you get the operation you want (move or copy) by always holding down Shift as you drag for a move and always holding down Ctrl as you drag for a copy. Alternatively, you can right-drag instead of dragging with the left mouse button. When you do so, a menu appears when you release the mouse button, enabling you to select a move or copy operation.

The Move to and Copy to commands (both on the Home tab) are unique to File Explorer, and provide an alternative to the other two methods just described. They enable you to move or copy using a dialog box interface.

If you want to move items to a removable drive such as a USB flash drive, there is yet another method available. Right-click the selected item(s) and select Send To from the context menu that is displayed, and then click the removable drive from the menu that appears.

Step by Step

Moving or Copying (Clipboard Method)

Follow these steps to move or copy selected files or folders using the Windows Clipboard:

1. In File Explorer, select the file(s) and/or folder(s) to be moved or copied.

2. Press Ctrl+C to copy, or press Ctrl+X if you want to move. Or, use one of the other methods from Table 5.1.

3. Navigate to the location where you want to paste the cut or copied item(s).

4. Press Ctrl+V to paste. Or, use one of the other methods from Table 5.1.

Moving or Copying (Drag-and-Drop Method)

Follow these steps to move or copy selected files or folders using drag-and-drop:

1. In File Explorer, select the file(s) and/or folder(s) to be moved or copied.

2. Open another File Explorer window (for example, click Start and click Computer) and navigate to the destination location.

3. Arrange the two windows so that both are visible at once.

4. Hold down Ctrl to copy, or hold down Shift to move. (See the note earlier in this section about the need to use those keys.)

5. Drag the selected item(s) from the original location to the destination.

Moving or Copying (Dialog Box Method)

Follow these steps to move or copy selected files or folders using the Move to Folder or Copy to Folder command:

1. In File Explorer, select the file(s) and/or folder(s) to be moved or copied.

2. On the Home tab of the ribbon, click Move to or Copy to. A menu of recently used locations appears.

3. If the desired location is on the list, click it, and skip the rest of these steps. Otherwise, click Choose Location. The Move Items or Copy Items dialog box opens.

4. Navigate to the desired destination location. Use the same navigation techniques you use in the folder tree in the navigation pane.

5. Click the Move (or Copy) button.

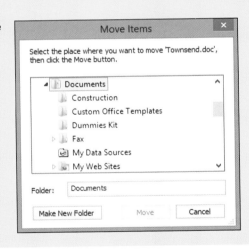

Working with Shortcuts

A shortcut is a link, or pointer, to the original file to which it refers. It allows a file or folder to appear to be in two or more locations at once, while maintaining a single original copy of it. For example, all the program names on the Start menu are shortcuts to the executable files that run those programs, as are the shortcut icons on the left end of the taskbar. You can also place shortcuts directly on the desktop.

Some shortcuts appear with a small arrow in the lower-left corner of the icon, indicating that the icon represents a shortcut rather than the original file, and some of them have the word "shortcut" in their name, as shown in Figure 5.20. However, not all shortcuts follow these conventions, so it is not a sure way to differentiate a shortcut from a regular file. A better method is to right-click the icon and choose Properties. If the dialog box that appears contains a Shortcut tab, the icon is a shortcut icon.

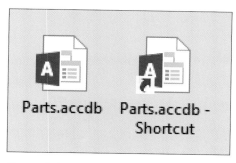

Figure 5.20 An original file (left) and a shortcut that refers to it (right).

To create a shortcut, right-drag the original file to another location. When you release the mouse button, a menu appears. On that menu, click Create Shortcuts Here. This works to create a shortcut almost anywhere. For example, you can use it to create a shortcut on the desktop for a data file in File Explorer.

You can work with shortcuts just like any other files. You can rename them, for example, in the same way you learned to rename files earlier in this chapter. You can move them and copy them freely. To delete a shortcut, delete it as you would any other file. Deleting a shortcut does not delete the file to which it refers.

Quick Review

1. How do you select multiple non-contiguous files?

2. Name two different ways of copying files from your hard drive to a USB flash drive.

3. What is a shortcut?

Summary

A Tour of Windows 8.1

The **Start screen** and the **desktop** are the heart of the Windows 8.1 interface. The Start screen is new in Windows 8, and replaces the Start menu. Windows 8.1 enables you to run a new, touchscreen-optimized type of application called a **Windows 8 app** (or Windows Store app). You can switch back and forth between the Start screen and the desktop. Press the Windows key to get to the Start menu from anywhere; click the Desktop tile on the Start menu to return to the desktop.

The key features of the desktop include the **taskbar** and **icons**. On the taskbar is the **Start button**, **pinned** icons, buttons for running application windows, the **notification area**, and the clock, from left to right. The Start screen holds tiles for applications that are pinned to it.

Starting Up and Shutting Down

Windows starts up automatically when you turn on the computer. You are prompted to sign in with your user ID and to type a password. A **cold boot** is one where the computer has been off; a **warm boot** is a restart with the computer already on.

Sleep mode is a power-saving mode that keeps RAM powered but turns off everything else. **Hibernate mode** saves the contents of RAM to the hard drive and then shuts down all power.

When a user is finished with the computer, he or she can **sign out**, which shuts down any running programs, closes open data files, and unloads that user's personal settings. To allow someone else to log in without the first user logging out, use **Switch User**. To return to a login screen without closing out of programs and applications, use the **Lock** command.

Running Applications

To start an application, choose it Start screen. If you don't see it on the Start screen, click the down arrow at the bottom of the Start screen to display the Apps list and find it there, or type its name and then click the name in the search results that appear.

A **window** is a movable rectangular block in which content appears, such as an application or file listing. Each window has a title bar at the top of it. In the right corner of the title bar are window control buttons: **Minimize**, **Maximize** (or Restore), and **Close**. To resize a window, drag one of its borders. To move a window, drag its title bar.

To navigate within an application, use its **menu bar**. Some commands have **keyboard shortcuts** for speeding up your work. Some commands open **dialog boxes** for providing more information. Programs with a menu bar sometimes have a **toolbar**, which is a row of clickable icons. A **ribbon** is a multi-page, more sophisticated version of a toolbar. Right-click for a **shortcut menu.**

To exit a desktop application, click the window's Close button, or open the File menu and choose Exit, or press Alt+F4.

To use a Windows 8 app, right-click to display a command bar. Use the Back arrow button to return to the top-level screen in an app. To exit a Windows 8 app, drag from the top of the screen down to the bottom or click the Close (X) button on its title bar. You can make the title bar appear by moving the mouse pointer to the top of the screen.

Managing Files

The parts of a File Explorer window include the **navigation pane**, ribbon, **address bar**, **status bar**, and **Search box**.

You can navigate to different locations using the shortcuts in the navigation pane in the **Favorites** list, or select one of the cloud-based folders from the **OneDrive** list. If you are connected to a network, you can browse network locations from the **Homegroup** or **Network** lists. Use the **This PC** list to browse local volumes. To change the view of a location, click a different view on the View tab.

Libraries are **virtual folders** that combine the contents of several locations into one window. The default libraries are Documents, Pictures, Music, and Videos for each user. You can create your own libraries too, and set up libraries to monitor additional folders. Each library has a **Save Location**, which is the folder that files are placed in when saved to the library. Libraries are not enabled by default in the navigation pane in File Explorer in Windows 8.1.

To select **contiguous** files and folders, hold down Shift as you click the first and last ones. To select **non-contiguous** files and folders, hold down Ctrl as you click each one individually. To create a new folder, click the New Folder button on the Home tab of the ribbon.

To rename a file or folder, select it, press F2, type the new name, and press Enter. To delete a file or folder, select it and press the Delete key. Deleted files go to the **Recycle Bin**; you can retrieve them from there.

You can move and copy files using the Clipboard, drag-and-drop, or use the Move to or Copy to command.

A **shortcut** is a pointer to a file or folder. To create a shortcut, right-drag an object to a new location and on the shortcut menu that appears when you release the mouse button, choose Create Shortcuts Here.

Key Terms

address bar
Apps list
Clipboard
cold boot
contiguous
desktop
dialog box
Hibernate mode
homegroup
icon
keyboard shortcut
library
lock
maximize
menu bar
minimize
non-contiguous
notification area
pinned
Recycle Bin

Restore
ribbon
save location
shortcut
shortcut menu
sign out
sleep
Sleep mode
Start button
Start screen
Switch User
system tray
taskbar
tiles
title bar
toolbar
virtual folder
warm boot
window
Windows 8 app

Test Yourself

Fact Check

1. Which of these is NOT a place where an application's icon can be placed or pinned?

    a. taskbar

    b. Start screen

    c. desktop

    d. status bar

2. If a program does not appear on the Start screen, click the _____ button at the bottom of the Start screen to see the Apps list

    a. Program

    b. Menu

    c. down arrow

    d. All

3. What mode turns off all components except RAM?

    a. Log off

    b. Hibernate

    c. Lock

    d. Sleep

4. Which window control button returns a window to its pre-maximized state?

    a. Restore

    b. Maximize

    c. Minimize

    d. Close

5. In a dialog box, which type of control selects only one of a group of mutually exclusive options?

    a. check box

    b. option button

    c. command button

    d. scroll box

6. To exit an application, open its File menu and choose

    a. Close

    b. Exit

    c. Quit

    d. End

7. There are four default _____: Documents, Music, Pictures, and Videos.

    a. journals

    b. navigation panes

    c. books

    d. libraries

8. To select multiple non-contiguous files, hold down the _____ key.

    a. Shift

    b. Alt

    c. Ctrl

    d. Home

9. To retrieve a deleted file, open the _____.

    a. Recycle Bin

    b. Trash folder

    c. Deleted Items folder

    d. Clipboard

10. Pressing Ctrl+V is one way to issue the _____ command.

    a. Copy

    b. Paste

    c. Cut

    d. Move

Matching

Match the feature to its function.

    a. hibernate

    b. lock

    c. sign out

    d. restart

    e. shut down

    f. sleep

    g. switch users

1. _____Shuts off all power except to memory.

2. _____Copies the content of memory to the hard drive and then powers off all components.

3. _____Exits Windows and turns the computer's power off.

4. _____Closes all open applications and files and unloads user-based settings.

5. _____Exits Windows and then restarts Windows.

6. _____Returns to a login screen without closing open applications, for security. The same user logs in to resume.

7. _____Returns to a login screen without closing open applications, so a different user may temporarily log in also.

Sum It Up

1. Describe the major features of the Start screen and desktop.

2. Explain the alternatives available to completely shutting down your computer at the end of your work session.

3. Explain how to start and exit a desktop application and a Windows 8 app.

4. Describe how to move, resize, minimize, maximize, and close a window.

5. Describe the controls used in dialog boxes.

6. Explain how to move, copy, rename, and delete files and folders.

7. Demonstrate how to navigate between storage locations using File Explorer.

8. Explain the difference between a user folder and a library.

Explore More

Sorting File Listings

File Explorer enables you to sort the file listing by name, date, or other characteristics. To do this, right-click a blank area of the file list, point to Sort By, and click the characteristic by which you want to sort. If you display the file list in Details view, you can also click one of the column headings to sort by that heading (for example, Type or Size). Try this out for yourself. Display the contents of the root directory of the C: volume in Details view, and sort the listing by Type. Sorting a file listing can make the files you want to work with contiguous, so you can use the Shift key method of selecting them that you learned about earlier in this chapter.

Looking at File Properties

Each file has properties that you can view by right-clicking it and choosing Properties from the menu. In a file's Properties box you will find a General tab that has file attributes on it and a Security tab that enables you to configure its security settings. Depending on the file type, there may also be other tabs, such as Details. If it's an application, there may be a Compatibility tab, on which you can configure the program to run with settings compatible for an earlier version of Windows. If it's a shortcut, a Shortcut tab offers settings for changing the shortcut's properties. Working on your own, open C:\ Windows in File Explorer and examine the properties of at least one folder and at least three files, and compare the tabs and settings that are available to view and adjust.

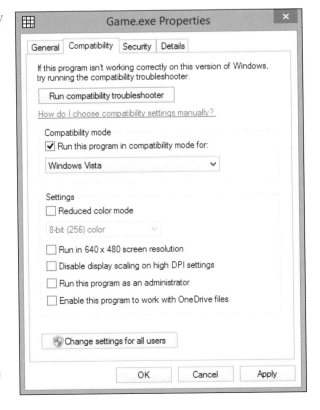

Compatibility Mode

Some older applications do not run well under Windows 8.1, but there's a workaround. You can set an application to run in Compatibility mode with settings that simulate an earlier Windows version of your choice. To set this up, follow these steps:

1. Browse the Program Files folder and find the executable file (look for an exe extension) that runs the application.

2. Right-click the executable file and choose Properties.

3. On the Compatibility tab, mark the check box next to the Run This Program in Compatibility Mode For.

4. Open the drop-down list of versions and choose an earlier Windows version. If you know which version the program was designed for, choose that. Otherwise, choose Windows XP (Service Pack 3). If that one doesn't work, you can come back later and try the next-latest version, and so on, until you find the one that works.

5. Click OK. Then try running the program again to see if the new settings help.

Think It Over

Desktop Shortcuts

Some people like to have shortcuts for all the applications they use on the desktop, so they can access them easily without having to use the Start screen. Their desktops become covered with dozens of icons over time. Other people prefer to keep the desktop clean, showing only the Recycle Bin, and they pin shortcuts only to the taskbar and Start screen. What is your preference, and why? Are there any drawbacks to pinning lots of icons to the desktop? To the taskbar? To the Start screen?

Security versus Convenience

How important is your privacy on your computer? Is it worth it to you in terms of privacy to have a separate user account from everyone else who uses your computer? Do you feel more comfortable stepping away from the computer while you are logged in if you use the Lock feature to password-protect it from others? Or would you rather have the computer be completely open to everyone in your family, with no private information?

New Applications

Suppose you bought a new application and it doesn't use either a ribbon or a menu system, at least not like the ones you have encountered before. How would you figure out how to use the program? What are some of the resources that might be available to you?

Chapter 6

Windows 8.1 Administration and Maintenance

Learning objectives

☐ Understand user accounts and how to manage them

☐ Use system utilities to provide information about your system and check for problems

☐ Identify and troubleshoot common Windows problems

Perhaps you would like to share your computer with family members or friends, and you would like those people to have individual accounts on the computer so you can keep your private documents separate. In this chapter, you will learn how to set up separate accounts for each user, and how to create an Administrator account so you can modify all aspects of Windows 8.1. You will also learn how to perform basic maintenance on your computer and how to fix common problems.

Managing User Accounts

user account An account associated with an individual person, used for authenticating the user when he or she logs into Windows.

When Windows 8.1 is installed on a computer, the installation program automatically creates a user account. It prompts you during the installation process for a username for that account. You can continue to use that account all the time, or you can create additional accounts.

As you learned in Chapter 5, "Introduction to Windows 8.1," when you turn on the computer, a lock screen appears, and then when you press a key, a sign-in screen appears with the names and pictures of each user account. You can click the one you want to sign in with, and then enter its password.

NOTE There is no fixed limit to the number of accounts you can have on a single copy of Windows. Keep in mind, however, that each account takes up a certain amount of hard drive space for its files, so make sure there is adequate hard drive space if several people use the same computer.

Help Desk Technician

If you enjoy working with Microsoft Windows settings, as you learn how to do in this chapter, you might like a career as a Help Desk technician. In this career, you might assist end users in making system changes, troubleshoot problems with their operating systems and help managers decide on appropriate computer usage policies that will allow users to do their work in safety and privacy. Depending on the position, a Help Desk technician might interact with users in person, on the telephone, or via email or instant messaging. To be a Help Desk technician, you should have at least an associate's degree in Computer Technology or a related field.

© iStockphoto.com/track5

Careers in IT

Accessing User Account Settings

You can make changes to an account from the PC Settings app (a Windows 8 app), or from the Control Panel. The Control Panel's Users and Family Safety section contains some account controls you can adjust, but in many cases it redirects you to PC Settings, which is a more modern way of making account changes. This chapter shows the PC Settings method. In this first set of steps, you will learn how to access account information, which you will need to do to complete many other procedures later in this chapter.

Accessing User Account Settings

Note that you must be logged in to an Administrator account to manage accounts other than your own. Use this procedure to access the screen where you can make changes to user account settings. Many of the upcoming procedures begin by following these steps.

1. Display the Charms bar. (To do so, point the mouse pointer to the lower right corner of the screen, or swipe in from the right on a touchscreen.)

2. Select the Settings charm. The Settings task pane appears.

3. Click Change PC Settings. The PC Settings app opens.

4. If some other section of the PC Settings app has been previously accessed, you might not see the main screen. If you see a Back arrow in the upper right corner, click it to return to the main screen.

5. Click Accounts. Information about your account appears.

Changing the Account Type

There are three types of Windows 8.1 accounts: Administrator, Standard, and Child. An Administrator account has full permission to do anything, including installing and removing software and changing system settings. Each system must have at least one Administrator account. A Standard account has fewer permissions. A Standard user cannot install or remove software and cannot make system changes that affect other users. For example, a Standard user could adjust his own desktop colors and change his own password, but could not delete someone else's user account or install a new version of an application. A Child account is a special type of account that can have limits placed upon it by an Administrator account through the Family Safety feature.

Charms bar A bar that appears on the right side of the screen when you swipe in from the right or move the mouse pointer to the lower-right corner of the screen, containing five charms.

charms Icons that appear in a Charms bar when it is activated. These icons open parts of the Windows interface, such as Search or Settings.

Administrator account A user account that has full permission to modify all aspects of Windows 8.1.

Standard account A user account that can only make changes to Windows 8.1 that do not affect other users.

malware Malicious software that consists of programs designed to disrupt the normal operation of computer systems.

Microsoft recommends that most people use Windows with a Standard account for their daily work and play, and log into an Administrator account(s) only when needed. Following this policy minimizes the risk of inexperienced users or malware making system changes that degrade the system's performance or cause it to stop working altogether. See Chapter 16, "Network and Internet Privacy and Security," for more information about malware.

TIP   If you are logged in as a Standard user and want to perform an action that requires an Administrator account, you do not always have to log out and back in again as a different user. In some cases, you can right-click the program or setting you want to access and choose Run as Administrator from the menu that appears. You can then select an account that has the needed permission and enter its password.

Step by Step

Changing the Account Type

If you are logged in with an Administrator account, use this procedure to change another user's account type. For example, you can promote a Standard user account to an Administrator account.

1. Follow the steps in "Accessing User Account Settings" earlier in this chapter.

2. Click Other Accounts. A list of accounts appears.

3. Click the account for which you want to change the type. Two buttons appear for the chosen account: Edit and Remove.

4. Click Edit. An Edit Account prompt appears.

5. Open the Account type drop-down list and choose a different account type.

6. Click OK.

Changing Your Account Picture

Each account has a picture that appears next to the name on the login screen. Windows automatically assigns a picture to the account when you create it, but you can change the picture to any one you like, including a photo of yourself.

Changing the Account Picture

To change the picture on an account follow this procedure.

1. Sign into Windows using the account for which you want to change the picture.

2. Follow the steps in "Accessing User Account Settings."

3. Under Account Picture, click Browse.

4. Select the picture to use, and click Choose Image.

Creating Accounts

When creating a new account, you must decide whether it will be a Microsoft account or a Local account.

By default in Windows 8.1, each user account is associated with a Microsoft account. A Microsoft account is a free account you can set up on Microsoft servers online; you use it to identify yourself when you are using Microsoft products such as Windows, Office, and OneDrive. When you create a new user account in Windows 8.1, you are prompted for an email address, and if that email address does not yet have a Microsoft account, one is created for you on-the-fly.

You can also create Local accounts on a Windows PC. A local account is not associated with a Microsoft account. Local accounts safeguard your privacy because they have no online presence, but they also don't have access to some of the convenient features that Microsoft accounts do, such as access to OneDrive storage.

Occasionally, you might need to delete an account that is no longer used. Deleting an account frees up hard drive space and also simplifies the login screen. When you delete an account, you have a choice of keeping the personal files associated with that account or deleting them. If you choose to keep them, the files are placed in a folder on the desktop, and you can relocate them where you want them from there.

Microsoft account user account that is registered with Microsoft, allowing use of online features such as OneDrive and social media connections.

local account A user account that exists only on a specific computer and is not linked to any online identity.

Creating a New Windows User Account with a Microsoft Account

Follow these steps to create a new user account. These steps create a Microsoft account (that is, an account associated with an email address that is registered with Microsoft), and create an account with Standard permissions.

1. Follow the steps in "Accessing User Account Settings" earlier in this chapter.

2. Click Other Accounts.

3. Click Add an Account. A prompt appears for an email address.

4. Enter an email address with which to associate the account, and then click Next.

5. Fill in the form provided to create a Microsoft account for that email address. You will need to specify a password for the Microsoft account, which is the password that person will use to sign in to Windows. Then click Next.

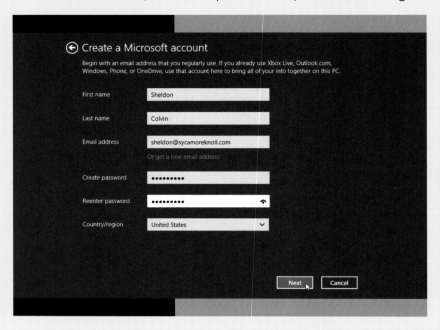

6. Fill in the security information requested. This information can help you recover your password later if you forget it. Then click Next.

7. On the Communication Preferences screen, enter the characters you see in the graphic shown. This step ensures that only humans, not machines, create new accounts. Then click Next.

8. Click Finish. The account is now created. By default it is a Standard account. If you would like it to be an Administrator account, do the following:

   a. Click the account name on the list of accounts.

   b. Click Edit.

   c. Open the Account Type drop-down list and choose Administrator.

   d. Click OK.

Creating a New Local Windows User Account

Follow these steps to create a new user account that is not associated with a Microsoft account.

1. Follow the steps in "Accessing User Account Settings" earlier in this chapter.

2. Click Other Accounts.

3. Click Add an Account.

4. At the bottom of the screen, click Sign in without a Microsoft Account (Not Recommended).

5. Click Local Account.

6. Fill in the prompts to create a user name, password, and password hint.

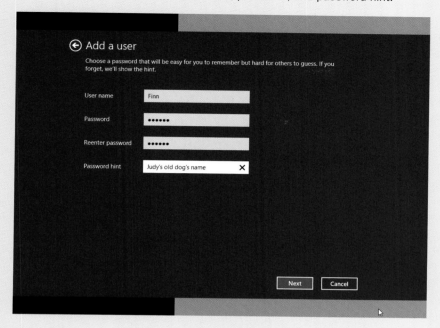

7. Click Next.

8. Click Finish.

Deleting Accounts

Occasionally you might need to delete an account that is no longer used. Deleting an account from your PC does not delete the Microsoft account; the Microsoft account still exists, and can be used to sign in to other computers on which it is set up as a valid user. Deleting an account does remove all that user's personal files from the local hard drive, however. Therefore, if there are any files you want to keep, make sure to back them up or move them to that Microsoft account's OneDrive cloud storage before deleting the account.

Step by Step

Deleting an Account

Follow these steps to delete an account.

1. Follow the steps in "Accessing User Account Settings" earlier in this chapter.

2. Click Other Accounts.

3. Click the account you want to delete.

4. Click Remove.

Manage other accounts

+ Add an account

Buddy
Child - Local Account

Pat Smith
studentcomp101@hotmail.com

Edit | Remove

Sheldon Colvin
Administrator - sheldon@sycamoreknoll.com

Manage Family Safety settings online

Set up an account for assigned access

5. Click Delete Account and Data.

Changing Account Passwords

password A word, phrase, or string of characters that a user enters in order to authenticate his or her identity.

Windows user accounts have passwords that protect the account from being used by unauthorized persons. Because they are associated with Microsoft accounts, they must be password protected so that the user will have security when accessing online resources. A local account can be set up without a password, but Microsoft recommends against it.

Changing the password on a Microsoft user account on one PC also changes it for that Microsoft account's sign-in on any other computer on which it is authorized. Microsoft does not allow the same password to be reused, so when you change to a new password, you can never use that same password again for that account. This restriction doesn't apply for changing the password on a local account.

New Technologies

Biometric Authentication

In the future, you may use some other method of logging into a computer than a password. For example, some computers have a biometric authentication system that determines the person's identity based upon some physical characteristic, such as fingerprints, facial appearance, hand dimensions, or retinal scan. This technology is available today and is becoming more and more popular as the price of the scanning hardware lowers. Some notebook computers have fingerprint readers built in. Another biometric authentication method is facial recognition, in which a camera (such as the computer's built-in webcam) takes a picture of the person sitting at the keyboard and compares it to the picture on file of the authorized user(s). Facial recognition software is built into Windows 8.

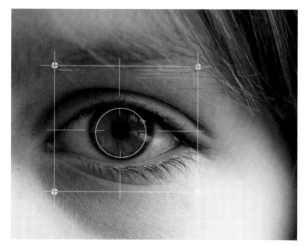

© iStockphoto.com/zmeel

To avoid problems with unauthorized people guessing your password and using it to access your computer without permission, use a strong password. Avoid using your name or the names of any of your friends, family, or pets as a password, and avoid using words found in the dictionary. The strongest passwords use a combination of uppercase and lowercase letters as well as numbers and symbols. If you find it difficult to remember a strong password, create one with a combination of letters and numbers that will make sense only to you. For example, you could start with a common word, such as *happiness,* and then substitute numbers for certain letters, like this: h2pp5n7ss. In this example, the numbers have been inserted in place of the vowels, and the number used is the position of the letter in the word. Make up your own system to create a password that is easy to remember but difficult to guess.

strong password A password that is difficult for others to guess.

Step by Step

Changing an Account Password

Follow this procedure to change the password for a Microsoft account. Making this change affects all other PCs on which this Microsoft account is used.

1. Sign in as the user for which you want to change the password.
2. Follow the steps in "Accessing User Account Settings" earlier in this chapter.
3. Click Sign-in Options in the navigation pane on the left.
4. Under the Password heading, click Change.
5. Type your current password to verify it, and click Next.
6. In the Old password box, type your old password. (Microsoft account only.)
7. In the Create password box, type your new password.
8. In the Reenter password box, type your new password again.

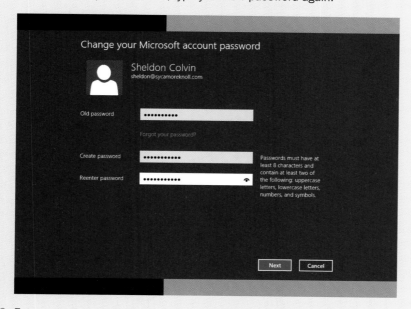

9. Enter a password hint in the Password Hint box (local account only).
10. Click Next.
11. Click Finish.

Enabling or Disabling the Guest Account

Guest account A special Windows account that has very few permissions, optionally offered at start-up so users who do not have an account on the computer can log in.

Windows has a Guest account that has no password. People who do not have a user account on your computer may use it to gain limited access to the computer, to carry out tasks such as use the Internet or run simple built-in programs like Calculator and Notepad. By default, the Guest account is disabled, but you can easily enable it if you want it to be available.

Enabling the Guest account is one of the new account-related activities that you must perform from the Control Panel rather than the PC Setting app, as described in the following Step by Step procedure.

Step by Step

Enabling or Disabling the Guest Account

Use this procedure to turn the Guest account on or off.

1. Open the Control Panel, and click the User Accounts and Family Safety heading.
2. Click the User Accounts heading.
3. Click Manage Another Account. A list of accounts appears, including the Guest account. Beneath the Guest account is a status message letting you know if it is off.

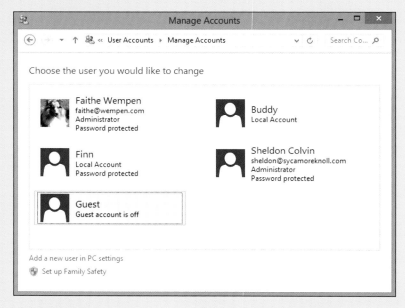

4. Click the Guest account.
5. If the Guest account was off, click Turn On.

    OR

    If the Guest account was on, click Turn Off the Guest Account.
6. Close the Control Panel window.

File and Folder Permissions

Using passwords on all the user accounts on your computer ensures that no unauthorized persons will be able to access your computer and view your personal data. However, it does not provide much privacy between users on the same computer. Administrator user accounts can browse the documents, music, videos, and other personal files in every other user's libraries. (Standard user accounts cannot.) In addition, if you store personal files in any other location besides your own libraries, such as in a new folder you create on the hard drive, all other users will be able to see and change whatever you put there.

To solve this privacy problem, Windows enables you to restrict permissions to do certain things to your folders and files, such as read them and modify them. You can set up these permissions on the Security tab in the Properties box for the folder or file. (Right-click the folder or file and choose Properties to display that dialog box.) This feature works only on drives that use the NTFS file system (the default for hard drives in Windows), so they won't work on writeable CDs or DVDs or on USB flash drives.

Do not confuse the Security tab with the Sharing tab in the Properties box. The Sharing tab is for network file sharing, not local file sharing.

NOTE

You can set permissions for files or folders, but many experts recommend that you set permissions only for folders, and then place the files into a folder that has the permissions you want the file to have. That way if you want to change the permissions for a group of files later, you can move them to a different folder with different permissions rather than having to change the permissions on each file individually.

CAUTION

On the Security tab of the folder's Properties box, you see group and usernames at the top. The Group or usernames list shows the current users or groups that have permission to access this resource. Figure 6.1, for example, shows four items: Authenticated Users, SYSTEM, the Administrators group, and the Users group. Notice that each of these has an icon to its left that shows two people's heads; that icon indicates a group rather than an individual.

Figure 6.1   The Security tab for a folder named Drivers.

To view the current permissions for a user or group, click it on the list. Then in the Permissions area at the bottom of the dialog box, examine the permissions that have been assigned. For example, in Figure 6.1, the Users group has been selected, and you can see that the group has Allow permissions three categories of operations.

Encrypting Folders

If you have Windows 8.1 Pro, for an extra measure of
security for especially sensitive files, you might choose
to encrypt the folder using Encrypting File System (EFS).
Encrypting the folder scrambles its contents for storage
on disk; the operating system holds the key that is able to
decrypt the folder whenever an authorized user accesses
it. Encryption makes it more difficult for someone to snoop
in a folder using a third-party utility designed to bypass the
normal folder permissions in Windows. To turn on encryption
for a folder, right-click the folder and choose Properties. On
the General tab, click the Advanced button. In the Advanced
Attributes dialog box, mark the Encrypt Contents to Secure
Data check box. If this option appears dimmed, the folder
cannot be encrypted for some reason. For example, perhaps
you do not have the Pro version of Windows 8.1.

When encryption is turned on the encrypted files and folders appear in green text in File Explorer. When you move
or copy data out of the folder, or when you move or copy
the folder itself, the encryption is removed. Encryption does not prevent files from being moved, copied, or deleted;
it only prevents them from being viewed. Therefore, encryption should be used in combination with the permissions
you are learning about in this section.

Bitlocker is another data security feature in Windows 8.1 Pro. It encrypts the entire hard drive to prevent it from
being read if it is physically removed from the computer in which it is installed. This prevents thieves from removing
a hard drive from a computer in one location and taking it to another location where they can try to access its data.
You can enable Bitlocker from the Control Panel. (If you don't have Windows 8.1 Pro, Bitlocker is not available.)
Before you do, though, balance the added security benefits against the difficulty you would have transferring your
hard drive's contents to a new PC if your existing PC became inoperable. Bitlocker should not be used on a system
where important data is not backed up frequently and regularly.

encrypt To scramble the contents of a file so it
cannot be read without the required permission
to decrypt it.

decrypt To reverse the encryption of a file so that
the file appears in its original form again.

Bitlocker A Windows feature (Pro edition) that
encrypts the entire hard drive so that it cannot be
read if it is moved to another computer.

To change the
permissions for a
user or group, or
to add or remove a
user or group from
the list, click the
Edit button in the
Properties dialog
box. A Permissions
dialog box opens,
in which you can
add and remove
users, and you
can mark and
clear Allow and
Deny check boxes
for each permis-
sion, as shown in
Figure 6.2.

Figure 6.2   Modify a folder or file's permissions from its
Permissions dialog box.

You can add other individual users or other groups to the Permissions list. To do so, click Add in the Permissions dialog box (Figure 6.2) to display the Select Users or Groups dialog box. From there, enter the user or group name in the text box provided, and then click Check Names to make sure that is a valid user or group. Some valid entries include:

- An individual account's username

- Everyone (to share with the Everyone group, which all accounts automatically belong to)

- Administrators (to share with the Administrators group, which all Administrator accounts automatically belong to)

Figure 6.3 shows both an individual username (Sheldon Colvin) and the Everyone group being added. Notice that when there are multiple entries, they are separated by semicolons. After adding users or groups to the list,

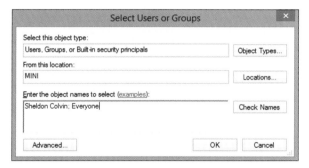

Figure 6.3   Add more users or groups to the Permissions list.

use the Allow check boxes in the Permissions dialog box to fine-tune which permissions that group will get.

Step by Step

Setting Folder Permissions for a User or Group
Use this procedure to set folder permissions:

1. In File Explorer, right-click the folder and choose Properties. The Properties dialog box opens.

2. Click the Security tab.

3. Click the Edit button. The Permissions dialog box opens.

4. If the user or group you want to work with appears, click it and then skip to Step 6.

   OR

   If the group or user does not appear, do the following:

   a. Click the Add button. The Select Users or Groups dialog box opens (refer to Figure 6.3).

   b. Type the user or group name desired into the Enter the Object Names to Select text box. If you enter multiple names, separate them with semicolons.

   c. Click the Check Names button. If the names check out, they appear in the text box with their names underlined.

      If they don't check out, an error appears; a Name Not Found dialog box opens. Correct the name or click the Remove *Username* from Selection option button, and then click OK.

   d. Click OK. The new user(s) are added to the Group or usernames list.

5. Click the desired user on the Group or usernames list.

6. Mark or clear the Allow check boxes to adjust the permissions.

7. Click OK to close the Permissions dialog box.

8. Click OK to close the Properties dialog box.

Removing Folder Permissions for a User or Group

To remove folder permissions, follow these steps:

1. In File Explorer, right-click the folder and choose Properties. The Properties dialog box opens.

2. Click the Security tab.

3. Click the Edit button. The Permissions dialog box opens.

4. Click the user or group for which you want to remove permissions.

5. Clear the Allow check box for the permissions to remove.

   OR

   To remove all permissions at once for the user or group, click the Remove button.

6. Click OK to close the Permissions dialog box.

7. Click OK to close the Properties dialog box.

Quick Review

1. What is the difference between an Administrator and a Standard user account?

2. What are the characteristics of a strong password?

3. On which tab of a folder's Properties box do you set local permissions?

Using System Utilities

Just as you don't have to be a mechanic to drive a car, you don't have to be a computer technician to use a PC. But just as everyone who drives a vehicle should be aware of its basic maintenance requirements, Windows users should understand how to assess and improve the computer's condition. In the following sections, you will learn how to use several utilities that can provide information about your system and check for any problems.

Getting Information about Your Computer

You can get information about your computer in Windows 8.1 in several ways. The most appropriate method depends on the information you are seeking.

To see the Windows version and edition, the processor, and the amount of RAM, use the System window, as shown in Figure 6.4. To open this window quickly, right-click the Start button on the taskbar and then click System. This window also contains the computer's network name, the workgroup to which it belongs, and the version of Windows 8.1 installed. These are all basic facts that a service technician might ask you when helping you diagnose a problem.

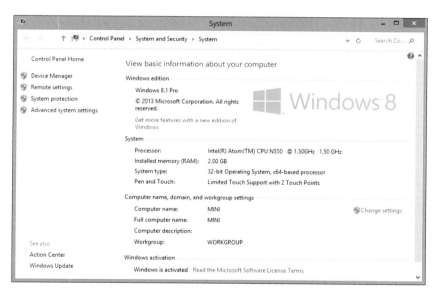

Figure 6.4   The System screen shows basic facts about your computer.

Looking for the Windows Experience Index and System Information utilities? They were present in Windows 7, but have been removed in Windows 8.1. If you need detailed configuration or performance information about your system, try a benchmarking utility, such as the free version of SiSoftware Sandra available at www.sisoftware.net.

TIP

Device Manager A Windows utility that provides detailed information about the hardware devices installed on the PC.

The Device Manager utility enables you to work with the drivers that control the PC's hardware devices. For example, you can update device drivers, disable devices, remove and reinstall devices, and see what system resources a device is using. Device Manager is also useful for identifying the exact model number of a device and its current driver revision number and date. You might need that information when searching online for an updated driver for the device.

You can access it by right-clicking the Start button and choosing Device Manager, or by choosing Device Manager from the System section of the Control Panel. To open the Properties dialog box for a device from Device Manager, double-click the device's name. Figure 6.5 shows the properties for a network adapter in Device Manager, with the Driver tab displayed, reporting, among other facts, the device's driver provider, date, and version.

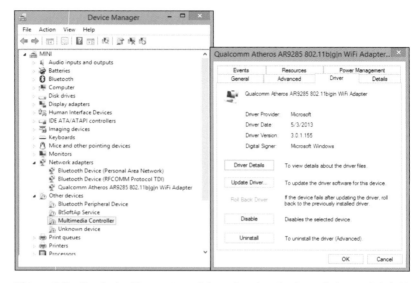

Figure 6.5　Use Device Manager to get information about hardware devices and their drivers.

Step by Step

Using Device Manager to View a Device's Details

Follow these steps to check the properties of a device:

1. Right-click the Start button, and click Device Manager. Device Manager opens.

2. Click the arrow sign beside a category to expand it.

3. Double-click a device to see its properties, as shown in Figure 6.5.

4. Click the tabs of the Properties dialog box to browse more properties of the device.

5. Click OK to close the device's Properties dialog box.

6. Close the open windows.

Checking for Disk Errors

Disk errors are not common anymore because today's hard drives are much more reliable than their predecessors, but errors do occur. Disk errors can cause Windows to crash or lock up, applications to stop working, and data files to be unreadable. When an error repeatedly occurs when you run a certain program or open a certain data file, error checking may help solve the problem.

There are two kinds of disk errors: physical and logical. A physical error occurs when there is an unreadable spot on the hard disk surface. If data is stored in that spot, some of the data may be lost. Windows may be able to read the data from that spot by repeatedly querying the disk for the information if the drive is having only sporadic problems; if Windows is able to read the data, it relocates it to another spot on the hard disk, which solves the problem.

A logical error occurs when the drive's table of contents, called the Master File Table (MFT), has an inconsistency in it. There are two copies of the MFT, and if the two copies don't agree, a logical error occurs. Logical errors also occur when the MFT expects to find data for a certain file in a certain location and it's not there, or when two different files claim the same physical spot as a part of them, or when data exists in a spot but no file claims it. You do not need to be able to differentiate between the types of errors, because Windows searches for them all automatically, correcting the problems where possible.

Error Checking A Windows utility that checks for disk errors and corrects them if possible.

physical error A hard drive error caused by a physically unreadable spot on the disk.

logical error A hard drive error caused by an inconsistency between the drive's actual content and the Master File Table.

Master File Table (MFT) The internal table of contents for a hard drive.

Once a hard disk drive begins developing physical errors, it is unreliable. Even if Windows is able to recover the file from a bad spot, more bad spots are likely to appear. The drive should be replaced soon, and essential information should not be stored on it anymore unless the data is backed up elsewhere.

CAUTION

Step by Step

Checking a Disk for Errors

To check a disk for errors, follow these steps:

1. Right-click the Start button and click File Explorer, or click the File Explorer shortcut on the taskbar.

2. Right-click the hard drive icon and choose Properties.

3. Click the Tools tab.

4. Click the Check button. The Error Checking dialog box opens.

5. Click Scan Drive. The error check starts. You can continue to use your computer while the error check is running.

6. When the check is completed, review the results and click Close to close the dialog box.

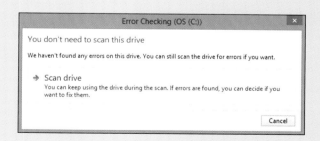

Error Checking (OS (C:))

You don't need to scan this drive

We haven't found any errors on this drive. You can still scan the drive for errors if you want.

→ Scan drive
You can keep using the drive during the scan. If errors are found, you can decide if you want to fix them.

Cancel

Optimizing a Hard Disk

sector The smallest addressable unit of storage on a disk drive, at 512 bytes.

cluster A grouping of sectors. The number of sectors in a cluster depends on the file system and the disk size.

A disk drive's storage system is organized by sectors, which are 512 bytes each, or by clusters (also called allocation units), which are groups of sectors. The cluster size depends on the file system (for example, Windows 8.1's file system for hard drives is NTFS) and the drive capacity. The default cluster size for most modern hard disk drives on a Windows system is 4,096 bytes (4 KB).

When a file is stored on disk, it is placed in the next available cluster. If a file is larger than the cluster size, it occupies multiple clusters. Typically when a file is written to the disk, it is stored in adjacent clusters. When a file's clusters are all adjacent, it is known as contiguous.

contiguous Physically adjacent to one another.

When a file is modified, it may increase in size so that it requires more clusters. There might not be clusters available that are adjacent to the original clusters for that file, so the new parts of the file are written to clusters somewhere else on the disk. The MFT keeps track of where the clusters are stored, and when the operating system asks for the file, the drive's read/write head moves to the different locations to pick up the data and assembles it into a whole file. A file that is stored non-contiguously is fragmented. Fragmented files work just fine, but the drive accesses them slightly more slowly because of the time required for the read/write head to move to the different locations.

fragmented A file whose clusters are not contiguous. In Windows 8.1, this is called *optimizing*.

defragment To relocate a fragmented file on a disk so that its clusters are contiguous.

Defragmenting relocates files so that they are once again stored in contiguous clusters. Defragmenting can slightly improve the speed at which the disk drive retrieves files. Windows 8.1 refers to defragmenting as *optimizing*.

NOTE Fragmentation is not an issue on solid state drives (SSDs) because there are no moving parts, and therefore no performance gain to be attained by files being stored contiguously.

Step by Step

Defragmenting a Hard Disk Drive

Use this procedure to defragment a hard disk drive:

1. Right-click the Start button and click File Explorer, or click the File Explorer shortcut on the taskbar.

2. Right-click the hard drive and choose Properties.

3. Click the Tools tab.

4. Click the Optimize button. The Optimize Drives dialog box opens.

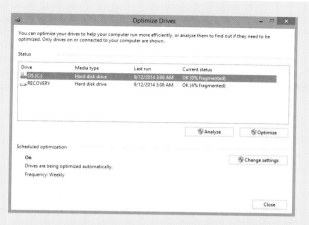

5. Click the main hard disk drive on the list and click Analyze. Then wait for a report to appear. It should take only a few minutes. The progress is shown in the Current Status column.

6. If the fragmentation is more than 5%, the drive may benefit from defragmenting. To defragment it, click the Optimize button. Otherwise, click Close to exit the utility without defragmenting.

7. If you chose to defragment in Step 6, wait for the utility to finish. It may take several hours. You can continue to use your computer while it works.

8. When the defragmentation process is complete, close the Optimize Drives dialog box.

Working with Printers

In most cases, the best way to add a printer is to run the Setup software that came on CD or DVD with the printer. However, there may be times when doing so is not possible. For example, perhaps you don't have the disc, or perhaps the printer is connected in a way that Windows can't automatically detect (such as a parallel port interface or certain types of network connections). In such cases, you can use the Add Printer Wizard to connect Windows to the printer and install a driver for it.

Installing a New Printer

Most printers use the USB interface, which is Plug and Play, so Windows detects them automatically and in many cases is able to install a usable driver from the set of drivers the printer comes with. However, allowing Windows to set up a printer automatically like that is not always the best method. Some printers come with a full-featured software suite that is installed when you run the setup CD that came with the printer, and if you let Windows detect the printer and install a driver for it, only the most basic driver is typically installed. It may be better to run the Setup software that comes with the printer before connecting the printer to the computer.

Put It to Work

A driver is a program that serves as a communicator between Windows and a device. So many devices are created by different companies that Windows can't maintain information about all the different languages they speak, so driver files are used to bridge the gap. When installing a printer in Windows, you are not literally installing the printer, but rather you are installing a driver for it. You can have multiple drivers for a single physical printer, each with its own settings.

driver A software interface between a device and the operating system.

After a printer has been installed, it appears in the Devices and Printers window. (To get to the Devices and Printers window, open the Control Panel, and under the Hardware and Sound heading, click View Devices and Printers.) From there, you can do any of the following:

- To see detailed information about the printer, double-click the printer's icon. Depending on the printer, a screen may appear with information or the printer's queue may open. If you see the information screen, you can click See What's Printing on that screen to view the queue.

- To set a printer as the default, right-click it and choose Set as Default Printer.

- To remove a printer's driver, select the printer's icon and press Delete, or click Remove Device on the toolbar at the top of the window.

- To see a printer's properties, right-click the printer's icon and choose Printer Properties.

NOTE Besides the Printer Properties command on the shortcut menu, there is also a Properties command; selecting it opens a different dialog box with a different set of properties for the printer. Experiment with both, if you like.

Step by Step

Adding a Printer

To add a printer to your system, follow these steps:

1. Right-click the Start button and choose Control Panel.

2. Under the Hardware and Sound heading in the Control Panel, click Devices and Printers. The Devices and Printers dialog box opens.

3. Click Add a Printer.

4. Wait for your printer to be detected and appear on a list. Then click Next.

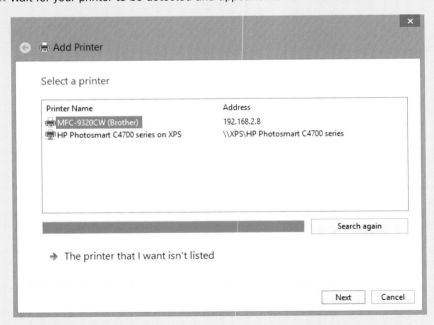

5. Change the printer's default name if desired, and then click Next.

6. If you want to share the printer with others on your network, click Share This Printer So That Others On Your Network Can Find and Use It. Otherwise leave Do Not Share This Printer selected. Then click Next.

7. (Optional) Click the Print a Test Page button. It is always wise to print a test page to ensure the installation is successful and the correct driver is installed.

8. Click Finish.

9. The new printer is automatically set to be the default printer. If you want some other printer to be the default, right-click that printer and choose Set as Default Printer.

Quick Review

1. What is the difference between a physical and a logical disk error?

2. What is disk defragmentation?

3. How do you add a printer to Windows?

Troubleshooting Common Windows Problems

Windows 8.1 operates trouble free most of the time, but sometimes a problem may occur with some software or with a device driver, and you may experience one or more of these problems:

- Windows might not start up correctly.

- Windows might run very sluggishly, taking a long time to open and close windows.

- Error messages might appear.

- An application might stop responding to commands.

The following sections explain how to troubleshoot some of these problems.

Troubleshooting Start-up and Performance Problems

Problems with Windows' configuration may cause Windows to not be able to start normally at all, or they may cause performance problems such as slow performance and frequent error messages. Windows 8.1 offers a variety of features to help you solve these problems.

Using Advanced Startup

If Windows fails to start normally, an Advanced Startup screen appears, offering you many different troubleshooting and repair options. You can check out this screen even when there is nothing wrong, so you will know what to expect in the future when you need the feature.

Starting Windows in Advanced Startup Mode

Follow these steps to start your computer in Advanced Startup mode. If your computer fails to start normally, Advanced Startup mode may load automatically; if it does, you do not have to go through these steps.

1. Display the Charms bar, and choose the Settings charm.

2. Click Change PC Settings.

3. Click Update and Recovery.

4. Under the Advanced Startup heading, click Restart Now.

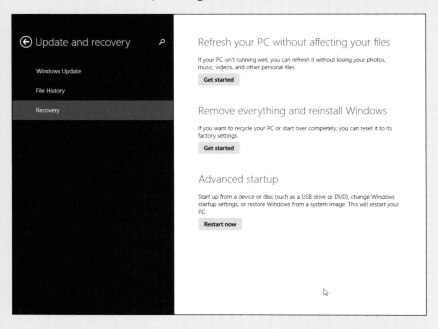

5. Wait for the PC to restart in Advanced Startup mode.

Using Advanced Startup Mode to Troubleshoot System Problems

Follow these steps after you have booted into Advanced Startup mode to explore the various troubleshooting tools that are available.

1. Click Troubleshoot.

2. Click Advanced Options.

3. Choose one of the troubleshooting options available. See Table 6.1 for details about them.

   - System Restore
   - System Image Recovery
   - Start-up Repair
   - Command Prompt
   - Start-up Settings
   - UEFI Firmware Settings

Table 6.1: Advanced Startup Options

Option	Purpose	Notes
System Restore	Returns your system files to an earlier version	This can often solve a problem that began recently, such as a problem that started after installing a new driver, application, or Windows update.
System Image Recovery	Restores a complete system image backup	This is useful only if you have a system image backup file (which you probably don't have). It returns the entire system to a previous state, not just the system files. Any data files that were created or changes since the image file was created are lost.
Startup Repair	Attempts to diagnose and repair system problems that are preventing your computer from starting normally	Worth a try; if it can't solve the problem, it will allow you to return to the Advanced Options menu to try something else.
Command Prompt	Opens a command line interface	This is useful if you are an advanced user with a solid understanding of command line commands and a specific idea of what you want to accomplish using command line utilities
Startup Settings	Allows you to restart to a Startup Settings menu, from which you can choose to enable Safe Mode or one of several other special boot modes	Sometimes if the system won't start up normally, it will start up in Safe Mode, and from there you can do some manual repairs, such as rolling back a driver (covered later in this chapter).
UEFI Firmware Settings	Allows you to boot into the BIOS Setup utility for the motherboard	This option is available only on systems where the motherboard supports UEFI.

Rolling Back a Driver Update

If problems occur with a device, sometimes the problem can be solved by installing an updated device driver. This file usually comes with its own setup program that you download from the manufacturer, and it installs itself with a few clicks. However, if there is a problem with the new driver, the device could stop working entirely or could cause Windows to not start up correctly or run sluggishly.

If you stick with signed drivers, you will seldom have problems with a driver that require a rollback. Unsigned drivers are more likely to cause the hardware to malfunction or to cause system problems.

NOTE

To return to a previous driver if the new one is causing problems, you use the Roll Back Driver feature. You can access this feature from Device Manager, as explained in the following steps. If Windows won't start (and therefore you can't get to Device Manager), use Advanced Startup and either do a System Restore (which will also undo any recently installed driver updates) or use Start-up Settings to start in Safe Mode so you can get to Device Manager to perform the following steps.

signed drivers Drivers that are certified to work with certain versions of Windows and certain hardware models.

Rolling Back a Driver Update

Use this procedure to roll back a driver update:

1. Right-click the Start button and choose Device Manager.

2. If needed, expand the category of the device. Then double-click the device to open its Properties box.

3. Click the Driver tab.

4. Click the Roll Back Driver button.

5. Follow the prompts that appear to roll back the driver.

6. Close all open windows.

Disabling a Start-up Program

Some programs load automatically when Windows starts. Sometimes this is very useful. For example, antivirus software should load at start-up so it can protect the system. However, not all the programs that load automatically are important. For example, some applications load a utility at start-up to check the company's web server for updates.

If a program that loads at start-up malfunctions, or uses a lot of memory, Windows performance can be negatively affected. If your system starts running more slowly after you install some new software that loads at start-up, you may be able to restore normal system performance by preventing that program from loading at start-up. You can still run the program manually whenever you need it.

> **TIP** If you don't know what is causing your system to run slowly lately, rather than trial-and-error to figure out what startup program is causing the problem, you might find it easier to do a System Restore, which will reverse all recent system changes at once. See "Restoring System Files to an Earlier State" later in this chapter.

First, try looking in the program itself to see if there is a setting that controls the program's start-up. If there is, turn that setting off. The program will then make the needed change to the system files automatically.

Task Manager A utility that shows the running applications and their processes, the programs set to load at startup, and several system performance measurements.

If that doesn't work, you can use the Task Manager to disable that program's automatic start-up. This utility lists all the programs that load at start-up, with check boxes next to the names; you can clear the check boxes for any programs you don't want to load.

> **NOTE** The Task Manager utility does not always make it obvious what program a certain line represents. If you are not sure about a start-up item, do a web search on its name.

Preventing a Program from Loading at Start-up

Follow these steps to prevent loading a specific program at start-up.

1. Right-click an empty area on the taskbar and choose Task Manager.

2. Click the Startup tab. The applications set to load at start-up appear on a list. If you don't see any tabs, click More Details to make them appear.

3. Click the item that you want to disable, and then click Disable. The button changes to Enable.

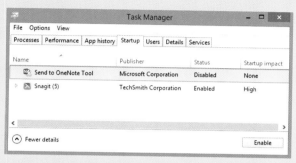

4. Close the Task Manager window.

5. Restart the computer to see if the problem is fixed.

Restoring System Files to an Earlier State

If you aren't sure what the problem is that is causing your system to not boot normally or to run sluggishly, System Restore may be able to help. System Restore automatically saves a copy of your system files every day. If a problem occurs, you can roll back the system files to a previously saved version that was created before the problem started. In many cases, doing so fixes the problem. The following steps explain how to use System Restore from within Windows; if you can't boot into Windows normally, use Advanced Startup to access System Restore, as explained earlier in this chapter.

Using System Restore

To return your system to an earlier version using System Restore, follow these steps:

1. Right-click the Start button and choose System.

2. In the navigation pane on the left, click System Protection. The System Properties dialog box opens with the System protection tab displayed.

3. Click the System Restore button. The System Restore utility opens.

4. Click the Next button.

5. Select the desired restore point. In most cases, the latest one is the best to use, but you might go back further if the problem started before the latest point.

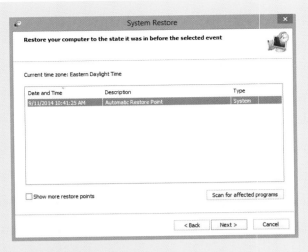

6. Click Next.

7. Click Finish.

8. Wait for the computer to reboot. When it does, the restore will have taken place.

Resetting or Refreshing Your PC

If none of your troubleshooting efforts solve the problem, you may need to **reset** or **refresh** your computer. Both of these operations require you to have the original installation discs or recovery discs for your computer. Your computer may have come with a Windows DVD, or it may have prompted you to create your own DVD recovery discs.

Reset To return Windows to its original state, removing all applications and data installed by the user.

Resetting your PC returns it to its original software configuration, with a clean copy of Windows and none of your applications or data. It's a last resort for fixing serious problems that don't respond to any other troubleshooting techniques.

Refresh To reinstall Windows system files without disturbing existing applications and data.

Refreshing the system is somewhat like reinstalling Windows except you don't lose any of your installed programs or data.

You can access Reset and Refresh from the Advanced Startup options you learned about earlier. You can also access them from within Windows (assuming Windows will start up, or that you can start it in Safe Mode). The following steps explain how to start them. Make sure you back up your data before performing either of these operations (if possible).

Step by Step

Reset or Refresh Your PC (within Windows)

1. Display the Charms bar, and choose the Settings charm.

2. Click Change PC Settings.

3. Click Update and Recovery.

4. Click Recovery.

5. To use Reset, under the Remove Everything and Reinstall Windows heading, click Get Started.

   OR

   To use Refresh, under the Refresh Your PC Without Affecting Your Files heading, click Get Started.

6. Wait for the computer to restart and the utility to load.

7. When a list of usernames appears, click your username.

8. If you are refreshing (not resetting), you will be prompted to click your username and then enter your password. Do so, and click Continue.

9. When prompted, insert your Windows installation or recovery media disc.

10. Follow the prompts to complete the operation. It may take an hour or more.

Reset or Refresh Your PC (from Advanced Startup mode)

1. Boot into Advanced Startup mode, as you learned earlier in this chapter. If your computer will not boot normally, it might start in Advanced Startup mode automatically.

2. Click Troubleshoot.

3. To use Reset, click Reset Your PC.

   OR

   To use Refresh, click Refresh Your PC.

4. Wait for the computer to restart and the utility to load.

5. When a list of usernames appears, click your username.

6. If you are refreshing (not resetting), you will be prompted to click your username and then enter your password. Do so, and click Continue.

7. When prompted, insert your Windows installation or recovery media disc.

8. Follow the prompts to complete the operation. It may take an hour or more.

Shutting Down an Unresponsive Program

Sometimes a program stops responding to commands. It may appear as if it has a white film over it, and an error message may appear, letting you know the program is not responding and offering to close it. If you see such a message, click Close the Program. You will lose any unsaved changes to data files you have made in that program.

If you don't see that message, you might need to manually shut down the unresponsive program. To do so, use Task Manager, which shows all the running applications and their underlying processes.

Task Manager A utility that shows the running applications and their processes and allows you to shut down unresponsive applications.

Step by Step

Using Task Manager to Shut Down an Unresponsive Program
Use this procedure to close a program using Task Manager:

1. Right-click the taskbar and choose Task Manager.

   OR

If Windows is not responding normally and you can't access the taskbar, press Ctrl+Alt+Delete and then click Task Manager.

2. If no tabs appear in the Task Manager window, click More Details.

3. On the Processes tab, in the Apps section of the list, click the application you want to shut down. It may show Not Responding in the Status column.

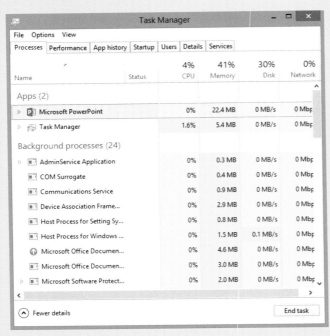

4. Click the End Task button.

5. Close the Task Manager window.

Using Help and Support

Windows 8.1 has an extensive Help and Support database built in, with instructions for almost every task you might want to complete in Windows. You can access the desktop version of it from the desktop by pressing F1 when no applications are active. (If you press F1 when an application window is active, the help that appears is for that application, not for Windows itself.) You can access the Windows 8 style version of Help from the Apps list by clicking Help+Tips. This chapter looks at the desktop version.

In the Windows Help and Support window, shown in Figure 6.6, you can type a keyword in the Search box to find related topics, or you can click Browse Help to browse the Help system by category. You can return to the home page of the Windows Help and Support window at any time by clicking the Help Home hyperlink.

To get more information about troubleshooting, click Browse Help and then click System Repair and File Recovery. Then click on one of the hyperlinks to read the associated help articles, as in Figure 6.7.

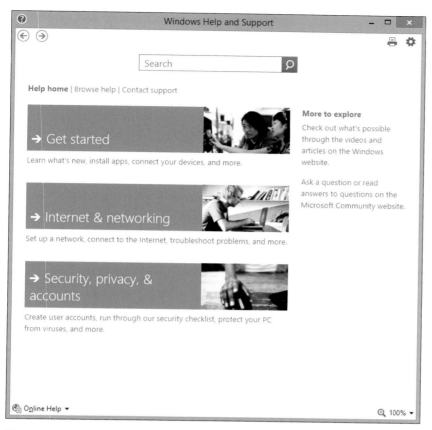

Figure 6.6   Windows Help and Support.

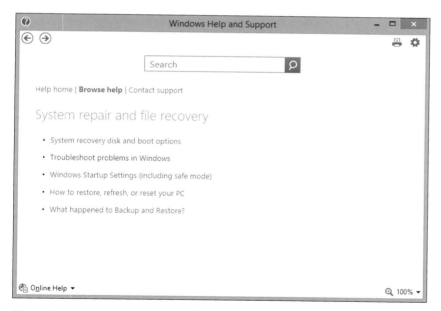

Figure 6.7   Browse troubleshooting articles to find the answers you need.

You can also access a variety of automated troubleshooting utilities via the Control Panel, as explained in the following Step by Step.

Using Troubleshooting Utilities

Use this procedure to browse the troubleshooting utilities available in Windows 8.1 via the Control Panel.

1. Open the Control Panel.

2. Open the View By drop-down list and choose Small Icons.

3. Click Troubleshooting.

4. Click a hyperlink under the heading that best represents the problem you are having.

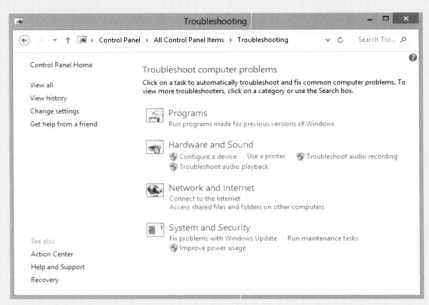

Quick Review

1. How do you start the System Restore process?

2. How do you boot to Advanced Startup mode if Windows does not display a message offering to do it for you?

3. How do you search for a topic in Windows Help and Support?

Summary

Managing User Accounts

To use Windows, you must log in using a **user account**. A **Standard account** can run programs and make simple customization changes that don't affect other users. An **Administrator account** can make any changes to Windows, including those that affect other users. Standard accounts are recommended for daily use because they pose fewer security risks. The **Guest account** is a limited account with no password; it is disabled by default.

User accounts have **passwords** assigned to them to prevent unauthorized use. A **strong password** is one that is difficult to guess; it may contain a combination of letters, numbers, and symbols.

You can prevent other users from looking at your personal files by changing the **permissions** for the folders they are in. On a per-user basis, you can set an Allow or Deny property for various activities, such as reading the file and changing its content.

Using System Utilities

Some of the utilities that can provide information about your system include the System section of the Control Panel and the **Device Manager**.

Disk errors can be either **physical errors** or **logical errors**. A logical error occurs when the **Master File Table (MFT)** does not match the disk's actual contents. A physical error is a bad spot on the disk surface. The Error Checking utility can find and fix both types.

Disks are organized by groups of **sectors** called **clusters**. When a file is stored in **contiguous** clusters, the drive can read it faster than when the clusters are **fragmented**. The Disk Defragmenter utility relocates files into contiguous clusters, **defragmenting** the drive and improving its performance.

A printer **driver** helps Windows communicate with a printer. You can install a printer driver from the software that comes with the printer or with the Add Printer Wizard.

Troubleshooting Common Windows Problems

When Windows can't start normally, it can sometimes be started up using **Avanced Startup mode**. You can use it to access troubleshooting tools that you might not otherwise be able to get to, such as System Restore, **Refresh**, and **Reset**.

To shut down an unresponsive program, right-click an empty area of the taskbar and choose **Task Manager**. Select the program on the Processes tab and click End Task.

To get help in Windows 8.1, click Help and Support on the Start menu or press the F1 key. You can also access troubleshooting tools from the Control Panel's Troubleshooting section.

Key Terms

Administrator account

Bitlocker

charms

Charms bar

cluster

contiguous

decrypt

defragment

Device Manager

driver

encrypt

fragmented

Guest account

local account

logical error

malware

Master File Table (MFT)

Microsoft account

password

physical error

Refresh

Reset

sector

signed drivers

Standard account

strong password

Task Manager

user account

Test Yourself

Fact Check

1. The _____ account is a limited user account that someone who does not have a regular account on the PC can use.

   a. Visitor

   b. Administrator

   c. Guest

   d. Standard

2. Which of these is the strongest password?

   a. JohnSmith

   b. @Columbus(1492)

   c. 1234567

   d. ChangeMe

3. Which of these utilities will check and fix all Windows system files but not cause you to lose data?

   a. Refresh Your PC

   b. Reset Your PC

   c. Driver Rollback

   d. System Restore

4. Set up the security permissions for a folder from the

   a. Control Panel

   b. folder's Properties dialog box

   c. Start menu

   d. desktop

5. Which utility would be most appropriate for finding out the version number of your network adapter's driver?

   a. Device Manager

   b. System Information

   c. Task Manager

   d. Windows Experience Index

6. The Optimize utility does what to files?

   a. Changes the number of sectors per cluster

   b. Fixes physical errors in them

   c. Fixes logical errors in them

   d. Stores them contiguously

7. From what utility do you disable programs from loading automatically at start-up?

   a. Control Panel

   b. Task Manager

   c. Device Manager

   d. System Restore

8. The _____ utility shows running applications and their processes.

   a. Task Manager

   b. System Information

   c. Check Disk

   d. Device Manager

9. What Windows 8 utility is used to manage user account settings?

   a. PC Settings

   b. Roll Back

   c. Device Manager

   d. People

10. What kind of account can make any and all system changes without any permission restrictions?

   a. Standard

   b. Microsoft

   c. Administrator

   d. Local

Matching

Match the term to its meaning.

a. System Restore

b. Device Manager

c. Error Checking

d. Advanced Startup Mode

e. Optimize

f. Task Manager

1. _____Enables you to view and manage hardware drivers.

2. _____Allows you to disable certain programs that normally would load automatically at start-up.

3. _____Returns system files to an earlier state.

4. _____Enables special startup utilities to be accessed even if Windows won't start normally.

5. _____Relocates non-contiguous data to be stored contiguously on a disk.

6. _____Finds and fixes disk errors.

Sum It Up

1. What are the two main types of user accounts in Windows 8.1? How are the Guest and Child accounts different from either of those two?

2. What are the characteristics of a strong password? Give an example of a very strong password and explain why it is strong.

3. Explain what to do if a program stops responding to commands.

Explore More

Biometric Authentication

Use the Internet to research how retina scans authenticate users. Find out how much it costs to get started using this technology and what its benefits and drawbacks are. Write a one-page report summarizing what you learned. Make sure you document your sources appropriately.

Think It Over

Balancing Security with Ease of Use

Each security measure you put in place has its drawbacks. For example, if you use a feature like Bitlocker on your hard drive and your computer breaks down, you have to go through special procedures to be able to get the data off your hard drive.

Think about the differences in appropriate security levels for different computer uses. What do you think is the appropriate balance between security and convenience for a home computer? For a computer used in the CEO's office in a large company? For a computer that a military officer with a high security clearance uses? For a computer used to store medical records in a physician's office?

The Risk of Unsigned Drivers

Suppose you are having a problem with the graphics in a game you are playing. A website says that there is a known problem that can be fixed with an updated display adapter driver. However, you cannot find a signed driver that is newer than the one you have. You find a driver on a website that contains drivers that amateur programmers have created and made available. When you try to install one of them, a warning message states that it has not passed Windows 8.1 compatibility testing, and asks if you want to continue anyway. What would you do from here? Explain your decision.

Chapter 7

Understanding Application Software

Learning objectives

☐ Identify the various types of application software

☐ Understand the basics of business productivity applications

☐ Explore graphics and photo-editing programs

☐ Understand system requirements and the installation and uninstallation processes

As you learned in Chapter 1, "Computer Basics," *software* is a broad term for any program that runs on a computer. This can include the operating system and all its helper files, utilities that keep the computer healthy and running well, and applications. Another name for software is a program.

Application software is software that enables you to perform a useful task on your computer. Some programs are classified as productivity software because they allow you to get things done. Other application software is designed to entertain you, or to help you learn something.

Business Productivity Software

Businesspeople typically use a collection of applications known as an office suite to perform the most common tasks involved in their jobs, such as writing reports and correspondence, performing numeric calculations, giving presentations, and maintaining databases of information. You will learn about each of those tools in more detail in later chapters, but the following section provides a general overview.

Understanding Word Processing and Desktop Publishing

application software Software that helps a human perform a useful task for work or play.

word processor A program used to create or view text-based documents.

The most popular type of productivity software is the word processor. This type of program is used to create text-based documents. A word processor contains many features designed to help improve text, such as spell-checking, grammar correction, and formatting tools. In fact, Microsoft Word is the world's most widely used word processor and one of the most advanced examples of this type of program.

In addition to creating and editing your own work, you can also open word-processing documents that other people have created. Word can open and save documents in a variety of formats, enabling you to exchange documents with people who use other word-processing applications. You will learn how to save and open files in Word and other Office applications in Chapter 8, "Understanding Microsoft Office 2013."

A word-processing program provides a wide variety of text formatting options. For example, you can make the text larger, change its color, or use different fonts. You can structure the page to emphasize important elements by using a larger type size. You can specify how the text is arranged, so that all the words start at the far left or far right of the page in a neat vertical arrangement. Figure 7.1 shows a document in Microsoft Word that includes several types of formatting, including shading, different fonts, and multiple columns. You will learn much more about Microsoft Word in the next two chapters.

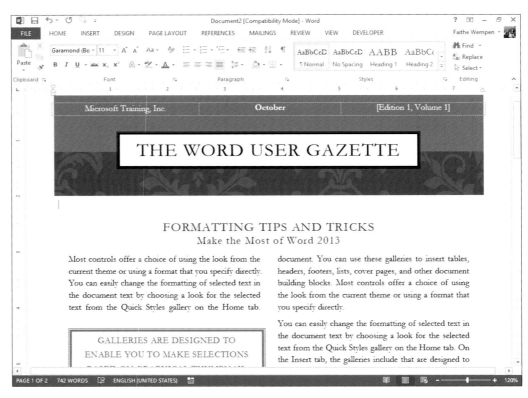

Figure 7.1 Word processing software provides strong formatting tools that are ideal for producing newsletters and reports.

For a detailed look at how to format a complete document and add images and charts, see Chapter 9, "Word Processing with Microsoft Word."

For even more control over page layout, you can use a desktop publishing program, sometimes called page layout software. Some popular desktop publishing programs include Microsoft Publisher for casual home users and QuarkXPress and Adobe InDesign for professionals.

Desktop publishing software enables users to precisely position the text and other elements on a page or across a double-page spread (facing pages) to create an attractive design. The text can be creatively wrapped around embedded images, and graphics can be made semi-transparent, or "ghosted," behind text so the words aren't obscured.

The main difference operationally between word processing and desktop publishing is that a word-processing program typically enables you to type directly on the page onscreen, and it flows the text automatically based on the margins, indents, and number of columns you specify. Desktop publishing, on the other hand, uses movable and resizable frames for everything, including text (see Figure 7.2). This gives you more control over the precise positioning of each element.

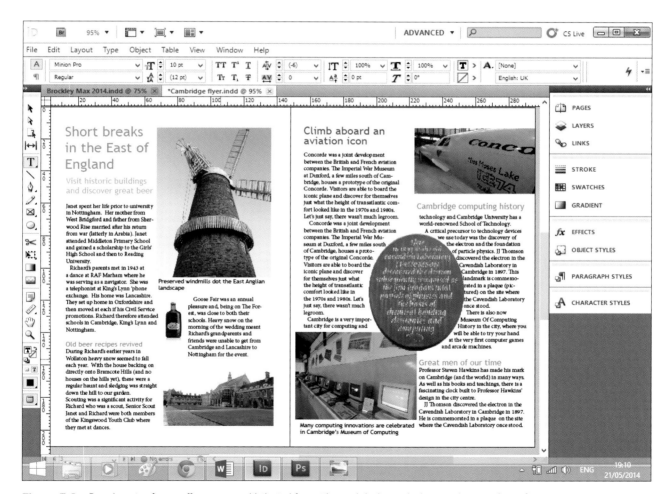

Figure 7.2   Page layout software offers more sophisticated formatting and design tools than word-processing software.

Administrative Assistant

An administrative assistant provides office and document support to a manager or executive. He or she is expected to know how to use a word processor to create and format documents. The templates supplied with word-processing software make the formatting and spell-checking processes much easier, but an administrative assistant should be familiar with how they work and be capable of producing neatly formatted reports with charts and graphs. An administrative assistant's duties may also include creating printed materials in other applications, such as Excel and PowerPoint, and combining content from multiple applications into reports and presentations.

All administrative support roles require a solid understanding of office productivity programs and strong organizational skills. A diploma in administration, information technology, or business management is also expected. A business administration or IT degree plus vocational courses will help progress your career into office management.

Understanding Spreadsheets

spreadsheet A program that presents rows and columns of figures and other items against which time and other variables can be plotted.

A spreadsheet program is used to analyze and present numeric data. For example, you might use a spreadsheet to create a budget, summarize sales data, or compare mortgages. Figure 7.3 shows a sales summary report with a chart created in Microsoft Excel, the most popular spreadsheet program available today. You will learn more about Excel in Chapter 10, "Creating Spreadsheets with Microsoft Excel."

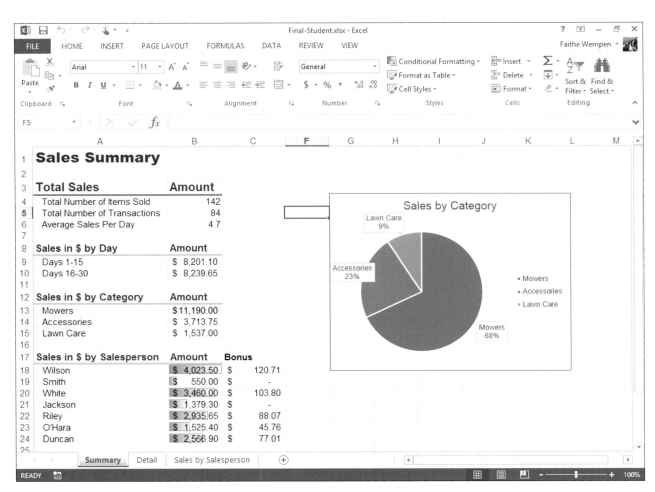

Figure 7.3 Use spreadsheets to record everyday expenses and make simple calculations.

Spreadsheet data is entered into cells in rows and columns. You can enter text, numbers, or a combination of the two. If you enter numbers, you can apply number formatting that makes the numbers appear as currency, percentages, or any of several other number types.

Spreadsheet software does more than just record lists of text and data, however. It also supports formulas that calculate and manipulate the numeric data. For example, in Figure 7.4, each of the expense figures in column B is summed in the formula in cell B9: =SUM(B3:B7). See Chapter 10 for detailed information on creating spreadsheets and working with formulas.

Figure 7.4 A formula is used in cell B9 to sum the values in cells B3 through B7.

Spreadsheets can produce a range of charts and graphs based on the data they contain, like the one shown in Figure 7.3. These charts can then be exported and used in a report such as a word processing document or a presentation.

Data Analyst

Accountants, tax advisors, business owners, and managers all depend on spreadsheets for their work. However, as with word-processing skills, it's likely you'll need to use spreadsheets in many different jobs. The ability to "crunch numbers" comes in useful for analysis, planning, and forecasting, too.

Spreadsheets are incredibly useful when working with a large amount of data. A data analyst must have the ability to categorize and process large volumes of information and draw meaningful conclusions from them. Databases and spreadsheets are both used to process data and extract meaningful information.

Data analysts may have a degree in statistics, mathematics, or business, but they also need an in-depth knowledge of spreadsheets in order to work with such large amounts of information and variables.

Careers in IT

Understanding Databases

database A collection of data stored in a structured format, with the same facts stored about each instance. A database stores data in a way that enables you to search and locate it quickly.

A database is a structured collection of data, such as the inventory of a store or a collection of personnel files. A database contains one or more **tables**, each of which contains records. For example, you might have a table called Employees that contains a record for each employee. A **record** is information about one instance of the data being stored, such as one employee, one inventory item, or one sales transaction. Each record contains one or more individual pieces of information, called a **field**. For example, in an Employees table, one of the fields might be Badge Number, and another might be Hire Date. The software used to create and control a database is a database management system (DBMS). For small, simple databases, many people use Microsoft Access, which is covered in Chapter 11, "Managing Databases with Access." For large-scale databases, a company might use an enterprise-level database system like Oracle.

database management system (DBMS) An application that helps users create and maintain databases.

A database program makes calculations and extrapolates information using combinations of data and varying instruction sets. You might use it to see how one item or person compares to another. For example, your school uses a database to keep track of how well you're doing in comparison to your classmates across different subjects. Extracting information from a database is known as data mining. Web searches make use of data mining to provide search results based on the search query the user enters.

data mining Extracting information from a database to zero in on certain facts or summarize a large amount of data.

relational database A spreadsheet-like database that shows how items in a database are connected or have attributes in common.

The most common type of database is called a relational database. In a relational database, there are multiple tables that have relationships to one another. For example, in a sales database, there might be a Customers table, an Orders table, and an Order Details table. Because an individual customer can have multiple orders, and an individual order can contain multiple items, the details about the customer are stored separately from the details about the order, and the order line items are stored separately from both. Figure 7.5 shows these tables and their relationships in Microsoft Access. Using related tables allows a salesperson to pull up the customer's shipping and payment information whenever he or she starts a new order, rather than having to reenter it each time. Microsoft Access, which you will learn how to use in Chapter 11, creates relational databases.

node The point of intersection in a diagram or in a database; where several items share a node, the node itself becomes important.

hierarchical database A way of organizing data from a single starting point or premise in a treelike parent and child relationship format. All records are shown in terms of how they relate to the originating point at the top of the tree.

A hierarchical type of database has a tree structure in which elements consist of nodes. The database starts from a single point, known as the parent node. The database branches out and has multiple levels. Items on a branch are known as child nodes. There may be one or several child nodes. A hierarchical database works by narrowing down a search starting with the entire set of records and successively excluding any that the search doesn't apply to. Family historians would use a hierarchical view to see all the descendants of a single ancestor.

For information on creating and querying databases, see Chapter 11.

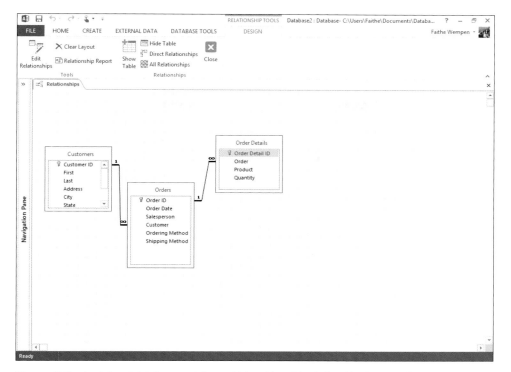

Figure 7.5   A relational database contains multiple tables with relationships between them.

How an Online Store Uses Databases

When you buy something online, the online store uses an application program to manage the purchase process that will connect to the database to check stock levels. When you arrive at the site and log in, the application will look for you in the customer database and check that your password and email address match the details for your account. When you add an item into your shopping cart, a database query is run to check the stock levels and, if applicable, the application places the requested item in your cart and instructs the database stock level to decrease by one. When you click Checkout to go the payment page, the site will ask you to confirm or revise your card payment details and then issue a request to your bank for the funds. Assuming the request is accepted, the online shopping application will confirm your purchase and send you an electronic receipt before issuing an instruction to the warehouse to send out your goods.

Put It to Work

Personal Information Management Software

It can be a challenge to keep track of where you need to be, what you need to do, and whom you need to contact. Personal information management (PIM) software helps people stay organized by providing a calendar, an address book, and a to-do list. Some PIM software also functions as an email program, and allows you to send, receive, store, and organize email messages.

Microsoft Outlook is a very popular email application that includes a full set of PIM capabilities. You can also get some of the individual PIM functions in other applications. For example, you can buy separate calendar, task list, and email applications, or use free versions online, such as Google Calendar and Gmail.

Software Suites

suite A group of applications by the same manufacturer purchased as a group.

Some software manufacturers, such as Microsoft, offer multiple related products that are designed to work well together. They are sometimes sold together as a suite, which is a collection of related applications. The Microsoft Office suite is a very popular suite of business applications; you will learn more about it in Chapters 8 through 12. It includes Word, Excel, PowerPoint, and Outlook, plus some extra applications in some versions such as Access and Publisher. All the applications in the Office suite have similar user interfaces and can exchange content freely. You can buy each application separately, but it is much less expensive to buy the suite.

Adobe also makes a well-known set of professional graphics and publishing tools, Creative Cloud Suite. In Creative Suite, the Photoshop, Dreamweaver, Illustrator, InDesign, Premiere Pro, and Director programs provide photo-editing, web design, vector graphics, desktop publishing, and video-editing capabilities. Each program in Creative Suite supports the proprietary file formats of the other programs, so a Photoshop file can be imported into Illustrator, where further elements can be added before the file is again opened for final edits to be completed in Photoshop.

Accounting and Personal Finance Software

accounting software Software that enables a small business to manage and track its financial health and transactions.

Whether you are doing the accounting for a small business or just keeping track of your own personal bank account, there is software available that can help you. Accounting software simplifies the entire process of managing a business's finances, including creating invoices and purchase orders, processing payments, and running reports. QuickBooks is one of the most popular accounting applications for small businesses; larger businesses may use their own proprietary accounting software. An online version is also available on a pay-as-you-go monthly fee plan. Other accounting programs include FreshBooks and Outright, both of which are web-based.

personal finance software Software that enables individuals to track and manage their bank accounts and investments.

If you are looking to track your own personal finances, you might want to consider a program such as Quicken, the most popular personal finance software. It can not only manage your bank accounts, but also your investments and loans. Microsoft also has a free online tool called Mint that can perform many of the same functions, and your bank may have its own web-based interface that you can use for free.

tax software Software that enables individuals and small businesses to calculate the taxes they owe and file the needed forms with the government.

If you live in a country where you have to file a yearly income tax statement, you may want to get help from tax software. TurboTax and H&R Block are two popular tax applications, each of which comes in various versions for different levels of tax filing complexity. This software can help you print the forms you need to mail, or in some cases to file the required forms electronically for you online.

Quick Review

1. What kind of software is useful for creating budgets and charts?

2. Explain how the following items are related: database field, database record, and database table.

3. What is a suite?

Graphics Software

Graphics software includes any application that enables you to create and manipulate visual images. This broad category includes drawing programs, photo manipulation programs, presentation creation programs, and video capture and editing software. The products available include both professional-quality software used in entertainment and advertising, and consumer-quality software that the average computer hobbyist might experiment with.

graphics software Software that enables you to create and manipulate visual images.

Desktop publishing software, which you learned about earlier in this chapter, can straddle the line between text and graphics software because it enables you to combine text and graphics to produce page layouts.

NOTE

Vector Image Drawing Programs

There are two main categories of graphic images: vector and raster. Although they may look similar, they are structured quite differently and require entirely different types of software to create them.

A vector-based illustration is created with math formulas, like in geometry class. A rectangle, an oval, a straight line—they all have a math formula that plots them on a two-dimensional grid. A three-dimensional vector graphic, such as a 3D representation of a cube or sphere, plots the image in a three-dimensional grid space. (The software does all the math, so you don't have to worry about that part—you just draw by dragging your mouse to create the lines and shapes you want.) Professional-quality programs such as Adobe Illustrator create very sophisticated vector graphics for commercial uses, such as technical drawings and architectural plans. At a much simpler level, Microsoft Office products like PowerPoint, Word, and Excel all come with basic vector drawing tools you can use in their data files. Vector graphics also figure prominently into many video games.

vector-based illustration A drawing that is constructed of mathematically created lines.

Vector images have many advantages. They do not take up much disk space to store because the information needed to display them is very simple and compact. They can also be resized to any size without any loss of quality, because the math formulas behind them are simply recalculated and the shape redrawn. The main disadvantage of a vector graphic is that even the best quality drawings don't look completely real. Most people would never mistake a character from a game like "Second Life" or "The Sims" for a video of a real person, for example.

Step by Step

Creating Vector Graphics

Follow these steps using Microsoft PowerPoint to explore the vector graphic tools in Microsoft Office 2013:

1. Open PowerPoint 2013, and press Esc to close the application's Start screen. A new presentation opens.

2. On the Home tab, click the Layout button, and click Blank.

3. On the Insert tab, click the Shapes button and then click one of the shapes in the Basic Shapes section of the menu.

4. Drag to draw the shape on the blank slide.

5. Drag one of the corners of the image's frame to resize the image. You can hold down Shift as you drag to maintain the aspect ratio (height to width proportion).

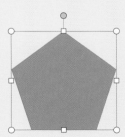

6. Drag the center of the image to move the image.

7. Draw at least three other shapes and at least one straight line (from the Lines section of the Shapes menu).

8. Select one of the shapes, and then on the Drawing Tools Format tab, click Shape Fill. On the palette of colors that appears, click a different color.

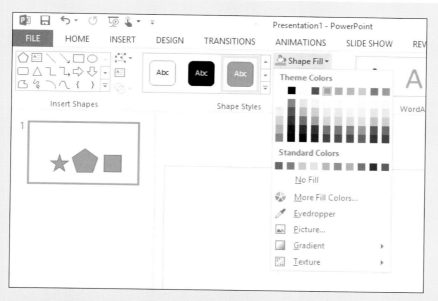

9. Close PowerPoint without saving your changes.

Raster (Photo) Editing Programs

A raster graphic, also called a bitmap image, is one that's composed of a grid of colored pixels. When you use a scanner or digital camera to capture an image or take a photo, the result is a raster graphic. Raster graphics can also be created from scratch using a program such as Paint (the free raster image-editing program that comes with Windows) or, on the higher end, Adobe Photoshop (or the consumer-level version, Photoshop Elements, shown in Figure 7.6).

raster graphic A graphic that consists of a grid of colored pixels that collectively form an image.

pixel An individual colored dot in a raster graphic or on a display screen.

Figure 7.6 Photoshop Elements, a simpler version of the popular Adobe Photoshop, can be used to create and edit raster graphics.

A raster graphic has a native size, known as its resolution. Resolution is measured in number of pixels horizontally by number of pixels vertically, like this: 1024 × 768. This is the same way monitor screen resolution is measured, as you may remember from Chapter 3, "Input, Output, and Storage." The higher the resolution, the better the picture will look when printed at a large size.

A raster image also has a color depth, which means the number of bits required to describe each pixel's color. A standard color depth is 24-bit, which uses 8 bits for red, 8 bits for green, and 8 bits for blue. There are 2^{24} (that is, 2 to the 24th power, or about 16 million) unique colors possible in 24-bit color. The human eye can only detect about 10 million different colors, so this is more than enough for full photorealism.

One disadvantage of raster graphics is that they take up a lot of disk space. Each pixel requires 24 bits to describe it, at a minimum, so a 1024 × 768 image would take up at least 2,359,296 bytes (about 2.3 MB) in an uncompressed file—maybe more, depending on the file format. Because raster images can be so large, some file formats employ compression.

Depending on the file format, compression can either be lossless (no loss of image quality) or lossy (some loss of image quality).

The other major problem with raster graphics is that they tend to lose their quality when resized—especially when enlarged beyond their original dimensions. This happens because when you enlarge a raster image, the pixels don't change size, so the software must simulate a particular pixel's color, taking up more space than it originally did. The trouble is, it's not nearly as simple as just adding another pixel of the same color next to the original, because resizing is often done in odd multiples, like 15%. Therefore, the image-editing software must do its best to simulate the enlargement by doubling some pixels but not others, and the result is a jagged or fuzzy image. In Figure 7.7, for example, see how this image, originally with crisp lines, becomes pixilated (that is, you can see the jagged edges of individual pixels) when it's enlarged.

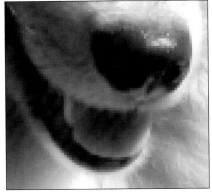

Figure 7.7 When you resize a raster image, jagged or fuzzy edges may appear.

Step by Step

Creating Raster Graphics

Follow these steps using Paint to experiment with raster graphic creation and editing:

1. Open the Paint program in Windows. (From the Start screen, type Paint, and then click Paint on the results list that appears.)

2. Click the Color 1 button and then click the color of your choice. This will be the outline color.

3. Click the Color 2 button and then click the color of your choice. This will be the fill color.

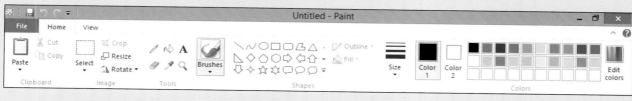

4. In the Shapes group, click the shape of your choice and then drag on the blank work area to create the shape.

5. Click the Fill button and then click Solid Fill. The shape receives a fill of the color you chose in Step 3, in the Solid style.

6. In the Tools group, click the Magnifier tool (the magnifying glass) and then click repeatedly on the image's border until the border looks jagged.

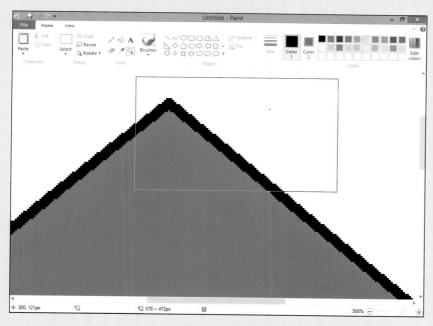

7. Right-click until the zoom returns to 100%. (The Zoom percentage appears in the lower-right corner of the window.)

8. Click the down arrow under the Brushes button and click a brush of your choice.

9. In the Tools group, click the Text tool (looks like an A). Then click in the center of the shape.

10. On the Text tab, in the Font group, change the font size to 48 and then type a question mark.

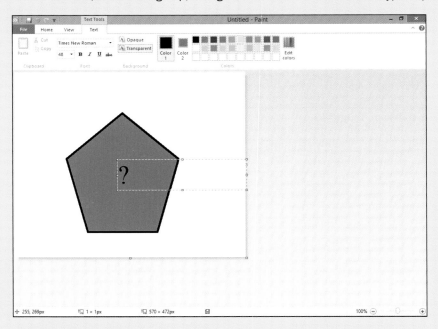

11. Click the Color 2 button and choose white as the color.

12. On the Home tab, in the Tools group, click the Eraser tool. Then drag the mouse pointer across part of the shape to erase it.

13. Close Paint without saving your changes.

Presentation Graphics Software

At various points in your working life, you're likely to be asked to give a presentation or make a speech. It's a daunting prospect. However, you can deflect some of the attention by giving your audience something else to look at. They will also find it easier to digest what you have to say if you provide a visual representation of key facts and figures you're discussing. Presentation graphics software is the ideal tool for this purpose. It enables you to create screen-sized slides containing a mixture of words and images that you can move through on demand as you deliver your presentation. You can incorporate audio and video clips, corporate branding such as company logos and color schemes, and other special elements and features. (See Figure 7.8.)

Most presentations are created and delivered using the Microsoft PowerPoint part of the Microsoft Office productivity suite. On an Apple computer, the equivalent program is Keynote; there is also a version of Microsoft Office available for Apple devices such as Macs and iPads.

presentation graphics software A program that combines charts, graphics, and bulleted lists of information as a series of slides that summarize a report or verbal presentation. Microsoft PowerPoint is the most widely used program.

slide A screen of information that is displayed in a static fashion while a presenter elaborates on its contents. Often, the slide will be part of an electronic presentation file and the presenter can move through successive files on demand.

Figure 7.8 A PowerPoint presentation is used to summarize the speaker's information.

Presentation graphics generally distill what the speaker says into bulleted summaries, and bar and pie charts. Such presentations may accompany a detailed report or be used as part of a marketing pitch—for example, showing why a company is better to do business with than its rivals. The most effective presentations have only a handful of slides and feature minimal details, allowing the audience to focus on what the presenter says. To make your point effectively, avoid creating long and boring presentations crammed with far too much information.

For a look at how to create and present a PowerPoint presentation, see Chapter 12, "Creating Presentation Graphics with PowerPoint."

Computer-Aided Design Software

Computer-aided design (CAD) software is used when designing any sort of item that has a physical form (rather than being flat like a photo). It uses the same basic idea as the two-dimensional vector graphics that you learned about earlier in this chapter, but it models them to have height, width, and depth. This is also known as *3D modeling*.

computer-aided design The process of using computer software to produce technical drawings that include the product's precise scale, simulate its textures, and show it in full three-dimensional detail.

wireframe A 3D vector drawing that consists only of drawn lines, without any surface textures applied.

Three-dimensional drawings are built around a wireframe. This is a sort of skeleton on which details of the computerized object or character are overlaid. The wireframe is created by extruding the flat shape to give it volume and depth.

The object is also given mass and assigned textures and properties such as skin, hair, bones, or fabric. Each of these elements has a predefined (but separately editable) set of attributes. For instance, the attributes of a brick wall would include strength, inflexibility, and resistance to wind and people bumping into it. The wireframe can be rotated so the designer can check that all the design elements and perspective are correct.

render To apply a surface texture and fill to a wireframe image to give it a solid appearance.

Once all the attributes have been added to an object created using a CAD program, the object is rendered to give it the appearance of a solid form by applying surface texture and color. For example, in Figure 7.9, which shows a rendered image in AutoCAD, notice how the image surface of the handheld vacuum includes two different surface textures: One looks like solid plastic, and the other looks semi-transparent.

Rendering can require huge amounts of computer power. Especially detailed designs can take many hours to render. If you want to design in 3D, you will need a powerful desktop computer with a multi-core CPU, lots of memory, and a high-quality graphics card.

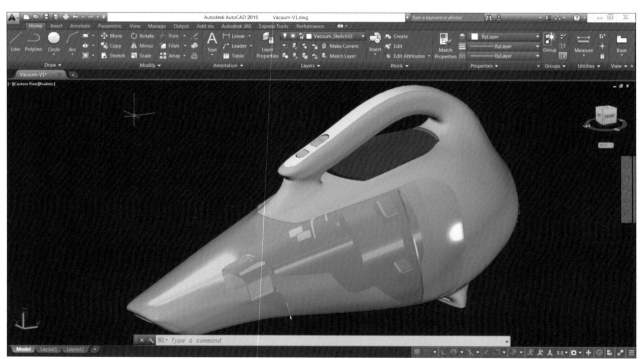

Image courtesy of Autodesk

Figure 7.9 Wireframe images are created in 3D vector modeling programs and then covered with surface textures to make them appear more realistic.

Computer-Aided Designer

Many creative industries depend on computers for their work. The computer games and film industries make extensive use of 3D design. Almost every new product that's created is prototyped using CAD software, too. A CAD designer needs strong technical drawing and creative graphics skills.

Developments in CAD software and a new type of printer have made it possible to prototype objects much more cheaply. A 3D printer uses plastic rather than ink to lay down layer upon layer in order to build up three-dimensional objects. Consequently, there is a greater demand for people who can produce the designs for the objects that will be printed in 3D. 3D printers such as the Makerbot Replicator 2X (pictured) are being used in classrooms and by hobbyists to create 3D models.

Photo courtesy of Makerbot.com

Quick Review

1. What are the advantages of vector graphics?
2. What are the advantages of raster graphics?
3. Explain the relationship between a wireframe and rendering in a CAD program.

Other Types of Software

Besides the big categories of software we've looked at so far in this chapter, there are many smaller categories, such as lifestyle and hobby programs, and educational software. The following sections only scratch the surface of what's available; you will want to explore the many types of applications available on your own.

Music and Video Players

If you have a Windows computer, you'll find that Windows Media Player can play music you've downloaded and any music CDs you insert. It will also play some video clips and movies. As an alternative to Windows Media Player, you might use iTunes, which is a free download from Apple's website (see Figure 7.10). iTunes can play music, videos, podcasts, audio books, and more. You can also use online services, such as Pandora, to listen to music.

Figure 7.10   iTunes is one example of an application that can play music and video clips.

Your computer may come with a DVD movie player application, or you might choose to buy one, such as RealPlayer Plus, WinX, or CyberLink PowerDVD. This software provides an interface you can use to watch movies on DVD and Blu-ray discs (provided, of course, you have an appropriate disc drive).

codec A translation file used to play back a certain audio or video format. An abbreviation of coder/decoder.

Troubleshooting

Can't Play DVDs?

If Windows Media Player won't play DVDs, it may be because you are missing a codec. A codec is a translation file; codec is short for *coder/decoder*. Different file formats require different codecs, and not all versions of Windows come with the one you need to play DVD movies. (If you have Windows 7 Home Premium, Ultimate, or Enterprise, you should have it already. It doesn't come with Windows 8.1 or Windows 8.1 Po.) You can choose to buy and install the needed codec. For Windows 7 and earlier, see `http://windows.microsoft.com/en-us/windows/windows-media-player-plug-ins`, or for Windows 8.1, upgrade to the Media Center Pack. But before you go to the expense of upgrading Windows, see whether there is some other application installed on your PC that will play DVD movies. Most PCs that come with a DVD drive also come with such software.

Audio and Video Editing Software

If you want to create your own videos and music, you'll need a camera and instruments to do so. You can easily capture video and record audio on a smartphone and then transfer them to your computer for editing.

Many applications are available for editing audio tracks. For example, the freeware program Audacity (`audacity.sourceforge.net`) lets you import multiple audio tracks, trim out the parts you don't require, and then splice everything together. Mac users can record and mix digital instruments such as piano, guitar, and drum tracks in the excellent GarageBand application. You can also buy more full-featured products, such as Adobe Audition.

Windows Live Essentials (`windows.microsoft.com/en-gb/windows-live/essentials`) contains a free Windows Movie Maker program that you can use to trim and combine video clips and photos and to add a sound track or commentary (see Figure 7.11). On a Mac, iMovie offers slick tools to quickly create your own mini movie. Neither of these programs will tax your computer's processor, but if you want to create professional-looking movies you'll need to use a dedicated video-editing program such as Sony Vegas Pro or Adobe Director, or a full-featured consumer level program such as Adobe Premiere Elements. As with the animation and 3D graphics programs described earlier, you need a powerful computer; a quad-core or eight-core processor and powerful graphics card are essential.

Figure 7.11   You can use a free video editor such as Windows Movie Maker to make video clips from your photos.

Personal Enrichment and Education Software

legal software Software that guides the user in creating legally binding contracts and forms.

Just about anything that you want to accomplish, you can find software to help you do it. For example, you can buy legal software that will help you draw up basic legal documents that are valid in your location, such as a will, a power of attorney statement, a lease, and a loan agreement.

reference software Software that provides access to established facts and information on a variety of topics.

You can also improve your life by using reference software, such as dictionary and encyclopedia programs. These are mostly found online these days because it is easier to keep them current that way; you might choose to use free resources or to pay for a subscription to an online encyclopedia with premium content.

NOTE With so many free online reference sources today, why would someone want a reference tool such as an online encyclopedia with premium content? One important reason is that a commercial source of reference materials offers more accuracy and higher quality because they can afford to pay full-time fact-checkers and professional writers. Online sources that are collaboratively maintained, such as Wikipedia, do not provide any assurance of accuracy, and the writing quality varies a great deal among entries.

educational software Software that teaches or trains an individual in a particular type of knowledge or skill.

Educational software can teach new skills and expand your knowledge on a variety of subjects. When you think of educational software, you might at first think of software designed for children, but there are many adult education programs too, such as Rosetta Stone for learning new languages (see Figure 7.12). Many colleges and universities offer online courses that have their own proprietary learning interfaces, including video lectures, interactive tutorials, and text and graphical lessons.

Figure 7.12   Learn a new language using Rosetta Stone software.

A Free Education

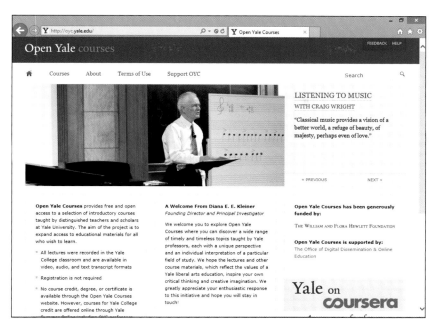

Do you know someone who would like to be better educated but doesn't have the money to spend on higher education? Direct her to Open Yale, a service of Yale University, at `http://oyc.yale.edu`. To quote from its website: "Open Yale offers free and open access to a selection of introductory courses taught by distinguished teachers and scholars at Yale University. The aim of the project is to expand access to educational materials for all who wish to learn. All lectures were recorded in the Yale College classroom and are available in video, audio, and text transcript formats. Registration is not required." This program does not issue any credit, degree, or certificate.

Put It to Work

Communication Software

Communication software provides various ways of communicating with other people, usually via the Internet.

An email application helps you send and receive email messages. You might choose a stand-alone application like Eudora, a combination email and PIM application like Outlook, or an online web-based service like Outlook.com or Gmail.

email application Software that assists in sending and receiving email.

Most operating systems come with a web browser application, but you can also download and install others, most of them for free. Popular browsers include Internet Explorer (which comes with Windows), Google Chrome (which comes with the Chrome OS), Safari (which comes with Mac OS X and iOS), Opera, and Firefox. Figure 7.13 shows the Google Chrome browser.

Figure 7.13 Versions of the Chrome browser are available for a variety of operating systems.

instant messaging Sending and receiving short text messages in real-time over the Internet.

Free instant messaging applications such as Yahoo! IM and AOL Instant Messenger enable you to have text conversations with your friends and family from your computer desktop. Some of these programs also have some video chat capabilities. Services such as Skype are designed specifically for video chat; they enable you to have person-to-person video chats with other people, provided you both have webcams and microphones on your computers. Windows 8.1 includes a Skype application.

video chat Having an online conversation that includes both audio and video.

videoconferencing A means of conducting a video conversation remotely using an Internet connection and the webcam or camera on your laptop, phone, or tablet.

Businesses use videoconferencing programs to hold meetings involving multiple people at multiple locations. These programs are the full-featured business version of video chat; they not only allow you to see and hear other participants, but also allow you to share computer screens, collaborate on documents in real-time, draw on a virtual whiteboard, and more. A company that does a lot of remote conferencing may have its own server with its own conferencing software.

groupware Software that helps people collaborate on business projects and work together in a team environment when they are not physically together.

Groupware helps people who are working on projects together to keep in touch. Users can post shared files that can be collaboratively edited, exchange messages, hold online meetings, and more in this environment. Microsoft SharePoint is one example of groupware software.

Web Authoring Software

Want to create your own website? There are many ways to do it. You can code your own files in HTML in a plain text editor like Notepad and then check your work in a browser, but most people (including most professionals) use web authoring software that provides a what-you-see-is-what-you-get (WYSIWYG, pronounced *wizzy-wig*) interface. Using this software, you don't have to constantly switch back and forth between your code and a browser window to see what you're doing. One

web authoring software Software that helps create website designs and content.

what you see is what you get (WYSIWYG) A feature in an application that allows users to see their work exactly as it will be when it is distributed to others, such as in print or online.

popular application that professionals use is Adobe Dreamweaver; there are many free and low-cost alternatives for the casual user, including tools found on websites that will host your web page for free or very cheaply.

Quick Review

1. What is a codec?

2. What is groupware?

3. What is WYSIWYG?

Managing Your Applications

In the following sections, you'll learn some important information that will help you choose the right software and manage your software collection.

Software License Agreements

Most software that you install is subject to copyright. This means that its design and content belong to somebody else and that person or organization has laid down rules governing how the program may be used. In order to install the software, you must agree to respect this copyright and to abide by the terms of use. The terms of use are also known as an End User License Agreement (EULA). Before you install the program, you are given the opportunity to read through the terms of this agreement in case there is anything you object to or there are any rights that you don't want to agree to.

End User License Agreement (EULA) The legal agreement between the owner of an application and the user who wants to install and use it

To learn about the different licenses that apply to different types of software, refer to the section "Software Licensing" in Chapter 17, "Legal, Ethical, Health, and Environmental Issues in Computing."

Application System Requirements

Before you purchase an application, you should check its system requirements. The system requirements represent the minimum hardware configuration required in order to successfully install and run the application. You can find the system requirements printed on the software box if you buy it at a retail store; if you buy it online, you can find them on the application's website. System requirements usually include a minimum CPU speed, a minimum amount of RAM, and certain standards for sound and video support. They may also specify Internet access, a particular type of input device (such as a joystick), and a certain amount of free hard drive space. Figure 7.14 shows the system requirements for the World of Warcraft video game under Windows, for example. It is common for the system requirements for games to be more restrictive than for business applications because of the intense graphic processing needed for games that have complex motion graphics. As you can see in Figure 7.14, this application has two sets of specs: one for the minimum requirements, and one that is recommended for best performance.

system requirements The minimum hardware required to install and run an application.

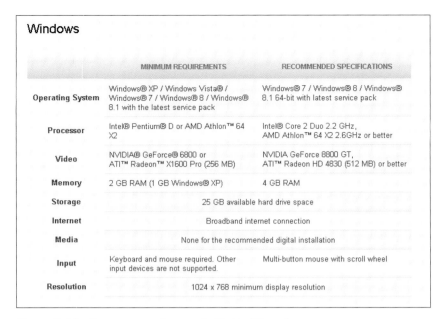

Windows

	MINIMUM REQUIREMENTS	RECOMMENDED SPECIFICATIONS
Operating System	Windows® XP / Windows Vista® / Windows® 7 / Windows® 8 / Windows® 8.1 with the latest service pack	Windows® 7 / Windows® 8 / Windows® 8.1 64-bit with latest service pack
Processor	Intel® Pentium® D or AMD Athlon™ 64 X2	Intel® Core 2 Duo 2.2 GHz, AMD Athlon™ 64 X2 2.6GHz or better
Video	NVIDIA® GeForce® 6800 or ATI™ Radeon™ X1600 Pro (256 MB)	NVIDIA GeForce 8800 GT, ATI™ Radeon HD 4830 (512 MB) or better
Memory	2 GB RAM (1 GB Windows® XP)	4 GB RAM
Storage	25 GB available hard drive space	
Internet	Broadband internet connection	
Media	None for the recommended digital installation	
Input	Keyboard and mouse required. Other input devices are not supported.	Multi-button mouse with scroll wheel
Resolution	1024 x 768 minimum display resolution	

Figure 7.14   The system requirements for World of Warcraft.

Installing and Removing Applications

Installing an application is easy. To install an application that came on CD or DVD, simply insert the disc into your computer. The Setup utility should run automatically. If it does not, browse the content of the drive in File Explorer and double-click the Setup.exe file. To install an application that you downloaded, double-click the downloaded file after it has finished downloading.

To remove an application in Windows 8.1, you use the Control Panel, as described in the following steps.

Step by Step

Uninstalling a Windows Application

Follow these steps to uninstall an application in Windows 8.1:

1. Right-click the Start button on the taskbar and click Programs and Features.

2. Click the program to uninstall on the list of programs that appears.

3. In the bar at the top of the list, click Uninstall.

4. Follow the prompts that appear to uninstall the application. They will vary depending on the application.

5. If prompted to restart the computer after the uninstall has completed, click Yes to do so.

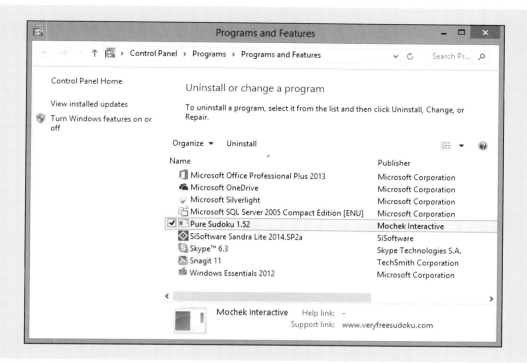

Updating Applications

Application developers frequently release free updates to their products. These updates may add new features, fix problems, or both. Some updates even patch security holes that make your computer vulnerable to online attack. It is almost always a good idea to install any available updates right away.

Some applications are set up to automatically notify you when an update is available. The notification may pop up in a dialog box, or as a balloon near the notification area. Click in the message that appears, and follow the prompts. Some Microsoft products, such as Microsoft Office, can update themselves automatically as needed through Windows Update.

Other applications must be checked manually for updates. For example, some applications have a Check for Updates command on the Help menu, as in Figure 7.15. Select the command to allow the program to check its home website for updates. Then follow the prompts that appear if an update is available. You might have to go to the website manually to look for updates.

Figure 7.15   Some programs require you to manually check for updates.

Quick Review

1. How do you install an application in Windows?

2. How can you tell whether your computer meets an application's requirements before you buy the application?

3. How do you uninstall a Windows application?

Summary

Business Productivity Software

A **word processor** is used to create text-based documents. **Desktop publishing** software provides more control over page layout than a word processor. A **spreadsheet** is a grid used to analyze and present numeric data in **cells**. Spreadsheets use **formulas** to perform calculations.

A database is a structured collection of data. The data resides in **tables**, each of which contains **records** and **fields**. An application that creates databases is a **database management system**. **Data mining** is the process of extracting useful information from a database. The most common type of database is a **relational database**, which has multiple tables with relationships between them; another type is a **hierarchical database**, which uses a tree structure made up of **nodes**.

A suite is a group of related applications, such as the applications in Microsoft Office. There are other suites too, such as Adobe Creative Cloud Suite.

Accounting software helps small businesses maintain their financial records. **Personal finance software** helps individuals and families do the same. **Tax software** helps individuals and businesses file their tax forms.

Graphics Software

Graphics software is software that enables you to create and manipulate visual images. **Vector graphics** are lines and shapes drawn mathematically, like in geometry. Vector graphics are small and easily resizable but not realistic.

Raster graphics, or bitmaps, are composed of a grid of colored **pixels**. They are large and don't resize well but can be photorealistic. A raster graphic's size is its **resolution** (number of pixels horizontally and vertically). It has a **color depth**, which is the number of bits required to describe each pixel's color. Some file formats support **image transparency**, **image animation**, and/or **compression**. When a raster image is resized, it may become **pixelated**.

Presentation graphics software enables you to create **slides** to use as visual aids in presentations.

Computer-aided design (CAD) software is used to design 3D objects using vector-based drawings. An object drawing starts out as a **wireframe** and then is **rendered** by having surface textures and colors applied to it.

Other Types of Software

Music applications such as iTunes can plan and manage not only music but also videos, podcasts, and audio books. DVD player software can play movies from DVD discs on your computer. For Windows Media Player to play DVDs, you must have a supported version of Windows or purchase a **codec**. To edit your own audio and video files, a variety of free and low-cost programs are available, as well as higher-end professional tools.

Legal software helps people draw up basic legal documents that are valid in their location. **Reference software** provides a collection of information, such as a dictionary or an encyclopedia. **Educational software** can teach new skills and expand your knowledge through lessons and tutorials.

Communication software includes **email applications**, **instant messaging**, and **video chat.** Professional-quality video chat for groups is called **video conferencing**. **Groupware** is software that helps people work together as a team from remote locations.

Web authoring software helps people create web pages and sites. Some are simple text editors, but most are **what-you-see-is-what-you-get (WYSIWYG)**, for easier viewing of the edits.

Managing Your Applications

The **End User License Agreement (EULA)** for an application spells out the terms of the license to use it.

The **system requirements** of an application explain the minimum hardware configuration required to run the application successfully. It may include specs for CPU, memory, graphics, and hard drive space.

To install an application, insert its CD/DVD or run its Setup file. To remove an application, use the Uninstall a Program feature in the Control Panel in Windows.

Some applications update themselves automatically; with others, you must locate and run a Check for Updates command in the software interface or visit the manufacturer's website to see if updates are available.

Key Terms

accounting software	personal finance software
application software	pixel
cell	pixilated
codec	presentation graphics software
color depth	raster graphic
compression	reference software
computer-aided design	relational database
data mining	render
database	resolution
database management system	slide
desktop publishing software	spreadsheet
educational software	suite
email application	system requirements
End User License Agreement (EULA)	tax software
formula	vector-based illustration
graphics software	video chat
groupware	videoconferencing
hierarchical database	web authoring software
instant messaging	what-you-see-is-what-you-get (WYSIWYG)
legal software	wireframe
node	word processor

Test Yourself

Fact Check

1. Which software creates page layouts by arranging text and graphics in movable frames?

    a. desktop publishing

    b. word processing

    c. spreadsheet

    d. DBMS

2. What does a spreadsheet use to do math calculations?

    a. macros

    b. formulas

    c. charts

    d. records

3. Which of these is *not* associated with a database?

    a. table

    b. record

    c. field

    d. formula

4. What kind of graphic can be resized without losing image quality?

    a. raster

    b. tabular

    c. vector

    d. pixilated

5. What is EULA an acronym for?

    a. End Underhand Licensing Agreements

    b. Extra User Licensing Arrangement

    c. End User Licensing Agreement

    d. End User Levy Arrangement

6. What are the individual dots that make up a raster image called?

    a. formulas

    b. pixels

    c. vectors

    d. hexagons

7. In CAD, a 3D object is first created as a _____ and then rendered to give it a surface.

    a. wireframe

    b. pixel

    c. vector

    d. record

8. _____ is software that enables team members to collaborate online.

    a. Freeware

    b. Groupware

    c. Shareware

    d. Teamware

9. _____ refers to applications by the same manufacturer purchased as a group.

    a. Legal software

    b. Desktop publishing software

    c. A suite

    d. System requirements

10. What does product activation do?

    a. registers the product with the manufacturer

    b. prompts you for a product key

    c. locks the product key to the computer on which the software is installed

    d. installs the software

Matching

Match the software type with an appropriate use for it.

    a. 2D vector drawing software

    b. CAD software

    c. database

    d. desktop publishing software

    e. presentation graphics software

    f. raster editing software

    g. spreadsheet

    h. word processor

1. _____Technical drawing of a building floor plan.

2. _____Retouching a photo.

3. _____Creating a 3D model of a new product being developed.

4. _____Creating a layout for a magazine.

5. _____Analyzing sales figures for the last three months.

6. _____Storing information about a company's inventory.

7. _____Writing a research paper for a class.

8. _____Creating slides to accompany a business presentation.

Sum It Up

1. For each of the following, name two types of work you could accomplish: word processor, spreadsheet, desktop publishing software, database.

2. What are the advantages of a software suite?

3. How is data stored in a relational database?

4. If a raster graphic had a resolution of 800 × 600, how would you determine the number of pixels in it?

5. Explain the process of rendering in a CAD application.

6. Explain the difference between instant messaging and video conferencing.

Explore More

Making Older Software Work in Windows 8.1

Applications originally written to run under earlier versions of Windows may not always perform well under Windows 8.1. One work-around is to set up Compatibility Mode for an application. Compatibility Mode can simulate any of several earlier Windows versions when interacting with that application. Using the Help and Support in Windows 8.1, look up information about Compatibility Mode to learn how it works and how to enable it.

With your instructor's permission, download a shareware or freeware game from `www.down-load.com`, where the system requirements do not include Windows 8.1, and install it on your computer. As you are locating a game to download, look at the system requirements for the game to find out the highest Windows version it supports. Then configure Compatibility Mode to emulate that version. Try the game to make sure it works with these settings. When you are finished, uninstall the game.

Other Software Types

There are many other software types besides the ones presented in this chapter. Using the Internet to help provide ideas, make a list of at least seven types of software that weren't covered in this chapter, and write a brief description of each type, including who might use it and what they might use it for. If you can't think of seven types, look at a website that sells software, such as Amazon.com, for ideas.

Think It Over

Paying for Application Software

Some types of software application cost hundreds of dollars, while other programs can be used for free. What are the advantages and disadvantages of paying for software? How do you think makers of free software make any money? What pricing model would you use if you were writing a program, and how would you make money from it? How would you provide customer support and make sure improvements to the program were made?

Sharing Software and Games

License agreements mean you aren't supposed to lend your friends the games you own. Do you think there is anything wrong with letting your friends make copies of the programs and games you've bought? Would you consider getting free copies of games you know normally cost money by downloading them from the Internet? Can you see any dangers or issues with doing so?

Part III
Microsoft Office

Chapter 8

Understanding Microsoft Office 2013

Learning objectives

☐ Identify the basic parts of an Office application's interface

☐ Use common features that all Office applications share

☐ Save, open, and create data files

☐ Print your work and email it to others

☐ Adjust the options of an Office application

Microsoft Office is the most popular suite of business applications in the world. Its core products—Word, Excel, and PowerPoint—are considered the standard tools in millions of offices. In many companies, newly hired business professionals and support staff are expected to come into their positions already knowing how to use these tools.

Upcoming chapters in this book cover the individual applications. However, because Microsoft Office is a suite, the applications share many common features. You will learn about the common features in this chapter, including using the interface, managing the application window, saving and opening files, creating new files, and distributing your work to others. These will be important skills to have already mastered when you get to later chapters.

Microsoft Office Specialist

After you have mastered the Microsoft Office products, you may want to pursue Microsoft Office Specialist certification. Candidates take a series of tests that show their mastery of the applications, and after passing the exams, earn a certificate. Potential employers will see this certification as proof that you can use Office applications productively to tackle whatever tasks are given to you.

There are three levels of certification. You can earn a Microsoft Office Specialist certification in each application. For Expert level certification, you must pass the Expert level exams for Word and Excel. For Master level, you must pass the Expert level exams for Word and Excel plus the basic level exam for PowerPoint and one other basic level exam of your choice (Outlook, Access, or SharePoint). See `http://www.microsoft.com/learning/en-us/mos-certification.aspx` to learn about the certification program.

© iStockphoto.com/cmcderm1

Understanding the Office 2013 Interface

Each Office 2013 application has the same basic controls, so once you have mastered one application, learning another application is easier.

The heart of each Office application's controls is a thick toolbar across the top called the Ribbon. The Ribbon has multiple tabs; click a tab to display a different set of controls. The Home tab is displayed by default when you open the application. Each tab of the Ribbon is organized into groups. A group is a named section; the group names appear at the bottom of each group. Some groups have a dialog box launcher in the lower-right corner. Clicking this button opens a dialog box or task pane with more extensive options than are shown on the Ribbon itself.

Some tabs are common to all applications, such as Home, Insert, and View; others are unique to a particular application, such as the Mailings tab in Word and the Formulas tab in Excel. Figure 8.1 shows the Ribbons in Word 2013 and Excel 2013.

To the left of the regular tabs is a File tab, which opens Backstage view. Within Backstage view, you can select a a category and then select commands on the right. The subcategories (if any) and commands change depending on which category you choose. For example, in Figure 8.2, the Share category has been selected, and the Email subcategory.

Ribbon The main toolbar in Office applications and some other Windows applications, consisting of multiple tabbed pages of commands.

tab A tabbed page of a Ribbon, or the name of a particular tabbed page.

group A named section of a Ribbon tab.

dialog box launcher An icon in the lower-right corner of a group on the Ribbon; when clicked, it opens a dialog box or task pane.

Backstage view The area of an Office application where you select commands that affect the entire active document or the application itself. Access it by clicking the File tab on the Ribbon.

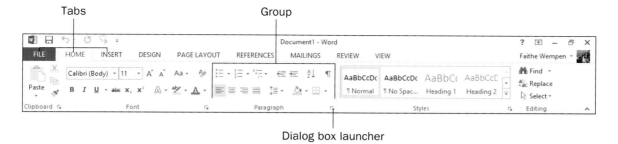

Tabs   Group

Dialog box launcher

Excel's first two groups are the same as in Word

Some of the buttons in Excel's Alignment group
are the same as those in Word's Paragraph group

Figure 8.1   The Ribbon in Word 2013 (top) and Excel 2013 (bottom).

Categories   Commands for saving, opening, and closing

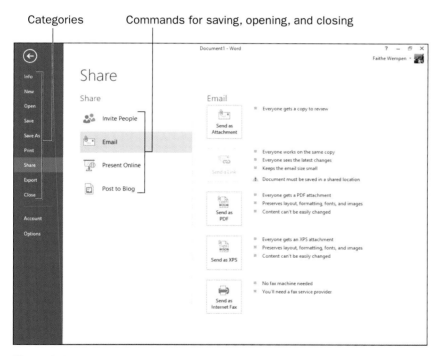

Figure 8.2   Backstage view provides access to commands and options that affect the entire file.

Above the Ribbon, on the left end of the title bar, is the Quick Access Toolbar (QAT). You can customize this toolbar by adding and removing commands from it. This toolbar remains constant no matter which tab is displayed, so you can keep your favorite commands close at hand on the QAT without having to remember which tab contains them. The down-pointing arrow at the right end of the QAT opens a menu of common commands that you can toggle on and off on the QAT by selecting them, as shown in Figure 8.3. You can also choose More Commands from that menu to add other commands to it that aren't on the list.

Quick Access Toolbar (QAT) The small, customizable toolbar above the Ribbon tabs in an Office application's interface.

To temporarily hide the Ribbon commands for more workspace onscreen, click the up-pointing arrow in the bottom-right corner of the Ribbon. The Ribbon will appear only when you click a tab name. You can also click the Ribbon Display Options button, which is the button just to the right of the Help (question mark) button in the upper-right corner of the application window. This button opens a menu of Ribbon states. The default is to show both tabs and commands, but you can show only tabs or you can auto-hide the Ribbon so that it doesn't appear at all unless you click at the top of the application.

Ribbon Display Options button

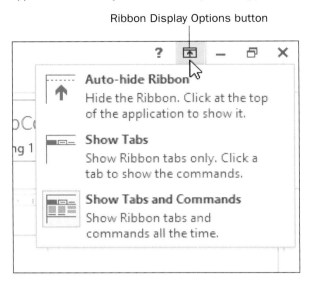

Quick Access Toolbar

Figure 8.3   Customize the QAT by selecting commands from its menu.

Ribbon Doesn't Look Right?

If the Ribbon in an application doesn't appear to have the same commands on it as your classmates' computers, yours may have been customized. To reset the Ribbon, right-click any button on the Ribbon and choose Customize the Ribbon. In the lower-right corner of the dialog box that appears, click Reset, and then click Reset All Customizations. Then click OK, and then click Yes to confirm. Your Ribbon will be back to its original state.

When you right-click, a short-cut menu appears (also called a *context menu*). Its commands depend on what you right-clicked. If you right-click a selected block of text, for example, commands appear that will help you format it, move or copy it, and check its spelling, as shown in Figure 8.4. If you right-click on a graphic, commands appear for formatting and positioning the graphic. The shortcut menu that appears when you right-click a button on the Ribbon offers an option to add that command to the Quick Access Toolbar.

When you hover the mouse pointer over a button or command on the Ribbon, a ScreenTip appears, telling you its name and purpose. In some cases, ScreenTips also contain keyboard shortcut prompts. For example, when you point at the Justify button on the Home tab, you find out that Ctrl+J is the keyboard shortcut setting that alignment, as shown in Figure 8.5. To use a keyboard shortcut, hold down the first key while you tap (press and release) the second key.

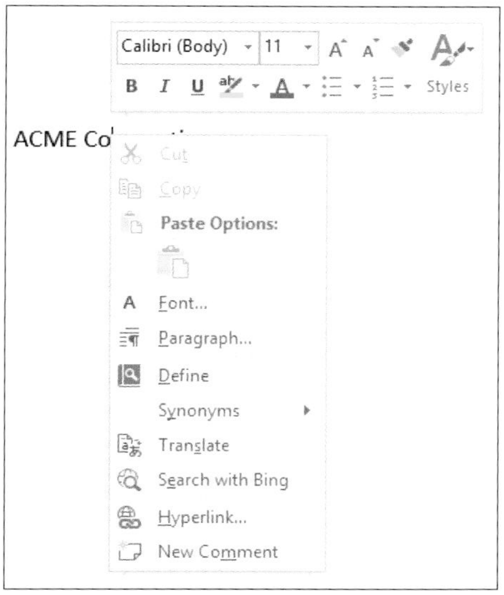

Figure 8.4 The shortcut menu is different depending on what you right-clicked. The menu shown here is displayed when you right-click a block of text.

shortcut menu A context-sensitive menu that appears when you right-click an object onscreen.

ScreenTip The information that appears about a command or button when you hover the mouse pointer over it.

keyboard shortcut Two or more keys that, when pressed in combination, issue a command.

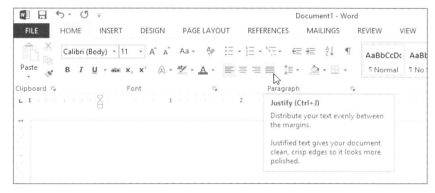

Figure 8.5 A ScreenTip provides information about a Ribbon command or button.

For a list of all the available keyboard shortcuts in an application, open the application's Help window (F1) and search for *keyboard shortcuts*. The status bar, at the bottom of the application window, provides several pieces of status-related information. In a Word document, for example, it tells you how many pages are in the document and what page number you are working with at the moment. It also tells you how many words are in the document. See Figure 8.6. The exact details the status bar provides depend on the application.

PAGE 1 OF 1   2 WORDS   ENGLISH (UNITED STATES)   📇   📖 📄 📄 - ──┼── + 120%

Figure 8.6   The Status bar in Word 2013.

status bar The bar at the bottom of an application's window that reports status information.

Zoom controls Controls at the right end of the status bar that adjust the magnification at which the data is displayed.

At the right end of the status bar are the Zoom controls. The Zoom controls enable you to zoom in and out to view your work at different magnifications. You can drag the slider, or you can click the - (minus) or + (plus) button on its ends to increment the zoom out (-) or in (+). The current zoom level is reported to the right of the Zoom slider; click the current Zoom level to open a Zoom dialog box in which you can set the zoom level more precisely. You can see the Zoom and View controls in Figure 8.6. The View tab also has Zoom controls that perform the same functions (plus a few others).

As with any window, you can adjust an Office application window's size. To resize a window, drag its border, and to move a window, drag its title bar. You can maximize it by clicking its Maximize button (in the upper-right corner of the window), and then restore it to pre-maximized size by clicking the Restore button, which replaces the Maximize button when the window is maximized. You can minimize the window down to a button on the taskbar with the Minimize button, and you can close the window (which closes the application and any open files) by clicking the Close button. Figure 8.7 points out the window controls in an Office application's window.

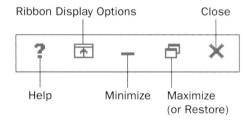

Ribbon Display Options   Close

Help   Minimize   Maximize
                           (or Restore)

Figure 8.7   Office application windows have the same window controls as other windows in your operating system.

Quick Review

1. What are the buttons above the tab names on the Ribbon?

2. What is Backstage view and what kinds of commands are found there?

3. How do you display a context-sensitive shortcut menu for an object?

Using Basic Features of Office Applications

Office applications have many commands and features in common. For example, the procedures for getting help, changing views, cutting and pasting, formatting text, and undoing mistakes are nearly identical. In the following sections, you will learn about some features that work the same way in each of the main Office applications.

Starting a New Blank Document

In Word, Excel, and PowerPoint, a Start screen appears each time you start the application. This Start screen enables you to select from recently used documents or choose a template on which to base a new document. You can bypass this Start screen by pressing the Esc key to start in a new blank document, or you can select a file to open or a template to use.

If you would prefer not to see the Start screen each time the application starts, choose File, Options, and on the General tab, clear the Show the Start Screen When This Application Starts check box.

TIP

Getting Help

To get help in any Office application, do one of the following:

- **Press the F1 key.** If you do this while a dialog box is open, the help provided is context-sensitive, with specific help on that dialog box.

- **Click the Help button.** It's the question mark above the right end of the Ribbon. You can see it in Figure 8.7.

In the Help window that appears, you can search for a particular topic by typing a keyword in the Search box, or you can browse the Help system by clicking on one of the hyperlinks on the home page of the Help system. Figure 8.8 identifies the buttons on the Help window's toolbar.

Changing Views

Each application has its own unique set of views that you can switch among while working with your data. Different views are useful in different situations. For example, in PowerPoint, you use Normal view for general slide editing and Slide Sorter view to reorder and organize the slides. In Word, you use Print Layout view for most editing, but you can switch to Outline view to organize sections of a document or Web Layout to see how a document will appear when saved as a web page.

To switch views, select the desired view from the View tab on the Ribbon. See Figure 8.9. You can also switch to certain views using the Views buttons on the status bar (just to the left of the Zoom controls).

Print

Forward | Font Size

Keep on Top

Back ——

Home ——

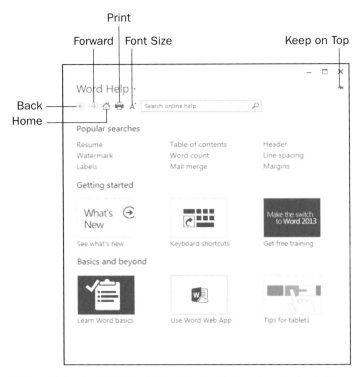

Figure 8.8   Use the Help window to look up information about using the active application.

Views

Zoom controls

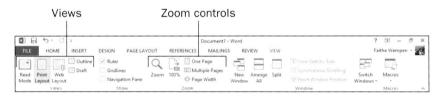

Figure 8.9   Choose an appropriate view for the task at hand from the View tab in the Views group.

Moving Around

As you create content in an application, you might have more content than you can see onscreen at once, so you might need to scroll to view different parts of it. You can scroll using the scroll bars with your mouse. Figure 8.10 shows a scroll bar.

scroll To page through the document so that a different part of it becomes visible.

scroll bar The horizontal or vertical bar to the bottom or right of the document, containing scroll arrows and a scroll box, which you can use to scroll.

In Excel, the vertical and horizontal scroll bars are always available. In Word and PowerPoint, the vertical scroll bar is always available, but the horizontal one only appears if the displayed document is wider than the screen width.

The size of the scroll box indicates how much content you can't see at the moment. For example, in Figure 8.10, the scroll box occupies about one-half of the scroll bar; that means that about one-half of the document's content is currently visible. In a very large spreadsheet or document, the scroll box might be very small.

You can also move around using keyboard shortcuts. As you gain experience with the applications, you might find using keyboard shortcuts more convenient than using the scroll bar. For example, pressing Ctrl+Home takes you to the beginning of the file in most Office applications.

Scrolling the display does not move the insertion point. To move the insertion point, click where you want it to go, or use the directional arrow keys on your keyboard to move it. In Excel, there is no insertion point, but a thick outline around the active cell shows the cell in which content will be entered.

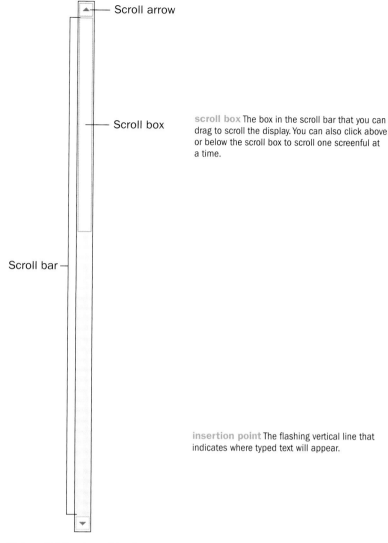

Scroll arrow

Scroll box

Scroll bar

scroll box The box in the scroll bar that you can drag to scroll the display. You can also click above or below the scroll box to scroll one screenful at a time.

insertion point The flashing vertical line that indicates where typed text will appear.

Figure 8.10 A scroll bar in Microsoft Word.

Here are some ways to use a scroll bar:

1. Click the arrow at the end of a scroll bar to scroll the display slowly in the direction of an arrow (a small amount each time you click).

2. Drag the box in the scroll bar to scroll quickly.

3. Click in the empty space on the bar to one side or the other of the scroll box to move one screenful at a time in that direction.

Selecting Content

Most of the commands you issue apply to whatever text or object is selected. For example, to italicize text, you first select the text to affect. Then when you click the Italics button, only the selected text is affected.

When you select in Excel, you usually want to select entire cells rather than individual characters of text. When a cell is selected, any formatting or other commands that you issue apply to everything in that cell. You can select a contiguous range (all in one rectangular block area) or a non-contiguous range (multiple cells are not adjacent to one another). To select an object (such as graphic), click it.

Step by Step

Selecting Text in Word or PowerPoint

Do any of the following to select text:

- Drag the mouse pointer across it (holding down the left mouse button).

- Click where you want to start and then hold down Shift as you press the arrow keys to extend the selection.

- Click where you want to start and then hold down Shift and click where you want to end the selection.

Selecting Cells in Excel

To select a contiguous range of cells:

- Drag the mouse pointer across the cells (holding down the left mouse button).

- Click the first cell to select it and then hold down Shift as you press the arrow keys to extend the selection.

- Click the first cell to select it and then hold down Shift and click the last cell.

To select a non-contiguous range of cells:

- Click the first cell to select it and then hold down Ctrl and click each individual cell to select.

Using the Office Clipboard

In the section "Moving and Copying Files and Folders" in Chapter 5, "Introduction to Windows 8.1," you learned about the Windows Clipboard. This temporary holding area enables you to cut or copy an item from one location and then paste it into another location, effectively moving or copying it. The Clipboard can also be used to cut, copy, and paste snippets of data from different applications and data files into a single file. For example, you can copy a paragraph from Word and paste it into an Excel worksheet or PowerPoint slide, or into a different location in Word (either in the same document or a different document).

Table 8.1 provides a quick summary of the ways to cut, copy, and paste in Office applications.

Table 8.1: Methods of Cutting, Copying, and Pasting in Office Applications

Action	Keyboard shortcut method	Ribbon method	Right-click method
Cut	Ctrl+X	Home ⇨ Cut	Right-click and choose Cut from the shortcut menu.
Copy	Ctrl+C	Home ⇨ Copy	Right-click and choose Copy from the shortcut menu.
Paste	Ctrl+V	Home ⇨ Paste	Right-click and choose Paste from the shortcut menu.

Microsoft Office has an enhanced version of the Clipboard called the Office Clipboard. It uses the Windows Clipboard as its basis, but adds the capability to store up to 24 objects at a time. (On the Windows Clipboard, when you cut or copy another object, the previously saved object is removed from the Clipboard.)

To display the Office Clipboard's task pane, click the dialog box launcher in the Clipboard group on the Home tab. Each time you cut or copy something to the Clipboard from an Office application, it is placed on the list in the task pane. If you want to paste the most recently cut or copied item, you can use the standard methods of pasting from Table 8.1. However, if you want to paste one of the earlier items, display the Clipboard task pane and then click the item you want to paste. Figure 8.11 shows the Clipboard task pane with several items on it. The Office Clipboard is shared between all Office applications, so you can, for example, copy several cell ranges or charts from Excel and have access to them in PowerPoint or Word on the Office Clipboard.

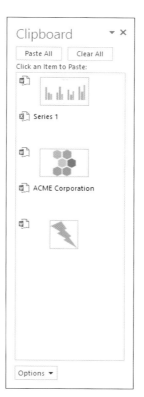

Office Clipboard The enhanced version of the Windows Clipboard that appears in Office applications. It can hold up to 24 items at once.

Figure 8.11 The Office Clipboard task pane enables you to store up to 24 items to be pasted.

Clearing the Office Clipboard

If you don't exit from all Office applications before stepping away from your computer, anyone who sits down at your computer can see the items on the Office Clipboard. If you have any concerns about privacy, click the Clear All button at the top of the Clipboard task pane to remove all items from it after you are finished using the Clipboard.

Privacy and Security

Using Undo and Redo

If you make a mistake in an Office application, you can easily undo your last action with the Undo command. You can either click it on the Quick Access Toolbar (see Figure 8.12) or press Ctrl+Z, its keyboard shortcut. You can do this multiple times in a row to go back multiple steps.

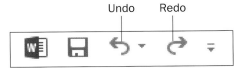

Undo   Redo

Figure 8.12   Undo and Redo buttons on the Quick Access Toolbar. The Undo button's menu enables you to go back multiple steps.

There's an easy way to undo multiple actions at a time. The Undo button has a down arrow to its right; click it for a drop-down list of recent actions, and then drag across the ones you want to undo.

After you have used Undo, a Redo button becomes available to its right on the QAT. Redo undoes the Undo operation. You can use Redo as many times in a row as you used Undo. For example, if you just clicked Undo three times to undo the last three actions, you can then click Redo three times to redo those actions. The shortcut for Redo is Ctrl+Y.

When Redo is not available, its button on the QAT turns into a Repeat button, which enables you to repeat the last action you took. If you aren't sure which button is active in that spot (Redo or Repeat), hover the mouse over the button and see what name appears in the ScreenTip.

Text Entry and Formatting

cell cursor The thick line around the active cell in Excel, indicating that this is where typed text will appear.

To enter text, click in an area that accepts text, moving the insertion point there, and begin typing. In Excel, you type in cells; in PowerPoint, you type in object placeholder frames. In Word, you can type text directly on the document page. To edit, use the Backspace key to delete the character to the left of the insertion point, or use Delete to delete the character to its right. You can also select blocks of text, or cells containing content, and press the Delete key to clear the text. See "Selecting Content" earlier in this chapter. In Excel, rather than an insertion point, there's a cell cursor, a thick outline that indicates the active cell.

Click and Type

In Word, when you start a new document, the insertion point is in the upper-left corner of the page. What if you want to type something in the center of the page, or at the bottom? One method is to press Enter until you get to the desired vertical position. An easier way is to use Click and Type. Move the mouse pointer to the spot where you would like to place the insertion point, so that the mouse pointer turns into an I-beam with an image of one of the alignment buttons next to it (from the Home tab's Paragraph group). Depending on where on the page horizontally you move, the alignment symbol changes to show how the text will be set to align if you click and type in that spot. Click, and the insertion point jumps to the spot you clicked, and Word automatically creates the needed paragraph breaks to get the insertion point to that spot. This only works in Word, not in Excel or PowerPoint.

All the Office applications have similar controls for text formatting. After you select some text, you can use the commands in the Font group on the Home tab to change the font, size, and color of text, as well as apply attributes like bold, italics, and underlining. Figure 8.13 shows the Font group in Word, and points out the buttons that are common to all the applications. To find out what the other buttons are in this group, point at each one to view the ScreenTip.

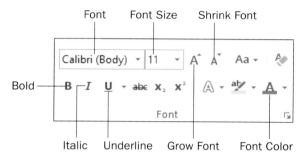

Figure 8.13   Use the Font group's commands to format text.

Understanding Themes and Color Palettes

Each application enables users to apply themes, which are groups of formatting presets. A theme contains definitions of three key formatting aspects: fonts, colors, and effects (applied to graphic objects). In some applications, a theme may contain additional elements; for example, in PowerPoint, a theme may contain a background image that is applied to each slide. You can override a theme's settings in one or more of those areas by applying a color theme, font theme, or effect theme (which are like themes but more limited, affecting only that one aspect of the formatting).

theme A named set of formatting presets, governing font, color, and object effect choices.

Each document, workbook, or presentation has a set of 12 color placeholders: ten colors for standard use, and two colors that define the colors for followed and unfollowed hyperlinks. The choice of theme (or color theme) dictates what those colors will be.

Commands for selecting colors (such as the Font Color button on the Home tab) open a color palette from which you can select a color, like the one shown in Figure 8.14.

color palette A grid of color choices that opens when you click a button for a feature that is color-related.

On this palette, you see the following choices:

- **Theme Colors:** The top row in this section contains theme colors, color swatches for the colors assigned to each placeholder position in the theme. Beneath the top row are variants of the theme colors, either lighter or darker than the original color by a specified amount. When you apply colors from this area, you are not choosing actual colors—you are choosing placeholder positions. If you change to a different theme or color theme, those colors will change.

theme colors The colors assigned to the color placeholders in a theme.

- **Standard Colors:** Standard colors are fixed and are not affected by the theme or color theme.

standard colors Fixed colors that are not affected by the theme in use.

- **More Colors:** If you want a fixed color but none of the color swatches in the Standard Colors section are right, choose More Colors to open a Colors dialog box from which you can select a color more specifically. On the General tab of this dialog box is a larger assortment of swatches. On the Custom tab, you can specify a color by number using one of the standard color models.

Variants of the theme colors   Theme colors

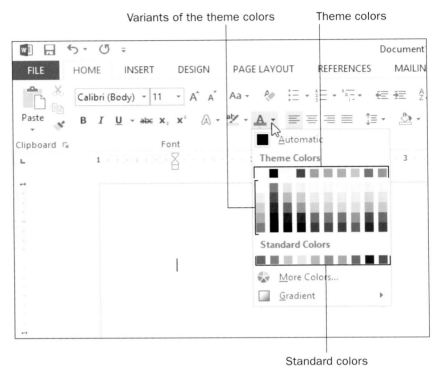

Standard colors

Figure 8.14   Select a color from a palette of choices.

There may be other choices at the bottom of the palette, depending on the object you are applying color to. For example, there may be a Gradient option for applying a blend of colors.

Moving and Resizing Objects

Each application includes the capability to insert content in movable and resizable frames that either float over the top of the regular content (as is the case in Excel) or interact with the text on the underlying page in a way you specify (as in Word). In PowerPoint, all content is in frames.

object An item that is separate from the rest of the document, with its own movable and resizable frame.

The content within one of these frames is known as an object. An object can be a graphic, a chart, a drawing, or any of several other items. A text box can also be an object.

selection handles The markers on the border of an object that allow the object to be resized.

To resize an object, drag one of its selection handles. A selection handle is a small square marker in a corner of the object's frame or at the midpoint along one side of the frame. Figure 8.15 shows the selection handles around a text box, for example.

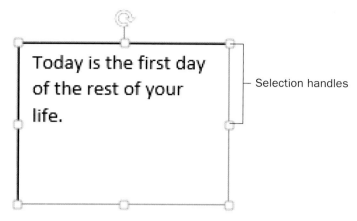

Figure 8.15 Drag a selection handle to resize an object.

As you resize an object, its aspect ratio (proportion of height to width) may change. If the object is a graphic, the graphic may become distorted. To avoid changing the aspect ratio when resizing an object, hold down the Shift key as you drag a corner selection handle. Some object types maintain their aspect ratio automatically when you drag a corner selection handle, even if you do not hold down the Shift key.

CAUTION

To move an object, drag it with the mouse. You can position the mouse pointer over any part of the object and then click and drag. (Exception: If the object is a text box, you must drag it by any part of its border that is *not* near a selection handle.)

Quick Review

1. How do you resize an object?
2. What key do you press to get help?
3. How do you change to a different view?
4. What is the difference between the Windows Clipboard and the Office Clipboard?

Saving, Opening, and Creating Files

Each application has similar procedures for working with data files. You can create, save, and open files in much the same way. In the following sections, you will learn the basic techniques for these operations.

Saving Files

As you work in an application, the content you create is stored in the computer's memory. This memory is only temporary storage. When you exit the application or shut down the computer, whatever is stored in memory is flushed away forever—unless you save it.

The steps for saving and opening data files are almost exactly the same in each application, so mastering it in one program gives you a head start in other programs.

One change in Office 2013 over earlier versions is that when you issue the command to save or open a file from the File menu, rather than a dialog box appearing immediately, a Backstage view page appears from which you can choose a general save location (your OneDrive or your local computer, for example) and optionally choose a shortcut to a recently used location. Figure 8.16 shows the Save As page in Backstage view, for example. Your OneDrive is the default save location that appears selected here. To save to your local computer, such as your hard drive, click Computer, and then click Browsed, or click one of the recent folders display.

Figure 8.16 Use the Save As dialog box controls to navigate to different locations.

After opening the Save As dialog box, you navigate to the drive and folder on which you want to save. Navigating the file system is the same in the Save As and Open dialog boxes as it is in File Explorer, which you learned to use in Chapter 5, "Introduction to Windows 8.1." You can move between volumes and folders, select favorite locations from the Favorites list, and so on. Figure 8.17 points out the navigation controls in the Save As dialog box in Word, for example.

Click a location in the navigation pane

Choose a path from the Address bar

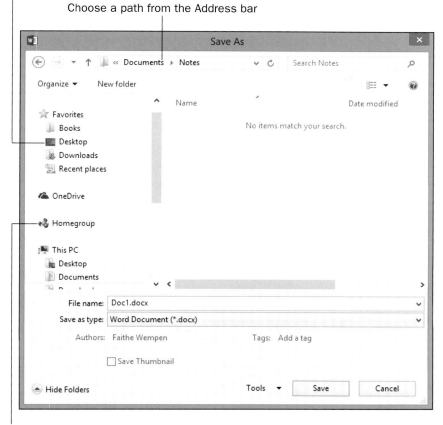

Choose a network location

Figure 8.17   Use the Save As dialog box controls to navigate to different locations.

Step by Step

Saving a File for the First Time

Use these steps the first time you save a new file:

1. Click the File tab and click Save, or click the Save icon on the QAT. The Save As page of Backstage view appears, as in Figure 8.16.

2. To save to your local computer, click Computer, and then click Browse.

   OR

   To save to your OneDrive, click Browse.

3. In the Save As dialog box, navigate to the desired location, as shown in Figure 8.17.

4. Type the desired filename in the File name box.

5. (Optional) Change the file type if desired.

6. Click Save.

Re-Saving a File Subsequent Times (Same Settings)

Do the following to save a file again using the same settings:

1. Click the File tab.
2. Click Save, or click the Save icon on the QAT. The file is immediately saved with the same settings as before.

Re-Saving a File Subsequent Times (Different Settings)

Follow these steps to save another copy of an existing file in a different location, or with a different name, or with a different file type:

1. Click the File tab and click Save As. The Save As page of Backstage view appears, as in Figure 8.16.
2. To save to your local computer, click Computer, and then click Browse.

   OR

   To save to your OneDrive, click Browse.
3. In the Save As dialog box (Figure 8.17), navigate to the desired location.
4. Type the desired filename in the File name box.
5. (Optional) Change the file type if desired.
6. Click Save.

Understanding Data Formats

Each application has its own data formats, summarized in Table 8.2. When you save a file, you can open the File type drop-down list and select a file format.

TIP When you don't have a reason to do otherwise, use the native file format for an application (the one where the extension ends in "x"). The resulting files are smaller and you ensure that you have access to the full set of application features that way. Some program features aren't supported in backward-compatible file formats, and you won't be able to use them (or save them) in a backward-compatible file.

Each application's native format is the default format in which new content is saved. Each application also has a macro-enabled option, for files that contain macros, which are recorded sequences of actions. (Most don't.) Making the general format non-macro-enabled cuts down on the risk of spreading macro viruses. Each application can also save and open files from earlier versions for backward compatibility. (Use the format that has 97-2003 in its name.)

Table 8.2: Office Application File Formats

Application	Native format	Macro-enabled format	Backward-compatible format (97-2003 format)
Word	docx	docm	doc
Excel	xlsx	xlsm	xls
PowerPoint	pptx	pptm	ppt

Password-Protecting Files

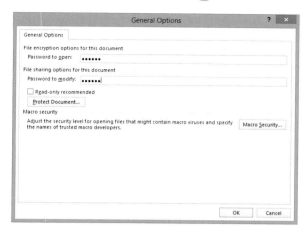

You can password-protect an Office application's data file as you save it. To do so, from the Save As dialog box, click the Tools button, and then choose General Options from the menu. In the dialog box that appears, you can assign a password to the file. There are two password prompts: Password to Open and Password to Modify. The former allows read-only access; the user cannot save changes back to the same file. The latter enables changes to be saved. You can assign two different passwords to allow some people one type of access and others the other type.

Privacy and Security

Opening and Closing Files

To open an existing file, click the File tab and click Open, click Browse, and then make your selection in the Open dialog box, after navigating to the location where the file is stored. After you have created a file and saved it, you can reopen the file to review or edit it.

You can also open files when you are not already in an application. In File Explorer you can double-click a data file to open it in its native application.

NOTE

If you want to open a recently used file, there's a quicker method. After clicking the File tab and clicking Open, click the shortcut for one of the recently used documents that appear on the list, as shown in Figure 8.18.

When you are finished with a file, you can close it by clicking the File tab and then clicking Close. Closing a file frees up some of your computer's memory for other uses. When you exit the application, all open files are automatically closed, and you are prompted to save any unsaved changes to them.

Creating New Files Using a Template

In each application, starting the program starts a new blank data file. You can start using this data file, or you can start another one using a template. A template is a file containing preset settings and, in some cases, sample content. Templates serve as shortcuts to creating documents with complex formatting, such as newsletters.

template A file containing preset layout and for-matting settings and sometimes sample content.

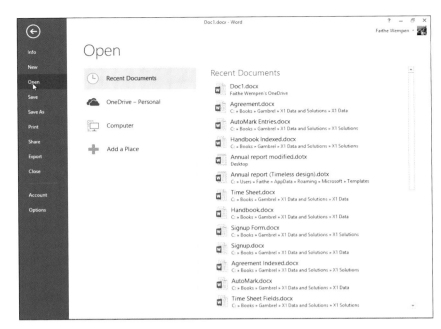

Figure 8.18 Select a file from the Recent list as an alternative.

Office.com provides hundreds of professional quality templates for each application, and you can access them from within each application, provided you have an Internet connection. You can also create and save your own templates for personal use. For example, you could modify one of the downloaded templates and then save a customized version.

TIP To start a new blank data file quickly, press Ctrl+N.

Step by Step

Starting a New File Based on a Template

Follow these steps to create a new file using a template:

1. Click the File tab and click New. Thumbnail images of some popular templates appear, along with a Search box for online templates.

2. Click one of the template thumbnails.

OR

Type a keyword in the Search box and press Enter, and then click one of the templates that appears on the search results list.

Depending on the template chosen, a new document may appear immediately or a dialog box may appear with information about the template.

3. If a dialog box appears for the template, click Create. If prompts appear, follow the prompts. (Some templates require a download or more information.)

Quick Review

1. Name two different ways of accessing the Save command.

2. How can you quickly reopen a recently used file?

3. How do you close an open document without exiting the application?

Printing and Sharing Files

Each application has a similar Print function that you can use to generate hard copies of your work. You can also share your work electronically with others by sending it to people via email.

Printing a File

To print a file, first set it up the way you want it in the application, including hiding or collapsing any content you don't want to show, setting font sizes and spacing, and so on. Then click the File tab and click Print, and make your selections of the options that appear.

The options are slightly different in each application; Figure 8.19 points out some of the common features. You can choose which printer to use, the number of copies to print, whether those copies should be collated, what page orientation to use, and more.

In the Pages text box, you can specify certain page numbers to print. To print individual pages, separate the numbers by commas, like this: 1, 3, 7. To print a range, use a hyphen, like this: 3-6. Other print options may be available, depending on the application; click the Print All Pages button to open a menu.

The largest portion of the Print screen consists of a Preview pane, on which you can see the document exactly as it will be printed. Use the arrow buttons below the preview to move between pages. If you don't like the preview, click any other tab to return to normal viewing and fix the document as needed before you print.

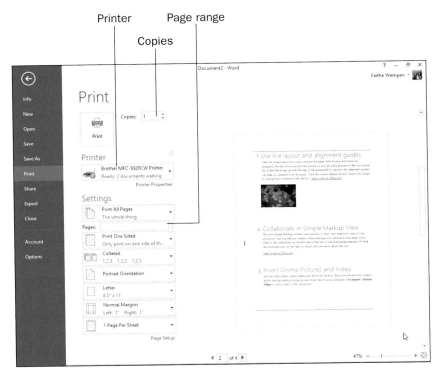

Figure 8.19   Print from the Print category in Backstage view.

Printing a File

Follow these steps to print a file:

1. Click the File tab and click Print. Options appear for the print job.

2. Adjust any settings as desired, including choosing a different printer, number of copies, and page range.

3. Click Print.

Sending a File as an Email Attachment

In your email software, you can attach files to your outgoing messages, but you can also attach and send files directly from within Office applications, without opening your email software separately. You can send a file in its native format (for example, docx for Word, pptx for PowerPoint, and so on), or you can choose to send it in some other format, such as PDF. When the recipient gets your attached file, he or she can double-click it to open it in whatever application is associated with that file type on his or her PC.

> **NOTE**   **PDF (Portable Document Format)** is a page layout format that is platform-independent; people often use it to send files to people who may not have the appropriate software to open the file in the application in which it was originally created. Sending a file as a PDF also makes it harder for others to make changes to the file, so it is useful for sending contracts and other official documents for review. XPS is the Microsoft equivalent of PDF. Office 2013 applications can save and send in either PDF or XPS. A PDF reader such as Adobe Reader or Adobe Acrobat is required to read PDF files. Windows comes with a free XPS reader.

Sending a File via Email

Follow these steps to send a file as an email attachment:

1. With the file open in its Office application, click the File tab and click Share.

2. In the center pane, click Email.

3. In the right pane, click the appropriate button to indicate the way you want the file sent. To send it in its native format, choose Send as Attachment.

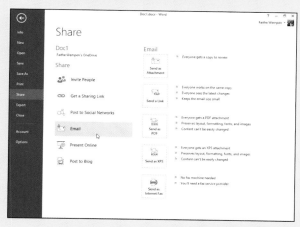

4. Follow the prompts to complete the send operation. The exact steps from this point depend on what format you chose in Step 3.

Quick Review

1. How do you preview a print job before it is actually printed?

2. How can you send a file to someone else as an email attachment?

Setting Application Options

Each Office application contains a similar Options dialog box, in which you can make some choices about how the application operates. Some options are unique to the specific application; others are the same (or similar) across all applications. In the following sections, you will learn about some of the options you can set.

To access the Options dialog box, click the File tab, and then click Options. Then click a category in the navigation bar at the left to see a certain page of options.

General Options

On the General options page are settings that control a few very basic things about the way Office appears:

- **Show Mini Toolbar on selection:** When this is enabled and you select some text and then point at the selection with the mouse or right-click the selection, a mini toolbar pops up containing some common formatting buttons for easy access.

- **Enable Live Preview:** When this is enabled, certain menus and galleries that contain formatting choices are "live," in that when you point at an option on the menu, you see it previewed in the document behind the open menu.

- **Username:** Put your name here so that the application can fill in your name when it uses a Name placeholder in certain templates.

- **Initials:** Put your initials here so the application can use your initials in certain features, such as identifying who made a certain comment.

- **Office Background:** Add a design in the title bar of the application with this option.

- **Office Theme:** Choose what color the Ribbon buttons will be. Your choices are White, Light Gray, and Dark Gray.

- **Show the Start Screen when This Application Starts:** Clear this check box to make the application start in a new blank document.

Proofing Options

Proofing options enable you to define how the spelling checker and related features work, such as AutoCorrect. AutoCorrect enables you to set up corrections for words that you commonly misspell, and contains a preset list of many common misspellings to get you started. For example, it can automatically correct *thier* to *their*. To access the AutoCorrect settings, click the AutoCorrect button on the Proofing page of the Options dialog box (File, Options).

For the other options, mark or clear the check boxes, as shown in Figure 8.20. For example, you can control whether or not the spelling checker ignores uppercase words (which can help you avoid having acronyms marked as misspellings). Word has more proofing options available than PowerPoint or Excel does.

Save Options

Save options, shown in Figure 8.21, define how the application saves files. You can choose whether to let it save AutoRecover information, for example, and at what intervals. AutoRecover automatically saves your work in progress in a temporary file; when you issue the Save command or exit the application, that temporary file is automatically deleted. However, if the program terminates abnormally, the temporary file persists, and you can use it to recover unsaved work.

AutoCorrect A feature that automatically corrects certain spelling errors.

AutoRecover A feature that automatically saves your work at specified intervals so you can recover it if the application terminates before you are able to save normally.

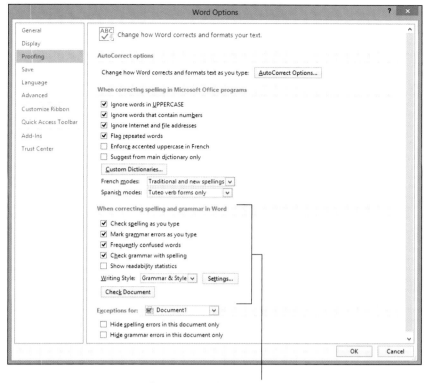

Grammar options are available only in Word

Figure 8.20   Proofing options define how the application's spelling check and AutoCorrect work.

Default location

Default file format

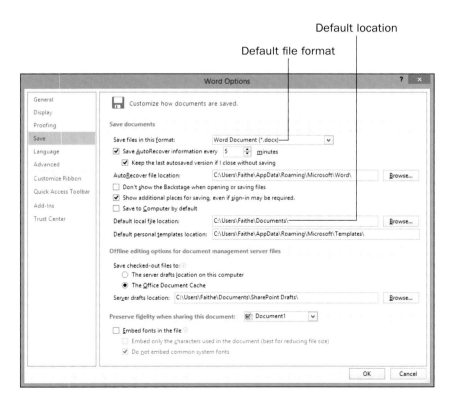

Figure 8.21   Save options define how Save operations work.

Another commonly changed option is to set a different default file format, in the Save Files in This Format drop-down list. For example, if you exchange files with someone who uses Office 2003, you will want to set each application to the 97-2003 file format for backward compatibility.

default file location The location where the Save As and Open dialog boxes start by default.

You can also specify a location (in path format) for the AutoRecover file location, as well as the default file location. The default file location is the default folder that appears in the Save As and Open dialog boxes the first time you open them in a work session. After the first time, the previously shown location appears, until you exit and restart the application, at which point the location is reset back to the default.

embed fonts To save the fonts used in the document along with the document itself, so others who view the document on another computer will be sure to have access to them.

You can also choose whether or not to embed fonts in the file when saving. Doing so makes the file larger than it would be otherwise, but it ensures that whoever opens it on another computer sees the presentation exactly as intended, even if that computer has different fonts installed.

Quick Review

1. How can you change what file format is used by default in the Save As dialog box?

2. How do you change your name and initials in an Office application?

3. How do you change the default save location?

Summary

Understanding the Office 2013 Interface

The **Ribbon** is the large, multi-tabbed toolbar at the top of each Office application window. It contains **tabs** (pages) of commands. Commands are organized in **groups** on each tab. A **dialog box launcher**, found in some groups, opens a dialog box related to that group.

When you click the File tab, **Backstage view** opens, which contains multiple categories in a navigation bar along the left side. Click a category to see a page of options relating to file management. The **Quick Access Toolbar (QAT)** is the small, customizable toolbar that appears above the Ribbon. When you right-click, a context-sensitive **shortcut menu** appears, from which you can select commands relating to what you right-clicked.

When you hover the mouse over a button, a **ScreenTip** appears explaining its name and purpose. Some ScreenTips contain **keyboard shortcut** prompts too. The **status bar** appears at the bottom of the application's window. **Zoom controls** adjust the magnification at which you see your work. Zoom controls appear on the right end of the status bar, and also on the View tab.

Basic Features of Office Applications

To open the Help system in an application, press F1, or choose Help from the File menu, or click the Help icon in the upper-right corner of the application window.

To **scroll** in the document, use the **scroll bars**. You can drag the **scroll box**, or click above or below the scroll box, or click one of the scroll arrows.

To select content, drag across it with the mouse, or click where you want the selection to begin and hold down Shift as you click at the other end or use the arrow keys to extend the selection area.

The **Office Clipboard** is like the Windows Clipboard except it has more features, and is available only in Office applications. It can hold up to 24 items.

Undo reverses the last action. Use the Undo button on the QAT or press Ctrl+Z. Redo reverses the reversal; press Ctrl+Y or use the Redo button on the QAT.

The **insertion point** is where text you type will appear. You can move it by clicking where you want it. In Excel, a **cell cursor**, a thick line around a cell, indicates that it is active, and text you type will be placed in it.

Office files can have **themes** applied, which are sets of formatting presets. They consist of font, color, and graphic effect choices. You can also apply each of those separately (color theme, font theme, effect theme). When you choose colors, you select from a color palette that contains **theme colors**, variants of theme colors, and **standard colors**.

A framed object within an Office document is called an **object**. Objects can include charts, graphics, and text boxes. Drag a **selection handle** on an object to resize it, or drag the object itself to move it. Drag the border to move a text box.

Saving, Opening, and Creating Files

To save a file, use the Save command on the File menu. The first time you save a file, you are prompted for a name, location, and type in the Save As dialog box. When you save subsequent times, you are not prompted. If you want to be prompted, use the Save As command instead.

To open a file, use the Open command on the File menu. Navigate to the location of the file in the same way you do in File Explorer. To close a file, use the Close command.

When you create new files, you can create a blank file or you can start with a **template**. Select a template from the New category on the File menu.

Printing and Sharing Files

To print your work, open the File menu and click Print. Then use the controls that appear to specify the options for the print job.

You can email a file to others in native format, or in PDF or XPS format. These are both page layout formats that people can read even if they do not have the original applications.

Setting Application Options

To set options for the application, open the File menu and click Options. An Options dialog box specific to that application appears. Some of the customization options are the same for all applications, such as identifying yourself and setting a save location. Others are specific to that application. Some of the settings you can adjust include **AutoCorrect, AutoRecover**, setting a **default file location**, and **embedding fonts**.

Key Terms

AutoCorrect	Ribbon
AutoRecover	ScreenTip
Backstage view	scroll
cell cursor	scroll bar
color palette	scroll box
default file location	selection handle
dialog box launcher	shortcut menu
embed fonts	standard colors
group	status bar
insertion point	tab
keyboard shortcut	template
object	theme
Office Clipboard	theme colors
Quick Access Toolbar (QAT)	Zoom controls

Test Yourself

Fact Check

1. What is found in the lower-right corner of some groups on the Ribbon?

    a. the status bar

    b. the dialog box launcher

    c. a list box

    d. the Close button

2. How do you enter Backstage view?

    a. Click the Home tab

    b. Press Ctrl+B

    c. Press Ctrl+X

    d. Click the File tab

3. How do you display a shortcut menu?

    a. Double-click

    b. Triple-click

    c. Right-click

    d. Press Ctrl+S

4. How do you display a ScreenTip?

    a. Hover the mouse over the item

    b. Double-click the item

    c. Right-click the item

    d. Triple-click the item

5. How do you display the Office Clipboard?

    a. Ctrl+K

    b. Click the Paste button

    c. Click the dialog box launcher in the Clipboard group

    d. Any of the above

6. Which of these is NOT stored in a theme?

    a. effect choices

    b. color choices

    c. font choices

    d. page size and orientation choices

7. In a color palette, what are the colors that appear below the top row of theme colors?

    a. variations on the theme colors

    b. standard colors

    c. fixed colors

    d. recently used colors

8. To resize an object, drag its

   a. border, but not on a selection handle

   b. selection handle

   c. rotation handle

   d. title bar

9. Which of these is the default file format for saving your work in Excel 2013?

   a. xlsm

   b. xls

   c. xlsx

   d. xlss

10. When sending a file as an attachment, you can send it in its native format, or you can send it as a formatted page description file in either XPS or _____ format.

   a. PNG

   b. MOV

   c. PDF

   d. MP3

Matching

Match the feature to its function.

   a. dialog box launcher

   b. object

   c. QAT

   d. ScreenTip

   e. selection handle

   f. shortcut menu

   g. theme

1. _____Toolbar that appears above the Ribbon

2. _____What you see when you right-click an item

3. _____The small icon in the lower-right corner of a group

4. _____Content that has its own resizable frame

5. _____What appears when you hover the mouse over a button on the Ribbon

6. _____A named set of formatting settings

7. _____What you drag to resize an object

Sum It Up

1. Explain how to save and open files in Office applications.

2. Describe the main features that the user interfaces of all Office applications have in common.

3. Describe how colors are arranged on a palette and how they relate to the active theme.

4. Name three things you can customize in an application via its Options dialog box.

5. Explain how to change the default save location.

6. Describe how to move the insertion point.

7. Contrast the Windows Clipboard to the Office Clipboard.

Explore More

Customizing the Status Bar

The status bar's content varies, not only between applications, but also with customization. Right-click the status bar in any application for a menu of items you can show or hide on it (see Figure 8.22).

Figure 8.22 Right-click the status bar to choose what information should appear there.

More Keyboard Shortcuts

Each application has an extensive set of keyboard shortcuts available. Open the application's Help system and search for *Keyboard Shortcuts* to see an article that lists the complete set. There are separate sets of shortcuts for various situations. For example, there are shortcuts for moving the insertion point, shortcuts for scrolling, shortcuts for selecting, shortcuts for commands, and so on.

Can't get enough of working with the keyboard? Each Ribbon tab and command has a keyboard equivalent too. To see them, press the Alt key, as shown in Figure 8.23. Key tips appear next to each tab and command name. Then press that key to choose that command. (You have to press Alt each time to use these shortcuts.) This is how people who can't use a mouse navigate in Office applications, by the way.

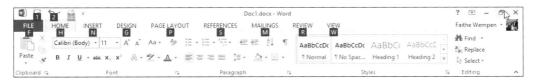

Figure 8.23   Press Alt to see keys you can use to select Ribbon tabs and commands.

More Application Options

For some of the more obscure settings in an application's options, check out the Advanced category in the Options dialog box. You might be surprised at some of the changes you can make. For example, in Word, you can set default behaviors for cutting, copying, and pasting data, and in PowerPoint you can disable right-clicking during a slide show as a security measure to keep people from stopping a slide show at an interactive kiosk.

Think It Over

Ribbon Customization

Some people may find an application easier to use when the Ribbon is customized, but if multiple people share a computer, customizations can be a problem. If you were in charge of your school's or workplace's computers, would you allow people to customize the Ribbon, or not? Explain your answer.

Theme Colors versus Standard Colors

When choosing colors for a project, would you rather use theme colors or standard colors? What are the trade-offs?

Sharing Files

You can share files in ways other than attaching them to email. What are some other ways you can share files, and how do they compare? What are the pros and cons of each method you identify?

Chapter 9

Word Processing with Microsoft Word

Learning objectives

☐ Learn how to edit and format text

☐ Learn how to format paragraphs

☐ Understand how to format pages and sections

☐ Learn how to insert pictures

☐ Demonstrate how to create tables

☐ Understand how to correct your work and collaborate with others

Editing and Formatting Text

Formatting Paragraphs

Formatting Documents and Sections

Working with Pictures

Working with Tables

Correcting and Collaborating

Who uses word processing? Just about everyone! Word processing is the most popular type of business productivity application, and Microsoft Word is the most popular program for doing it. In almost any workplace, you will be expected to know how to use Word to type letters and reports, and depending on your job, you might also need to know how to create more complex documents that include graphics and tables.

This chapter covers the basic Word skills that you need for success in a modern office setting, regardless of your specific job title. You'll find out how to edit and manipulate text, format documents in various ways from individual characters to entire pages, insert pictures and tables, and correct your spelling and grammar errors. By the time you reach the end of this chapter, you will have all the basic information you need to create a variety of documents.

Word Processing Specialist

Although anyone can learn the basics of word processing, some people take that extra step to become really proficient in all aspects of the software. A word processing specialist is able to create consistent, professional looking documents, including memos, forms, legal reports, letters, and technical articles, in a variety of formats. Word processing specialist may be a full-time career in itself, or the duties may be combined with those of a general administrative assistant or receptionist. To prepare for this career, you should have at least a high school education, and have specialized word processing training. Microsoft Office Specialist certification in Microsoft Word at the Expert level is recommended.

Editing and Formatting Text

In Microsoft Word, you can type directly onto a blank page. Just position the insertion point and start typing. As you type, the text wraps to a new line automatically when you come to the right margin. To start a new paragraph, press Enter. To start a new line without starting a new paragraph, press Shift+Enter.

Pressing keys like Enter and the spacebar generates characters, but you can't see them by default. Click the Show/Hide ¶ button on the Home tab to toggle the display of non-printing, hidden characters onscreen. In Figure 9.1, for example, each space appears as a small dot and each paragraph break appears with a paragraph symbol (¶), and each manually created line break (Shift+Enter) appears with a bent arrow symbol.

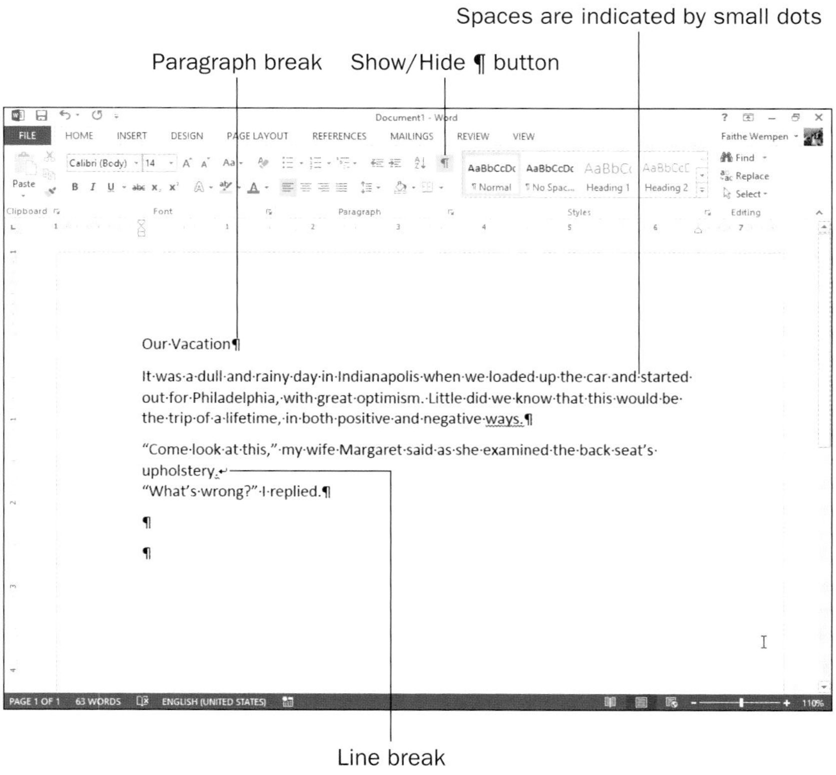

Figure 9.1 Hidden (non-printing) characters are displayed when you click the Show/Hide ¶ button on the Home tab.

Editing Text

To edit text, you can click or use the arrow keys to position the insertion point and then use Backspace to delete to the left of the insertion point or Delete to delete to its right. Or, you can select a block of text and then press the Delete key to remove it. As you type, the text to the right of the insertion point moves over to make room for the new text.

You can move text using the Office Clipboard (by cutting and pasting), or you can drag and drop with the mouse to move text. Both techniques were covered in Chapter 8, "Understanding Microsoft Office 2013."

Changing the Text Font

As you learned in Chapter 8, you can change the text font from the Font drop-down list on the Home tab. On the Font drop-down list, you'll find all the fonts listed that are available on your computer. Office comes with many fonts, so that's where most of them came from. Others may be installed on your PC from Windows itself or from other applications.

Before you choose a specific font from the Font drop-down list, however, consider whether you might prefer instead to use font placeholders and allow Word to apply a consistent font throughout the document, as explained next.

At the top of the Font list are two special fonts, marked (Headings) and (Body). These are not actual fonts, but placeholders. Every document has a default heading font and a default body font. The actual fonts assigned to those placeholders are subject to change. In Figure 9.2, the fonts assigned are Calibri Light for headings and Calibri for body.

Recall from Chapter 8 that a theme defines three formatting properties for the entire document: theme colors, theme fonts (for Heading and Body defaults), and theme effects (for graphics). Choosing a different theme or theme fonts from the Page Layout tab is one way to redefine which fonts are used as the Headings and Body fonts. Look back at the section "Understanding Themes and Color Palettes" in Chapter 8 for more information.

Another way to redefine the font set is to choose a different style set. A style is a named, preset combination of formatting. Word's default template for blank documents includes several styles, including Normal (for body text), Heading 1 and Heading 2 (for headings), and Title (for document titles). The text in your document appears in Calibri 11-point font by default because the Normal style is defined that way. A style set is an alternative set of style definitions for the basic built-in styles such as the ones

style A named, preset combination of formatting.

style set An alternative set of style definitions for the basic built-in styles.

just mentioned. You can quickly change the look of the entire document by applying a different style set. The style definitions in a style set include not only font choices but also line spacing and indentation for paragraphs.

Figure 9.2 To allow Word to control which font is used based on the theme or style set, choose the (Heading) or (Body) font from the Font drop-down list.

NOTE Why are some styles treated as body paragraphs and some styles are treated as headings? It all depends on the style's outline level. If it's set to Body Text, the (Body) font is applied to it; if it's set to any of the heading levels, the (Heading) font is applied. To check and change a style's outline level, click the dialog box launcher in the Styles group on the Home tab to open the Styles pane, and then right-click a style and choose Modify. In the Modify Style dialog box, in the lower-left corner, click Format, and click Paragraph. In the Paragraph dialog box, set the Outline Level setting to the desired value on the Indents and Spacing tab.

You will learn more about styles later in this chapter, in the section "Working with Styles."

Step by Step

Changing to a Different Style Set

Use these steps to change the style set:

1. On the Design tab, click the More arrow in the Document Formatting group. The Style Set gallery opens.

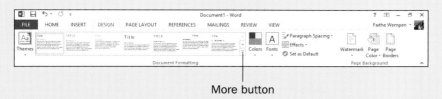

More button

2. Point to a different style set, and observe the formatting change to the document behind the open menu.

3. Click the desired style set to apply it.

Changing to a Different Theme

Use these steps to change the theme:

1. On the Design tab, click the Themes button.

2. Point to a theme, and see its formatting previewed on the document behind the open menu.

3. Click the desired theme.

Changing to a Different Theme Fonts

Use these steps to change only the font aspect of the theme:

1. On the Design tab, click the Fonts button. A list of font themes opens. This list corresponds to the overall themes on the Themes list.

2. Point to a theme font set, and see the fonts previewed on the document behind the open menu.

3. Click the desired theme fonts.

Fonts Don't Change

If the fonts don't change when they ought to—that is, when you apply a different style set, theme, or theme fonts—it's probably because the text has been manually formatted. To strip off manual formatting, select the text and then either press Ctrl+spacebar or click the Clear Formatting button in the Font group on the Home tab.

Troubleshooting

Changing Font Size

Select a font size from the Font Size drop-down list on the Home tab (see Figure 9.3). As the font sizes get larger on the list, they start skipping numbers; for example, 20 and 22 are both on the list, but 21 isn't. You can type an exact font size in the Font Size text box above the drop-down list to use a size that isn't on the list. You can also change the font size by clicking the Grow Font or Shrink Font button in the Font group (see Figure 9.3). Each time you click one of those buttons, the font increases or decreases by one position on the Font Size list. (As pointed out earlier, that's not necessarily one point; with the larger sizes, the increase or decrease could be several points.)

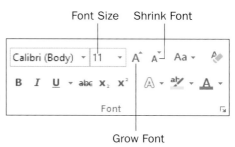

Figure 9.3 Choose a font size, type an exact font size, or use the Grow Font or Shrink Font button.

Formatting Text

Most people find it simplest to apply formatting from the Font group on the Home tab. Word has a few more commands there than the other applications because Word's specialty is text. Figure 9.4 points out the text formatting commands in the Font group.

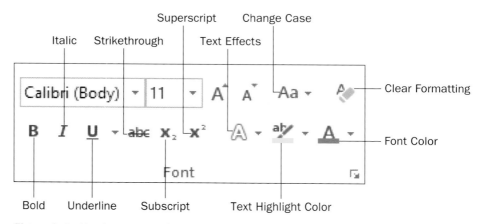

Figure 9.4 Use these commands to apply formatting to text in Word.

text effects A set of special effects you can apply to text, such as outline, shadow, and glow.

Some of the commands in the Font group deserve some extra explanation because their functions are not obvious. Text effects, for example, opens a menu of types of special effects you can apply to the text, such as Outline, Shadow, and Glow. Superscript makes the text smaller and moves it above the baseline, as in X^2. Subscript makes it smaller and moves it below the baseline, as in H_2O. You also can select some presets. Figure 9.5 shows the Shadow submenu open from this button.

You can access additional effects from the Font dialog box. Display the Font dialog box by clicking the dialog box launcher in the Font group, and then click the Text Effects button at the bottom of the dialog box to open a Format Text Effects dialog box.

Text Effects

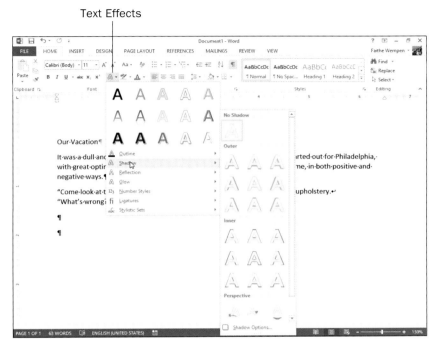

Figure 9.5 Select special effects for text from the Text Effects button's menu.

The Change Case button opens a menu from which you can choose different text cases. This feature enables you to quickly switch blocks of text from uppercase to lowercase without having to retype. See Figure 9.6.

Clear Formatting

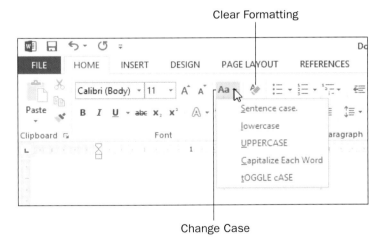

The Clear Formatting button strips off all manually applied text formatting (such as any formatting you applied using any of the other buttons in the Font group). It leaves any formatting that was applied via a style or theme.

Change Case

The Text Highlight Color enables a high-lighter, like a highlighting marker you might use on a paper copy. You can select from 15 different highlighter colors. After you turn on the feature, the mouse pointer changes to a highlighter; drag across the text you want to highlight, and then press the Esc key or click the button again on the toolbar to turn the feature off.

Figure 9.6 Use the Change Case button to shift the letter cases without retyping.

For more font formatting choices, click the dialog box launcher in the Font group, opening the Font dialog box (see Figure 9.7). Here you can select a font, font style (regular, bold, italic, or both bold and italic), and size, as well as a font color, underline style, and underline color. You can also apply a variety of text effects. Some of

Figure 9.7 Apply text formatting in the Font dialog box.

these, like Small Caps and Double Strikethrough, are not available on the Ribbon, but only in this dialog box.

NOTE In the Font dialog box, two of the font choices on the Font list are +Body and +Headings. These correspond to the (Headings) and (Body) fonts on the Font drop-down list, described earlier.

Quick Review

1. What is the significance of (Body) and (Heading) next to certain fonts on the Font drop-down list?

2. How do you choose a font size that is not on the Font Size drop-down list?

3. How would you apply Small Caps text formatting?

Formatting Paragraphs

paragraph formatting Formatting that applies to entire paragraphs, not to individual characters.

Paragraph formatting, as the name implies, is formatting that applies to entire paragraphs, not to individual characters. For example, line spacing, indentation, tab stops, and bulleted and numbered lists are all types of paragraph formatting. In the following sections you will learn about the paragraph formatting capabilities in Word.

Creating Bulleted and Numbered Lists

Bulleted and numbered lists are both ways of making certain paragraphs stand out. Use bulleted lists for lists where the order is not important, like a grocery list; use numbered lists where the order is significant, such as a set of instructions for making a recipe.

To make a bulleted or numbered list, select the paragraphs to include and then click the Bullets or Numbering button on the Home tab (in the Paragraph group). For the default style, click the face of the button. To choose from a gallery of other styles, click the down arrow to the right of the button. Figure 9.8 shows the choices from the Bullets button's menu, for example. You can also choose Define New Bullet from that library to use any character you like for the bullets.

Numbering

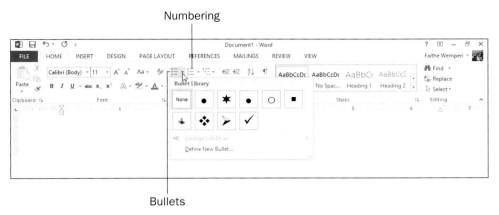

Bullets

Figure 9.8   Open the Bullets button's library for other bullet character choices.

Creating Tab Stops

When you press the Tab key, the insertion point moves to the right until it encounters a tab stop. By default, body paragraphs have tab stops every half inch, but you can set custom tab stops for any paragraph at any positions.

tab stop A non-printing marker in a paragraph that stops the insertion point when the Tab key is pressed.

Tab stops are left-aligned by default, meaning that when the insertion point stops at the tab stop, the text that you type at that point is left-aligned with the tab stop. Tab stops can have several other alignments, though. Figure 9.9 shows some examples of the various tab stop types. Tab stops can be aligned to the left or right, centered, or decimal—that is, aligned with the decimal place in the entry. There is one other type of tab stop, called Bar, which places a vertical line between the tabbed columns of text at the tab stop position.

Tab stop indicators appear on the horizontal ruler above the document, as shown in Figure 9.9. (If you don't see the horizontal ruler, mark the Ruler check box on the View tab.) You can place a tab stop on the ruler by clicking on the desired spot. If you want a type other than Left, click the Tab Type icon at the far left end of the ruler until the desired type appears, and then click on the ruler to place it. You can remove a tab stop by dragging it downward off the ruler. You can change a tab stop's position by dragging it from side to side.

You can also create tab stops using the Tabs dialog box. The dialog box method has the advantage of enabling you to create tab leaders. A leader is a repeated character between the text before the tab stop and the tab stop. Leaders are sometimes used in tables of contents to help the eye follow across to the page number, as in Figure 9.10.

Click here to change tab stop type, and then click on the ruler

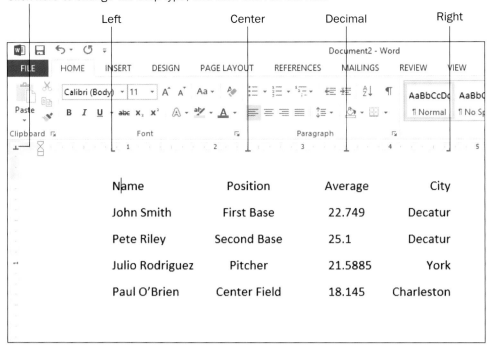

Figure 9.9   Examples of tab stop types.

Figure 9.10   A tab leader.

Step by Step

Setting Tab Stops with the Tabs Dialog Box

Use these steps to create a tab stop using the dialog box method:

1. Click anywhere in the paragraph to affect, or select multiple paragraphs to affect.

2. Click the dialog box launcher in the Paragraph group on the Home tab.

3. In the Paragraph dialog box, click the Tabs button. The Tabs dialog box opens.

4. In the Tab Stop Position box, type a numeric value representing the tab stop's position on the ruler, in inches.

5. In the Alignment section, select the tab type.

6. In the Leader section, if desired, select a leader character.

7. Click Set.

8. If you want to set another tab stop, repeat Steps 4 through 7. Otherwise click OK.

Modifying a Tab Stop with the Tabs Dialog Box

Follow these steps to modify an existing tab stop using the Tabs dialog box:

1. Double-click the tab stop on the ruler. The Tabs dialog box opens.

2. Make any changes as needed to the tab's settings in the dialog box.

3. Click OK.

Indenting Text

Indentation is the amount that a paragraph is offset from the left and right margins. If the document has a 1 inch margin on the left, and the paragraph has a 0.5 inch left indent, the paragraph will start 1.5 inch from the left edge of the paper.

indentation The amount that a paragraph is offset from the document margins.

You can set indentation for selected paragraphs by dragging the indent markers on the ruler to the left or right. On the left end of the ruler are three markers: two triangles and a rectangle, as shown in Figure 9.11. The top triangle is the first-line indent marker. It controls the indent for the first line of the paragraph. The bottom triangle is the marker for all the subsequent lines of the paragraph (other than the first one). You can drag it to adjust the indent for just those lines. The square is the left indent marker; dragging the rectangle moves both triangles at once, keeping them in the same relational position to one another. At the right end of the ruler is a single triangle, representing the right indent for the paragraph.

A quick way to increase or decrease the left indent for a paragraph is to click the Increase Indent or Decrease Indent button on the Home tab (in the Paragraph group).

TIP

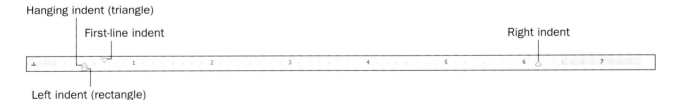

Hanging indent (triangle)

First-line indent

Right indent

Left indent (rectangle)

Figure 9.11   Indent markers on the ruler.

You can also set indentation from the Paragraph dialog box. The dialog box method has the advantage of being able to set an exact numeric value for the indents. The settings available there are Left, Right, and Special. The Special indent has a drop-down list containing two options: First Line and Hanging. They are both technically first-line indents, but the First Line setting indents the first line more than the general Left indent for the paragraph, and Hanging indents the first line by less than the general Left indent.

First-line indents are commonly used in publishing to make paragraphs easier to read. The first paragraph below a heading is not usually first-line indented, but all the subsequent ones are.

NOTE

Setting Paragraph Indents Using the Paragraph Dialog Box

Use these steps to set paragraph indents using the dialog box method:

1. Click anywhere in the paragraph to affect, or select multiple paragraphs to affect.

2. Click the dialog box launcher in the Paragraph group on the Home tab. The Paragraph dialog box opens.

3. On the Indents and Spacing tab, in the Indentation section, set indentation settings for Left and Right indents.

4. (Optional) If you want the first line indents to be different, open the Special drop-down list and choose First Line or Hanging and then enter an amount of additional indentation for the first line.

5. Click OK.

NOTE The Mirror Indents check box enables different left and right indents depending on whether the page is odd or even. It is used in situations where you are binding double-sided pages at the left and you want to leave extra indentation on one side or the other depending on whether the selected paragraph(s) fall on the right or left side of the binding.

Setting Line Spacing

line spacing The amount of vertical space between the lines of a paragraph.

Line spacing is the vertical blank space between each line of a paragraph. A paragraph can also have extra spacing before or after it. In Figure 9.12, notice that the paragraphs have a smaller amount of space between their individual lines than they do between them.

NOTE Documents created using the default settings have a line spacing of 1.08 and an After setting of 8 pt.

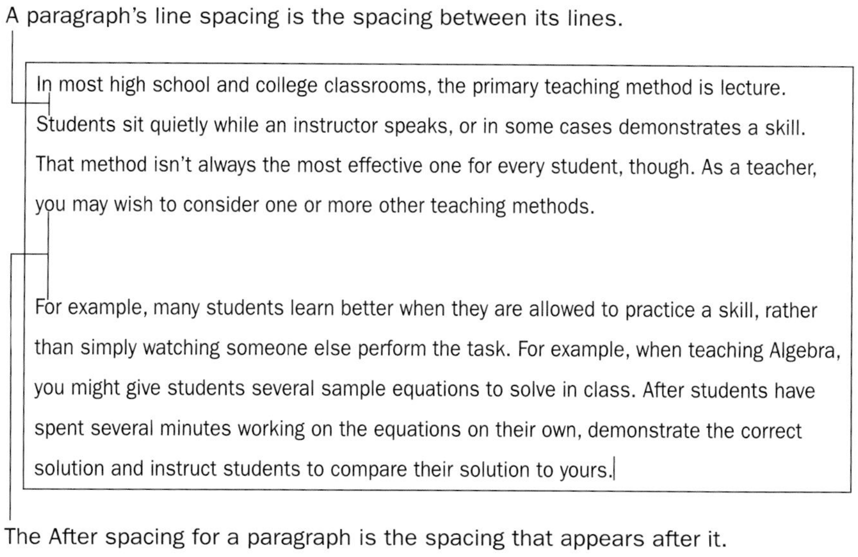

A paragraph's line spacing is the spacing between its lines.
In most high school and college classrooms, the primary teaching method is lecture. Students sit quietly while an instructor speaks, or in some cases demonstrates a skill. That method isn't always the most effective one for every student, though. As a teacher, you may wish to consider one or more other teaching methods.
For example, many students learn better when they are allowed to practice a skill, rather than simply watching someone else perform the task. For example, when teaching Algebra, you might give students several sample equations to solve in class. After students have spent several minutes working on the equations on their own, demonstrate the correct solution and instruct students to compare their solution to yours.
The After spacing for a paragraph is the spacing that appears after it.

Figure 9.12 A line spacing example.

If you want to choose one of the line spacing presets, you can do so from the Line and Paragraph Spacing button's menu on the Home tab, as shown in Figure 9.13. For example, you could increase the line spacing slightly by choosing 1.15, or go for even more spacing with 1.5. You can also add or remove space before or after the paragraph from this menu.

Line Spacing
Document2 - Word
FILE
HOME
INSERT
DESIGN
PAGE LAYOUT
REFERENCES
MAILINGS
REVIEW
VIEW
Calibri (Body)
11
Paste
AaBbCcDc
¶ Normal
AaBbCcDc
¶ No Spac...
Clipboard
Font
1.0
1.15
1.5
2.0
2.5
3.0
Line Spacing Options...
Add Space Before Paragraph
Remove Space After Paragraph

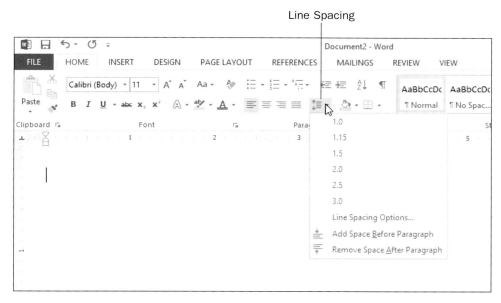

Figure 9.13 Choose line spacing settings from the Line and Paragraph Spacing button on the Home tab.

For even more control over line spacing, use the Paragraph dialog box, as in the following steps.

Setting Line Spacing Using the Paragraph Dialog Box

Use these steps to set paragraph spacing using the dialog box method:

1. Click anywhere in the paragraph, or select multiple paragraphs.

2. Click the dialog box launcher in the Paragraph group on the Home tab. The Paragraph dialog box opens.

3. On the Indents and Spacing tab, in the Spacing section, open the Line Spacing drop-down list and select Single, 1.5 Lines, or Double if you want one of those presets.

   Or, select a unit of measurement, and then set a value in the text box to the right of it. The units of measure available are:

   - *At Least:* Specifies a minimum spacing, in points. The spacing might increase depending on the font size.

   - *Exactly:* Specifies an exact spacing, in points. The spacing will not increase or decrease with font size changes.

   - *Multiple:* Specifies a multiple of 1 (which is single spacing). The number is expressed as a multiple of single spacing, whatever spacing that entails based on the font size. For example, you could specify 1.15 or 1.75.

4. If desired, change the values in the Before and After boxes. For best results, use only one or the other, because the paragraphs above and below this one will have their own Before or After settings that, when combined with this one, might produce results different from your preferences.

5. Click OK.

Working with Styles

As you learned earlier in the chapter, a style is a named collection of formatting attributes that you can apply simultaneously. For example, the default Heading 1 style consists of the font assigned to the (Headings) placeholder, 14 points in size, bold, and blue in color, with 24 points of space before the paragraph and no space after the paragraph.

Each template comes with a set of styles. The default Normal template comes with several heading styles, named Heading 1, Heading 2, and so on, as well as a Normal style (used for body text) and a Title style (for the document title).

Storing Styles in a Template

Using styles in your documents can save a great deal of time because you can apply the same formatting over and over, not only within the same document, but across multiple documents. Start a new blank document, and create all the styles in it that you want. Then use the Save command (covered in Chapter 8) to save the document as a template. (To do that, set the document type to Word Template.) Then whenever you want to create a document that employs those styles, start the new document based on that template, and the styles will be there waiting for you.

Put It to Work

To apply a style, click in the paragraph you want to affect, or select the text you want to affect if you want more or less than one paragraph. Then choose a style from the Styles group on the Home tab. If you don't see the style you want, click the More button (⊽) to open the Styles gallery. Not every style appears in the gallery, though. For a full list of all available styles, click the dialog box launcher in the Styles group to open the Styles pane, as shown in Figure 9.14.

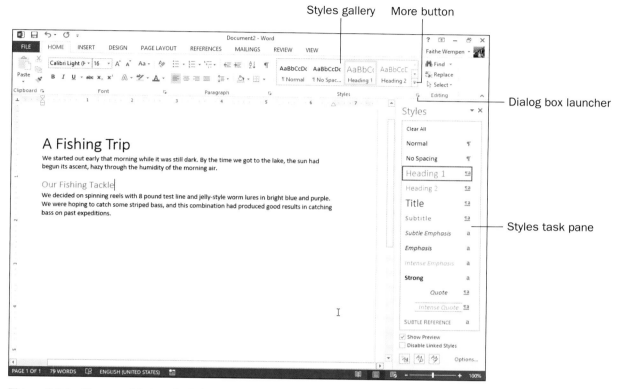

Figure 9.14 Choose a style from the Styles gallery or open the Styles task pane to select one.

To modify a style, apply the style to some text, and then change that text's formatting. Then right-click the style in the Styles pane and choose Update *stylename* to Match Selection.

You can also create new styles of your own. To do so, use the following steps.

Step by Step

Creating a New Style

Use these steps to create a new style:

1. Format a paragraph exactly the way you want the new style to be, and select the paragraph.

2. At the bottom of the Styles pane, click the New Style button (![icon]). The Create New Style from Formatting dialog box opens.

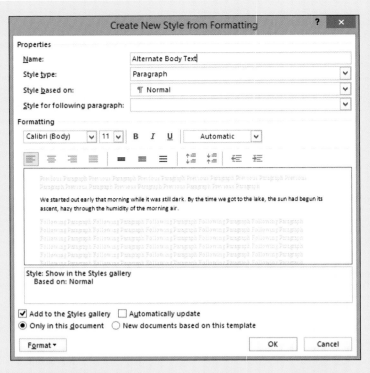

3. Type a name for the style in the Name box. Be as descriptive as you can, while still being concise.

4. Click OK to create the style.

Deleting a Style

Use these steps to remove a style that you have previously created. You cannot remove the built-in styles.

1. In the Styles pane, right-click the style to be removed.

2. Choose Delete *stylename,* where *stylename* is the style's name.

3. At the confirmation box, click Yes.

Quick Review

1. How do you remove the vertical space that follows a paragraph?

2. What is a tab leader?

3. What do the triangles represent on the horizontal ruler?

4. How do you modify the definition of a style?

Formatting Documents and Sections

Some types of formatting, such as margin settings, number of columns, and paper size, apply to the entire document. They aren't relevant to individual paragraphs or characters because they deal with entire pages or groups of pages. In the following sections, you will learn how to apply settings that affect the document as a whole.

Creating Page Breaks

When you reach the bottom of a page, Word starts a new page automatically. That's called a soft page break. If you add or remove text so that a change to the break point is required, Word makes it automatically. You can also insert a hard page break, which is a manually placed break. To do so, press Ctrl+Enter, or on the Page Layout tab, click the Breaks button and click Page.

soft page break A page break made automatically by the application when the current page is full.

hard page break A page break created by the user in order to force a page break in a certain place.

section break A divider in a document that allows settings that are normally document-wide to be applied differently in parts of the document.

Creating Section Breaks

As mentioned earlier, certain settings apply to the entire document. What if you want to have two different values for one of these settings that are normally document-wide? For example, suppose you wanted a business letter and its envelope to be stored in the same document file, and the envelope has different dimensions than the letterhead paper. In a case such as that, you would create a section break. A section break divides the document, allowing you to have different document-wide settings on each side of the break.

Section breaks can be Continuous (which means Word doesn't start a new page at the break), Next Page (which does include a page break with the section break), Even Page, or Odd Page. Those latter two not only insert a page break but also make sure that the text that follows the break begins on either an even or odd page number, and it inserts a second page break if needed to ensure that. To insert a section break, from the Page Layout tab, click Breaks, and then click the desired section break type from the Section Breaks section of the menu. See Figure 9.15.

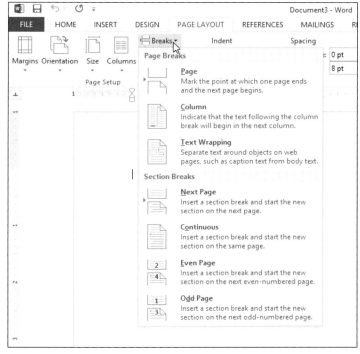

Figure 9.15   Choose a section break type from the Breaks button's menu.

NOTE

In some circumstances, Word creates sections breaks automatically. For example, if you select one or more paragraphs and then issue one of the document-wide commands found in the Page Setup group on the Page Layout tab, such as Columns, Size, or Orientation, Word automatically adds a section break before and after the selected paragraphs, and applies the settings only to the section between them (that is, the text you have selected).

Step by Step

Creating a Section Break

Use these steps to insert a section break:

1. Position the insertion point where you want the section break, or select the text that you want to be in its own section.

2. On the Page Layout tab, click Breaks and then click the desired section break type.

Deleting a Section Break

Use these steps to remove a section break:

1. On the Home tab, click the Show/Hide ¶ button if hidden characters are not already displayed. The section break becomes visible.

....Section Break (Continuous)...

2. Select the section break and press the Delete key, or position the insertion point to the right of (or below) the section break and press the Backspace key.

orientation The direction that the text runs in relation to the paper. Can be either portrait or landscape.

portrait The page orientation in which the text runs parallel to the narrow edge of the paper.

landscape The page orientation in which the text runs parallel to the wide edge of the paper.

Changing the Paper Size and Orientation

You can set the Size setting in Word to accommodate any paper size you have and that your printer can accommodate. You can also set the orientation of the page. The orientation is either portrait (the default) or landscape. On a portrait page, the text runs parallel to the narrower edge of the paper; on a landscape page, the text runs parallel to the wider edge.

TIP If you choose a paper size that's smaller than your actual paper, Word prints on only part of the paper, and you can trim the paper down to the desired size later.

Size and orientation are both controlled from the Page Layout tab, in the Page Setup group. On the Size menu, shown in Figure 9.16, you can choose from many popular paper sizes, or you can choose More Paper Sizes to open the Page Setup dialog box and create a custom size.

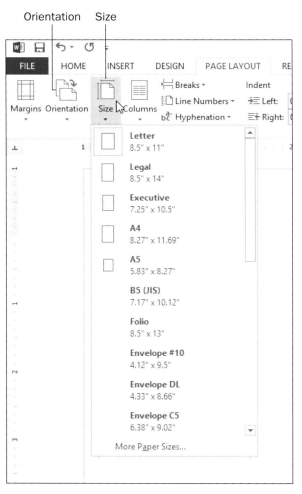

Figure 9.16 Choose a paper size from the Size button's drop-down list.

Setting Margins

The margins of a document represent the amount of blank space between the edge of the paper and the printable area of the document. On the Page Layout tab, you can click the Margins button to open a menu of margin presets, or you can choose Custom Margins to open the Page Setup dialog box, from which you can select exact margin settings for each side of the page, as shown in Figure 9.17.

margins The blank space between the edge of the paper and the document's content.

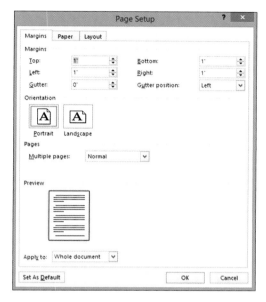

Figure 9.17   You can set custom margins in the Page Setup dialog box.

Another way to open the Page Setup dialog box is to click the dialog box launcher in the Page Setup group on the Page Layout tab.

TIP

Step by Step

Set the Page Margins

Use these steps to set the margins for the document:

1. On the Page Layout tab, click Margins.

2. Click one of the presets. Or, do the following to set custom margins:

    • Click Custom Margins. The Page Setup dialog box opens, as in Figure 9.17.

    • Enter the exact settings desired in the Right, Left, Top, and Bottom text boxes.

    • Click OK.

Numbering Pages

Numbering pages can help you make sure the pages are in order after they are printed. It's easy to drop a stack of papers and lose their original order, but page numbering can make the work of putting them back together easier. Page numbering can also enable you to refer to a certain page when discussing the document with others.

Page numbers are placed in the header or footer, which you will learn about later in this chapter, but you don't have to access the header and footer in order to set up page numbering. On the Insert tab, click the Page Number button, and then choose the desired position and style, as shown in Figure 9.18. Word places an appropriate page numbering code in the header or footer automatically.

Working with Headers and Footers

header The area at the top of each page that contains consistent or repeated information.

footer The area at the bottom of each page that contains consistent or repeated information.

The header and footer areas hold the text that repeats on each page of the document, such as the document's name, a copyright notice, or page numbers. The header is at the top of the page, and the footer is at the bottom.

NOTE You can have a different header/footer for the first page of a document, and different headers/footers for even- and odd-numbered pages. Each section can also have its own header/footer.

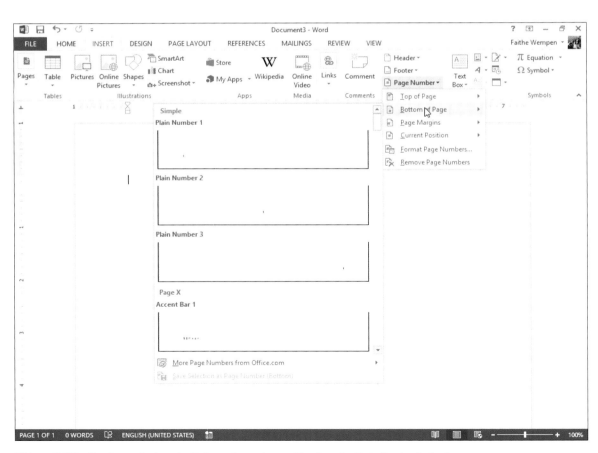

Figure 9.18 Number pages by selecting a page number position from the Page Number button's menu.

Each document has a header and footer area, but it is empty by default. When you use the Page Numbers feature, as in the preceding section, it places a code in the header or footer. You can also display the header and footer and manually type your own content into it, or insert codes into it. When the header and footer are open, you can type only in those areas; the rest of the document is dimmed and inaccessible until you close the header and footer, as shown in Figure 9.19. A special tab on the Ribbon also appears, containing commands for working with the header and footer.

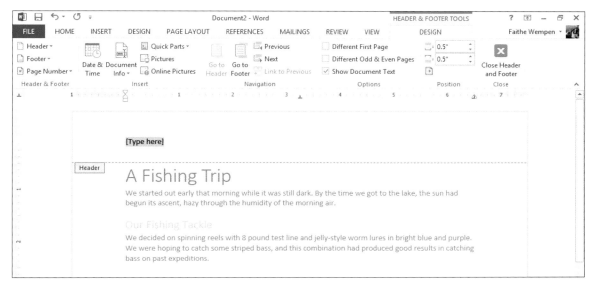

Figure 9.19   When the header or footer is active, the rest of the document is dimmed and uneditable.

To open the header and footer, you can do any of the following:

- From Page Layout view, double-click the top or bottom of the page.

- On the Insert tab, click Header and then click Edit Header, or click Footer and then click Edit Footer. This opens the header or footer without putting any content into it automatically.

- On the Insert tab, click Header and then click one of the sample header layouts that appear. Or, click Footer and then click one of the sample footer layouts.

To discard the contents of the header or footer, click the Header button and click Remove Header, or click the Footer button and then click Remove Footer.

After you have opened the header or footer, you can format it using the tools on the Header & Footer Tools tab on the Ribbon, shown in Figure 9.19. For example, you can insert a page number code or a date and time code, you can set up a different first page, you can set up different odd/even pages, and you can adjust the divider between the main document and the header or footer.

When you are finished working with the header and footer, double-click the main body of the document, or click the Close Header and Footer button on the Ribbon.

Using Multiple Columns

A document can have multiple newspaper-style columns. These columns can all be the same width, or can be custom widths. And, thanks to section breaks, you can have different numbers of columns in certain sections of the document.

To switch the entire document to multiple columns, click anywhere in the document and then on the Page Layout tab, click the Columns button and select a number of columns. Or, choose More Columns from the menu and then set up the columns in the Columns dialog box, as shown in Figure 9.20.

To set only part of a document in multiple columns, select the paragraphs to affect before choosing a number of columns. Word will insert continuous section breaks on both sides of the selection. If you want some other type of section breaks, insert the section breaks manually first, and then position the insertion point in the desired section and choose a number of columns.

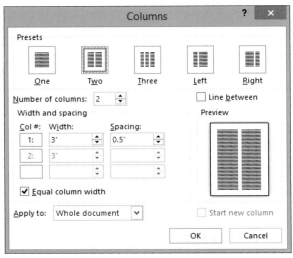

Figure 9.20 Configure column usage in the Columns dialog box.

Newsletters and Multiple Columns

One common use for a continuous section break is to have a newsletter masthead (title) that stretches across the entire page, followed by a multi-column layout of articles beneath it, as shown here:

Continuous Improvement Newsletter

Volume 1   Issue 1

Improvement Efforts Pay Off

Section 7 has had a dramatic increase in productivity this month, due to the efforts of Shift Supervisor Mark Bennett, who has successfully implemented a new Quality First program there. "I had hoped for a 20% improvement," said Bennett, but I was thrilled to find out that our initiative had done even better, and had increased productivity by 30% in a 6-month period. As a result, many of Bennett's improvements are set to be implemented plant-wide starting in February.

Employee Appreciation Dinner

The annual employee appreciation dinner will be held this year at Shula's Steakhouse, 344 Capital Point, in the village of New Macon on February 1, starting at 6 p.m. Please RSVP with the number of people in your family who will be attending to Sheila Rhodes in Human Resources no later than January 15.

To create this layout, start by typing and formatting the newsletter title. Then insert a section break after it. Then position the insertion point below the section break and set the number of columns to 2, 3, or whatever you want. The text above the section break remains in single-column layout.

Quick Review

1. How do you set document margins?

2. What is the purpose of a section break?

3. How can you make certain parts of the document use a different number of columns than the rest?

Working with Pictures

Pictures can add meaning to your documents, and can also make them more attractive and interesting. You can insert pictures from your own computer, such as those you have taken with a digital camera, and you can insert images from Office.com via the Clip Art feature. This is true of Excel and PowerPoint too; the skills you learn in the following sections will also apply to those applications.

Inserting a Picture

To insert a picture that you already have, position the insertion point where you want the picture and then on the Insert tab, click Pictures. In the Insert Picture dialog box, select the desired picture, and then click the Insert button to place it in the document. If it's the wrong size, or in the wrong place, see "Moving and Resizing a Picture" later in this chapter.

Finding and Inserting Clip Art

There are two meanings to the term clip art. In a generic sense, clip art is line art drawing in a vector format. A vector-based illustration is a line drawing constructed of mathematically created lines, like in geometry. (You don't have to do the math yourself; you use drawing tools to create the images. The math is all behind the scenes.) Because they are vector graphics, clip art images can be resized to any size without loss of quality, and they do not add much to the file size. The other meaning of *clip art* is a piece of art that has been acquired through the Office.com Clip Art feature in an Office application, regardless of the picture's actual type. It could be a vector graphic, a photo, a video (or animated graphic), or a sound file.

clip art 1) A vector-based line drawing. 2) An image inserted via the Clip Art feature in Office programs.

vector-based illustration A drawing that is constructed of mathematically created lines.

The Office.com Clip Art feature in Office applications relies on your Internet connection to communicate with Office.com, where most of the clip art library is stored. When you search for a clip by keyword in an Office application, the application checks to see if you are connected to the Internet, and if you are, it includes Office.com images in the search results.

Finding and Inserting an Image from Clip Art

Use these steps to locate an image that matches a keyword and insert it in your document:

1. Position the insertion point where you want the image.

2. On the Insert tab, click Online Pictures. The Insert Pictures dialog box opens.

3. In the Search box next to Office.com Clip Art, type a keyword.

4. Press Enter. Search results appear in the dialog box.

5. Click the clip you want to insert and then click the Insert button. The picture appears in the document.

6. Close the task pane.

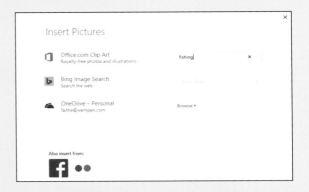

Moving and Resizing a Picture

After you insert a picture, it may not be exactly the way you want it. It might be the wrong size, or in the wrong position. You can move and resize pictures in just the same way you move and resize any other content in a frame, as you learned in Chapter 8. To move the picture, drag it by any part of it (other than a selection handle). To resize a picture, drag one of its selection handles. To resize it proportionally, drag a corner handle, or hold down the Shift key as you resize. You can also specify an exact size on the Picture Tools Format tab, in the Size group.

Adjusting a Picture's Wrap Text Setting

Wrap Text The feature in Office applications such as Word that enables you to specify how the graphic should interact with any adjacent text.

Text and pictures that occupy adjacent spots in a document interact in different ways based on the picture's Wrap Text setting. The default is In Line with Text, which means the picture is treated like a big character of text would be treated.

To treat the picture like a floating object and have the text wrap around it, set the Wrap Text setting to one of the other settings, like Square, Tight, or Top and Bottom. Make your selection from the Picture Tools Format tab, from the Wrap Text button's menu, as shown in Figure 9.21. Figure 9.22 shows examples of some of the wrap types.

Cropping a Picture

crop To cut away the unwanted parts of a picture from one or more sides.

To crop a picture is to cut away the unwanted parts of the picture from one or more sides. You can then enlarge the picture if desired, resulting in a zoomed-in effect. Cropping is more commonly performed on photos than on clip art.

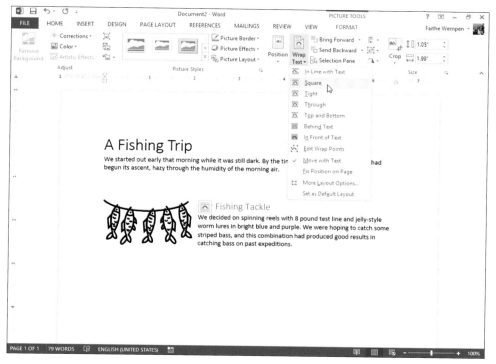

Figure 9.21   Set the text wrap setting for the selected picture.

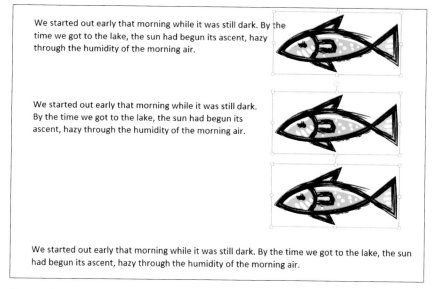

Figure 9.22   Text wrap setting examples. From top to bottom: Tight, Square, and Top and Bottom.

To crop a photo, use the Crop tool on the Picture Tools Format tab, as described in the following steps.

Cropping a Photo

Use these steps to crop a photo that has already been inserted into a Word document:

1. Select the photo.

2. On the Picture Tools Format tab, click the Crop button. Black crop handles appear adjacent to the selection handles.

3. Drag one of the crop handles inward to decrease the area of the photo. The areas to be excluded appear gray. Repeat if needed for another selection handle.

4. Click the Crop button again to finalize the cropping.

Uncropping a Photo

Use these steps to revert cropping on a photo that has already been inserted into a Word document:

1. Select the photo.

2. On the Picture Tools Format tab, click the Crop button. Black crop handles appear over the edges of the cropped picture. The parts you cropped out before are still visible in gray.

3. Drag the crop handles to different locations to re-crop, or drag them all out to the edges of the picture to uncrop.

TIP The Crop button's menu contains several additional options, which you can access by clicking the button's arrow below it. For example, you can crop to a shape, which changes the shape of the picture to any shape you choose from Word's Shapes gallery.

Rotating a Picture

There are three ways to rotate a picture. One way is to drag its rotation handle to rotate it manually, as shown in Figure 9.23. The rotation handle is the arrow circle that appears above a picture when it is selected. This method works well when you know the look that you want to achieve but you don't care what the numeric value of it is.

rotation handle The arrow circle at the top of a selected picture that, when dragged, rotates the picture.

The second way of rotating a picture is to open the Rotate Objects button's menu from the Picture Tools Format tab (Arrange group) and choose to rotate the image to the right or the left by 90 degrees. This method is the quickest, but is only good if you happen to want rotation in increments of 90 degrees. (For example, you could use it twice in a row to rotate 180 degrees.)

Mouse pointer while rotating

Rotation handle

Figure 9.23   Drag the rotation handle to rotate a picture.

The third way is to open the Rotate Objects button's menu and choose More Rotation Options, opening the Layout dialog box and click on the Size tab, as shown in Figure 9.24. From there, you can set a rotation amount in the Rotation text box, from 0 to 359. This method is best when you need a precise amount of rotation.

Enter rotation amount in degrees here

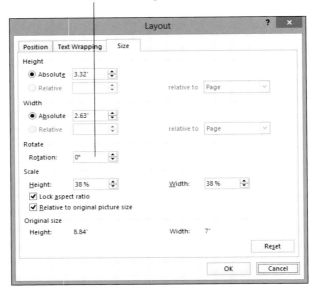

Figure 9.24   Adjust a picture's rotation from the Rotation text box on the Size tab of the Layout dialog box.

Quick Review

1. How do you restrict a clip art search to a certain type of image, such as only photos or only illustrations?

2. How do you crop a picture?

3. How do you change how text wraps around the picture?

Working with Tables

The term *table* has different meanings in different applications. As you will see in Chapter 10, "Creating Spreadsheets with Microsoft Excel," an Excel table is a range of cells grouped together to manage structured data stored in them. In Word and PowerPoint, however, a table is much more informal than that. A table in Word and PowerPoint is simply a grid of cells into which you can place data to help organize it and present it in orderly rows and columns. Figure 9.25 shows an example of a document that benefits from using a table.

Two contextual tabs are available when working with a table. The Table Tools Layout tab, shown in Figure 9.25, contains commands for changing the structure of the table—for example, adding and removing rows and columns. The Table Tools Design tab, which you will work with later in this chapter, contains commands for changing the formatting of the table, such as the cell background color and the width of the border lines.

Notice the small box in the upper-left corner of the table in Figure 9.25, containing a four-headed arrow. This is the table selector. You can click it to select the whole table. This is useful to do before you apply a formatting command that should affect the whole table, for example.

table In Word or PowerPoint, a grid of cells into which you can place data to help organize and present it in orderly rows and columns.

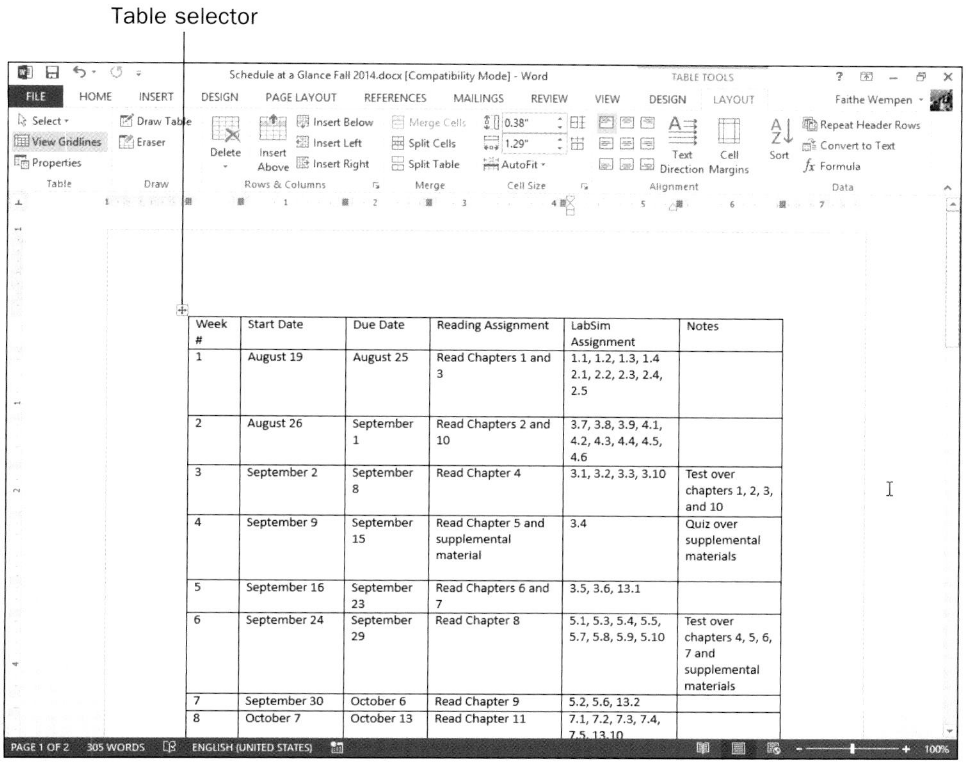

Figure 9.25 A table organizes information in rows and columns.

Creating a Table

To create a table, use the Table button on the Insert tab. When you click the button, a menu appears containing several different tools for creating tables. At the top of the menu is a grid of squares. You can drag across the grid with your mouse to select a certain number of rows and columns, as shown in Figure 9.26. When you release the mouse button, a table appears in your document.

If you prefer, you can use a dialog box to create a table instead. On the Table button's menu (refer to Figure 9.26), select Insert Table, and then you can select a number of rows and columns from a dialog box.

For maximum flexibility, you can draw your own table. From the Table button's menu, choose Draw Table, and your mouse pointer turns into a pencil. Drag to draw a rectangular frame that will form the outside of the table, and then drag to draw each vertical and horizontal line in the table. This method works well when you need a table with a complex split of row and column dividers in different parts of the table, as in Figure 9.27. To access the Draw Table command for an existing table, click the Draw Table button on the Table Tools Layout tab. To erase a line, click Eraser on that same tab and then click the line to erase.

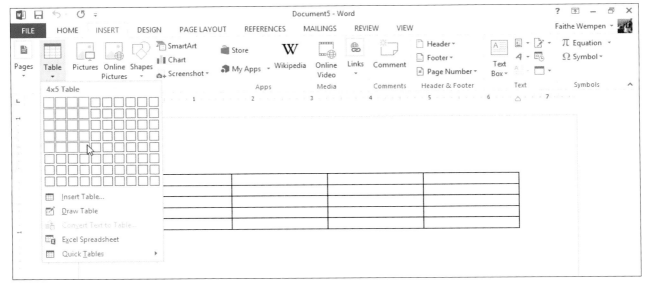

Figure 9.26   Create a table by dragging across the squares on the Table button's menu.

Draw Table

Eraser

Mouse pointer

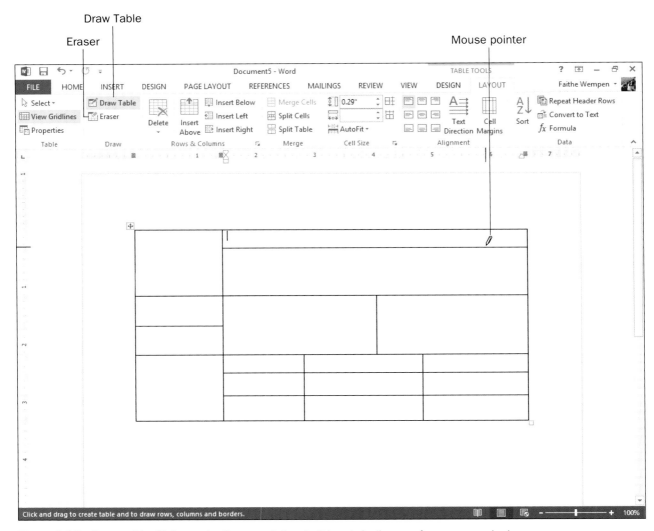

Figure 9.27   Draw a table with the exact cells you want; they don't have to be the same for every row and column.

Even if you create the table with one of the other methods, you can still use Draw Table to modify the table whenever you like. The Draw Table and Eraser buttons are available on the Table Tools Layout tab.

TIP

Typing in a Table

To type in a table, just click in a cell and begin typing. Text automatically wraps to another line when it reaches the edge of the cell. You can use most of the same text entry techniques as with any other text, such as Enter for a paragraph break and Shift+Enter for a line break.

To move to the next cell, you can click in it, or you can press the Tab key to move to it. The next cell is the one to the right of the active cell, or if the active cell is the rightmost one in a row, the next cell is the leftmost cell on the next row. If you press the Tab key in the rightmost cell in the bottom row, Word starts a new row. To go back to the previous cell, press Shift+Tab.

Adjusting Column Widths

To adjust a column width, position the mouse pointer over the border between two columns and drag. What happens to the other columns in the table when you change one column's width? It depends on what key you press, if any, as you drag. Table 9.1 summarizes the differences.

Table 9.1: Adjusting Column Width

Hold Down	Result
No key	The columns to the left and the right change their relative sizes, but the amount of space they take up collectively does not change. No other columns change, and the overall size of the table does not change.
Ctrl key	The column to the left of the divider you are dragging is resized; all other cells in the table are adjusted proportionally to maintain the same relative ratio between the sizes. The overall size of the table does not change.
Shift key	The cell to the left of the divider you are dragging is resized. No other cells change size; the overall size of the table changes.

You can also change the size of a row or column by specifying an exact value in the text boxes on the Table Tools Layout tab in the Cell Size group, as shown in Figure 9.28. Also in this group are Distribute Rows and Distribute Columns buttons, which equalize the height of the rows or the width of the columns in the table without changing the table's overall dimensions.

You can also AutoFit the column width to the widest entry in that column. To do so, double-click the divider between the column to AutoFit and the one to its right.

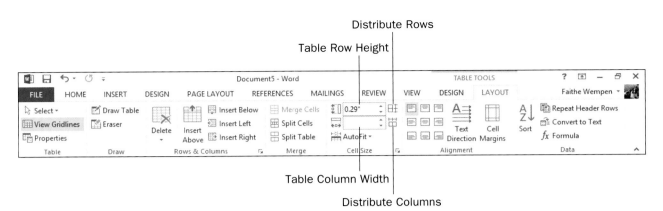

Figure 9.28   Set an exact size for cell height or width in the Cell Size group.

Selecting Rows, Columns, or Cells

Before you issue certain commands, such as commands that apply formatting, you must select the cells you want to affect. You can select entire rows and columns, individual cells, or ranges (rectangular groups of cells).

To select an entire row, position the mouse pointer to the left of the row (outside of the table), so the mouse pointer becomes a white arrow that points slightly to the right ( ), and then click.

To select an entire column, position the mouse pointer above the column (again, outside of the table), so the mouse pointer becomes a down-pointing black arrow ( ), and then click.

To select certain cells, drag across them with the mouse. To select one individual cell, move the mouse pointer to the left border of a cell, so that the pointer turns into a black, right-pointing arrow, and then click.

Inserting and Deleting Rows and Columns

To insert a new row at the bottom of the table, click in the last cell (bottom right) and press the Tab key.

If you want a row in some other position, or a new column, use the Table Tools Layout tab. In the Rows & Columns group are buttons for inserting new rows or columns either before or after the active cell's row or column. (Refer to Figure 9.28.) If you want to insert multiple rows or multiple columns, select a corresponding number of rows or columns in the table before clicking one of these buttons.

To delete a row or column, select the row or column and then click the Delete button in the Rows and Columns group, on the Table Tools Layout tab.

TIP   As an alternative method of inserting or deleting rows or columns, you can right-click a selected row or column and choose Insert or Delete commands from the shortcut menu that appears.

Merging and Splitting Cells

As you saw earlier in the chapter, you can use the Draw Table and Eraser tools to add and remove borders in your table. This is one way of merging and splitting cells. Click Draw Table and then drag a dividing line to split a cell into two pieces by drawing another line. Repeat as many times as needed. Click Erase and then click any dividing line to merge two cells.

Another way to merge and split cells is with the Merge Cells and Split Cells buttons on the Table Tools Layout tab.

Step by Step

Merging Cells

Use these steps to merge two or more cells:

1. Select the cells to merge.

2. Click the Merge Cells button on the Table Tools Layout tab.

Splitting Cells

Use these steps to split a cell:

1. Select the cell(s) to split.

2. Click the Split Cells button on the Table Tools Layout tab. The Split Cells dialog box opens.

3. Specify a Number of Columns and Number of Rows.

4. Click OK.

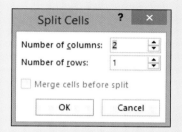

Formatting a Table

You can format each individual cell of a table with a certain background color (fill) and your choice of borders around each side of it (color, style, and thickness). However, it is often easier to apply a *table style* to the entire table, which applies preset combinations of formatting chosen to work well together. See Figure 9.29.

table style A style that applies to an entire table, formatting it with a set of preset formatting, including borders and sharing.

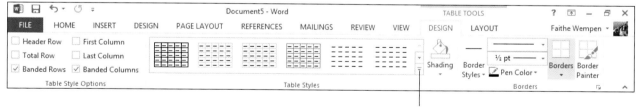

Click More to see more styles

Figure 9.29 Select a table style to format the entire table at once.

To choose a table style, open the gallery in the Table Styles group on the Table Tools Design tab and make your selection of colors and styles. The colors are from the theme colors currently applied. (See Chapter 8 for more information about themes and theme colors.)

You can set certain cells to be differently formatted by marking or clearing the check boxes in the Table Style Options group, as shown in Figure 9.29. For example, you can make the first row (Header Row) or last row (Total Row) different, or the first or last column different. You can also specify whether or not you want rows or columns to be banded (alternating in color).

To manually format certain cells, select them and then use the Shading or Borders button in the Table Styles group to apply different borders or shading to only the selected cells.

Quick Review

1. How do you widen a column to fit the longest entry in that column?

2. How do you apply a table style?

3. How do you erase individual lines in a table?

Correcting and Collaborating

In most business environments, more than one person has input on a document. You might create a document initially on your own, but your supervisor and coworkers may review it and add comments, or you may collaborate with multiple teammates throughout the process. In the following sections, you will learn about some features that make it easy to correct your work and collaborate with others.

Finding and Replacing Text

You might sometimes need to find certain words or phrases in an existing document, and you might also need to replace them with some other words or phrases. For example, if the contact person changes for a company to which you are selling products, you might need to find and replace all instances of the previous representative's name in a contract or bid proposal. You could also use Find and Replace to repurpose an existing document for a new customer or product.

Word has two different Find methods. The first one is easy, and involves the navigation pane. The other one has more options, and uses the Find and Replace dialog box.

Finding Text Using the Navigation Pane Method

Use these steps to find a text string in a document using the navigation pane:

1. On the Home tab, in the Editing group, click Find, or press Ctrl+F. The navigation task pane appears.

2. In the Search Document text box, type the text for which to search. Search results appear immediately in the pane.

3. Click the first instance found to jump to it in the document. Click each additional instance to jump to it as needed.

4. When you are finished, close the navigation pane.

Finding Text Using the Dialog Box Method

Use these steps to find a text string in a document using a dialog box:

1. On the Home tab, in the Editing group, click the down arrow on the Find button, and on the menu that appears, click Advanced Find. The Find and Replace dialog box opens with the Find tab displayed.

2. In the Find What box, type the text you want to find.

3. (Optional) To set options, click the More button to expand the dialog box, and then specify any options desired, such as matching the case of the text, finding whole words only, or using wildcards.

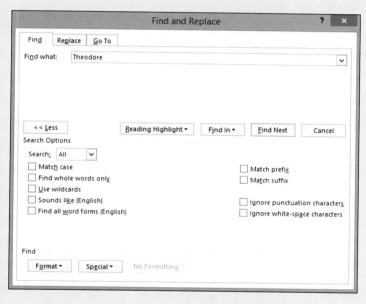

4. (Optional) To find only text with certain formatting, click the Format button in the dialog box and select a type of formatting, and then set the specifications that the found text must have.

5. (Optional) To find some special character, click the Special button in the dialog box and select the desired character. For example, you might search for section breaks using this option.

6. Click Find Next. The first instance appears.

7. Continue clicking Find Next until you have found all instances, or click Cancel to close the dialog box.

Replacing is a lot like finding using the dialog box method; in fact, it uses the same dialog box, but a different tab in it. The Replace tab has all the same features as the Find tab, but it also has a text box in which you can type the text that should replace the found text.

Step by Step

Replacing Text

Use these steps to find a text string in a document using the navigation pane:

1. On the Home tab, in the Editing group, click Replace, or press Ctrl+H. The Find and Replace dialog box opens to the Replace tab.

2. (Optional) If the advanced options don't already appear, and you want to use them, click the More button.

3. Set any advanced options for the Find portion of the operation, as described in the previous steps.

4. In the Replace With box, type the text string you want to replace the found string with.

5. Click Find Next. The first instance is located.

6. If you want to replace this instance, click Replace; otherwise, click Find Next. You can also click Replace All to replace all instances at once.

7. Continue working through all instances, or click Cancel to close the dialog box.

Correcting Spelling and Grammar

Everyone makes spelling and grammar errors now and then, even if they are just typographical errors. Word has tools for helping correct these before anyone else sees them, including both Spelling and Grammar checkers.

As you type, Word points out any words that are not in its dictionary with a red wavy underline. You can right-click the wavy-underlined word or phrase to see a shortcut menu of possible fixes. As shown in Figure 9.30, you can do any of the following:

- **Accept a suggested correction:** One or more suggested spellings appear at the top of the menu; click one to instantly make the correction.

- **Ignore the error:** You can choose Ignore All to ignore all instances of the word within this document only.

- **Add the word to the dictionary:** You can add the word to Office's list of accepted words, so the word will not be flagged as misspelled in any document in the future.

- **A wavy blue underline indicates a possible grammar error.**
Check the entry carefully, and make a correction if needed. Keep in mind, however, that Word's Grammar feature sometimes makes mistakes, so do not rely on it over your own judgment. If you want to know more about the error, choose Grammar from the shortcut menu, or click the Spelling & Grammar button on the Review tab, to open the grammar task pane, as shown in Figure 9.31.

Add this word to the dictionary

Choose a correction

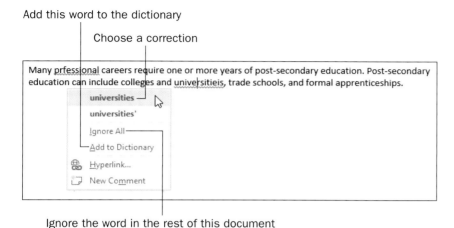

Ignore the word in the rest of this document

Figure 9.30   Right-click a word with a wavy red underline to see a menu of correction choices.

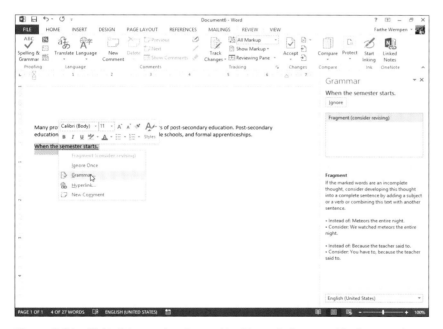

Figure 9.31   Right-click a word or phrase with a blue underline to see Word's suggestions for correcting grammar.

If you want to review the entire document at once, instead of scanning through it looking for wavy underlines, on the Review tab click Spelling & Grammar. A task pane opens, displaying the first error found. (If it's a spelling error, the Spelling task pane appears; if it's a grammar error, the Grammar task pane appears.)

The controls in the task pane depend on whether it is a spelling error or a grammar error; Figure 9.31 shows the task pane for a grammar error, and Figure 9.32 shows it for a spelling error. All the options from the shortcut menus are available, plus additional options. For example, you can ignore individual instances or all instances, change one or all instances, and choose a different dictionary language.

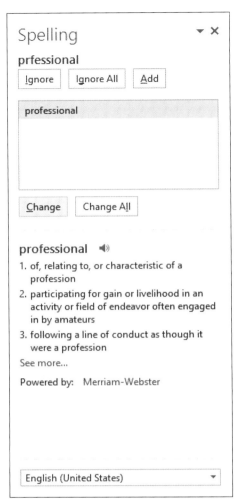

Figure 9.32 You can also check spelling from the Spelling task pane.

TIP To adjust the spelling and grammar options, click the File tab, click Options, and then click Proofing. You can choose which grammar rules will be checked, use custom dictionaries, and more.

Tracking and Accepting Changes

When editing someone else's work, you might want to mark your changes so that they can be reviewed easily. Word's Track Changes feature enables you to track each person's changes individually, marking each one with a different color, so multiple people's suggestions and changes can be reviewed in a single copy without losing any information about what the document originally contained. Figure 9.33 shows an example of a document with tracked changes. Depending on Word's settings, some or all changes may also appear in balloons, which appear to the right of the document. Figure 9.33 shows one balloon. By default, only comments (covered later in this chapter) and formatting changes appear in balloons.

balloon A rounded text box appearing in the space to the right of the document, containing a comment or a tracked change.

Most professional careers require one or more years of *post-secondary education*. Post-secondary education can include not only traditional colleges and universities, but also trade schools and formal apprenticeships. Selecting a post-secondary educational institution requires ~~careful~~ diligent planning to ensure you find the school that will best prepare you for your future goals.

Faithe Wempen A few seconds ago
Formatted: Font: Italic

Figure 9.33   A document with tracked changes.

Step by Step

Enabling or Disabling Change Tracking

Use these steps to begin or stop tracking changes:

1. On the Review tab, in the Tracking group, click the Track Changes button.

Setting Change Tracking Options

Use these steps to customize the way change tracking works:

1. On the Review tab, in the Tracking group, click the dialog box launcher. The Track Changes Options dialog box opens.

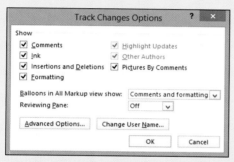

2. Make any changes to the settings as desired.
3. Click the Advanced Options button. The Advanced Track Changes Options dialog box opens.

4. Make any change to the settings as desired.

5. Click OK.

6. Click OK to close the Track Changes Options dialog box.

Changing the Username

Word shows each user's changes in a different color. If you want to change to a different username, follow these steps:

1. On the Review tab, in the Tracking group, click the dialog box launcher. The Track Changes Options dialog box opens.

2. Click the Change User Name button. The Word Options dialog box opens.

3. Change the name in the User Name box.

4. Change the initials in the Initials box.

5. Click OK.

6. Click OK to close the Track Changes Options dialog box.

Also in the Tracking group on the Review tab, you'll find these buttons for controlling what you see onscreen when tracking changes:

- **Display for Review drop-down list:** From here, you can change what you see onscreen in terms of the changes:

  - *Simple Markup* shows the edited form of the document with most markup hidden, but with short vertical bars in the left margin next to lines that contain changes. This view is designed for easy viewing of a document that contains a lot of changes.

  - *All Markup* shows the document in its edited form with all the changes tracked.

  - *No Markup* shows the document in its edited form with the tracked changes hidden.

  - *Original* shows the document in its original form and hides the tracked changes.

- **Show Markup drop down list:** You can specify which types of changes you want to see when markup is displayed. For example, if you don't care about formatting changes, you choose Formatting from this list to clear its check box.

- **Reviewing Pane drop-down list:** Enables you to choose between a vertical or horizontal reviewing pane. The reviewing pane lists all changes in the document, so you can jump to a change easily. To turn the reviewing pane on or off, you can click the face of the Reviewing Pane button rather than opening its drop-down list.

One way to review the tracked changes in the document is to manually browse through and look at each one. Right-click a change and then choose Accept or Reject from the shortcut menu. The exact wording depends on the type of change. Figure 9.34 shows Accept Insertion and Reject Insertion, for example.

You can also use the Review tab to review the changes. In the Changes group, use the Next and Previous buttons to move among the changes, and then use the Accept or Reject button to specify how to handle each one.

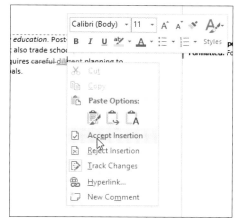

Figure 9.34 Accept or reject a change individually by right-clicking it and making your selection.

To accept or reject all the remaining changes at once, open the drop-down list for the Accept or Reject button and choose Accept All Changes in Document or Reject All Changes in Document.

Locking Revision Tracking

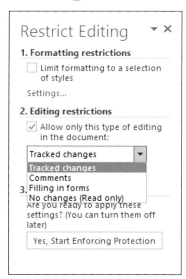

If you don't want others to be able to make untracked changes, or accept or reject changes without your permission, you can password-protect the feature. To do so, click the Restrict Editing button on the Review tab. (Depending on the width of the application window, you might have to click the Protect button and then click Restrict Editing.) In the Restrict Editing task pane, mark the Allow Only This Type of Editing in the Document check box, and then open the drop-down list and choose Tracked Changes. Then click Yes, Start Enforcing Protection. In the Start Enforcing Protection dialog box, type and retype a password and click OK. Now all changes will be tracked, and only those who know the password will be able to make untracked changes.

Making and Reviewing Comments

comment A non-printing note inserted into a document to share information or an opinion about the document with others editing it.

When you want to make a note in a document without changing its contents, you can use a comment. A comment is like a sticky note that you attach to a certain spot in the document. It doesn't print (unless you configure Word to print the comments). You can leave comments for other people who are working on the document to let them know your ideas and opinions. You can read other people's comments and then make changes to the document, make your own comments in response, and/or delete the comment.

Step by Step

Inserting a Comment

Follow these steps to create a new comment in a document:

1. Place the insertion point where you want the comment to be attached, or select the text or other object to which you want it attached.

   You can attach a comment to one spot in a paragraph, to an individual word, sentence, or paragraph, to multiple paragraphs, to a graphic, or to just about anything else.

2. On the Review tab, click New Comment. A new comment balloon appears to the right of the main document.

3. Type the comment in the balloon.

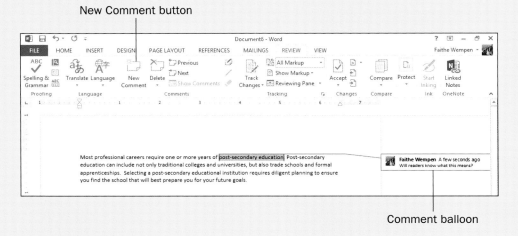

New Comment button

Comment balloon

Moving Among Comments

Follow these steps to find the next or previous comment in the document:

1. Click the Review tab on the Ribbon.

2. In the Comments group, click Next to go to the next comment or Previous to go to the previous comment.

Deleting a Comment

Follow these steps to delete a comment:

1. Right-click the comment balloon.

2. Click Delete Comment.

   OR

1. Click to place the insertion point in the comment.

2. On the Review tab, in the Comments group, click Delete.

Protecting a Document from Changes

After you have spent a lot of time on a document, you might want to make sure that nobody makes unauthorized changes to it. There are several ways to protect a document, each with its own features and benefits.

Password Protection

The most basic protection is password protection. You can assign two separate passwords for a document: Password to Open and Password to Modify. When prompted for the password, the document either opens normally or in Read-Only mode, depending on which password the user enters.

Step by Step

Password-Protecting a Document

Follow these steps to password-protect a Word document:

1. Click File and then click Save As. Select a save location and then click Browse if needed to open the Save As dialog box.

2. At the bottom of the dialog box, click Tools. On the menu that appears, click General Options. The General Options dialog box opens.

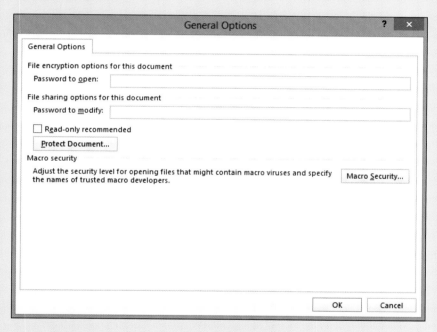

3. In the Password to Open box, type the password a user must know in order to open and view the document.

4. (Optional) If you want to assign a password to edit, type it in the Password to Modify box.

5. Click OK. The document is now password-protected.

Removing a Password

Follow these steps to stop password-protection on a document:

1. Click File, and then click Save As. The Save As dialog box opens.

2. At the bottom of the dialog box, click Tools. On the menu that appears, click General Options. The General Options dialog box opens.

3. Clear the text in the Password to Open and Password to Modify boxes.

4. Click OK.

Word offers a couple of protections that are very weak, in that users may circumvent them at will. They exist in order to warn users that the document should not be edited without a good reason, but they do not prevent the user from overriding the warnings.

You can recommend read-only access to users so that a warning appears when someone opens the document, as shown in Figure 9.35. Users may bypass this warning.

Figure 9.35   When read-only access is recommended, this warning box appears when you open the file.

You can also mark a document as Final. When you do so, a notice appears at the top of the document letting users know that the document is finalized, as shown in Figure 9.36, so that they hopefully will hesitate before making gratuitous changes. This warning, like the read-only warning, is easy to override, so it is not to be considered a type of security.

Figure 9.36   When a document has been marked as final, this warning appears when you open it.

Step by Step

Recommending Read-Only

Follow these steps to discourage changes in a Word document:

1. Click File and then click Save As. The Save As dialog box opens.

2. At the bottom of the dialog box, click Tools. On the menu that appears, click General Options. The General Options dialog box opens.

3. Mark the Read-Only Recommended check box.

4. Click OK.

Marking a Document as Final

Follow these steps to mark a document as final:

1. Click File and then click Info.

2. Click the Protect Document button.

3. Click Mark as Final.

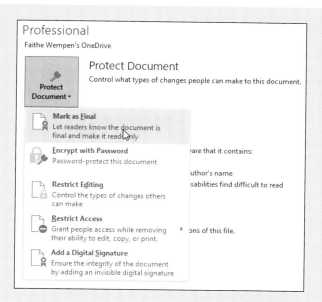

You can also restrict editing for a document to allow certain types of changes but not others. To experiment with this feature, click the Restrict Editing button on the Review tab.

NOTE

Quick Review

1. How do you display the Find tab of the Find and Replace dialog box?

2. How do you turn on change tracking?

3. How do you insert a comment?

4. What is the purpose of marking a document as final?

Summary

Editing and Formatting Text

Choose a font from the Font drop-down list, or use the (Headings) and (Body) fonts at the top of that list to stick with consistent body and heading fonts. **Style sets** and **themes** can apply the same fonts to all heading and body paragraphs in the entire document. To apply a different font size, choose it from the Font Size drop-down list, or type an exact size in the associated text box. For effects such as Bold, Italic, and Underline, use the buttons in the Font group on the Home tab.

Formatting Paragraphs

Paragraph formatting applies to entire paragraphs. For example, you can assign bulleted or numbered list formatting to a series of paragraphs. You can set **tab stops** using the ruler or the Tabs dialog box. You can **indent** a paragraph from the left and right margins, and set the first line indent separately from the rest of the paragraph. You can set **line spacing**, which is the amount of vertical space between the lines of a paragraph.

A **style** is a named collection of formatting attributes you can apply simultaneously. Word has built-in styles in the Normal template (and in other templates), and you can also create your own.

Formatting Documents and Sections

An automatically occurring page break is a **soft page break**. Press Ctrl+Enter to create a **hard page break**. A **section break** divides the document, allowing you to have different settings for different parts of the document that would otherwise be document-wide settings, like margins and paper size.

A page's **orientation** is either **portrait** or **landscape**. The **margins** of a document represent the amount of blank space between the edge of the paper and the printable area of the document. All of those features can be set up from the Page Layout tab.

To number the pages, place a page numbering code in the header or footer. You can use the Page Number command in the Insert tab. The **header** holds repeated information for the top of each page, and the **footer** holds it for the bottom of each page.

A document or section can have multiple newspaper-style columns, set up on the Page Layout tab.

Working with Pictures

The term **clip art** can refer generically to line art in **vector** format, or to art placed using the Online Pictures feature in an Office application.

To move a picture, drag it where you want it. To resize a picture, drag one of its selection handles. By default, a picture is an inline image; you can make it float so you can drag it freely by changing its **Wrap Text** setting.

To **crop** a picture, use the Crop tool on the Picture Tools Layout tab. To rotate a picture, drag its **rotation handle**, or use the Rotate Object button's menu.

Working with Tables

A **table** in Word is a grid of cells into which you can place data. To create a table (using any of several methods), click the Table button on the Insert tab. Click in a cell and type; press Tab to move to the next cell, or Shift+Tab to move to the previous cell.

Drag the border between columns to resize a column. The behavior of the other columns depends on whether or not you hold down Shift, Ctrl, or neither as you drag.

To select rows, columns, or cells, drag across them. To select a row, you can also click to the left of that row; to select a column, you can click above that column outside the table border. To insert or delete rows or columns, use the Rows and Columns group's buttons on the Table Tools Layout tab. To merge or split cells, use the Draw Table and Eraser buttons, or use the Merge Cells and Split Cells buttons.

To format a table, you can apply a **table style** from the Table Tools Design tab, or you can select individual cells and apply border and shading format to them from that same tab.

Correcting and Collaborating

Use Find and Replace to locate a text string and optionally replace it with another text string. The navigation pane method of Find shows all instances in a list in the pane. The dialog box method allows options to be set.

Spelling errors are marked with a wavy red underline and grammar errors with a blue wavy underline. Right-click an error and select a correction, or choose to ignore the error. You can also click Spelling on the Review tab to do a full check with a dialog box.

You can track changes by clicking the Track Changes button on the Review tab. Changes may appear in a **balloon**, depending on your settings; they also appear in the Reviewing pane. Changes are tracked by user name, so change the user name if you want to represent a different author.

A **comment** is a non-printing note inserted into a document. Insert a comment using the New Comment button on the Reviewing tab. To delete a comment, right-click it and choose Delete.

To protect a document, you can assign passwords to it for opening and/or editing. You can also mark a document as final or suggest read-only, although those latter two are not true security measures.

Key Terms

balloon
clip art
comment
crop
footer
hard page break
header
indentation
landscape
line spacing
margins
orientation
paragraph formatting

portrait
rotation handle
section break
soft page break
style
style set
tab stop
table
table style
text effects
vector-based illustration
Wrap Text

Test Yourself

Fact Check

1. What does the ¶ symbol represent when hidden characters are displayed?

   a. line break

   b. paragraph break

   c. non-breaking space

   d. tab

2. To change the fonts assigned to heading and body paragraphs, change the

   a. tab stops

   b. font size

   c. font color

   d. style set

3. _____ is the amount that a paragraph as a whole is offset from the left margin.

   a. Hanging indent

   b. First line indent

   c. Left indent

   d. Right indent

4. When you press Ctrl+Enter, you insert a

   a. line break

   b. section break

   c. soft page break

   d. hard page break

5. To create a document with a different number of columns for certain paragraphs than for others, insert _____ before and after the section that should be different from the rest.

   a. section breaks

   b. paragraph breaks

   c. tab stops

   d. hard page breaks

6. Portrait and landscape are both _____.

   a. table styles

   b. page orientations

   c. paper sizes

   d. margin presets

7. Page numbering codes are placed where?

    a. header or footer

    b. header only

    c. footer only

    d. document title

8. Square, Tight, and In Line with Text are all types of _____ for a picture.

    a. preset positions

    b. preset sizes

    c. text wrap settings

    d. frame types

9. What is the arrow circle above a picture when it is selected?

    a. sizing handle

    b. selection handle

    c. rotation handle

    d. moving handle

10. What would you use to insert a non-printing note in a document?

    a. tracked changes

    b. tab stops

    c. comments

    d. warnings

Matching

Match the keyboard shortcuts to their purposes.

    a. Ctrl key

    b. Ctrl+Enter

    c. Ctrl+F

    d. Ctrl+H

    e. Shift key

    f. Shift+Enter

1. _____Press this while dragging a column divider to resize a cell so that other cells in the table adjust size proportionally to maintain the same relative ratio.

2. _____Press this while dragging a column divider so that only the cell to the left of the divider is resized, and the overall size of the table changes.

3. _____Press this to insert a hard page break.

4. _____Press this to start a new line without starting a new paragraph.

5. _____Press this to open the Navigation task pane so you can find a certain text string.

6. _____Press this to open the Find and Replace dialog box to the Replace tab.

Sum It Up

1. List five different ways of changing the formatting of individual characters.

2. Explain how to create a numbered list.

3. Describe how to change a document's margins.

4. Explain how to find and insert clip art.

5. Describe how to password-protect a document.

6. Describe two different ways of inserting a table.

Explore More

Advanced Text Formatting

On the Advanced tab of the Font dialog box, you can set some advanced options for character formatting that professional typesetters use. For example, you can change the Scale, Spacing, and Position, set up kerning, and use ligatures. Research what these features are (use the Word Help system or other web resources), and write a one-page paper explaining each feature, showing examples of each.

Modifying a Custom Dictionary

Suppose you add a word to the custom dictionary in Word and then realize that it was a mistake to do so. How would you edit the custom dictionary to remove it? Research this, either in Word's Help system or online, and write a step-by-step procedure as if you were describing that process to a friend.

Text Wrap versus Position

On the Picture Tools Layout tab are buttons that open menus for Wrap Text and for Position. They both change the position of the selected picture, but in different ways. Research both of these buttons to identify the purpose of each one, and write a one-page summary that includes scenarios of when each feature would be most appropriate.

Think It Over

Page Orientation

Make a list of some documents that are most appropriate for landscape orientation, and another list of documents that work best in portrait orientation. For example, which orientation is better for business letters? Wide tables with many columns? Certificates of achievement? Newsletters?

Setting Margins

What are good guidelines for the margins to use for documents? For example, what margins would you use for an academic report? What margins would you use for a letter to a friend, or a tightly packed sheet of study notes for a test? What are the upper and lower limits for margin settings before the document begins to look strange?

Header and Footer Content

What types of information would be appropriate to place in a document's header or footer? Give some examples of information that works well there, and some examples of information that would not work well there.

Chapter 10

Creating Spreadsheets with Microsoft Excel

Learning objectives

☐ Explain the features of the Excel interface

☐ Demonstrate how to navigate in a workbook and enter text

☐ Show how to change the structure of a worksheet

☐ Explain how to use formatting to improve a worksheet

☐ Demonstrate the use of formulas and functions

☐ Show how to summarize and illustrate data with charts

☐ Understand how Excel uses tables to organized structured data

Understanding the Excel Interface

Moving Around in a Worksheet

Changing the Structure of a Worksheet

Formatting Cells

Entering Formulas and Functions

Creating Charts

Working with Data Tables

Spreadsheets help us to organize, calculate, and make sense of numeric data. Like the orderly row-and-column format of a paper ledger, a spreadsheet enables users to organize large amounts of data so that it is easy to understand and easy to refer to.

In businesses everywhere, Microsoft Excel is the most commonly used application for creating and managing spreadsheets. In this chapter, you will learn the basics of Excel, including how to enter data, how to calculate it, how to format it, and how to summarize it to find its meaning.

Project Manager

A project manager makes things happen. Project managers keep all the workers, equipment, locations, and materials on track for a building project, an event, a manufacturing process, or any other rollout that requires advance planning. Project managers need training in a variety of fields, including accounting, logistics, people management, and, of course, office productivity software. Excel is the go-to tool for project managers because it has so many different uses. You can store financial data in Excel to calculate a project's budget, lists of items and their prices and availability, and scheduling constraints for multiple departments. You can use "what if" analysis to determine the optimal solution to a problem with multiple variables, and you can produce charts that graphically summarize a project's status.

Understanding the Excel Interface

As you learned in Chapter 8, "Understanding Microsoft Office 2013," each Office 2013 application has the same basic controls, including a tabbed Ribbon, a title bar, a status bar, scroll bars, and Backstage view. Turn back to Chapter 8's section "Understanding the Office 2013 Interface" if you need a reminder about these elements. The following sections describe some of Excel's unique features.

Workbooks and Worksheets

workbook An Excel data file, containing one or more worksheets.

Excel calls a data file a workbook. Each workbook, by default, contains one tabbed page, and you can add more as needed. Each page is a worksheet. The tabs along the bottom of the Excel window represent the worksheets; Figure 10.1 shows a workbook with two sheets. Click the New Sheet button (the plus sign) to add new sheets.

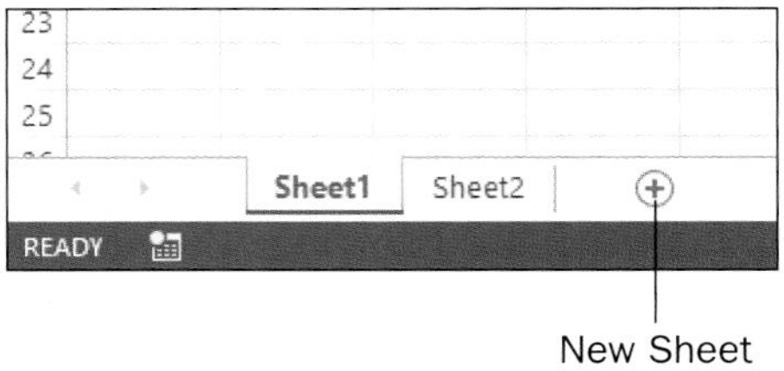

worksheet A tabbed page of a workbook, containing a grid of rows and columns.

New Sheet

Figure 10.1 Worksheet tabs at the bottom of the Excel window.

You can switch to a different worksheet by clicking its tab. If there are so many tabs that you can't see them all at once, use the arrow buttons to the left of the tabs to scroll through them.

TIP You can change the name of a worksheet by double-clicking the tab and typing a new name.

Rows, Columns, and Cells

cell The intersection of a row and a column in a worksheet.

cell address The column letter and the row number that intersect to form the cell, such as A2 or BB6.

Name box The box above cell A1 where the name of the active cell appears.

Each worksheet consists of a grid of rows and columns. Each row has a number, listed along the left side of the screen, and each column has a letter, listed along the top of the screen. At the intersection of each row and column is a rectangular area called a cell, into which you can type content. Together the column letter and the row number form a cell address, such as A1. When the letters increment past Z, they begin with double letters, AA through AZ, BA through BZ, and so on. The Name box, which appears above column A, shows the address of the active cell.

The active cell is the one with the cell selector (the dark green outline) around it. For example, in Figure 10.2, the active cell is C4.

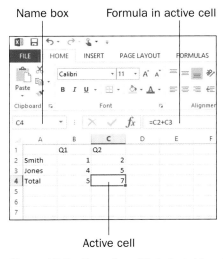

Figure 10.2   The active cell is indicated by a thick dark green outline called the cell selector.

Formula Bar

When a cell contains a formula, the result of the formula appears in the cell itself. The formula appears in the formula bar, above the column headings. For example, in Figure 10.2, the formula in cell C4 is =C2+C3. Because that cell is active, you can see the formula in the formula bar. Cell C4 itself shows the result: 7. Notice that the Name box shows the cell's address: C4. If the cell contains a numeric value or a text string, the formula bar shows the same content as the cell itself.

Quick Review

1. Give an example of a valid cell address.

2. Under what circumstances does the formula bar display something different than what's displayed in the active cell?

3. Which cell's address appears in the Name box?

Moving Around in a Worksheet

To type in a cell, you must make it the active cell, either by clicking it or by using one of the keyboard methods of moving the cell selector. Table 10.1 summarizes the keyboard methods.

Moving the cell selector is not the same as scrolling. When you scroll the worksheet, you change which cells are visible, but you do not change the active cell. Use the scroll bars to scroll, as you learned in Chapter 8.

NOTE

Table 10.1: Keyboard Shortcuts for Moving the Cell Selector

Press This . . .	To Move . . .
Any arrow key	One cell in the direction of the arrow
Tab	One cell to the right
Shift+Tab	One cell to the left
Ctrl+arrow key	To the last or first non-empty cell in the direction of the arrow
Ctrl+End	To the bottommost, rightmost cell in the worksheet that contains data
Ctrl+Home	To the beginning of the worksheet
Home	To the beginning of the active cell's row
Page Down	One screen down
Page Up	One screen up
Alt+Page Down	One screen to the right
Alt+Page Up	One screen to the left
Ctrl+Page Down	To the next sheet in the workbook
Ctrl+Page Up	To the previous sheet in the workbook

Typing and Editing Cell Content

To enter content in a cell, make the cell active by moving the cell selector to it, as you learned in the preceding section, and then just start typing. When you are finished, move to another cell. For example, press Enter to move to the cell below the current one, or press Tab to move to the cell to its right. You can also click any other cell to save your entry and move on. If you want to cancel what you typed, press Esc.

To edit a cell's content, make the cell active and then do any of the following:

- To replace the cell's content with a new entry, type the new entry.

- To edit the cell's content without replacing it entirely, click in the formula bar and make your edits there, as shown in Figure 10.3, or double-click the cell to move an insertion point into it and then edit the text directly in the cell.

- To clear all the text from the cell, press the Delete key.

- To clear both the text and the formatting from the cell, click the Home tab, click the Clear button, and click Clear All.

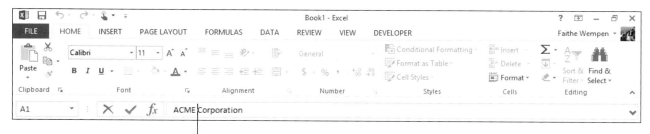

Click to move insertion point into the formula bar

Figure 10.3   Click in the formula bar to move the insertion point into it and then edit as you would text in a word processor.

Just like in Microsoft Word, you can move the insertion point in the cell or in the formula bar by using the arrow keys. You can press Backspace to remove the character to its left, or Delete to remove the character to its right.

Working with Ranges

A range is one or more cells that are selected at the same time. A range can be a single contiguous rectangular block or multiple cells or groups of cells from different locations, including on different worksheets.

range A logical grouping of one or more cells that function as a single unit while selected.

Describing a Range

When a range is a contiguous rectangular block, its name is written with the upper-left cell address, a colon, and the lower-right cell address, like this: B2:C8. When a range contains non-contiguous cells or blocks, the pieces are separated by commas, like this: B2:C8,E2:E8. Figure 10.4 shows that non-contiguous range. Notice that even though multiple cells are selected, there is still only one active cell: E2. If you type something with this range selected, the typed text will appear in E2.

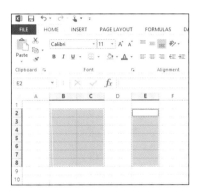

Figure 10.4   A non-contiguous selected range: B2:C8,E2:E8.

When an entire row or column is included, the row number or column letter appears twice, separated by a colon, like this: 10:10 or B:B. When multiple entire rows or columns are selected, the range is the row numbers or column letters, like this: 10:12 or B:D.

Selecting a Range

To select an entire row, click its row number. To select an entire column, click its column letter. You can select multiple rows or multiple columns by dragging across the row numbers or column letters.

You can drag across a contiguous range to select it. To select a non-contiguous range with the mouse, hold down the Ctrl key as you drag across the blocks of cells to select and click the individual cells to select. Release the Ctrl key when you are done choosing cells to include.

You can also use keyboard shortcuts to select a range, as shown in Table 10.2.

Table 10.2: Selecting a Range with the Keyboard

Press This . . .	To Extend the Selection to . . .
Ctrl+A	The entire worksheet
Ctrl+spacebar	The entire column of the active cell
Shift+spacebar	The entire row of the active cell
Ctrl+Shift+arrow key	The last nonblank cell in the same column or row as the active cell, or if the next cell is blank, to the next nonblank cell
Ctrl+Shift+End	The last non-empty cell on the worksheet (lower-right corner)
Ctrl+Shift+Home	Cell A1
Ctrl+Shift+Page Down	The current and next sheets in the workbook
Ctrl+Shift+Page Up	The current and preceding sheets in the workbook

Filling in Content in Multiple Cells

fill handle The small dark green rectangle in the lower-right corner of the cell selector, used to extend the selection to other cells by dragging.

AutoFill The feature that enables content to be filled into adjacent cells by dragging the fill handle from the active cell.

If you need to fill in the same value in multiple adjacent cells, you can use the fill handle to do so. The fill handle is the small dark green square in the lower-right corner of the cell selector. Drag it in any direction from the active cell to fill the same entry into the adjacent cells, as shown in Figure 10.5. This feature is called AutoFill.

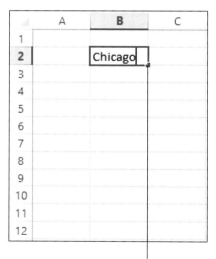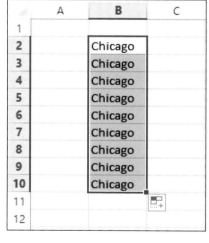

Fill handle

Figure 10.5   Drag the fill handle (left) to extend the selection to adjacent cells (right).

You can also AutoFill a series, such as days of the week, months of the year, or any sequence of numbers. To do so, enter data in the first two cells of the series, establishing the pattern you want. For example, to fill days of the month, you might type **Monday** and **Tuesday** in the two cells. To fill a numeric series, type the first two numbers in the series.

For example, to count by 10 starting with 2015, type 2015 and 2025. Then select both cells and drag the fill handle to continue the series. See Figure 10.6.

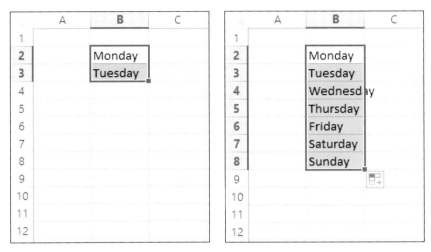

Figure 10.6   AutoFill a series by entering and selecting the first two values before dragging the fill handle.

Create Your Own Series

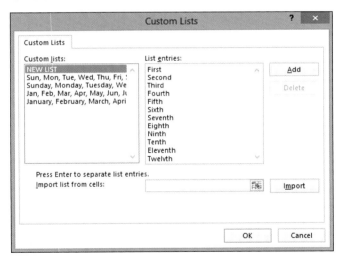

To create new series for Excel to AutoFill, choose File⇨Options, click Advanced, and then scroll down to the bottom of the dialog box and click Edit Custom Lists. From here, you can create your own custom lists that Excel will use to AutoFill. Click NEW LIST and then type the list entries in the List Entries pane, as shown here. Click Add to add the series and then click OK to close the dialog box.

Quick Review

1. Give an example of a valid non-contiguous range.

2. What is the purpose of the fill handle, and where is it located?

3. What key do you hold down as you press arrow keys on the keyboard to extend the selection?

Changing the Structure of a Worksheet

As you input your worksheet's content, changing the structure of a worksheet is easy. You can add and delete columns, rows, and even individual cells, merge multiple cells into one big cell, and move and copy data from one range to another.

Inserting and Deleting Rows and Columns

As you build a worksheet's content, you might realize that you need more or fewer rows or columns between some existing ones. It's easy to insert and delete rows and columns; the others shift over to make room (if adding) or to close up the space (if deleting).

Deleting is different from erasing/clearing. The Delete key on the keyboard clears the contents of the rows or columns you select, but it does not remove them. To remove the rows or columns entirely, use the Delete command on the Home tab or on the context menu that appears when you right-click the selected row or column.

Step by Step

Inserting Rows or Columns

Use these steps to insert one or more rows or columns:

1. Select the row that the new row should appear above or the column that the new column should appear to the left of.

   If you want to insert multiple rows or columns, select multiple rows or columns. For example, to insert three rows above row 10, you would select rows 10, 11, and 12.

2. On the Home tab, click Insert.

Deleting Rows or Columns

Use these steps to delete one or more rows or columns.

1. Select the row(s) or column(s) to delete.

2. On the Home tab, click Delete.

   OR

   Right-click the selected range and choose Delete from the context menu.

Inserting and Deleting Cells

Inserting individual cells can be a layout challenge because the existing cells have to go somewhere to make room for them. When inserting cells, you specify whether the existing cells should shift down or to the right.

Similarly, deleting individual cells can be challenging because their deletion leaves a "hole" in the spreadsheet that the surrounding cells must fill by shifting their positions either up or to the left.

Inserting Cells

Use these steps to insert one or more cells:

1. Select a range where you want the new cells to be inserted. It doesn't matter if that range already contains data.

2. On the Home tab, click the down arrow adjacent to the Insert button and click Insert Cells. The Insert dialog box opens.

3. Click the option button to describe what should happen to the cells in the selected range.

4. Click OK.

Deleting Cells

Use these steps to delete one or more cells:

1. Select a range of cells that you want to delete.

2. On the Home tab, click the down arrow to the right of the Delete button. The Delete dialog box opens.

3. Click the option button to describe what surrounding cells should shift to fill in the vacated space.

4. Click OK.

Preventing Others from Changing the Worksheet Structure

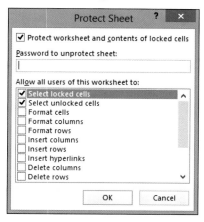

Once you get the worksheet the way you want it structurally, you can prevent others from changing it. On the Review tab, click Protect Sheet. Then in the Protect Sheet dialog box, make sure that the check boxes are cleared for Insert Columns, Insert Rows, Delete Columns, and Delete Rows. If you want to include a password, do so by typing it in the Password to Unprotect Sheet text box. Then click OK.

Privacy and Security

Merging and Unmerging Cells

The orderly grid format of a worksheet means that you have the same number of rows in each column, and the same number of columns in each row—usually. For special layout effects, you can merge two or more cells into a single cell that occupies the same space as the two would have taken up separately. Merging is often done to center a title or heading across the top of a set of columns, as in Figure 10.7.

merge To combine two or more cells into a single cell.

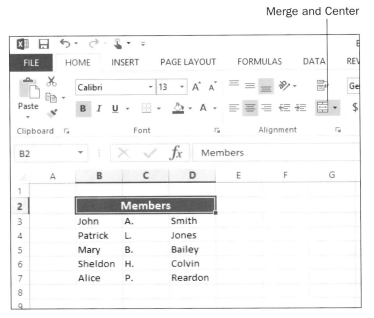

Merge and Center

Figure 10.7 You can merge and center a title over multiple columns.

Step by Step

Merging Cells

Use these steps to merge contiguous cells:

1. Select the cells to merge. Keep in mind that only the text in the upper-left cell will remain after the merge; its text will appear as the text in the merged cell, and its name will appear in the Name box when the merged cell is selected.

2. On the Home tab, click the Merge and Center button.

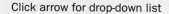
Click arrow for drop-down list

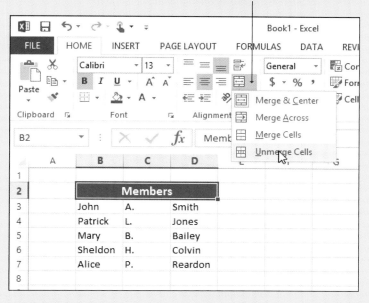

Unmerging Cells

Use these steps to unmerge a merged cell:

1. Select the merged cell.

2. On the Home tab, click the down arrow to the right of the Merge & Center button.

3. On the menu that appears, click Unmerge Cells. Note that any text that was deleted as a result of the merge will not return when the cell is unmerged.

Moving and Copying Cells and Ranges

To move or copy a cell, or a range of cells, first select the cell(s) to be copied. From there you can use the Office Clipboard, as you learned in Chapter 8, or you can use drag-and-drop. To drag and drop content, position the mouse pointer on the border of the selection so the pointer turns into a four-headed arrow, as shown in Figure 10.8. Then drag to a new location to move, or hold down the Ctrl key and drag to a new location to copy. (If you hold down the Ctrl key, the mouse pointer changes to an arrow with a + (plus) sign on it, indicating you are copying rather than moving.)

When you move or copy cells that contain references to other cells, the references can be either relative or absolute. See "Understanding Absolute References" later in this chapter for information about that.

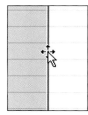

Figure 10.8
Position the mouse pointer over the border of the selection and then drag to move the selection.

Quick Review

1. What happens to the surrounding cells when you delete an individual cell?

2. How can you copy a range using drag-and-drop?

3. How can you insert multiple rows at a time?

Formatting Cells

Formatting the cells in a worksheet can make it much easier for people to read and understand. For example, you could make certain data labels stand out by applying background shading to them or making their font bold and italic. Formatting can also include making columns and rows different sizes to accommodate their contents better, and applying number formats that can, for example, distinguish currency amounts from percentages, or dates and times from quantities. In the following sections, you will learn some ways to format cells.

Resizing Rows and Columns

Sometimes a cell is too narrow to hold its contents. When this situation occurs, Excel handles it in different ways:

- If the cell contains a numeric value and no number format has been applied to the cell, Excel displays the number in scientific format, which represents the number in a more compact format. For example, it would change the number 223456898 to 2E+08. The actual number still exists in the cell and will be used in any calculations that refer to this cell.

- If the cell contains a numeric value and a specific number format has been assigned to the cell (besides General, the default), a series of # symbols fill the cell instead of the number itself, like this: #####.

- If the cell contains text and the cell to the right is empty, the text display overflows into the next cell's space.

- If the cell contains text and the cell to the right is not empty, the text appears truncated.

You can widen the column to make the entry appear normally again. There are several methods of changing a column's width. You can **AutoFit** a column width (resizing the column's width to accommodate the widest entry in it) or make the column a certain size that you specify. You can do the same thing with row heights.

AutoFit Automatically resizing a column width or row height to fit the largest entry.

When you specify an exact column width, the number you use refers to the number of characters that will fit in the cell using the default font and font size. For example, the default column width in a blank worksheet is 8.43 characters, and the default font is Calibri 11 point. If you use a different font or size in that column, the numbers will not match the actual number of characters that fit in each cell.

point The measurement used to describe font height; one point equals $\frac{1}{72}$ of an inch.

When you specify an exact row height, the number you use is the number of points of font height. A *point* is $\frac{1}{72}$ of an inch. The default font size is 11 point. A row will automatically expand its height to accommodate the largest text in it, so you normally do not have to worry about adjusting row height. However, if you have previously specified or adjusted the row height for a row and then you change the font sizes used in that row, the row will no longer auto-adjust, and you will have to adjust the row height manually.

When specifying an exact row height, add about 30% to the size of the largest font used in that row so the letters will not be tight up against the top of the cell. For example, for an 11-point font, use 15 as the row height, and for a 16-point font, use 21 as the row height. That's what Excel does when it automatically resizes row heights.

Step by Step

AutoFitting Column Width or Row Height

Use these steps to adjust a column's width or a row's height to fit the largest content in it:

1. Position the mouse pointer between two row letters or between two column numbers. The column to the left or the row above will be the one adjusted.

2. Double-click. The column width or row height is adjusted.

OR

1. Select the rows or columns you want to AutoFit.

2. On the Home tab, click Format and then click AutoFit Column Width or AutoFit Row Height.

Setting an Exact Column Width or Row Height

Use these steps to set the column width or row height to an exact amount:

1. Select the rows or columns you want to affect.

2. On the Home tab, click Format and then click Column Width, or click Row Height. A dialog box opens.

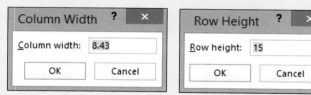

3. Enter the desired column width (in characters) or row height (in points).

4. Click OK.

Setting Horizontal and Vertical Alignment

By default, text is left-aligned in a cell and numbers are right-aligned. There's a good reason for this custom: Text is read from left-to-right (at least in English and most European languages), and the eye is accustomed to each line starting at the left margin. Numbers, however, are generally lined up on the right, so that numbers with different numbers of digits can be more easily compared. Figure 10.9 shows some text and numbers in cells with the default alignments.

City	Sales
New York	$2,500
Chicago	$52,000
Toronto	$115,000
Mexico City	$1,230,500
London	$7,000
Paris	$16,500,000

Figure 10.9 Text aligns to the left by default, and numbers align to the right.

You might sometimes want to change these defaults. For example, you might want a text label to right-align so that it is closer to the number it is labeling, or you might want the column headings to be centered over each column.

By default, each cell has a bottom vertical alignment, but most people don't notice it because Excel automatically sizes row height to fit the text. Therefore, you won't notice the vertical alignment unless the text in the cell is smaller than text in some other cell in that row, or unless the row's height has been manually changed.

To change a cell's horizontal or vertical alignment, select the cell(s) and then use the buttons in the Alignment group on the Home tab, as shown in Figure 10.10.

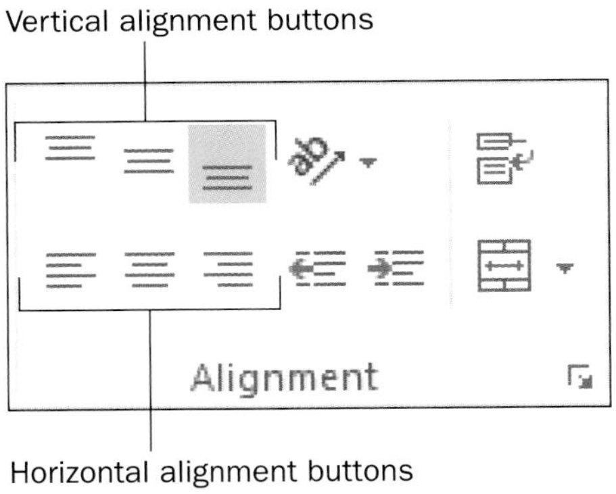

Vertical alignment buttons

Horizontal alignment buttons

Figure 10.10 Buttons for controlling alignment in cells.

Specifying a Number Format

Number formats specify how a number will be represented in the cell. In the Number group on the Home tab are buttons for the three most common number formats: Accounting, Percent, and Comma.

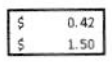

Accounting Style: Uses a currency symbol appropriate for the country set up in the Windows Region and Language settings (see Appendix A, "Customizing Windows 8.1"). It aligns the currency symbol with the left margin of the cell, and aligns the rest of the number with the right margin. It uses two decimal places, even if the original number had none, and shows negative numbers in parentheses. It uses commas as separators between each three digits to the left of the decimal point.

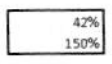

Percent Style: Uses a percent symbol to the right of the number. Because a percentage is, by definition, 1/100th of a whole value, the decimal point in the number is moved two places to the right, so 0.42 becomes 42%. This format does not show any digits after the decimal point, so 0.3% (.003) would appear as 0%.

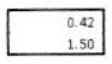

Comma Style: This format is identical to the Accounting format except it does not have a currency symbol.

You can select other number formats from the drop-down list in the Number group, or click the dialog box launcher in the Number group to open the Format Cells dialog box to the Number tab, and fine-tune number formatting from there. Many of the number formats can be customized, including changing the number of decimal places displayed and changing the way negative numbers are represented. For example, the options shown in Figure 10.11 are available for the Number format (yes, there is a format named Number), which is for general numbers that do not fall into one of the other categories.

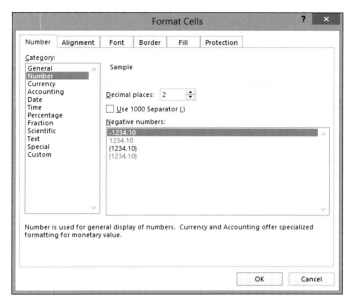

Figure 10.11   Choose a number format on the Category list and then fine-tune it on the right.

The difference between the Accounting and Currency formats is that Accounting left-aligns the currency symbol and Currency right-aligns it.

NOTE

Step by Step

Modifying a Number Format

Use these steps to select and then modify a cell's number format:

1. Select the cell(s) to affect.

2. On the Home tab, open the Number Format drop-down list (in the Number group) and select a format, or click the Accounting, Percent Style, or Comma Style button.

Number Format
drop-down list   Decrease indent

Comma style

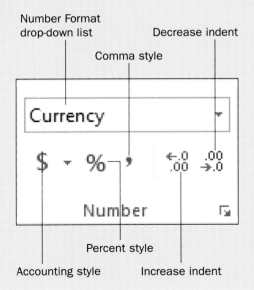

Accounting style   Increase indent

Percent style

3. If you want to change the number of decimal places, click the Increase Decimal or Decrease Decimal button in the Number group.

4. (Optional) If you want to make other changes to the number format, click the dialog box launcher in the Number group to open the Format Cells dialog box (see Figure 10.11).

5. Make any additional number formatting selections as needed.

6. Click OK.

In addition to normal number formats, Excel also supports Date and Time number formats. Excel stores dates as numbers. January 1, 1900, is represented by 1, and each day since then is incremented by one whole number. January 1, 1901 is 367, for example (366 because it's a leap year, and then one more because it's the day after 1900 ended). January 1, 2014, is 41640, for example (365 x 114 years, plus 29 for the extra days in the leap years, plus 1 because it's the new year).

Times are represented by numbers that follow the decimal point in the number. For example, 41640.5 is 12:00 noon (half of the day) on January 1, 2014, and 41640.75 is 6:00 p.m. (three-fourths of the day) on that date.

Applying Cell Borders and Shading

gridlines The lines around each cell, which may be visible or not depending on settings.

Gridlines are the lines around each cell. They are always there, but they don't always show. On the Page Layout tab, mark or clear the View and/ or Print check boxes in the Sheet Options group under the Gridlines heading to control whether gridlines appear onscreen and/or on print-outs. See Figure 10.12.

View gridlines onscreen

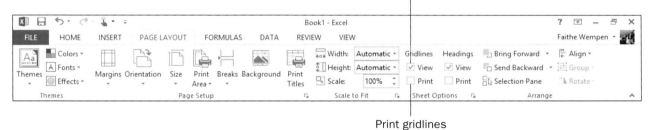

Print gridlines

Figure 10.12   You can choose whether or not gridlines display onscreen and print.

borders Decorative lines used to enhance the appearance of a worksheet by outlining certain cells.

You can optionally set up borders for one or more sides of certain cells. Borders are decorative lines used to enhance the appearance of the worksheet and make its meaning clearer. Borders can be different colors and widths, and can be solid, dotted, or dashed lines. A cell can have different borders on different sides. Figure 10.13 shows some data in which borders have been used to make the data easier to interpret.

To apply a border preset, select the cells to affect, and then open the Borders button's drop-down list on the Home tab (in the Font group) and select a border pre-set, as shown in Figure 10.14. Note that your choice will apply to the range as a whole, not to each individual cell. So, for example, if you choose to apply a bottom border, only the bottom of the bottommost row in the range will receive the border. From this same menu you can also choose a line color and a line style (such as dashed or double). If you want to make one of those choices, do it first, before selecting the preset from the top portion of the list.

City	Sales
New York	$2,500
Chicago	$52,000
Toronto	$115,000
Mexico City	$1,230,500
London	$7,000
Paris	$16,500,000
Total	$17,907,000

Figure 10.13 Apply borders to make a worksheet more attractive and easier to understand.

If you want to fine-tune the borders even further, choose More Borders from the bottom of the list, opening the Border tab of the Format Cells dialog box. See the following Step by Step procedure to learn how to use this dialog box.

Border button

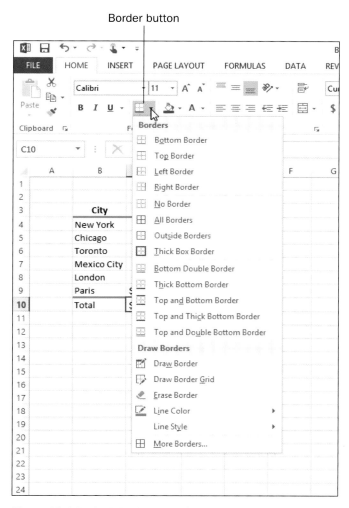

Figure 10.14 Apply border presets from the Border button's drop-down list.

Step by Step

Customizing Cell Borders

Use these steps to apply custom borders to a range of cells:

1. Select the cell(s) to affect.

2. On the Home tab, open the Borders drop-down list from the Font group and choose More Borders. The Format Cells dialog box opens with the Border tab displayed.

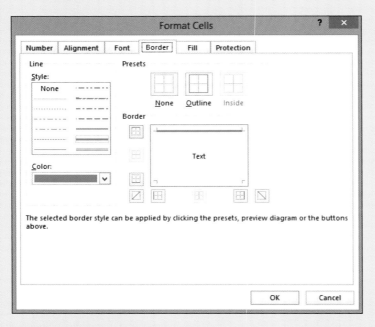

3. Select a style from the Style section.

4. Open the Color drop-down list and select a color.

5. In the Presets area, click one of the presets (None, Outline, or Inside) if desired.

6. In the Border area, click one or more of the buttons representing a certain side of the range.

7. Click OK to apply the border.

fill A background color, such as in a cell or graphic object.

You can also apply a fill to certain cells to help them stand out from others. A fill is a background color. You can select a fill from the Fill Color button's palette on the Home tab (Font group). The color palette works just like the color palettes you learned about in Chapter 8; select a theme color or a standard color. See Figure 10.15.

TIP If you apply a fill color from the Fill tab of the Format Cells dialog box, you have the option of selecting a gradient or pattern fill. Use the dialog box launcher in the Font group to open that dialog box and then click the Fill tab.

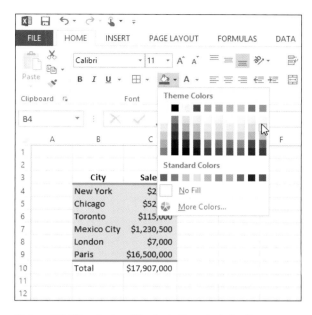

Figure 10.15   Apply a fill color to the selected cells.

Formatting Cell Text

Cell text can be formatted just like text in any other Office application; you learned about text formatting in Chapter 8. Recall that the Home tab contains tools for applying text formatting in its Font group; Figure 10.16 labels these controls for your reference. You can choose different fonts, sizes, and colors here. You can also click the dialog box launcher for the Font group to open the Font tab of the Format Cells dialog box.

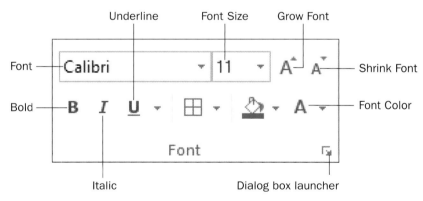

Figure 10.16   Use text formatting tools on the Home tab to format the text in cells.

Quick Review

1. What is the difference between gridlines and a border?

2. What is the difference between Accounting and Currency number formats?

3. How do you AutoFit a column's width to its content?

formula A math calculation to be performed in an Excel cell. It may refer to other cells for its values.

Entering Formulas and Functions

A formula is a math calculation to be performed, like =2+2. In Excel, formulas provide the instructions to perform calculations. A formula begins with an equals sign (=), which signals to Excel that what follows it is an instruction, not a literal entry.

A formula can contain both numbers and cell addresses. For example, the formula =A6+10 adds 10 to whatever value it finds in cell A6. The formula =A2*B2 multiplies the value in A2 by the value in B2.

order of operations The order in which math operators in a formula are calculated: exponentiation, and then multiplication/division, and then addition/subtraction.

Understanding Order of Operations

Formulas use math operators to express what needs to be done, and these math operators have an order of operations, just like in regular math. Exponentiation is done first (represented by the ^ symbol), followed by multiplication and division (* and / respectively), and then finally addition and subtraction (+ and –).

NOTE Exponentiation is the process of taking one number to the power of another. For example, =3^2 is the same as 3 to the 2nd power (3 x 3), which is 9. =3^3 is three to the third power (3 x 3 x 3), which is 27.

If you want a formula to calculate in some other order than the default, use parentheses to indicate what should be done first. For example, the formula =1+2*3 would normally produce a result of 7 because you would first multiply 2*3 and then add 1 to it. However, the formula =(1+2)*3 would produce a result of 9 because 1+2 would first be added, and then the result of 3 would be multiplied by 3. Figure 10.17 provides a few additional examples to review.

Order of Operations Rules

Rule	Example	Steps	Result
Exponentiation comes first	=4*2^3	2^3=8 4*8=32	32
Multiplication and division occur before addition and subtraction	=4*2+3/3	4*2=8 3/3=1 8+1=9	9
Parentheses override all other rules, and inner parentheses are executed before outer ones	=2^(2*(3+1)/2)	3+1=4 2*4=8 8/2=4 2^4=16	16

Figure 10.17 Review these order of operations rules for creating formulas in Excel.

Understanding Functions

A function is a named math operation, such as AVERAGE, SUM, or COUNT. Functions are traditionally written in all uppercase, but are not case sensitive. A function name is followed by a set of parentheses, and within the parentheses are arguments. An argument is a variable that tells the function what data to act upon and in what way. Most functions have one or more required arguments, along with one or more optional ones. For example, the SUM function has one required argument: the range of data that you want to sum, like this: =SUM(C1:C10). You can optionally specify other data ranges to include by adding more arguments, separating each one with a comma. For example, you could add the range F1:F10 to the previous example like this: =SUM(C1:C10,F1:F10).

In functions, you can refer to ranges of cells, like C1:C5. You can't do that in formulas that are not functions. For example, to sum the range C1:C5, if you use the SUM function you can structure it like this: =SUM(C1:C5). However, if you do the same with a regular formula using math operators, you must write out each individual cell, like this: =C1+C2+C3+C4+C5.

NOTE

Some functions' complicated arguments have to be listed in a certain order, and it can be difficult to remember which arguments you need. Excel offers several ways of helping you remember. The simplest is the ScreenTip. When you start typing a function into a cell, a ScreenTip appears prompting you for its arguments, as shown in Figure 10.18.

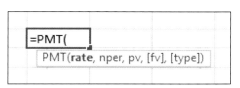

Figure 10.18   A ScreenTip appears to help with a function's arguments.

If you need more help than that, such as needing to know what those abbreviations stand for in the ScreenTip, you can use the Insert Function feature, as described in the following Step by Step.

Step by Step

Entering a Function

Follow these steps to use Insert Function to create a function:

1. Click the cell into which you want to enter the function. (Select only one cell.)

2. On the formula bar, click the Insert Function icon. The Insert Function dialog box opens.

Insert Function

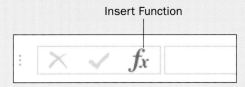

3. If you know the name of the function you want, select it from the Select a Function list, or select a category and then select the function. If you don't know, type a description of what you want to do, and then click a function in the results to read about its purpose below the list. For example, in the following screen I am looking for a function that will calculate an interest rate, and RATE is one of the functions that Excel recommends.

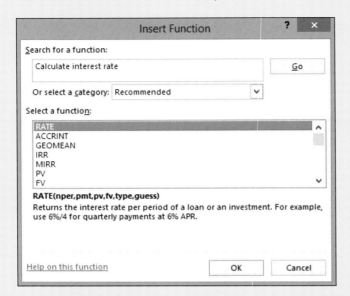

4. Click OK. The Function Arguments dialog box opens.

5. In each argument box, either fill in a number or a cell reference. The arguments with boldface names are required, and the others are optional.

   To find out the meaning of a particular argument, click in its text box and read the description that appears. For example, in the following figure, information about the Pv argument appears.

   If you need to check the worksheet to see what cell to reference, you can either drag the dialog box to the side or click one of the Collapse Dialog buttons to temporarily shrink the dialog box so you can select the desired cell.

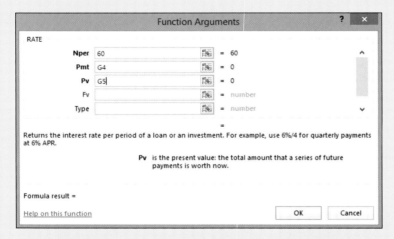

6. When you have finished filling in all the arguments, click OK to complete the function. It is entered into the cell.

Fixing Errors in Formulas and Functions

Here are some of the most common errors in worksheet formulas and functions:

- **Circular reference:** Occurs when a cell refers to itself, such as =A2+1 being in cell A2.

- **#VALUE error:** Occurs when a formula can't calculate a valid result.

- **#NAME error:** Occurs when the formula references a named range or cell address that is invalid.

You can use the Error Check feature to find and correct these types of errors and more. On the Formulas tab, click Error Checking in the Formula Auditing group, and then work your way through the errors it finds, correcting each one.

```
Error Checking                                    ?   [x]

Error in cell D10
   =SUM(D4:D8)                        [ Update Formula to Include Cells ]
Formula Omits Adjacent Cells               [     Help on this error     ]
The formula in this cell refers to a range that
has additional numbers adjacent to it.     [       Ignore Error         ]

                                           [    Edit in Formula Bar      ]

[ Options... ]                         [ Previous ]      [ Next ]
```

Understanding Absolute References

When you move or copy cells that contain references to other cells, such as a formula that references another cell, those references are relative. Excel will change the cell references to match the relative positioning in the new location. An example will make this clearer. Suppose, as shown in Figure 10.19, you have a function in cell C7 that adds up the amounts in cells C3 through C6. The function looks like this: =SUM(C3:C6).

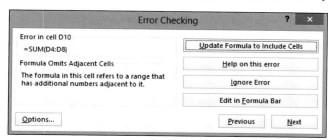

C7	▼	⋮	✕ ✓ *fx*	=SUM(C3:C6)		
	A	B	**C**	D	E	F
1						
2			North	South		
3		Q1	25	28		
4		Q2	24	21		
5		Q3	13	25		
6		Q4	15	19		
7		Total	77	93		
8						

Figure 10.19   The formula in cell C7 is going to be copied to D7.

Now suppose that you click the Copy button on the Ribbon, click cell D7, and click the Paste button on the Ribbon. The formula is copied to D7. However, the copied version appears like this: =SUM(D3:D6). Excel has assumed that the references to the cells in column C in the original formula were context-sensitive. It assumed that what you really wanted was to sum the values in the four cells immediately above D7, rather than to sum the cells in column C. And, in this case, it is right. That's called a relative reference.

relative reference In a formula or function, a reference to another cell that changes if that formula or function is moved or copied to another cell.

absolute reference In a formula or function, a reference to another cell that does not change if that formula or function is moved or copied to another cell.

The alternative to a relative reference is an absolute reference, which never changes no matter where you copy it. For example, in Figure 10.20, cell D4 contains a formula that multiplies the base amount in C5 by the bonus percentage in C2. When that formula is copied into D6:D8, you want the copies to update the references to the base amounts, but you don't want the reference to the bonus amount to change. Therefore, you make the reference to C2 an absolute reference by placing dollar signs before the column letter and before the row number, like this: C2. An absolute reference does not change, no matter where you copy it.

D5		:	$\times$	$\checkmark$	$f\!x$	=C5*C2

	A	B	C	D	E
1					
2		**Bonus Amount**	2%		
3					
4		**Salesperson**	**Base**	**Bonus**	
5		Smith	$45,000	$900	
6		Jones	$32,000		
7		Frederickson	$15,000		
8		Clark	$41,000		
9					
10					

Figure 10.20 The formula in D5 will be copied to D6, D7, and D8. When copied, the reference to the base amount will change for each copy (C6, C7, and C8, respectively), but the reference to C2 will not change because it is marked as an absolute reference by the dollar signs.

mixed reference A reference that is partly absolute and partly relative. For example, the row number may be relative and the column letter may be absolute.

A mixed reference is a reference that is partially absolute and partially relative. For example, $C2 makes the column absolute but keeps the row number relative, and C$2 does the opposite.

TIP You can press F4 to toggle among the reference types (absolute, mixed, and relative) for a selected reference.

Quick Review

1. In the formula =1+2*3^2, what will be the result? How would the result change if you add parentheses like this: 1=(2*3)^2?

2. How does an absolute reference change when it is copied or moved?

3. In the function =AVERAGE(A2:A6), what is the argument?

Creating Charts

A chart can help show the meaning of data in a graphical way. For example, suppose you were presented with the data shown in Figure 10.21. This data represents the sales quantities for several products, but it is difficult to gain any useful summary information by browsing it. When some of this data is presented in charts, as in Figure 10.22, you can immediately discern some useful facts.

chart A graphic that illustrates and summarizes worksheet data. Examples include pie chart, line chart, and bar chart.

	A	B	C	D	E	F
1	Product	Units Sold	Price	Wholesale	Per Item Profit	Total Profit
2	Bath towel	120	$18	$10	$8	$960
3	Hand towel	75	$8	$4	$4	$300
4	Shower caddy	24	$19	$12	$7	$168
5	Soap dish	125	$5	$2	$3	$375
6	Soap dispenser	100	$8	$3	$5	$500
7	Washcloth	50	$4	$2	$2	$100

Figure 10.21   This raw data is so detailed that the overall meaning is not obvious.

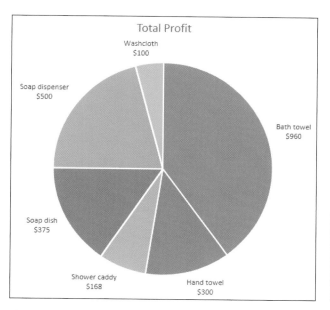
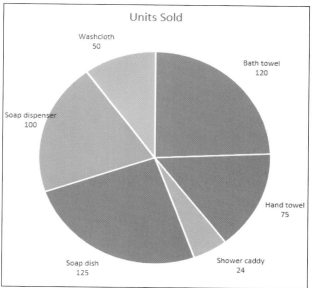

Figure 10.22   When the data from Figure 10.21 is charted, more meaningful information becomes clear. Each chart extracts a different meaning from the data.

Types of Charts and Their Uses

Excel can create many types of charts. The pie charts in Figure 10.22, for example, are useful for showing the relationship of parts to a whole. In each case in Figure 10.22, the whole represents the total sales (one chart showing the profit earned and one chart showing the units sold), and the pie slices are proportionally sized to represent each item's contribution toward that whole.

pie chart A chart that represents the data as slices of a pie, or parts of a whole.

data series The data representing one row or column in the data used to create the chart.

column chart A chart that uses vertical bars to represent values.

bar chart A chart that uses horizontal bars to represent values.

A pie chart is a single-series chart; it plots only one data series and its associated labels. The series in the first pie chart in Figure 10.22 is total profit per item, and the series in the second pie chart in Figure 10.22 is units sold per item. Other chart types plot multiple series at once. For example, the column chart in Figure 10.23 shows sales quantities for three different periods, inviting the reader to compare each item's performance in one month against the other months. Charts can be two-dimensional, like the ones in Figure 10.22, or three-dimensional, like the chart in Figure 10.23. When a chart's bars run horizontally instead of vertically, it is called a bar chart. Variants of both bar and column charts are available with cylindrical or pyramid-shaped bars.

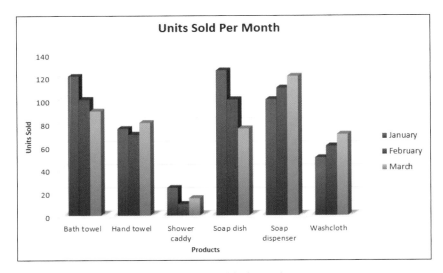

Figure 10.23   A column chart can plot multiple data series.

scatter chart A chart that plots data in patterns of dots scattered on the plot area. Scatter charts are useful for showing the results of experiments or studies where the results may not be repeatable or absolute.

trend line The straight line that runs through the data, showing the overall trend that the data represents.

legend The key that tells what each color or pattern represents.

data label A label telling the exact value of a particular data point.

A scatter chart can be useful in seeing a pattern in data, especially data from an experiment that is not absolute or repeatable. In Figure 10.24, for example, the charted data indicates that there is a relationship between bird sightings and the average daily temperature. The straight line that runs through the data is a trend line; it shows the overall trend that the data represents.

The key that tells what each color or pattern represents (as in Figure 10.23) is called a legend. Any chart can have a legend, but some charts don't need one. For example, the pie charts in Figure 10.22 don't need legends because the information the legend would provide is already in the data label for each slice. The scatter chart shown in Figure 10.24 doesn't need a legend because there is only one data series.

You can create a chart by selecting the data for it and then choosing a chart type from the Charts group on the Insert tab. A newly created chart appears as a floating object on the active sheet, in its own frame. You can drag it around, resize it, or move it to its own Sheet tab.

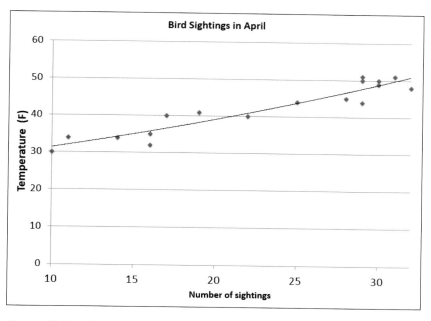

Figure 10.24   A scatter chart helps find trends or patterns in data.

TIP

Placing a chart on its own Sheet tab is a good way of making a complex chart large enough to see clearly without obscuring any worksheet cells. It is also useful to place a chart on its own sheet if you want to be able to print the chart separately from the data it represents.

Stock Charts

A stock chart is a special chart type used to show stock prices. Depending on the sub-type, it contains different information. An Open-High-Low-Close chart, for example, shows four values for each date: the stock's opening value, high value, low value, and closing value. You must structure the data in that order in the worksheet before selecting the range and making the chart. Another sub-type is High-Low-Close, which contains only three values per date. Yet another is Volume-Open-High-Low-Close, which has five values per date.

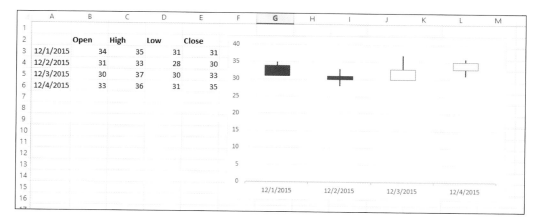

Put It to Work

The most important thing when creating stock charts is to make sure the data appears in the specified order.

Creating a Chart

Use these steps to create a chart from data in a worksheet range:

1. Select the data you want to plot. Include any row or column labels that you want to be part of the chart.

2. On the Insert tab, click one of the chart type buttons in the Charts group.

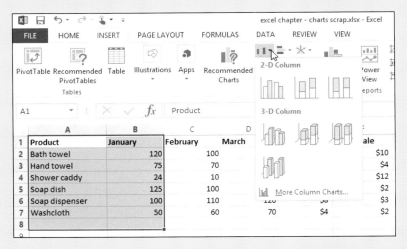

3. On the menu that appears, click the desired sub-type. The chart appears in a floating frame over the active sheet.

Resizing a Chart

Use these steps to resize a chart:

1. Position the mouse pointer on a selection handle on the border of the chart frame, so the pointer becomes a double-headed arrow. The selection handles on a chart frame are located in the corners and in the center of each side.

2. Drag the border to resize the chart's frame.

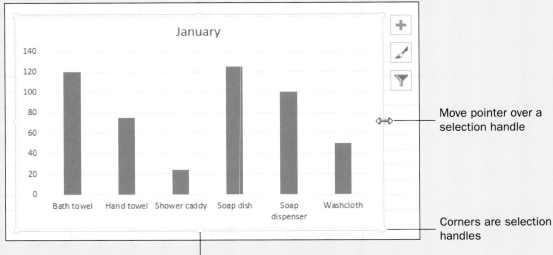

Move pointer over a selection handle

Corners are selection handles

The center of each side is a selection handle

Moving a Chart

Use these steps to move a chart:

1. Position the mouse pointer over the border of the chart, but not over a selection handle, so that it changes to a four-headed arrow.

2. Drag the border to move the chart.

Moving a Chart to a Separate Sheet

Use these steps to move a chart to a separate sheet:

1. Right-click the chart's frame, and choose Move Chart on the menu that appears.

2. In the Move Chart dialog box, click New Sheet.

3. Type a name for the new sheet, replacing the default name.

4. Click OK.

Adding and Removing Chart Elements

Each chart consists of a number of elements, and each element can be selected and formatted separately. Figure 10.25 points out a number of chart elements that you should be able to identify and select on a chart.

The totality of a chart (all its elements) is referred to as the chart area. When you apply certain formatting to the chart area, the entire chart is affected. The portion of the chart where the actual data is plotted is known as the plot area. Within the plot area are the data points, which are the individual pieces of data, represented by bars, lines, dots, or whatever marker the chosen chart type uses. Data points may be divided into multiple data series. A data series is all the data points of a certain type, such as all the bars of one color on a bar chart.

chart area The entire chart.

plot area The part of the chart on which the data is plotted.

data point A single point of plotted data.

data series The data representing one row or column in the data used to create the chart.

The large text at the top of the chart is the chart title. The numbers along the vertical axis are the vertical axis labels, and the product names along the horizontal axis are the horizontal axis labels. The explanatory labels along each axis (*Units Sold* and *Products* in Figure 10.25) are the vertical axis title and horizontal axis title. Depending on the chart, they might or might not be helpful. In Figure 10.25, they are mostly superfluous because the chart's title and horizontal axis labels make the axes' purposes clear. A data table shows the data on which the chart was based. Data tables are useful if you are going to distribute the chart separately from the worksheet on which the data appears.

chart title The overall label for the chart, usually at the top of the chart area.

axis labels The text on the axes of the chart that shows the values.

axis titles The text on the axes of the chart that shows the meaning of the axis labels.

data table An optional table that appears below the chart showing the values on which it is based.

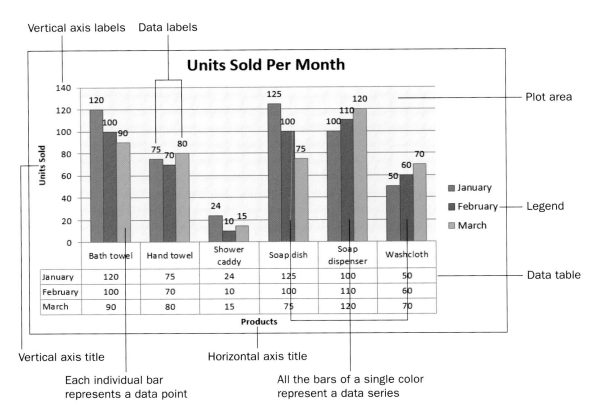

Vertical axis labels   Data labels

Units Sold Per Month

Plot area

Legend

Data table

Units Sold

Products

	Bath towel	Hand towel	Shower caddy	Soap dish	Soap dispenser	Washcloth
January	120	75	24	125	100	50
February	100	70	10	100	110	60
March	90	80	15	75	120	70

Vertical axis title

Horizontal axis title

Each individual bar represents a data point

All the bars of a single color represent a data series

Figure 10.25   Parts of a typical chart.

Each of these elements can be enabled or disabled from the Chart Tools Design tab by clicking Add Chart Element, as shown in Figure 10.26. This button has a complex submenu system with separate submenus for enabling and configuring each element. For example, in Figure 10.26, you can see the choices for data labels. To turn off an element, you can choose None from its menu, or you can select the element on the chart and then press the Delete key on the keyboard. Each of the elements has a More command at the bottom of the submenu. You can choose it to open a task pane for that element with more controls in it.

TIP   Excel comes with several preset combinations of chart elements called Quick Layouts. You can choose a chart layout from the Chart Tools Design tab, in the Chart Layouts group.

New in Excel 2013, you can also click the Chart Elements button (the plus sign) to the right of the chart to access a menu system similar to the one provided by the Add Chart Element button. You can mark or clear the check box for each chart element, as shown in Figure 10.27, or you can point to an element and then click the right-pointing triangle that appears to open a submenu from which you can fine-tune the settings.

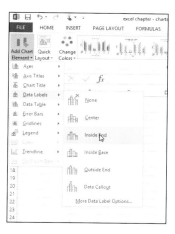

Figure 10.26 Configure the settings for chart elements from the Add Chart Element button on the Chart Tools Design tab.

Chart Elements button

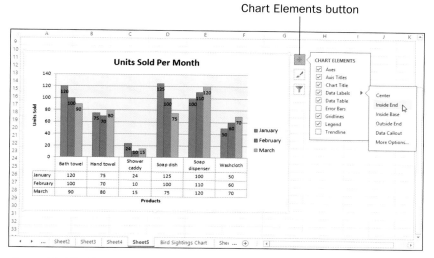

Figure 10.27 Use the Chart Elements button adjacent to the chart to turn elements on and off and configure them.

Step by Step

Adding and Positioning a Legend

Use these steps to add a legend to a chart and/or change its position:

1. Select the chart, and then on the Chart Tools Design tab, click Add Chart Element, and then click Legend. A submenu opens.

2. Choose one of the legend positions from the menu. An overlay legend is one that overlaps the plot area.

Adding and Configuring Data Labels

Use these steps to use data labels on a chart and to change what is shown on those labels:

1. Select the chart, and then on the Chart Tools Design tab, click Add Chart Element and then click Data Labels. A submenu appears.

2. Choose one of the presets on the menu, or choose More Data Label Options to open the Format Data Labels task pane. This task pane may look different from the one shown, depending on the chart type.

3. Click the Label Options icon (looks like three vertical bars), and if needed, click the Label Options heading to expand its options.

4. In the Label Contains section, mark or clear the check boxes to define what you want to appear on the labels.

5. In the Label Position section, select a position.

6. If you want the legend key in the label, mark the Legend Key check box. If you do this, you might not need to have a legend on your chart.

7. If you chose more than one item in Step 3, open the Separator drop-down list and choose the way the items will be separated.

8. Close the task pane.

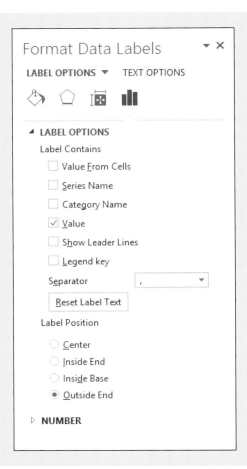

Changing the Chart Type

To change a chart's type, select the chart and then click the Change Chart Type button on the Chart Tools Design tab. In the Change Chart Type dialog box that appears, make your selection of one of the types from the list on the left and then choose a sub-type from the choices across the top. Finally, select one of the samples in the center. See Figure 10.28.

Switching the Plot Orientation

You can switch the chart between plotting by rows versus by columns in your data. For example, in the chart shown in Figure 10.25, you could switch the chart so that it shows the months along the horizontal axis and uses different colored bars for each item. To switch the plot orientation, select the chart and click the Switch Row/Column button on the Chart Tools Design tab.

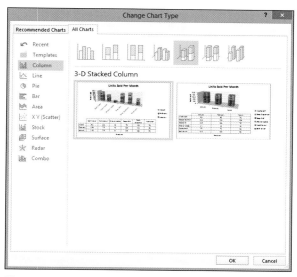

Figure 10.28   Change the chart type from the Change Chart Type dialog box, accessed from the Chart Tools Design tab.

Formatting a Chart

You can format each element of a chart individually, for precise control over its look. You can also format a chart using chart styles, which apply preset combinations of formatting to the entire chart at once.

To format individual chart elements, right-click the desired element and choose Format *element*, where *element* is the element name. For example, when you right-click the chart title, the command on the menu is Format Chart Title. An appropriate task pane opens for the selected element.

You don't have to close the Format task pane for the chart element in order to do other things in the worksheet or chart. Any changes you make to the settings in it are applied immediately; Excel doesn't wait for you to click an OK button as it does in a dialog box. Click a category on the left and then make your formatting selections on the right. The categories depend on the element chosen. Each task pane has multiple categories, and in some cases multiple levels of categories. For example, in Figure 10.29, in the Format Legend task pane, there are two main headings at the top: Legend Options and Text Options. After clicking one of those, several icons appear. Click an icon to select the next level of subcategory. Below the icons are one or more expandable headings with options below them.

chart style A set of formatting applied to a chart as a whole.

To format the entire chart at once, select a chart style from the Chart Tools Design tab in the Chart Styles group. Click one of the styles shown, or click the More button [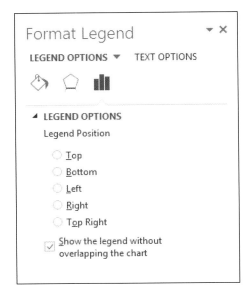] to open a gallery of styles, as shown in Figure 10.30.

Format Legend

LEGEND OPTIONS ▼   TEXT OPTIONS

◢ LEGEND OPTIONS
Legend Position

○ Top
○ Bottom
○ Left
○ Right
○ Top Right
☑ Show the legend without overlapping the chart

Figure 10.29   Use the Format task pane for a certain element to make changes to its formatting.

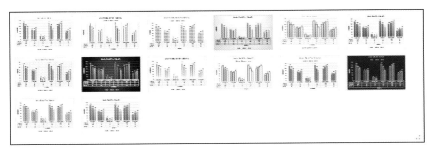

Figure 10.30   Select a chart style from the Chart Styles gallery, from the Chart Tools Design tab.

Quick Review

1. From which tab on the Ribbon do you insert a chart?

2. How do you change the chart type after creating it?

3. How do you change the formatting of a certain chart element?

Working with Data Tables

In addition to its calculation capabilities, Excel can also store structured data. Structured data is data that has a consistent pattern to it, with the same type of information in every row, as in a database. For example, in Figure 10.31, Excel is shown storing phone numbers.

Phone Contacts

	A	B	C
1	**Phone Contacts**		
2			
3	**First**	**Last**	**Phone**
4	John	Albertson	317-555-0102
5	Tom	Baker	317-555-0104
6	Chris	Corleone	317-555-0106
7	Parker	Davis	317-555-0108
8	Marilyn	Epperson	317-555-0110
9	Marnie	Franck	317-555-0112
10	Phyllis	Goswin	317-555-0114
11	Jean	Higgins	317-555-0116
12	Patrick	Ibanez	317-555-0118
13	Mary	Jones	317-555-0120
14	Sara	Kelly	317-555-0122
15			

Figure 10.31 Excel can be used to store structured data like this phone list.

structured data Data that has a consistent pattern to it, with the same type of information in every row, as in a database.

Converting a Range to a Table

When you are working with structured data, you might decide to convert the data range into a table. A table is a group of cells that work together as a data storage unit. When you convert a range to a table, certain extra tools become available for working with structured data, such as the capability to easily sort and filter the list using drop-down menus. For example, in Figure 10.31, notice the down arrows to the right of each column heading. Clicking one of those arrows opens a menu from which you can sort and filter the data.

table A group of cells that work together to store structured data.

If you don't want to see the arrows on each field name onscreen, click the Data tab and then click the Filter button to toggle them off. Click Filter again to turn them back on again when you need to work with them.

TIP

There are two methods of converting a range to a table, as described in the following Step by Step. One applies the default table style, and the other allows you to pick a table style. After the table has been created, you can change the table style from the Table Tools Design tab.

Step by Step

Converting a Range to a Table (Default Style)

Use these steps to convert a range to a table and apply the default table style to it:

1. Select the range.
2. On the Insert tab, click Table. The Create Table dialog box opens.
3. Click OK.

Converting a Range to a Table (Your Choice of Style)

Use these steps to convert a range to a table and apply your choice of table style to it:

1. Select the range.
2. On the Home tab, click Format as Table.

3. Select a style. The Format As Table dialog box opens.

4. Mark the My table has headers check box, if appropriate.

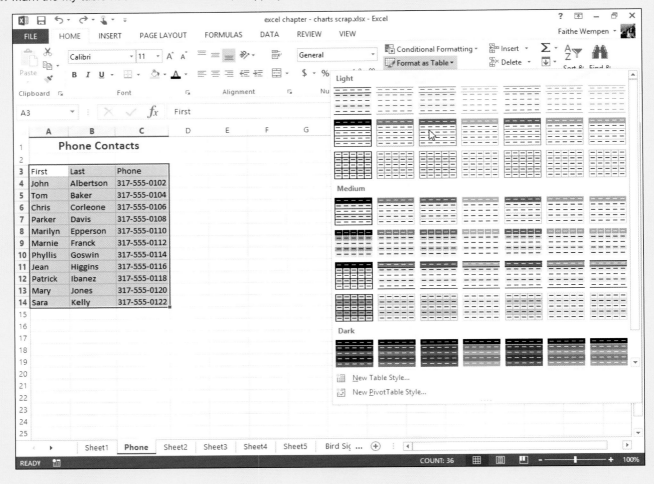

5. Click OK.

Sorting a Table

field A column in a table, storing one particular kind of information, such as Phone or Name.

record A row in a table, storing information about a specific person, place, or thing.

sort To put records in a specific order according to the entry in a certain field.

ascending sort An A to Z sort, or a sort from smallest to largest.

descending sort A Z to A sort, or a sort from largest to smallest.

In a table, each column is known as a field. A field contains a specific type of structured data, such as Phone or Address. Each row is a record, containing all the fields for a specific instance. To sort means to put records into a specific order according to the entry in a certain field. For example, you might sort a list by Last Name or by City.

To sort a table, click the down-arrow button to the right of the field by which you want to sort, opening a menu, and on that menu, click Sort A to Z or Sort Z to A, depending on whether you want an ascending sort or descending sort. See Figure 10.32. If the field contains something other than text (for example, numbers or dates), the choices of sort order may be different. For example, with numeric values your choices might be Sort Smallest to Largest or Sort Largest to Smallest.

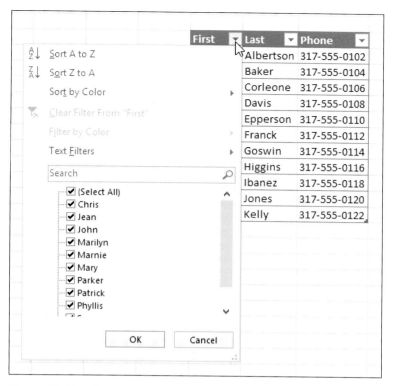

You can also sort a table in the same way you would sort a range: using the Sort buttons on the Data tab. Use the AZ button there for an ascending sort or the ZA button for a descending sort, or click the Sort button to open a Sort dialog box in which you can set up a multi-field sort. A multi-field sort is useful if you have some duplicates in the field by which you are sorting, because the secondary field you specify will break any ties.

Filtering a Table

To *filter* means to hide certain records according to criteria you specify. You can filter a table in several ways:

filter To hide certain records according to criteria you specify.

- If you want to exclude records that contain a certain value in a certain field, open a field's menu, as in Figure 10.32, and at the bottom of the menu, clear the check boxes for any entries that you do not want to be included.

- If you want to filter to include only records that contain a certain value in a certain field, find a record that should be included in the results, and in its row, right-click the field by which you want to filter. On the shortcut menu that appears, point to Filter and then choose Filter by Selected Cell's Value.

- If you want to filter by criteria you define, open a field's menu, point to Text Filters (or Number Filters, or whatever appears, depending on the field data type) to open a submenu, and then choose a filtering criterion, such as Equals, Does Not Equal, Begins With, or Ends With. Then in the dialog box that appears, specify the criterion, as shown in Figure 10.33.

Figure 10.33 Define a filter using criteria of your choice.

After you have applied a filter, the down arrow to the right of the field's name changes to a symbol that looks somewhat like a funnel. Clicking that symbol opens the field's menu, the same as if it were the regular down-pointing arrow.

To clear a filter, display the Data tab and click Clear, or open the field's menu and choose Clear Filter from *Fieldname*.

Converting a Table to a Range

You may decide that you want the table to be a regular range again, so you can more easily separate the data and work with it in other ways (for example, perform calculations on it rather than treating it as structured data). When you convert a table back to a range, it keeps the formatting applied to it.

Step by Step

Converting a Table to a Range

Use these steps to convert a table to a range:

1. Click anywhere within the table.

2. On the Table Tools Design tab, click Convert to Range.

3. Click Yes to confirm.

Quick Review

1. How do you convert a range to a table?

2. How do you sort a table by a certain field?

3. How do you remove a filter?

Summary

Understanding the Excel Interface

An Excel data file is a **workbook** and can contain multiple **worksheets**. You can switch between worksheets with the tabs at the bottom of the window. A worksheet is organized in rows and columns; the intersection of a row and column is a **cell**. A cell's **address** is its column letter and row number, like this: B9. The active cell is the cell that contains the **cell selector** (the thick dark green outline). You can move the cell selector by clicking or by using the arrow keys.

The **formula bar** is the bar above the column headings where the contents of the active cell appears. If the active cell contains a formula, the formula appears here and the result of the formula appears in the cell.

Moving Around in a Worksheet

To bring different parts of the worksheet into view, use the scroll bars. To move the cell selector, use the arrow keys or click the cell you want, or use keyboard shortcuts, as shown in Table 10.1.

To enter data in a cell, select it and then type. To edit a cell's content, you can replace its entry completely or move the insertion point into it and then edit text directly in the cell or in the formula bar. To clear all text from the cell, press the Delete key.

A **range** is one or more cells selected at the same time. Ranges are described by the address of the upper-left and lower-right cells, like this: C3:F10. When a range is not contiguous, the additional parts of the range are added with commas, like this: C3:F10,F12:F13. Drag across a range to select it, or hold down Shift and use the arrow keys to expand the selection from the active cell.

The **fill handle** is the small dark green rectangle in the lower-right corner of the cell selector. Drag it to fill the data into adjacent cells from the selected cell(s). The **AutoFill** feature allows you to fill a series, such as days of the week or a sequence of numbers.

Changing the Structure of a Worksheet

You can insert rows or columns as needed. To insert rows or columns, use the Insert button on the Home tab. To delete rows or columns, select them and then use the Delete button on the Home tab. When you insert individual cells, the surrounding cells must move down or to the right. You can specify which action you prefer in the Insert dialog box. The opposite is true when you delete cells: Surrounding cells must move up or to the left.

When you **merge** cells, you make one big data entry area out of the space occupied by multiple cells. Use the Merge & Center button on the Home tab to merge contiguous cells.

To move a cell or range, select it and then use the Office Clipboard, as described in Chapter 8, or use drag-and-drop. Hold down the Ctrl key if you want to copy rather than move.

Formatting Cells

To resize rows or columns to fit the content (**AutoFit**), double-click between the row numbers or column letters. You can also manually resize them by dragging the divider between the row numbers or column letters.

To set the horizontal or vertical alignment for a cell, use the buttons in the Alignment group on the Home tab. Vertical alignment is not obvious unless the cell is taller than the text it contains requires it to be.

Number formats make the numbers in a cell appear in a certain way, such as currency or percentage. You can apply number formats from the Number group on the Home tab. Number formats also include Date and Time; Excel represents dates and times as numeric values.

All cells have **gridlines**, which are usually non-printing. You can also apply **borders** around certain cells to set them off from the rest. Use the Borders button on the Home tab, or use the Format Cells dialog box. You can also apply a **fill** (a background color) to cells using the Home tab or the Format Cells dialog box.

Entering Formulas and Functions

A **formula** is a math calculation in a cell. It may refer to other cells for its values, such as =A1+A2, or it may refer to literal numbers, such as =2+3. Formulas calculate using the same **order of operations** as in standard math: first exponentiation, then multiplication and division, and finally addition and subtraction.

Functions are named calculations such as AVERAGE or PMT. Functions have **arguments**, which are variables placed in parentheses after the function name. When there are multiple arguments, they are separated by commas, like this: =PMT(A2,A3,A4).

References to cell addresses in formulas and functions can be absolute, relative, or mixed. An **absolute reference** does not change when the formula is copied or moved; a **relative reference** does change. Absolute references are indicated with dollar signs, as in A1. A **mixed reference** uses an absolute reference for one part but not the other, such as $A1 or A$1.

Creating Charts

A **chart** is a graphic that illustrates and summarizes worksheet data. Many types of charts are available in Excel, including **pie chart**, **column chart**, and **bar chart**. A pie chart uses only a single **data series**; other chart types can have multiple data series. A scatter chart can help find the trends in non-repeatable data. A **trend line** helps find the overall meaning in the **data points**.

A **legend** is a color key that tells what each color in the chart represents. A chart can also have **data labels** on each data point to show its exact value. The entire chart is the **chart area**. The area on which data is plotted is the **plot area**. The **chart title** describes the chart's overall purpose. Vertical and horizontal **axis labels** show the values on axes, and **axis titles** describe what those values mean. A **data table** shows the values from the worksheet that are plotted in the chart.

To format a chart, you can apply a different **chart style**, or you can format individual elements by right-clicking them and choosing the Format command.

Working with Data Tables

Excel can store **structured data** in tables. A **table** is a group of cells that work together as a data storage unit. Converting a range to a table makes it easier to sort and filter the data.

In a table, each column is a **field** and each row is a **record**. You can sort the data by a particular column in **ascending** or **descending** order. You can also **filter**, which means to hide records according to criteria you specify.

Key Terms

absolute reference	fill handle
active cell	filter
argument	formula
ascending sort	formula bar
AutoFill	function
AutoFit	gridlines
axis labels	legend
axis titles	merge
bar chart	mixed reference
borders	Name box
cell	number format
cell address	order of operations
cell selector	pie chart
chart	plot area
chart area	point
chart style	range
chart title	record
column chart	relative reference
data label	scatter chart
data point	sort
data series	structured data
data table	table
descending sort	trend line
field	workbook
fill	worksheet

Test Yourself

Fact Check

1. Where does the active cell's address appear?

   a. Name box

   b. address bar

   c. formula bar

   d. cell selector

2. Which of these is a valid cell name?

   a. 4AB

   b. 145

   c. 12A

   d. BZ12

3. What is the small dark green rectangle in the bottom-right corner of the cell selector?

   a. function helper

   b. absolute reference indicator

   c. fill handle

   d. formula box

4. To insert a row or column, select a row or column and then click the Insert button on the _____ tab.

   a. Home

   b. Insert

   c. Data

   d. Review

5. To copy a range of cells, select the range and then hold down the _____ key as you drag the range to a different location.

   a. Alt

   b. Shift

   c. Ctrl

   d. Insert

6. To make a number appear with a currency symbol, apply the Currency _____ to its cell.

   a. attribute

   b. table style

   c. font

   d. number format

7. Which of these is a valid formula in Excel?

   a. =2A+B

   b. =A2+B2

   c. =A2:B8

   d. =AVERAGE-B8

8. Which of these is a valid function in Excel?

   a. =SUM

   b. =SUM(A2+A3+A4*5)

   c. =SUM(A1:A6)

   d. =SUM=A1:A6

9. Which of these is a relative reference?

   a. A$1

   b. A1

   c. A1

   d. $A1

10. What kind of chart is used to show how parts relate to a whole?

   a. pie

   b. bar

   c. scatter

   d. column

Matching

Match the parts of an Excel chart to its function.

a. chart area

b. data label

c. data point

d. data table

e. legend

f. plot area

g. trend line

1. _____A line on a scatter chart that helps interpret the data.

2. _____The key that tells what each color or pattern on a chart represents.

3. _____Numeric values that appear next to each data point.

4. _____A single piece of data represented on a chart.

5. _____A grid below a chart that shows the values from which the chart is built.

6. _____The section of a chart that contains the data points.

7. _____The entire chart.

Sum It Up

1. Describe how cell addresses are determined.

2. Explain how to select both contiguous and non-contiguous ranges.

3. Describe how colors are arranged on a palette and how they relate to the active theme.

4. Explain how to merge two or more cells, and give an example of a situation in which it would be useful to do so.

5. Give an example of an absolute reference.

6. List and describe three elements of a chart that you can turn on/off and format.

7. Explain why you might want to convert a range into a table.

Explore More

Working with Named Ranges

You can name ranges (and remember, a range can be as small as one cell) in Excel, and use those names in formulas. To name a range, select the range and then type a name in the Name box, or use the buttons in the Defined Names group on the Formulas tab to create and manage ranges.

To try out named ranges, create the worksheet shown in the figure:

	A	B	C
1			
2		Pay Calculator	
3			
4		Rate	$20.00
5		Hours	40
6		Total	
7			

Name cell C4 *Rate*, and name cell C5 *Hours*. Then enter the following formula in C6: =Rate*Hours. If it correctly calculates the result as $800.00, you have named the ranges correctly.

Using Excel to Create Forms

You can use Excel to create business forms that people can fill out onscreen. By combining borders, fills, and merged cells, you can use Excel's basic grid to create a variety of form types.

To get started, create a new document using a template that creates a business form, such as an invoice. (Search for Invoice when searching for a template.) See how the template uses fills and borders, along with varying row heights and column widths. Then start with a new blank document and create a form of your own, such as a time card or a change-of-address form.

Exploring Other Number Formats

In a new worksheet, type the same number in cells A1 through A11. Format each of the cells using a different number format (from the drop-down list in the Number group on the Home tab), and compare the formats. Think of an example scenario in which each format might be useful.

Think It Over

Financial Functions

What financial functions would be useful for the average consumer? For example, what functions would someone use when comparing mortgage rates? When determining the payments on a personal loan made to a friend or family member? When calculating the interest earned on an investment? When determining the future value of an investment at a certain rate of return for a certain number of years? Browse the functions available in Excel and decide on the best functions to use for each activity.

Making Meaning with Charts

The same data can be used to draw very different conclusions, depending on how it is presented. For the chart shown below, how would you modify the chart for the following scenarios?

- You want to make it easier to compare the values for each region from month to month. (Hint: What would make it easier to do so visually?)

- You want to minimize the differences between the regions. (Hint: How would you change the scale of the numbers on the vertical axis to do this?)

- You want to emphasize teamwork and show how each region contributes to the whole. (Hint: What about a different chart sub-type?)

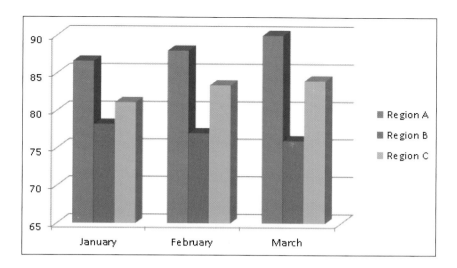

Excel versus a Database

Excel works fine to store a single data table, as you learned in this chapter, but what about when your data storage needs are more complicated? Suppose, for example, you wanted to store information about customers and their orders. How could you set that up in Excel tables to be most useful? Or would it be better to use a relational database application such as Microsoft Access (see Chapter 11)?

Chapter 11

Managing Databases with Access

Learning objectives

☐ Understand how a database differs from a spreadsheet

☐ Demonstrate how to create databases and tables

☐ Create queries

☐ Create and explain the benefits of forms and reports

Understanding Access Databases

Creating Databases and Tables

Creating Queries

Creating Forms and Reports

A database is a collection of structured data—that is, data in a consistent format. For example, your address book is a database, as is a catalog of items for sale, because the same facts are stored about each instance. In Chapter 10, "Creating Spreadsheets with Microsoft Excel," you learned how to store structured data in an Excel table, but in many cases the complexity and size of the database make Excel an impractical tool for storing and maintaining it. A better tool is Microsoft Access, which is also part of some editions of the Microsoft Office suite.

In this chapter, you will learn some basics about databases, and you'll find out how to use Microsoft Access to create and store a simple database.

Understanding Access Databases

Microsoft Access is a popular application for creating and managing small to medium-sized databases. This type of application is called a database management system (DBMS). A DBMS can not only store data, but can also use helper objects such as forms and reports to make the data easier to enter, summarize, and understand.

database A collection of data stored in a structured format, with the same facts stored about each instance. A database stores data in a way that enables you to search and locate it quickly.

database management system (DBMS) An application that helps users create and manage databases.

Database data is stored in one or more tables. You worked with some basic tables in Excel in Chapter 10, in the section "Working with Data Tables." At its most basic level, a table is a collection of fields into which users can input records. Recall from Chapter 10 that a field is a type of information to be collected, such as Name or Phone, and that a record is a stored instance, such as an individual person, place, or thing.

Datasheet view A view of a table in which the table's data appears in a structured grid or rows and columns.

An Access table can be displayed in Datasheet view, which makes its data appear in a two-dimensional grid that looks a lot like an Excel table. See Figure 11.1. As in an Excel table, the field names appear across the tops of the columns and the data records appear in rows beneath those column headings.

You can enter new data into the first empty row at the bottom of a table datasheet, as you would enter it in an Excel table or worksheet. There is another option, however; in Access, you can create forms for data entry. A form makes the process of data entry more user-friendly by displaying only one record at a time, as shown in Figure 11.2. The form itself contains no data; it merely funnels data into the table(s) with which it is associated.

form A database helper object that simplifies data entry to presenting a user-friendly form in which to enter data.

relationship A connection between two tables based on a shared field.

One of the benefits of using Access is that you can have two (or more) tables in the same data file, and you can create a relationship between the tables. For example, you could have Customers and Orders tables for your business. In the Customers table, you could store the full contact information for each customer, and in the Orders table, you could store information about each order placed. The Orders table could have a Customer ID field that has a relationship to the Customer ID field in the Customers table, so that each order is tied to a particular customer's record. You could also have a table called Order Details that contains each line-item of each order, with an Order ID field that is related to the Order ID field in the Orders table. Figure 11.3 shows these tables and relationships plus several others. Creating relationships between tables is very useful, and is one of the main benefits of using Access rather than Excel for a multi-table database.

Columns are fields   Rows are records

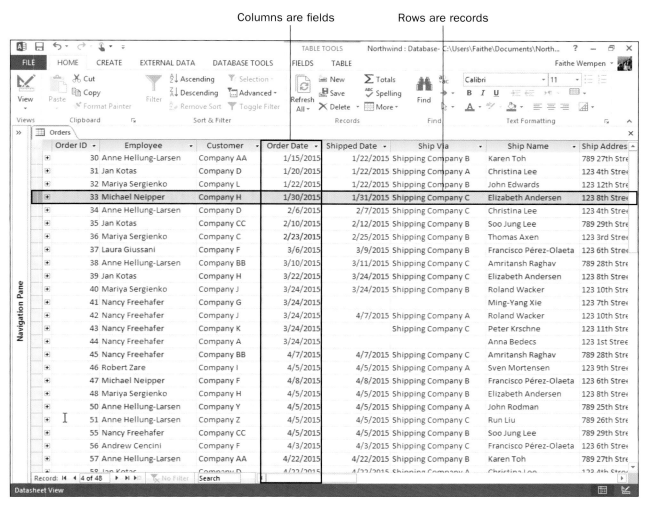

Figure 11.1   Column headings are field names, and records appear in rows beneath them.

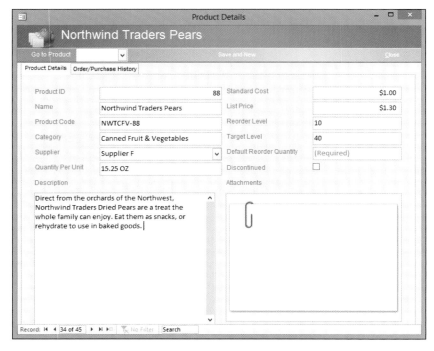

Figure 11.2   A form makes data entry into a table more user friendly.

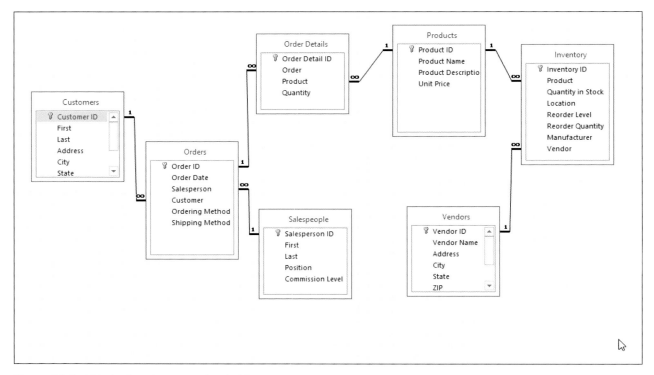

Figure 11.3 This database has seven related tables.

In Chapter 10, you learned how to use Excel to sort and filter data in a table in a basic way, but in Access, the sorting and filtering capabilities are much stronger. You can create a query, which is a set of saved specifications for sorting, filtering, and other data manipulation. A query's results display in a datasheet, like a table does, but may include a subset of the fields and/or records from the table on which it is based. A query can also be used to combine the data from multiple related tables. For example, looking back at the relationships in Figure 11.3, you could create a query that shows a record for each order placed on a certain date and the postal code to which it was shipped. The order number and order date would come from the Orders table, and the postal code would come from the Customers table.

A query can help you find key information quickly, such as in the preceding example, but the results it generates will be presented in a plain-looking datasheet. When you want to present data in a more attractive format, you can generate a report. A report takes data from a table or query and lays it out for printing with a title and page headers/footers. Reports can also optionally summarize data rather than presenting the full set of records. Figure 11.4 shows a sample report.

Using Access for Web-Based Applications

Access databases are not just for personal computer use; you can also make them available on web pages. For example, you can use Access Services, which is a component of Microsoft's groupware application SharePoint, to build a web application that others can use to enter and view data. For more information, read the article and watch the videos at `http://office.microsoft.com/en-us/access-help/build-an-access-database-to-share-on-the-web-HA010356866.aspx`.

Monthly Sales Report

June, 2015

Product	Sales
Northwind Traders Boysenberry Spread	$2,250.00
Northwind Traders Dried Apples	$1,590.00
Northwind Traders Fruit Cocktail	$1,560.00
Northwind Traders Chocolate	$1,020.00
Northwind Traders Dried Pears	$900.00
Northwind Traders Cajun Seasoning	$660.00
Northwind Traders Coffee	$230.00
Northwind Traders Clam Chowder	$96.50
June Sales Total	$8,306.50

Page 1 of 1

Figure 11.4   A report presents data in an attractive format suitable for printing.

Quick Review

1. How is storing data in Access different from storing it in an Excel table?

2. Besides a datasheet, what other object can be used to help users enter data?

3. What does a query do?

Creating Databases and Tables

A database file starts with one or more tables. A table is the only database object that can hold data, so you must construct your tables before you can do any data entry or create any other objects. In the following sections, you will learn how to start a new database file, find your way around the Access 2013 interface, and create the tables you need.

Creating a Database

When you start Access, the application's Start screen appears, as shown in Figure 11.5, and from here you can start a new database based on a template or start a new blank database. You can also click Open Other Files to open an existing database, or choose one of the shortcuts to recently opened database files.

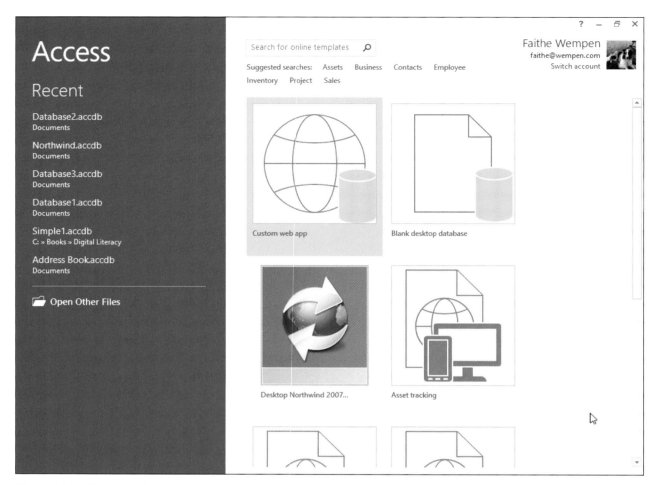

Figure 11.5 Start a new database or open an existing one.

For the purposes of this chapter, we will start with a new blank database. Doing so will give you a chance to create all the database objects from scratch, so you will learn how to do it. You may choose to start with one of the templates when you work with Access on your own in the future.

Step by Step

Creating a New Blank Database

Use these steps to start a new database:

1. On the Access Start screen (Figure 11.5), click Blank desktop database.

   If you do not see the Access Start screen, click the File tab to open Backstage view and then click New in the navigation pane at the left.

2. In the File Name box, change the generic name there (Database1, or some other number) to a filename of your choice.

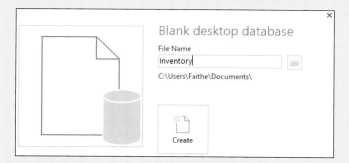

Blank desktop database

File Name

Inventory

C:\Users\Faithe\Documents\

Create

(Optional) If you want to save the database file somewhere other than your default Save location for Office documents, click the folder icon to the right of the File Name box and select a different location.

3. Click Create. The database is created, and a new blank table appears in Datasheet view.

You will learn what to do with this new table as this chapter progresses. You don't have to do anything with it for now. Just leave it onscreen.

You might notice that in the Access application's title bar, *Database (Access 2007-2013 file format)* appears. This refers to the format in which the database file is stored. Access 2007-2013 is the most recent format available; some databases may be stored in earlier Access formats, such as 2003 or 2000, for backward compatibility.

NOTE

Understanding the Access Interface

Microsoft Access has the same basic elements as other Office applications, such as the Ribbon, the status bar (with View buttons in the right corner), and a File menu that opens Backstage view.

Along the left side of the screen is the navigation pane, which contains a list of all the database objects. You can create a variety of database objects, including tables, forms, reports, and queries, and you can switch among them by selecting them from this navigation pane. Right now, as shown in Figure 11.6, there is only one object there: Table1, the automatically created table placed there when you created the database file.

navigation pane The pane along the left side of the Access window that lists and organizes database objects.

Because a table is open in Figure 11.6, the Table Tools contextual tabs appear: Fields and Table. These tabs contain commands for working with the table. Other contextual tab sets may appear when you are working with other object types.

Figure 11.6 shows the table in Datasheet view, which displays the fields in columns and the records in rows. In Figure 11.6, there are no records yet, and only one field: ID. The ID field is automatically generated; it will contain a unique value for each record entered into the table. To switch to another view, such as Design, click its button in the status bar, or click the View button on the Ribbon.

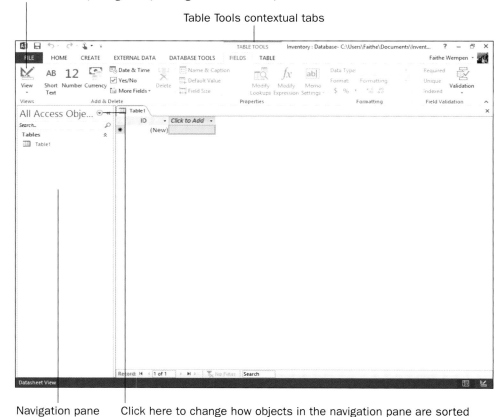

Views button (changes depending on current view)

Table Tools contextual tabs

Navigation pane   Click here to change how objects in the navigation pane are sorted

Figure 11.6   The Access 2010 application window with a table displayed in Datasheet view.

NOTE   The View button on the Ribbon changes depending on what view is currently displayed; in Figure 11.6, since you are in Datasheet view, it shows the Design view graphic on the button face.

Creating a Table in Datasheet View

You can create or modify a table in Datasheet view or in Design view. In Datasheet view, you can define the fields in a basic way, while still looking at the table in its familiar row-and-column format.

When you create a new blank database, it starts out with a new table in Datasheet view, as you saw earlier. Use this table as your first table, naming and structuring it as needed with the fields you want. You can add more tables later from the Create tab.

When you are finished modifying a table's structure, you must save it. Use the Save button in the Quick Access Toolbar, or use the Save command on the File menu. You will be prompted to save it when you close the table or switch to another view of the table. Give the table a descriptive but short name, such as Customers, Orders, or Inventory.

Creating a New Table

Use this procedure to start a new table (other than the one that Access creates automatically with a new database file):

- On the Create tab, click Table to create the table in Datasheet view.

    OR

- On the Create tab, click Table Design to create the table in Design view.

Create a new table in Datasheet view

Create a new table in Design view

Adding a Table Field in Datasheet View

Follow these steps to create a new field to the right of all existing fields in the datasheet:

1. Click the Click to Add heading. A drop-down list of field types appears.

2. Select the desired field type. (Text is the most common.) A generic field name appears in the column heading. The field name is highlighted, ready to be changed.

3. Type the new field name, replacing the generic name, and press Enter. For best results, use short field names.

    OR

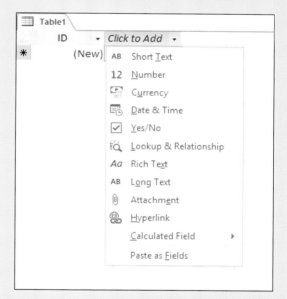

Follow these steps to insert a new field between two existing fields:

1. Click the column heading for the field that the new field should appear to the right of.

2. On the Table Tools Fields tab, in the Add & Delete group, click the button that corresponds to the type of field you want to add. A generic field name appears in the column heading. The field name is highlighted, ready to be changed.

3. Type the new field name, replacing the generic name, and press Enter. For best results, use short field names.

Renaming a Field in Datasheet View

Follow these steps to rename a field in Datasheet view:

1. Right-click a field name and choose Rename Field.

2. Type the new field name, replacing the previous name, and press Enter.

Changing a Field's Type in Datasheet View

Follow these steps to change a field type in Datasheet view:

1. Click the column heading for the field to change.

2. On the Table Tools Fields tab, in the Formatting group, open the Data Type drop-down list and select a different field type.

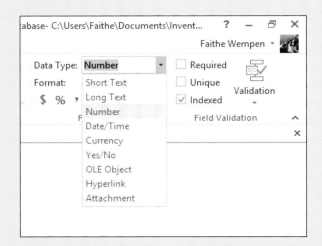

Reordering Fields in Datasheet View

Follow these steps to reorder fields in Datasheet view:

1. Click the column heading for the field to change.

2. Drag and drop the field to a different position. A thick vertical line shows the destination as you drag.

Saving a Table

Follow these steps to save a table:

1. Click the Save button on the Quick Access toolbar. If you have not saved the table before, the Save As dialog box opens.

2. In the Save As dialog box, type a name for the table.

3. Click OK.

Renaming a Table

Follow these steps to rename a table:

1. Close the table if it is open. To close a table, right-click its tab and choose Close.

2. Right-click the table's name in the navigation pane and choose Rename.

3. Type the new name and press Enter.

Creating a Table in Design View

Design view A viewing mode for a database object that enables you to modify the object's structure and properties.

Design view provides more options and more control over the fields in your table. Many database professionals prefer to work with table structure and properties in Design view because it shields them from the data so they can focus on the table itself.

NOTE When you switch from Datasheet view to Design view, you will be prompted to save the table if you haven't already done so.

Step by Step

Displaying a Table in Design View

Do any of the following to display a table in Design view.

- If the table is already open in Datasheet view, right-click its tab and choose Design View.

- Right-click the table's name in the navigation pane and choose Design View.

- Click the Design View button at the right end of the status bar.

In Design view, the field names appear in the top section of the screen, in the order they appear in the datasheet, as in Figure 11.7. The data type appears to the right of each field name. You can modify the field names and data types freely here. The Data Type column uses a drop-down list from which you can select the data type. Table 11.1 summarizes the available field types and their recommended uses.

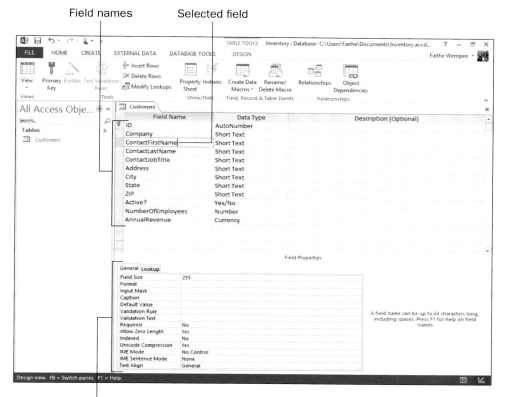

Figure 11.7   A table in Design view.

Table 11.1:   Field Types in Access Tables

Field Type	Recommended Uses	Comments
Short Text	Fields that contain only text, or a mixture of text and numbers	This is also used for fields that contain numbers that are treated as text, such as postal codes and phone numbers.
Long Text	Fields that will need to be able to hold a large amount of text	This field type can hold up to 65,536 characters, but it lacks some of the benefits of a text field.
Number	Fields that contain a general numeric value (not currency)	Use this field for quantities and other numbers that you might need to calculate.
Date/Time	Fields that report a date and/or time	This field type is technically a numeric type, but it formats the numbers as dates or times.
Currency	Fields that contain monetary values	This type is similar to Number except it uses the currency symbol and two decimal places in its default format.
AutoNumber	Use this type for only one field in a table; it automatically assigns a unique numeric value to each record	You don't enter data in this field; Access enters it for you. Use this field when each record should have a unique identifier but you don't care what it is.

continued

Table 11.1 continued

Field Type	Recommended Uses	Comments
Yes/No	Fields that contain logical conditions such as True/False, Yes/No, or On/Off	Users will select from a two-item drop-down list when entering data into this field.
OLE Object	Fields that store external content from other programs, such as an Excel workbook or Word document	Use for attaching Office documents to records, such as attaching a person's resume to his or her personnel file. The advantage of OLE Object over Attachment is that you can more easily open and edit the document if you use the OLE Object type.
Hyperlink	Fields that store a web address or an email address	By using the Hyperlink field type, you make the address clickable in Datasheet view.
Attachment	Fields that store external files from other programs	The advantage of Attachment over OLE Object is that it supports more file formats and you can have more than one attachment per record.
Calculated	Fields that store the calculated values from one or more other fields in the same table	You don't enter data into this field; Access populates it automatically based on the calculation you specify.
Lookup Wizard	Fields that should display a drop-down list of choices from a list you create or generate from another table	This is not a true field type, but a means of accessing the Lookup Wizard feature for setting up a lookup.

Troubleshooting

Using Lookups

One of the biggest headaches for database administrators is that users make typographical errors when entering and editing data. One way to minimize the typos is to use lookups for fields. A lookup is a menu of choices that users select from; they don't have to type the entry, so they don't make typing errors. Lookups are useful for fields in which there are a fixed number of valid values, such as Marital Status. You can choose Lookup Wizard as the field type to open a series of dialog boxes that walk you through the process of creating a lookup.

lookup A menu of choices for entering data into a field.

In Design view, you can enter a Description for each field. This description does not appear in most other views (including Datasheet view), so you can use it for your own internal notes about the field.

In the lower part of Design view are the field properties for the active field. You will learn about these in the next section.

Step by Step

Adding a Table Field in Design View

Follow these steps to create a new field after all existing fields in the datasheet:

1. Click in the first empty row of the field list in Design view.

2. Type a field name in the Field Name column.

3. In the Data Type column, open the drop-down list and select a type (refer to Table 11.1).

4. (Optional) Enter a description of the field in the Description column.

Follow these steps to insert a new field between two existing fields:

1. Click the field name that the new field should appear above.

2. On the Table Tools Design tab, click Insert Rows.

3. Type a field name in the Field Name column.

4. In the Data Type column, open the drop-down list and select a type (refer to Table 11.1).

5. (Optional) Enter a description of the field in the Description column.

Renaming a Field in Design View

- Edit the name in the Field Name column.

Changing a Field's Type in Design View

- Open the Data Type column's drop-down list and choose a different type.

Reordering Fields in Design View

1. Click the selector (the blank gray box) to the left of the field name to select that row in the field list.

2. Drag and drop the field up or down to a different position. As you drag, a horizontal line appears between fields to show the destination.

Modifying Field Properties

Each field has properties that determine how it looks (such as how numbers are formatted, if it's a Number field), what kind of data it accepts (for example, a character limit), whether it is required, and what its default value is, if any. Different types of fields have different properties. Numeric fields can be assigned a format, for example, that dictates whether there will be any helper symbols (like currency or percentage) and how many decimal places will show.

To set a field's properties in Datasheet view, as shown in Figure 11.8, click anywhere in that field's column and then use the buttons on the Table Tools Fields tab to change the properties as desired.

Figure 11.8   Set field properties in Datasheet view.

To set a field's properties in Design view, as in Figure 11.9, select the field at the top part of the screen, and then modify the fields on the General tab in the Field Properties area at the bottom of the screen.

General	Lookup	
Field Size	255	
Format		
Input Mask		
Caption		
Default Value		
Validation Rule		
Validation Text		
Required	No	
Allow Zero Length	Yes	
Indexed	No	
Unicode Compression	Yes	
IME Mode	No Control	
IME Sentence Mode	None	
Text Align	General	

Figure 11.9 Set field properties in Design view.

Setting the Primary Key

primary key The field that is unique for all records in the table, by which records in the table will be referenced in other tables.

The primary key for a table is the field used to distinguish one record from another. All the other fields in the table can have the same value in multiple fields except this one. Access recommends that you have a primary key defined in each table, and if you try to save the table without choosing one, a warning appears.

TIP

If there are no unique fields in your table that would be suitable to be the primary key, consider adding an ID field for this purpose. Set the ID's field type to AutoNumber so you don't have to assign a value to it for each record.

Step by Step

Setting the Primary Key

Follow these steps to specify which field should be the primary key:

1. Display the table in Design view.

2. Select the field that should be the primary key.

3. On the Table Tools Design tab, click the Primary Key button to select it. A key symbol appears to the left of the field name.

Primary Key button

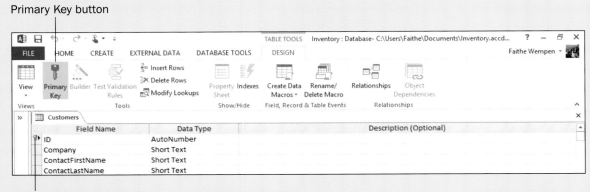

This symbol marks which field is the primary key

Creating a Relationship between Tables

Creating relationships between tables has many benefits. It allows you to run queries and create reports that pull information from multiple tables, for example, and to create data entry forms that enter data into multiple tables simultaneously.

A relationship usually links the primary key field in one table with the corresponding foreign key in another table. A foreign key is a field that contains the same information as its related primary key field but is not unique for each record. For example, in the Customers table, the ID field is the primary key, and each record has a unique ID. In the Orders table, the Customer field—the foreign key—contains customer ID numbers that correspond to those in the Customers table. In the Orders table, multiple records can have the same value for that field, because a single customer might place multiple separate orders. This is called a one-to-many relationship.

foreign key A field that has a relationship to the primary key field in another table.

You can create relationships between tables in the Relationships window, as shown in Figure 11.10. In Figure 11.10, there are three tables. In two of them, the primary key field has a relationship with the corresponding foreign key field in the other table. Notice the tiny 1 and ∞ symbols on the line. These symbols are present because this relationship enforces referential integrity in the one-to-many relationship between the tables. Referential integrity means that the data on the "many" side must have a corresponding value on the "one" side. In Figure 11.10, that means that there can be no orders placed for customers who do not appear in the Customers table, and there can be no order details entered for orders that do not appear in the Orders table. You can create relationships without referential integrity if you choose, but your database will not be as error-proof that way.

one-to-many relationship A relationship in which the connected field is unique in one table and not unique in the other table.

referential integrity A requirement that the data in related tables be matched, so that an entry in the "many" side of the relationship (the foreign key) must have a corresponding entry in the "one" side of the relationship (the primary key).

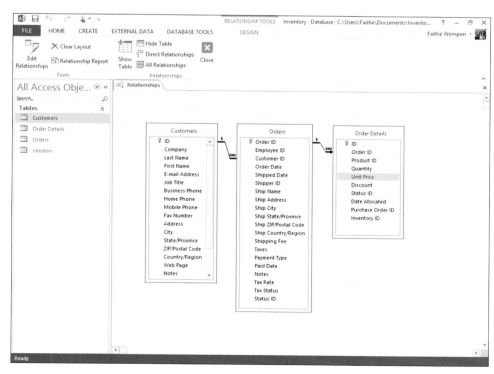

Figure 11.10   A simple example of database relationships.

Referential integrity has two options: Cascade Update Related Fields and Cascade Delete Related Records. Cascade Update Related Fields changes the entry in the foreign key table when the entry in the primary key table changes. For example, if a customer's ID number changes in the Customers table, her ID will be automatically updated for each of her records in the Orders table.

Cascade Delete Related Records deletes the entry in the foreign key table when the entry in the primary key table is deleted. For example, suppose a customer is removed from the Customers table for some reason (for example, the customer dies, or asks to be removed). If Cascade Delete is enabled, all records in the Orders table from previous orders that customer placed would be deleted.

Step by Step

Creating a Relationship between Tables

Follow these steps to create a relationship:

1. Ensure that the fields to be related have the same data type.

Note: For Step 1, AutoNumber should be considered a Number data type. If you are creating a relationship between an AutoNumber field and a foreign key field, that foreign key field's type must be set to Number.

2. On the Database Tools tab, click Relationships. The Relationships window opens.

3. If the table(s) you want to work with do not appear, click the Show Table button. Click a table to show, and click the Add button. Repeat this for each table you want to show, and then click Close.

Show Table button   Select the tables to include

4. Drag and drop the primary key field from one table onto the foreign key field that matches it in the other table. The Edit Relationships dialog box opens.

5. (Recommended but optional) Mark the Enforce Referential Integrity check box.

6. (Optional) Mark the Cascade Update Related Fields and/or Cascade Delete Related Records check boxes if appropriate.

7. Click Create to create the relationship.

Editing a Relationship

Follow these steps to edit a relationship:

1. When viewing the Relationships window, double-click the line between the two tables. The Edit Relationship dialog box opens.

2. Edit the relationship as needed.

3. Click OK.

Deleting a Relationship between Tables

Follow these steps to remove a relationship:

1. When viewing the Relationships window, click the line between the two tables to select it.

2. Press the Delete key on the keyboard. A confirmation box appears.

3. Click Yes.

Closing the Relationships Window

Follow these steps to close the Relationships window:

1. On the Relationship Tools Design tab, click Close. A box appears asking if you want to save the changes.

2. Click Yes.

Entering Data in a Table

It is a good idea not to enter any data until you have finalized the tables and their relationships, because changing a table's fields and properties may change the rules for what data a field will accept. For example, if you change a field's type from Text to Number, text-based data in that field will become invalid.

You can enter data directly into a table in Datasheet view. Click in the first cell in the first blank row of the datasheet, and start typing. Press Tab to move to the next field, just like you did in Excel in Chapter 10, or press Shift+Tab to go back to the previous field. When you reach the final cell in the row, pressing Tab moves to the beginning of the next row and starts a new record. If you don't want to tab all the way to the end of the row, just click the mouse to move the insertion point outside of that row, or click the Save button in the Records group on the Home tab. Records are saved automatically when you navigate away from them; you don't have to click the Save button after each one to save it.

There are several ways to delete a record. Select it (by clicking the selection box, which is the gray blank box to the left of the record), and then do any of the following:

- Press the Delete key.
- Right-click the record and choose Delete Record.
- On the Home tab, in the Records group, click the Delete button.

Quick Review

1. What is the purpose of setting a primary key field for a table?

2. What is referential integrity?

3. How do you change a field's name?

Creating Queries

A query is a view of a table that shows it in a different way. A query can hide certain fields, hide certain records, show records sorted in a certain order, and more. Queries are useful for cutting out the unimportant data to find an answer to a question, and for extracting data that helps make sense of a situation. For example, a query could answer the question "What orders did customer X place in January?" or "What were the top 10 best-selling products in the Northeast region?" A query can also be used to make the data from two or more related tables appear together in a single datasheet. That query can then be used as the basis for a report, allowing you to create reports using data that spans multiple tables.

select query A query that selects certain fields and records from one or more tables.

You can create a query using the Query Wizard, which walks you step-by-step through the process of creating a query, or you can use Design view. This chapter briefly explains both.

Creating a Query with the Simple Query Wizard

The Simple Query Wizard is a good place to start for your first query because it makes the process very simple. The Simple Query Wizard enables you to create a query that includes fields from one or more related tables, and that includes only certain fields. It can either show all the records (a detail query) or show a summary of them (a summary query).

The drawback to the Simple Query Wizard is that it does not allow you to filter the records. In other words, it shows all the records (or a summary of all the records). You could not, for example, show only one customer, or only one date range of orders.

detail query A query that shows all records in the dataset.

summary query A field that totals or summarizes the data from the records rather than listing each record.

Step by Step

Creating a Detail Query with the Simple Query Wizard

Follow these steps to create a detail query with the Simple Query Wizard:

1. On the Create tab, click Query Wizard. The New Query dialog box opens.

2. Click Simple Query Wizard and click OK. The Simple Query Wizard runs.

3. Open the Tables/Queries list, and choose the table from which to pull fields.

4. In the Available Fields list, click a field you want to include and click the > button to add it to the Selected Fields list. Do this for each field to include. Or, to add all the fields from the query, click the >> button.

    To remove any fields selected in error, click the field to remove and click the < button.

5. If you want another table's fields to be included, repeat Steps 3 and 4. Otherwise click Next to continue.

6. If you included one or more fields that can be calculated, such as a Number or Currency field, a screen appears asking if you want a detail or summary query. Choose Detail, and then click Next.

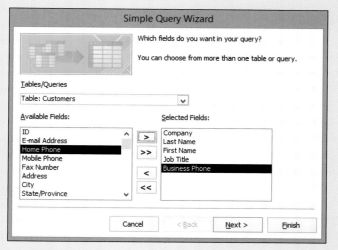

7. If desired, change the default name of the query in the What Title Do You Want for Your Query? text box.

8. Click Finish. The query opens in Datasheet view. The query's name appears in the navigation pane.

Creating a Summary Query with the Simple Query Wizard

Follow these steps to create a query with the Simple Query Wizard:

1. On the Create tab, click Query Wizard. The New Query dialog box opens.

2. Click Simple Query Wizard and click OK. The Simple Query Wizard runs.

3. Open the Tables/Queries list and choose the table from which to pull fields.

4. In the Available Fields list, click a field you want to include and click the > button to add it to the Selected Fields list. Do this for each field to include. Or, to add all the fields from the query, click the >> button.

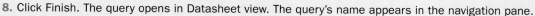

Note: Make sure that you include at least one field that can be calculated, such as a Number or Currency field.

5. If you want another table's fields to be included, repeat Steps 3 and 4. Otherwise click Next to continue.

6. When prompted whether you want a Detail or Summary query, click Summary, and then click the Summary Options button. A list of all the calculable fields in the selected list appears, with Sum, Avg, Min, and Max check boxes for each one.

7. Mark the check boxes for the calculations you want to appear in the query.

8. Click OK, and then click Next.

9. If you included any Date/Time fields, you are asked how you want to group the dates in your query. Choose any grouping as desired, and then click Next.

10. If desired, replace the generic query name with a different name. Then click Finish. The query results appear in Datasheet view. For any calculations you requested, a calculated field (column) appears in the datasheet.

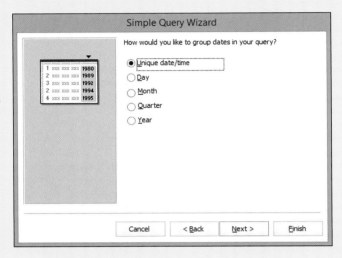

Creating a Query in Design View

When you create a query in Design view, you have full control over the query. You can filter out certain fields and/or records by the criteria you specify.

In Query Design view, the top section shows the fields from the tables that you add to the grid. The bottom section is the Query By Example (QBE) grid; you drag individual fields here and then set properties to configure how they will appear in the query results. For example, in Figure 11.11, five fields are included: Company (from the Customers table), Order Date (from the Orders table), and Product ID, Quantity, and Unit Price (from the Order Details table). The query is sorted first by Company and then by Order Date, and filtered to show only orders with a date between 3/1/2015 and 3/31/2015. Table 11.2 explains the syntax used to define the filtering criteria.

NOTE For more detailed examples of writing query criteria, see `http://office.microsoft.com/en-us/access-help/examples-of-query-criteria-HA010066611.aspx`.

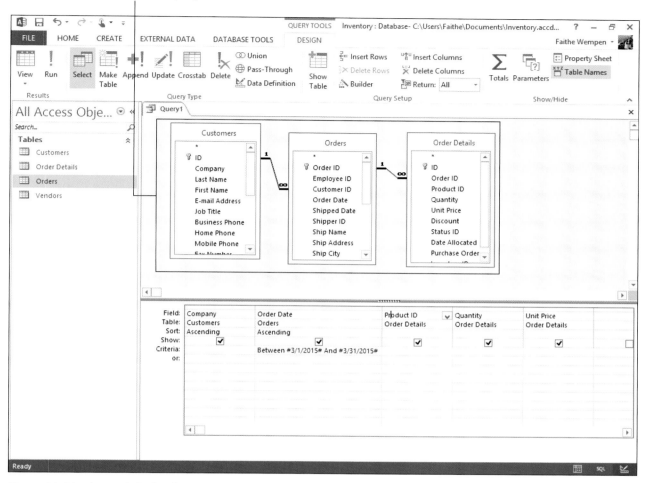

Tables used in the query

Figure 11.11 A query in Design view that extracts certain fields and certain records and sorts them first by Company and then by Order Date.

Table 11.2: Writing Criteria in the QBE Grid

Data Type	Instructions	Example
Text	Place in quotation marks	"Chicago"
		Finds only records that contain exactly that value
	Exclude values with NOT	NOT "Chicago"
		Finds records that do not contain exactly that value
	Begin with the specified string with Like	Like "Chi"
		Finds records that begin with that string (Chicago, China)
	Exclude beginning with a specified string with Not Like	Not Like "Chi"
		Excludes records that begin with that string
	Include the specified string with Like and a wildcard character *	Like "*Chicago*"
		Finds records that have that string anywhere in that field (Old Chicago, Chicago Heights)
	Use OR to include any of a short list of values	"Chicago" OR "New York"
		Finds records that have one or the other of those two values

continued

Table 11.2 continued

Data Type	Instructions	Example
	Use IN to include any of a longer list of values	In ("Chicago","New York","Philadelphia","Seattle")
		Finds records that have any of the listed values
Empty or Non-Empty Fields	Use Is Null to find empty fields or Is Not Null to find non-empty fields	Is Null finds empty fields
		Is Not Null finds non-empty fields
Number or Currency Fields	Use the numbers without any special characters	12
		Finds records that have an exact value of 12
	Use NOT to exclude a value	NOT 12
		Finds records that do not have an exact value of 12
	Use > and < for greater than and less than	>6
	Use >= for greater than or equal to	Finds records where the value is greater than 6
	Use <= for less than or equal to	
	Use Between to specify a range	Between 0 and 12
		Finds records where the values are greater than 0 and less than 12
	Use IN to include any of a longer list of values	IN ($5, $10, $15, $20)
		Finds records that contain one of the listed values
Date and Time Fields	Use # around an exact date	#12/21/2014#
		Finds records that contain exactly that date
	Use > and < for greater than and less than	>#12/21/2014#
	Use >= for greater than or equal to	Finds records where the date is after the specified date
	Use <= for less than or equal to	>#2/1/2014# and <#2/28/2014#
		Finds values that fall within the specified date range
		<#2/1/2014# or >#2/28/2014#
		Finds values that fall outside of the specified date range

NOTE For a query that just selects data, like the ones you create in this chapter, switching to Datasheet view and clicking the Run button do the same thing. For other types of queries that you might create, though, the buttons serve differently: Run executes the instructions in the query to actually modify the data, whereas switching to Datasheet view does not.

Figure 11.12 shows the results of the query from Figure 11.11 in Datasheet view. To switch to Datasheet view, you can either click the View button or the Run button on the Query Tools Design tab.

Company ▾	Order Date ▾	Product ▾	Quantity ▾	Unit Price ▾
Company A	3/24/2015	81	25	$2.99
Company A	3/24/2015	43	25	$46.00
Company A	3/24/2015	1	25	$18.00
Company BB	3/10/2015	43	300	$46.00
Company F	3/6/2015	8	17	$40.00
Company G	3/24/2015	43	300	$46.00
Company H	3/22/2015	48	100	$12.75
Company J	3/24/2015	19	10	$9.20
Company J	3/24/2015	4	10	$22.00
Company J	3/24/2015	6	10	$25.00
Company J	3/24/2015	81	200	$2.99
Company K	3/24/2015	81	50	$2.99
Company K	3/24/2015	80	20	$3.50

Figure 11.12   The query from Figure 11.11 shown in Datasheet view.

Step by Step

Creating a Query in Design View

Follow these steps to create a detail query in Design view:

1. On the Create tab, click Query Design. A blank QBE grid opens, and the Show table dialog box opens.

2. Click a table from which you want to use fields, and click Add. Repeat for each additional table you also want to use fields from, and then click Close to close the dialog box.

3. Drag a field from a table to the QBE grid at the bottom of the screen. Do this for each field you want to include, in the order they should appear in the query results.

Note: If you make a mistake in the order, you can drag a field to reposition it. Select it by clicking the thin gray bar above the field name in the QBE grid, so that the column for that field turns black, and then drag to the left or right.

4. To sort by a certain field, click in the Sort line for that field, so that a drop-down list arrow appears. Open the drop-down list and choose Ascending or Descending.

Note: If more than one field has sorting enabled, data will be sorted from left to right; the leftmost field marked for sorting will be the primary sort.

5. To filter by a certain field, enter the criteria in the Criteria line for that field. Table 11.2 summarizes the way to enter different types of data.

6. (Optional) If you want to hide a certain field from the results, clear the check box in its Show line. You might filter by a certain field but then hide that field from the results, for example.

7. Click the Run button on the Query Tools Design tab to see the query results, or switch to Datasheet view.

Quick Review

1. How do you create a query that contains data from multiple tables?

2. How do you enter selection criteria for a query?

3. How do you specify that records should be included where a particular field is not empty?

Creating Forms and Reports

Forms provide data entry assistance by displaying the records in a more attractive and accessible onscreen format. There are many ways to create forms, as you can see in the Forms group on the Create tab. In this section, you'll use the easiest method, which is the Form button. Just by clicking the button, you get a fully developed form. If there is a related table, the related table's data appears as a sub-form. See Figure 11.13.

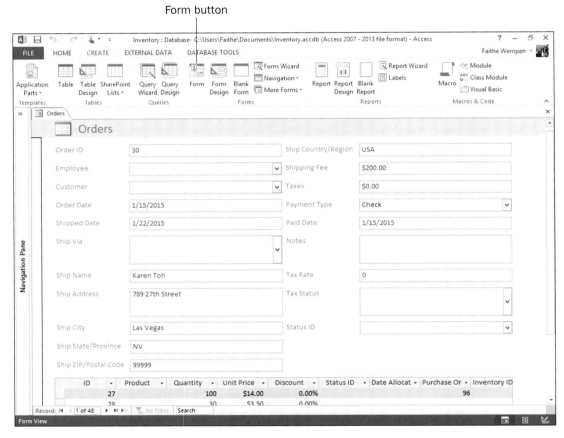

Figure 11.13   A form created with the Form button.

Setting Program Options

Access has a large array of customizable options, both for the individual database you are working with and for the program in general. Click File⟿Options to open the Access Options dialog box and explore what's available. Here are just a few highlights:

- On the Current Database page, if you want a certain form to open when the database opens, select it from the Display Form drop-down list. You can create forms with buttons on them that users can click to open specific forms and tables, creating a very user-friendly environment.

- On the Datasheet page, you can change the default font size for text that appears in the datasheet. For example, you could increase the font size for someone with limited vision.

- On the Object Designers page, you can change the defaults for new fields, such as choosing a different field type or default field size.

- On the Client Settings page, you can change the way Access behaves when users are entering and editing data. For example, you can choose what happens when they press Enter or an arrow key and whether or not to display a confirmation box when performing certain activities.

Step by Step

Creating a Quick Form

Follow these steps to quickly create a form for a table:

1. In the navigation pane, select the table on which to base the form.

2. On the Create tab, click Form. The form opens in Layout view.

3. Switch to Form view to start using the form, or edit the form in Layout or Design view as needed.

There are three views for forms:

- **Form view:** This is the view in which you use the form to work with the data. The form itself is not editable in this view.

- **Layout view:** This is an editable view of the form that looks almost exactly like Form view: what you see is what you get (WYSIWYG). In this view, you can add and remove fields and other basics, and the existing fields move over to make room or close up the space when something is deleted. Layout view is simple for beginners.

- **Design view:** This is a fully editable view of the form, on which you can make the full range of changes. You can drag fields around to position them exactly here, add calculated controls, and much more beyond the scope of this chapter. Design view provides the detailed level of control that professionals want to have. Figure 11.14 shows the form from Figure 11.13 in Design view.

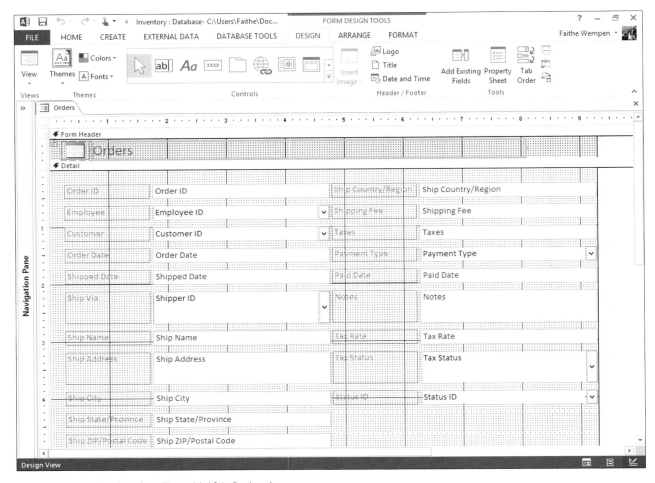

Figure 11.14 The form from Figure 11.13 in Design view.

TIP Another easy way to create a form is the Form Wizard, which you can access from the Forms group on the Create tab. The Form Wizard enables you to select only certain fields to include on the form, and also allows you to choose among several layouts and formatting styles.

Whereas forms are designed to be used onscreen, reports are designed to be printed. Forms and reports have much in common in terms of how they are created and edited. Reports also have Layout and Design views as two different ways of modifying them: Layout for simple edits that a beginner can make, and Design for precise control.

To create a report, use the Report button in the Report group on the Create tab to create a default-styled report with all the fields from the selected table or query, or try out the Report Wizard for a few more choices.

For reports, a Report view and a Print Preview view are both available. Report view is designed for reading the report onscreen, whereas Print Preview view is designed for seeing how the report will look when printed, but they are very similar.

Creating a Quick Report

Follow these steps to quickly create a report from a table or query:

1. In the navigation pane, select the table or query on which to base the report.

2. On the Create tab, click Report. The report opens in Layout view.

Printing a Report

Follow these steps to print a report:

1. Switch to Print Preview view.

2. Click the Print button on the Print Preview tab. The Print dialog box opens.

3. Change any printer settings as desired.

Print button

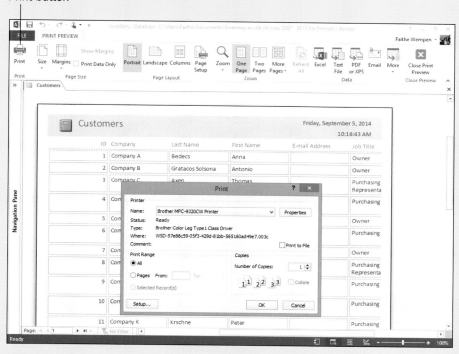

4. Click OK.

Quick Review

1. What is the difference between a form and a report?

2. What are the three views in which you can view a report?

3. How do you make a certain form automatically open when the database opens?

Summary

Understanding Access Databases

Microsoft Access is a **database management system (DBMS)**. It stores not only data but also helper objects such as **forms**, **reports**, and **queries**. Tables and query results are typically displayed in **Datasheet view**, which looks like a spreadsheet. A **query** is a saved specification for sorting and filtering the data in one or more tables. By creating **relationships** between tables, you can connect the data from multiple tables, such as connecting customers to orders.

Creating Databases and Tables

A database file starts with one or more tables; a table is the only database object that can store data. The tables and other objects in the database appear in the **navigation pane**. You can create a table in either **Datasheet view** or **Design view**. A table consists of one or more fields, each of which has a field type (text, number, and so on) that dictates what data can be placed in it. You can adjust the properties of a field to further define it, such as assigning a default value or making it required.

The **primary key** is the field that is used to distinguish one record from another. When creating **relationships** between tables, the primary key field in one table is usually related to a **foreign key** in another table. You can optionally enforce **referential integrity** on a relationship to prevent data from being entered that does not work with the relationship.

You can enter data directly into a datasheet. Click and start typing, and use Tab to move to the next field, just like in Excel. You don't have to save a record; it is saved automatically when you leave it.

Creating Queries

A query is a view of a table that shows it in a different way, such as hiding certain fields or records and sorting the records in a certain order. One way to create a query is with the Simple Query Wizard. It enables you to select a subset of fields from multiple tables and show either details or a summary of the data (a **detail query** or **summary query**, respectively).

You can also create a query in Design view. You can add tables, and then select fields from those tables. You can choose to sort by certain fields, and enter criteria to filter the record set.

Creating Forms and Reports

Forms provide data entry assistance by displaying records in a more attractive and accessible onscreen format. Use the Quick Form feature by clicking the Form button on the Create tab. You can work with forms in Form view (for data entry), Layout view (for simple form changes), and Design view (for more complicated form changes).

A report is designed to be printed. You can create a Quick Report with the Report button on the Create tab, or try out the Report Wizard for more choices.

Key Terms

database
database management system (DBMS)
Datasheet view
Design view
detail query
foreign key
form
lookup
navigation pane

one-to-many relationship
primary key
query
referential integrity
relationship
report
select query
summary query

Test Yourself

Fact Check

1. In what view does data from a table appear in a spreadsheetlike grid?

   a. Design

   b. Datasheet

   c. Grid

   d. Layout

2. What database object is useful for data entry?

   a. report

   b. query

   c. form

   d. relationship

3. What database object is useful for recalling a saved sort-and-filter operation?

   a. report

   b. query

   c. form

   d. relationship

4. Where is the navigation pane located in Access?

   a. top

   b. bottom

   c. left

   d. right

5. What field type holds a large amount of text—up to 65,536 characters?

   a. short text

   b. long text

   c. OLE object

   d. hyperlink

6. What is the purpose of the primary key?

   a. Identifies the first field

   b. Identifies the unique field

   c. Identifies the last field

   d. Identifies the longest field

7. When you create a relationship, the primary key in one table is usually related to the _____ in another table.

   a. report key

   b. foreign key

   c. master key

   d. secondary key

8. Cascade Update Related Fields and Cascade Delete Related Records are available options only when you enforce _____ in a relationship.

   a. indexing

   b. numeric integrity

   c. the Required property

   d. referential integrity

9. What object enables you to define filtering criteria?

   a. form

   b. table

   c. relationship

   d. query

10. What type of database object is designed to be used for printing?

    a. report

    b. query

    c. table

    d. form

Matching

Match the terms to their meanings.

   a. referential integrity

   b. query

   c. form

   d. relationship

   e. report

   f. table

1. _____ Sorts and filters data from one or more tables.

2. _____ Provides a user-friendly interface for working with records onscreen one at a time.

3. _____ Provides an attractive layout of data that is ready for printing.

4. _____ Connects the primary key in one table to the foreign key in another.

5. _____ Stores data.

6. _____ Prevents data in one table from being entered without a corresponding value in another table.

Sum It Up

1. Explain the purpose of each of the following objects: table, form, query, and report.

2. List at least four field types, and give an example of data that could be stored in each.

3. Describe what happens when you delete a record in a table that has a relationship with another table in which Cascade Delete Related Records is enabled.

4. Explain two ways of creating a new table.

5. Explain two ways of creating a query, and list one benefit of each method that the other method lacks.

Explore More

Normalization

Part I: A database is said to be *normalized* when certain design requirements are met. Use the web to research database normalization and write a one-page paper that explains the first two normalization rules: First Normal Form (1NF) and Second Normal Form (2NF).

Part II: Plan a database (table names, field names, and relationships) in which 1NF and 2NF are enforced, and explain why you made the choices you made.

Form and Report Editing

After creating a form or report, modify it in Layout view. Make at least three edits, including reordering the fields, changing the title, and changing the font color of the data labels. Close it without saving your changes.

Next, do the same thing to the same form or report, but do it in Design view. Make the same edits you made before.

Write a one-page paper or an email discussing the experience. Which view did you find easier to use? Which view would you probably use in the future to make changes to forms and reports?

Northwind Traders

Microsoft provides a sample database called Northwind that contains many different objects along with example data. It is a good database to look through to see the scope of what can be accomplished with Access. To see it, start a new database using the Northwind template. Examine several of each type of object (table, form, query, and report). Make notes about what you see and what types of objects you might be interested in incorporating in your own databases.

Think It Over

Excel or Access?

Now that you have studied both Excel and Access, go through the following list and state which application you think would be more suitable for the project: Excel or Access, and why.

- An inventory management system for a warehouse
- A home budget
- A detailed financial proposal with many calculations
- A single-table list of a baseball team's members and their contact information
- Personnel records for a small business

Securing a Database

When creating a database to which multiple people will have access, security and data integrity become concerns. Make a list of the problems that could occur, and briefly note how you might address them.

Creating Reports

Suppose you had a database that tracked the product sales in a retail showroom for lighting fixtures. At the end of the week, the owner would like some reports to help him understand the week's revenues. Describe the report(s) you would create for him to provide that information. What fields would you include, from what tables? What fields would you calculate or summarize?

Chapter 12

Creating Presentation Graphics with PowerPoint

Learning objectives

☐ Build a basic PowerPoint presentation

☐ Format a presentation

☐ Create and insert multiple types of content on slides

☐ Apply transitions and animation effects

☐ Present a live slide show using a PC

Presentation graphics refers to the visual aids used with public speaking activities, including academic classroom lectures, business presentations, and organizing meetings for hobby groups and clubs. Microsoft PowerPoint is the most popular program in the world for creating presentation graphics. With PowerPoint, you can create and deliver live slide shows, and also distribute recorded shows in a variety of ways, including email, web pages, CDs, and videos.

Presentation graphics Graphics designed to accompany a public speaking activity, a lesson, or a business presentation.

Many of the techniques you learned in Chapter 9, "Word Processing with Microsoft Word" also apply to PowerPoint, such as formatting text and inserting clip art and photos. This chapter won't go over those skills again; instead, it forges ahead to teach you about other content types that haven't been covered yet, like SmartArt and audio/video clips.

By the time you reach the end of this chapter, you will be able to create a simple but effective PowerPoint presentation that includes formatting, multimedia content, transitions, and animations.

Careers in IT

Building a Basic Presentation

The PowerPoint interface is in some ways very similar to that of Word and Excel. It contains the same type of Ribbon, and a File menu with the same types of commands on it.

PowerPoint's default view is Normal view, and it's divided into three main panes, as shown in Figure 12.1. At the left is the navigation pane, also known as the *Slides pane*. It shows thumbnail images of each slide in the presentation. The large center pane is the Slide pane. This is where you create and edit the content of the active slide. (Only one slide is active at a time.) At the bottom is the Notes pane, where you can type notes to yourself or other authors or deliverers of the presentation; the notes don't display to the audience, and they don't print unless you specifically indicate that you want them printed. If you don't see the Notes pane in Normal view, click the Notes button on the status bar to make it display.

If you Outline view is identical to Normal view except it shows the text of each slide rather than thumbnail images of the slides in the navigation pane.

As in Word and Excel, you can change to different views on the View tab, or by using the view buttons on the status bar. Each view is designed for a certain range of activities. For example, Slide Sorter view, shown in Figure 12.2, is designed for viewing and arranging all the slides in the presentation. There are other views too for special situations, such as Notes Pages view for editing speaker notes.

Normal view The default PowerPoint view, in which you can edit the content of individual slides.

navigation pane The pane on the left side of the screen in Normal or Outline view in PowerPoint, showing thumbnail images or text of the presentation.

Slide pane The main editing pane for a slide in Normal view in PowerPoint.

Notes pane The pane in which you type speaker notes in Normal view in PowerPoint.

Outline view A view similar to Normal view except it shows the text of each slide in the navigation pane.

Slide Sorter view The PowerPoint view in which you can browse thumbnail images of all the slides in the presentation and easily rearrange them.

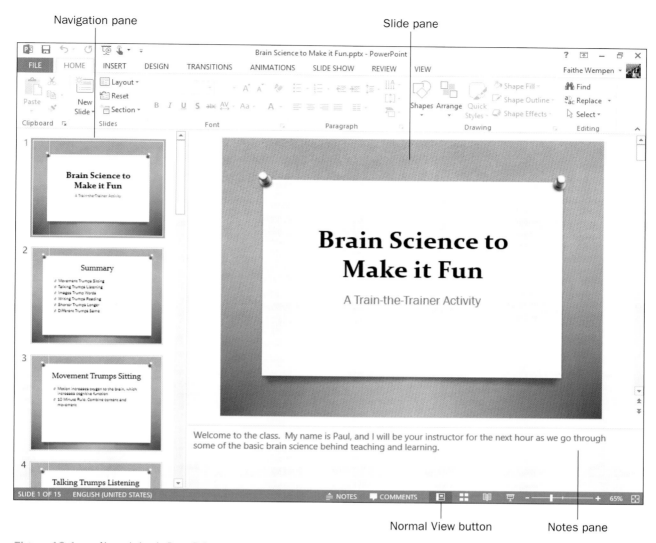

Figure 12.1   Normal view in PowerPoint.

Entering and Editing Text

In PowerPoint, everything you enter (text, graphics, and so on) appears in a movable frame on a slide. You can't type anything directly onto a slide the way you type directly into a Word document.

After starting PowerPoint, press Esc for a new blank presentation, or click the Blank Presentation tile. You can also start using a template if you prefer, as you learned to do with Word in Chapter 9.

When you start a new blank presentation, it has a single slide in it, one that uses the Title Slide layout. A layout is an arrangement of place-holders on a slide. The Title Slide layout contains two placeholders: one for the presentation title, and one for the presentation subtitle. See Figure 12.3. Click in a placeholder and type the desired text.

layout A preset arrangement of placeholders on a PowerPoint slide.

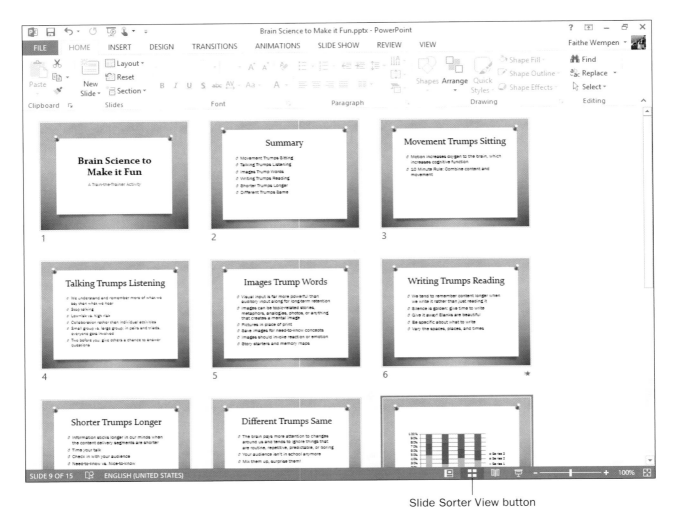

Slide Sorter View button

Figure 12.2 Slide Sorter view in PowerPoint.

To add another slide, click the New Slide button on the Home tab. (Click the button face, not the text beneath the button.) This creates a slide with a layout called Title and Content. As the name implies, it has two placeholders: one for a title, and one multi-purpose placeholder that can accept any type of content. See Figure 12.4. In the content placeholder are six icons representing the six most common types of graphical content; you can click one of those icons to start inserting that content, or you can click in the content placeholder and then type text into it. A content placeholder can hold only one type of content at a time, so if you put text in it, for example, you can't also put a graphic into it; you must either place the graphical content manually on the slide or switch to a different layout that contains more than one content placeholder. If you want the new slide to have some other layout than Title and Content, click the New Slide text below the button's face to open a menu of layouts.

New Slide button

Figure 12.3   The Title Slide layout contains two placeholders.

Insert Chart

Type text here   Insert Table   Insert SmartArt Graphic

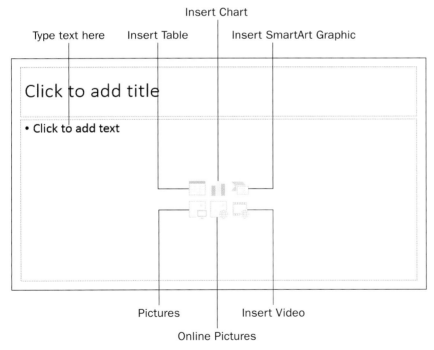

Pictures   Insert Video

Online Pictures

Figure 12.4   The Title and Content layout contains a multi-purpose placeholder.

Changing a Slide's Layout

The layout determines what placeholders appear on the slide and in what positions. Each template comes with a variety of preset layouts, and you can also create your own. To switch an existing slide to another layout, click the Layout button on the Home tab, and then click the desired layout from the gallery, as shown in Figure 12.5.

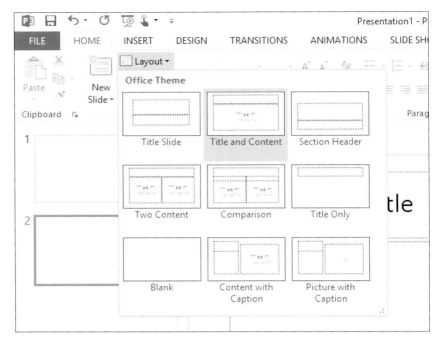

Figure 12.5   Switch to a different layout.

Inserting and Deleting Slides

As you learned in the earlier section, "Entering and Editing Text," one way to insert a new slide is to click the New Slide button on the Home tab. Doing so places a new slide immediately after the active slide. The active slide is the one that appears in the Slide pane, the one that is currently editable. You can change which slide is active by clicking a different slide in the navigation pane.

active slide The slide that currently appears in the Slide pane in Normal view in PowerPoint.

Here are some other ways to create a new slide:

- Press Ctrl+M to insert a new slide after the active slide.

- On the Home tab, click the arrow below the New Slide button to open a gallery of layouts. Click the desired layout to create a new slide based on it.

- In the navigation pane in Normal or Outline view, click between two slides to place a horizontal line between them. Then press Enter to create a slide that uses the same layout as the slide above it.

- In Outline view, in the navigation pane, click to place the insertion point at the beginning of the title line for a slide, and then press Enter to create a new blank slide immediately before that slide.

- To promote a paragraph on an existing slide to be the title of its own slide in Outline view, position the insertion point at the beginning of that line in the navigation pane and press Shift+Tab, or right-click the paragraph and choose Promote.

- Right-click any part of any slide in the navigation pane in Normal or Outline view and choose New Slide from the shortcut menu.

To delete a slide, select it in the navigation pane, and then do either of the following:

- Right-click the slide in the navigation pane and choose Delete Slide.

- Press the Delete key on the keyboard. (If working in Outline view, make sure all the text for the whole slide is selected before pressing Delete.)

Reordering Slides

You can reorder slides from either Normal view or Slide Sorter view, but most people find Slide Sorter view easier. From Slide Sorter view, drag and drop the slides where you want them. Use the Zoom controls on the status bar as needed to zoom in so you can see the slide content better or zoom out so you can see more slides at once.

In Normal view, you can reorder slides by dragging them up and down on the list in the navigation pane. Drag the thumbnail images as you could in Slide Sorter view; the only difference is that the slides appear in one column in Normal view.

In Outline view, click the icon to the left of the slide's title in the navigation pane to make sure the entire slide is selected before dragging up or down.

You can also right-click a selected slide in the navigation pane and then click Move Up or Move Down to rearrange slides.

TIP

Quick Review

1. Which method of inserting a new slide allows you to choose its layout?

2. Why would you want to use Slide Sorter view?

3. What are the six types of content you can insert using the icons in a content placeholder?

Formatting a Presentation

When formatting a presentation, it's important to maintain consistency between slides as much as possible, for a polished and professional look. It is possible to apply separate manual formatting to certain text or objects, as you learned to do in Chapter 9 in Word, but you should have a specific reason for doing so, such as to make certain text stand out or emphasize a point.

The following sections explain several ways to change the formatting of the presentation as a whole.

Setting the Slide Size and Orientation

You can set a size in inches for the presentation's slides, but when you deliver an onscreen presentation, the slide fills the entire screen, regardless of the slide size. That said, it's more useful to think about slide size as a ratio of width to height (an aspect ratio) rather than as a literal measurement.

The aspect ratio to choose depends on the aspect ratio of the monitor on which the presentation is going to be shown. For a standard monitor (like an older-style CRT or a standard-definition TV), choose a ratio of 4:3. For a widescreen monitor, choose a ratio of 16:9. (See Figure 12.6.)

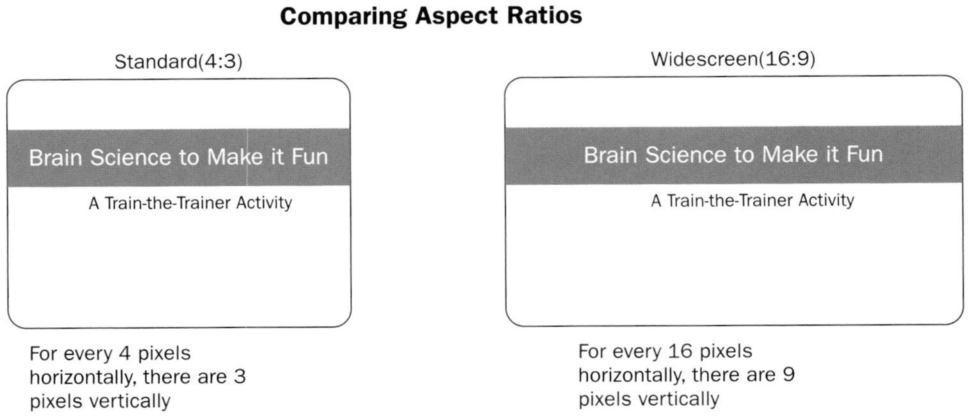

Comparing Aspect Ratios

Standard(4:3)   Widescreen(16:9)

Brain Science to Make it Fun   Brain Science to Make it Fun

A Train-the-Trainer Activity   A Train-the-Trainer Activity

For every 4 pixels   For every 16 pixels
horizontally, there are 3   horizontally, there are 9
pixels vertically   pixels vertically

Figure 12.6   Aspect ratios for standard versus widescreen monitors.

If you are planning to distribute the presentation on paper rather than showing it onscreen, slide size does make a difference. You can specify an exact height and width for the slides, or you can choose from among many presets for different paper types, such as Letter, A3, Overhead, and Banner.

You can also set a slide orientation. By default, presentations are in Landscape orientation, which means the slides are wider than they are tall. You can reverse that by changing to Portrait orientation for special situations, such as when you are presenting on a monitor that is rotated 90 degrees.

Step by Step

Changing the Slide Aspect Ratio
Use these steps to change the slide size to the Standard or Widescreen preset.

1. On the Design tab, click Slide Size.

2. Click Standard (4:3) or Widescreen (16:9).

Changing the Slide and Orientation

Use these steps to change the slide size and orientation to a custom setting.

1. On the Design tab, click Slide Size.

2. Click Custom Slide Size. The Slide Size dialog box opens.

3. Open the Slides Sized For drop-down list and select a size or aspect ratio.

   OR

   Enter an exact width and height in the Width and Height text boxes.

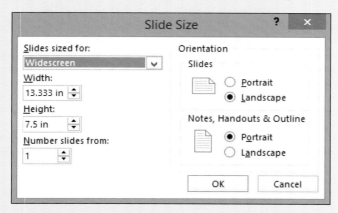

4. Under Orientation, click the Portrait or Landscape button for Slides.

5. Click the Portrait or Landscape button for Notes, Handouts & Outline.

6. Click OK.

Changing the Presentation Theme

You learned about themes, theme fonts, and theme colors in Chapters 8 ("Understanding Microsoft Office 2013) and 9 ("Word Processing with Microsoft Word"). Recall that a theme is a preset combination of formatting that you apply to an entire document, workbook, or presentation. At a minimum, a theme contains font choices, color choices, and effect choices. When applied to a presentation in PowerPoint, the theme also supplies other formatting information, such as a background image (in some cases) and a set of slide layouts with placeholders positioned in certain spots on each layout. Because different layouts are associated with different themes, applying a theme can change the presentation's look in more dramatic ways than it does in Word and Excel files. For example, Figure 12.7 shows the same slide with four different themes applied to it.

Figure 12.7   A theme can change the placement and appearance of content on a slide.

 **TIP**   If you don't like the background graphics in a theme but you like the other features of it, apply the theme and then on the Design tab, click Format Background to display the Format Background task pane and mark the Hide Background Graphic check box there.

New in PowerPoint 2013, you can apply variants for certain themes. Any available variants appear in the Variants group on the Design tab. A variant might consists of different background graphics and/or different colors, for example.

If you like the colors from one and the background from another, feel free to mix up theme colors, fonts, and effects. First apply an overall theme and then click the More button in the Variants group on the Design tab to open a menu system in which you can choose different Colors, Fonts, Effects, and Background Styles.

Step by Step

Changing the Theme and Variant
Use these steps to choose a different theme, colors, fonts, and/or effects for a presentation:

1. On the Design tab, click the More button in the Themes group to open the full gallery of themes.

More button for Themes   More button for Variants

2. Scroll through the list of themes, and click the desired theme.

3. (Optional) Click a variant in the Variants group, or click the More button in the Variants group to open the complete gallery of variants and click the desired variant.

4. (Optional) Click the More button in the Variants group, point to Colors, and choose a different set of theme colors.

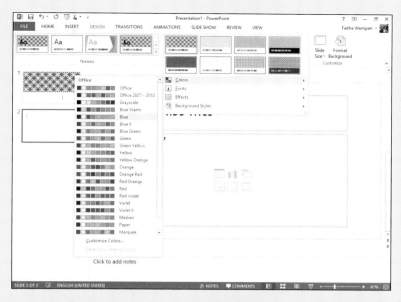

5. (Optional) Click the More button in the Variants group, point to Fonts, and choose a different set of theme fonts.

6. (Optional) Click the More button in the Variants group, point to Effects, and choose a different set of theme effects.

Theme Applies Inconsistently

If certain text doesn't conform to the font and/or font size settings supplied by the theme, that text might have had manual formatting applied to it earlier. Manually formatted text doesn't change when you choose a different theme or theme fonts. To remove manual formatting from text, select the text and press Ctrl+spacebar, or click the Clear All Formatting button ( ) in the Font group of the Home tab.

Working in Slide Master View

Slide Master view is the view in which you can view and modify the slide layouts on which you base individual slides. The slide master is the overall guide for slides using the currently selected theme. Subordinate to the slide master are multiple layout masters, each of which defines the exact content and positioning for a particular layout (such as the Title and Content layout you worked with earlier). To enter Slide Master view, as shown in Figure 12.8, click Slide Master on the View tab. To exit Slide Master view, click the Close Master View button on the Slide Master tab.

In Slide Master view, thumbnail images appear in the navigation pane on the left. The image at the top of the pane is the slide master itself. Changes made to it affect all layouts based on it. Below the slide master are the individual layout masters. Masters that contain content placeholders that accept text include multiple levels of bulleted lists. Changes you make to one of these levels affects all paragraphs that have that level in the hierarchy of a slide. For example, make changes to the topmost bulleted list item to change first-level bulleted paragraphs.

Slide Master view The PowerPoint view in which you can make changes to the slide master.

slide master The template slide that controls the appearance and repeated elements for all slides in a presentation.

layout master The template slide that controls the appearance and repeated elements for all slides that use a certain layout in a presentation.

Slide Master

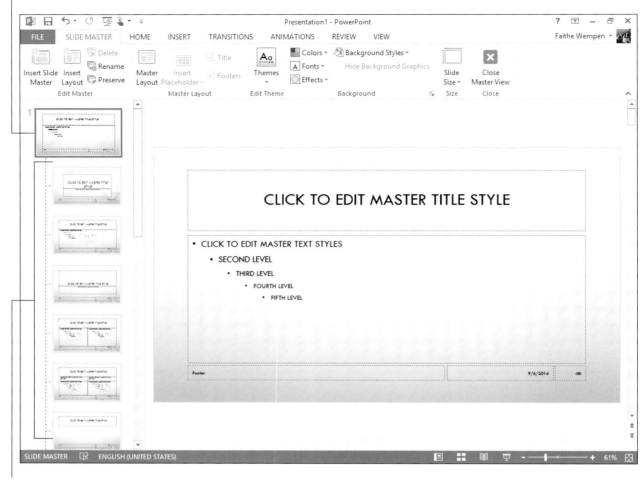

Layout Masters

Figure 12.8   Slide Master view.

TIP

The Footer, Date/Time, and # text boxes on slide masters and layout masters determine where the footer, date, and slide number elements will appear if they are enabled. (They're not enabled by default.) Rather than typing text into these text boxes in Slide Master view, just position the text boxes where you want that information to appear on the slide. Then after exiting Slide Master view, on the Insert tab, click Header & Footer, and enable the desired repeating elements in the dialog box that appears.

Some of the changes you might make to a slide master or layout master include:

- Changing text font, size, color, and attributes for certain paragraph levels. Use the tools on the Home tab's Font group, as you learned in Chapters 8 and 9.

- Moving or resizing the placeholders, the same way you learned to move and resize objects in Chapter 8.

- Adding a graphic or text box that should repeat on every slide. Use the Insert tab to insert various types of content.

■ Adding or removing placeholders. To add a placeholder, use the Insert Placeholder button in the Master Layout group on the Slide Master tab. To remove a placeholder, select its border and press Delete.

Quick Review

1. What is the difference between a slide master and a layout master?

2. How do you apply a different theme to a presentation?

3. How do you change the aspect ratio of the presentation's slides?

Creating and Inserting Content

PowerPoint slides can accept many types of content, so you can use PowerPoint to showcase information in a variety of forms. For example, a slide can include tables, graphics, videos, and charts, in combination with explanatory text.

Each content type can be inserted manually on a slide using the commands on the Insert tab. When you manually place an object on a slide, it appears in the center of the slide, and from there you can move and resize it as needed. When you apply different layouts to the slide, the manually placed content does not move.

You can also put content into content placeholders. When you do this, the content becomes part of the slide's layout, and if you change to a different layout that positions the content placeholder differently, the item moves to the new position. If the new layout does not have a placeholder appropriate to that type of content, the content is converted over to a manually placed object and becomes disassociated with the layout.

Inserting a Text Box

Besides the text placeholders on slides, you can also manually place text boxes on a slide. The content of these text boxes does not appear in the navigation pane in Outline view, nor when printing or exporting a text outline for the presentation, so limit such text boxes to non-essential text, such as an identifying label near a graphic or a tip or caution.

You can insert a text box in two ways; each results in a text box with different settings:

■ On the Insert tab, click Text Box and then click where you want the text box to begin. Then start typing. The text box expands horizontally as needed for the text you enter. It doesn't start a new line unless you press Enter (or Shift+Enter) to force it.

■ On the Insert tab, click Text Box, and then drag a rectangle where you want the text box. The box takes on the width you specified. As you type, if the cursor reaches the edge of the text box, it moves to the next line.

You can move, resize, and format a text box just like any other object in an Office application. Chapter 8 covered object placement, sizing, and formatting.

Changing Text Box Settings

Troubleshooting

If the text box isn't behaving the way you want, you can change its settings. Select the text box, and then on the Drawing Tools Format tab, click the dialog box launcher in the WordArt Styles group to open the Format Shape task pane with the Text Options displayed. Click the Textbox icon (the rightmost icon) and then change the text box's settings in the controls that appear. For example, the Wrap Text in Shape check box toggles on/off the capability for text to wrap to the next line when it reaches the edge of the text box. You can also set the text box to Autofit, which shrinks the font size in a text box or text placeholder to make it continue to fit at the box's current size.

Creating a Table

A table in PowerPoint is a grid of rows and columns, with cells at their intersections. You type text into cells to organize the text into an orderly grid. Tables in PowerPoint are much like tables in Word, except somewhat simpler. To insert a table, click the Insert Table icon in a content placeholder box, or use the Table button on the Insert tab to insert a table manually. If you use the Table button, you can choose from among several methods, just like in Word, including dragging across a grid of squares to specify table size and drawing a table with the mouse pointer as a pencil tool.

Step by Step

Inserting a Table in a Content Placeholder

Use these steps to place a table in a slide's content placeholder:

1. On the slide, click the Insert Table icon in the content placeholder. The Insert Table dialog box opens.

2. Specify a number of columns in the Number of Columns text box.

Insert Table

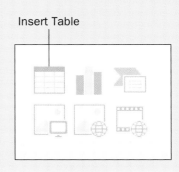

3. Specify a number of rows in the Number of Rows text box.

4. Click OK to insert the table.

5. Type text in the table as desired.

Inserting a Table without a Placeholder

Use these steps to place a table on a slide that may not have a content placeholder available to hold a table:

1. Display the slide on which you want to create a table.

2. On the Insert tab, click the Table button.

3. Drag across the grid to select the number of rows and columns you want, and then release the mouse button to complete the table.

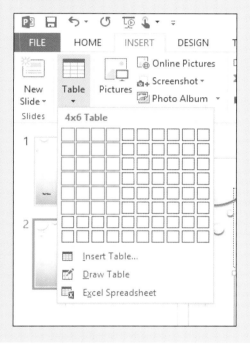

Inserting Audio and Video Clips

An audio clip is a file that contains sound, such as music, narration, or a sound effect. A video clip is a file that contains motion video. You can insert audio and video clips directly onto a slide, so that they play automatically or when clicked as part of the slide show.

audio clip A file that stores a sound, narration, or music.

video clip A file that stores motion video.

You can also incorporate sound clips in other ways too. For example, you can assign a sound clip to a transition or animation effect, so that the sound happens whenever that event occurs. You can also attach a sound to a graphic object on the slide, so that when that object is clicked, the sound plays.

There are three different ways to insert an audio clip on a slide:

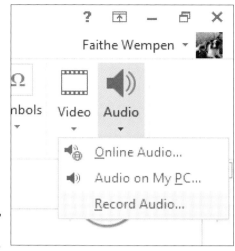

Figure 12.9 Record an audio clip to include in the presentation.

- **You can record your own audio clip from within PowerPoint.** To use this method, on the Insert tab, click the down arrow under the Audio button and then click Record Audio. See Figure 12.9.

- **You can insert an audio clip from a file that you already have.** To use this method, on the Insert tab, click the Audio button and then choose Audio on My PC to open the Insert Audio dialog box and then choose the desired clip.

- **You can locate an audio clip using the Internet.** Office.com provides hundreds of audio clips you can use royalty-free. To use this method, on the Insert tab, click the Audio button, and click Online Audio. Then search for an audio clip the same way you search for clip art (as described in Chapter 9).

Regardless of the method used for inserting the clip, you can work with it the same way after insertion. The clip appears on the slide, as shown in Figure 12.10, and controls for it appear on the Audio Tools Format and Audio Tools Playback tabs on the Ribbon. The Audio Tools Format tab contains commands for making the clip's icon appear a certain way, and the Audio Tools Playback tab contains commands for controlling how and when the clip will play.

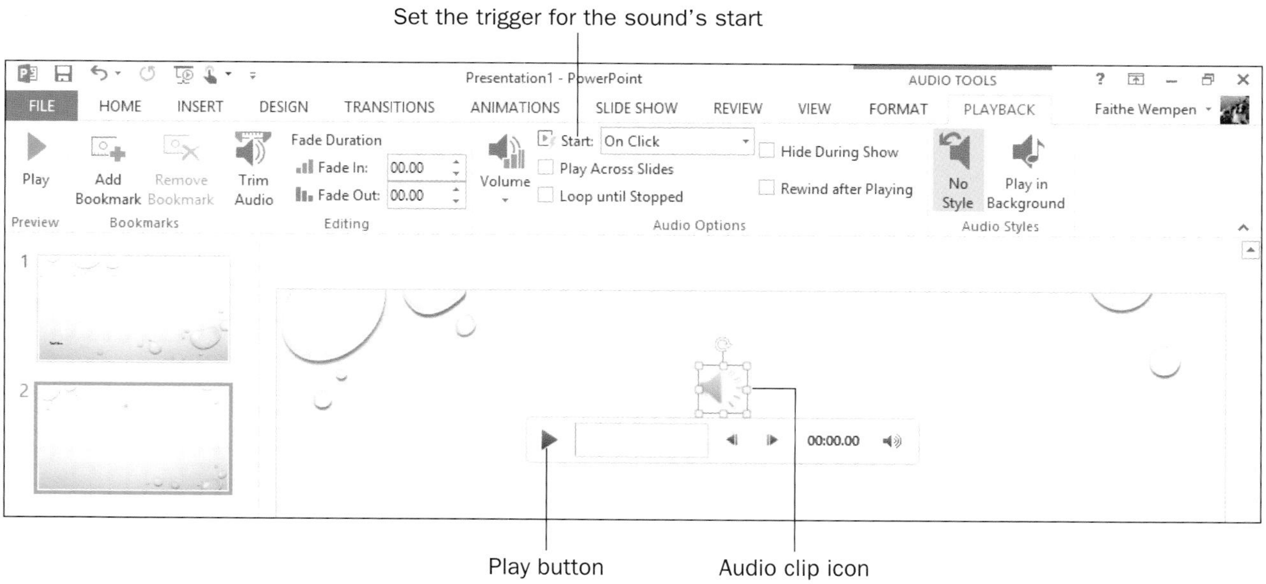

Set the trigger for the sound's start

Play button   Audio clip icon

Figure 12.10 Control an audio clip's playback and appearance.

Inserting a video clip is similar to inserting an audio clip except you don't have the option of recording new ones from within PowerPoint. Click Video button on the Insert tab to choose whether you want Online Video or Video on My PC. You can also click the Insert Video icon in a content placeholder.

You can control whether a clip should play automatically when the slide appears or wait until it is clicked to play. You can find that setting on the Playback tab (Audio Tools Playback or Video Tools Playback, depending on the clip type). Open the Start list and choose Automatically or On Click.

Inserting Pictures

Inserting pictures in PowerPoint is similar to inserting them in Word, which you learned about in Chapter 9. To insert a manually placed image, use the Insert tab's Pictures button to insert from a file you already have, or use the Online Pictures button to find an image from an online source. Or, to fill a placeholder, click the Pictures or Online Pictures icon in the placeholder box.

Drawing Shapes

Using the Shapes feature, you can draw your own vector-based lines and shapes on a slide in PowerPoint, for all kinds of reasons. You might construct your own simple drawings out of these lines and shapes, or you could use them as accents for the other content on the slide, such as an arrow to point out a certain area of a photo or chart.

Shapes The drawing feature in Office applications that enables users to create vector-based lines and shapes.

To draw a line or shape, click the Shapes button on the Insert tab, as shown in Figure 12.11, click the desired shape, and then drag across the slide to draw the line or shape. You can move, resize, and format lines and shapes just like any other content. You can also type text into shapes, creating impromptu text boxes.

A text box is the same element as a drawn rectangle shape, and can be formatted in all the same ways. To convert a rectangular text box to some other shape with text in it, select the shape and then on the Drawing Tools Format tab, in the Insert Shapes group, click the Edit Shape button, point to Change Shape, and select one of the drawing shapes.

TIP

Inserting a Chart

To start a chart in PowerPoint, use the Insert Chart icon in the content placeholder, or use the Chart button on the Insert tab.

Excel's charting feature is integrated with Excel, so that when you start a new chart in PowerPoint, an Excel window opens into which you can enter the data for it. In the Excel window, some placeholder data appears, as shown in Figure 12.12. A blue outline appears around the range that will be charted; you can drag the small triangle in the lower-right corner of that outlined range to change the range area to have more or fewer rows or columns included. Change the generic labels in the sample data as needed.

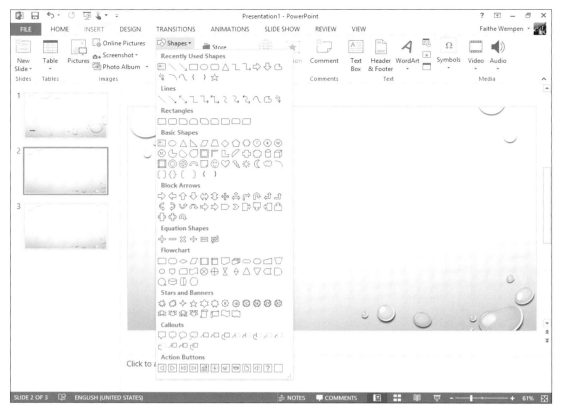

Figure 12.11 Choose a line or shape and then drag on the slide to create it.

Inserting a Chart

Use these steps to place a chart on a PowerPoint slide:

1. Click the Insert Chart content placeholder icon, or on the Insert tab, click Chart. The Insert Chart dialog box opens.

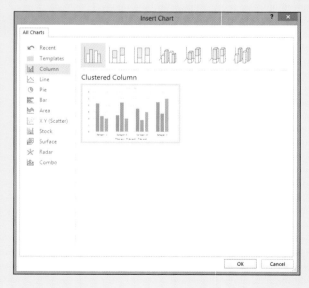

2. Select the chart type on the left, and then the subtype across the top, and then a template in the center (if there is more than one for the chosen subtype), and then click OK. Excel opens (refer to Figure 12.12).

3. Replace the generic data with your own data and then close the Excel window.

   If you later need to reopen the Excel window to edit the data further, click the Edit Data button on the Chart Tools Design tab.

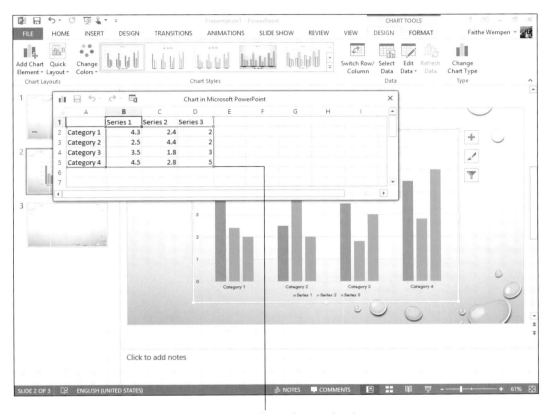

Drag the small blue triangle to change the data range

Figure 12.12   Excel opens when you start constructing a chart in PowerPoint.

Formatting a chart works the same in PowerPoint as it does in Excel. Refer to Chapter 10, "Creating Spreadsheets with Microsoft Excel," for information about chart formatting.

Creating SmartArt

SmartArt combines the visual interest of a graphic with the information of text. This type of object is available in multiple Office applications, but it is especially well suited for PowerPoint because of the focus on delivering information conceptually. Figure 12.13 shows several examples of SmartArt graphics. SmartArt not only can present text, but also can show relationships between ideas, illustrate processes, and outline an organization's structure.

SmartArt A tool in Office applications that combines shapes with text listings to create informative and visually interesting graphics.

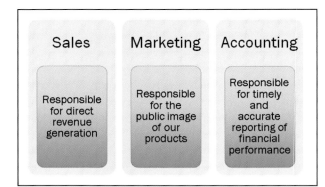
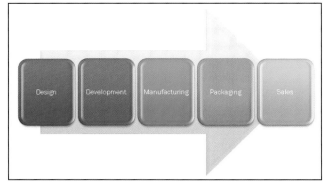
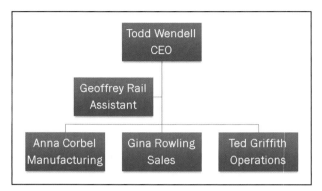

Figure 12.13   SmartArt helps deliver text information in a graphical way.

You can use the Insert a SmartArt Graphic icon in a content placeholder to start some SmartArt, or you can use the SmartArt button on the Insert tab. You can also convert existing text (for example, an existing bulleted list on a slide) to SmartArt by selecting the text and then clicking the Convert to SmartArt Graphic button in the Paragraph group of the Home tab.

Step by Step

Creating a New SmartArt Graphic

Use these steps to create a SmartArt graphic:

1. Click the Insert a SmartArt Graphic icon in a content placeholder, or on the Insert tab, click the SmartArt button. The Choose a SmartArt Graphic dialog box opens.

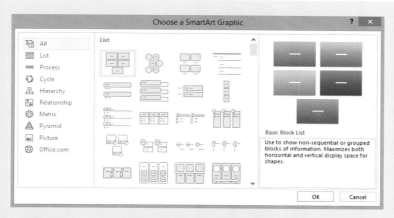

2. Select the category from the left and then select the layout from the right pane. You can change layouts later if desired.

3. Click OK. The graphic appears on the slide.

4. Type text into the text placeholders.

Converting a Text List to a SmartArt Graphic

Use these steps to convert an existing text list to SmartArt:

1. Select the text to be converted.

2. On the Home tab, in the Paragraph group, click the Convert to SmartArt Graphic button.

Convert Text to SmartArt Graphic

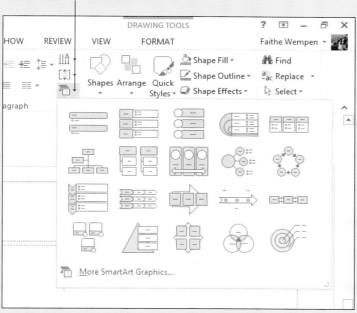

3. On the menu that appears, click a layout type, or click More SmartArt Graphics to see a dialog box.

4. If you chose to open the dialog box, make your selection and click OK.

After creating the SmartArt, you can modify it using the tools on the SmartArt Tools Design tab. You can add and remove shapes, apply a different layout, reorder shapes, and choose a different style. On the SmartArt Tools Format tab, you can choose formatting for individual shapes to make one or more stand out from the rest.

For easier text editing, you might choose to use the text pane. To display it to the left of the graphic, on the SmartArt Tools Design tab click Text Pane, or click the arrow button on the left edge of the graphic's frame. See Figure 12.14.

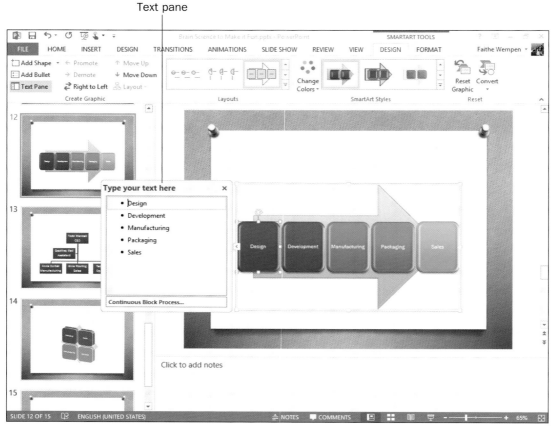

Figure 12.14 Modify a SmartArt graphic with the tools on the SmartArt Tools Design tab.

Step by Step

Modifying a SmartArt Graphic's Layout and Style

To modify a SmartArt Graphic's layout and style, follow these steps:

1. With the SmartArt graphic selected, display the SmartArt Tools Design tab.

2. If you want to change to a different layout, select one from the Layouts group.

3. If you want to change the colors, click the Change Colors button and then select a different color set.

4. If you want to change styles, select one from the SmartArt Styles group.

Adding a Shape

To add a shape to the SmartArt graphic, follow these steps:

1. With the SmartArt graphic selected, display the SmartArt Tools Design tab.

2. Click the shape on the SmartArt that the new shape should follow.

3. Click Add Shape to add a shape of the same level.

   OR

   To add a shape subordinate to the selected one, click the down arrow on the Add Shape button and click Add Shape Below.

Deleting a Shape

To delete a shape, follow these steps:

1. Select a shape.

2. Press the Delete key.

Quick Review

1. How can you convert an existing bulleted list to SmartArt?

2. What other application is used when creating a chart in PowerPoint?

3. How would you insert a video clip from a file?

Applying Transitions and Animations

Transitions and animations add movement to an otherwise static presentation. A transition is a movement effect between one slide and another; an animation is a movement effect of a particular object on a slide.

transition A movement effect between one slide and another.

animation A movement effect of an object on a slide.

Applying Transitions

To select a transition, first select the slides to which it should apply. You can do this in the navigation pane of Normal view or in Slide Sorter view. Or, if you want to affect only one slide, just make it the active slide. (If you want to apply the same transition to all the slides, apply it to one slide and then click Apply to All.)

Then, on the Transitions tab, click the desired transition in the Transition to This Slide group. You can click the More button to open the gallery for more choices. Some transitions have options you can set. If the chosen effect has options available, the Effect Options button becomes active, and you can click it to choose an option. For example, many of the transitions have directional options, such as in Figure 12.15.

Choose a transition   Effect Options button

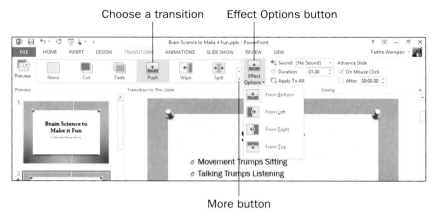

More button

Figure 12.15   Select a transition from the Transitions tab.

In the Timing group, you can control the timing of the transition. The Duration setting indicates how long the transition will take to execute, from start to finish. Transitions are set by default to Advance Slide On Mouse Click, but you can optionally set an After value to make the slide advance automatically after a certain amount of delay.

Applying Animations

Each slide has only one transition, so it's simple to set up, as you saw in the preceding section. Animations, however, are more complicated because you can have multiple animations per slide. You can animate each object separately, and a single object can have multiple animations applied to it.

You can apply four types of animations to an object:

- **Entrance:** Controls when and how the object enters the slide.

- **Emphasis:** Controls what the object does between its entrance and its exit.

- **Exit:** Controls when and how the object exits the slide.

- **Motion path:** Technically a type of emphasis effect but set up separately, a motion path moves an object along an invisible line (a path) that you set up, at a time and speed that you specify.

To sequence the animations on a slide, you can display the Animation pane. (Click the Animation Pane button on the Animations tab to do so.) On the Animation pane, you can move animation effects up or down on the list to change their order, and you can set options and timings for each effect individually. The different animation types appear in different colors in the Animation pane: green for entrance, yellow for emphasis, red for exit, and blue for motion paths. Figure 12.16 shows a sequence of animation effects that includes at least one of each of those.

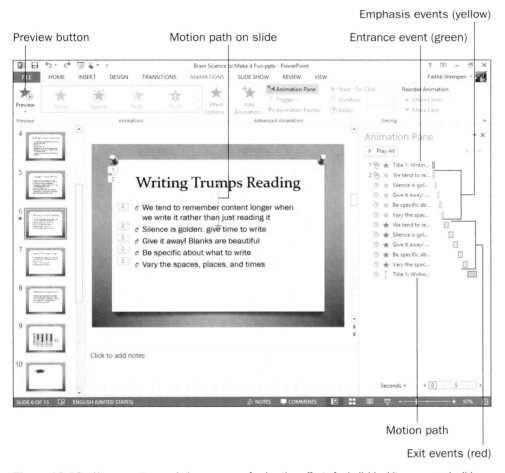

Figure 12.16 You can set up a whole sequence of animation effects for individual items on each slide.

Adding an Animation Effect

To add an animation effect, follow these steps:

1. Select the object to animate.

2. On the Animations tab, click Add Animation.

3. Click the animation effect you want (and then skip the rest of these steps).

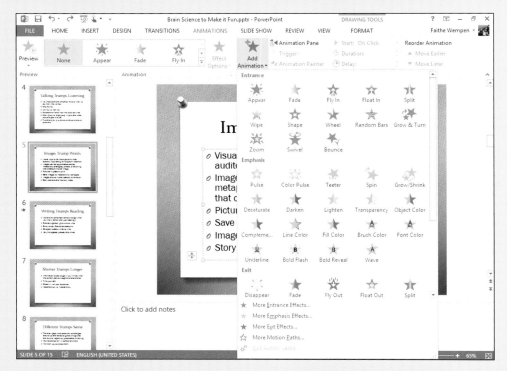

OR

If you don't see the effect you want, choose the More command that matches the type of animation you want (for example, More Entrance Effects).

4. Select the effect from the dialog box that appears. (The name of the dialog box varies.)

5. Click OK.

Adjusting the Animation's Timing

To adjust the animation timing, follow these steps:

1. In the Animation pane, click the animation event to change.

2. On the Animations tab, in the Timing group, open the Start drop-down list and choose a start setting (With Previous, After Previous, or On Click).

Start setting

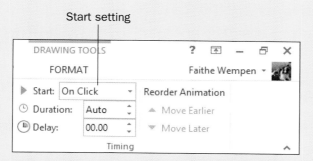

3. In the Duration box, enter the number of seconds for the duration. The lower the number, the more quickly the animation happens.

4. In the Delay box, enter the number of seconds of delay between the previous event and this animation. The previous event is the item above this one in the Animation pane, or if none, the previous event is the transition to the current slide from the previous one.

Changing an Effect's Options (Basic)

To change the animation event, follow these steps:

1. In the Animation pane, click the animation event to change. If the Animation pane does not appear, click the Animation Pane button on the Animations tab.

2. On the Animations tab, click Effect Options and then select an option. The options vary depending on the effect.

Changing an Effect's Options (Advanced)

For more advanced options to change an animation event, follow these steps:

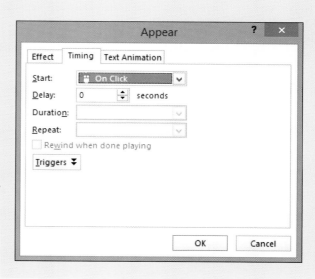

1. In the Animation pane, click the animation event to change.

2. On the Animations tab, click the dialog box launcher in the Animation group, opening a dialog box for the animation. The dialog box name varies.

3. On the Effect tab, set any options as needed. For example, you can choose an accompanying sound effect.

4. Click the Timing tab, and adjust the timing of the animation effect. These are the same controls as on the Animations tab but with a few more options available.

5. Click OK.

Quick Review

1. What is the difference between a transition and an animation?

2. How do you change the direction of a transition?

3. What do the colors of animation events mean in the Animation pane?

Presenting a Slide Show

When you are ready to show your presentation to others, you can use Slide Show view to project a full-screen image of each slide on your screen, one at a time.

To enter Slide Show view, do one of the following:

- Click the Slide Show icon in the status bar.
- On the Slide Show tab, click From Beginning or From Current Slide.

To exit the slide show, press the Esc key, or right-click anywhere on the slide in Slide Show view and choose End Show.

Locking Down Slide Show View

If you leave a presentation running on an unattended computer, you might want to take steps to prevent unauthorized users from stopping the presentation. You can disable some of the ways that normally work to control the presentation in order to make the computer more secure. For example, you could give users only the mouse to navigate with and then prevent the right-click menu and the navigation icons from appearing, so all the users could do would be to click to move forward.

For basic security, on the Slide Show tab, click Set Up Slide Show and then choose Browsed at a Kiosk (Full Screen) as the show type. This disables Presenter View and also sets the show to loop continuously until Esc is pressed. If you hide the keyboard so only you can press Esc, the show remains on.

For even more security, click the File tab and click Options, and then click Advanced. Scroll down to the Slide Show section of the options, and clear the Show Menu on Right Mouse Click and Show Popup Toolbar check boxes.

Slide Show

☑ Show menu on right mouse click ⓘ

☑ Show popup toolbar ⓘ

☑ Prompt to keep ink annotations when exiting

☑ End with black slide

When in Slide Show view, PowerPoint shows navigation icons in the lower-left corner of the screen. The icons appear semitransparent and dimmed until you move your mouse over them; then they become brighter. Figure 12.17 shows the navigation icons. They include Previous and Next buttons for moving between slides, and also these icons:

- **Pen:** Opens a menu of choices for changing the mouse pointer to various types of pens and pointers. You can use the pen tool to draw on the slide using your mouse to emphasize certain points. See Figure 12.18.

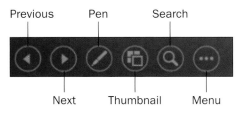

Figure 12.17 The Presentation toolbar in Slide Show view, appearing in the bottom-left corner of the slide.

- **Thumbnails:** Displays thumbnails of the slides in the presentation; you can then jump to a certain slide by clicking its thumbnail.

- **Zoom**: Allows you to zoom in on the content of the active slide.
- **Menu:** Opens a menu of commands for controlling the presentation. See Figure 12.19.

Figure 12.18   The Pen button's menu.

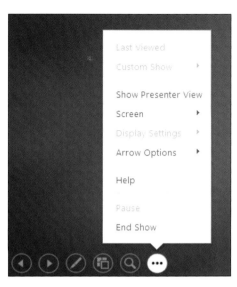

Figure 12.19   The Menu button's menu.

You can also right-click in Slide Show view for a shortcut menu that contains commands from both of the other two menus.

Presenter View

If you have more than one monitor, you might choose to use Presenter view. It is a special mode that applies only to Slide Show view; it shows the presentation on one monitor and shows a special control panel on the other one that includes presenter notes, a preview of what slide is coming up next, and other tools. Presenter view can give you more control of a live presentation by giving you information that your audience doesn't have (or need).

To set up Presenter view, on the Slide Show tab click the Set Up Slide Show button. Mark the Use Presenter View check box, and then specify which monitor to use for the slide show in the Multiple Monitors section of the dialog box.

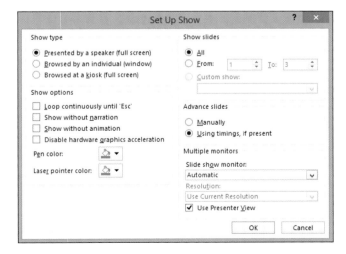

Advancing to the Next Slide

Do any of the following to advance the slide show to the next slide:

- Click the left mouse button.

- Press the spacebar, the right arrow key, or the down arrow key.

- Click the right mouse button, and choose Next on the menu that appears.

- Click the Next icon in the presentation toolbar.

Returning to the Previous Slide

Do any of the following to return to the previous slide:

- Press the Backspace key or the left or up arrow key.

- Click the Previous icon in the presentation toolbar.

- Click the right mouse button and then click Previous.

The Last Viewed command on the shortcut menu returns you to the last slide you viewed, which may or may not be the slide previous to the current one in the presentation's order, because you can jump to a different slide at any time, as in the following steps.

Displaying a Specific Slide

To display a specific slide, follow these steps:

1. Right-click to display the shortcut menu.

2. Point to See All Slides.

3. Click the desired slide.

4. Click the right mouse button and then click Previous.

Quick Review

1. How do you start showing the presentation beginning with the active slide?

2. How do you activate the Pen feature while in Slide Show view?

3. How do you quit Slide Show view and return to PowerPoint?

Summary

Building a Basic Presentation

Presentation graphics are visual aids used in public speaking activities, and PowerPoint is an application that creates them. PowerPoint's default view is **Normal view**, in which you can edit slides individually. It contains a **navigation pane**, a **Slide pane**, and a **Notes pane**. **Outline view** is just like it except the slide text appears in the navigation pane. **Slide Sorter view** is good for rearranging slides.

Each slide has a **layout**, which is an arrangement of placeholders. You can choose a different layout from the Layout button on the Home tab. You can also choose a layout when inserting new slides with the New Slide button.

The **active slide** is the one that appears in the Slide pane. You can change which slide is active by clicking a different one in the navigation pane.

To reorder slides, drag their thumbnail images in the navigation pane (Normal or Outline view) or in Slide Sorter view.

Formatting a Presentation

Slide size and orientation are set for the entire presentation, not for individual slides. Set these on the Design tab. Choose an aspect ratio of standard (4:3) or widescreen (16:9) for on-screen viewing.

You can apply a different theme from the Design tab's Themes group. You can then optionally choose a different set of theme fonts and theme colors.

Slide Master view enables you to modify the **slide master** and the **layout masters**. Choose Slide Master view from the View tab. The slide master is the topmost slide in the navigation pane in Slide Master view, and the smaller thumbnails beneath it are its layouts.

Creating and Inserting Content

In addition to the text placeholders, you can manually insert extra text boxes, but their text will not appear in the outline. Use the Text Box button on the Insert tab. You can click and begin typing, or you can drag to create a text box of certain dimensions.

To create a table, use the Table button on the Insert tab or use the Insert Table icon in the content placeholder. To insert **audio clips**, use the Audio button on the Insert tab. To insert a **video clip**, use the Video button, or use the Insert Video icon in the content placeholder.

To insert a picture from a file, use the Pictures button on the Insert tab or the Picture icon in a content placeholder. To insert clip art, use the Online Pictures button on the Insert tab or the Online Pictures icon in a content placeholder.

To draw **shapes**, click the Shapes button on the Insert tab, choose a shape and then drag on the slide.

To insert a chart, use the Chart button on the Insert tab or the Insert Chart icon on a content placeholder. Excel opens when you insert a chart, and you enter the data in the worksheet that appears for it.

SmartArt combines the visual interest of a graphic with the information of text. Use the SmartArt button on the Insert tab or the Insert a SmartArt Graphic icon in a content placeholder to start a new piece of SmartArt, or use the Convert to SmartArt button on the Home tab to convert an existing list.

Applying Transitions and Animations

A **transition** is a movement effect between slides; an **animation** is a movement effect of an object on a slide. They have separate tabs from which to create them: the Transitions tab and the Animations tab. There are four types of animation effects: Entrance, Emphasis, Exit, and Motion Path. You can manage multiple animations on a single slide using the Animation pane.

Presenting a Slide Show

To enter Slide Show view, you can click the Slide Show button in the status bar or choose From Beginning or From Current Slide from the Slide Show tab.

To move between slides, you can click to move forward, or use the navigation icons in the lower-left corner of the slide, or the arrow keys on the keyboard. Right-click and choose See All Slides to jump to a particular slide. Press Esc to end the slide show.

Key Terms

active slide
animation
audio clip
layout
layout master
navigation pane
Normal view
Notes pane
Outline view

presentation graphics
Shapes
slide master
Slide Master view
Slide pane
Slide Sorter view
SmartArt
transition
video clip

Test Yourself

Fact Check

1. What view is best for rearranging slides?

    a. Normal

    b. Slide Sorter

    c. Notes Pages

    d. Outline

2. A _____ is an arrangement of placeholders on a slide.

    a. template

    b. slide master

    c. theme

    d. layout

3. 16:9 is an example of a(n):

    a. aspect ratio

    b. slide size (in inches)

    c. banner type

    d. template

4. Which of these is NOT included in a theme in PowerPoint?

   a. font choices

   b. background images

   c. color choices

   d. sample content

5. The _____ is the overall guide for slides using the currently selected theme.

   a. layout master

   b. slide master

   c. template

   d. Notes pane

6. From which tab of PowerPoint are most types of graphic objects inserted?

   a. Object

   b. Design

   c. Insert

   d. Page

7. Which of these is NOT one of the icons in a content placeholder?

   a. Table

   b. Picture

   c. Media Clip

   d. Audio Clip

8. You can specify when and how a video clip plays on a slide from the Audio Tools _____ tab.

   a. Playback

   b. Format

   c. Design

   d. Layout

9. _____ can present text graphically and show relationships between ideas and processes.

   a. Text boxes

   b. SmartArt

   c. Clip Art

   d. WordArt

10. What type of animation effect enables you to move an object along a path you specify?

   a. Effect

   b. Emphasis

   c. Motion Path

   d. Movement

Matching

Match the keyboard shortcuts to their purposes.

a. transition

b. animation

c. emphasis

d. layout master

e. pen

f. slide master

1. _____A movement effect between slides.

2. _____A movement effect of an object on a slide.

3. _____A type of animation that makes the object move without entering or exiting the slide.

4. _____The feature that allows the mouse pointer to be used to draw on a slide in Slide Show view.

5. _____The template for all the slides in a particular theme.

6. _____The template for all the slides that use a particular layout.

Sum It Up

1. Explain the difference between a slide master and a layout master and how to enter Slide Master view.

2. Describe the parts of the presentation's formatting controlled by a theme and how to apply a theme.

3. List the seven types of content that can be inserted into a content placeholder. (**Hint:** One of them doesn't have an icon.)

4. Define SmartArt and describe how it might be used to present information.

5. Explain how to draw a shape on a slide.

6. Explain the difference between a motion path animation and an exit animation.

Explore More

Templates

Try out several of the templates available from Backstage view in the New section. Based on these experiments, what does a template offer that a theme does not?

More Views

Open an existing presentation and try out Reading view and Notes Page view. Summarize what each of those views looks like and what it might be useful for. Try out the Handout Master and Notes Master views, too, and compare and contrast them to Slide Master view.

Inserting Content from Word

Create an outline in Word using Outline view and then open it in PowerPoint. After doing that, close the file, and start a new blank Presentation. On the Home tab, click the down arrow below New Slide, select Slides from Outline, and choose the Word document to import slides from it. Was there any difference between the two methods of importing Word content?

Think It Over

Lots of Layouts

Suppose you need to create a presentation that has many different arrangements of content. Do you think it would be advantageous to create a lot of different layouts? Or would it be better to stick to just a few layouts and manually move the placeholders on each slide? Explain the pros and cons of each.

Sound Effects

What would you think of a speaker who used a lot of different wacky sound effects in his presentation? Would you find it entertaining, or would you think he was unprofessional? Would the topic of the presentation make any difference?

Consistency or Variety?

Which would be more appealing for an audience to view: a presentation that was consistent in its use of themes, layouts, and transitions, or a presentation that mixed all of those things up, with different slide background colors, different transition effects, and different fonts on every slide? Explain your answer.

Part IV
Connectivity and Communication

Chapter 13

Networking and Internet Basics

Learning objectives

☐ Identify communications networks in daily life

☐ Distinguish between types of networks

☐ Identify common types of network hardware

☐ Understand the Internet and choose a connection method

☐ Troubleshoot common network and Internet connectivity problems

Our Connected World: Communication Systems

Ways of Classifying Networks

Network Hardware

Understanding and Connecting to the Internet

Troubleshooting Network and Internet Connections

When computing first began, each computer was separate, and data was moved between computers only with difficulty. Today, however, computers connect to both local and global networks that make information sharing easy, whether you're sharing data with your brother's computer in the next room or with a file server halfway around the world.

This chapter explains the basics of modern networking, both large and small networks, both wired and wireless, and both private and public. You will learn how networks are structured, how network resources are identified, and how network security helps keep your data safe. You'll also learn how to troubleshoot some common network-related problems.

Our Connected World: Communication Systems

Networking is nearly everywhere, and many of our everyday activities are enabled or assisted by computer networking, even the activities that might not on the surface seem to have anything to do with it. For example, when you withdraw funds at your local bank branch, the bank verifies your account balance on the bank's main server at the home office. When you buy an item at your local discount chain store and pay for your purchase with a credit card, the digital cash register's software checks a credit card verification server to make sure your card is valid before charging your purchase. It then sends the information to the store's internal inventory management system via the local network. The local server then sends an updated inventory report to the company's web server, so that someone ordering from the store's website will know that the item is no longer in stock. When you call your mother on your cell phone on the way home to tell her about your purchase, your call goes through the wireless network for your cell phone provider.

Let's start out this chapter by looking at some of the large-scale networks that make up our connected world.

Public Telephone and Data Networks

The first worldwide network ever created was the telephone network, predating computers by many decades. This network is an example of a circuit-switched network. It works by creating a point-to-point circuit between the two locations, as shown in Figure 13.1. The telephone network creates a pathway between the two points, and that pathway remains open for the duration of the phone call. Networks can be public or private. The public telephone system—the whole of the world's circuit-switched telephone networks—is known as the public-switched telephone network (PSTN).

circuit-switched network A network that creates a point-to-point connection between locations that remains open for the duration of the communication.

public-switched telephone network (PSTN) The worldwide network of circuit-switched telephone lines.

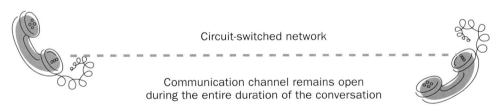

Circuit-switched network

Communication channel remains open
during the entire duration of the conversation

Figure 13.1   A circuit-switched network maintains a single constant line of communication.

packet-switched network A network that transfers data by breaking it up into separately transferred packets.

In contrast, computer networks are packet-switched networks. A communication channel does not remain open between two points for an entire conversation; instead, the data is broken up at the sending end into small packets, each with an electronic envelope around it that states the source and the destination, and sent individually to the receiver. Depending on the network traffic, each packet may take a different route to the destination, but when they arrive they are unpacked and reassembled into the original message, as in Figure 13.2.

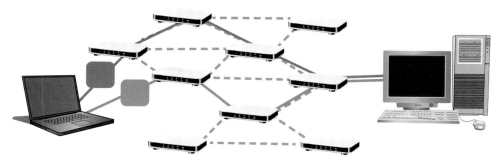

Packet-switched network

Different packets in the same communication
session take independent routes to the destination

Figure 13.2 A packet-switched network allows each packet to find the best route to the destination independently.

The Internet

The Internet is the world's largest computer network. It is not owned or maintained by any one company; instead, it is a cooperative effort among many companies and governments, with multiple standards organizations managing the rules for its operation. The Internet is a packet-switched network with a worldwide addressing system. The Internet uses various protocols (rules) that all participating computers have standardized on, so that services like the web, email, and instant messaging work the same everywhere. Most companies and individuals don't connect directly to the Internet; instead, they connect to an Internet service provider (ISP), which in turn connects to the Internet. For example, if you have cable Internet at home, your ISP is your cable provider.

The Internet is based on a protocol stack (a set of protocols) called Transmission Control Protocol/Internet Protocol (TCP/IP). TCP/IP provides a common set of standards by which data can be sent and received. It is used not only on the Internet, but in most private networks today as well. One of the key features of TCP/IP is IP addressing, which is a means of uniquely identifying each connected computer on the network by a numeric value.

Internet A global packet-switched network created cooperatively by multiple companies, governments, and standards organizations.

protocol A rule or custom that governs how something is done. In a computer context, it refers to a standard for transferring data.

Internet service provider (ISP) A company that maintains a direct connection to the Internet and leases access to it to individuals and companies.

protocol stack A related group of protocols—for example, TCP/IP.

Transmission Control Protocol / Internet Protocol (TCP/IP) The protocol suite (set of rules) that defines how data will move on the Internet and on most other modern networks.

Private Digital Networks

Many companies maintain high-speed connections between their locations. They can do so by leasing a line running their own, or using the existing pathways of the Internet. Using the Internet is the most cost-effective method, but not the most reliable method, because the connection can be affected by Internet traffic problems and connections that other companies control and maintain.

Using the Internet is also not very secure; it's an open system, and data being sent and received can easily be snooped. To tighten the security when using the Internet as a conduit, many companies use a software technology called virtual private networking (VPN). VPN technology creates a secure, tamper-resistant data tunnel between two points on the Internet, so that sensitive information can be exchanged securely, as in Figure 13.3. A VPN allows an employee who is working outside of the company's main building to connect to any of the internal network resources, just as if he or she were in the building.

virtual private networking (VPN) A method of creating a secure, private communication tunnel using a public communications channel such as the Internet.

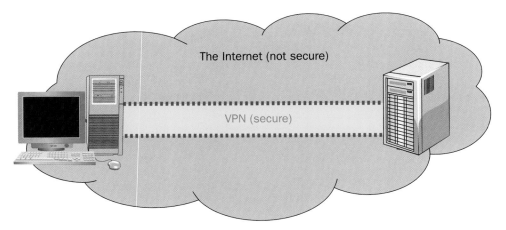

The Internet (not secure)

VPN (secure)

Figure 13.3   A VPN creates a secure connection between two points using the Internet's infrastructure to physically carry the data.

Satellite Data Networks

satellite A data transmitter/receiver in geosynchronous orbit with the Earth.

A satellite is a transmitter/receiver unit that orbits the Earth, more than 22,000 miles up. Satellites are in geosynchronous orbit (that is, their orbit is synchronized with the Earth's orbit), so they do not appear to change in position compared to any location on Earth. A satellite contains transponders, which are two-way radios that communicate with stations on the ground. Satellites are used to quickly send information between two points on Earth that are physically separated by a great distance. For example, when the Olympics are held in one country, satellites are used to broadcast the video of each competition nearly instantly to every other country. Satellites are also used for services like satellite radio (Sirius/XM, for example) and satellite TV broadcasts such as DirecTV and Dish Network (see Figure 13.4). Some Internet services also use satellites to provide Internet access to areas where other high-speed connection technologies are not available.

© iStockphoto.com/Petrovich9

Figure 13.4   Satellites can be used for broadband communications.

Cell Phone Networks

Cellular telephone companies have their own data networks, using a combination of satellites, cables, and on-ground towers with transmitters and receivers on them. Calls connect to the cell tower that is closest to the phone's current location, and that cell tower then taps into the larger telecommunications network via satellites and cables.

Some cell phone networks can also be used to access the Internet (see Figure 13.5). You can access the Internet on a smartphone (a cell phone that includes computer functionality), and you can tether (connect) a smartphone to a computer and use the phone as a modem to allow the computer Internet access.

© iStockphoto.com/amete

Figure 13.5 Cell phone networks can carry both voice and data.

smartphone A cellular phone that includes computer applications and Internet access capability.

tether To connect a smartphone to a computer so that the computer can use the smartphone's Internet access.

Tethering a Computer to a Smartphone for Internet Access

© iStockphoto.com/a_Taiga

If your phone has Internet access, you can probably share its Internet access with a notebook or tablet computer. The exact steps depend on you phone's operating system. On an iPhone, the feature is called Personal Hotspot. On a Windows Phone, it's called Internet sharing. On Android, it's called Tethering & Portable Hotspot. Check out your phone now and see whether that feature is available. It's not cost-effective as a long-term Internet access solution, but it works great when you don't have other access available, such as in a car or boat.

Put It to Work

1. How does a circuit-switched network differ from a packet-switched network?

2. What is an ISP?

3. What is the benefit of creating a VPN as opposed to sending data directly over the Internet?

Ways of Classifying Networks

As you learned in the previous section, the world is full of networks of various types. Most of the rest of this chapter, however, focuses specifically on networks that help personal and business computers connect with one another.

There are several ways to classify computer networks. You can look at them according to their geographical scope, the way the network is physically laid out, the way data travels through the network, and whether the network is wired (that is, connected with cables) or wireless. In the following sections you will look at networks in several of these ways.

Geographical Range

One way to classify networks is according to the geographical range that they cover, from a few feet within a single person's office to a huge area that covers multiple countries or even multiple continents. Figure 13.6 provides a graphical explanation of some of these ranges.

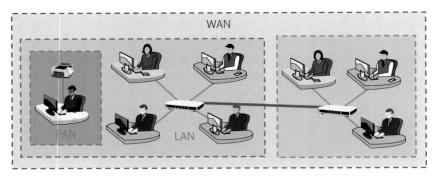

Figure 13.6 The geographical range of linked devices determines the type of network that connects them.

Personal Area Networks

personal area network (PAN) A network formed when devices are connected to an individual computer.

A personal area network (PAN) consists of devices that directly connect to a single computer. For example, if you are showing a presentation in a conference room during a business meeting, you might connect your notebook PC to the projector in the room. You might also form a PAN by connecting your smartphone to your computer.

Local Area Networks

local area network (LAN) A network that connects devices housed in the same physical location.

A local area network (LAN) is a network in which all the devices are located within the same physical location, such as a single building or a group of adjacent buildings. A key characteristic of a LAN is that it is contained within a relatively small area. For example, your home network is a LAN, and so is the network at your school.

Metropolitan Area Networks

A metropolitan area network (MAN) is a network that spans an entire town or city—or, as the name implies, a metropolitan area that might span a major city and its suburbs. A city might invest in a network infrastructure, for example, and then businesses and individuals within that area might sign up to use the network.

Wide Area Networks

A wide area network (WAN) is a geographically dispersed network, usually consisting of at least two LANs connected together by an external link. A business or college with multiple separate campuses might link all the individual LANs together to form a WAN, for example. A WAN is not necessarily managed by a single organization and may include architecture and communications hardware from several different service providers. In this sense, the Internet is a form of global WAN.

Peer-to-Peer and Client/Server Networks

Another way to classify networks is to look at whether or not a server is involved in their management. As you learned in Chapter 1, a *server* is a computer that is dedicated to providing network and sharing services to the other computers on the network. Very small networks (10 computers or fewer) can get by without a server by operating as a peer-to-peer (P2P) network, also called a *workgroup*. In a P2P network, each computer shares in the administrative burden of maintaining the network, as shown in Figure 13.7. Each computer is responsible for authenticating other users who want to share its resources (files and printers) and for making those resources available. A P2P network slows down each computer slightly because of the overhead involved in the network. It is not usually noticeable with just a few computers, but the more computers there are, the greater the slowdown.

Peer-to-Peer Networking

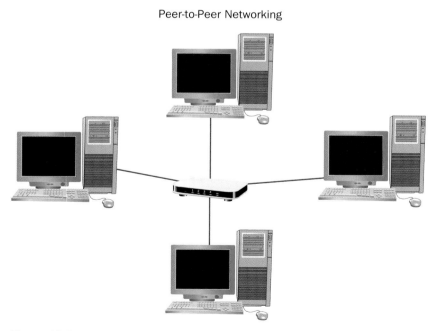

Figure 13.7 Every computer shares administrative responsibilities on peer-to-peer networks, which have no servers.

For larger networks, a client/server model is more effective. A client/server network, such as the one shown in Figure 13.8, is a network that consists of one or more servers plus one or more clients—that is, computers with which individuals run applications. Client/server networks can be any size, and can have multiple servers. Each server may perform a different type of network task, such as a file server or a print server. Each server may also serve a subset of the total pool of clients.

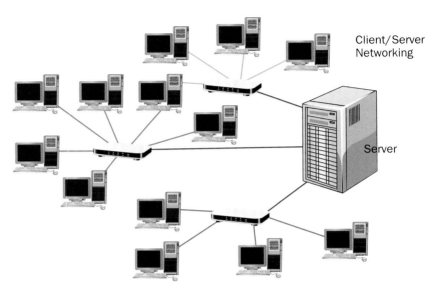

Client/Server Networking

Server

Figure 13.8 Client/server networks have one or more servers through which multiple computers can perform various tasks.

Intranets and Extranets

Some organizations have a part of the network that can only be accessed from within the organization. This sub-network is known as an intranet. The network administrator may enable intranet users to share message board items, link to external web pages, and comment on photos or news items that are posted. The intranet cannot be accessed by anyone outside the organization and can't be accessed when staff are not physically located in the office unless they are given specific permission for remote access.

In contrast, a company may maintain an extranet, a separate network that is specifically intended for people outside the organization. An extranet may be used by the company's business partners, contract employees, or customers to get real-time information, such as about products they supply that might soon need restocking.

Ethernet

Over the years since networking began, there have been several popular networking technologies—that is, different sets of standards for networking hardware and software. Each of these technologies has involved different hardware and software installed in each computer, different connection hardware, and different types of cables. Some of the early networking technologies included Token Ring, Banyan Vines, and Ethernet. All of those technologies have become obsolete except Ethernet. Most network hardware that you buy in stores today can be assumed to be Ethernet-compatible unless it specifies otherwise.

Ethernet can technically be either wired or wireless, but it is becoming increasingly common to refer to only the wired type as Ethernet; wireless Ethernet is popularly called Wi-Fi. (See the following section for more information about Wi-Fi.)

Ethernet devices have a certain maximum speed. For example, 1000BaseT Ethernet, which is common in most residential and business networks, transfers data at up to 1000 Mbps (1 Gbps). The "T" in the name refers to the twisted-pair cables used; you will learn more about cables in the "Network Hardware" section later in this chapter. The Ethernet standard also allows fiber optic cable and very high rates of data transfer (such as 10-Gigabit Ethernet, which transfers data at up to 10 Gbps).

Ethernet The current dominant standard for local area networking devices.

1000BaseT A type of Ethernet that transfers data at up to 1000 Mbps over twisted-pair cables.

Wireless Networking Technologies

A network can connect devices using either wired or wireless connections. A wired connection runs a cable between the points, whereas wireless connects the two points via radio frequency (RF) or infrared.

Wireless communications have two main uses. The first use is at the endpoints of network connectivity, where a device such as a smartphone or laptop computer connects wirelessly to a router or other device that provides network and/or Internet access. The second use is as a source of transferring data between locations when using cables is not practical, such as with satellite and microwave systems.

A single network can contain a mixture of wired and wireless connections, as long as they are the same network technology. For example, if you have a router in your home through which all the computers share an Internet connection, some of the computers can connect to it with wired Ethernet and others can connect to it via Wi-Fi. Because they all share a common network technology (Ethernet), they work together seamlessly. However, networks using different technologies cannot communicate with one another. For example, you can't use a Bluetooth device to connect to an Ethernet network.

NOTE

Wi-Fi

Wi-Fi is the common name for the wireless networking technology that's used for almost all home and business networks today, often referred to by its standard number: IEEE 802.11. Whenever you use wireless networking to access the Internet at your home or workplace or in a public location such as a cafe or library, you are using Wi-Fi.

Wi-Fi Wireless Ethernet. A means of connecting computers and other devices wirelessly. Another name for it is IEEE 802.11, its technical standard.

IEEE is the Institute of Electrical and Electronics Engineers. It publishes the standards for many different technologies. IEEE 802.11 is the standard that governs Wi-Fi, but there are also many other standards too. For example, 1394 is the standard for FireWire, and 802.15 is the standard for Bluetooth (although nobody calls Bluetooth by its standard number).

NOTE

There have been different versions of the Wi-Fi standard since its original development. The popular version today is 802.11n, which can carry up to 600 Mbps of data over a range of up to 230 feet indoors or 840 feet outdoors. An update to it called 802.11ac has recently been approved; it may already be incorporated into networking devices you can buy in stores by the time you read this. 802.11ac has a maximum throughput of 1.3 Gbps, more than doubling the capacity of 802.11n. Table 13.1 lists the different Wi-Fi standards and their speeds and distances.

Table 13.1: Wi-Fi Standards

Standard	Distance (indoors/outdoors)	Speed	Backward compatible with
802.11a	115 feet / 390 feet	54 Mbps	
802.11b	115 feet / 390 feet	11 Mbps	
802.11g	125 feet / 460 feet	54 Mbps	802.11b
802.11n	230 feet / 860 feet	Up to 600 Mbps	802.11b and g
802.11ac	230 feet / 860 feet	Up to 1.3 Gbps	802.11b, g, and n

Bluetooth

Bluetooth An inexpensive short-range networking technology used for computer-to-device connections such as computer-to-printer or phone-to-headset.

Bluetooth is a wireless technology used to connect individual devices to one another in close proximity. It is most commonly used to connect a computer to an input or output device. For example, you might have a Bluetooth headphone that you use with your smartphone, or you might have a Bluetooth-enabled printer that you can use with your notebook PC. A personal area network (PAN) forms when the devices are within range of each other and they are paired (by using software to authenticate them to one another). When the devices are no longer in range of one another, the PAN stops. Bluetooth is limited to about 20 feet in range, so it isn't a practical technology to use for wireless networking in general (such as to share an Internet connection with computers all over a home or office).

pair To connect a Bluetooth input or output device to a computer.

Pairing Bluetooth Devices

To connect devices via Bluetooth, you must pair them. Pairing can take several different forms, depending on the devices. For example, one device might generate a PIN code and the other one might prompt you to type that PIN code to confirm. Obviously, that works only if both devices have a display screen on which a PIN code could display, of course. For a device without a display, such as a Bluetooth mouse, the device will have a button you can press to make it temporarily discoverable. Press the button (you may have to hold it for a few seconds), following the directions in the device's documentation to make it discoverable, and then select it on the screen of the device with which you want to pair it. In Windows, you can access the Bluetooth controls via the Control Panel.

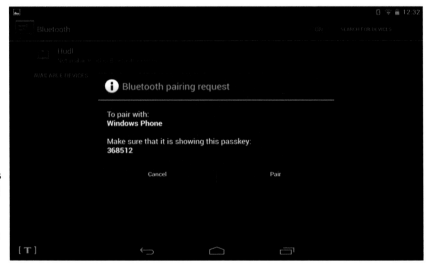

Infrared

Infrared technology uses light waves to "beam" information from device to device. Infrared was the method of choice for connecting wireless peripherals a decade or so ago, but Bluetooth has mainly superseded it today. However, infrared is still used for most remote controls for TVs and other home theater components. The main drawback of infrared transmission is that it must have a clear line of sight between the two points. The standard for an infrared connection is IrDA (short for Infrared Data Association, the organization that created and manages the standard).

infrared Older type of wireless communication that used light waves to pass simple information between nearby devices.

Microwave

Microwaves are high-frequency radio waves. A microwave communication system allows two locations to be wirelessly connected by using a high-frequency communication band, much higher than that used for Wi-Fi or Bluetooth. The points can be miles apart (up to about 25 miles), but as long as there are no visible obstructions between them, they can exchange data. Because line of sight is so critical for microwave communications, the transmitters are often placed high up on towers or buildings. Microwave technology is not as widely used today as it was prior to the development of satellite networking systems, but it still has some special uses; for example, military forces use it to quickly set up communications in areas where the terrain is too rugged to support wired connections and security is critical. (A point-to-point microwave connection is more secure than a connection that goes through a satellite.)

microwave communication system A secure, point-to-point wireless networking technology that requires a line of sight between the two points.

Quick Review

1. What is the difference between a LAN and a WAN?
2. Name three different wireless networking technologies.
3. What is a client/server network?

Network Hardware

Network connectivity requires both hardware and software. The software portion is handled by the operating system; all modern operating systems include network support. However, not all computers include networking hardware, and some network hardware is independent of any one computer, so you may at some point find yourself shopping for networking hardware. In the following sections, you will learn about several common network hardware devices.

Network Installer

Technicians who install networks have an active work environment. Rather than sitting at a desk all day, as most IT professionals do, installers are out crawling around in the ceilings and basements of buildings, running cables and mounting satellite dishes. They set up closets with stacks of switches and routers in them, configure network security settings, and make sure all network hardware is installed correctly and functioning well. To install networks, you should have at least a high school diploma, plus a technical certification such as CompTIA Network+. To learn more about Network+ certification, see `http://certification.comptia.org/ getCertified/certifications/network.aspx`.

© iStockphoto.com/805promo

Network Adapters

Each network client device (computer, tablet, printer, and so on) must have a network adapter. A network adapter enables the computer to participate in the local area network. Most desktop and notebook computers come with a wired Ethernet adapter built in, and notebook computers almost always include a built-in wireless adapter as well.

network adapter A hardware component that enables a computer to connect to a network.

When a network adapter is not built into the motherboard, but instead installed as an expansion board, it is called a network interface card (NIC). Although it is not technically accurate, the term NIC (pronounced "nick") has come to refer to any network adapter, not just an add-on card. Most portable computers (notebooks, tablets, smartphones) have a Wi-Fi network adapter built in. A portable device may also have other built-in network adapters, such as a Bluetooth adapter.

network interface card (NIC) A network adapter that is on an expansion card, rather than built into the computer's motherboard. Sometimes used informally to refer to any network adapter.

You can configure a device's network adapter via the Settings or Control Panel in the operating system. You can turn the various wireless adapters on or off on a tablet or smartphone, for instance. Many people choose to keep Bluetooth and Wi-Fi turned off to save battery life when those adapters are not being used.

Step by Step

Checking Device Manager for Network Devices

Not sure what network adapters are installed on your PC? Follow these steps to find out:

1. In Windows, right-click the Start button and click Device Manager.

2. Click the arrow to the left of Network Adapters to expand that category. The available network adapters appear. For example, in the example screenshot below, there are three network adapters. You can deduce from their names what kind of networks they support.

3. Double-click the network adapter with Ethernet or WiFi in its name. Its Properties box appears.

4. Click each of the tabs in the dialog box to review its settings, and then click Cancel.

5. Close the Device Manager window, and close the Control Panel window.

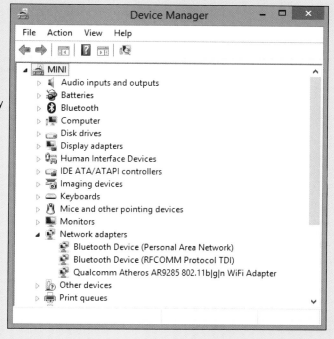

Each network adapter has a hardware address, called a media access control (MAC) address, that is unique in all the world. It has nothing to do with Macintosh computers, despite the similar name. This address, also called a physical address, is hard-coded into a chip on the adapter and never changes, regardless of the network being used. Low-level networking software uses the MAC address to ensure it is delivering data to the right device. The MAC address is separate from the network-specific address, such as the IP address (covered in Chapter 15, "Web Basics").

media access control (MAC) address A unique hardware address for a network adapter.

Step by Step

Finding Your MAC Address

Follow these steps to find your network adapter's MAC address:

1. Right-click the Start button and click Command Prompt. A command prompt window appears.

2. Type **ipconfig /all** and press Enter. Information about all your network hardware and its connections appears.

3. Scroll through the information and find the Physical Address. This is the MAC address.

4. Make a note of the MAC address and then close the command prompt window.

```
                          Command Prompt              _  □  ×

Microsoft Windows [Version 6.3.9600]
(c) 2013 Microsoft Corporation. All rights reserved.

C:\Users\Faithe>ipconfig /all

Windows IP Configuration

   Host Name . . . . . . . . . . . . : MINI
   Primary Dns Suffix  . . . . . . . :
   Node Type . . . . . . . . . . . . : Hybrid
   IP Routing Enabled. . . . . . . . : No
   WINS Proxy Enabled. . . . . . . . : No
   DNS Suffix Search List. . . . . . : Belkin

Wireless LAN adapter Local Area Connection* 3:

   Media State . . . . . . . . . . . : Media disconnected
   Connection-specific DNS Suffix  . :
   Description . . . . . . . . . . . : Microsoft Wi-Fi Direct Virtual Adapter
   Physical Address. . . . . . . . . : 12-B9-A5-12-09-CD
   DHCP Enabled. . . . . . . . . . . : Yes
   Autoconfiguration Enabled . . . . : Yes

Ethernet adapter Bluetooth Network Connection:

   Media State . . . . . . . . . . . : Media disconnected
   Connection-specific DNS Suffix  . :
   Description . . . . . . . . . . . : Bluetooth Device (Personal Area Network
   Physical Address. . . . . . . . . : 48-5D-60-AE-23-87
   DHCP Enabled. . . . . . . . . . . : Yes
   Autoconfiguration Enabled . . . . : Yes
```

Switches and Hubs

switch A gathering point for the computers in a LAN to connect with to participate in the network.

A switch is a box that provides a central gathering point for all the computers in an Ethernet LAN. Each computer's network adapter connects to the switch, either via a cable or wirelessly. (Bluetooth and infrared wireless networks don't use switches because they only connect individual devices to one another, not groups of devices.) The switch manages the data traffic between the devices. If one device wants to send something to another device on the same network, it sends its request to the switch, and the switch delivers the message to the proper destination. Figure 13.9 shows a switch for a wired network, with eight ports into which you can connect cables from network adapters. A wireless switch is called a wireless access point (WAP).

wireless access point (WAP) A wireless switch.

© iStockphoto.com/schamie

Figure 13.9   A switch connects the computers in the LAN.

hub A primitive version of a switch that lacks the capability to read packet addresses and route them to the appropriate port.

A switch is able to read the addressing information on a packet and intelligently route it to the right port so it will reach its destination. An earlier version of a switch, called a hub, was not so intelligent. Rather than sending the message only to the correct port, it would send all traffic to all ports and rely on each computer to ignore anything that wasn't addressed to it. Using a hub placed a performance drain on each computer because it had to spend so much time checking network packets; switches are much better for network performance and are much more commonly used today.

Routers

A router performs all the same functions as a switch, but it also has an added bonus: It can direct traffic into and out of the LAN. For example, suppose you have two separate groups of computers, each group connected to its own switch, and you want their computers to be able to communicate with one another. If you use a router instead of a switch for each group, the routers will be able to transfer data packets that belong to the other group. Each router has an output port called a default gateway that enables data to leave the local network to be delivered. On some routers, the port may be labeled Uplink, WAN, or Internet.

Routers serve an important role in home networks because they enable multiple computers to share a single Internet connection. The broadband modem connects to the router's output port, and the router directs all Internet requests from each of the computers to that port. When data comes in from the Internet, the router directs it to the computer that requested it. The type of router used for this purpose is sometimes called a broadband router. A broadband router can be wired or wireless; Figure 13.10 shows a small wireless router suitable for home use. Like most wireless routers, it has several ports for plugging in Ethernet cables, so it can serve for both your wired and wireless devices. You can tell it's a wireless router because it has an antenna.

© iStockphoto.com/bedo

Figure 13.10 A router manages traffic into and out of your LAN.

Routers also make the Internet possible. The Internet consists of a mesh of interconnected commercial-grade routers that pass data back and forth between them. To deliver a packet from one point to another on the Internet, the packet is routed through a series of hops, from one router to another, until it reaches its destination.

Gateways, Bridges, and Repeaters

The term *gateway* has two meanings. At the software level, as you learned in the previous section, the default gateway is an output port on a router. At the hardware level, a gateway is a connector box that enables you to connect two dissimilar networks by translating the data requests between them and providing the correct physical connectors for each network type. For example, a gateway might join an Ethernet-based LAN to a mainframe computer. A bridge is a device that connects two similar networks, such as Ethernet networks in two different buildings.

router A connection box for Ethernet networks that physically joins the devices in the network (wired) or provides wireless connectivity (wireless), and enables a connection to an outside network such as the Internet.

default gateway The port on a router that connects to external networks.

gateway A connector box that enables you to connect two dissimilar networks.

bridge A connector box that enables you to connect two networks of similar types.

repeater A device that receives and retransmits a network signal.

A repeater does just what the name implies—it repeats a network signal. As network traffic travels a long distance, the signal weakens and errors may be introduced. A repeater reads the incoming data and then rebroadcasts it.

Network Cables

Wired communication media consists mainly of various types of cables. Data can be carried efficiently and reliably through cables, and some cables can carry data at very high speeds. Here are the most common types of network cables you may encounter.

Twisted-Pair Cable

twisted-pair cable Cable that transfers data via pairs of copper wires that are twisted around each other to reduce electromagnetic interference.

electromagnetic interference (EMI) The corruption of data as it is passing through a cable due to the magnetic field generated by a nearby cable.

unshielded twisted pair (UTP) A type of twisted-pair cable that does not have an outer sheath that protects against external EMI.

shielded twisted pair (STP) A type of twisted-pair cable that has an outer sheath that protects against external EMI.

Most of the Ethernet cables in business and residential buildings are twisted-pair cable. It gets its name from the pairs of copper wires inside the cable. The wires twisting around each other help reduce electromagnetic interference (EMI) caused by the magnetic field generated when electricity passes through the cable.

Most twisted-pair cable is unshielded-twisted pair (UTP). Shielding is an optional copper mesh in the lining of a cable that cuts down on EMI getting through to the cable from external sources. Shielded-twisted pair (STP) contains this extra lining and is used in environments where EMI is a problem, such as in cables run through ceilings with fluorescent light fixtures in them.

category 3 cable A type of UTP cable used in telephone systems.

RJ-11 A connector used on one-line UTP telephone cables.

RJ-14 A connector used on two-line UTP telephone cables.

category 5e cable A type of UTP cable used in 1000BaseT Ethernet networking.

There are different types of UTP cable, which have different numbers of wire pairs and can carry data reliably at different maximum speeds. When you connect a telephone to a phone jack in a home or business wall outlet, for example, you use Category 3 (Cat3) cable, which contains either one or two pairs of wires (for a one-line or two-line phone system). The connector for a telephone cable is either an RJ-11 (two wires) or RJ-14 (four wires). The cable used in Ethernet networking (the most common type of networking, used in most homes and businesses) is an 8-wire type called Category 5e (Cat5e) that can carry data reliably at up to 1000 Mbps (which, you may remember from the Ethernet section earlier in this chapter, is the same maximum speed as 1000BaseT Ethernet). It has a wider connector than that of a phone cable, called an RJ-45 connector, shown in Figure 13.11.

© iStockphoto.com/Henrik5000

Figure 13.11 An RJ-45 connector on a UTP Ethernet cable.

RJ-45 A connector used on UTP cables designed for Ethernet networking.

Coaxial Cable

Coaxial cable is the type of cable used for cable TV connections; if you have cable Internet, it's the cable that runs from the wall to your cable modem. Like twisted-pair cable, it carries data in electrical signals. It's a more expensive cable than twisted pair, but it can carry much more data and at faster speeds. Coaxial cable consists of a single copper wire in the center, surrounded by insulation, with a plastic jacket on the outside. See Figure 13.12. Coaxial cable is not normally used for networking within a building anymore, although some older, now-obsolete forms of networking used it.

coaxial cable Cable that consists of a solid copper core with an insulated sleeve around it.

© iStockphoto.com/tacojim

Figure 13.12   A coaxial cable has a solid copper core in the center, surrounded by insulation.

Fiber Optic Cable

Whereas the cables you've learned about so far carry data electrically, fiber optic cable carries data in pulses of light along a glass fiber (see Figure 13.13). Each fiber is very tiny—about the thickness of a human hair. Each cable contains hundreds of fibers, and can carry billions of bits per second. Fiber optic

fiber optic cable Cable that carries data using light pulses through a bundle of glass fibers.

© iStockphoto.com/zentilia

Figure 13.13   A fiber optic cable contains multiple thin strands of glass fiber.

cable is often used as the backbone (the central part) of a network, such as to move large amounts of data between points on the Internet. It's reliable, fast, and not subject to EMI; it's also very hard to snoop or hack into, making the connection more secure than other cable types. Fiber optic cable isn't widely used at the consumer level, though, because it is expensive and difficult to install and maintain. It's also not compatible with most consumer-level networking equipment.

Quick Review

1. How is a router different from a switch?

2. What kind of cable should you buy for an Ethernet network?

3. Name two advantages of fiber optic cable over other types.

Understanding and Connecting to the Internet

The Internet began as a way of enabling schools, research institutions, and the military to share information. Today, however, it is used not only by schools and governments but by businesses, non-profit organizations, and individuals in every country and of every profession. You can use the Internet to look up information on the web, send and receive email, exchange instant messages, upload and download files, and much more. You will learn more about the uses of the Internet in Chapter 14, "Online Communication," and Chapter 15, "Web Basics."

Internet Structure

Structurally, the Internet is a mesh of routers and servers connected to one another at multiple points, as illustrated in Figure 13.14. This makes the Internet very fault-tolerant. If any single router or server goes down, network traffic is simply routed around the point of failure.

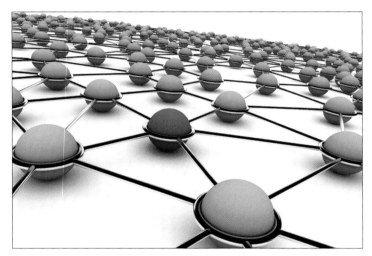

© iStockphoto.com/iSergey

Figure 13.14 A mesh network does not rely on any one point being active; traffic can easily route around any blockages.

At the beginning of this chapter you learned about packet-switched networks. The Internet is a packet-switched network, which means each message sent is broken up into multiple data packets and each packet is sent individually across the network. When the packets arrive at the destination computer, they are opened and the data is reassembled into the original message. In this description, the term *message* is generic, and can refer to any data sent or received, such as the request to display a web page, the information you enter in an online form, or an email you send.

Internet Speed

The Internet itself does not have a fixed speed. Data travels through the Internet as fast as it can go on whatever cable it travels through, and a single data packet may travel at different speeds during different parts of its journey. At the heart of the Internet are high-capacity, high-speed data pathways that are like superhighways for data. These pathways form the Internet's backbone. The backbone is made up mainly of fiber optic cables that can carry data very fast—literally at the speed of light! Large ISPs have entire buildings full of servers that are connected directly to the Internet off of this main backbone. From the ISP's servers to the individual neighborhoods and individual homes and businesses, the connection speeds are lower because the cheaper copper-based cables used in those areas carry data at a lower rate. Some ISPs charge different prices for different speeds of Internet connection, and they throttle the connection speed (usually at the broadband modem) for customers who have signed up for a slower connection.

> **backbone** The central connection pathways of a network, where connection speeds are high and the data pathway is wide.

The Internet service that you subscribe to has two speeds, both measured in megabytes per second (Mbps). The first is its theoretical maximum speed, which is what your ISP tells you that it is delivering under optimal conditions. The second is your actual speed, which will be lower.

Some of the factors that affect actual performance speed include:

- Internet traffic: During peak hours of the day, when more people are using the Internet, overall speeds may be slower.

- Local traffic: If you have cable Internet, you share bandwidth with your neighbors. If someone is using a lot of bandwidth, such as streaming multiple movies at once into his or her home, your connection's performance may suffer.

> **bandwidth** The amount of data that can be transmitted at a sustained rate by a communication channel or device.

- Server issues: Individual websites that you try to view may be located on a server that has a slow connection to the Internet or is located in an area where Internet traffic is currently heavy, or the server may be experiencing problems such as overloading (when too many people try to access the same server at once).

- Throttling: If you have used more data than your Internet service provider allows you to use for a certain time period, the ISP may temporarily throttle the speed of your connection for a certain amount of time (usually 24 hours) as a penalty. This is common on satellite Internet service, but uncommon on other service types.

Testing Your Internet Connection Speed

How fast is your connection? To find out, use an online speed test. Open your web browser and go to a site that offers free testing. You can search for a free testing site, or try one of these:

- `http://speedtest.comcast.net`

- `www.cnet.com/internet-speed-test`

- `www.dslreports.com/speedtest?flash=1`

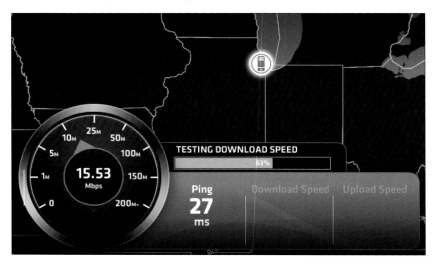

Types of Internet Connections

When choosing Internet service for your home or business, there are a variety of factors to consider. Speed is important, of course—faster is better. However, faster may also be more expensive. It's also important to look at availability, and evaluate any package deals you may be able to get with other services such as cable TV or phone service.

In the following sections, you'll learn about the major types of Internet connections available to consumers today. All of these types except dial-up are always-on broadband connections. The word broadband literally means *wide path*, but when referring to Internet connectivity it refers to a connection with a speed higher than 256 Kbps. Many of today's broadband Internet options are much faster than that.

broadband A fast, always-on network connection.

Dial-Up Internet

In the early days of the Internet, dial-up access was all that was available. A dial-up connection uses a telephone line to connect to an ISP at a maximum speed of around 44.8 Kbps. Dial-up connections have many drawbacks. You cannot use the phone line for telephone calls while you are connected to the Internet, and the Internet connection is not always on; you must connect to the Internet when you want to use it, and then disconnect when you are finished. The speed is very slow (less than 1/100th of a more modern connection, on the average), resulting in frustrating waits for every operation.

dial-up modem A device that converts between analog and digital data so computer data can be sent over analog phone lines.

A dial-up connection is established using a dial-up modem. The word modem is short for modulator/demodulator. A modem converts the digital data from the computer to an analog (sound) signal for delivery over the phone line. Then at the receiving end, another modem converts the analog signal back to digital for the computer's use at that end. The modems go on converting between analog and digital for one another as long as the connection is active.

A dial-up modem can either be internal (built into the computer) or external (a separate device you connect to one of the computer's ports). Most dial-up modems have two phone jacks. You connect your phone cable from the wall to one of them, and you can optionally connect your phone to the other one so that when the modem is not in use, you can continue to use your phone normally.

To use a dial-up modem, you issue a command in the operating system or in a communication software application that tells the modem what number to dial. You get the phone number from your ISP. The modem makes some noises as it is connecting, but then the noises stop when the connection is made.

Cable Internet

At the other end of the speed spectrum from dial-up is cable Internet access. Cable is currently the fastest type of commercially available Internet access for residential customers, theoretically delivering top speeds of more than 100 Mbps (although most connections top out at around 30 Mbps).

Cable Internet is delivered through the same coaxial cable as the cable TV programming. You connect a splitter to the cable coming in from the wall, to allow the cable to go to both your TV and to a cable modem (which may be provided by the cable company for a monthly lease fee). Figure 13.15 shows one model of cable modem; there are many different models. You can connect one computer directly to the cable modem via an Ethernet cable to receive high-speed Internet on that computer.

ble modem A broadband modem designed to rk with a cable Internet connection.

You can also optionally share the Internet connection with other computers in your home or office by using a broadband router. You connect an Ethernet cable from the cable modem to the broadband router's Uplink port, and the router sees the Internet connection as an external network and allows all the computers connected to the router to participate in it. Some cable modems are dual-purpose units, with a router built in.

© iStockphoto.com/blue_iq

Figure 13.15   A cable modem provides broadband Internet to a home or business.

If you have one of these, you do not need a separate router. Sharing an Internet connection with a router works the same way with most other broadband Internet connection types too, including DSL and satellite (covered next).

DSL Internet

digital subscriber line (DSL) A broadband Internet technology provided by the telephone company.

Digital subscriber line (DSL) is a high-speed Internet connection from your local land-based telephone company. There are two types of DSL: asynchronous DSL (ADSL), in which the download speeds are higher than the upload speeds, and synchronous DSL (SDSL), in which the upload and download speeds are the same. Ordinary DSL uses the same twisted-pair cable to provide Internet that it does to provide voice service, with a splitter used to separate the data and voice signals so you can use them both at once. This type of DSL has a speed ranging from 256 Kbps to 20 Mbps depending on the distance between the service address and the phone company's connection box. It can also deliver high-definition TV and phone service, all on a single line. The main drawback to DSL is that it is geographically limited. For top speeds, the service address must be within 1,000 meters of a phone company service box.

Some newer types of DSL, such as AT&T's U-Verse system, use a new technology called Very High Bit Rate DSL (VDSL). It can deliver up to 52 Mbps download and 16 Mbps upload on copper wires and up to 85 Mbps (both download and upload) on coaxial cable.

Satellite Internet

satellite Internet A broadband Internet technology that uses satellites and a transmitter/receiver to provide Internet access.

Satellite Internet service uses the same communication satellites that you learned about earlier in this chapter. Satellite Internet service involves using a satellite dish for receiving and a satellite transmitter for sending data. Because the transmitter positioning is important and improper positioning may violate communication laws, professional installation is usually required.

latency A period of waiting for another component to deliver data needed to proceed.

Satellite service is not likely to be anyone's first choice as a broadband Internet connection. It is relatively slow (around 1 Mbps) and suffers from significant latency (delay) issues that make it unsuitable for performance-sensitive online activities like video conferencing and playing action-based games. Satellite Internet providers also typically place usage caps on user accounts, and penalize subscribers either by charging more or temporarily throttling connection speed for using too much data. However, satellite is available just about anywhere, even in the most rural of areas, as long as there is a clear view of the southern sky (in the northern hemisphere). When faced with the choice of dial-up modem connection or satellite, people who need a broadband connection will go with satellite.

Internet over Cell Phone Networks

Modern cell phone network providers such as Verizon and AT&T not only offer telephone service, but also Internet service. This service is mainly offered to be used to access the Internet via smartphones, but it can also be used to connect other devices as well, such as tablets, notebooks, and even desktops to get Internet access in situations where Wi-Fi and other Internet connection methods are not available, such as when riding in an automobile.

Not all areas of cell phone networks worldwide have the appropriate technology and speed to access the Internet. There have been many different cell phone standards and technologies over the years, and it has only been recently, with the development of 3G, that cell phone networks have become fast enough to support Internet use. 3G, which stands for 3rd Generation, supports download speeds of up to 14 Mbps. An even newer and faster technology, 4G, can support up to 100 Mbps downloads. Cell phone companies provide coverage maps that show the areas in which they provide 3G or 4G service.

3G Digital technology for moving data through a cell phone network at up to 14 Mbps.

4G Digital technology for moving data through a cell phone network at up to 100 Mbps.

If your cell phone data plan is not unlimited, be aware of how much you are using the Internet via your cell phone, to avoid extra charges for going over your data limit. Your cell phone provider may have a website or a phone utility that enables you to see how much data you have used on the current billing cycle.

CAUTION

Quick Review

1. What are the drawbacks of using a dial-up modem?

2. Name three factors that may potentially affect the actual performance of an Internet connection.

3. Which Internet connection technologies offer the fastest service?

Troubleshooting Network and Internet Connections

The Internet has become such an essential part of many people's computing experience that when the connection goes down, or slows to a crawl, it can be a very frustrating experience. In the following tables, you will learn about some problems that commonly occur with network and Internet connections and how to solve them.

Several of the solutions proposed in Tables 13.2 and 13.3 involve using the Windows Network Diagnostics troubleshooter. This utility checks your network connection for several common issues and corrects any problems that it can, recommending fixes for problems you must correct on your own.

You can start the Windows Network Diagnostics troubleshooter by right-clicking the network icon in the notification area and choosing Troubleshoot Problems. Then just follow the prompts by answering the questions presented to you, as in Figure 13.16.

Table 13.2: Troubleshooting General Networking Issues

Symptom	Try this
No network icon appears in the notification area.	Check in Device Manager to make sure you have a correctly installed network adapter and that an appropriate driver is loaded for it. If the network adapter is new, you may need to run the setup software that came with it.
A wireless network icon appears in the notification area with a red X on it.	The wireless network adapter is disabled. You might have accidentally pushed a button on the computer that disabled it. Re-enable it in Device Manager, or run the Windows Troubleshooter by right-clicking the icon and choosing Troubleshoot Problems.
A wireless network icon appears in the notification area with a yellow star on it.	Wireless networks are available, but you aren't connected to any of them yet. Click the icon to see a list of networks, and then click the one to connect to.
A wireless network icon appears in the notification area with a yellow triangle and an exclamation point on it.	There is a problem with the wireless network to which you are connected; the network may be working but not providing Internet access. Try disconnecting from it and reconnecting. If that doesn't work, right-click the icon and choose Troubleshoot Problems.
You appear to have network access, but you can't browse other computers on your local area network.	Check that those other computers have file and printer sharing enabled.
A computer connected directly to the broadband modem with a cable has Internet access, but computers that connect via the router don't.	Power cycle your router by unplugging it, waiting 15 seconds, and plugging it in again.

Table 13.3: Troubleshooting Common Internet Problems

Symptom	Try This
You can browse other computers and resources on your network, but you can't access web pages or email.	Check that your Internet connection is up and running. Look at the lights on your broadband modem to see if there are any clues about the connection's status. Try power cycling the broadband modem by unplugging it, waiting 15 seconds, and plugging it in again.
	Try a different computer on your network if possible. If none of the computers can access web pages or email, contact your ISP for help.
You have Internet access but it is extremely slow.	Close all unnecessary applications that are open. Close and reopen your web browser. If that doesn't help, power cycle both the router and the broadband modem and restart the computer. If the problem persists for more than a few hours, contact your ISP for help.
You have web access but no email.	Your mail server may be temporarily down. Suspect this if you get an error message in your email program when you attempt to send or receive mail. Restart your email program. If that doesn't help, wait a few hours to see if the problem resolves itself, and then contact your ISP for help.
You have email access but no web access.	Close and reopen your web browser. Try a different web browser. If the other web browser works, remove and reinstall the web browser that doesn't work (if other than Internet Explorer), or check for updates available to Internet Explorer and install them if possible. If no other browsers work, see "Certain applications can't access the Internet."
One particular website is not loading.	Wait a few hours to see if the problem resolves itself. This is probably not your computer's fault, and there is nothing you can do about it.
Certain applications can't access the Internet.	Temporarily disable the firewall and see if the problem clears up. If it does, adjust the firewall settings to allow the application to go online.

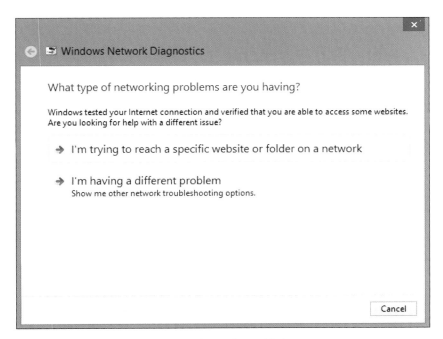

Figure 13.16   The Windows Network Diagnostics troubleshooter.

Quick Review

1. How do you start the Windows Network Diagnostics troubleshooter utility?

2. What should you do if a certain application can't access the web?

3. What should you do if the network icon in the notification area shows a red X on it?

Summary

Our Connected World: Communication Systems

Networking is nearly everywhere, and many of our everyday activities are enabled or assisted by computer networking. For example, the **public-switched telephone network (PSTN)** is a world-wide network that predates the Internet. It is an example of a **circuit-switched network**, one that creates a connection between two points and maintains it for the duration of the communication. In contrast, a **packet-switched network** is one that sends and receives data in packets that may take different routes to the destination.

The **Internet** is the world's largest computer network. It uses various standard **protocols**, so that services like the web and email work the same everywhere. Most companies don't connect directly to the Internet; instead they connect to an **Internet service provider (ISP)**.

The Internet is based on a **protocol stack** (a set of protocols) called **Transmission Control Protocol/Internet Protocol (TCP/IP)**. TCP/IP provides a common set of standards by which data can be sent and received. It is used not only on the Internet, but in most private networks today as well.

To tighten security when using the Internet as a conduit, many companies use a software technology called **virtual private networking (VPN)**. VPN technology creates a secure, tamper-resistant data tunnel between two points on the Internet.

A **satellite** is a transmitter/receiver unit that orbits the Earth, thousands of miles up. Satellite networks are used to deliver services such as TV and video broadcasts, satellite radio, and satellite Internet service. Cellular telephone companies have their own data networks, using a combination of satellites, cables, and on-ground towers with transmitters and receivers on them. Some cell phone networks can also be used to access the Internet. You can access the Internet on a **smartphone** (a cell phone that includes computer functionality), and you can **tether** (connect) a smartphone to a computer and use the phone as a modem to allow the computer Internet access.

Ways of Classifying Networks

There are several ways to classify computer networks. One way is according to the geographical range that they cover: **personal area network (PAN)**, **local area network (LAN), metropolitan area network (MAN)**, or **wide area network (WAN)**. Another way is to look at whether or not a server is involved. In a **peer-to-peer network**, there is no server; in a **client/server network** there is at least one server.

An **intranet** is a network accessible only from inside a company. An **extranet** is a network that is for the use of those outside the organization.

Ethernet is the most popular Internet technology, having outlived many competitors such as Token Ring and Banyan Vines. Ethernet can be wired or wireless; the wireless version is also called **Wi-Fi**. Ethernet devices have a certain maximum speed. For example, **1000BaseT** Ethernet, which is common in most residential and business networks, transfers data at up to 1000 Mbps (1 Gbps).

A wired connection runs a cable between the points, whereas wireless connects the two points via radio frequency (RF) or infrared. **Wi-Fi** is the common name for the wireless networking technology that's used for almost all home and business networks today, often referred to by its standard number: IEEE 802.11. **Bluetooth** is a wireless technology used to connect individual devices to one another in close proximity. It is most commonly used to connect a computer to an input or output device. When the devices are within range, they are **paired**. **Infrared** technology uses light waves to "beam" information from device to device. Infrared was the method of choice for connecting wireless peripherals a decade or so ago, but Bluetooth has mainly superseded it today.

A **microwave communication system** allows two locations to be wirelessly connected by using a high-frequency communication band, much higher than that used for Wi-Fi or Bluetooth.

Network Hardware

A **network adapter** enables a computer to participate in the local area network. When a network adapter is not built into the motherboard, but instead installed as an expansion board, it is called a **network interface card (NIC)**. Each network adapter has a hardware address, called a **media access control (MAC) address**, that is unique in all the world.

A **switch** is a box that provides a central gathering point for all the computers in an Ethernet LAN. A wireless switch is called a **wireless access point (WAP)**. An earlier version of a switch, called a **hub**, was not so intelligent. A **router** performs all the same functions as a switch, but it also has an added bonus: It can direct traffic into and out of the LAN. Each router has an output port called a **default gateway** that enables data to leave the local network to be delivered.

A **gateway** enables you to connect two dissimilar networks. A **bridge** connects two similar networks. A **repeater** does just what the name implies—it repeats a network signal to strengthen it on its way to its destination.

Most of the Ethernet cables in business and residential buildings are **twisted-pair cable**. The wires twisting around each other helps reduce **electromagnetic interference (EMI)** caused by the magnetic field generated when electricity passes through the cable. Most twisted-pair cable is **unshielded twisted pair (UTP)**. **Shielded twisted pair (STP)** contains this extra lining, and is used in environments where EMI is a problem. **Cat3** cable is used for telephone networks and has an **RJ-11** or **RJ-14** connector. **Cat5e** cable is used for modern Ethernet networks and uses an **RJ-45** connecter. **Coaxial cable** is the type of cable used for cable TV connections. It is also used for some networking, such as delivering cable Internet to a home. **Fiber optic cable** carries data in pulses of light along a glass fiber.

Understanding and Connecting to the Internet

The Internet began as a way of enabling schools, research institutions, and the military to share information. Structurally, the Internet is a mesh of routers and servers connected to one another at multiple points.

At the heart of the Internet are high-capacity, high-speed data pathways that are like superhighways for data. These pathways form the Internet's **backbone**.

The Internet service that you subscribe to has two speeds, both measured in megabytes per second (Mbps): the theoretical maximum speed and the actual speed. Many factors can prevent an Internet connection from achieving its top speed, including local and Internet traffic and problems with your own broadband modem or router.

Types of Internet connections include dial-up and broadband. A dial-up connection is established using a **dial-up modem**. It is a very slow and inconvenient connection. Broadband connections are usually always on. Types of broadband connections include **cable modem**, **digital subscriber line (DSL)**, **satellite Internet,** and cell phone networks with **3G** and **4G** service.

Troubleshooting Network and Internet Connections

The Windows Network Diagnostics troubleshooter can find and fix most network-related problems. To start troubleshooting a network issue, look at the network icon in the notification area; its icon's appearance may give you a clue as to what is wrong. For Internet connection problems, restarting the router, broadband modem, and/or computer can often fix the problem.

Key Terms

1000BaseT
3G
4G
backbone
bandwidth
Bluetooth
bridge
broadband
cable modem
category 3 cable
category 5e cable
circuit-switched network
client
client/server network
coaxial cable
default gateway
dial-up modem
digital subscriber line (DSL)
electromagnetic interference (EMI)
Ethernet
extranet
fiber optic cable
gateway
hotspot
hub
infrared
Internet
Internet service provider (ISP)
intranet
latency
local area network (LAN)

media access control (MAC) address
metropolitan area network (MAN)
microwave communication system
network adapter
network interface card (NIC)
packet-switched network
pair
peer-to-peer (P2P) network
personal area network (PAN)
protocol stack
protocol
public-switched telephone network (PSTN)
repeater
RJ-11
RJ-14
RJ-45
router
satellite
satellite Internet
shielded twisted pair (STP)
smartphone
switch
tether
Transmission Control Protocol/Internet Protocol (TCP/IP)
twisted-pair cable
unshielded twisted pair (UTP)
virtual private networking (VPN)
wide area network (WAN)
Wi-Fi
wireless access point (WAP)

Test Yourself

Fact Check

1. Which type of network would you use to copy a photo from your smartphone to your laptop?

   a. personal area network

   b. local area network

   c. wide area network

   d. metropolitan area network

2. What does it mean when a wireless network icon appears in the notification area with a yellow star on it?

   a. There are no networks available.

   b. You have no networking hardware installed.

   c. Networks are available, but you are not connected to any yet.

   d. You are connected to a network.

3. The Internet is based on what protocol stack?

   a. Token Ring

   b. TCP/IP

   c. WPA

   d. HTML

4. What type of network creates a secure tunnel through the Internet?

   a. virtual private network

   b. Ethernet

   c. infrared

   d. Bluetooth

5. Which type of network has no servers?

   a. Ethernet

   b. P2P

   c. client/server

   d. VPN

6. What kind of network is only for the use of people within the company?

   a. P2P

   b. extranet

   c. intranet

   d. Ethernet

7. Which of these is *not* a type of wireless networking?

   a. 802.11

   b. microwave

   c. Bluetooth

   d. bridge

8. In what type of device would a wireless network adapter be found?

   a. notebook computer

   b. keyboard

   c. mouse

   d. monitor

9. Every NIC has a unique _____.

   a. router

   b. access point

   c. MAC address

   d. server name

10. What type of cable is not subject to EMI?

   a. fiber optic

   b. Cat3

   c. coaxial

   d. UTP

Matching

Match the term to its description.

   a. bridge

   b. gateway

   c. hub

   d. repeater

   e. router

   f. switch

1. _____A gathering point for network connections that is unable to route any packets.

2. _____A gathering point for network connections that can route packets only to devices directly connected to it.

3. _____A gathering point for network connections that can route packets out of the local network, such as to the Internet.

4. _____A network device that strengthens and rebroadcasts a signal.

5. _____A network device that connects dissimilar networks.

6. _____A network device that connects similar networks.

Sum It Up

1. List three types of wireless connection.

2. How do a switch and a router differ?

3. Explain the difference between STP and UTP cable.

4. What kind of cable would you need for a 1000BaseT network?

5. What is TCP/IP?

6. List four ways to connect to the Internet.

7. List two things to try if your computer is connected to a network but can't access the Internet.

8. Why is satellite Internet not more popular?

Explore More

Finding a Fast Internet Connection

Suppose a neighbor wanted to know what the best Internet connection available in your neighborhood is. Use the Internet to research this topic, and find the fastest service available at your home address. Collect all the information you can about this service, including:

- What company is providing it?

- What is the advertised speed of the connection? Are the download and upload speeds different?

- Is there a limit on data usage per day or per month?

- What connection technology does it use?

- How much does it cost per month?

- Is a wireless router included?

- Are there any startup costs involved?

Think It Over

Virtual Private Networking

With a VPN, a company can use the Internet to establish a secure communication channel between two points without going to the expense of leasing a data line. There are some people who say that it's unfair, though, that large companies can use so much bandwidth, making the whole Internet run slower for everyone else, without paying for it. Do you agree? Do you think companies that transfer a large amount of data on an everyday basis should pay more, or should be forced to lease their own lines?

Metropolitan Area Networks

Suppose you are the mayor of a small town, and it has been suggested that the town install a metropolitan area network that will provide low-cost, high-speed Wi-Fi to all citizens who want it. Proponents say that it will encourage people to move to the town and will encourage highly educated young adults to stay in town instead of moving away. Opponents argue that the town will go into debt paying for such a system with no guarantee that enough people will sign up for the service to make it pay for itself. What questions would you want answered in order to help you make up your mind?

Chapter 14

Online Communication

The way we communicate with friends and business associates has changed dramatically in the last decade, thanks to the Internet. Our communication channels are increasingly shifting toward computer-assisted technologies, many of which are not only more immediate but also less expensive to use than the non-computerized alternatives. For example, a business can save a great deal of money by sending its advertisements to customers by email rather than postal mail and by meeting with clients through videoconferencing rather than having employees travel to the client site, and families can keep in touch using video chat services, as in Figure 14.1.

With all these new technologies for communication available, though, it can be a challenge to select the appropriate communication medium for a situation. In addition, each new form of communication comes with its own social conventions about the type of language to use, the format messages should take, and the appropriate level of formality. Whether or not you conform to these communication rules directly affects how well your message is received.

In this chapter, we will review the many different types of computer-assisted communication technologies available in today's world. You'll learn about their pros and cons and accepted uses, and you'll learn some of the etiquette rules and customs that will enable you to get your message across effectively.

© IStockphoto.com/arekmalang

Figure 14.1 The Internet has changed the way people communicate by offering technologies such as video chatting, email, and instant messaging.

Internet Communication Types

The Internet in its original form was for the transfer of data between computers over a network. Email was one of the first Internet applications and is one of the most popular means of communication. Many more ways of communicating online are now available, including:

- Instant messaging
- Social networking
- Blogs and microblogs
- Newsgroups
- Forums
- Voice over IP (VoIP)
- Video chat/videoconferencing

Many of these communication options require little more than a web connection and a username and password for the particular service. This chapter explains how some of these systems work and helps you choose appropriate communications tools.

Email

Email (short for electronic mail) is the computer equivalent of postal mail. Billions of email messages are exchanged every day through a worldwide system of email servers.

Email is a store-and-forward system, as shown in Figure 14.2, not an instant communication medium. When you compose and send an email, your provider's outgoing mail server forwards it to the recipient's incoming mail server. The message is stored there until the recipient logs in and picks it up. Each ISP or organization that provides email service has its own mail servers that participate in this global network for mail

email A computer-based system for exchanging messages through mail servers.

store-and-forward A message delivery system in which messages are forwarded between servers and then stored on those servers until they are picked up.

mail server An online server that sends and/or receives email messages on behalf of the email addresses it supports.

delivery. To access your messages on your incoming mail server, you can use a mail client (email software installed on your computer) or you can log into a web-based interface maintained by your email provider.

mail client Software installed on a computer that is used to compose and manage email.

Email Delivery

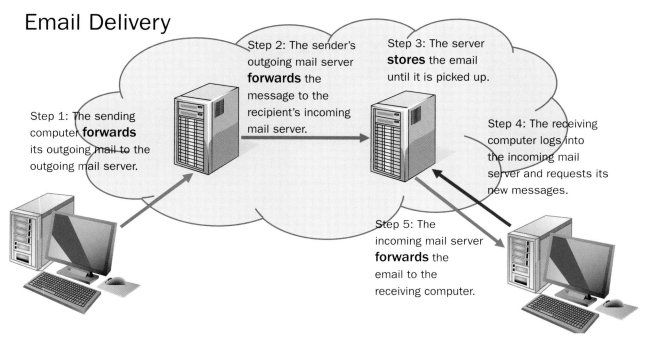

Step 1: The sending computer **forwards** its outgoing mail to the outgoing mail server.

Step 2: The sender's outgoing mail server **forwards** the message to the recipient's incoming mail server.

Step 3: The server **stores** the email until it is picked up.

Step 4: The receiving computer logs into the incoming mail server and requests its new messages.

Step 5: The incoming mail server **forwards** the email to the receiving computer.

Figure 14.2 Email is a store-and-forward system involving mail servers on the Internet. Mail is forwarded from one mail server to another, and then is stored until the recipient picks it up.

Most providers that offer free email services, like Google, Yahoo!, and AOL, are primarily web-based. These types of email accounts are sometimes referred to as HTTP email accounts. HTTP (Hypertext Transfer Protocol) is a protocol for web content transmission. You might be able to set up certain mail clients to work with those accounts, but it is generally expected that you will use the web interface.

HTTP email account An email account that is designed to be used with a web interface, and that uses web technology for email management.

On the other hand, a mail client is customarily used for most email accounts that someone pays for, either directly or indirectly. For example, the email accounts at your workplace, the accounts that your ISP provides to you, and the accounts that you have through a web-hosting service (for example, if you own a domain name) are all designed to be used with a mail client.

Two kinds of email accounts are designed to be used with mail clients: a POP account and an IMAP account. Each uses a different protocol for receiving mail, and offers slightly different advantages.

POP account An email account that is designed to be used with an email client and that uses POP protocol for receiving mail.

IMAP account An email account that is designed to be used with an email client and that uses IMAP protocol for receiving mail.

- Post Office Protocol (POP) is a literal store-and-forward protocol. It holds the messages until you pick them up, but it doesn't maintain any direct communication with your email client. You can choose to leave the messages on the server or delete them from the server after you pick them up, but what you do with them after that point is of no concern to the server. For example, you could delete an email from your email client, and the message would continue to persist on the server. POP accounts work well for people who always work with their email from the same computer.

Post Office Protocol (POP) A protocol for receiving email through a mail client.

Internet Mail Access Protocol (IMAP) A protocol for receiving email through a mail client.

■ Internet Mail Access Protocol (IMAP) is a modified version of store-and-forward. It continues to hold your messages even after you pick them up, and anything you do in your email client is reflected on the server. For example, if you delete a message, or create a new folder for storing messages, that change is automatically reflected in the email clients of every device that you use. The drawbacks are that you may not be able to access old mail without an Internet connection and not every email provider offers IMAP accounts.

Simple Mail Transfer Protocol (SMTP) A protocol used for sending email for a POP3 email account.

The POP and IMAP protocol are used only for receiving email; a complementary protocol called Simple Mail Transfer Protocol (SMTP) is used for sending email from a POP or IMAP account.

The line between HTTP, POP, and IMAP accounts has become blurry in recent years, as more email providers have attempted to give customers more options without making them change email account types. Most providers allow customers the option of a web-based interface no matter what type of email account they have, and some email clients can send and receive mail from HTTP accounts, either natively or with some special setup. In addition, some free web-based email services offer customers the option of paying a small amount for an upgrade to an account that can be used as a POP or IMAP account.

Instant Messaging, Texting, and Chatting

instant messaging Sending and receiving short text messages in real-time over the Internet.

Instant messaging (IM) is another type of written message that is sent over the Internet. As its name suggests, the message is sent immediately rather than waiting for the recipient to log on to the service to retrieve his messages. In many cases, the recipient will be online at the same time as the sender and may respond immediately. The immediacy of IM makes it more like having an online chat.

push technology A technology that sends information to a recipient without the recipient asking for it each time.

pull technology A technology that sends information to a recipient only when the recipient requests it.

Instant messaging is a push technology. That means that the messages are pushed out to the recipient if he or she is logged in; it doesn't require the recipient to do anything to check for new messages. In contrast, email is a pull technology, because the recipient must actively check for messages in order to pull the new messages to his computer. (The email client can be set to automatically check for new messages at certain intervals, so the email messages may seem to be arriving on their own, but it is actually the client software pulling them.)

Instant messaging requires you to have IM client software installed for the service you are using. For example, Yahoo! Messenger's client software for Windows appears in Figure 14.3. Other instant messaging clients include AOL Instant Messenger (AIM) and Microsoft Lync (formerly known as Microsoft Office Communicator). IM client software is available for Mac, Windows, and Linux operating systems, plus several smartphone and tablet operating systems.

Some instant messaging services include voice and even video chat capabilities, as well as picture sharing. Including these features takes the applications beyond simple instant messaging, into the realm of Voice over IP (VoIP) and videoconferencing, both of which are covered later in this chapter.

You can also send and receive instant messages on smartphones using a technology called Short Message Service (SMS), which goes through your cell phone provider's network. This type of messaging is called texting.

The differentiation between SMS and IM messages can get blurry because services are available that can cross the platforms. For example, some IM services offer clients for certain smartphone operating systems, and there are computer-based applications that can send and receive SMS messages. If you use one of these services, it may not be obvious how the message delivery will be billed (that is, whether the messages count as SMS messages toward your cell phone plan's text message allowance, or whether the messages use the phone's Internet data plan), so monitor your usage carefully until you are sure.

Short Message Service (SMS) The text messaging technology used on cell phone networks.

texting Sending and receiving short text messages in real-time over a cell phone network.

Figure 14.3 Yahoo! Messenger's client software for Windows enables you to have one-on-one text chats with others.

WhatsApp

Depending on your cell phone plan, you may only get a certain number of SMS text messages per month. If you find yourself running out of SMS messages each month, consider using WhatsApp Messenger, a cross-platform smartphone application that can send text messages using your phone's Internet data plan, bypassing the phone's SMS service. You are still sending text messages, but you're doing so through an Internet server, so you aren't charged per message, but only for the small amount of Internet data used. WhatsApp is available for iPhone, BlackBerry, Android, Windows Phone, and Nokia. WhatsApp was originally developed by a very small company, but was purchased by Facebook in February 2014, giving it a much broader audience and greater financial backing for future development.

New Technologies

Some IM clients allow group chats, but they are normally with people whom you specifically invite. In contrast, many public or semi-public chat rooms enable you to have group conversations with people you may not know. Many websites include chat room software on some of their web pages that anyone can log into to participate in a group chat. For example, a recovery support site for alcoholics might have a group chat every night at a certain time.

chat room An online virtual room in which you can meet and talk to other people.

Internet Relay Chat (IRC) An online system of public chat servers.

channel An individual chat room on a chat server such as IRC.

social network An Internet-based system that enables users to interact in real-time and by using messaging programs.

tag A topic or subject assigned to a social networking post. Also called a **hashtag**.

Instagram A social network for posting and sharing photos.

Vine A social network for posting and sharing video clips.

Reddit A social network for posting new snippets.

YouTube A social network for posting and sharing videos.

Facebook A social network for posting interesting updates, web links, and photos, and for chatting with friends.

Twitter A microblogging platform used to post frequent updates and to comment on events as they happen.

The largest system of public chat rooms is Internet Relay Chat (IRC), with about 400,000 users worldwide. IRC is a system of chat servers that users log into using IRC client software. The user can then select a channel, which is a chat room for a particular subject of discussion, and enter the channel to join the conversation.

Social Networking

Social networking is an umbrella term for sites such as Facebook, Twitter, LinkedIn, and Google+, in which users can post information about themselves and create groups of people with shared interests with which to chat and exchange ideas and web links.

Each user creates a profile, which can include details about her location, job, family, and interests. Social networks grow organically by friends inviting friends who in turn invite or include their own friends. Users are able to post and comment on photos and videos published to the network, share links, send each other emails, and conduct web chats.

Some social networks make extensive use of tags. These are searchable labels that can be added to posted content allow other people to find like-minded users and join interest groups, fan pages, and more. However, these self-applied tags are also useful to marketers and enable them to target potential customers far more accurately. Information sharing and access to people's private information has thus become an important area of debate. On Twitter and some other services, tags are preceded by hash symbols (#) and are referred to as hashtags.

Some social networks are specialized. You might use Instagram to share photos, Vine for video clips, Reddit for news snippets, YouTube for video-sharing, and **LinkedIn** for business networking. Other networks, such as Facebook and Twitter, are more general but allow you to cross-post updates to and from other social network sites.

One reason social networks are so successful is that they have accompanying mobile apps, so it's easy for users to post updates and read posts from their smartphones or tablets. Many apps let you log in using your existing Twitter or Facebook details. This makes for a convenient user experience and is also useful to the app developers and Facebook/Twitter as a mechanism for promotion.

Social Media Marketer

A social media marketer specializes in helping companies promote themselves using social networking tools such as blogs, social networks, and microblogs, including Twitter. Their purpose is to increase public awareness of the company and its products. The role requires marketing expertise and a thorough understanding of how search tools work and how to call attention to the client companies. Using this knowledge, the social media marketing person adds keywords and hashtags to the content they create. This helps the client company's web pages appear more prominently and frequently in search results and rank higher in page rank indexes. The process of writing content in this way is known as search engine optimization (SEO). Marketing and business skills and professional courses in SEO marketing are expected for such a role. A successful social media marketer will demonstrate her expertise by maintaining her own use of social networks.

Careers in IT

Blogs and Microblogs

A blog (originally called *weblog*) is a web page where an individual or group publishes stories, essays, or articles that are generically referred to as posts. Blog posts differ from websites that contain news stories and marketing information in that they are personal and often opinionated in nature. Whereas a news story is objective, a blog post may put forth a point of view or an extended commentary. Some blogs are similar to personal diaries, but others are run by users with specialist knowledge of a topic they want to share with other people. A blog owner is likely to engage directly with readers who comment on the topic and follow the blog.

Popular blogs with lots of followers and comments can be highly influential in their sphere of expertise. Social media tools such as Twitter and Facebook (www.facebook.com) are used to promote posts and get more people to contribute to the commentary.

Companies often use blogs to share news about forthcoming product launches and ideas they are working on. A blog of this type may be part of a company's website. For example, Microsoft hosts several official blogs written by employees in various departments to let the public know informally about what its teams are working on for future products and services. Figure 14.4 shows the Blogging Windows blog, for example, found at http://blogs.windows.com/bloggingwindows, which highlights new and interesting apps and technologies for Windows.

search engine optimization (SEO) The process of writing web content so as to increase a page's ranking in online search results.

blog A web page containing the author's personal experiences and opinions.

post An article published on a blog.

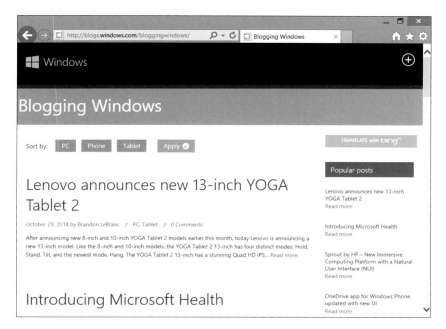

Figure 14.4 Although blogs are best known for containing individual writers' personal stories and opinions, some blogs are corporate-sponsored, like this one.

Many individual bloggers use a blog platform, which is a free or low-cost blog-hosting website. Some of the most widely used blog platforms are WordPress, Typepad, and Blogger. These platforms act as the web host and offer customizable design templates as part of the blog. For a small additional fee, extra features are available, such as the capability to use your own domain name.

blog platform A web server that hosts the blogs of individuals, either free or for a small fee.

microblog A service that allows the posting of short messages.

Microblogging is a form of blogging that allows users to post brief text commentary or post photos and audio clips. On Twitter (the best-known microblogging platform), each post (called a "tweet") can be no longer than 140 characters. This restriction is intended to keep updates interesting and make people think about the essence of what they're trying to say. Some updates are used to link to blog posts the users have written or to online articles they've found interesting and want to share or discuss, as in Figure 14.5, while others serve as a means for people in the public eye to communicate with their fans.

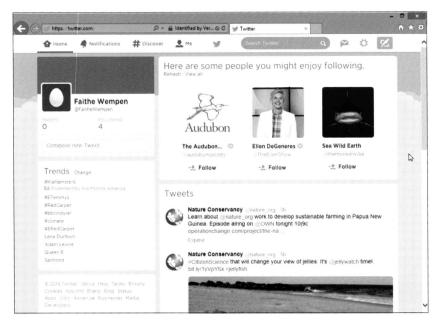

Figure 14.5   Twitter is used by all sorts of people and organizations to promote themselves and to comment on events.

Unlike email, microblogs can be seen by anyone and can be commented on by anyone, though people must usually register with the service to comment. To address a post to someone, put an @ sign in front of the username. To find a topic of interest, you can search within the blogging platform. To make a post more likely to be found, you can add a # (hashtag) indicating the topic. Figure 14.6 shows a search for items tagged "Gardening."

The best-known microblogging platforms are Twitter, Tumblr, and Google+. Video and photo-sharing sites Vine and Instagram can also be thought of as microblogs, because users generally post a photo or a video clip with a caption and then invite comments.

Smartphone and tablet apps for microblogging sites enable users and followers to view new posts and get notifications about them or about replies to their own posts. Relevant and interesting posts are reposted by followers to their own followers, thereby helping to promote the original post. A particularly significant tweet from a prominent public figure might be retweeted thousands of times.

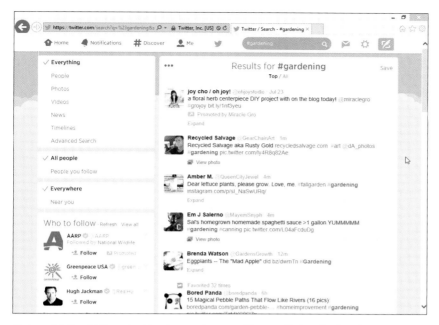

Figure 14.6   Adding a hashtag to a post ensures it's more likely to be found.

Wikis

A wiki is an online database of information that any user can copy or amend using a web interface. Wikis are usually set up so users can collaborate and share information and knowledge. If someone has additional information related to the wiki's content, he can add it to the wiki. Wikipedia is the best-known example of a wiki; it is a form of online encyclopedia created by and edited by web users. Figure 14.7 shows the Wikipedia web page that describes a wiki.

wiki A web-based application that can be edited by anyone and that is usually informational or instructive in nature.

Figure 14.7   A wiki is an online database used for collaborative projects.

Newsgroups

Newsgroups were created long before the web and were the forerunners to the web-based forums we use today. These groups are part of a system called Usenet, which is a global distributed discussion system. Usenet users read and post messages to various categories known as newsgroups. Discussions are stored as threads, which follow a particular topic. Posts are not stored on individual servers; they are stored on a set of distributed servers that form part of the Usenet network. Newsgroup servers are connected to each other to form a network. Newsgroups have their own protocol for accessing the posts, called NNTP (network news transport protocol), which transports news articles between news servers and clients reading and posting articles. The client computer needs an application called a newsreader to read Usenet articles, or needs to use an email client that supports news reading.

Newsgroups usually focus on a particular topic of interest, but some groups allow postings on any topic. Discussions are not held on the servers indefinitely and typically will disappear after a few months. Newsgroups have declined in popularity as other forms of online communication have come to prominence, but there are still more than 100,000 active groups.

Forums

Web forums are a more sophisticated type of newsgroup. A forum is hosted on a standard website and can be accessed using any web browser. Many forums have a question-and-answer format in which members request advice from other forum members. Comments and replies to a post create a forum thread. Forum threads are saved and archived so that other users can easily find the answer to the same or similar question in future. You don't always need to become a forum member in order to find useful advice on a forum or to search its threads, but you must join in order to create a new post and ask a question or start a discussion.

If you're looking for advice on a brand or product, try typing that product name plus the word **forum** into a search engine. For example, if you wanted to buy a new digital SLR camera, you might use a search engine to find answers to the question *Which DSLR camera under $500 shall I buy?* Your search results may include a link to a forum thread covering this topic at `www.photography-forum.org` (see Figure 14.8). You could then read everyone's comments and advice on the matter, but you would need to join the forum to contribute to the discussion.

Forums are often set up by interest groups and cover every aspect of life—from hobbies to transport, technology, health, and so on. Other forums are hosted on a company's website so customers can request help with support issues and get advice from other customers and from technicians within the company. On many forums, users can give a thumbs-up to a post to show appreciation for it and to increase the poster's forum rating. Some forums are moderated, meaning a leader or administrator approves each message before it is posted, to cut down on inappropriate postings such as advertisements.

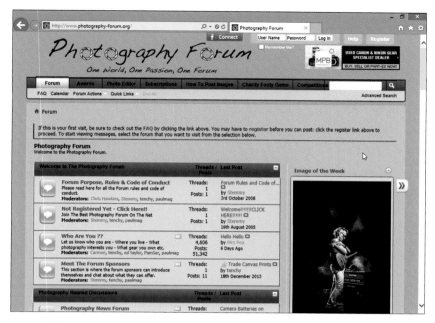

Figure 14.8 The home page of a photography forum.

VoIP

Voice over Internet Protocol (VoIP) is used to make voice calls via the Internet by turning the voice message into small packets of data. IP, short for Internet protocol, is used to identify individual devices that are connected to the Internet and to route calls between them. For more detail at how IP addresses work, refer to Chapter 15, "Web Basics."

Making VoIP calls requires a reliable web connection with plenty of bandwidth. This bandwidth is needed in order to translate your voice into bits of data, transmit it to your friend, and then reassemble it in the correct order so what you said makes sense. On slower web connections, this process may not work so smoothly and the caller's speech may sound garbled or have delays.

VoIP calls can be made from your computer using a SIP (session Internet protocol) client and a URI (unique resource indicator), but it's far easier—and much more common—to use a VoIP service such as Skype, FaceTime (on Apple devices), or an IM client that also allows you to make voice calls, such as Yahoo! Messenger. VoIP calls can also be made from a tablet or smartphone using a VoIP app. Skype, Facebook Chat, and Truphone are popular VoIP apps. Google users in some countries can also make calls from their Google accounts just by clicking on the name of the person they want to call.

VoIP was originally designed for making web-based phone calls, but the advent of much faster broadband and fixed-line Internet connections has made it possible for the web to carry video calls too. Not only has VoIP become so dependable that many offices have replaced their telephone systems with VoIP-based ones, but it is now also routinely used for corporate videoconferencing.

Voice over Internet Protocol (VoIP) A means of providing web-based telephony. The best-known example is Skype.

Skype A Microsoft-owned VoIP service used to make phone calls and sometimes video calls over a broadband, Wi-Fi, or cellular mobile web connection.

FaceTime An app installed on Apple devices such as the iPhone and iPad that is used to make video calls between Apple device owners.

Skype is the most popular VoIP service in the world. Skype began as a VoIP service for making free computer-to-computer calls, but can also now be used to make cheaper international calls from a smartphone and for one-to-one video calls. Other VoIP services work in a similar way to Skype, but they don't all have video calling options.

To use Skype, download the software client from www.skype.com. Then use the software to create a user profile for inclusion in the Skype database so others who might want to call you can find you. You can also use your email contacts list and call anyone on it who also uses Skype. Skype is part of Microsoft, so if you already have an Outlook, Messenger, or Hotmail account, you can sign in with those credentials. You can also sign in with your Facebook account details. A commercial version of Skype enables you to add a Skype phone number that non-Skype subscribers can use to call you.

To use Skype for VoIP calls on a computer or laptop, you need built-in speakers and a microphone, or to use an external microphone and speakers or a headset. To make video calls using Skype, you also need a webcam. You can also make calls using a Skype app on your tablet or smartphone.

Videoconferencing

videoconferencing A means of conducting a video conversation remotely using an Internet connection and the webcam or camera on your laptop, phone, or tablet.

Most video calls you make using Skype or another video calling app involve one person at each end of the line. Videoconferencing is a multi-party version of the video call, as in Figure 14.9. An advantage of videoconferencing is that meetings can be held without the need for participants to travel, saving travel time and associated costs. Videoconferencing is also becoming prevalent in education: Online lectures can be delivered, backed up with video-call–based mentoring sessions.

© iStockphoto.com/Blend_Images

Figure 14.9 Videoconferencing enables multiple people to video chat at the same time.

Videoconferencing uses the same underlying protocols as VoIP uses, but it requires much more bandwidth. Corporate videoconferencing facilities can cost many thousands of dollars to set up, but the costs are quickly recouped because hotel bills, travel expenses, and time out of the office are not required. Companies such as Cisco and Polycom provide video-conferencing telephony equipment. Microsoft Lync provides a phone and laptop-based videoconferencing service that companies can sign up their employees to use.

Videoconferencing can be far more effective than phone-based meetings because relevant graphics can be shown and because participants can see each other and interact in real-time.

Quick Review

1. Which protocols are used for sending and receiving email?
2. What distinguishes a microblog from other blogs?
3. Which type of communication uses hashtags (#)?
4. What is VoIP used for?

Communicating Appropriately

The way you express yourself online is just as important as choosing the best means of communicating. The language and tone you use can be chatty, friendly, respectful, or persuasive. You should always choose the appropriate medium and tone to fit the occasion and relationship with your intended recipient.

Professional versus Personal Communication

As the use of social media plays an increasingly larger role in our lives, it's easy to fall into the trap of being overly familiar in your communication. When corresponding with people you don't know well, or who are older or in a position of authority, address them formally and use polite language. Avoid jargon and slang. Emoticons such as smiley face characters are also inappropriate in professional communication.

When sending professional communications, use a sincere but not overly friendly tone and diplomatic language. Avoid unnecessary capitalization and exclamation marks. Read through what you've written before sending the document. Check spelling and grammar. Microsoft Word and other word processors have automatic spell-checkers and grammar checkers, but keep in mind they are not foolproof. If the document is a job application or a letter asking for a work experience placement, your written material will be scrutinized on these elements in addition to the content.

Personal communication also involves a measure of good judgment. Remember that jokes aren't always appreciated; something you think is funny and friendly may inadvertently upset someone else. Emails and text messages can come across more negative than the writer intended.

Emoticons can help, but they can also be misinterpreted. If possible, talk to the person face-to-face or chat online. Verbal communication and IMs can be a lot friendlier and allow your tone of voice or, in the case of video calls or face-to-face chat, gestures and facial expressions, to help convey your meaning.

For any type of digital communication, avoid language that could offend on the basis of race, religion, disability, sexuality, or gender. A good rule for any form of communication is to ask yourself if you would be happy to see the message printed in a newspaper or another public outlet.

Verbal versus Written Communications

Online communication has become the standard contact method for many people, but a phone call or face-to-face conversation can sometimes be the better choice. When deciding between written and verbal communication, consider these factors:

- With whom am I communicating? If you know someone well and the two of you regularly chat face-to-face and by email, a less formal means of communicating, such as an instant message or a Facebook message, could be fine.

- What is the context or subject of the communication? If you want to discuss something serious or enlist someone's help and support, verbal communication is often the best approach. Verbal communication may also be best for confidential matters.

- Am I likely to need a record of the communication? Written communications are generally best when you need a record of proof. An email may suffice, but a legal document or formal notification or application may require a typed letter sent by regular mail service. For business communication, address the recipient formally, using a courtesy title such as Mr., Mrs., or Ms., and use polite, respectful language.

- Is the speed of communication important? Some people check their email and social media messages frequently; other people do so much less often. Check whether the person you want to communicate with uses online communication regularly.

In any medium, stay calm and moderate your language, even if someone is criticizing you. Slang and profanities undermine any argument.

Choosing the Appropriate Online Medium

Using the right means of online communication shows you understand what message you want to get across and whom you are corresponding with.

The following checklist can help you choose the right medium for the particular occasion.

Email
- Suitable for most types of communication, especially if they are not time-sensitive.
- Good for formal messages and communication with strangers.
- Provides a permanent record of outgoing and incoming messages (unless, of course, you delete them).

Instant messaging
- Ideal to get a quick answer to a question or for passing small amounts of information between colleagues.
- Useful for quick updates with friends.

Social networking—personal
- Appropriate mainly for your personal world.
- Useful for informing your network of friends what is happening in your life, not necessarily work related.
- Good for posting photos and videos of recent events you've been involved in.

Social networking—business
- Increasingly used for advertising and business promotion.
- Many social networking sites are dedicated fully or in part to matching job-seekers with potential employers.

Blogs
- Ideal for expressing personal opinions and providing updates about yourself publicly as well as to your friends.

Microblogs
- Best for very short summary updates you want existing followers to see and that can also be found by anyone searching for you or for the topic you cover.

Forums
- Best for discussing topics of shared interest and communicating as part of a community.

VoIP calls
- Useful for chatting with friends or business associates. Requires a reliable, high-speed web connection and use of the same VoIP service. Works well for families keeping touch around the globe using phone or video.

Videoconferencing
- Appropriate mainly for the workplace or schools and colleges so groups can interact visually.

Choose your communication method carefully, understanding the benefits and drawbacks of each channel. Tailor your communication to what you need to accomplish and with whom you communicate.

Quick Review

1. What would be an appropriate medium for quickly checking with someone to confirm an appointment time?

2. Under what conditions is a forum the best method of communication?

3. In what ways should using social networks for personal use differ from using them for business communication?

Using and Managing Email

Email is the online communication method you will probably use the most in your daily work, school, and personal life. As you learned earlier in this chapter, you can access your email using a web interface or you can use an email client application. In the following sections, you'll learn how to use Microsoft Outlook 2013, the email client that comes with the Microsoft Office suite of applications that you have studied in earlier chapters. The general principles are the same no matter which email client you use, though, such as setting up accounts, sending and receiving mail, and organizing messages into folders.

Setting Up Email

When you install an email client, the Setup utility offers to set up your email account. You can add more email accounts later, though, in the same email client so that you receive messages from multiple accounts in a single Inbox folder. Each time you send an email, you can choose which account it will be sent from. If you are using a web-based email interface, you do not have to set up your account; logging in with your correct email address and password is all that's needed.

CAUTION When you sign up for an email account, you will be asked what password you want to use. Make sure you choose a strong password. A strong password is one that is difficult to guess; it may include a combination of uppercase letters, lowercase letters, numerals, and symbols. A strong password should be fairly long (at least eight characters) and should not match any word in the dictionary or any common phrase or number sequence.

---

strong password A password that includes a combination of uppercase letters, lowercase letters, numerals, and symbols, making it difficult to guess.

Some email clients can automatically configure some types of accounts without your having to enter the technical settings for them (such as the incoming and outgoing mail server names and the account type). When you set up an email account, Outlook attempts to determine the correct settings for that account automatically. It doesn't always succeed, so you may need to manually configure the account settings. The following Step by Step exercise shows the steps for setting up a new account in Outlook 2013.

NOTE These steps assume that Outlook is already configured for at least one account, or has been opened previously. The first time you open Outlook on a PC, a wizard appears that starts the process rolling for setting up a new account; if that's the case for you, pick up the following steps at step 2.

Setting Up a New Account Automatically in Microsoft Outlook 2013

Follow this procedure to set up a new account in Outlook 2013 by allowing Outlook to automatically detect the correct settings to use. Try this method first:

1. Click File, and click Add Account fom the Info tab. The Add Account dialog box opens.

2. Fill in your name, email address, and password in the fields provided. Then click Next.

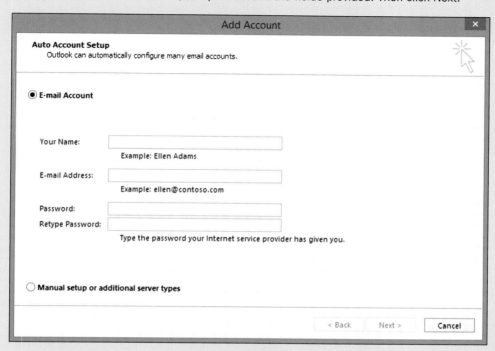

3. If you see a box asking whether to allow a website to confirm server settings, click Allow.

4. If a message appears that the account has been successfully configured, click Finish, and you're done. If, on the other hand, a message appears that the account cannot be automatically configured, click Cancel and then see the next section.

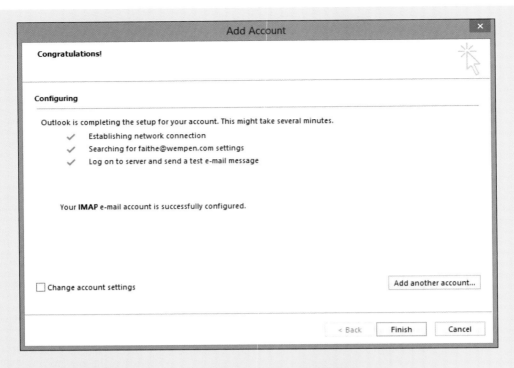

Setting Up a New Account Manually in Microsoft Outlook 2013

Follow this procedure to set up a new account in Outlook 2013 manually. Use this method if the previous method has failed, or if your account has some special settings that email clients in the past have failed to detect.

1. Click File, and click Add Account. The Add Account dialog box opens.
2. Click Manual Setup or Additional Server Types, and click Next.
3. On the Choose Service screen, choose the server type and click Next. Most email accounts for home use are POP or IMAP, so the rest of these steps will assume that you chose POP or IMAP. If you are setting up some other type of account, follow the prompts that appear.
4. On the POP and IMAP Account Settings screen, fill in all the requested information. You will need to know the incoming and outgoing mail server names; if you don't know these, get that information from your email provider.

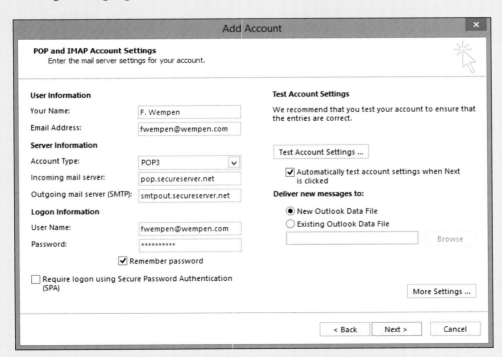

Note: By default Outlook creates a new data file for each email account you set up. If you want the new email account to use an existing data file (for example, outlook.pst), select the Existing Outlook Data File option button and then browse for the data file. This is an issue only for POP3 accounts, IMAP accounts store the mail on the server.

5. Click Next. Outlook tests the settings by sending and receiving a message. If both incoming and outgoing tests show Completed, click Close and then click Finish; your settings are correct.

   If, on the other hand, you see a message that Outlook cannot connect to either your incoming or outgoing mail server, click Close and then click More Settings to open the Internet Email Settings dialog box.

6. Use the options in the dialog box to configure your settings as directed by your email service provider. For example, here are some common settings you might need to change:

   ■ On the Outgoing Server tab, select the My Outgoing Server (SMTP) Requires Authentication check box.

   ■ If your email provider has told you that you need an SSL connection, on the Advanced tab, mark the This Server Requires an Encrypted Connection (SSL) check box.

   ■ On the Advanced tab, change the port numbers for the incoming and/or outgoing servers to the numbers that your email service provider has specified.

7. Click OK, and then return to Step 5 to recheck your settings.

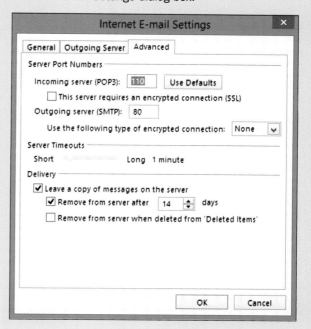

Receiving Email

Once the account is set up, your email client will automatically start using it. Your email address and password are stored, and you will not have to enter them again.

If you are using Outlook, and if you followed the Step by Step exercise in the preceding section to set up the account, the first message you will probably receive is the test message you sent yourself. You may also receive other messages too, and you can send yourself additional test messages for practice.

The navigation pane in an email client typically appears on the left and shows a list of mail folders, with one of them being Inbox. The Inbox folder is where incoming mail appears by default. Nearly all email clients work this same way, with a navigation pane at the left. There are also folders there for Outbox (where outgoing messages wait to be sent), Sent (where copies of the messages you send are stored), and Trash (where deleted messages are stored). There may also be a Junk Email folder, where incoming messages that the email client classifies as junk mail are placed. Figure 14.10 shows these in Outlook 2013. Note that unread messages appear in bold in the list of messages.

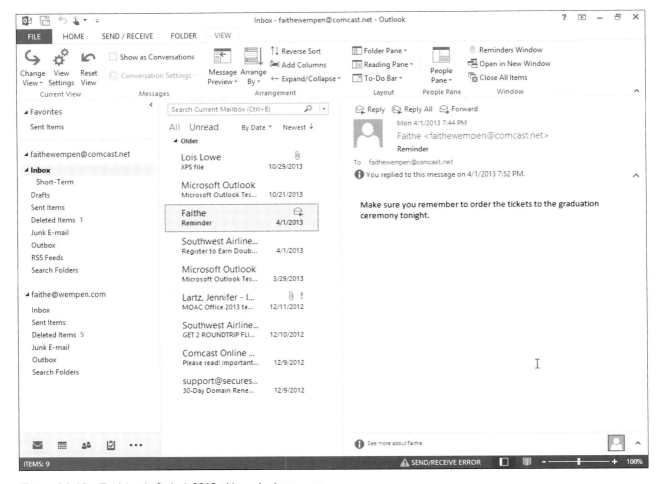

Figure 14.10 The Inbox in Outlook 2013 with received messages.

reading pane A pane in a mail client that pre-views the content of the selected message.

Also in Figure 14.10, notice that Outlook 2013 provides a reading pane, which shows the content of the selected message. When you use a reading pane, you do not have to open a message (by double-clicking it) to read its contents; you can preview that content just by selecting the message in the list. The Reading pane can appear either on the right or at the bottom of the window; you can control its setting on the View tab. Other email clients typically also have a reading pane. A web interface may or may not have one.

Your email client is probably set to send and receive message automatically at certain intervals, such as every 10 minutes. If so, messages will appear in your Inbox throughout the day, as long as your email client is running. You can also manually initiate a send/receive operation. To do so in Outlook 2013, click the Send/Receive All Folders icon on the Quick Access Toolbar (above the File tab).

Sending Email

To send a message in Outlook 2013, click the Home tab and click New Email. Or, in another email client, click the equivalent button, which may have a slightly different name (like New or Compose). A message composition screen appears. Fill in the information as prompted, as shown in Figure 14.11, and then click the Send button.

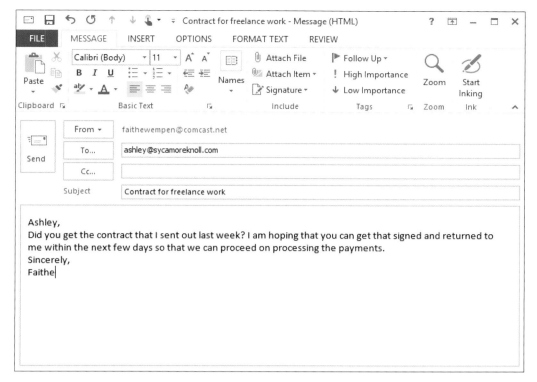

Figure 14.11 An email message being composed in Outlook 2013.

- **From:** This field might or might not appear. If you have multiple email accounts set up in your mail client, you may be prompted to choose which account the message will be sent from.

- **To:** Put the recipients' email addresses here. If there is more than one recipient, separate the names with semicolons. You can also look up recipients from a stored address book in your mail client; in Outlook, addresses are stored in the Contacts list.

- **Cc:** If you want to send an informational copy of the message to someone, put that person's email address in the **Cc** field.

- **Bcc:** This field might or might not appear. A **Bcc** is a blind copy—in other words, a copy that other recipients are not aware is being sent. In Outlook 2013, this field doesn't appear by default, but if you click the To or Cc button, a dialog box appears in which you can select or enter Bcc recipients along with To and Cc recipients.

- **Subject:** This is the title of the message, which will appear in the recipient's Inbox list. The subject should be short but descriptive; avoid general subject likes like "Hi" or "Info."

- **Body:** This is the area where you type the main part of the message.

Working with Attachments

Email you receive may have attachments, which are files that travel along with the text of the email. You can also send attachments with emails you send yourself.

attachment A file that travels along with a text email to a recipient.

When you receive a message with an attachment, a symbol may appear on the message in your Inbox to indicate its presence. In Outlook 2013, the symbol is a paperclip, as shown in Figure 14.12.

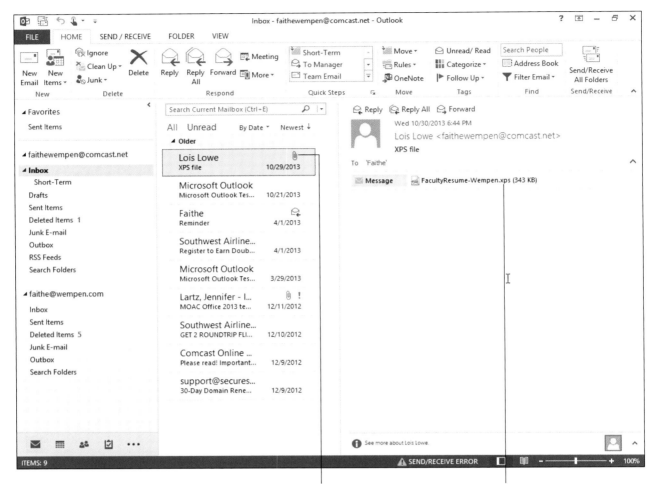

Paperclip icon indicates an attachment   Attachment name appears in preview pane

Figure 14.12 A received email with an attachment.

To open an attachment, double-click it. To save it to your hard drive, right-click it and choose Save As (for one) or Save All Attachments (for all).

To send an attachment yourself, as you are composing the message, look for an Attach button or command. In Outlook 2013, an Attach File button appears on the Ribbon. Click it and then follow the prompts to attach the file(s).

The following Step by Step explains how to compose and send a message in Outlook 2013 that contains an attachment.

Composing and Sending an Email that Contains an Attachment in Outlook 2013

Follow this procedure to use Outlook 2013 to send an email that contains an attachment:

1. Click the Home tab, and click New Email. A new message composition window appears.

2. Enter the recipient(s), the subject, and the message in the fields provided.

3. Click the Attach File button on the Ribbon. The Insert File dialog box opens.

4. Select the file(s) to insert and then click the Insert button.

5. Click Send to send the message.

Working Around Attachment Size Limitations

Email providers have specific (but varying) limits to overall size of emails and their attachments. Larger files (such as video clips) will be rejected and prevent the email containing them from being delivered. If you want to send a large file, try compressing it first. You can do this by right-clicking the file in Windows Explorer and choosing Send To ⇨ Compressed folder. If it still exceeds your email provider's limit, it's better to send a link for your friend to download the item. You can use an FTP service or upload a file to OneDrive, iCloud, or Dropbox (online storage services you can use for free) and send your friend a link to download it. This can also be preferable because large emails take longer to send and use up a large chunk of the recipient's mailbox.

Troubleshooting

Working with Stored Contacts

Outlook 2013 is a full-featured contact management application, and it includes separate sections for email handling, contact management, and calendars. All these sections are connected, though, so you can use them together. The contact management section is called Contacts. To view it, click the People icon in the lower-left corner of the Outlook 2013 screen. Figure 14.13 shows the Outlook 2013 Contacts list with three contacts in it. When you first open the Contacts list, you may not have any contacts there. You can create some if you like by clicking the New Contact button and filling out the form that appears.

Contacts The section in Outlook that stores people's contact information.

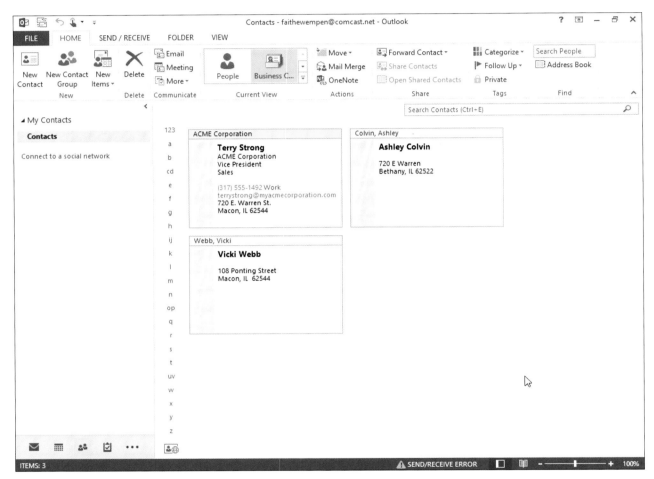

Figure 14.13 The Contacts list in Outlook 2013. You may have many more contacts, and they may be arranged differently. Use the View tab to change how the contacts appear.

When addressing an email message, if you know the person's email address, you can type it directly into the To, Cc, or Bcc field. As you start typing, the email client's autocomplete feature may offer to fill in the address for you. You can also select from your Contacts list, as shown in the following Step by Step.

Addressing an Email Message from the Contacts List in Outlook 2013

Follow this procedure to look up email addresses in the Contacts list as you are composing a new email in Outlook 2013:

1. If you are already in the Mail area of Outlook, click the Home tab, and click New Email. Or, if you are in some other area, such as Contacts or the Calendar, click the Home tab, click New Items, and click E-mail Message. A new message composition window appears.

2. Click the To button. The Select Names: Contacts dialog box opens.

3. Click the name of the person to whom you want to address the email.

4. Click one of the buttons at the bottom of the dialog box to indicate the appropriate field in which to place the person's email address: To, Cc, or Bcc.

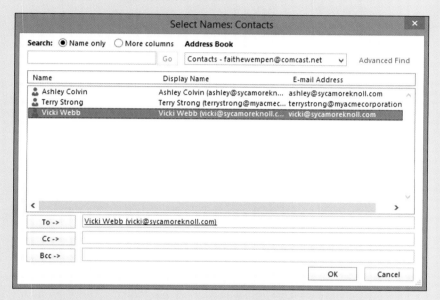

5. Repeat Step 4 to add more recipients if desired.

6. Click OK to return to the message composition window and complete the email as you would normally.

Make sure you don't share others' contact information without permission. If you're sending an email to multiple people, and you don't want them to see each other's addresses, put your own email address in the To field and then put all the recipients' addresses in the Bcc field.

CAUTION

Responding to and Forwarding Emails

When you receive an email, you can choose to reply to it by creating a new message, but it is often easier to use the Reply feature in your email client. When you select a message and then choose Reply, the mail client starts a new message for you that is pre-addressed to the original sender, with the original subject in the Subject line preceded by RE: and the original message quoted in the message body. This saves time because all you have to enter is your reply. Figure 14.14 shows a reply being composed in Outlook 2013. Notice that it appears in the Reading pane area, and not in a separate window. If you want it to appear in a separate window, click Pop Out.

Reply A message that is sent back to the original sender.

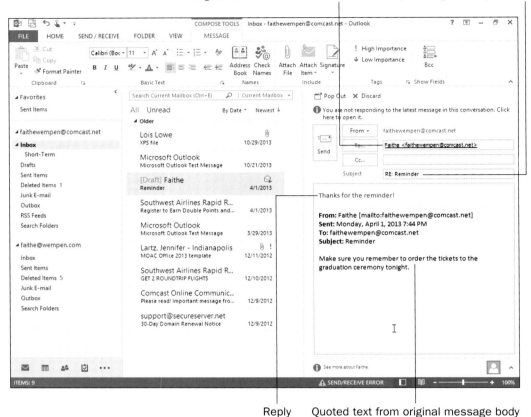

Original sender's email address   RE: plus original subject line

Reply   Quoted text from original message body

Figure 14.14   A reply includes the original subject and message body, and the original sender is set as the recipient.

Reply All A message that is sent back to the original sender plus to any other recipients.

The Reply All feature works just like Reply except it addresses the message not only to the original sender but also to any co-recipients on the original message. (It does not include recipients who got their copies through Bcc.)

Forward A copy of a message sent on to someone other than the original sender.

To send a message you've received from one person to someone else, use the Forward feature. When you forward a message, the original subject appears in the Subject line, preceded by FWD:. The original message body appears in the body area, and if the original message contained any attachments, they are included as attachments in the forwarded email too. Everything is filled in for you except the new recipient. Fill in the new recipient in the To box and send the message.

Out of Office/Automatic Replies

out-of-office message A message that people receive when you are unable to personally answer your email for a certain time.

If you know you won't be responding to emails for a few days, it's polite to set up an out-of-office message. When people send you an email, they'll get an automatic response explaining that you are out of email contact at present but will attend to their messages as soon as you return.

A good out-of-office message should include the dates that you will be gone and an alternative contact person who can be reached in case of an urgent matter.

For example, here is a typical message:

I will be out of the office from March 1 to March 15 and will not be checking messages. If this is an urgent matter, please contact my supervisor, Mary Clark, at 317-555-2811 or mary@sycamoreknoll.com. Otherwise, I will respond to your message when I am back in the office.

Sincerely,
Ashley Colvin

Out-of-office messages are set up on your mail server, not in your email client. That's because when you are out of the office, your email client software won't be running, so you can't count on it to handle the automatic reply.

automatic reply A feature on a mail server that automatically sends a message back to each one received when it is enabled.

In some cases, you may be able to set up automatic replies through your email client. It depends on the incoming mail server. If you are using a Microsoft Exchange mail server (for example, through your company's network at work), you can use the Automatic Replies feature in Outlook 2013. Click File, and click Automatic Replies. If you don't see that command after clicking File, you can't use automatic replies in Outlook.

To set up an automatic reply on your mail server, log into your mail provider's website, or log into your hosting account if the email account you are working with is part of a domain you own. In the provider's configuration pages online, you will find a feature that will enable you to set up an out-of-office message. You may also be able to set up an automatic reply in the web-based interface for your account, as shown in Figure 14.15.

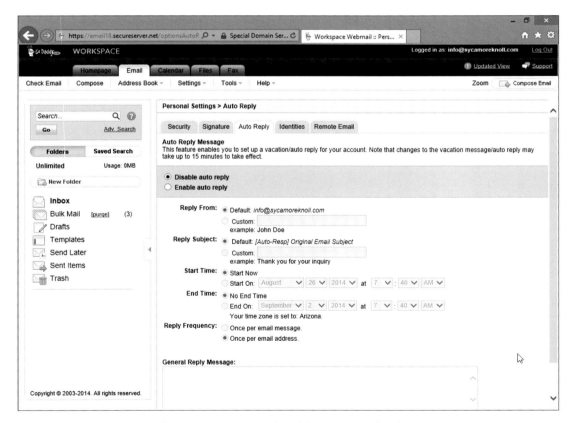

Figure 14.15 It may be possible to set up an automatic reply in the web interface for your email account.

Signatures

signature Text that is automatically appended to outgoing messages.

Rather than typing your name at the end of each email you send, you can append a signature that is added automatically. This can include your Skype name, mobile phone number, Twitter handle, blog address, or other information. You set up a signature in your email client. The following Step by Step section shows how to set one up in Outlook 2013.

CAUTION Be conservative with the information you put in a signature line if you are using the same email account for both business and personal email. You might write a formal email address to a business client, for example, and forget that you have something very informal and silly in your signature.

Step by Step

Creating a Signature in Outlook

To create a signature in Outlook, follow these steps:

1. Select File ⇨ Options ⇨ Mail. Under Compose Messages, choose Signatures. A Signatures and Stationery dialog box appears.

2. Click New, type a name for a new signature, and click OK.

3. Type the text for the signature in the Edit Signature area. Use the formatting tools above the text entry area to format the text as desired.

4. Repeat Steps 2 and 3 as needed to create additional signatures if you want different signatures for different accounts or situations.

5. Open the E-mail Account drop-down list and choose an email account for which you want to set a signature.

6. Open the New Messages drop-down list and choose the signature you want to use for that email for new messages, or choose (none) to turn off signatures.

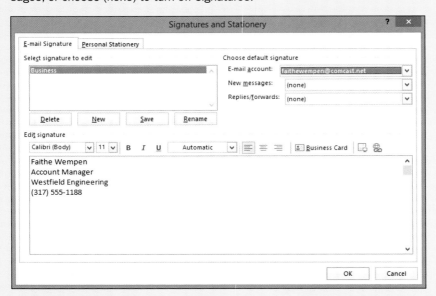

7. (Optional) If you want to use a signature for replies and forwards, open the Replies/Forwards drop-down list and choose the signature you want to use, or choose (none) to turn off signatures.

8. (Optional) Repeat Steps 5–7 to configure additional email accounts if desired.

9. Click OK.

Archiving Emails

Your email client keeps emails indefinitely, so over time the data file for your email client may become very large. The larger the data file, the longer it takes for the application to open, and the longer it takes for some operations, such as searching. A large data file also takes longer to back up.

One solution is to delete the old emails, and it's a good idea to do so if there are emails that you know you will never want to refer to again. However, there's another way to keep your email data file small: You can archive old messages to a separate data file. That way, you can open that archive any time you need to refer to older mail, but your old mail isn't in your mail client taking up space on a daily basis.

archive To move items from the current location to another for backup purposes; a useful way of storing old messages while freeing up space for new ones.

Some email clients have an Archive command that you can use to automatically archive items that meet certain criteria. Other clients require you to create archive files manually and move content into them manually by dragging and dropping content from existing folders to the archive folders. Outlook 2013 has a very good archiving feature, explained in the following Step by Step.

Step by Step

Setting Up AutoArchiving in Outlook

To set the defaults for automatic archiving, follow this procedure:

1. Click File, and click Options.

2. Click Advanced.

3. In the AutoArchive section, click the AutoArchive Settings button.

4. In the AutoArchive dialog box, adjust the default settings as desired. For example, you can choose where to move old items to, and how old an item must be before it is archived.

5. Click OK.

Opening an Archive

To review archived content, follow these steps:

1. Click File, click Account Settings on the Info tab, and click Account Settings.

2. Click the Data Files tab, and click Add.

3. Select the data file containing the archive and click OK.

4. Click Close. Now the archive data file appears in the navigation pane at the left, below your main Outlook data file's folders.

Setting up AutoArchiving for Specific Folders

To set the AutoArchiving options for specific mail folders, follow these steps:

1. Right-click the folder in the navigation pane and choose Properties.

2. Click the AutoArchive tab.

3. Choose Archive the Items in This Folder Using the Default Settings.

   OR

   Choose Archive This Folder Using These Settings, and then adjust the settings as desired.

4. Click OK.

Manually Archive (One-Time Operation)

If you would prefer to retain control over archiving, do it manually, rather than setting up automatic archiving. Follow these steps:

1. Click File, click Cleanup Tools on the Info tab, and click Archive.

2. In the Archive dialog box, select a folder to archive, or to archive all folders, select the parent folder at the top of the list.

3. Choose a date from the Archive Items Older Than pop-up calendar.

4. Confirm the archive file name in the Archive File text box.

5. Click OK.

Managing Junk Mail

spam Unsolicited "junk" mail, typically containing offers (some legitimate, some not) of products or services to buy.

Junk email, also called spam, is sent out by the millions of messages every day on the Internet. By some estimates, it accounts for more than 80 percent of all email sent. Mail filtering software helps cut down on the number of unsolicited ads you receive by analyzing your incoming messages and applying message sorting rules and filtering to them to determine which ones are ads and which ones are legitimate correspondence. Using mail filtering software can save you lots of time because you don't have to go through large amounts of junk mail to find the important messages sent to you.

There are several ways to filter junk mail. Many email applications include a junk mail filter that automatically moves messages it suspects to be spam into a Junk Mail folder. You can periodically look through that folder to see if there is anything you want, and then delete the rest.

Many ISPs also offer junk mail filtering. This type of filtering is typically invisible to the end user; the mail that's filtered out never even reaches your email client software. Because of the danger of missing a legitimate message, this type of filtering is usually very conservative in its targeting of junk mail.

Third-party junk mail filtering programs can work with your email client and can be fine-tuned for the level of filtering you are most comfortable with. Some people prefer to get more junk mail in order to be assured they aren't missing any legitimate messages, whereas other people prefer to enable the most aggressive junk mail filtering settings. Some filtering software can even get better over time by learning from the choices you make.

When you identify a piece of junk mail, you can add its sender to a *blacklist*. Any further mail from that sender will be automatically discarded upon receipt. If you want to make sure that you always receive mail from a certain recipient, regardless of your junk mail settings, you can add that address to a *whitelist*, also called a *safe list*. Whitelisted senders will always have their mail delivered to your inbox.

blacklist A list of prohibited email senders.

whitelist A list of allowed email senders; also called a safe list.

In Outlook 2013, you can control your junk mail options by clicking the Junk button on the Home tab and then choosing Junk E-mail Options from the menu. In the dialog box that appears (see Figure 14.16), you can choose a level of filtering and choose whether junk mail will be deleted or stored in a Junk E-mail folder.

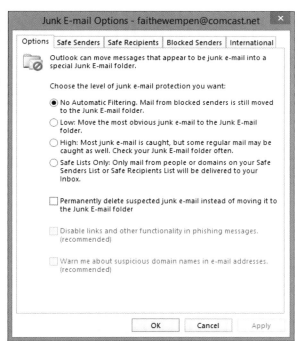

Figure 14.16 Manage junk email settings in Microsoft Outlook 2013.

Quick Review

1. What is the benefit of using a signature?

2. How do you include an attachment in an email?

3. How do you set up an automatic response when you are out of the office?

4. What is archiving, and what is its advantage over deleting messages?

Summary

Internet Communication Types

The Internet has fostered many means of communication, and it is important to choose the correct medium for a situation. **Email** is like postal mail for computers; it is not instantly delivered, using a **store-and-forward** system that employs **mail servers** to move the mail from place to place and a **mail client** to pick up one's mail.

Some email accounts are web-based, also called **HTTP email accounts**. Most people use them via web interfaces. There are also **Post Office Protocol** (**POP**) and **Internet Mail Access Protocol** (**IMAP**) accounts, which are both designed for use with mail clients. POP and IMAP protocols are only for receiving email; they are both paired with the **Simple Mail Transfer Protocol** (**SMTP**) for sending mail.

Instant messaging (IM) consists of instant text messages sent over the Internet. When instant messages are sent over phone systems, it is called **texting** or **Short Message Service (SMS)**. IM is a **push technology**, whereas email is a **pull technology**.

Chat rooms are like group instant messaging. You signal your willingness to participate by entering a chat room, such as a **channel** in an **Internet Relay Chat (IRC) server**.

Social networking is an umbrella term for sites such as Facebook, Twitter, LinkedIn, and Google+. Users can post their own text and pictures and express their opinions. **Tags** (hashtags) are used to identify topics. Some common social networks are **Instagram**, **Vine**, **Reddit**, **YouTube**, **Facebook**, and **Twitter**.

A **blog** is a web page where an individual or group publishes **posts,** which may contain news, opinions, photos, and essays. Blogs can be either personal or commercial. A **blog platform** is a service that enables people to create their own blogs and hosts the blogs on its server. **Microblogging** allows users to post brief text commentary, photos, and audio clips. Twitter is the best-known microblogging site.

A **wiki** is a collaboratively managed database of information. Wikipedia is the largest and most popular wiki. **Newsgroups** are no longer very popular, but used to be extremely so; they are public message forums exchanged through a service called **Usenet**. To read in newsgroups, you use **newsreader** software. A **forum** is a web-based public discussion area.

Voice over IP (VoIP) is a technology for making voice calls over the Internet. These calls can also include video, through services such as **Skype** and **FaceTime**, or an IM client that includes video chat capabilities. **Videoconferencing** is a multi-user version of video chat.

Communicating Appropriately

Because there are so many means of online communication, the appropriate tone and language need to be chosen for each. More formality is typically expected in business communication than in social networking. Poorly written communications send out the wrong message and can be misinterpreted, leading to conflict. Face-to-face communications and phone calls are preferable to online exchanges in some circumstances because non-verbal communications methods, including gestures and tone of voice, can be used to ensure the message is correctly conveyed.

Using and Managing Email

Email is sent and received through an email client or a web interface. Microsoft Outlook is one of the most popular email clients. When you set up a new email account, make sure you choose a **strong password**, which is a password that is not easy for someone to guess.

To get started with an email client, you set up your account(s) in that program. Your messages then appear in the Inbox, and you can compose your own messages from that program's interface. The Inbox may include a **reading pane**, which shows the content of the selected message.

When composing email, you must enter a recipient, a subject, and a message body. You may optionally include an attachment. When addressing email, the To box is for the main recipients, **Cc** is for those who will receive a copy, and **Bcc** is for those who will receive an undisclosed copy. You may optionally select recipients from the **Contacts** list in Outlook (or equivalent in your email application).

Most email clients enable you to save email addresses of people with whom you correspond and use them when addressing messages. In Outlook, this is the Contacts list.

You can reply to a received message by clicking the **Reply** button; other options include **Reply All** and **Forward**.

An **out-of-office message** sends an **automatic reply** to anyone who emails you while you are away. You can set this up in Outlook only if you use an Exchange server. Otherwise, you must set it up with your mail provider. You may be able to configure it from the web-based interface that the provider supplies for your email account.

A **signature** is text that is automatically appended to outgoing emails. You can set this up in your mail client.

To avoid having your mail file get too big, you can periodically **archive** messages, which means to transfer messages to an auxiliary storage folder based on criteria you specify.

Unsolicited junk mail, also known as **spam**, can be minimized using mail filtering software, which may include both **blacklists** and **whitelists**.

Key Terms

archive
attachment
automatic reply
Bcc
blacklist
blog
blog platform
Cc
channel
chat room
Contacts
email
Facebook
FaceTime
forum
forum thread
Forward
HTTP email account
IMAP account
Instagram
instant messaging (IM)
Internet Mail Access Protocol (IMAP)

Internet Relay Chat (IRC)
mail client
mail server
microblog
newsgroup
newsreader
out-of-office message
POP account
post
Post Office Protocol (POP)
pull technology
push technology
reading pane
Reddit
Reply
Reply All
search engine optimization (SEO)
Short Message Service (SMS)
signature
Simple Mail Transfer Protocol (SMTP)
Skype
social network

spam

store-and-forward

strong password

tag (also hashtag) (social media)

texting

Twitter

Usenet

videoconferencing

Vine

Voice over Internet Protocol (VoIP)

whitelist

wiki

YouTube

Test Yourself

Fact Check

1. Which of the following systems limits the size of any message you post?

   a. social networks

   b. blogs

   c. microblogs

   d. forums

2. What would be the most appropriate communication to use when submitting your resume?

   a. Post to a forum.

   b. Post onto your blog.

   c. Add it to your Facebook profile.

   d. Attach it to an email.

3. The _____ system is used by newsgroups.

   a. Facebook

   b. Usenet

   c. FTP

   d. Twitter

4. Which would be an appropriate use of a forum?

   a. Check to see if there are known problems with a device.

   b. Request a refund for a purchase.

   c. Transfer a file.

   d. Communicate privately with a teacher.

5. Which of the following is a collaborative online information database?

   a. VoIP

   b. wiki

   c. IMP

   d. forum

6. You want to send a copy of an email to someone without the main recipient being aware you have sent that other copy. Which address field do you use when composing the mail in Outlook?

   a. Acc:

   b. Bcc:

   c. Cc:

   d. Dcc:

7. Which of the following communication systems is the best channel for you to publish your thoughts and feelings onto a website for all to see?

   a. forum

   b. blog

   c. Skype

   d. newsgroup

8. Which of these is a push technology?

   a. texting

   b. forums

   c. wikis

   d. email

9. Out-of-office messages can be set up in Outlook only if:

   a. you have Signatures enabled.

   b. you are using an Exchange server.

   c. you have a POP account.

   d. you have an IMAP account.

10. Where are archived messages sent?

    a. online storage area

    b. desktop

    c. Recycle Bin

    d. specified archive file

Matching

Match the term to its description.

   a. microblog

   b. post

   c. forum

   d. videoconferencing

   e. FaceTime

   f. tags

1. _____An app installed on Apple iPhone and iPad devices that is used to make video calls between Apple device owners.

2. _____A web-based discussion and advice-sharing site.

3. _____A means of conducting a video conversation remotely using an Internet connection and the webcam or camera on your laptop, phone, or tablet.

4. _____An article published on a blog.

5. _____Labels that can be added to posted content on social networks to allow people to find content of interest to them.

6. _____A service that allows the posting of short messages.

Sum It Up

1. Name four online communication options available for talking with a friend who lives in another city.

2. Give two examples of situations where email should be used to communicate rather than texting or instant messaging.

3. Name two video chat clients.

4. Explain the purpose of an email signature.

5. What are the advantages of archiving your email?

Explore More

Following the Trail in Outlook

Try looking at the email headers in Outlook to get an idea of what happens to an email in transit.

1. Open Outlook and highlight an email in your Inbox.

2. Double-click the mail to open it in a new window.

3. Click the File tab, and under Info, select Properties at the bottom. The Properties box for the mail opens and at the bottom is a box titled Internet Headers. In that box, you can see the history of the mail.

4. From the information in the Properties box, can you work out how many mail servers the email went through and how long it took to arrive?

Think It Over

The Impact of Social Networking

Social networking has become a major player in Internet communication and is now moving into the workplace. Look at your environment, school, college, or workplace and consider the impact of allowing social networking on the internal network. Ask yourself the following questions:

- Would being able to use social networking during working hours affect productivity?

- Can social networking replace existing communications in the workplace?

- Are there disadvantages to using social networking in the workplace?

Discuss these questions with your colleagues and compare their views with yours.

Chapter 15

Web Basics

Learning objectives

☐ Identify the components that make up the web

☐ Use the basic functions of a web browser

☐ Search the Internet

☐ Understand the need for security and recognize secure connections

In the span of a single generation, the Internet and World Wide Web have revolutionized our lives. Using these technologies, we can connect with others—whether they are next door or halfway around the globe—more easily than ever before. The Internet also makes it possible to engage in electronic commerce, and to expand our knowledge of topics far and wide.

But how does this technology work? What components and technologies are necessary to facilitate this communication? How does one find the information one needs online? These topics are the focus of this chapter.

How the Web Works

Internet A global packet-switched network created cooperatively by multiple companies, governments, and standards organizations.

World Wide Web (WWW) A network of interconnected pages of information stored on publicly accessible servers.

The Internet is a global network of millions of computers that can communicate with each other. Provided that two computers are connected to the Internet, they can share information between them. The World Wide Web (WWW), often referred to as "the web," is part of the Internet; it is a network of interconnected pages of information stored on publicly accessible servers using a consistent page layout and formatting language.

Web Browsing Components

Web browsing involves these three components:

- **Web servers:** Store and provide access to websites.
- **Web browsers:** Request and display information to individuals.
- **Web pages:** The individual documents that web servers store and web browsers request.

Web Servers

When someone connects to the Internet, he typically uses a personal computer or mobile device such as a tablet or smart phone. The information accessed by that person, however, is stored on a different type of computer, called a web server. As you learned in Chapter 13, "Networking and Internet Basics," a server is a powerful computer that exists in order to provide data or services to other computers. A web server is a server on which web pages are stored and made available to the public.

web server A server that receives requests for web page data and supplies it by sending it over the Internet.

Careers in IT

Web Designer

A web designer creates websites for businesses, schools, organizations, and individuals. Web designers not only have a strong background in programming tools like HTML, Java, and ASP, but also an eye for what makes a page not only functional but attractive and easy to use. If you are interested in being a web designer, you will want to study computer technology, programming, user interface design, and computer graphics.

Web Browsers

web browser An application used to access websites and to retrieve or upload information. Often referred to as a **browser**.

platform-independent An interaction between two computers in which the type of hardware and the operating system that each one uses is irrelevant.

A web browser, often referred to simply as a browser, is an application used to access websites and to retrieve or upload information. The browser runs on an individual user's computer and provides a communication interface to web servers.

NOTE The relationship between a web browser and a web server is platform-independent, meaning that the hardware and operating systems that each of them are using are irrelevant. They communicate using standardized languages such as HTML, so Windows, Mac, and Linux computers running a web browser can all communicate equally well with a web server running UNIX, Linux, or Windows Server.

The most popular ones include Internet Explorer, Firefox, Chrome, and Safari. All these browsers work in a similar fashion. Typically, if you know how to use one, you'll be able to find your way around any of the others.

Internet Explorer comes preinstalled on computers that run the Windows operating system. To use a different browser, simply download it from the manufacturer's website and install it. Note that certain web applications prefer certain browsers, so you may want more than one. You can have multiple browsers installed in Windows, and even have more than one open at a time. You'll learn more about using a browser later in this chapter.

Web Pages

A web page is a file that is formatted for use on the World Wide Web. The content of a web page is displayed in a browser. Web pages can contain a variety of content, including text, graphics, audio, and video.

web page A file formatted for use on the World Wide Web.

Most Web pages are written in HyperText Markup Language (HTML), which defines the layout of a web page by using a variety of tags and attributes. Figure 15.1 shows some sample HTML code. When a web page is downloaded into a browser, the browser uses the instructions in the markup language to display the page as the page author intended. The codes in angle brackets, such as <title> in Figure 15.1, are tags. A tag tells the web browser how to treat the text that follows. Most tags are two-sided, meaning that whatever is between them will be formatted a certain way. For example, in <title>Wiley: Home</title>, the text Wiley: Home will be treated as the page title because it is surrounded by an opening tag <title> and a closing tag </title>.

Hypertext Markup Language (HTML) A language for encoding data and graphics for display in a web browser.

tag A bracketed code in HTML that tells a browser how to handle the text that follows it.

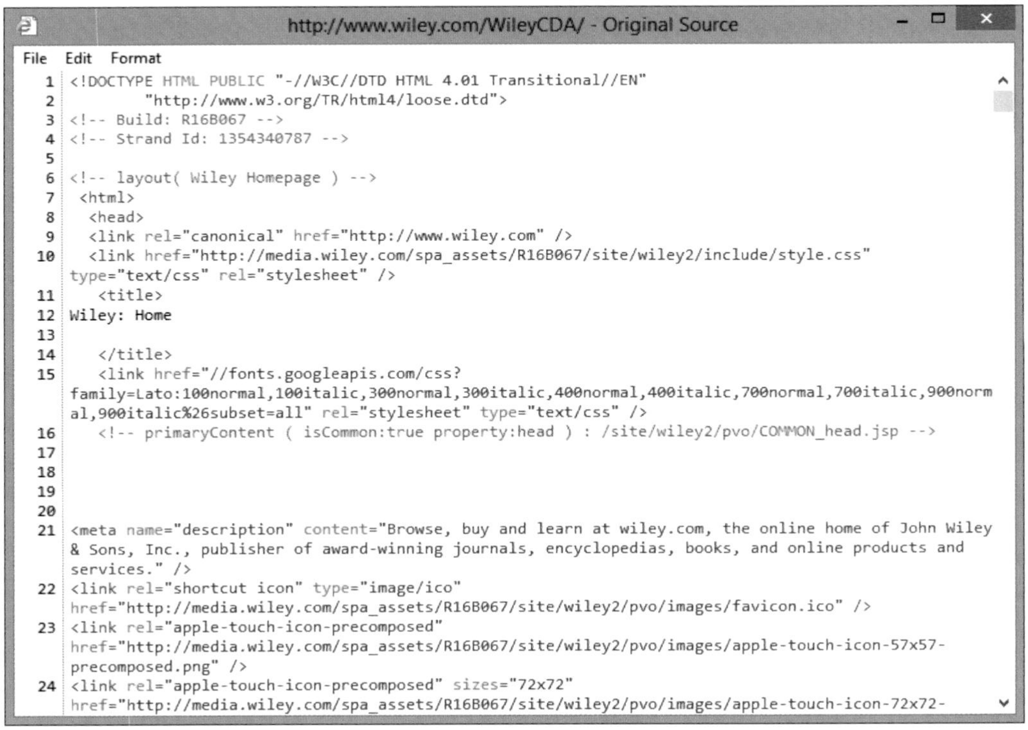

```
                    http://www.wiley.com/WileyCDA/ - Original Source          _  □  ×
File  Edit  Format
  1  <!DOCTYPE HTML PUBLIC "-//W3C//DTD HTML 4.01 Transitional//EN"
  2          "http://www.w3.org/TR/html4/loose.dtd">
  3  <!-- Build: R16B067 -->
  4  <!-- Strand Id: 1354340787 -->
  5
  6  <!-- layout( Wiley Homepage ) -->
  7   <html>
  8    <head>
  9    <link rel="canonical" href="http://www.wiley.com" />
 10    <link href="http://media.wiley.com/spa_assets/R16B067/site/wiley2/include/style.css"
      type="text/css" rel="stylesheet" />
 11      <title>
 12  Wiley: Home
 13
 14      </title>
 15      <link href="//fonts.googleapis.com/css?
      family=Lato:100normal,100italic,300normal,300italic,400normal,400italic,700normal,700italic,900norm
      al,900italic%26subset=all" rel="stylesheet" type="text/css" />
 16      <!-- primaryContent ( isCommon:true property:head ) : /site/wiley2/pvo/COMMON_head.jsp -->
 17
 18
 19
 20
 21  <meta name="description" content="Browse, buy and learn at wiley.com, the online home of John Wiley
      & Sons, Inc., publisher of award-winning journals, encyclopedias, books, and online products and
      services." />
 22  <link rel="shortcut icon" type="image/ico"
      href="http://media.wiley.com/spa_assets/R16B067/site/wiley2/pvo/images/favicon.ico" />
 23  <link rel="apple-touch-icon-precomposed"
      href="http://media.wiley.com/spa_assets/R16B067/site/wiley2/pvo/images/apple-touch-icon-57x57-
      precomposed.png" />
 24  <link rel="apple-touch-icon-precomposed" sizes="72x72"
      href="http://media.wiley.com/spa_assets/R16B067/site/wiley2/pvo/images/apple-touch-icon-72x72-
```

Figure 15.1 Sample HTML code.

Most web pages contain hyperlinks. A hyperlink, sometimes simply called a "link," is a clickable link to another page (or another spot on the same page). The hyperlink is the main mechanism for navigating through a website. Each page on a website might have any number of links to content stored elsewhere on the site or even on another site altogether. When the mouse cursor changes from an arrow symbol to a hand, that indicates the presence of a hyperlink.

Some web pages are static. That is, its content does not change until its owner updates it manually. Other web pages are dynamic, providing frequently updating information, such as a current stock price or weather report. The site news.google.com, shown in Figure 15.2, provides news headlines that automatically update. If you open this page and keep it open, you will notice that the page reloads itself with updated headlines every few minutes.

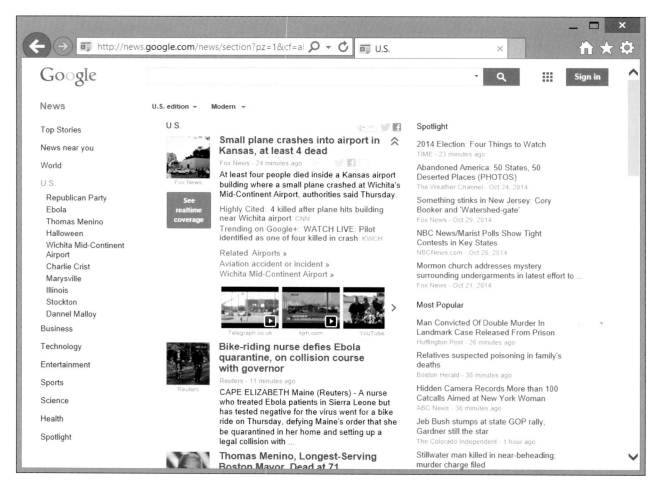

Figure 15.2 The Google News page updates headlines automatically.

Understanding URLs and IP Addresses

You know what the main components of the Internet are. But how do users actually access the web pages they need online? This happens in large part due to the use of URLs and IP addresses.

A uniform resource locator (URL), sometimes called a web address or a uniform resource identifier (URI), is the set of characters you enter into your web browser's address bar to navigate to a specific web page. An example of a URL is **http://www.microsoft.com**. If you type this URL in your browser's address bar, your browser will display the home page of Microsoft's website.

What makes up a URL? The full string of a URL is composed of three components:

■ **The protocol:** A protocol is a set of rules that govern the transmission of data between two devices. On the Internet, the HyperText Transfer Protocol (HTTP) is commonly used for this purpose— hence the presence of **http://** in most URLs. Another example of a protocol used on the Internet is the Internet Protocol (IP).

■ **The destination server (domain name):** This is indicated by a domain name, such as **bbc.co.uk** (you'll learn more about domain names in a moment). In most cases, this domain name is preceded with the letters **www** followed by a period.

uniform resource locator (URL) A string of characters that identifies the location of a resource on a website.

HyperText Transfer Protocol (HTTP) The protocol used to send and receive web pages on the Internet.

The letters preceding the domain name (such as www) represent the subdomain; they indicates the server (or area of the server) the data is on within the company or organization that owns the domain name. For a company with only one web server, it is customary to use www as the subdomain for a web server. However, companies with multiple servers may point to them by using different letters before the domain. For example, Google uses news.google.com, maps.google.com, images.google.com, and so on.

NOTE

■ **The path:** This is the exact location of the file you are requesting on the server. For example, the document might be stored in a folder on the web server called **news**. A path might also include a specific filename, such as **news/story24871.htm**. If no filename is included in the path, a default page from the specified folder location loads.

A full URL would be **http://www.bbc.co.uk/news/story24871.htm**. Figure 15.3 identifies each portion of the URL.

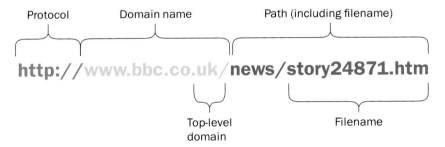

Figure 15.3   The URL explained.

Notice the use of the forward slash as a separator. This is in contrast to the backslash used in Windows to describe a file path.

NOTE

A domain name is a name that identifies an entity on the Internet. It's a key part of a URL. A company or individual can register for a domain name. That name can then act as an identifier for that company or person.

In its basic form, a domain name consists of an identifier followed by an extension, like **microsoft.com**. The extension, also called the top-level domain, is often used to identify the type of organization that the name represents. For example, the **.com** extension represents a commercial organization, whereas the **.edu** extension is reserved for educational institutions, like **harvard.edu**.

Table 15.1 shows a list of the more common top-level domains. (Note that the list of available top-level domains is growing. For example, if you own a restaurant, your domain name could include the .food extension. Or if you are a doctor, your domain name could include the extension .doctor. For a list of available top-level domains, visit http://data.iana.org/TLD/tlds-alpha-by-domain.txt.)

Table 15.1: Top Level Domains

Name	Identity	Description
.com	Commercial	Commercial businesses
.mil	Military	Reserved for the U.S. military
.gov	Government	Government organizations
.edu	Educational	Educational institutions, colleges, schools, and so forth
.org	Organization	Nonprofit organizations
.net	Network	Usually used by Internet or technology companies

Some domain names also include a two-letter country code—for example, **.uk** for the United Kingdom, **.ca** for Canada, and **.sa** for Saudi Arabia. Domain names can also include sub-domains—for example, **training.microsoft.com** or **marketing.microsoft.com**.

TIP   Companies that are global in nature should register their domains in multiple countries. For example, if you type **www.microsoft.se**, you receive Microsoft's home page in Swedish.

Registering a Domain Name

For any company wanting to do business on the Internet or just have an online presence, choosing the right domain name is critical. Ideally, the domain name will match the company name as closely as possible. An exact match may not be possible, however, because the name may already be taken. If your company needs a specific name that is already taken, you may be able to buy the rights to that name from the current owner, or you may be able to register the name with a different top-level domain. For example, instead of a .com address, you might be able to get the .net or .biz version.

Anyone can register a domain name, as long as it doesn't belong to an existing company or organization. You can register a domain name with a domain registrar company such as GoDaddy.com or 1&1.com. The exact cost varies with the registrar, but is generally between $10 and $30 USD a year.

The name registration must be renewed on a yearly basis, but you can pay for multiple years at a time. When the owner of a domain name fails to renew it, it becomes available for someone else to claim and register.

Put It to Work

Every computer that connects directly to the Internet has its own unique numeric address, called its IP address. IP stands for Internet Protocol, one of the protocols in the TCP/IP suite of protocols. A protocol is an agreed-upon rule or standard; the Internet is based on TCP/IP rules. Most networks today, including the Internet itself, use IP addressing to identify computers. If you connect to the Internet through an Internet Service Provider (ISP), your ISP assigns you an IP address automatically. Depending on the ISP, that address may be a static IP address (that is, permanently assigned to your modem) or a dynamic IP address (that is, temporarily assigned to your modem as long as it is connected to the ISP).

IP address A numeric address by which a particular computer is known on a network.

static IP address An IP address that is permanently assigned to a device.

dynamic IP address An IP address that is temporarily assigned to a device.

Network Address Translation

Suppose your family has a single account with your ISP, but you have several computers that all need to share it. Your ISP assigns your modem (probably cable or DSL) a single IP address. Then you connect a router to the modem in your home. The router assigns its own private IP addresses to each computer, for them to use to communicate with one another, and it sets up the Internet connection as a gateway. When requests that should go out to the Internet reach the gateway, the router uses network address translation (NAT) to change the IP address on the outgoing message so that it appears to be coming from the IP address assigned to the modem. Then when the reply comes back from the Internet, the router changes the IP address back again to the address of the local PC. This is how many computers can share a single Internet IP address.

Put It to Work

There are two types of IP addresses currently in use. Their functionality is similar, but the addresses look completely different.

- **IPv4 address:** An IPv4 address is a binary number made up of 32 bits (binary digits). It is represented in dotted decimal notation. That is, the 32 bits are split into four groups of 8 bits, and each block of 8 bits is converted to a decimal number and separated by dots, like so: **131.107.23.100.** There are more than 4 billion possible IPv4 address combinations. Although this number was deemed adequate when the Internet first appeared in 1969, it is no longer sufficient—hence the development of a new addressing scheme, discussed next.

IPv4 address An addressing system made up of 32 binary digits, represented as four decimal numbers separated by dots like this: 131.107.23.100.

- **IPv6 address:** An IPv6 address is a much larger number. Made up of 128 binary bits, it has a maximum address space of 340,282,366,920,938,463,374,607,431,768,211,456 addresses— somewhat larger than the 4 billion with IPv4. Hopefully, with this scheme, we won't run out of addresses again. The size of an IPv6 address makes it impractical to write it in the dotted decimal format. Instead, IPv6 addresses are displayed in eight groups of four hexadecimal numbers separated by colons (:), like so: **2001:0:0:635:7b62:12ab:34c2:1038.** (A hexadecimal number is one that has 16 as its base rather than 10.)

IPv6 address An addressing system made up of 128 binary bits, represented as eight groups of hexadecimal numbers.

Identifying Your Computer's IP Address

To discover your computer's IP address, follow these steps:

1. From the desktop, right-click the Start button and click Command Prompt. A command prompt window opens.

2. At the command prompt, type **ipconfig** and press Enter.

```
                                    Command Prompt                    –  □  ✕
Microsoft Windows [Version 6.3.9600]
(c) 2013 Microsoft Corporation. All rights reserved.

C:\Users\Faithe>ipconfig_
```

3. Look for the line that includes "Local Area Connection." or "Wireless" or "Wi-Fi." You should see the two addresses allocated to your computer—IPv6 first, followed by IPv4.

```
                                    Command Prompt                    –  □  ✕
Wireless LAN adapter Wi-Fi:

    Connection-specific DNS Suffix  . : Belkin
    Link-local IPv6 Address . . . . . : fe80::8cc8:ff62:64aa:f341%3
    IPv4 Address. . . . . . . . . . . : 192.168.2.6
    Subnet Mask . . . . . . . . . . . : 255.255.255.0
    Default Gateway . . . . . . . . . : 192.168.2.1
```

Running the **ipconfig** command displays your computer's IP address, which is the private address assigned to it by your router. If you want to see your computer's public address—that is, the one it uses on the Internet—visit http://whatismyipaddress.com. The main page will display your computer's public IP address. There is also a map that shows the geographical location of your Internet service provider.

How Domain Names and IP Addresses Are Related

Suppose you want to visit a website on the Internet. That website—like all websites—is accessible via its IP address. For example, suppose you want to visit Microsoft's website. To do so, you could type its IP address—if you happened to know it. You probably don't know it, though. Instead, you may know Microsoft's site as www.microsoft.com, its domain name.

If you enter an IP address in your web browser, the browser goes directly to that site. If you enter a domain name, though, it goes to a Domain Name System (DNS) server on the Internet, which is a directory lookup that converts domain names into their corresponding IP addresses. Looking up a name and finding the IP address is known as name resolution, or resolving the address. Your browser does this for you automatically.

The Internet contains thousands of interconnected DNS servers which collectively hold the entire Internet address directory. (Each server holds only a subset.) When you type a URL into your browser, your browser contacts a DNS server and finds out what the IP address is. It then uses the IP address to open up that page for you.

Domain Name System (DNS) The naming system employed to enable users to access websites using their domain names or URLs rather than their IP addresses.

name resolution The process of translating domain names to numerical IP addresses. A DNS server is used to resolve a name to an address.

DNS server A server on the Internet that provides DNS services, translating between domain names and IP addresses.

Quick Review

1. What are the three main components of the Internet?

2. What are the three main components of a URL?

3. What are the two types of IP addresses?

4. What type of server is used to resolve (convert) domain names or URLs to IP addresses?

Accessing the Web with a Browser

As mentioned, you use a web browser to access content on the Internet. In this section, you'll learn how to start your browser, access websites, navigate those sites, bookmark your favorite sites, and more.

> **NOTE**
>
> This section assumes you're using the Internet Explorer browser, which is included with the Windows operating system. Browsers are constantly being updated. The version shown in this book, which comes with Windows 8.1, is Internet Explorer 11. If you have Windows Updates enabled (refer to Chapter 16, "Network and Internet Privacy and Security"), your system likely has the latest version.

Starting Your Browser

There are two versions of Internet Explorer installed in Windows 8.1—a traditional desktop version and a touch-optimized app. In this chapter the examples assume that you are using the desktop version, which is more full-featured.

To start the desktop version of Internet Explorer, click the Internet Explorer shortcut that is pinned to the taskbar on the desktop, as in Figure 15.4.

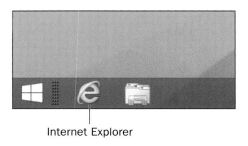

Internet Explorer

Figure 15.4   Use the Internet Explorer shortcut on the taskbar to start the browser.

NOTE

The Internet Explorer shortcut that is pinned to the Start screen by default points to the app version, not the desktop version, so you must access IE from the taskbar in order to get the desktop version. However, if you set that IE tile on the Start screen to be pinned to the taskbar (for example, if it has become unpinned and you need to repin it), the result is a shortcut that opens the desktop version of IE.

Why does that work? Because there is only one application for Internet Explorer; it opens in either the desktop or the app version depending on the context. When accessed from the Start screen, it opens the app version; when accessed from the taskbar, it opens the desktop version.

You can also start Internet Explorer (or your default browser, if not IE) by clicking a web hyperlink in an email address or document. In some programs, such as Microsoft Word, you have to hold down the Ctrl key as you click on a hyperlink to open it in a browser.

home page The page that is displayed when you launch your web browser.

When Internet Explorer opens, it takes you to your home page. Your home page is the page that is presented every time you open the browser. By default, the browser's home page is **msn.com.** You can set your home page to the site of your choice, however. If you use a particular site all the time, you can set that site as your home page. This makes browsing more efficient.

Step by Step

Changing Your Internet Explorer Home Page

To change your Internet Explorer home page, follow these steps:

1. Open Internet Explorer using one of the methods listed previously.

2. Type the address of the website you want to set as your home page into the address bar and allow it to load.

3. Click the Tools button (the one that looks like a gear wheel in the upper-right corner of the browser screen). A menu appears.

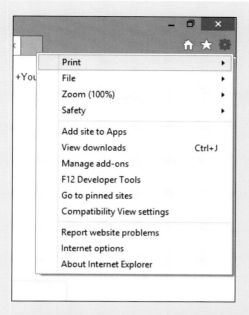

4. Select Internet Options. The Internet Options dialog box opens, with the General tab displayed.

5. In the Home Page section of the General tab, click the Use Current button. The box above it should now contain the URL of the current site.

6. Click the Apply button. The next time you launch the browser, the home page you selected will be displayed.

Accessing a Website

After you launch your web browser, you simply type a URL in the address field to visit the site associated with that URL. DNS will resolve the URL to an IP address, and you will be presented with the page you specified. You can then click on hyperlinks on that page to see additional pages and information, or to visit other sites.

Identifying Secure Sites

When you browse a website that uses the HTTP protocol, everything is transmitted and received in clear text. That means someone using a packet sniffer (discussed in Chapter 16, "Network and Internet Privacy and Security") could easily intercept the information. This is okay for normal browsing, but not when carrying out financial transactions that involve entering credit card information or other personal details.

To prevent criminals from acquiring your information, a secure encrypted connection is required when you are sending sensitive data. HyperText Transfer Protocol Secure (HTTPS) provides an encrypted connection between the web browser and the web server. With HTTPS, the two endpoints exchange an encryption key, enabling the encryption of all future communication between them. When a connection uses HTTPS, the URL starts with **https://** rather than **http://**, as shown. In addition, a padlock appears in the browser's address bar, and in some browsers the address bar may appear with a green background. A secure connection happens automatically when you log into a secure site; you do not have to do anything special to initiate it.

All sites that use HTTPS have a digital certificate that validates them as being trustworthy. This certificate is issued by a third-party certificate authority, such as Verisign. Certificates must be renewed on an annual basis, and can be revoked if questions about the company that holds it arise. To view certificate details for a site that uses HTTPS, click the padlock symbol displayed in the browser's address bar and choose View Certificates from the menu that appears.

Going Back, Going Forward, and Refreshing

Suppose that while visiting a website, you've clicked several hyperlinks to view many different web pages. Or maybe you've viewed additional websites during the same browser session. Either way, it may be that you want to revisit a page that you viewed previously. To do so, simply click the Back button in the upper-left corner of the browser window. (It's the button with a left-pointing arrow on it.) This returns you to the page you viewed last. Click the button multiple times to cycle back to additional viewed pages.

When you click the Back button, the Forward button becomes active (that is, it turns blue). The Forward button is next to the Back button and features a right-pointing arrow. If, after clicking the Back button, you want to return to the original page, you can click the Forward button.

You can also refresh a web page. You might do so to make sure you are viewing the most current version of the page. (Sometimes, if you've visited a web page before, your browser saves it and reloads it the next time you visit. This helps to speed downloads but may result in an outdated page being displayed.) To do so, click the Refresh button. It's the clockwise circular arrow at the right end of the address bar. Figure 15.5 shows the Back, Forward, and Refresh buttons.

Back   Forward   Refresh

Figure 15.5   The Back, Forward, and Refresh buttons.

Engaging in e-Commerce

One of the most important and culture-changing uses for the Web is as a means of conducting online financial business, also known as e-commerce. E-commerce can be business-to-business (B2B), business-to-consumer (B2C), or consumer-to-consumer (C2C). E-commerce can include a business ordering supplies or materials from another business, a consumer buying a book from an online bookstore, and a friend sending money to a friend.

From the consumer perspective, e-commerce is a win-win. Thanks to e-commerce, consumers have many more choices. Because e-commerce is global, people can buy from retailers all around the globe 24 hours a day, without leaving the comfort of their homes.

E-commerce makes economic sense for retailers as well. With e-commerce, there's no need to maintain a brick-and-mortar storefront. Online retailers can work from one or more large warehouses, selling and shipping a wide range of items.

With e-commerce, you aren't limited to purchasing goods online. E-commerce covers all aspects of business and life. For example, many governments now offer services online, enabling citizens to pay their taxes, sign up for government services, and license their vehicles online.

When engaging in e-commerce, be sure you buy from secure sites. You'll learn more about how to tell whether a site is secure in Chapter 16.

Put It to Work

Working with Tabs

tab A web browser feature that enables users to have multiple pages open at once within the same browser window.

A tab enables you to have multiple web pages open at once within the same browser window. When you launch Internet Explorer, it displays your home page on a tab. To open another tab—leaving the page on the first tab accessible—click the New Tab button (the gray box to the right of the existing tab). A second tab opens, again with your home page displayed. You can then type a URL in the address bar to visit a different page as normal.

Perhaps even more useful, Internet Explorer enables you to open pages via a hyperlink on a separate tab. To do so, right-click the hyperlink and choose Open in New Tab from the menu that appears. Internet Explorer opens a second tab and displays the linked page on it. Figure 15.6 shows a browser window with multiple tabs open.

Figure 15.6 Multiple tabs open, with the New Tab button highlighted.

Adding Favorites (Bookmarks)

favorite A website or page that you visit frequently, and to which you want easy access.

If you frequently visit a website, you might want to store it in your browser so you don't have to type its URL every time you visit it. To do so, you can save it as a Favorite (also called a Bookmark). A favorite is a website or page that you visit frequently, and to which you want easy access.

Step by Step

Adding a Website to Your Favorites List

To add a website to your Favorites list, follow these steps:

1. Click the View Favorites, Feeds, and History button in the upper-right corner of the browser screen. (It's the one that looks like a star.) The Favorites Center pane opens. It has three tabs: Favorites, Feeds, and History. The Favorites Center pane also contains an Add to Favorites button.

2. Click the Add to Favorites button. The Add a Favorite dialog box opens.

3. Click the Add button to add the website to the Favorites tab.

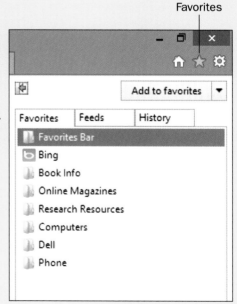

Accessing Your Favorites

To access a website on your Favorites list, follow these steps:

1. Click the View Favorites, Feeds, and History button to open the Favorites Center pane.

2. If necessary, click the Favorites tab to view your Favorites list.

3. Click the link for the site you want to visit. Internet Explorer opens the site.

Organizing Your Favorites in Folders

If you collect a lot of favorites, you might like to organize them in the Favorites Center pane to make them easier to find. One approach is to place them into folders. For example, you could place all your news-related favorites in one folder, all your cooking-related favorites in another folder, and so on.

To create a folder for your favorites, follow these steps:

1. With a site you want to add to your new folder open, click the View Favorites, Feeds, and History button to open the Favorites Center pane.

2. Click the Add to Favorites button. The Add a Favorite dialog box opens.

3. Click the New Folder button. The Create a Folder dialog box opens.

4. Type the name of your new folder and specify the folder's location. (You can nest folders—create them inside one another—if required.) Then click the Create button.

5. Click Add. The folder is created and includes a link to the website you have open.

Another option is to add frequently visited websites to the Favorites bar. If enabled, the Favorites bar appears along the top of your browser window, just below the address bar. To enable it, right-click the title bar and choose Favorites Bar.

You can click a site in the Favorites bar to access it. Every new site you add to the Favorites bar will appear on the far-left end. When the bar is full, two small chevrons will appear on the right side of the bar, as shown in Figure 15.7. Click the chevrons to display a menu containing additional Favorites not visible on the Favorites bar.

Add to Favorites

Figure 15.7   The Favorites bar.

Adding a Site to the Favorites Bar

To add a site to your Favorites bar, follow these steps:

1. Click the View Favorites, Feeds, and History button to open the Favorites Center pane.

2. Click the down arrow to the right of the Add to Favorites button. A menu appears.

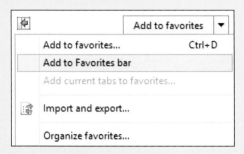

3. Choose Add to Favorites Bar. A link to the site appears on the Favorites bar.

 An even faster way to add a site to your Favorites bar is to click the Add to Favorites Bar button on the left side of the Favorites bar (see Figure 15.7).

To remove a Favorites from your Favorites list, simply right-click it in the Favorites list or Favorites bar and choose Delete from the menu that appears.

Viewing Your Browser History

By default, Internet Explore stores a list of recently visited websites, called the **browser history**. If you forget the URL of a site you've visited recently, you may be able to access it from this list.

To view your recent browser history, click the down arrow on the right side of the address bar. A menu of previously visited sites appears. (See Figure 15.8.) Simply click the site you want to visit, and the browser will reload it.

To view even more sites visited, you can open the Favorites Center pane and click the History tab. There, you can choose to view sites by date— that is, from the current day, current week, one week ago, two weeks ago, or three weeks ago. (See Figure 15.9.) Or, you can open the drop-down menu at the top of the pane and choose to view sites in alphabetical order (choose View By Site), by frequency of visit (choose View by Most Visited), or in the order they were visited today (choose View By Order Visited Today). You can also search your history list by choosing Search History from the drop-down list, typing a search term, and clicking the Search Now button.

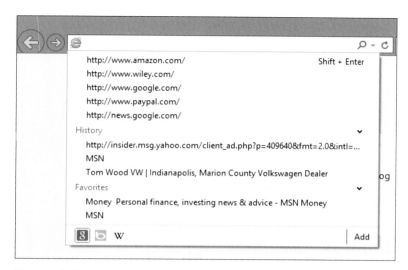

Figure 15.8   Using the Browser History feature.

Figure 15.9   Using the browser History feature to View by Date.

Internet Explorer automatically saves your browsing history for 20 days. If you like, you can change this setting. The maximum is 999 days.

Step by Step

To change the History settings, follow these steps:

1. Click the Tools button in the upper-right corner of the browser screen. A menu appears.

2. Select Internet Options. The Internet Options dialog box opens, with the General tab displayed.

3. Click the Settings button in the Browsing History section. The Website Data Settings dialog box opens.

4. Click the History tab.

5. Change the number of days the history is kept and click OK.

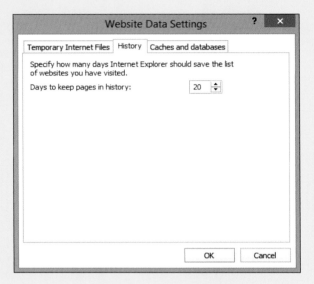

If you'd prefer not to store information about your browsing history, open the Internet Options dialog box as described. Then, in the Browsing History section of the General tab, select the Delete Browsing History on Exit check box. Finally, click OK. Every time you exit the browser, all history will be erased.

Downloading and Uploading Content

Internet is a vast repository of data in the same way that a library is full of books. Some data is for onscreen consumption only, but much of the data is also downloadable.

When you click a hyperlink that points to a downloadable file, a dialog box may appear automatically inviting you to specify a file name and location on your local computer in which to save the file. You can also right-click the hyperlink and choose Save Target As (or an equivalent command, depending on the browser you are using). Some browsers automatically download files to a default Downloads folder, using the file's default name, so you are not prompted for a name or location.

You can also upload content—that is, copy it from a desktop computer to a server on the Internet. You might do this to back up your data, storing it online on a personal storage site such as Microsoft OneDrive or Dropbox (also known as **cloud storage**). You can also use these sites to share data with others.

Step by Step

Uploading Files to OneDrive

Follow these steps to use a web interface to upload a file to your OneDrive, if you have one. If you don't, go to www.onedrive.com and create a free Microsoft account before doing these steps.

1. Launch Internet Explorer and go to www.onedrive.com. Sign in if needed using your Microsoft ID.

2. Click the Upload button.

3. In the Choose File to Upload dialog box, select the file to upload.

4. Click Open. The file is uploaded and appears in your file listing.

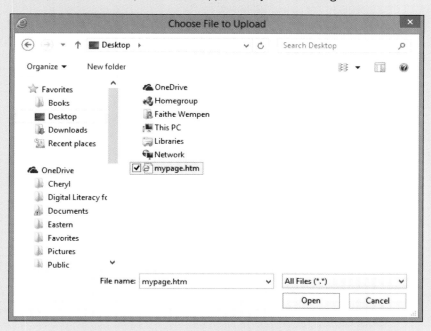

Another way to upload files for storage or sharing is to use the File Transfer Protocol (FTP). FTP is used solely for the transfer of files online. In the same way that there are web servers on the Internet, there are also FTP servers, maintained by businesses and individuals to enable users to upload and download files. Some of these are private, requiring a user ID and password; others are public, for distributing files that anyone may access.

You access an FTP site using a web browser in much the same way as a website; the main difference is that the address you enter into the browser starts with **ftp://** rather than **http://**. You can also access an FTP site using an FTP application. FileZilla (www.filezilla-project.org) is a free FTP client that anyone may download and use. It is shown in Figure 15.10.

Figure 15.10   FileZilla is an FTP application, used for uploading and downloading files from an FTP server online.

Managing Plug-ins (Add-ons)

plug-in A piece of software added to a web browser to give it additional functionality.

A plug-in, also called an add-on, is a piece of software that can be added to a web browser to give it additional functionality, like the capability to view movies or Flash content. Two of the most common plug-ins are Adobe Shockwave Flash Object and Java.

In most cases, you do not have to search for or manually install plug-ins. If one is needed, your browser will display a message offering to find and install it for you, or will direct you to a web page where you can download and install it.

Managing Installed Add-ons

To view and manage currently installed add-ons, follow these steps:

1. Click the Tools button in the upper-right corner of the browser window. A menu appears.

2. Choose Manage Add-ons. The Managed Add-ons window appears, displaying currently installed add-ons, organized by type.

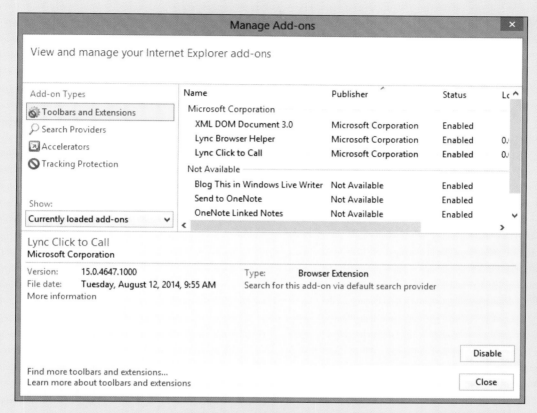

3. Click on any of the installed add-ons to view further details. When the add-on's details are displayed, you have the option of enabling or disabling that add-on.

4. Click Close to close the dialog box.

Using Web-Based Applications

These days, developers can use a number of programming languages to run web-based applications within a web browser. A web-based application is software that is downloaded and run within the web browser rather than being installed directly on the user's computer.

A good example of a web-based application Outlook.com (previously called Hotmail). You use this program to read and write email messages. All the messages are stored on the server, not on your computer.

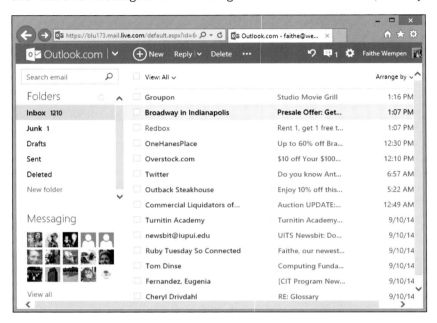

Web-based applications offer developers increased flexibility. Because they are browser-based, developers can build applications that work regardless of operating system. Web-based applications also alleviate concerns about local data storage. Finally, web-based applications are easier to update; there is no need to install and maintain applications on the local level. To capitalize on this new technology, many companies are moving to a subscription-based model, where users pay a monthly fee to use it rather than purchasing it outright.

Quick Review

1. Why might you choose to change your browser's home page?

2. Why might you save a site as a Favorite?

3. By default, how long does Internet Explorer save your browsing history?

4. What is a plug-in?

web-based application Software that downloads to your computer and then runs within a web browser.

search engine A software tool used to locate information on the web.

Using Web Search Tools

The answer to just about any question you may have is likely available on the Internet. The problem is knowing where to look to find it. This is where search engines come in. A search engine is an application that builds an index of sites on the Internet. Users can then search that database using keywords or phrases to find sites that contain the information they need.

Top Search Engines

This book uses Google as the basis for its examples, but you are free to try out other search engines too. Here are some of the most popular search engines that provide English-language results. To try out one of these, type its name (followed by .com) in the Address bar of your browser.

Google	Wow
Bing	WebCrawler
Yahoo!	MyWebSearch
Ask	Infospace
AOL	Info

Conducting a Search

To conduct a search in Google, you type a keyword or phrase into the Search field and click the blue magnifying glass button on the right. Google returns a list of sites that contain information matching the word or phrase you typed. It also shows you how many matches Google found, and how long it took Google to conduct the search.

As shown in Figure 15.11, each entry in the list contains three pieces of information:

- **The title:** This indicates the source of the information.
- **The URL:** This is the web address for the page containing the information.
- **The text:** Google shows an excerpt of the information, with the search words highlighted in bold.

To access a site that appears in the results, simply click it in the list.

The order in which the results are displayed depends upon multiple factors. One is relevance. The topmost result is, in Google's estimation, the site that best matches the keyword or phrase your typed and is likely to provide the most informative answer. Subsequent results are likely to be less relevant. The excerpt shown for each result will help you decide which entry is most likely to provide the information you need.

Another factor that determines the order of results is money. Companies pay Google to ensure that when users conduct a search that's relevant to their business, their page appears at (or closer to) the top of the list. Why? Because people who use search engines typically view only the first page of results. By ensuring their sites appear near the top of that page, companies increase the likelihood that their sites will receive more traffic.

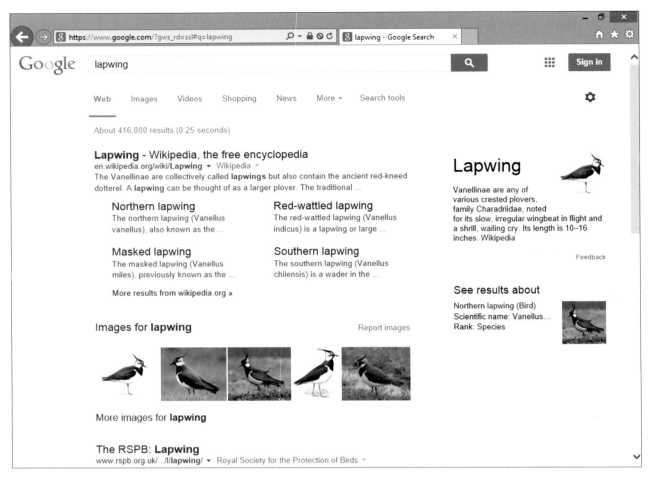

Figure 15.11   The results of a Google search for "lapwing."

Narrowing Your Search

Sometimes, you may find that a search yields too many results to be useful. To pare things down, try adding words to your search string. For example, if you type search for **lapwing**, Google finds over 416,000 results. If you search instead for **lapwing nesting habits**, the number of results drops to 42,900, as shown in Figure 15.12. The longer the search phrase, the more likely it is to narrow down the results to a manageable number.

Advanced Search Options and Features

Some search engines offer advanced search features, and Google is no exception. To access these features, type **http://www.google.com/ advanced_search** in the browser's address bar. You'll see a screen like the one shown in Figure 15.13. Fill in any of the relevant fields to narrow your search. For example, fill in the This Exact Word or Phrase field if you want to find pages that contain that text verbatim. Or, fill in the None of These Words field if you want Google to omit pages that contain that word from your search results. You can also narrow results by language, region, and more. After you enter all your search criteria, click the Advanced Search button near the bottom of the page to see a list of results.

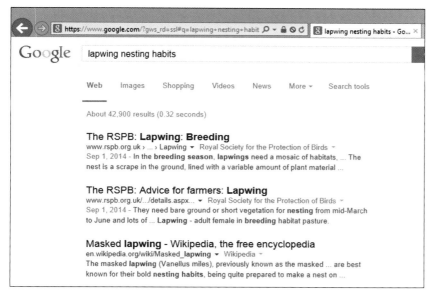

Figure 15.12   Search engine results, reduced by making the search term more specific.

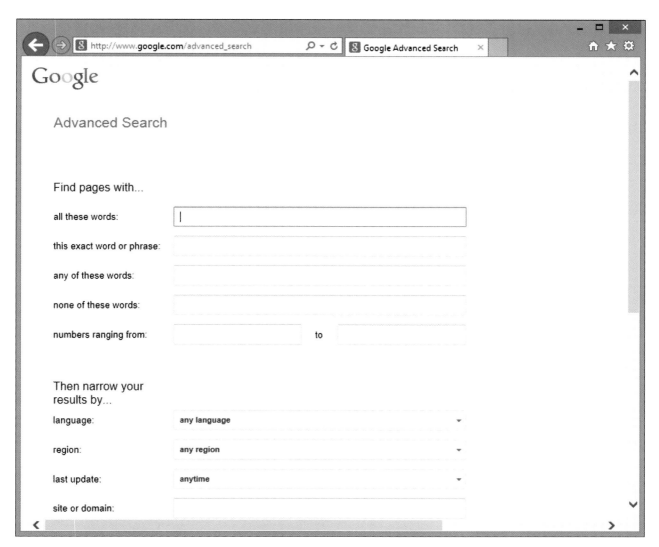

Figure 15.13   The Google Advanced Search page.

search operator A word or symbol that has a specific function when carrying out a search.

Another way to narrow your search is to enter specific search operators in the Search field. A search operator is a word or symbol that has a specific function when carrying out a search. These operators tell the search engine to follow specific instructions when it carries out the search. Table 15.2 outlines the most commonly used search operators.

Table 15.2: Common Search Operators

Operator	Result
site:	Gets results from only the site or sites listed
inurl:	Limits the search to words contained in the URL string
allinurl:	Returns entries that contain all the words specified in the URL
intitle:	Returns entries that contain one of the specified words in the title
allintitle:	Returns entries that contain all the specified words in the title
author:	Returns entries or articles by a specific author
- (minus sign)	Excludes what follows from the query

To use a search operator, simply type the operator, including the colon, followed by the keyword or phrase, and then click the Search button. Figure 15.14 shows the results achieved by entering the following query: **site: microsoft.com accounting**. Notice that all the entries returned are from Microsoft, and either they contain the word "accounting" or pertain to finance and accounting.

TIP You can enter more than one advanced search operator into a search query.

Evaluating the Accuracy of Web Information

The wonderful thing about the web is that anybody can create a website and publish her own information. The bad thing about the web is that anybody can create and publish her own information.

The web can provide answers to your questions, but how do you know how accurate or reliable this information is? To gauge this, consider the source of the information. If the information appears on a website hosted by a university, respected institution, or reputable company, it is likely that the information is accurate. If not, it's possible that the information is accurate, but there is no way of knowing for certain. The information is only as good as its source. Information on an individual's blog, for example, is not usually reliable information.

Keep in mind that many websites are created with an agenda in mind that may conflict with providing objective facts. For example, someone selling a product may exaggerate the product's benefits or post fictitious reviews, and someone promoting a certain political agenda may twist or intentionally misinterpret data to create an impression that supports his or her position.

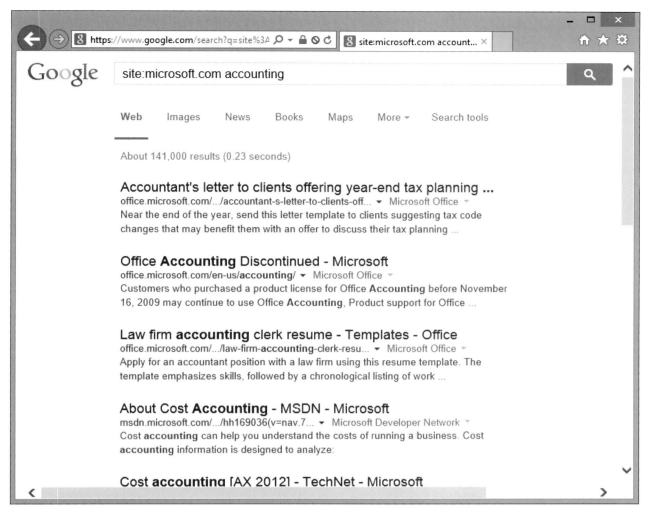

Figure 15.14   Using search operators.

Many web pages contain ads, and the ads are not always sectioned off separately from the main text; they may appear between the paragraphs of an article and might trick you into thinking they are part of the article. An ad is never a reliable source of information. Similarly, sponsored links are mini-ads that contain hyperlinks to other websites. Do not assume that a sponsored link is relevant to the topic of the article or that the author of the article even knows that the sponsored link is placed there.

sponsored link A hyperlink that is placed on a page because a payment has been made.

Forums are public message boards that you access via websites. They may be sponsored by a particular company, such as a support forum for a certain kind of hardware or software, or they may be created and managed by an individual. Because the posts on a forum are made by the general public, not by known experts, you must be cautious about applying any advice you read in forums. For example, a forum post might recommend that you download and install a certain file, but that file might have a virus or might cause compatibility problems on your computer. Some forums are monitored by official or unofficial representatives of the hosting company.

forum A web-based discussion and advice-sharing site.

knowledge base A set of articles provided and maintained by a company or government agency about their products.

A knowledge base more reliable source of information. It is a set of articles provided and maintained by a company or government agency about their products. For example, Microsoft has a knowledge base in which you can look up officially approved articles about various Microsoft products.

Encyclopedia sites vary in their accuracy and reliability. Well-known encyclopedias such as Encyclopedia Britannica and World Book Encyclopedia may generally be thought of as accurate. However, many sites that appear to be encyclopedias at first glance are actually wikis. A wiki is a knowledge base in which content is user-generated, so that anyone can post or edit entries, even someone who is not an expert on the topic or who has an agenda to promote. The best-known wiki is Wikipedia (www.wikipedia.org/). While Wikipedia is a good source of basic information on a topic, it cannot be trusted as a reliable source by itself, because of its nature; verify any information you learn from Wikipedia or any other wiki with other sources.

wiki A web-based application that can be edited by anyone and that is usually informational or instructive in nature.

Wikipedia A free, online encyclopedia. Wikipedia is an example of a wiki.

virtual private network (VPN) A method of creating a secure, private communication tunnel using a public communications channel such as the Internet.

Virtual Private Networks

Suppose you work for a company that has a head office and several remote sites. The company wants to connect the sites to form one network, and also to allow staff to work from home using the company network. However, they don't want to go to the expense of running secure dedicated network cables between each person's home and the company headquarters.

Virtual private networking (VPN) enables a user to create a secure connection to a remote server by going through the Internet. A VPN creates a secure tunnel, or pipeline, between a VPN-enabled web server and an individual computer. This tunnel is very difficult to hack, so the connection is safe enough to use for sensitive data.

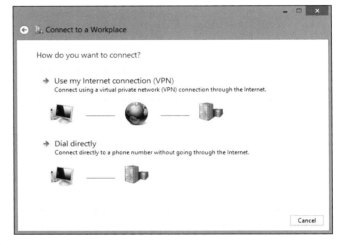

To connect to a VPN using Microsoft Windows, open the Network and Sharing Center (right-click the network icon in the notification area and choose Open Network and Sharing Center, or go through the Control Panel). From there, click Set Up a New Connection or Network, and double-click Connect to a Workplace. Choose Use My Internet Connection (VPN), and then follow the prompts to set up the connection, using the settings provided to you by the owner of the VPN server (your employer or school, for example).

Quick Review

1. What is a search engine?

2. What are the three pieces of information contained in a result returned by a search engine?

3. Why is it a good idea to narrow your search results?

4. What is the purpose of a VPN?

Summary

How the Web Works

The **Internet** is a global network of millions of computers that can communicate with each other. The **World Wide Web (WWW,** or the **web)** is one part of the Internet; it is network of interconnected pages of information stored on publicly accessible servers. Web pages are stored on web servers, and accessed by web browsers. A **web page** is a file that is formatted for use on the web. A **web server** is a server on which web pages are stored and made available to the public. A **web browser** is an application that can display web pages. The relationship between a web server and a web browser is **platform-independent**.

Most web pages are written in **HyperText Markup Language (HTML),** a coding language that includes bracketed **tags** that tell the browser how to display the content. A **hyperlink** is a clickable link to another page.

A **uniform resource locator (URL)** is the address you enter into your web browser's address bar to navigate to a specific web page. A URL consists of a protocol, a domain name, and, optionally, a path following the domain name.

A **domain name** is a name that identifies an entity on the Internet. It's a key part of a URL. In its basic form, a domain name consists of an identifier followed by an extension, like **microsoft.com**. The extension, also called the **top-level domain**, is often used to identify the type of organization that the name represents. Some domain names also include a two-letter country code.

Every computer that connects to the Internet has its own unique numeric address, called the **IP address**. Two types of IP addresses are currently in use: IPv4 addresses and IPv6 addresses. An **IPv4 address** is a binary number made up of 32 bits. It is represented in dotted decimal notation. There are more than 4 billion possible IPv4 address combinations. An **IPv6 address** is made up of 128 binary bits, and has a maximum address space of 340,282,366,920,938,463,374,607,431,768,211,456 addresses.

Domain Name System (DNS) is the naming system employed to enable users to access websites using their domain names or URLs rather than their IP addresses. The process of mapping domain names to IP addresses is called **name resolution** and is done by DNS servers.

Accessing the Web with a Browser

To open Internet Explorer (IE), use the shortcut on the Start menu or the taskbar, or click a web hyperlink in a document. The page that opens by default is the **home page**. Click on a hyperlink to go to a web page. Use the Forward and Back buttons to navigate between pages you have recently visited. Use the Refresh button to reload a page, or use the Stop button to stop a page from completing its loading. Internet Explorer enables you to have multiple **tabs** open at once, each displaying a different page.

To store a URL so you can easily recall it later, save it as a **Favorite**. IE maintains a list of recently visited sites called **History**. To access both favorites and history, click the View Favorites, Feeds, and History button (which look like a star).

When you click on the hyperlink for a downloadable file, your browser downloads it, or prompts you for a filename and location to download it. To upload a file to a server, you can use a web-based uploading interface, such as with Microsoft OneDrive, a type of **cloud storage**. You can also use the FTP protocol in your web browser (on some sites) or use a separate FTP application.

A **plug-in** (also called an add-on) is a piece of software that can be added to a web browser to give it additional functionality, like the capability to view movies or Flash content. If you need a plug-in to play a certain type of content, your browser will prompt you to install it.

Using Web Search Tools

A **search engine** is an application that builds an index of sites on the Internet. Users can then search that database using keywords or phrases to find sites that contain the information they need. Examples include Google, Bing, and Yahoo!.

Sometimes, you may find that a search yields too many results to be useful. Search using multiple keywords to narrow down a search, or use **search operators.** Different search engines support different operators.

To gauge the accuracy of information you find on the web, consider the source of the information. Forums, ads, sponsored links, and blogs are all unreliable sources. Knowledge bases and official company sites are generally more reliable. A wiki may contain accurate information or not; it is not reliable.

Key Terms

DNS server
domain name
Domain Name System (DNS)
dynamic IP address
Favorite
home page
hyperlink
HyperText Transfer Protocol (HTTP)
Internet
IP address
IPv4 address
IPv6 address
name resolution
plug-in

search engine
search operator
server
static IP address
tab
top-level domain
uniform resource locator (URL)
virtual private network (VPN)
web-based application
web browser
wiki
Wikipedia
World Wide Web (WWW)

Test Yourself

Fact Check

1. Which of the following is the correct format for an IPv4 address?

    a. 192:168:32:3

    b. 192.168.32.3

    c. 192,168,32,3

    d. 192-168-32-3

2. What is the name of the process that changes the domain name into an IP address?

    a. name conversion

    b. name translation

    c. name changing

    d. name resolution

3. What do you call software that adds functionality to a browser such as Internet Explorer?

    a. extension

    b. plug-in

    c. browse tool

    d. socket

4. What kind of online server translates between IP addresses and domain names?

    a. DNS

    b. IPSec

    c. SSL

    d. PPTP

5. Which numbering scheme is used to display an IPv6 address?

    a. binary

    b. octal

    c. decimal

    d. hexadecimal

6. A(n) _____ indicates that a website is trustworthy.

    a. digital certificate

    b. DNS certificate

    c. certificate authority

    d. IP certificate

7. The latest version of Internet Explorer can access only websites that use IPv6 addresses. True or False?

    a. true

    b. false

8. If you wanted to visit a web page that you looked at last week, where would you look for a link to it?

    a. Favorites

    b. History

    c. Forums

    d. Feed

9. What is the name of the object on a web page that you can click to open another page?

    a. hyperlink

    b. hypertext

    c. hypervisor

    d. web connector

10. Internet Explorer is the only browser that can be used on Windows. True or False?

    a. true

    b. false

Matching

Match the following words to the correct phrase:

   a. web server

   b. home page

   c. IP address

   d. web-based application

   e. search engine

   f. domain name

   1. _____An application that runs within a web browser

   2. _____A name that identifies an entity on the Internet

   3. _____A unique numeric address for a computer on the Internet

   4. _____A software tool used to locate information on the web

   5. _____A computer that responds to requests for web content

   6. _____The page that is displayed when you first launch your web browser

Sum It Up

   1. What is the relationship between the Internet and the World Wide Web?

   2. What does a hyperlink do?

   3. What type of server is used to resolve domain names and URLs to IP addresses?

   4. What browser feature enables users to open multiple web pages in a single browser window?

   5. What function does a search engine serve?

   6. What is a VPN?

Explore More

Identifying the Path from Source to Destination

To see happens when you type a URL into a web browser to visit a web page, you can use the **tracert** command. It traces the path from the browser to the website, noting all the devices it goes through en route.

   1. Right-click the Start button and click Command Prompt. A command prompt window opens.

   2. At the command prompt, type **tracert** followed by a space and then the URL for the website of your choice (for example, **www.bbc.co.uk**) and press Enter. The command prompt window will list all the devices that your request travels through before it gets to the chosen destination. The program will also list the IP address of each device. When the process completes, the window will say "Trace Complete."

As you can see, when you send the request, it leaves your computer, goes through your router, and then passes through a series of other devices between your browser and the destination. Notice that your request can probably get from one side of the world to the other in about 15 stages or hops—sometimes fewer.

Decoding URLs

When you visit a website, look at the complete path of the URL, including any folder names. Try different pages on the site and see if you can map how the site is laid out based on the different folder names you see.

Exploring DNS Name Resolution

DNS name resolution is a process that happens automatically whenever you type a URL into the web browser. This exercise enables you to see which DNS server you are using:

1. Right-click the Start button and click Command Prompt. A command prompt window opens.

2. At the command prompt, type **nslookup**, followed by the URL for the website you want to visit (for example, type **nslookup www.google.com**) and press Enter. The command prompt window lists the name and address of the DNS server you are using, followed by Google's IP address. If you see more than one address in this part of the results, it means the DNS knows about five different Google servers. Your browser usually will go to the first one in the list, but if it is not available, your browser will go to the second, and so on.

Think It Over

Evaluating Web Browsers

Imagine you are working for an organization that uses Windows computers and notebooks. Users have been allowed to download any software they like onto these computers, including different browsers. This creates a problem for the support department, so your supervisor has asked you to evaluate possible web browsers so that all computers can be standardized with one program. What browsers might you evaluate? What features might you consider most important?

Chapter 16

Network and Internet Privacy and Security

Learning objectives

☐ Understand the basic concepts of computer security

☐ Identify common threats when using a computer on a network

☐ Identify various malware programs

☐ Recognize the importance of securing personal data

☐ Develop strategies to make a computer more secure

Network and Internet Security Concerns

Network and Internet Privacy Concerns

Strategies for Improving Security

You learned how computers are connected via networks and the Internet in Chapter 13, "Networking and Internet Basics." Computers connected in this way are vulnerable to a range of malicious activities. These machines are at risk for attacks that can cause poor performance or destroy data, or can cause users to become victims of fraud or identity theft.

In this chapter, you will learn about some of the threats that exist when using networks and the Internet, and about some of the precautions you can take to protect yourself and your computers from exposure.

Security Specialist

Computer security is among the biggest growth areas in IT. With this comes a growing demand for engineers who have the skills to protect computers and networks. Security specialists are responsible for ensuring that all the security devices in a company are correctly configured. These specialists must also be able to spot different types of attacks and know how to respond to each one.

To work in this area, you will need to master skills such as understanding operating systems and networks. You will also need good computer qualifications from a college or university, plus industry certifications from companies like CompTIA and EC Council. Finally, you will need experience in other areas of IT, such as troubleshooting and support, before you can move into this role.

© iStockphoto.com/baranozdemir

Network and Internet Security Concerns

Computer crime is becoming increasingly common. It is relatively easy to attack computers to cause disruption or steal data. In fact, this can be carried out over a network or the Internet with low risk of the crime being traced back to the perpetrator.

Because of the ease with which attacks can be launched, it is essential that you remain aware of security and take the necessary steps to secure your data and online identity.

Computer security is built around upholding three basic goals:

- **Confidentiality.** Your data should be visible and accessible only to those whom you choose to see it.

- **Integrity.** The data you see and store should be reliable and accurate, and should not be tampered with. You need to be able to trust this data.

- **Availability.** Your data should be accessible when you want it, including after a mishap or disaster.

The threat assessment and security measures discussed in this chapter center around the need to uphold these three goals.

Security Threats Posed by Computer Criminals

Computer criminals engage in many types of activities that can compromise your computer system, your data, and your online identity.

Phishing

One of the common threats—and one that is also easy to carry out—is phishing. In a phishing attack, offenders send email messages to unsuspecting users in an attempt to trick them into giving away personal information such as login details or credit card information. The attackers then use this information to conduct fraudulent activity. This type of attack is often successful because the email messages appear to be from a trustworthy source, such as a bank or other reputable organization.

How does phishing work? Often, you will receive an email that appears to be from your bank. The email states that there is a problem with your account and it has been suspended. To reinstate your account, you must fill in the online form and submit your personal details. If you look closely, however, you'll find that the email is *not* from your bank and the link to the form does not take you to the bank website—although it may appear as though it does. This is a very easy way for criminals to acquire information about account holders and, once they have it, to remove money from their accounts.

Such emails are not always sent under the guise of banks. They may appear to be from mobile phone providers, computer companies, or any other organization you may have an account with.

phishing The act of attempting to acquire information such as usernames, passwords, credit card information, and so forth, by pretending to be from a genuine, trustworthy source such as a bank.

Legitimate banks and other companies will *never* send an email asking you to submit sensitive personal information online. Never click on the links in such emails. As a good Internet citizen, you should report the emails to the bank or other company to make them aware of the phishing attempts.

CAUTION

Phishing emails are getting more sophisticated and harder to recognize, but here are some considerations that will help you identify them:

- Do you actually have an account with that bank or company? If not, then it's reasonable to assume the message is an attempt at phishing.

- Check the source of the email. Does the email address match the organization's standard email address? Check not only the address that appears as text in the message, but also the address that appears as a ScreenTip when you point the mouse at it.

- If you hover over the link to the company website with your mouse, it shows you the true URL. Is the address correct?

- Are there grammar and spelling mistakes? Does the message appear in the language you would expect? Even if the body text is in the expected language, are there buttons or other details with text from another language? These are all indications of a possible attempt at phishing.

- Check for the presence of the security padlock icon in the address bar. The presence of the security padlock icon is an indication that the message may be genuine—although it is not a guarantee.

Finally, remember that real companies and banks *never* ask for personal information in this way.

In April 2014, security experts discovered a security bug that affected Internet users worldwide. Called "Heartbleed," the bug placed around half a million of the world's secure servers—the ones indicated by the aforementioned security padlock icon—vulnerable to attack, placing the servers' private keys and users' session cookies and passwords at risk. Most sites quickly patched the problem, but sensitive data for many users was vulnerable in the interim.

Figure 16.1 shows an example of a phishing email. The message claims to be from Apple, telling a user that his Apple account has been suspended.

Figure 16.1 An example of a phishing email.

Notice that the email is from service@id-appactivate.com. The address doesn't end in @apple.com. If you were to click on the link to `http://facturation-apple.org` (which you should not do if you suspect you have received a phishing email), you would see what initially appears to be the Apple login screen, as shown in Figure 16.2. The page may look authentic, but it is not the official Apple website.

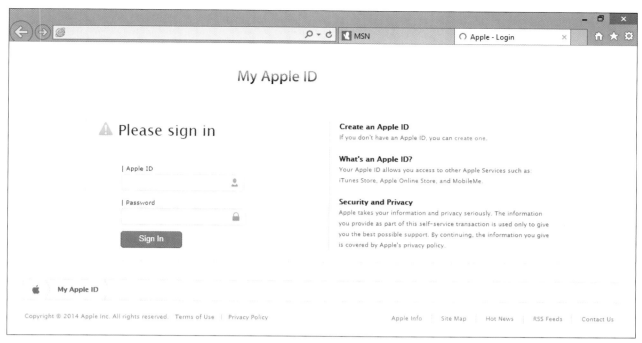

Figure 16.2 Fake credentials screen. (Note that this screen includes another clue that you have fallen prey to a phishing email: a mention of MobileMe, which was discontinued in June 2012.)

If you were to type your Apple username and password to log in (which, again, you should not do if you suspect the email is a phishing attempt), you would be taken to a page where you are asked to provide all your personal information, including your address, birth date, and full credit card details. (Do not be fooled into thinking that this screen is genuine by the presence of the padlock icon and the word "secure"; as noted, the presence of the padlock icon is no guarantee that the page is truly secure.) This gives the thief a complete, legitimate identity plus a credit card to use for illegal purchases.

Recipients of phishing email should delete them without opening them. If they do open the mail, they should not click on the embedded link.

CAUTION

Spoofing

When a computer connects to a network, it has several identities that are unique within that environment. It has a name and an Internet address, also known as the Internet Protocol (IP) address. In addition, the network chip in the computer has an address (known as a media access control, or MAC, address). A computer is granted access to a network as a legitimate device because its IP address is among those authorized for that network.

In a spoofing attack, the attacker's computer assumes a false Internet address in order to gain access to a network. This type of attack is typically used by people who want to gain access to data but do not have a legitimate username or password to the network where the data resides. In that case, the attacker waits for a legitimate user to log in, and then hijacks that user's IP address and takes over.

spoofing An attack in which a user pretends to be another by providing false IP address data.

Packet Sniffing

When data is sent over a network, it is sent in multiple small packets rather than one large file. When you download a web page, you see the completed item on the screen, but in reality that one page might be composed of several hundred packets of data. The same applies to an Internet telephony program such as Skype. It takes upwards of 50 packets of data to carry one second of speech.

Sniffing is the capability to capture copies of data packets as they travel across the network and decode their content. Often, data sent over a network or the Internet is unencrypted, so someone with the right software can capture and copy the packets that made up the data and decipher the contents.

In simple terms, the sniffer software draws a picture of what it sees and stores this data in a file. Figure 16.3 shows an extract from a sniffing program called Wireshark. The snapshot identifies the address of the website that the user is visiting (Google.co.uk), the operating system (Windows), and the browser (in this case, Firefox). That's a lot of information from just a few lines.

```
0030   40 3d e2 71 00 00 47 45   54 20 2f 20 48 54 54 50   @=.q..GE T / HTTP
0040   2f 31 2e 31 0d 0a 48 6f   73 74 3a 20 77 77 77 2e   /1.1..Ho st: www.
0050   67 6f 6f 67 6c 65 2e 63   6f 2e 75 6b 0d 0a 55 73   google.c o.uk..Us
0060   65 72 2d 41 67 65 6e 74   3a 20 4d 6f 7a 69 6c 6c   er-Agent : Mozill
0070   61 2f 35 2e 30 20 28 57   69 6e 64 6f 77 73 20 4e   a/5.0 (W indows N
0080   54 20 36 2e 31 3b 20 57   4f 57 36 34 3b 20 72 76   T 6.1; W OW64; rv
0090   3a 32 38 2e 30 29 20 47   65 63 6b 6f 2f 32 30 31   :28.0) G ecko/201
00a0   30 30 31 30 31 20 46 69   72 65 66 6f 78 2f 32 38   00101 Fi refox/28
```

Figure 16.3   A data sample captured by the Wireshark sniffer.

Password Cracking

When you log in to a computer or connect to an account on the Internet, you identify who you are with a username or number and you authenticate your identity, typically with a password. Passwords are the most common method of authentication because they are easy to use and maintain. Most systems and programs allow users to choose their own passwords, provided the passwords satisfy the system or program's security policy.

It may be relatively easy to determine someone's username. However, finding out someone's password is often much more difficult. People who want to break into a system or account often attempt password cracking—that is, they attempt to identify a user's password. Password cracking can be accomplished in several ways:

- **Guessing:** The more you know about a user, the easier it is to guess his password. The most common passwords are based on the names of family members, but pets' names, football clubs, birthdays, and other words are also common. People often choose passwords they can easily remember, but this practice can weaken security and help crackers.

- **Keylogger:** A keylogger is a piece of hardware or a software program that captures every keystroke a user types. A hardware keylogger (see Figure 16.4) can be used to capture keystrokes sent from a physical keyboard to a computer, while a software keylogger can capture keystrokes from a virtual keyboard or other input device. When a user enters a password, the keystrokes are logged, and the password is captured for the attacker to use to gain access to the user's account.

- **Social engineering:** Social engineering is the art of obtaining someone's password either by befriending her or tricking her into sharing it. Two classic social engineering methods are pretending to be an administrator who needs to know a password to fix a problem and sending a phishing email asking a user to fill in a form that requires her username and password.

Figure 16.4 A hardware keylogger. This model looks similar to a flash drive.

- **Sniffing:** As mentioned, sniffing is the practice of capturing data packets on the network. In many cases, when people enter their passwords, data packets contain those passwords in clear text. If the packets can be captured, the password can be discovered.

- **Password-cracking tools:** Dozens of software programs are designed for password cracking. Different types of passwords (Windows logon passwords, Adobe document passwords, and website passwords, for example) require different password-cracking tools.

Malicious Programs

As noted in the preceding section, computer criminals engage in a wide variety of activities to compromise your computer system, data, and online identity. They are aided in their efforts by various types of malicious software, grouped together under the title malware. This section outlines the main types of malware programs.

Viruses

A virus is a piece of malicious software that is installed without the user's knowledge or consent. When executed, the virus program replicates and spreads to "infect" other computer programs, data files, or even the boot sector of the hard drive.

Viruses often carry a malicious payload. For example, a boot-sector virus might stop the computer from loading the operating system. Some viruses might delete all files of a certain type—for example, Word documents. Other viruses may simply have annoying consequences—perhaps opening and closing the CD drawer. Some viruses hide as long as they can so they can do as much damage as possible before being discovered. New viruses appear virtually every day, so it is vital that you take precautions and protect yourself from them.

The most common way for a virus to spread is for a user to open an infected email attachment or Internet link without having virus protection in place. This allows the malicious software to gain access to the system. If the infected file is sitting in RAM memory and you run another program, the virus attaches a copy of itself to the second program—and so on and so forth.

Worms

worm A malicious computer program that spreads itself to other computers over a network or the Internet.

A worm is similar to a virus in that it may have a malicious payload. However, worms are designed to automatically spread from computer to computer over a network or the Internet. Like viruses, the consequences of worms range from destructive to annoying. A worm might delete files or direct users to a fake website, or it might just do something annoying like swapping left and right mouse button actions. At the very least, a worm will consume network bandwidth.

CAUTION Some worms are designed to compromise the user's email address book and send itself to all the user's contacts. If you receive an odd or unexpected message from one of your contacts, it could indicate that her address book has been infected by a worm. Before opening the email, contact the sender to determine whether the email is legitimate and to alert her to the possibility that her machine has been infected.

Trojans

According to Greek mythology, the Greeks conquered the city of Troy through trickery. They constructed a large wooden horse, which they presented to the Trojans as a gift. Unbeknownst to the Trojans, however, the Greeks had hidden a select team of soldiers inside the horse. After the Trojans dragged the horse inside the city walls, the Greek soldiers emerged from the horse and opened the city gates, enabling the rest of the Greek army to swarm the town.

Trojan A piece of malicious software that looks harmless but has a detrimental effect on a computer when it runs.

It is after this horse, called the Trojan horse, that Trojans are named. A Trojan is a piece of software, such as a game or utility, that may look innocent but has a malicious purpose. Typically, the user knowingly installs the game or utility, but doesn't realize there's a Trojan inside. When the user runs the program, the Trojan starts running in the background, often without the user's knowledge.

A Trojan can do nasty things to a computer, but more likely it is there to gather information. For example, many Trojan programs are keyloggers. As described, a keylogger records all the keys the user presses on the keyboard and saves them in a file. It then sends the file with the user's keystrokes to the person or group who sent the Trojan. In this way, whoever sent the Trojan can learn what the user does on the computer. More importantly, they can uncover the user's username and password, enabling them to log in themselves.

A common type of Trojan is one that displays a screen that recommends that you purchase and download some type of anti-malware software, as shown in Figure 16.5. In this case, however, the software is fake and will probably put more Trojans on your computer. Worse, if you buy it, the thieves will then have your credit card details.

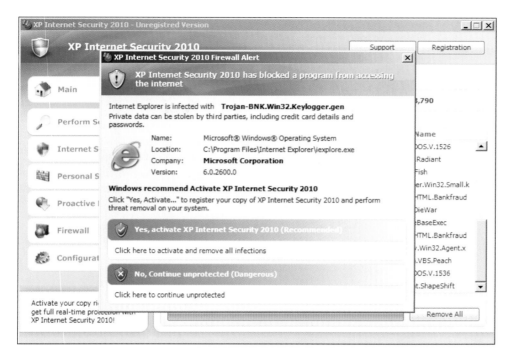

Figure 16.5   A Trojan advertising fake anti-virus software.

Ransomware

Some new, very nasty Trojans are called ransomware. These Trojans encrypt files on the system, such as photos, music, and documents. The Trojan then displays a message describing how to get the files back. Retrieval inevitably involves sending a payment over the Internet to an unknown destination with the promise that once the money is received, you will receive the key to unlock your files. The key doesn't exist and the damage is already done, however. You will not get your files unlocked. Your best protection against ransomware is to frequently back up your system on an external hard drive. That way, if you fall prey to this type of Trojan, you can simply copy the files from your backup drive. You'll learn more about backing up your system later in this chapter.

Another type of Trojan runs spyware. Spyware is software that monitors what the user does on the computer without her knowledge. It then sends the information it gathers to a third party, which uses it to target the user with pop-up advertisements—often for fake products.

Protecting Yourself against Malware

The earliest anti-virus programs were designed to detect and protect against viruses, but have improved over the years into broader security solutions that can detect viruses, worms, Trojans, and sometimes more complex threats. A good anti-virus package provides a wide range of protective measures and may include firewall management (discussed later in this chapter) and anti-spyware as well.

An anti-virus program aims to protect a computer against viruses in two ways. First, it contains a database of all known viruses; it can then compare the code in a program that your computer attempts to execute against this database. If the anti-virus software finds a match, it raises an alert and either removes the virus or puts the infected file in a special area where it cannot be accessed, or *quarantines* it. Second, the anti-virus program looks at a program that is attempting to run and makes an intelligent guess as to whether it could be a virus. If the software thinks a program is a virus, it quarantines or cleans it, but this solution is not perfect. Sometimes anti-virus software raises a false alarm and removes a legitimate file, so you have to recover it manually. Still, this is a small price to pay for reliable protection.

Many good anti-virus products are in the marketplace: Symantec, Sophos, Kaspersky, and McAfee are among the most popular security solutions. They all work in a similar way and produce similar results. In addition, Microsoft has its own product, called Security Essentials. You can also find free anti-virus software, such as AVG (see Figure 16.6) or ClamWin. Free products usually have a more limited range of services than the commercial choices, but in some cases, you can upgrades to a paid version for expanded offerings.

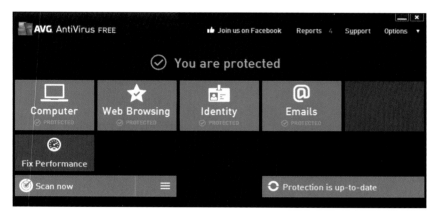

Figure 16.6   Free anti-virus software.

When an anti-virus product is installed, it provides real-time protection that checks files every time a user wants to run a program. The program will also do periodic scans of hard drives, checking every single file. See Figure 16.7. Most systems will carry out automatic scans and also allow manual scan runs at any time.

Figure 16.7   An anti-virus scan in action.

DoS Attacks and Zombies

In a denial of service (DoS) attack, the attacker floods a website or service with thousands of requests for access—so many that it cannot deal with them all. As a result, legitimate users are prevented from accessing the site or service. DoS attacks often involve many thousands of computers from all over the world, all launching multiple requests against the target website or service, making them difficult to prevent. Once an attack is started, it can render the target site unavailable very quickly.

denial of service (DoS) attack A coordinated attack in which the target website or service is flooded with requests for access, to the point that it is completely overwhelmed.

The computers that launch these attacks are called zombies. A zombie is a computer that has been infected with a particular type of Trojan called a bot. Initially, the bot runs in the background, doing very little beyond communicating with its master over the Internet every now and then, awaiting instructions. One day, it, along with thousands of other bots, receives instructions to bombard a particular website as part of a DoS attack. This is called a botnet. Millions of computers around the world are part of multiple botnets, all used for DoS attacks.

zombie A computer used to conduct a DoS attack.

bot A type of Trojan, used to infect a zombie computer to conduct a DoS attack.

botnet A network of zombie computers infected with bots, often numbering in the thousands. Computer criminals use botnets to conduct DoS attacks.

Wi-Fi Networks

Hackers frequently target Wi-Fi networks. When Wi-Fi networks are not properly secured, it is easy to steal data on them with little chance of being caught. Hackers don't even need any special equipment to penetrate such a Wi-Fi network.

When people use their devices to locate and connect to a wireless network, they see a list of available networks, as shown in Figure 16.8. Some of these networks may be open access, meaning you don't need a password to connect. Others may require a password and will provide users with a secure connection. Insecure networks are identified with a small exclamation mark; the other networks have encrypted connections.

Some wireless networks appear to be genuine, but in fact attempt to intercept your traffic. These types of Wi-Fi networks are called rogue Wi-Fi. These Wi-Fi networks usually seem authentic, often with a name that is similar or the same as a legitimate network. The difference? This network "sniffs" all your traffic, making a copy of everything you type—including any usernames, passwords, and credit card numbers.

Figure 16.8 Visible wireless networks.

rogue Wi-Fi A wireless network that "sniffs" traffic, making a copy of everything users type—including usernames, passwords, and credit card numbers.

Public places where many people are looking for Wi-Fi, such as coffee shops, restaurants, and airports, are common locations for rogue Wi-Fi connections. How can you tell whether a Wi-Fi network to which you want to connect is in fact rogue? It's not easy. If you are directed to a "Terms of Service" page after you connect, that's a good indication that the network is legitimate. A time limit is another sign that the network may be genuine. But your best bet is to simply ask someone who works at the location whether it offers Wi-Fi, and if so, the name of the network.

Wireless Network Authentication

A wired network typically doesn't have any special security that prevents someone from physically connecting to it. The switch or router to which someone might connect a cable is usually locked down in a closet or a special room in the facility to which only IT professionals have access, so it would be difficult for an unauthorized user to connect without permission.

With a wireless network, however, it's a different story. Anyone within range of a wireless network may be able to see and connect to it. For that reason, there are several methods of protecting a wireless network from unauthorized usage.

A wireless network may be open (no security), or secure (having some type of encryption). If a network is secure, the first time a computer connects to the wireless access point, a password prompt appears. The user must type the correct encryption key (password) in order to connect to the network. The encryption key is assigned and can be changed in the wireless access point's setup utility.

NOTE

To access the wireless access point's setup utility, use your web browser. Enter the IP address of the access point, and its configuration page will appear. If you don't know its IP address, consult its documentation, or visit the support website for the device online.

Several systems of wireless network security have been developed over the years, each one an improvement over earlier systems in terms of security level. Here are the most common ones, in order of oldest to newest (and most secure):

- **Wired Equivalent Privacy (WEP):** An older and weaker form of wireless encryption. It is available in both 64-bit and 128-bit encryption key versions. (The more bits, the greater the security.)

- **Wi-Fi Protected Access (WPA):** A security system designed to overcome the weaknesses of WEP, providing an improved 128-bit encryption key.

- **WPA2:** An improved version of WPA that provides even stronger protection with a 128-bit or 256-bit encryption key.

To make it easier for devices to connect to home networks that use encryption, some wireless access points include a feature called Wi-Fi Protected Setup (WPS). This feature enables a user to connect a device to a trusted network by pressing a button on the wireless access point to temporarily place it into a mode that allows new connections, and then clicking an onscreen button in the operating system to complete the connection.

Another way to make a wireless network more secure is to set the wireless access point not to broadcast its service set identification (SSID), which is its name. By default, a wireless access point constantly broadcasts its name so that computers that want to connect to it can find it. That makes it easy for computers to select it from a list of available networks. If you set it to not broadcast its name, only those who know its name will be able to find it and connect to it. You can set the wireless network's SSID and choose whether or not to broadcast it from the wireless access point's setup utility.

Wired Equivalent Privacy (WEP) An older and less secure form of wireless encryption.

Wi-Fi Protected Access (WPA) A form of wireless encryption providing a 128-bit encryption key.

WPA2 An improved version of Wi-Fi Protected Access that provides stronger protection with a 128-bit or 256-bit encryption key.

Wi-Fi Protected Setup (WPS) A feature available on some wireless access points that enable a user to connect a device to a trusted network.

service set identification (SSID) The name assigned to identify a wireless access point so that other computers can find it.

Quick Review

1. What are the three goals of computer security?

2. What are two ways to detect a phishing attack?

3. What are the three main types of malware?

4. What is the best protection against malware?

Network and Internet Privacy Concerns

The Internet has changed the way people live, learn, and communicate. While the Internet offers enormous power to communicate and to find information, it also makes us more vulnerable to invasions of privacy. The Internet consists of vast amounts of data spread globally across millions of websites; thanks to the sheer size and scope of the Internet, it's impossible to know how all this information is stored and how private it is!

Here are just a few of the ways in which using networks and the Internet can put your privacy at risk:

- When you use a search engine, the search engine site can gather information about you based on the terms you search for and the questions you ask.

- When you provide personal information on the Internet—such as your name, address, email, and so forth—to a website, that website can store the information and perhaps use it for purposes other than those you intended.

CAUTION Be aware of the personal information you make available online. That information may spread far beyond the sites you contact directly!

- Your computer has a unique identity. Someone who knows this unique identity can access your computer via a network and view, change, or delete your personal data.

Data Storage

When you store data on your computer, you store it as files. As the number of files grows, it becomes harder to locate the data you want. This is where databases come in. A database stores data in a way that enables you to search for and locate it quickly.

database A collection of data stored in a structured format, with the same facts stored about each instance. A database stores data in a way that enables you to search and locate it quickly.

There are millions of databases worldwide that, together, store billions of files. Often, these files contain information about individuals. For example, large companies have databases that contain information about their customers. Similarly, social networks like Facebook have huge databases to store the information about their users. If these networks are vulnerable to unauthorized access, sensitive data for many people may be compromised.

Most of this data is stored by private companies, and we rely upon them to handle personal data with care. Everything should be based on the principle of least privilege—that is, you give people minimum access for the jobs they have to do. If you request data about yourself, that is all you should see—no one else's details.

Privacy Laws

To protect people's privacy, there are rules to govern how personal information is handled. Most countries have data protection and privacy laws to control the access and distribution of this personal information. These laws are needed to regulate the companies that hold our personal information and to ensure that all our information is properly protected.

Different countries have different rules, but most require that any personal information stored is:

- Used only for the intended purpose
- Accurate
- Sufficient for the purpose, with no unnecessary information held
- Accessible by the owner
- Obtained legally
- Kept secure from unauthorized access
- Deleted when no longer needed

Privacy Laws in the United States

The United States has more than 25 data privacy laws, each dealing with different categories of data. Here are a few of those important privacy laws:

- **Health Insurance Portability and Accountability Act (HIPAA):** This law includes provisions to ensure the privacy of medical records.
- **Gramm-Leach-Bliley Act:** This law governs the collection, disclosure, and protection of consumers' nonpublic personal information in financial institutions.
- **Electronic Communications Privacy Act (ECPA):** This law prevents unauthorized government access to private electronic communications.

Similar laws exist in different countries. More than 100 nations have specific privacy laws. Thanks to these laws, companies are prohibited from giving your information away to anyone who asks for it.

Of course, just because there are laws designed to protect your privacy online does not mean that you shouldn't take additional steps to keep yourself safe. For more information, read on.

Step by Step

Checking Your Online Identity

When you start using the Internet, you create an online identity. To get a sense of your online identity, try the following:

1. Open your web browser and type **www.google.com** or the address of your favorite search engine.
2. Type your name in the Search box and see what results you get. Do you see links to pages that contain information about you?
3. Click the Images link if the search engine provides one. Are there any pictures of you online?

The results may surprise you. Perhaps you find information about yourself that you would prefer were kept private. If you can see this information about yourself, so can anyone else!

Understanding Social Networking Risks

A social network is an Internet-based system that enables users to interact in real time and by using messaging programs. With a social network, users can share every aspect of their lives with others. Examples of social networks include Facebook, Twitter, and Instagram.

While sharing information via social networks can be wonderful, it is not without its risks. It is easy to get carried away on social networks and publish information about yourself that would be better kept private. Before you publish too much information about yourself, you must consider just who can see that data. After you have published it, it is very difficult—if not impossible—to remove it from the Internet.

CAUTION Never leave a computer or laptop without logging out of any social network sites you have open. If you remain logged in, someone else could post information while pretending to be you.

Social networks pose another risk—namely, that some of the "friends" you make online may not be who they say they are. Be careful how much you reveal about yourself to such people. Remember: A social network is global, your new "friends" could be anywhere, and some of them may ask you to do things you shouldn't.

CAUTION Never agree to meet someone you've met online in person unless you bring a friend with you for protection.

Cyberbullying

Social networks have become part of our everyday lives—particularly among young people. Indeed, millions of young people spend time on sites such as Facebook, Twitter, Instagram, and other social network sites, often to stay in touch with friends.

Sometimes, however, what starts as a fun activity—interacting with friends online—turns ugly. Someone makes unpleasant comments about you online. Others join the conversation. People might even post rumors or altered images of you in an attempt to harass you. This is called cyberbullying—and it's a growing problem.

What should you do if you are being cyberbullied? The most important thing is to tell someone who can help. If you are being bullied at school or in the workplace, then your instructor or employer needs to know about it. He or she may be able to take action to stop it. Of course, telling others about the cyberbullying may be difficult because some of the comments may be hurtful or embarrassing. But it is important to let people know it is happening. You can't just ignore it and hope it will go away. All that does is empower the bullies.

Deleting Cookies

When you visit some websites, they place a cookie on your computer. A cookie is a small file that stores information about your interaction with the website. When you revisit the site, the site reads the cookie on your computer to identify you. Just one visit to a website can result in the installation of several cookies on your computer.

Privacy and Security

While this can sometimes be handy—for example, for sites that you've personalized—it's not always a good thing. For example, some cookies contain personal information that a hacker could use to gain access to a website while pretending to be you. The hacker could then use your PayPal or credit card information in a fraudulent manner, for example. Or, a hacker could trick you into downloading a Trojan that steals your cookies and sends them to the hacker's computer, enabling him to use them at will.

To prevent this, you can delete cookies, and prevent your computer from storing them in the future. If you do so, the next time you go to a website, it will not be able to identify you because there will be no cookies on your computer. While this may be frustrating on occasion—you may have to input information all over again—it can be a safer way to use the Internet. When you delete or disable cookies, you no longer leave a trail of information that others could use for malicious purposes.

Step by Step

Deleting and Disabling Cookies in Internet Explorer

To delete and disable cookies in Internet Explorer, follow these steps:

1. Open Internet Explorer.

2. Click the Tools button (the one with a cog wheel icon, located in the upper-right corner of the window) and choose Internet Options from the menu that appears.

3. The Internet Options dialog box opens with the General tab displayed. Under Browsing History, click the Delete button.

4. The Delete Browsing History dialog box opens. Ensure that the Cookies and Website Data check box is checked and then click the Delete button. This deletes all cookies currently stored on your system.

5. To prevent your system from storing additional cookies, select the Delete Browsing History on Exit check box in the Internet Options dialog box.

6. Click the Apply button. Then click OK.

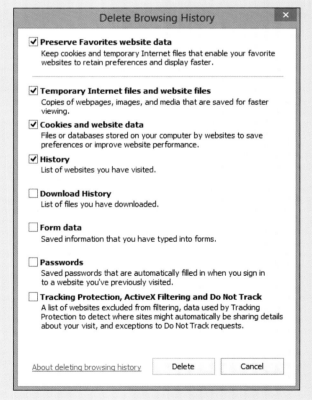

NOTE   If you do not use Internet Explorer as your web browser, search your browser's Help files for the phrase "delete cookies."

Quick Review

1. What is a social network?

2. What should you do if you are being cyberbullied?

3. What is a cookie?

4. What happens if you delete a cookie from your system?

Strategies for Improving Security

How can you improve security? Some of the work is done for you by operating system vendors, who typically add security features when they produce new versions of an operating system. For example, Microsoft Windows now has a built-in firewall, and Microsoft offers its own anti-virus security products. The operating system is also more secure thanks to better login mechanisms and the presence of fewer vulnerabilities. There is still some work you can do, however. For example, you can restrict access to data, use encryption, protect against data loss, install security-related updates, and more.

Restricting Access

Perhaps the easiest and most effective security measure you can take is to restrict access to the data on your computer. You can do this by using passwords, applying permissions, and enabling firewalls.

Using Passwords

When Windows is installed on a computer with only one user account, it does not require the use of a password to log in to the operating system. When you start the computer, it takes you straight to the desktop or Start screen. That means anybody could start the computer and see what is stored on it as well as run programs without permission. This is not a good practice. What if someone rifled through your files until he found sensitive information you'd rather keep quiet? Or what if someone were to use your computer to hack into a government network?

All this is to say that it's critical to create a strong password for your computer. That way, no one who does not know the password can log in. A strong password should contain a mix of uppercase and lowercase letters, numbers, and special characters such as @ or #, and be difficult or impossible for other people to guess. An example of a weak password might be "manchester." You could easily strengthen the password, however, by changing out some of the letters for other characters, like this: "M@nch35Ter." You should, of course, create a password that you can remember, and also change the password on a regular basis.

You should create similarly strong passwords for any accounts you create on the Internet. That way, you ensure no one "cracks" your password and accesses your online accounts.

Locking the Computer

If you're logged in to a computer, you should never leave it unattended, even for a few minutes. If you do, someone could easily access your files, install a Trojan, or send an improper email as if it was from you. One simple security measure you can take to prevent this is to lock your computer when you are away from the machine.

You can lock your computer in one of three ways. One is to press the Ctrl+Alt+Del keys at the same time. You will be presented with an options screen; select the Lock option to lock the computer. An even faster way to lock the computer is to press the Windows+L keys at the same time. To unlock the computer, simply press any key to display the password prompt and then enter your Windows password. You can also click your user name on the Start screen in Windows 8.1 and choose Lock.

Sharing Folders with Permissions

If your Windows computer will have more than one regular user, you can create a user account for each person. Each person's data—his pictures, music, movies, documents, and so on—will be stored in his own user folder. Only a folder's owner can access the contents of his user folder. This is to help keep the data secure. A user can, however, choose to share some of his folders with other users on the computer, without granting access to all the data in his account. You can also share folders and files with other users over a network. This is done through the use of *permissions*.

Before you start assigning permissions to share data with others, you should consider what you wish to share and how much access to allow. For example, you can set a folder's or file's permissions to give others access to its contents, but not allow them to change the contents. Or, you could set a folder's or file's permissions such that others can add, change, and/or delete items.

Step by Step

Setting Permissions on a File or Folder

To set permissions on a folder or file, follow these steps:

1. Open File Explorer.

2. Select the folder or file you want to share.

3. Right-click the selected folder or file and choose Share With. A submenu appears.

4. In the submenu, choose Specific People.

5. The File Sharing window opens. Click the drop-down menu at the top of the window and choose Everyone, or choose a certain person's name.

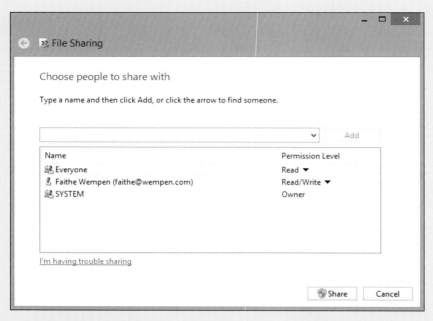

6. Click Add. Windows applies the default level of permission. To change it, click the appropriate entry in the list and choose Read or Read/Write from the menu that appears.

7. Click Share to share the folder or file.

Be cautious when sharing folders and files with others. Give people only the level of access they need—and no more.

Using a Firewall

firewall A security barrier on your computer or network that controls what traffic is allowed to pass through.

A firewall is a security barrier on your computer or network that controls what traffic is allowed into and out of your computer or network. The barrier is designed to separate your computer or network, which you trust, from an external network, which you might not.

The firewall works from a set of instructions, or rules. It looks at every packet of traffic that attempts to travel through the firewall in either direction and decides whether to allow it or block it. Most firewalls come with a set of default rules, but they can be adjusted, enabling you to configure yours to allow or deny whatever traffic you choose. If you play computer games, for example, you may need to configure the firewalls on your router and your computer to allow the gaming traffic through. Windows includes a free firewall application called Windows Firewall.

Step by Step

Changing the Settings on Windows Firewall

To adjust the settings of Windows Firewall, follow these steps:

1. Right-click the Windows Start button and choose Control Panel.

2. In the Control Panel window, click the System and Security option.

3. In the System and Security window, click Windows Firewall. Windows displays the current status of your firewall. If the networks have green check marks, you are protected. If you see red X's instead of the green check marks, your firewall is not running.

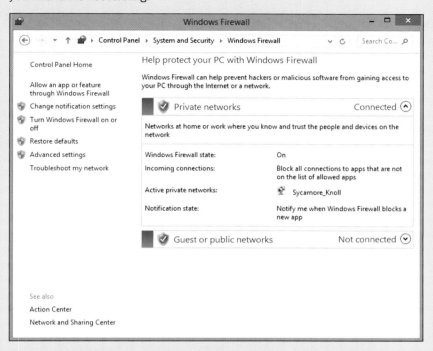

4. To change the settings, click the Allow a App or Feature Through Windows Firewall link on the left side. Windows will display a list of programs and note whether they are allowed or not.

5. Click Change Notification Settings to modify the list.

Encrypting Data

When you store data on a hard drive, the data is written such that it can be read by anyone who has access to the drive. That means if someone were to steal your computer, that person would have access to the data on your hard drive. Even if she did not have the password required to log on to your system, she could still access the contents of your hard drive simply by removing it from your computer and installing it on another machine.

encrypt To scramble the contents of a file so it cannot be read without the required permission to decrypt it..

decrypt To reverse the encryption of a file so that the file appears in its original form again.

Your data is vulnerable! Fortunately, there are ways to protect your data so that only you can access it. One method is to use encryption. Encryption involves using a mathematical process to scramble data to such an extent it is impossible to read . . . unless you have the key. The key unscrambles or decrypts the data so that it is readable again. When you use encryption on your computer, you work as normal; the encryption and decryption processes take place in the background.

As an extra layer of security, the NTFS file system can encrypt files. Encryption stores the files in a scrambled format, so that anyone browsing them from outside the operating system will see nothing useful. When an authorized user attempts to access them from within the operating system, the files are automatically decrypted (de-encrypted) and shown to the user as if they were not encrypted at all. NTFS's compression and encryption features are mutually exclusive; you cannot enable both at once for the same file or folder. Encryption is available only in the Pro and Enterprise versions of Windows 8.1 , so if you are using the standard Windows 8.1 edition, it will not be available.

BitLocker A whole-drive encryption utility provided with some editions of Windows.

Windows 8.1 Pro and Enterprise editions also offer a feature called BitLocker, a whole-drive encryption feature that makes a certain volume inaccessible if the physical drive is removed from its current computer and placed in a different computer. BitLocker prevents thieves from stealing data by taking the entire hard drive out of a computer.

CAUTION A risk of data loss exists whenever you use an encryption system; the data cannot be restored without the key, and if you lose the key, you lose your data. Therefore, if you use either of these systems, you should make sure you back up the data before encrypting it, and then the encryption keys after encryption. Check the documentation for that feature to find out how. Many people decide that the risk of data loss is more serious than any benefit they might get from enhanced privacy and decide not to use encryption.

Step by Step

Encrypting Individual Files Using EFS

If you only want to encrypt certain files, you can follow this process:

1. Open File Explorer.

2. Navigate to the file (or files) that you want to encrypt.

3. Select the file you want to encrypt. To select multiple files, use the Shift or Ctrl key as described in the section "Selecting Files and Folders" in Chapter 5, "Introduction to Windows 8.1."

4. Right-click one of the selected files and choose Properties from the menu that appears. The Properties dialog box opens.

5. In the General tab of the Properties dialog box, click the Advanced button. The Advanced Attributes dialog box opens.

6. Select the Encrypt Contents to Secure Data check box.

7. Click OK to close the Advanced Attributes dialog box.

8. Click OK again to close the Properties dialog box. A confirmation dialog box appears.

9. Choose Apply Changes to This folder Only, or choose Apply Changes to This Fold, Subfolders and Files.

   If you look in File Explorer, you'll see that the files you encrypted are now shown in green rather than black.

Encrypting the Hard Drive Using BitLocker

You can use the BitLocker program (in the Enterprise edition of Windows 7) to encrypt the entire hard drive. Follow these steps:

1. Right-click the Windows Start button and choose Control Panel.

2. In the Control Panel window, click the System and Security option.

3. In the System and Security window, click BitLocker Drive Encryption. You will see a list of all the hard drives in your system. If you have any USB drives plugged in, they will also be shown here.

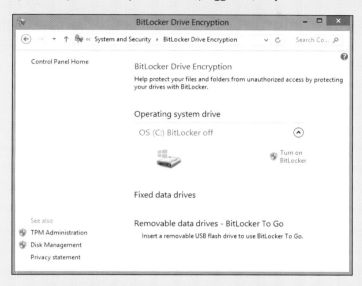

4. Click the Turn On BitLocker link next to the drive you want to encrypt. BitLocker will start.

5. When prompted, supply the password you want to use to decrypt the drive.

6. The system will generate a recovery key that can be used if you lose or forget the password. Print this key and save it somewhere safe, or save it to a file on another drive or device.

7. Click Next. The system is ready to encrypt the drive.

8. Click Start Encrypting, sit back, and wait. The bigger the drive, the longer it will take to encrypt. When the process is complete, the list of drives in the Control Panel will show your encrypted drive as "On" rather than "Off."

CAUTION   Don't save the recovery key on the hard drive you have just encrypted. You won't be able to read it if you lose the password!

Encrypting Internet Communications

In addition to encrypting your hard drive and the individual files on it, some websites enable you to encrypt your Internet communications. To determine whether an Internet connection is secure, check to see whether the URL starts with https rather than http and look for a padlock icon in the web browser's address bar. In some browsers the address bar might also appear with a green background when viewing a secure site. Those are all indicators of a secure connection between your computer and the website; data captured between the two points will be unreadable. (That said, see the Caution about the Heartbleed virus earlier in this chapter.)

Installing Operating System Updates

When you buy a computer, it usually comes with an operating system pre-installed so you can start work straightaway. The version of the operating system that is installed is typically the version that was available when the computer was manufactured. Operating systems are constantly being updated, however. For example, Microsoft is always looking for ways to improve its products. That means the version of the operating system installed on your computer might not be the most recent version available.

This would not necessarily be a problem, were it not for the fact that many of the improvements made to operating systems after their initial release pertain to fixing bugs and patching security holes—hence, the use of the word "patches" to describe these fixes. It's critical that you install updates to your computer's operating system (and to the programs that run on it) to ensure that all the most recent patches are applied.

service pack A collection of patches, released in a single package.

Software manufacturers can distribute a patch as a single update to a program or as a group of updates to several programs. Periodically, Microsoft groups several patches together and produces a package called a service pack. A service pack contains all the patches released either since the product was launched or since the last service pack was released. To determine whether any service packs have been installed on your Windows computer, open the Control Panel and click the System and Security option. Then click System to see the current status of your operating system. (See Figure 16.9.) If you do not see "Service Pack" as part of the Windows edition, you do not have any service packs installed.

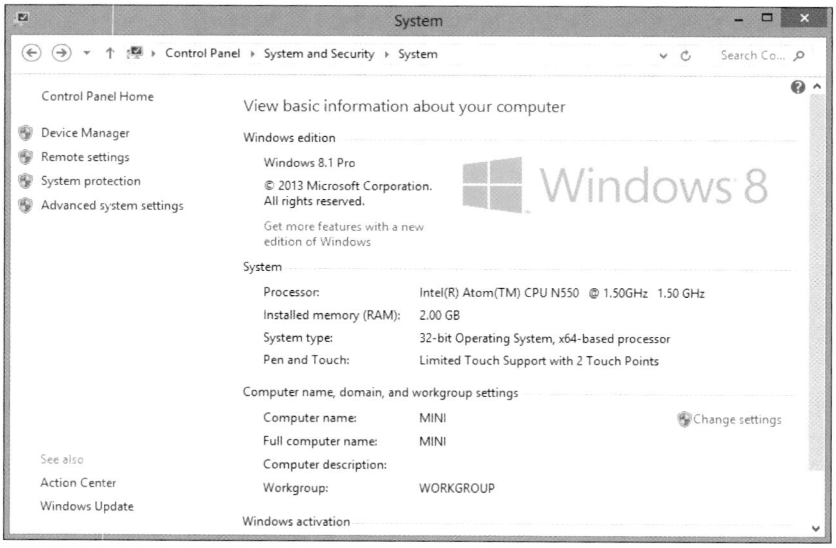

Figure 16.9   Windows 8.1 Pro.

Windows Update: A feature in Windows that automatically downloads and installs updates to Windows and optionally to some Microsoft applications.

To make it easier for you to keep your system up to date, Microsoft offers the Windows Update tool. To access it, open the Control Panel, click System and Security, and choose Windows Update. As shown in Figure 16.10, you can click on the links to choose from the following options:

- **Check for Updates:** Select this option to perform an immediate check for new updates.

- **Change Settings:** Choose this option to specify how and when updates are installed.

- **View Update History:** To see when updates were installed, select this option.

- **Restore Hidden Updates:** This option enables you to install updates that you have chosen not to install previously.

Figure 16.10   Using Windows Update to keep your system up to date.

The simplest way to manage updates is to allow your system to install them automatically; you can select that option by choosing Change Settings in the navigation bar at the left and then adjusting the settings on the Choose Your Windows Update Settings screen that appears. The default settings are to install updates automatically, at whatever time is indicated by the maintenance window. By default this is 2 a.m. If your computer is not powered up at that time, Windows will perform the update the next time you turn it on.

maintenance window The time specified for Windows to perform its daily maintenance tasks.

Step by Step

Changing the Maintenance Window

If you want your PC's maintenance window to be a time other than the default, follow these steps:

1. Right-click the Start button and choose Control Panel.

2. Click System and Security, and then click Action Center.

3. Click to expand the Maintenance heading's options if it is not already expanded.

4. Under Automatic Maintenance, click Change maintenance settings.

5. Change the Run maintenance tasks daily at setting.

6. Click OK.

Wiping Old Drives

In Chapter 5, "Introduction to Windows 8.1," you learned how to delete files. You may not have realized, however, that when you delete files from a computer, you do not delete the data in those files. Instead, you delete the information about where to find the data on the hard drive. Many software programs can recover files that have been deleted. That's good news if the files were deleted by mistake. But it's bad news if someone in possession of your hard drive—for example, someone who obtains it after you have disposed of it—uses one of these programs to recover files you deleted on purpose.

To permanently remove files from your hard drive, you must use a software program that erases the hard drive permanently and securely. These programs work by writing a series of patterns over the entire disk so that all existing data is overwritten and cannot be recovered. Several good programs perform this task. Some are even available free of charge, such as Active@ KillDisk for Windows (see Figure 16.11) and Eraser.

If you want to dispose of a hard drive, even if only to give it to a friend, it's important to remove all traces of personal information from the drive by running one of these programs on it beforehand. That way, you can be sure that the hard drive is blank, and there is no chance that anyone else could recover your data.

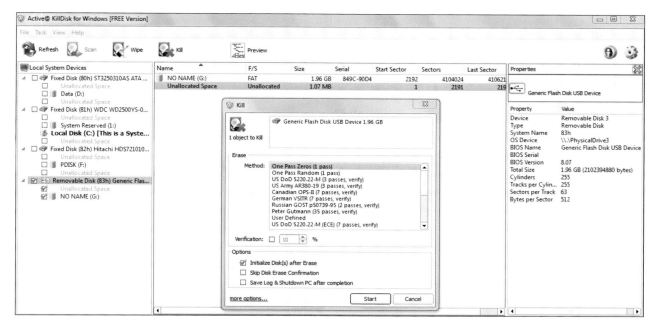

Figure 16.11   Using a disk eraser program.

Before you erase your hard disk, copy all the data on it to a new hard drive unless you are sure you no longer want this data. Once you start the overwriting process, you can't retrieve the data.

CAUTION

Quick Review

1. What are the characteristics of a strong password?

2. What level of access should you give others to your files and folders?

3. What does a firewall do?

4. What is needed to decrypt encrypted data?

Summary

Network and Internet Security Concerns

Computer crime is becoming increasingly common. It is essential that you be aware of computer security and take the necessary steps to secure your data and online identity.

Computer criminals engage in many types of activities that can compromise your computer system, your data, and your online identity. One of the common threats is **phishing**. In this type of attack, nefarious users try to trick unsuspecting users into giving away personal information such as login details or credit card information. Another threat is **spoofing**. In this type of attack, the attacker's computer assumes a false Internet address in order to gain access to a network. Attackers also use **sniffing** to capture copies of data packets as they travel across the network and decode their content.

Often, the goal of hackers or crackers is to obtain a user's password. To do so, they often attempt **password cracking**—that is, they attempt to identify a user's password. Password cracking can be accomplished in several ways, including guessing, using a **keylogger** to record the user's keystrokes, **social engineering**, sniffing, or using any one of a variety of password-cracking tools.

Many computer criminals employ **malware**—that is, malicious software—in their efforts to compromise a user's computer system, data, and online identity. There are several types of malware, including **viruses**, **worms**, **Trojans**, **spyware**, and **ransomware**. To protect yourself against malware, you must run a security program. Although these programs are often called "anti-virus programs," they have evolved over the years into a broader security solution that can detect and protect against viruses, worms, Trojans, and sometimes more complex threats. A good anti-virus package provides a wide range of protective measures and may include firewall management and anti-spyware. Many good anti-virus products are in the marketplace, including Symantec, Sophos, Kaspersky, and McAfee.

Anti-virus programs are less effective against **denial of service (DoS)** attacks. In this type of attack, the attacker floods a website or service with thousands of requests for access—so many that the site or service cannot deal with them all. As a result, legitimate users are prevented from accessing the site or service. The computers that launch these attacks are called zombies. A **zombie** is a computer that has been infected with a particular type of Trojan called a **bot**.

Users should also be wary of Wi-Fi networks. When Wi-Fi networks are not properly secured, it is easy to steal data on them with little chance of being caught. It's not just un-secure networks that pose a risk, however. Some wireless networks *appear* to be genuine, but in fact attempt to intercept your traffic. These types of Wi-Fi networks are called **rogue Wi-Fi**. Public places where many people are looking for Wi-Fi, such as coffee shops, restaurants, and airports, are common locations for rogue Wi-Fi connections.

Network and Internet Privacy Concerns

Using networks and the Internet can put your privacy at risk in a number of ways. For example, search engine sites can gather information about you based on the terms you search for and the questions you ask. In addition, websites for which you provide personal information, such as your name, address, email, and so forth, can store that information and perhaps use it for purposes other than those you intended. Finally, someone who ascertains the unique identity of your computer can use this information to access your computer via a network and view, change, or delete your personal data.

To protect people's privacy, most countries have data protection and privacy laws to control the access and distribution of this personal information. These laws regulate the companies that hold our personal information and ensure that all our information is properly protected.

Of course, just because there are laws designed to protect your privacy online does not mean that you should not take additional steps to keep yourself safe. As a first step, you should determine what personal information is available online by conducting a search for your name. You should also take care when using **social media** to avoid sharing information about yourself that would be better kept private. Another strategy is to delete **cookies** from your computer. That way, no one can use your cookies in a malicious way.

Strategies for Improving Security

You can take many steps to improve security. One step is to restrict access to your computer and data by using strong passwords, applying permissions, and enabling **firewalls**. You can also use **encryption** to scramble the data on your hard drive, thereby preventing others from being able to read it.

It's important that you run the most up-to-date version of your operating system. That way, as manufacturers fix bugs and patch security holes, you ensure that all the most recent patches are applied. To make it easier for you to keep your system up to date, Microsoft offers the Windows Update tool, which performs automatic updates to the operating system. Using this tool, you can check for new updates, change the automatic update settings, view your update history, and more.

If you want to dispose of data you have on a hard drive, even if only to give your computer to a friend, you must remove all traces of personal information from the drive. To do so, simply run a special software program that is designed to permanently erase the contents of your hard drive. These programs work by writing a series of patterns over the entire disk so that all existing data is overwritten and cannot be recovered.

Key Terms

bot	service pack
botnet	service set identification (SSID)
cookie	sniffing
cyberbullying	social engineering
database	social network
decrypt	spoofing
denial of service (DoS) attack	spyware
encrypt	Trojan
firewall	virus
keylogger	Wi-Fi Protected Access (WPA)
maintenance window	Wi-Fi Protected Setup (WPS)
malware	Windows Update
password cracking	Wired Equivalent Privacy (WEP)
phishing	worm
ransomware	WPA2
rogue Wi-Fi	zombie

Test Yourself

Fact Check

1. Which of the following describes a computer falsely reporting its identity to gain access to another computer?

   a. phishing

   b. sniffing

   c. spoofing

   d. spamming

2. Which of the following types of malware is likely to use your address book to spread itself to other computers?

   a. virus

   b. Trojan

   c. spam

   d. worm

3. Which of the following would be the strongest password?

   a. August23

   b. birmingham

   c. NewYork

   d. M3rll n@t

4. Which of the following programs can be used to encrypt certain files within the file system?

   a. TPM

   b. Drivecrypt

   c. BitLocker

   d. Encrypted File System (EFS)

5. An email that requests you provide personal information but is not from the company it represents itself to be from is an example of _____.

   a. phishing

   b. spoofing

   c. logging

   d. sniffing

6. _____ is the practice of trying to get information from people using non-technical means.

   a. Sniffing

   b. Spoofing

   c. Encrypting

   d. Social engineering

7. Which of the following is the best approach to controlling access to data?

   a. Give users as much access as they need.

   b. Only give users the minimum access they need.

   c. Allow users to decide how much access they need.

   d. Don't give users any access.

8. A _____ attack is an attempt to prevent users from accessing a website.

   a. denial of service

   b. social engineering

   c. phishing

   d. spoofing

9. True or False: Your computer should have anti-virus software and a firewall installed.

   a. true

   b. false

10. What is the safest way to ensure your privacy when disposing of an old computer?

   a. Ensure you have a copy of all the files before disposal.

   b. Copy your files and then pass the computer on to a friend you trust.

   c. Copy your files to the new computer and then delete the files on the old one.

   d. Copy your files and then erase the disk using a suitable program.

Matching

Match the security threat to its definition.

   a. spoofing

   b. phishing

   c. password cracking

   d. virus

   e. Trojan

   f. worm

   g. rogue Wi-Fi network

1. _____The act of attempting to acquire information such as usernames, passwords, credit card information, and so forth, by pretending to be from a genuine, trustworthy source such as a bank.

2. _____A malicious computer program that spreads itself to other computers over a network or the Internet.

3. _____A wireless network that "sniffs" traffic, making a copy of everything users type—including usernames, passwords, and credit card numbers.

4. _____The act of attempting to identify a user's password in order to gain access to a system or program.

5. _____A piece of malicious software that looks harmless but has a detrimental effect on a computer when it runs.

6. _____Malicious software that copies itself (replicates) to other programs on the same computer to "infect" them.

7. _____An attack in which a user pretends to be another by providing false IP address data.

Sum It Up

1. List four types of activities that computer criminals engage in.

2. Why is it important to have an active firewall either on your computer or at the edge of your network (or both)?

3. How many different types of threats can be detected by security solution software products?

4. Why do you need to be careful when using Wi-Fi in public places?

5. Why is sniffing a threat?

6. What are the effects of a denial of service attack?

Explore More

Keeping Your System Up to Date

Explore your computer to check how up-to-date it is. Does it have a service pack installed? Run the Windows Update process to see if there are any uninstalled updates. Is there a reason why you have not installed them?

Protecting Yourself against Malware

Identify what type of anti-virus solution you have in place. Every package has its own control panel for administration. Open this panel and see how often the software checks the Internet for updates. Carry out a manual scan of your computer.

What Are the Latest Threats?

Visit the website of one of the anti-virus software providers and look at what the latest threats are and how recent they are. Identify how many pieces of malware have been discovered in the last seven days.

Think It Over

Planning for Security

Imagine that you are going to purchase a new computer running a Windows operating system. Thinking of security, what steps would you take to ensure that the computer is secure from unauthorized users and that your data is protected against loss or damage? Think of any software programs you may install to provide additional protection and compare the features of the different products to identify which would be best for your situation.

Chapter 17

Legal, Ethical, Health, and Environmental Issues in Computing

Learning objectives

☐ Be aware of the legal issues that arise from using computers and the Internet

☐ Understand how to use the Internet in an ethical manner

☐ Understand the potential impact on health when using a computer

☐ Be aware of what to consider when disposing of a computer

This chapter moves beyond the technical aspects of working with computers and software to examine the legal and ethical issues related to computer use. These issues range from the legal ownership of online content to the ethical options for acquiring and using software, as well as what is appropriate (and inappropriate) online activity. This chapter also covers various health risks posed by computer use and the appropriate methods for disposing of computer hardware.

Legal Issues in Computing

Nearly everything we do in life is governed by laws of one sort or another. Not surprisingly, these laws extend to cover our use of computers and the Internet. Legal issues in computing are complex, however. Whereas we are usually governed by the laws of the country in which we reside, the Internet is global, and different countries have different laws. That means you might access Internet content in your web browser that is regulated by local law, but the content itself is hosted on a server in another jurisdiction, and as such is governed by another set of rules. What is legal in one country is not necessarily legal in another, so you could end up unwittingly being guilty of an offense. For example, in some countries, online gambling is legal, and citizens may both participate in online gambling and host their own gambling sites. In other countries not only is it illegal to host an online gambling site, but it is also illegal for citizens of that country to use an online gambling site hosted in a country where it is legal.

Intellectual Property

Intellectual property (IP), also called intellectual property rights (IPR), is a legal term that grants people the exclusive rights to the ownership of content that they have created. "Created" is the important word here. This can apply to tangible items, such a book, as well as to ideas that have been documented, such as patents, artistic works, photographs, and music.

IP has evolved over many years and can now be applied to certain aspects of computing and the Internet. For example, suppose you design a web page or produce some written material for a website. Depending on the nature of the material (and on any agreements you have in place with others), you may have the exclusive rights to use it because you created it. In effect, it belongs to you. Intellectual property provides protection for the owner of the material.

Copyright Laws

Copyright is a subset of intellectual property but differs in interpretation and use. Copyright is a legal protection that usually gives the creator of a work—be it written or artistic—exclusive rights to its use and distribution for a limited time period. For example, when an author writes a book, he might choose to obtain the copyright for that book. Then, the author (and his descendants) will be entitled to royalties from the sale of the book until the copyright expires. In many countries, a work's copyright lasts for the duration of the creator's lifetime plus an additional 50 years after his death. (Note that in some cases, a book's publisher might hold the copyright on the work, depending on the agreement struck by the author. Note, too, that copyright can be limited to geographical boundaries unless there is some form of international agreement between the parties.)

There is no symbol to identify IP, but when something is copyrighted, you will usually see the © symbol along with the copyright owner's name and sometimes a year. For example, if you look inside the front cover of this book, you will see the following copyright: ©2014 John Wiley & Sons, Ltd. Copyright has become difficult to enforce with the advent of digital media and the Internet, which make it easy to download and redistribute material. Unless some form of digital rights management (DRM) is in use, it is impossible to enforce copyright law over so many jurisdictions. (You'll learn more about DRM in the next section.)

Digital Rights Management

Digital rights management (DRM) involves the use of technology to control access to copyrighted material. It is a practical attempt to address the growing problem of the unauthorized copying and distribution of material. The practice of distributing digital content over the Internet via file-sharing networks has made the enforcement of traditional copyright laws difficult.

Imagine you want to download a copyrighted music track. Normally, you would do so by purchasing it. In essence, when you purchase the track, you pay for the right to access it, with part of the purchase price being paid to the author or artist in the form of royalties. If you were to instead download the track illegally from a free peer-to-peer sharing site, you would defraud the author or artist of her royalties.

DRM helps to prevent such illegal downloads. DRM allows for access verification to protected material. To access DRM-protected material, the user needs a username and password, which are stored in a database. When the user attempts to access the material, his credentials are checked against the database, and the user is granted or denied access accordingly. Once access is granted, the user can access the content, but there may be restrictions on what actions he can carry out.

In other cases, DRM helps to prevent already downloaded files from being widely shared with others. For example, iTunes downloads can be burned to an audio CD a limited number of times, can be placed only on portable devices that are registered to the signed-in user, and will not play if manually copied to another computer.

Some software vendors use DRM to allow document authors to protect content created with the software. Access to a document may be restricted by requiring anyone who opens the file to log into a DRM server online. Figure 17.1 shows an example of such a login screen.

digital rights management (DRM) The use of technology to control access to copyrighted material.

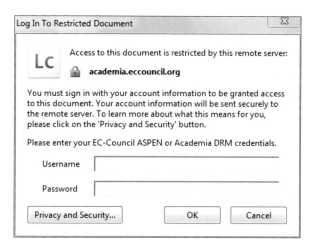

Figure 17.1 Using digital rights management.

Opponents of DRM

DRM is not without controversy. Indeed, many organizations and computer scientists are opposed to the practice. Some argue that the use of DRM restricts users' access from using content they have rightfully purchased as they see fit. For example, DRM prevents legitimate users from making personal copies of materials, lending copies to friends, and so on. In addition, DRM may on occasion prevent legitimate users from accessing their content. Finally, many argue that the use of DRM is pointless, as more often than not, users are able to crack the codes used to secure content.

Software Licensing

When you install an operating system or software program, one of the first stages of the process is to agree to its terms and conditions. These terms and conditions are presented in a legal document called an End User License Agreement (EULA), the end user being you. The EULA defines what you as a user can and cannot do with the product you are about to install.

End User License Agreement (EULA) A legal document that grants you permission to use a piece of software.

These agreements, when displayed, often take up more than one screen. That means you'll often need to use a scroll bar to read the entire agreement. When you get to the bottom of the screen, you will typically see a check box or option button, as shown in Figure 17.2, which you select to accept the agreement. You will not be able to proceed to the next stage of the install until you accept the agreement. If you choose not to accept the terms and conditions, you won't be permitted to install the software. It may take a few minutes to read through the terms and conditions, but it's a good idea to do so, so you will know what you can and cannot legally do with the software.

Figure 17.2   A typical end user license agreement.

What are you agreeing to? This depends on the nature of the product and the terms the vendor defines. Here are a few points to keep in mind:

- Usually you are "granted the rights to use" a particular software program, not necessarily "granted ownership" of the software in question.

- Sometimes when you purchase software, you may be required to pay an annual fee to use it. In this case, your license would grant you access to the product only until the renewal date. For example, Adobe CC and Office 365 are both subscription-based.

- You normally have explicit use of one copy of the software. That means you can download and run it, but you cannot make copies and install it on another computer, nor can you make copies and distribute them to your friends.

For most vendors, licensing is a way of ensuring that they collect revenue for the products they offer. Vendors also use licensing to ensure that if people use the software to break any laws, it is the user who is in trouble, not the vendor.

NOTE

Product Activation

During installation, some products require you not only to agree to the terms and conditions, but also to enter a license code or key to activate the product. This key can be sent by email as part of the registration process. Alternatively, it could be provided on a printed card as part of a physical software package.

Many products, particularly the more expensive ones like Microsoft Office, also require online activation. This calls for an active Internet connection. Online activation adds the license key to a database of active licenses, maintained by the software vendor. This prevents someone from using the same code again to license the software more than once, thus breaking the terms of the single user license.

Types of Software and Licensing

Software vendors offer different types of software. Some software vendors offer proprietary software—that is, software you can use but do not own, and whose source code is kept private. Other vendors offer open-source software—that is, software that is free to use, and whose source code is accessible and can be altered by any user with the appropriate programming skills. For more information about each of these types of software and their legal ramifications, read on.

Proprietary Software

Proprietary software is software you can use but do not own. The vendor retains ownership; you simply have the right to use one or more copies of the software after purchasing it and agreeing to the EULA. The source code used in this type of software is kept private. That is, users are not permitted to access and/or change the code.

proprietary software Software to which the vendor retains ownership rights. Users merely have usage rights.

Products such as Microsoft Office are licensed in this way. For example, if you purchase a copy of Microsoft Office Home and Student, you are allowed to run one licensed copy of the software on a single computer for the life of the PC. It is possible to transfer the license to another computer, but there are restrictions.

Even with a basic computer—one that you use at home or at college—you must consider how you manage the licensing. For example, to use a computer with Microsoft Office, you would need to have the following:

- A valid license to use the operating system
- A valid license to use Microsoft Office

Fortunately, the process of agreeing to licenses is usually automatic, so it is not something you have to spend too much time on.

Trial Software

Some vendors enable users to download a free trial version of a proprietary software program. When you do, you still have to agree to the terms and conditions, and you only get to use the software for a short period of time—typically from 7 to 30 days. You may also find that the trial version is a scaled-down version of the full program, without all the features. In other words, certain aspects of the full-version software don't function. The idea behind the trial software is for you to evaluate the software and see if it is the right product for you. At the end of the trial period, if you want to continue using the software, you will be asked to purchase a license. If so, you will be sent a code to activate the product.

Open-Source Software

open-source software Free access to a software program and the source code that produced the program.

There is a growing movement toward producing open-source software—that is, software that is not only free to use, but also whose source code is accessible to users to modify and redistribute. You may be wondering, why is it free? What's in it for the software developers? The answer is simple: The open-source movement is all about promoting freedoms and removing licensing restrictions. The theory is that by allowing the free distribution of software that can be enhanced by others, the computer world benefits from having consistently improved products—and from that, we *all* benefit.

General Public License (GPL) A license used for many types of open-source software, allowing the software to be legally copied and modified.

Although open-source software is about removing licensing restrictions, many types of open-source software do carry a license, called the General Public License (GPL). The GPL—developed by an organization called the Free Software Foundation, that exists to support the creation and distribution of free software—is a simply worded license that enables individuals and companies to legally copy and modify software. This gives users much greater freedom with the product, allowing them to make as many copies as they like, installing it on all their computers, distributing it to friends, and, of course, making changes to the source code if they so desire.

Software Piracy

Software piracy is the unauthorized copying of software programs. There are various types of software piracy:

software piracy The unauthorized copying and distribution of software.

- **Counterfeit software.** Counterfeit software is a copy of a legitimate product that is made and marketed as an original. With counterfeit software, the media and packaging may look genuine, but only because the software has been copied and packaged to look like the original. It is sometimes difficult to tell the difference between the genuine article and a fake. Counterfeit software is even easier to sell over the Internet—particularly software that is downloadable rather than distributed on a physical disc. This type of software is often sold on sites that appear to be authorized, but if you look closely, you can usually spot clues that the site is not legitimate, such as a slightly different spelling in the URL, grammar or usage errors that indicate a non-native speaker may have created the page, or blurry or incorrect logos.

- **Corporate piracy.** Often, a company or organization will purchase software in a legitimate way, but install the software on more machines than it is supposed to. For example, a company might buy software with 50 licenses but install it on 100 computers. This practice, which can save corporations many thousands or even millions of dollars, is called "corporate piracy." It may seem benign, but it is in fact a form of theft.

- **Unbundling packages.** When you purchase a computer or notebook, it frequently comes as an original equipment manufacturer (OEM) bundle. For example, the operating system comes preloaded on the computer and is licensed to that particular computer. If the bundle comes with a backup copy of the operating system on DVD and the owner sells that copy to someone else, this breaks the terms of the license and is a form of piracy.

- **Internet piracy.** There are many Internet sites where copyrighted software can be illegally downloaded free or at low cost. These sites even give users guidance on where to obtain the license key information necessary to use the program, or produce fake keys themselves. This is Internet piracy. With so many sites and so much software available, Internet piracy is virtually unstoppable. Much of the illegal software is published in countries where the necessary laws are not strongly enforced. Sites that offer these illegal activities sometimes contain malware that can infect your computer when you download from them.

Next time you accept an offer of some software from a friend, ask yourself these questions:

CAUTION

1. Has it come from a genuine source?
2. Is it okay to share this software with others?
3. Is it licensed for more than one computer?

You could quite easily break the law by accepting the software and using it. Remember, though, that ignorance is not a legal defense.

Quick Review

1. What is the difference between intellectual property and copyright?

2. When you have purchased proprietary software, who owns the software?

3. What is the advantage of using open-source software?

Ethical Issues in Computing

With computing comes several ethical issues—particularly with regard to the Internet. These range from plagiarism to censorship, libel, slander, and beyond.

Plagiarism

plagiarism The act of copying someone else's work and pretending that it is your own.

Plagiarism is the practice of copying someone else's work and pretending that it is your own. Thanks to the Internet, it is all too easy to download a document from an obscure website and submit or republish it as yours.

Plagiarism comes in several forms:

- Copying work produced by someone else word for word and presenting it as your own

- Inserting portions of someone else's work into your own and claiming full credit

- Changing a few words and phrases of a piece of work so it looks different but is based on someone else's work

- Taking material from multiple sources and putting it all together as your own work

Plagiarism has become a big problem in colleges and universities. Often, when students receive assignments, they simply research on the Internet, copy large blocks of text from various sources, stitch them together into a single document, and pass the result off as their own work. Even worse, some students patronize any one of several Internet-based companies that write assignments for them.

Using Citations

citation A reference to a source—that is, to the author and name of a published or unpublished work—following a quotation from said source.

It is not always wrong to use someone else's work. In many cases, you can quote or paraphrase (discussed next) someone else's work in your own piece—provided you include a reference to the source (in other words, to the author and name of the work). This is called a citation. Including a citation to give credit to the original author of a piece of work is the only way to avoid plagiarism.

footnote Information about the source of a quote, which is marked with a number and appears at the bottom of the page.

Citations generally appear in footnote form. A footnote contains information about the source of the text being quoted, appearing at the bottom of the page that contains the text in question. The quote is marked with a small number, which is then repeated next to the footnote. This enables the reader to match the footnote with the quote. Another way to cite sources is with a bibliography, which is a list of the sources you reference.

bibliography A list of the sources referenced in a document, commonly used in academic writing.

As an alternative to footnotes, there are endnotes. These appear at the end of a chapter or document rather than at the bottom of a page. They contain the same content as footnotes, however.

Step by Step

Inserting a Footnote in a Word Document

To insert a footnote in a Microsoft Word document, follow these steps:

1. Click at the end of the quoted or paraphrased material in your document. Then click on the References tab. Finally, click the Insert Footnote button. This adds a superscript numeral to the right of the quoted material and moves the cursor to the bottom of the page, where the number is repeated.

2. Type the citation, including the author's name and the name of the work being quoted. (Note that the format of the citation may vary. If you are working on an assignment, ask your professor or supervisor for details.)

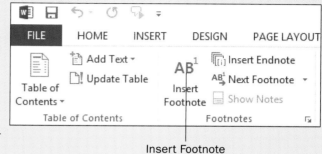

Insert Footnote

3. To insert additional footnotes, repeat Steps 1 and 2. As you do, the footnote number will increment.

You can also use footnotes to supply other information about the text. For example, you might use a footnote to supply the full title of a book to which the text refers, as shown in Figure 17.3, or to fill in additional details about the topic at hand.

> Any number of shutter speeds and apertures will get you a "correct" exposure of 0. Which one should you use? The book Understanding Exposure [1] by Bryan Peterson is a great resource. After you've mastered Aperture Priority and Shutter Priority modes, get this book and read it cover to cover. It gave me a
>
> ---
> [1] Understanding Exposure 3rd Edition (2010)

Figure 17.3 A footnote example.

Paraphrasing

In addition to quoting an author directly, you can paraphrase what he or she writes. When you paraphrase, you use different words to convey the same idea. Even so, you still must include a citation to acknowledge that the original idea came from someone else.

paraphrase To use different words to convey the same idea.

Combating Plagiarism

Recent years have seen the development of a range of anti-plagiarism software products, such as turnitin (www.turnitin.com). These programs compare a submitted document against a large database of quotes and texts. Mathematical processes check not only for actual word-for-word plagiarism, but also for paraphrased text where it can identify the original source. The results then highlight any suspect or copied areas in text and state where citations should be applied.

Using software like this, it takes only a few seconds to examine a document. Some educational institutions use this type of software as standard practice for all work handed in by students. Students can also use this type of software before turning in an assignment to ensure they have not inadvertently plagiarized.

Censorship and Filtering

censorship The act of suppressing speech or not allowing certain communications to be made public.

Censorship is the act of preventing something from being printed or heard. Historically, censorship has been used to prevent important information from reaching the population at large by controlling what can be printed or broadcast. Censorship is sometimes implemented by governments so they can control the flow of information for political or military reasons. For example, writing that is deemed to be obscene or advocates that citizens break the country's existing laws might be censored. Individuals or companies can also apply forms of censorship by not allowing certain types of information to be published. For example, if you post a negative review of a product on the manufacturer's website, your view may be deleted; this is an example of corporate censorship.

filtering Preventing something from getting through—in this case, content.

Filtering is a form of censorship performed by software. Filtering means to prevent something from getting through. For example, when you filter water, you remove all the impurities, making it safe to drink. Similarly, when you filter the Internet, you exclude certain categories of content from general access. For example, a parent might install web filtering software on a child's computer to prevent the child from accessing websites with graphic violent content, or a coffee shop might use filtering to prevent its patrons from accessing adult-themed sites when using the store's Internet connection. Companies also may filter their employees' web usage at work, such as blocking social networking sites like Facebook to improve productivity.

proxy server A server that sits between the user's web browser and the Internet that intercepts all requests for web pages and processes those requests.

Web filtering is accomplished by using a proxy server—that is, a server that sits between the user's web browser and the Internet and manages all requests for content. Proxy servers work as follows:

1. The user types a URL or clicks a link in her web browser in an attempt to visit a web page.

2. The web browser sends a request for the page to the proxy server.

3. The proxy server fetches the requested page on the Internet and passes it back to the user's web browser, or lets the user know that the page cannot be displayed, depending on the proxy server's filtering settings.

When users attempt to access a filtered site, a message is displayed in their browser, notifying them that the request is denied. Figure 17.4 shows a list of blocked site categories on a proxy server.

Search URL blacklist

☑ ads	☑ adult	☑ aggressive	☑ antispyware	☑ artnudes	☑ astrology	☑ audio-video	☑ banking
☑ beerliquorinfo	☑ beerliquorsale	☑ blog	☑ cellphones	☑ chat	☑ childcare	☑ cleaning	☑ clothing
☑ culinary	☑ dating	☑ desktopsillies	☑ dialers	☑ drugs	☑ ecommerce	☑ entertainment	☑ filehosting
☑ financial	☑ frencheducation	☑ gambling	☑ games	☑ gardening	☑ government	☑ hacking	☑ homerepair
☑ hygiene	☑ instantmessaging	☑ jewelry	☑ jobsearch	☑ kidstimewasting	☑ mail	☑ marketingware	☑ medical
☑ mixed_adult	☑ mobile-phone	☑ naturism	☑ news	☑ onlineauctions	☑ onlinegames	☑ onlinepayment	☑ personalfinance
☑ pets	☑ phishing	☑ porn	☑ proxy	☑ radio	☑ reaffected	☑ religion	☑ ringtones
☑ searchengines	☑ sexual_education	☑ sexuality	☑ shopping	☑ socialnetworking	☑ sportnews	☑ sports	☑ spyware
☑ test	☑ updatesites	☑ vacation	☑ verisign	☑ violence	☑ virusinfected	☑ warez	☑ weapons
☑ weather	☑ webmail	☑ whitelist					

Figure 17.4   A list of blocked categories on a proxy server.

You can apply filtering using any or all of the following criteria:

- Block access to certain websites based on their URLs

- Block access to certain websites based on the actual content of the web pages

- Prevent certain users from accessing certain websites

- Restrict access based on time of day

- Restrict access based on categories of content

Flaming

Most likely, when you use chat rooms or social networks or comment on websites, you interact quite happily with other users. Occasionally, however, you may find that some users become quite hostile. This happens frequently on sites like YouTube, which gives users the option to post comments, and on social networking sites like Facebook. Some of the comments become negative and personal, complete with insults and swear words. This is called flaming. When the negativity escalates as more comments are posted, it is known as a flame war.

flaming Where Internet users interact in a hostile way with each other.

Libel and Slander

Libel and slander are similar in that both are statements that can cause damage to someone's reputation.

Libel is the act of putting a false and defamatory statement in writing. Any false statement that could damage the reputation of an individual or organization could be considered to be libel. Because it is written, it can have a lasting effect on the individual or company being libeled. For example, a libelous comment published on Twitter and then retweeted to others could spread quickly. It would be difficult to control the spread and to undo the damage caused. In most countries, libel is a civil offense. That means the person or organization being libeled would have to take

libel Putting in writing a defamatory statement that could damage a person's or organization's reputation.

legal action to obtain any form of compensation or redress. For libel to be upheld, it must be proved that the statement is untrue.

Slander is the verbal version of libel. Slander might consist of negative comments about an individual or group that are made as part of a phone or face-to-face conversation; in the digital world, it may include slanderous comments made on an online-published video or in a group video conference. The effect is just as damaging to the reputation of the target individual.

slander Making a defamatory verbal statement that could damage a person's or organization's reputation.

Spamming

Spam—that is, unsolicited or "junk" email, typically containing offers (some legitimate, some not) for electronic goods, drugs, software, and so on—is a major problem on the Internet. These emails are sent in bulk, bombarding thousands if not millions of users at a time. There are varying estimates of how much email is spam, but most put the number at 80% or more. Although most email programs include a junk email filter, many of these emails still slip through to fill users' inboxes, as shown in Figure 17.5. As a result, users waste valuable time reading and deleting unwanted messages.

spam Unsolicited "junk" mail, typically containing offers (some legitimate, some not) of products or services to buy.

☐ SpeedDate	View pics of singles - chat with ... ↓	27/04/2014
☐ Prime Scrat...	Your account has been credited ...	25/04/2014
☐ Prime Scratch Cards	Your account has been credited ...	22/04/2014
☐ Jenna	Hello Shelagh, I have some mor... !	21/04/2014
☐ Match.com	See Who's on Match.com - It's ... ↓	20/04/2014
☐ First PREMIER Bank	First PREMIER Bank MasterCard ... ↓	18/04/2014
☐ Houzz Updates	Elements of Contemporary Bathr...	16/03/2014
☐ Paul Asadoorian	Webcasts: Expose the monsters l...	27/02/2014
☐ Houzz Updates	Kitchen Backsplash 101	Create...	16/02/2014

Figure 17.5   Examples of spam.

Typically, spammers use mailing lists to send these unwanted messages. A mailing list is simply a list of email addresses. Sending an email to a mailing list is no more difficult than sending it to a single recipient. You don't have to type all the individual email addresses in; you just type the name of the mailing list. Often, spammers purchase these mailing lists from companies that sell them. Additionally, software programs, called mail harvesters, also collect email addresses over the Internet, which spammers then compile into mailing lists.

Not all email received from a business is spam. Businesses with whom you have a previous relationship, such as a store where you have ordered before, might send you promotional emails because you have given them your email address. You can unsubscribe from such emails with the Unsubscribe link provided in the email. Beware, however, of using the Unsubscribe link in a generic mass email that you get from a company that you have no relationship with. Sometimes unscrupulous spammers use the Unsubscribe link to confirm that their message has reached an active email address, and trying to unsubscribe will only get you added to more spammers' lists.

Is spamming legal? It depends on what country you are in. In the United States, spam is legal, provided the message conforms to certain formats. What is most definitely *not* legal is when spam encourages recipients to visit fake websites and share personal information. That's when spam becomes phishing.

Quick Review

1. Why do people use citations?

2. What is the difference between libel and slander?

3. What role does a proxy server play?

Health Issues in Computing

Using computers brings with it a host of health issues, from eyestrain to back and limb problems. The stress and strain placed on a human body while using a computer can cause discomfort and pain and can lead to long-term medical conditions if not addressed. To confront these problems, users can pay special attention to their work environment, using good posture, ergonomic furniture, and appropriate lighting.

Combating Eyestrain

When you use your computer, your eyes focus at a fixed distance on a small area (your screen) for a considerable period of time. They were not designed to do this, however. As a result, many computer users end up with eyestrain, which can lead to blurring or headaches.

Here are a few tips for combating eyestrain:

- Have regular eye examinations. If you have corrective eyewear, use it while working at the computer.

- Situate your computer monitor such that it is 20 to 40 inches (50 to 100 centimeters) from your face, with your eyes just above the center of the screen. If necessary, adjust the angle of the screen. (Adjusting the height and angle of your monitor will also help to protect your neck and shoulders.)

- Use incandescent rather than fluorescent lighting in your work area, because fluorescent lighting tends to flicker more. If you cannot avoid fluorescent lighting, avoid working directly underneath the light fixture if possible.

- Position your monitor so that bright light does not shine directly on it, to reduce glare.

- Use a flat-screen LCD monitor instead of the older CRT type. If you cannot avoid using a CRT, set its refresh rate to at least 100 Hz in the display settings in your operating system.

- Take frequent breaks. Avoid sitting in front of your monitor for more than an hour at a time.

- When you take a break, exercise your eyes. That is, look at items at different distances so your eyes get used to focusing normally again. Another way to exercise your eyes is to follow the 20-20-20 rule. That is, every 20 minutes, look away from the screen at something 20 feet away for 20 seconds. This prevents the eye muscles from being in the same position for too long.

In addition, to prevent eyestrain, opt for as large a screen as possible (19 inches, or 48 centimeters, is a good bet), and decrease the screen resolution so that icons and text appear larger. That way, you won't have to strain to see them. A lower resolution may make the display on an LCD monitor appear fuzzy, so you may have to balance between resolution and sharpness. However, in Windows 7 and higher, you can increase the size of icons and text without decreasing the display resolution. You can also adjust the brightness and contrast of your display to reduce eyestrain.

Step by Step

Changing Your Screen Resolution

To change your screen's resolution, follow these steps:

1. Right-click the desktop in Windows and choose Screen Resolution.

2. Click the Resolution drop-down list. Then, drag the slider that appears to adjust the resolution.

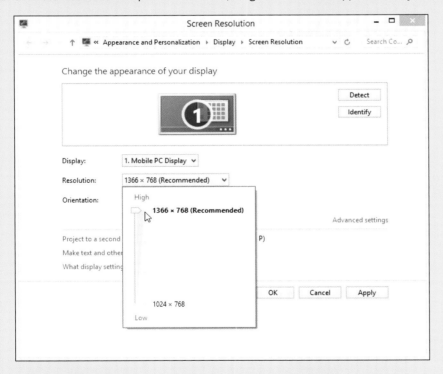

3. To see how the selected resolution looks, click the Apply button.

4. If you like the change, click the Keep Changes button in the dialog box that appears. Otherwise, click Revert, and repeat Steps 3 and 4 as needed.

5. When you are satisfied with the resolution, click the OK button to close the Screen Resolution screen.

Changing the Size of Icons and Text

To change the size of icons and text without changing your screen's resolution, do the following:

1. Right-click the desktop and choose Screen Resolution.

2. Click the Make text and other items larger or smaller hyperlink.

3. Mark the Let me choose one scaling level for all my displays check box.

4. Click one of the available option buttons to change the size of text and other items. (Here, Smaller is chosen.) Then click the Apply button. You'll be prompted to log off your computer and log back on to implement the change.

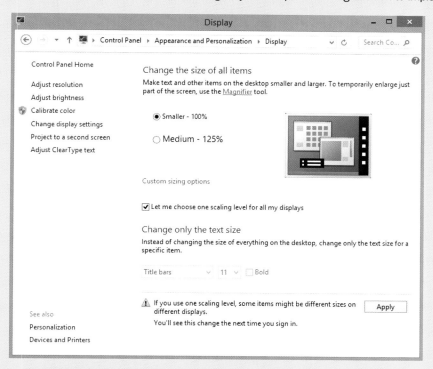

Adjusting the Screen Brightness

To adjust the screen's brightness, follow these steps:

1. Right-click the Start button and choose Control Panel to open the Control Panel window.

2. In the Control Panel window, click the Hardware and Sound heading.

3. Click the Power Options heading.

4. Drag the Screen Brightness slider, located at the bottom of the window, to adjust the brightness.

5. Close the Control Panel window.

Easing Your Back and Upper Limbs

Everything we do depends on our back. If our back is injured or out of alignment, it affects our ability to perform even the most mundane tasks. And yet, the back is arguably the most abused part of the body. This is because we fail to adopt the correct position when we perform certain activities, such as lifting heavy items. Even sitting down must be done correctly to ensure back health.

Unfortunately, too many computer users suffer from back problems because they fail to care for their back while they work. Computer users are also subject to sore fingers, aching shoulders, tired arms, and injured elbows. Often, permanent damage is done. For help preventing this, read on.

Using Good Posture

posture How a person sits or stands. When someone has good posture, the body is straight and the spine is correctly aligned.

Posture refers to how we sit or stand. When using your computer (or doing anything else), it's critical that you use good posture. Otherwise, you put too much strain on your body.

A good working posture is one in which the body's position can be maintained with minimal physical effort. Your body should be relaxed. This allows you to maintain your position for longer, without putting strain on the body. Here are some hallmarks of good posture:

- The lower back is supported by the shape of the chair.
- The head is up and level.
- The upper arms are relaxed.
- The forearms are at a right angle with the upper arms.
- The wrists are in a straight line with the hands and forearms.
- The knees are level with the hips and the thighs are horizontal.
- The feet are flat on the floor (or resting on a platform or footrest).

For best results, obtain an adjustable chair. Then use it to adjust your position while seated—leaning slightly backward for a while, and then slightly forward. Moving around in this way will help reduce strain on your body. (Regardless of how good your posture is, it is not wise to sit in the same position for too long!) An adjustable table or monitor stand can also help, enabling you to position the monitor correctly, as well as promote the correct placement for your forearms and wrists.

TIP To prevent neck strain, position your monitor directly in front of you on the desk, not at an angle off to one side.

Compare Figure 17.6 with Figure 17.7. The person in Figure 17.6 is leaning forward, with his feet dangling in an unnatural position. This puts strain on the rest of his body. In contrast, the person in Figure 17.7 is more upright, and his feet are resting on the floor. His spine is in correct alignment.

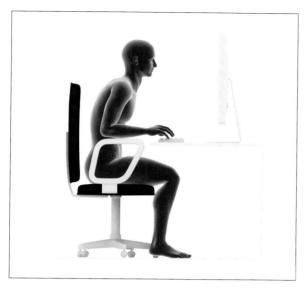

© iStockphoto.com/angelhell

Figure 17.6   Poor posture.

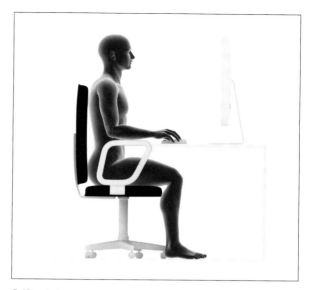

© iStockphoto.com/angelhell

Figure 17.7   Correct posture.

Even if you use perfect posture, you should take frequent breaks to maintain back health. Get up and stretch every 1-2 hours, at a minimum. Taking frequent breaks will also help you minimize stress and fatigue.

TIP

Positioning Your Desk and Chair

Desk and chair height can make a big difference in your body's comfort. For best results, think parallel lines. Adjust the desk and chair height so that when you sit up straight at the desk, your thighs are parallel to the floor and both feet are flat on the floor. Adjust the keyboard and mouse heights so that your forearms are parallel to the floor when you are using them. You may need to install a keyboard tray below the desk's main surface to achieve this.

Ergonomic Input Devices

Even with the proper vertical positioning of your keyboard and mouse, you may still experience some wrist strain when you use them for a long time. Repetitive stress injuries such as Carpal Tunnel Syndrome can make the tendons in your hands and wrists swollen and painful and cause burning or tingling.

One way to further protect your hands and wrists is to use ergonomically designed input devices. These special keyboards, mice, and trackballs are designed to reduce the strain placed on your body when you use them. For example, the keyboard shown in Figure 17.8 has a split design, so that your hands extend straight from your wrists when typing, rather than curving inward. This keyboard also has a built-in wrist rest in front. Figure 17.9 shows an ergonomically designed mouse; notice how the hand and thumb fit naturally on it at rest.

© iStockphoto.com/webphotographeer

Figure 17.8 An ergonomic keyboard.

© iStockphoto.com/photosoup

Figure 17.9 An ergonomic mouse.

Quick Review

1. What can you do to prevent eyestrain?

2. Why is it important to adopt a correct posture when sitting at a computer?

3. What are two ways to reduce your risk of hand and wrist pain when using a mouse and keyboard?

Environmental Issues in Computer Disposal

Computers are made of more than just their metal or plastic case. They contain components such as a motherboard, hard drive, display, and peripherals. These components contain all sorts of different materials, some of which may be toxic to the environment.

To avoid damaging the environment, it's imperative that you dispose of your computer properly when you no longer want it. Dumping a computer in a landfill could cause heavy metals and poisons such as arsenic from the components to enter the area's water supply, putting the population at risk. Similarly, incinerating a computer could release elements such as mercury and cadmium into the atmosphere, which could be harmful to those nearby.

Many countries now have regulations that govern the disposal process. In some cases, these regulations require computer retailers and manufacturers to contribute toward having the computer recycled. This makes the disposal process much safer and easier.

Rather than disposing of an old computer, consider harvesting the components and using them elsewhere. Here are a few ideas:

- **Hard drive:** Consider reusing the hard drive in another computer, as an additional drive for yourself or someone else. Or, keep it as a spare. If you opt to give the drive away, be sure to wipe your data from it using a program such as Active@ KillDisk (discussed in Chapter 16, "Network and Internet Privacy and Security").

- **Memory:** If the RAM is still usable and of a suitable capacity and speed, you could use it in another computer.

- **Keyboard and mouse:** These are pretty universal and could be used with any computer. It's always worth keeping old keyboards and mice as spares!

- **Display:** If the monitor is of the CRT variety, it is probably at the end of its life and should be disposed of. If it's a more modern, flat-screen monitor, you may be able to use it with another computer. Alternatively, you could use it as a second monitor on your primary computer, running dual displays.

- **Removable components:** A desktop computer may contain removable components such as a display adapter, sound card, or network interface card that could be saved for use in another computer.

- **Notebooks:** There is not much you can remove and reuse from a notebook computer other than the hard drive and possibly the RAM, so this is likely to be disposed of intact.

Alternative Uses for an Older Computer

Before you dispose of your old computer, consider whether there is an alternative, environmentally friendly way of dealing with it—especially if the computer still has some life left in it. Here are a few ideas:

- **Sell it:** If there's nothing wrong with the computer, why not see if you can sell it—for example, on eBay or some other market place? (If you go this route, again, be sure you wipe the hard drive clean. See Chapter 16 for details.)

- **Give it away:** It may be that some deserving person or organization could make good use of your old computer. Why not donate it?

- **Assign it a new role:** Even if your old computer is a bit slow running newer versions of Windows, it's probably fast enough to run an alternative operating system, such as Linux. Try installing such an operating system on your old computer if you want an extra computer to play with!

- **Keep it as a spare:** It's not a bad idea to keep the old computer as a spare, just in case you have a problem with your new one. That way, if your main computer needs repairs, you'll still have a computer to use in the interim.

Put It to Work

Quick Review

1. What are two environmental problems associated with disposing of a computer improperly?

2. What should you do with a hard drive before giving it to someone else to use?

3. What are two alternative uses for an old computer when you have a new one?

Summary

Legal Issues in Computing

Intellectual property (IP) is a legal term that grants people the exclusive rights to the ownership of content that they have created, such as books, artistic works, photographs, music, software, and patents. **Copyright** is a legal protection that usually gives the creator of a work exclusive rights for a specified time period.

Digital rights management (DRM) involves the use of technology to control access to copyrighted material in an attempt to prevent the unauthorized copying and distribution of material. When you install an operating system or software program, you must agree to legal document called an **End User License Agreement (EULA)**. The EULA defines what a user can and cannot do with a product.

Open-source software is software that is not only free to use, but whose source code is accessible to users to modify and redistribute. Although open-source software is about removing licensing restrictions, many types of open-source software do carry a license, called the **General Public License (GPL)**. The GPL enables individuals and companies to legally copy and modify software.

Software piracy is the unauthorized copying of software programs. There are various types of software piracy, including counterfeit software, corporate piracy, unbundling packages, and Internet piracy.

Ethical Issues in Computing

Plagiarism is the practice of copying someone else's work and pretending that it is your own. To avoid plagiarism, use **citations** when referencing the work of others. One way to site a source is using a **footnote**. You can also reference your sources in a **bibliography**. You must cite not only the source of exact wording, but the source of **paraphprased** ideas.

Censorship is the act of preventing something from being printed or heard. Governments, companies, or individuals can apply forms of censorship by not allowing certain types of information to be published or distributed.

Filtering means to prevent something from getting through. When you filter the Internet, you exclude certain categories of content from general access. A **proxy server**—that is, a server that sits between the user's web browser and the Internet—is used to filter web content.

Sometimes, online communications become hostile, with personal attacks and insults. This is called **flaming**. **Libel** is the act of putting a false, defamatory statement in writing. **Slander** is the verbal version of libel. Slander might consist of negative comments about an individual or group that are made as part of a conversation.

Spam is unsolicited junk email. Although most email programs include a junk email filter, many of these emails still slip through to fill users' inboxes, wasting users' valuable time.

Health Issues in Computing

To combat eyestrain, situate your computer so it is 20 to 40 inches (50 to 100 centimeters) from your face, with your eyes just above the center of the screen. If necessary, adjust the angle of the screen. Work in incandescent lighting rather than fluorescent when possible, and position your monitor so that light does not shine directly on it. Use an LCD monitor if possible rather than a CRT; if you must use a CRT, set its refresh rate to at least 100 Hz. Use as large a monitor as possible, and take frequent breaks from looking at it.

A good working **posture** is one in which the body is relaxed and can maintain its position with minimal physical effort. Even if you use perfect posture, you should take frequent breaks to maintain back health. Position your desk and chair so that your thighs and forearms are parallel to the floor as you work.

Repetitive use of the mouse and keyboard can strain on the hand and wrist muscles, causing them to become swollen and painful. To help prevent this, ensure that your arms and wrists are correctly positioned. Use ergonomic input devices if they are available to further reduce strain.

Environmental Issues in Computer Disposal

To avoid damaging the environment, it's important to dispose of your computer properly. Many countries now have regulations that govern the disposal process.

Rather than disposing of an old computer, consider harvesting the components and using them elsewhere. You could also sell the computer, donate it to a deserving person or charity, repurpose it, or keep it as a spare.

Key Terms

censorship
citation
copyright
digital rights management (DRM)
End User License Agreement (EULA)
filtering
flaming
footnote
General Public License (GPL)
intellectual property (IP)

libel
open-source software
paraphrase
plagiarism
posture
proprietary software
proxy server
slander
software piracy
spam

Test Yourself

Fact Check

1. Is it legal to send spam?

   a. Yes, you can send spam in any country.

   b. No, it is illegal to send spam from anywhere.

   c. It depends on what country you are in.

   d. Yes, provided you only send it to your friends.

2. _____ is the practice of insulting users during a conversation on the Internet.

   a. Spamming

   b. Phishing

   c. Flaming

   d. Filtering

3. What is it called when someone posts untrue written statements about you on a website?

    a. flaming

    b. bullying

    c. slander

    d. libel

4. What is the purpose of copyright?

    a. It gives you the right to copy material regardless of owner.

    b. It is a software tool that ensures copies are accurate.

    c. It protects the rights of the author of a piece of work.

    d. It allows for material to be distributed freely to others.

5. What is the purpose of a citation?

    a. It ensures credit is given to the author.

    b. It acknowledges you as the author of a piece of work.

    c. It prevents software piracy.

    d. It prevents the author from being credited for the work.

6. Which type of software license allows you to modify a program and republish it?

    a. proprietary license

    b. trial license

    c. modification license

    d. General Public License (GPL)

7. What is the purpose of a proxy server?

    a. To allow unlimited access to websites

    b. To restrict access to undesirable content

    c. To check documents for plagiarism

    d. To act as a spam filter

8. How far away from your face should your monitor be positioned?

    a. 20 to 40 inches

    b. 12 to 14 inches

    c. 6 to 10 inches

    d. 30 to 60 inches

9. A split keyboard is an example of a(n) _____ design.

    a. space-saving

    b. ergonomic

    c. high-efficiency

    d. wireless

10. What should you do before disposing of a computer?

    a. Make sure the computer is completely intact.

    b. Ensure all personal data has been removed and the hard drive erased.

    c. Replace all the original components.

    d. Ensure you have the original packaging.

Matching

Match the following words to the correct phrase:

    a. flaming

    b. paraphrase

    c. citation

    d. filtering

    e. spamming

    f. plagiarism

1. _____The act of passing off someone else's work as your own.

2. _____Acknowledging the source of your work.

3. _____The process of controlling access to websites.

4. _____Using different words to describe something.

5. _____The act of interacting in a hostile way online.

6. _____The process of sending bulk unsolicited emails.

Sum It Up

1. What non-technical issues must be considered when using computers and the Internet?

2. How is software protected from illegal copying and piracy?

3. What steps must Internet users take to behave ethically when it comes to using work that has been published by others?

4. In what ways can using computers be bad for your health?

5. What steps must be taken to ensure that computers are disposed of properly?

Explore More

Assessing Your Work Environment

Examine the physical environment where you use computers at home, at school, and at work. Look at the furniture you are using—the desks, chairs, and so forth—and see what improvements you can make to provide a healthier work environment. Are there any cost-free measures you can take? Or do you need to purchase new items to create a better environment?

Think It Over

Studying Software Licenses

Software licensing is an important issue for computer software vendors. Look at some of the license agreements for some of the software you have installed, or install some trial software so you can view the terms and conditions. Can you understand the terms being using? If not, where could you get help? Is the license agreement too complex and difficult to understand? Could you reword a license agreement so that it is understandable to nearly anyone and is only as long as it needs to be?

Customizing Windows 8.1

Customizing the Interface

Changing Location-Based Settings

Windows 8.1 requires very little maintenance. Once it is installed, you can use it productively every day without putting much thought into what is happening behind the scenes. You are free to focus on the applications you run for work, education, or play.

However, there may be some times when you want to make a change to the way Windows operates. You might want to change a system setting, such as adjusting the mouse pointer speed, or customize the interface by changing the monitor resolution or the background color. This appendix shows you some simple ways you can customize Windows 8.1 so that it looks and behaves just as you would like it to.

Customizing the Interface

user interface (UI) The interface that a human uses to communicate with a computer.

The user interface (UI) enables you to communicate with the computer. It includes the input devices that convey your commands and enter data, such as the keyboard and mouse, and also the display that you see on the screen.

You can customize the UI in several ways. You can adjust the way the input devices work, for example, and you can control many aspects of the display screen—not only the colors and fonts that it uses, but also the tools and features it includes. You will learn about some of the most common settings in the following sections.

Adjusting the Keyboard and Mouse Settings

The keyboard and the mouse are the two most popular computer input devices. Most of them work well with the default settings, but you might find that adjusting how one or both of them operate can make the user interface more comfortable for you to use. See "Changing the Keyboard Layout" later in this appendix for information about using a different keyboard layout (for example, for typing in a different language).

To customize the keyboard, open the Keyboard Properties dialog box from the Control Panel. To open the Control Panel, right-click the Start button on the desktop taskbar and choose Control Panel. The easiest way to find the Keyboard settings is to type **keyboard** in the Search box in the upper-right corner of the Control Panel window.

repeat delay The amount of time between when a key is held down and when it starts repeating.

repeat rate The speed at which a key repeats after the repeat delay period has passed.

cursor Also called the insertion point, the blinking vertical line that appears in a text box or other area that can accept text input.

Some of the settings you can change for the keyboard pertain to a feature called Repeat. When you hold down a key, after a certain amount of time the character represented by that key begins repeating on the screen rapidly. This feature enables you to create a row of dotted lines by holding down the period key, for example. The repeat delay setting determines how long Windows delays after you start holding down the key before the character beings repeating. The repeat rate determines how quickly the character repeats once it gets started doing so. You can also adjust the cursor blink rate, which determines how fast the cursor blinks.

You can also make many adjustments in how the mouse operates. The most commonly customized settings for a mouse are:

- **Button configuration:** You can switch the functions of the right and left mouse buttons. This might be useful for someone who is left-handed and prefers to use the mouse on the left side of the computer.

- **Double-click speed:** You can change the minimum threshold for how quickly the two clicks need to be in succession to be considered a double-click instead of two separate clicks.

- **Pointers:** The default mouse pointer scheme in Windows 8.1 uses a small white arrow as the main pointer. It also defines graphics for many other pointer situations too, such as the graphic to appear while Windows is busy, when the pointer is over a clickable hyperlink, and when the pointer is over the border of a resizable window. You can choose a different scheme, or you can customize each of the pointers individually.

- **Motion:** You can control how far the pointer onscreen moves in relation to the amount of mouse movement. This setting is adjusted on the Pointer Options tab.

If you have a custom pointing device installed that has its own software, the Mouse Properties dialog box may look different from the one described and shown in this appendix, and you may have some different settings.

Step by Step

Changing Keyboard Settings

Follow these steps to change your keyboard settings:

1. Right-click the Start button on the desktop taskbar and click Control Panel.

2. In the Search box, type **keyboard,** and press Enter. In the search results that appear, click Keyboard. The Keyboard Properties dialog box opens.

3. Drag the Repeat Delay slider to adjust the setting as desired.

4. Drag the Repeat Rate slider to adjust the setting as desired.

5. Click in the text box and hold down a key to test your settings in Steps 3 and 4. Readjust as needed.

6. Drag the Cursor Blink Rate slider to adjust the setting as desired. The cursor sample to the left of the slider shows the current setting.

7. Click OK to close the dialog box.

Switching Right and Left Mouse Buttons

Use this procedure to switch the functions of the right and left mouse buttons:

1. Right-click the Start button on the desktop taskbar and click Control Panel.

2. Click the Hardware and Sound heading. (In some Windows 8.1 editions, you don't have to do this; Mouse is at the top level of the Control Panel.)

3. Under the Devices and Printers heading, click Mouse. The Mouse Properties dialog box opens.

4. Mark the Switch Primary and Secondary Buttons check box.

5. Click OK to close the dialog box.

Adjusting Mouse Settings

Follow these steps to adjust your mouse settings:

1. Right-click the Start button on the desktop taskbar and click Control Panel.

2. Click the Hardware and Sound heading.

3. Under the Devices and Printers heading, click Mouse. The Mouse Properties dialog box opens.

4. On the Buttons tab, drag the Speed slider to adjust the double-click speed as needed. To test your setting, double-click the folder icon to the right of the slider.

5. Click the Pointers tab.

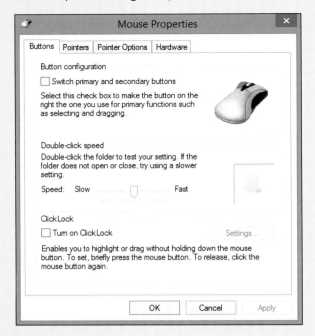

6. Open the Scheme drop-down list and select a different pointer scheme if desired.

7. Click the Pointer Options tab.

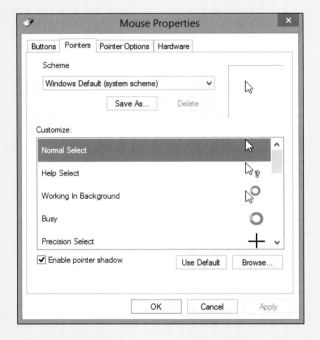

8. Drag the Motion slider to adjust the pointer speed. Click Apply and then move the mouse to test the setting. Adjust as needed and click Apply again.

9. Click OK to close the dialog box.

10. Close the Control Panel window.

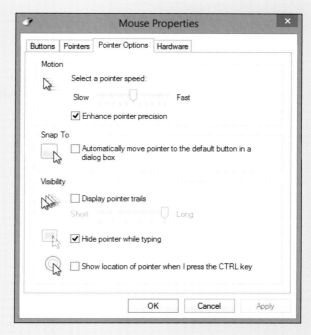

Customizing the Taskbar

As you learned in Chapter 5, "Introduction to Windows 8.1," the task-bar is the bar across the bottom of the desktop. The Start button is at the left end, and the clock is at the right end. In between them are various icons and shortcuts.

To customize the taskbar, right-click the taskbar, click Properties, and then click the Taskbar tab. Here are some ways you can customize the taskbar:

■ **Lock the taskbar:** You can lock or unlock the taskbar. When it's locked, it can't be moved or resized and the toolbars on it can't be resized. Keeping it locked except when you want to make changes ensures that there are no accidental changes made.

You can lock or unlock the taskbar by right-clicking it and choosing the Lock the Taskbar command. **TIP**

■ **Auto-hide the taskbar:** You can auto-hide the taskbar. When this option is enabled, the taskbar disappears when you aren't using it. To make it reappear, move the mouse to the bottom of the screen and it pops into place. Auto-hiding the taskbar provides a little more room for application windows.

■ **Change the icon size:** You can choose an icon size (small or large) for the icons on the taskbar. When the Use Small Icons option is enabled, the icons on the taskbar are smaller than when the option is disabled. Smaller icons take up less space, but the icons may be easier to see at the larger size. Figure A.1 compares the two sizes.

Figure A.1   Small icons on the taskbar (above) versus large ones (below).

Taskbar Location: You can change the taskbar location. By default, it is at the bottom of the screen but you can move it to the top, left, or right.

Combine Buttons for the Same Application: You can choose whether or not to combine buttons for different items in the same application on the taskbar. The default is to combine them only when the taskbar is full, but you can choose to always or never combine. Figure A.2 shows a full taskbar with the icons for all the Word documents combined. Pointing at the combined icons produces a jump list of the names of the documents and thumbnail images of them; you can click one of those names or images to quickly jump to that document.

jump list A list of files that appears when you hover the mouse pointer over a program icon on the taskbar.

Thumbnail images of each of the open documents appear

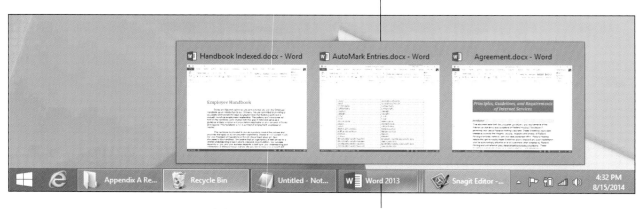

Point at a button for an application with multiple open documents

Figure A.2   Combined icons on the taskbar. Point at the combined stack to see thumbnail images of the documents in the stack.

Choose Notification Area Icons: You can customize which icons appear in the notification area. As you learned in Chapter 5, the notification area is the area just to the left of the clock, where icons appear for programs that run in the background. Certain icons appear there all the time, whereas others are hidden until you click the up-pointing arrow to display them, as shown in Figure A.3. You can choose one of three settings:

Show icon and notifications: The icon will always appear. Use this setting for applications you interact with frequently, such as the volume control and your instant messaging program.

Hide icon and notifications: The icon will not appear even if the program wants to show you a message. Use this for programs you never want to interact with.

- **Only show notifications:** The icon will not appear unless the program has a message to show you, in which case it will appear in the notification area until you have read the message. Use this for programs that you usually don't interact with but that you want to be made aware of if there is a problem.

You can also enable or disable each of the system icons that can potentially appear in the notification area: Clock, Volume, Network, Power, and Action Center.

- **Show Windows Store apps on the taskbar:** You can choose whether or not Windows 8 applications (that is, applications acquired from the Windows Store, or that came with Windows 8 or 8.1) will appear with buttons on the taskbar when they are running.

- **Display or Hide Taskbar Toolbars:** You can display a number of optional toolbars on the taskbar. Some of them can be useful, but each one takes up space that could otherwise be used for the buttons for running programs. For example, the Address toolbar, shown in Figure A.4, enables you to enter commands or searches without opening the Start menu. You can choose to display or hide each available toolbar individually.

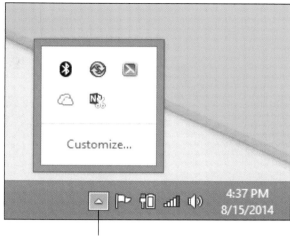

Click here for the pop-up list

Figure A.3   You can specify which programs appear in the main part of the notification area and which programs are on the pop-up list.

Figure A.4   The Address toolbar shown here is one example of the several optional toolbars you can display on the taskbar.

- **Resize the Taskbar:** The taskbar is one row high by default. You can make it thicker so that it can display more rows (useful if you have a lot of windows open at once).

- **Pin and Unpin Items on the Taskbar:** The icons to the right of the Start button are pinned to the taskbar. By default, Internet Explorer and FIle Explorer are pinned there, but you might have other programs pinned there, too. You can pin shortcuts there for quick use, or unpin shortcuts for items you don't use much.

pin To attach a shortcut to a program or data file to a certain menu or toolbar.

Customizing the Taskbar

Use this procedure to set up the taskbar to work best for your needs:

1. Right-click the taskbar and choose Properties. The Taskbar and Navigation Properties dialog box opens.

2. On the Taskbar tab, mark or clear the following check boxes as desired:

   a. Lock the taskbar

   b. Auto-hide the taskbar

   c. Use small taskbar icons

3. Open the Taskbar Location on Screen drop-down list and select the desired location. Bottom is the default. If the Taskbar is unlocked you can click the bar and drag it to the desired location, then release the mouse button.

4. Open the Taskbar Buttons drop-down list and select a behavior for combining taskbar buttons.

5. Click OK to close the dialog box.

Customizing the Notification Area

Follow these steps to adjust the Notification Area to your preferences:

1. Right-click the taskbar and choose Properties.

2. On the Taskbar tab, click the Customize button for Notification Area. The Notification Area Icons screen appears (a part of the Control Panel).

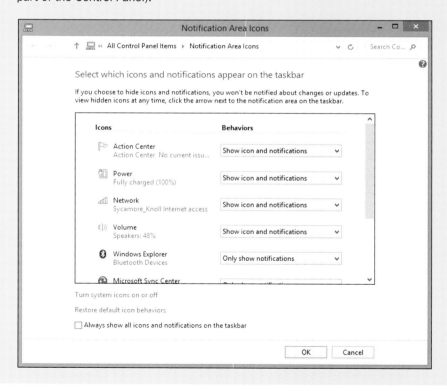

3. For each icon, open the drop-down list and select a setting.

OR

To always see all icons, mark the Always Show All Icons and Notifications on the Taskbar check box.

4. Click the Turn System Icons On or Off hyperlink.

5. For each system icon, open the drop-down list and choose On or Off.

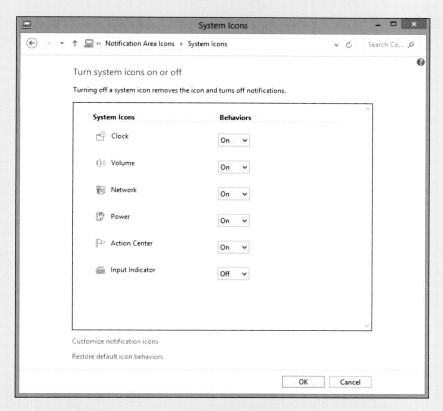

6. Click OK to accept the settings for system icons.

7. Click OK to accept the settings for notification area icons.

Displaying or Hiding Taskbar Toolbars

Use one of the following methods to show or hide the toolbars:

Dialog Box Method:

1. Right-click the taskbar and choose Properties.

2. Click the Toolbars tab.

3. Click to mark or clear the check box for each toolbar.

4. Click OK.

Shortcut Menu Method:

1. Right-click the taskbar and point to Toolbars. A pop-up menu appears of the toolbars. Toolbars already displayed have a check mark next to the name.

2. Click the toolbar to enable or disable.

Resizing the Taskbar

Follow these steps to resize the taskbar:

1. Right-click the taskbar and if Lock the Taskbar has a check mark next to it, click it to toggle that option off.

2. Position the mouse pointer over the upper edge of the taskbar until the symbol changes to a double-headed arrow.

3. Drag upward or downward to adjust the size.

Pinning a Program to the Taskbar

Use this procedure to pin an item to the taskbar:

1. Display the Start screen, and click the down arrow button at the bottom to display the Apps list.

2. Right-click the program you want to pin, and choose Pin to Taskbar.

Removing a Pinned Program from the Taskbar

To unpin a program, follow these steps:

1. Right-click the pinned program on the taskbar.

2. Click Unpin This Program from Taskbar.

Customizing the Start Screen

The Start screen is like a bulletin board on which you can pin shortcuts for the applications and locations you use most often. It comes with a few locations already pinned there, but you can easily make changes. You can also change the Start screen's appearance by choosing different colors and designs for its background.

For each tile on the Start screen, you can adjust by doing any of the following:

- You can reposition it by dragging it where you want it to go.

- You can right-click it and choose Unpin from Start to unpin it. You can still access the application from the Apps list (which appears when you click the down arrow at the bottom of the Start screen).

- You can change its size by right-clicking it and choosing Resize and then selecting a size.

To pin applications to the Start screen that aren't already there, display the Apps list and then right-click the application and choose Pin to Start.

To change the appearance of the Start screen, select the Settings charm (from the Start screen, not from the desktop) and then choose Personalize. A Personalize pane appears, from which you can select a background image, background color, and accent color. See Figure A.5.

Figure A.5   You can select an image, a background color, and an accent color for the Start screen.

Step by Step

Unpin an App from the Start Screen

To unpin an app from the Start screen, follow these steps:

1. Right-click the app on the Start screen.

2. Click Unpin from Start.

Pin an App to the Start Screen

To pin an app to the Start screen, follow these steps:

1. From the Start screen, click the down arrow to display the Apps list.

2. Right-click the desired app.

3. Click Pin to Start.

Move an App Tile on the Start Sreen

To move an app's tile, follow these steps:

1. From the Start screen, click and hold on the tile to move.

2. Drag the tile to a different location.

Resize an App Tile on the Start Sreen

To resize an app's tile, follow these steps:

1. From the Start screen, right-click the tile to resize.

2. Point to the Resize command.

3. Click the desired size.

Customize the Start Screen Appearance

To change the colors and background graphic on the Start screen, follow these steps:

1. From the Start screen, display the Charms bar and select the Settings charm.

2. Click Personalize.

3. Click the desired background graphic in the top section (see Figure A.5).

4. Click the desired color in the Background color section. First select a basic color in the color palette, and then select a shade of that color.

5. Click the desired color in the Accent color section. First select a basic color in the color palette, and then select a shade of that color.

6. Click away from the pane to close it.

Changing the Screen Resolution

screen resolution The number of pixels used to form the display image, expressed as width × height, like this: 1024 × 768.

Screen resolution is the number of pixels horizontally and vertically that comprise the display. For example, most screens shown in this book use 1024 × 768 screen resolution. At higher resolutions, the icons and text on the desktop appear smaller in proportion to the desktop background. Figure A.6 compares two resolutions.

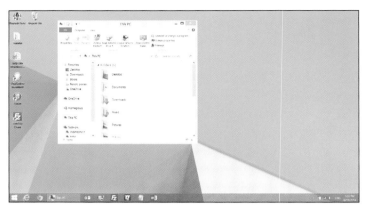 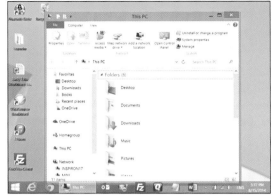

Figure A.6 A desktop display at 1920 x 1080 (left) and 1024 x 768 (right).

aspect ratio The ratio of width to height in the number of pixels in a display.

Different screen resolutions can have different aspect ratios. A widescreen display like the one shown on the left side of Figure A.6 has an aspect ratio of 16:9. In other words, for every 16 pixels horizontally there are 9 pixels vertically. A standard aspect ratio like the one shown on the right side of Figure A.6 has an aspect ratio of approximately 4:3.

Put It to Work

Choosing the Right Resolution

When selecting a screen resolution, keep your monitor's aspect ratio in mind; if you choose a screen resolution with a different aspect ratio than your monitor, the display might be distorted. If you aren't sure what aspect ratio a particular screen resolution represents, divide the larger number by the smaller one. If it comes out to approximately 1.78, it's a widescreen aspect ratio. If it comes out to approximately 1.3, it's standard. Or if you don't want to pull out your calculator and do the math, you can just try different aspect ratios until you find one that seems to fit your monitor well.

On most flat-screen monitors, the display looks best at the maximum resolution. At lower resolutions, the display may appear fuzzy and the text may not be crisply defined. Fortunately, Windows has a setting that enables you to make the text and icons on your screen larger without changing display resolutions. In the Control Panel, under Appearance and Personalization, there is an option to make text and other items larger or smaller. As shown in Figure A.7, Smaller – 100% is the default size. You can choose Medium – 125% or Larger – 150% to increase the text and icon size. There is a drawback, however; some items may not fit on your screen at the higher settings, or may look strange, because the application they are associated with is not aware of Windows having made the size change. The only way to know how it will affect your screen and the applications you use is to try it out; it's easy to reverse the setting if you are not happy with the results.

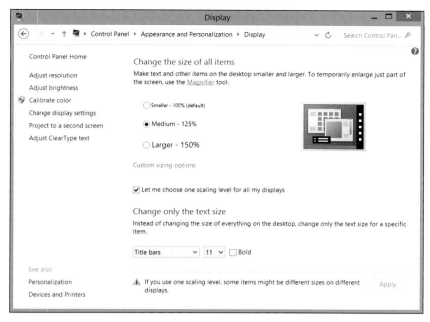

Figure A.7 You can make text and other items on the screen larger without decreasing the screen resolution.

For instructions on changing the screen resolution, see Chapter 17, "Legal, Ethical, Health, and Environmental Issues in Computing."

Step by Step

Changing the Text and Icon Size

To change the size of your text and icons, follow these steps:

1. Right-click the desktop and choose Screen Resolution.

2. Click the Make Text and Other Items Larger or Smaller hyperlink.

3. Click Smaller, Medium, or Larger. Larger may not be available on all systems.

If you see a Smaller/Larger slider instead of the option buttons shown in Figure A.7, you can drag the slider to adjust the size, or you can mark the Let me choose one scaling level for all my displays check box to make the option buttons appear. **NOTE**

4. Click Apply.

5. If prompted to log off, click Log Off Now. When you log back in, the new text and icon size will be in effect.

Personalizing the Desktop

You work with the desktop a lot when working in Windows, so you will probably want to adjust its appearance to be pleasing to you. You can make several changes to the desktop. For example, you can change the background image to your favorite photo, an abstract design, or a solid color. You can also change the window color, the sounds that Windows makes as it operates, and the screen saver. To access the interface for changing the desktop right-click the desktop and choose Personalize. The Personalization screen appears, as shown in Figure A.8.

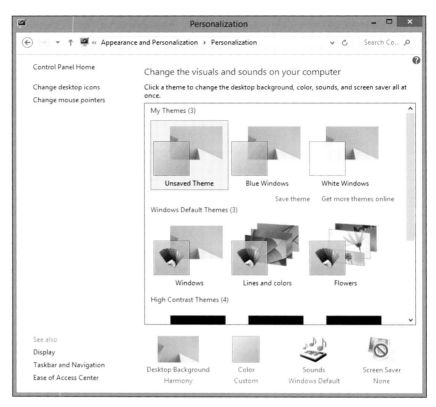

Figure A.8   Personalize the Windows desktop in one or more ways.

theme A named set of formatting presets, governing font, color, and object effect choices.

high-contrast theme A theme that uses starkly contrasting colors for adjacent items, such as window borders and the Windows desktop, to make them easier to see.

As a time-saver, Windows 8.1 provides themes, which are preset combinations of formatting features. A theme specifies one or more background graphics plus window color settings; some themes also specify system sounds. You can create your own themes by saving your current Windows settings as a new theme. A number of high-contrast themes are also included along with the basic themes; high-contrast themes are often useful to people with limited vision.

Step by Step

Applying a Theme

Follow these steps to apply a theme:

1. Right-click the desktop and choose Personalize. The Personalization screen appears (see Figure A.8).

2. Click the desired theme. It is applied immediately.

3. Close the window.

Windows 8.1 comes with many interesting and attractive desktop background photos and abstract graphics. You can choose any of those, or you can use your own photos. Select the location to browse from the Picture Location drop-down list in the Desktop Background window, as shown in Figure A.9.

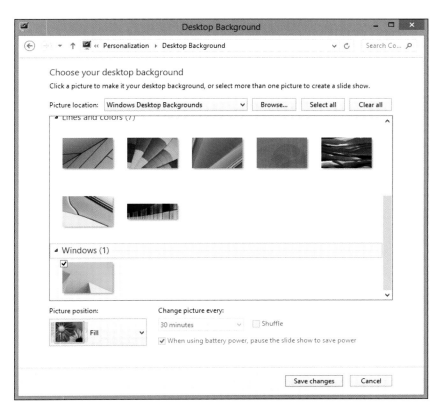

Figure A.9   Select one or more images for the desktop background.

If you select only one desktop background, that's the one that stays on all the time. However, if you select multiple backgrounds, Windows will cycle through them, changing the background at the interval you specify. To choose multiple images, click to place a mark in the check box in the upper-left corner of each image you want. To show them in random order, mark the Shuffle check box.

After selecting an image as the background, you must specify how it will appear if it is not exactly the same size (that is, the same resolution) as the current desktop resolution. Table A.1 summarizes the choices available on the Picture Position drop-down list. Some of the choices involve a background color behind the image. The default is black; if you want a different color, click the Desktop Background hyperlink at the bottom of the window (see Figure A.8) to open a dialog box from which you can choose some other color.

If you don't want any image at all—just a solid color on the desktop— then choose Solid Colors from the Picture Location drop-down list and choose the desired color.

Table A.1: Image Placement as a Desktop Background

Setting	Result
Fill	If the image is larger than the desktop, the center of the image appears and the edges are truncated. If the image is smaller than the desktop, the image enlarges to fill the desktop completely. Image quality may suffer.
Fit	The image enlarges or shrinks to match the screen resolution vertically. If the image is not as wide as the screen, a solid color appears on the sides of the image. The image's aspect ratio does not change.
Stretch	The image expands to fill the entire screen, changing its aspect ratio as needed. The image may be distorted.
Tile	If the image is smaller than the desktop, the image repeats itself in any remaining space. This setting sometimes works well for small pictures that can repeat many times onscreen.
Center	A single copy of the image appears in the center of the desktop, with a solid color filling the remainder of the space.

Step by Step

Changing the Desktop Background

Use this procedure to change your desktop background:

1. Right-click the desktop and choose Personalize.

2. Click the Desktop Background hyperlink at the bottom of the window. The Desktop Background screen appears (see Figure A.9).

3. Open the Picture Location drop-down list and choose a picture location. Alternatively, you can click Browse and choose a different location.

4. Click the desired picture.

5. (Optional) To select additional pictures, point at the additional picture so that a check box appears in its upper-left corner and then click the check box to mark it.

6. Open the Picture Position drop-down list and select one of the available positions.

7. If more than one picture is selected, open the Change Picture Every drop-down list and select an interval.

8. (Optional) To display pictures at random, mark the Shuffle check box.

9. Click the Save Changes button to accept the new settings.

---

window color The color of the window title bar and border.

hue The color being represented, such as red, green, or blue.

saturation The intensity of the color. A highly saturated color is vivid; a minimally saturated color looks close to gray with only a pale tint of the color.

brightness The degree of light or dark in a color.

Selecting a Window Color

Window color refers to the color of the title bar and border of the windows. A theme provides a window color, but you can change it.

Click Color at the bottom of the Personalization window (Figure A.8). Some color swatches appear. Click the one you like best as a starting point, and then drag the Color Intensity slider to fine-tune its intensity. You can also click the Show Color Mixer button to display additional sliders for hue, saturation, and brightness, as shown in Figure A.10.

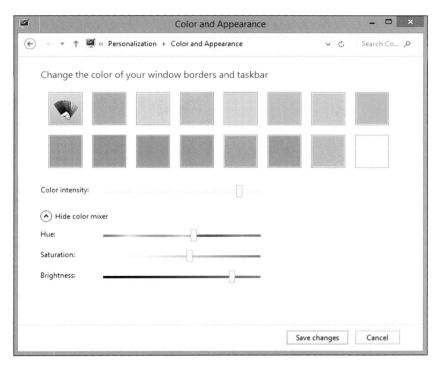

Figure A.10   Select a color swatch and adjust its intensity, hue, saturation, and brightness.

Step by Step

Changing the Window Color

To change the window color follow these steps:

1. Right-click the desktop and choose Personalize.

2. Click Color.

3. Click the desired color.

4. Drag the Color Intensity slider to adjust the window color as desired. The color is previewed on the active window.

5. (Optional) Click Show Color Mixer and then drag the additional sliders to further adjust the color.

6. Click Save Changes.

Selecting a Sound Scheme

As Windows operates, it makes sounds (provided the computer has sound support and the speakers aren't muted). For example, there is a Windows log-off sound, an Exit Windows sound, and sounds made when windows open and close.

The process of choosing individual sounds to be associated with each system event can be tedious, so Windows provides sets of sounds called sound schemes. A sound scheme includes a sound clip pre-selected for each system event. Some themes include a sound scheme, and some use the Windows default sounds or the current sound scheme setting.

sound scheme A set of sounds that are used to indicate common events.

Step by Step

Choosing a Sound Scheme

Follow these steps to select a sound scheme:

1. Right-click the desktop and choose Personalize.

2. Click Sounds. The Sound dialog box opens.

3. Open the Sound Scheme drop-down list and choose a scheme.

4. (Optional) To preview a sound, select the event and then click Test.

5. Click OK to close the dialog box.

screen saver A utility that displays a moving object or changing pattern on the screen after there has been no user interaction for a specified amount of time.

Selecting a Screen Saver

Screen savers were necessary in the early days of computing because if the same image remained on the screen for a long time there was the likelihood of damage to the screen because the static image could end up being "burned in" and would always be visible in the background. The moving image of the screen saver prevented this from happening. Monitor technology has changed now, and screen savers are no longer necessary for this purpose. However, the screen-saver feature remains in Windows, partly because some people enjoy them, and partly because a screen saver provides a certain level of privacy by obscuring your screen after a certain period of inactivity so that passersby cannot see what you were doing when you stepped away from the PC. You can also set the screen saver to display the logon screen when the computer wakes up from a screen saver operation, providing some extra security.

Some screen savers have options you can set. For example, the Photos screen saver enables you to choose the location from which the photos will be used and the speed at which the photos will change.

Choosing a Screen Saver

To select a screen saver follow these steps:

1. Right-click the desktop and choose Personalize.

2. Click Screen Saver at the bottom of the window. The Screen Saver Settings dialog box appears.

3. Open the Screen Saver drop-down list and choose the desired screen saver.

4. Click the Settings button. Depending on the screen saver, a dialog box containing additional options or a message may appear that it has no options you can set. Adjust any settings available and click OK.

5. (Optional) Click the Preview button to preview the screen saver. Move the mouse or press any key to return.

6. Change the Wait value to the number of minutes you want to wait after the computer is idle before the screen saver starts.

7. (Optional) If you want a password to be required when waking up from the screen saver, mark the On Resume, Display Logon Screen check box.

8. Click OK to close the dialog box.

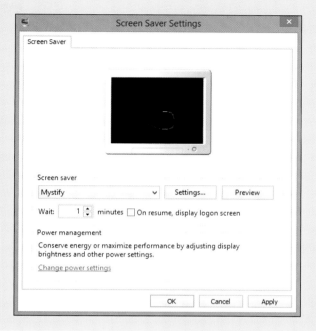

Saving Your Settings as a New Theme

After making all your desktop appearance selections, you may want to save those settings as a new theme so you can quickly reapply the same settings later if you temporarily switch to some other theme. When there are unsaved changes to the current theme, an Unsaved Theme entry appears in the Personalization window in the My Themes area. You can save Unsaved Theme as a new theme with a name that you specify.

You can also save the theme in a file that can be shared with other people. You might do this if you wanted all the PCs in your home or office to have exactly the same settings, for example.

Saving Settings as a New Theme

Use these steps to save your settings as a new theme:

1. Right-click the desktop and choose Personalize.

2. Right-click Unsaved Theme and choose Save Theme. The Save Theme As dialog box opens.

3. Type a theme name in the dialog box.

4. Click Save.

Saving a Theme to Share with Others

To save a theme so you can share it, follow these steps:

1. Right-click the desktop and choose Personalize.

2. Right-click the theme to save and choose Save Theme for Sharing. The Save Theme Pack As dialog box opens.

3. Navigate to the location where you want to save the file.

4. Type a name for the file in the File name box.

5. Click Save.

Adjusting Accessibility Features

accessibility features Features that help people with disabilities use Windows more easily.

Accessibility features are utilities and settings that make Windows easier for people with disabilities to use. Windows contains a broad array of accessibility options that can help people with visual, hearing, and movement impairments.

New Technologies

Controlling a Computer with Your Brain?

People with disabilities who have some movement that they can control can operate a computer using some form of adaptive input device, such as a joystick, a special keyboard, or a laser pointer mounted on the forehead. But what about people who can't control any movements at all? Researchers are working on a type of computer input device that uses brainwaves for control. People can be trained to use thought patterns to fire certain neural pathways in the brain voluntarily, and a sensor can pick up that pathway activity and use it to control an on-screen pointing device. Clinical trials and studies are in progress now that could improve and refine this technology to make it available to everyone who can benefit from it. For more information about this technology, read the article at `http://www.alsa.org/assets/pdfs/fyi/fyi_brain_computer_interface.pdf`.

© iStockphoto.com/agsandrew

The easiest way to set up accessibility features in Windows 8.1 is to use the Ease of Access Center, a section in the Control Panel. There you will find links to all the accessibility tools and features that Windows offers. Table A.2 provides a summary of what's available.

Table A.2: Accessibility Features

Type of Disability	Feature	Function
Visual	Magnifier	Magnifies the section of the screen near the mouse pointer
Visual	Narrator	Reads the text in the active window aloud
Visual	High Contrast	Changes the Windows colors and window appearances so they are easier to see
Visual	Audio Description	Enables descriptions of what's happening in videos (when available)
Visual	Large mouse pointers	Makes the mouse pointer easier to see
Movement	On-Screen Keyboard	Makes a virtual keyboard available onscreen; keys can be pressed by pointing and clicking

Type of Disability	Feature	Function
Movement	Speech Recognition	Enables users to control Windows with voice commands.
Movement	Mouse Keys	Enables the mouse pointer to be moved by pressing keys on the numeric keypad.
Movement	Sticky Keys	Enables shortcut key combinations to be entered one key at a time.
Movement	Toggle Keys	Plays a tone when Caps Lock, Num Lock, or Scroll Lock is pressed, to alert the user.
Movement	Filter Keys	Ignores brief or repeated keystrokes and adjusts the repeat rate.
Sound	Sound Sentry	Provides visual notifications when system sounds play.
Sound	Text Captions	Turns on text captions for spoken dialog (when available).

The most popular accessibility tools appear at the top of the Ease of Access Center: Magnifier, On-Screen Keyboard, Narrator, and High Contrast. Click any of those and then follow the prompts to get started with it. See Figure A.11.

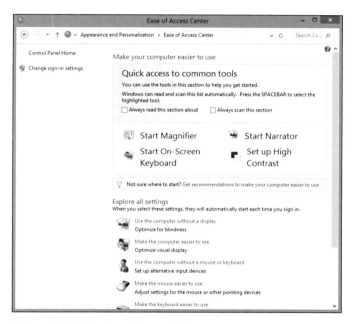

Figure A.11   The Ease of Access Center.

If you aren't sure which settings you want to change, start with one of the scenarios in the Explore All Settings section in the Ease of Access Center. For example, if you have a visual impairment but are not completely blind, you might choose Make the Computer Easier to See. From there, a screen appears, containing links to Ease of Access features that might be useful for your situation, as shown in Figure A.12.

An even easier way to set up for accessibility is to fill out an accessibility questionnaire and let Windows suggest the tools you might want. At the end of the questionnaire, a Recommended Settings list appears with options for turning on the features that might be right for you.

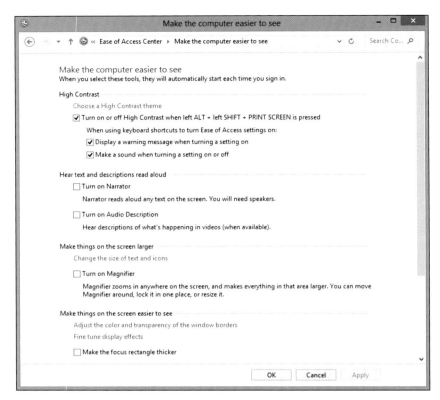

Figure A.12 Select one of the scenarios to see suggestions for features you may want to enable.

Step by Step

Opening the Ease of Access Center

Follow these steps to display the Ease of Access Center:

1. Right-click the Start button and click Control Panel.

2. Click the Ease of Access heading.

Completing the Accessibility Questionnaire

Follow these steps to fill out the questionnaire:

1. Right-click the Start button and click Control Panel.

2. Under the Ease of Access heading, click Let Windows Suggest Settings. Statements appear with check boxes next to them.

3. Click to mark the check boxes for statements that apply to you. Then click Next for the next page of statements.

4. Continue working through the statements until the last page appears; then click Done. A Recommended Settings page appears.

5. Mark the check boxes for any features you want to enable.

6. Click OK.

Using Magnifier

Follow this procedure to access and use the Magnifier:

1. From the Ease of Access Center, click Start Magnifier. A magnified panel appears at the top of the screen.

2. Move the mouse normally; the magnified area follows the mouse pointer.

3. A magnifying glass icon appears floating on the desktop; click it to open a Magnifier toolbar, and use it to change the magnification level if desired.

4. (Optional) To increase the height of the magnified pane, drag the border downward between the main desktop window and the magnified pane.

5. To turn Magnifier off, right-click its button in the taskbar and choose Close Window.

Using Narrator

Follow this procedure to access and use the Narrator feature:

1. From the Ease of Access Center, click Start Narrator. A Microsoft Narrator pane opens in the lower-left corner of the screen, and Narrator reads its contents aloud.

2. Adjust any of Narrator's settings as needed and then minimize its window.

3. To turn Narrator off, right-click its button in the taskbar and choose Close.

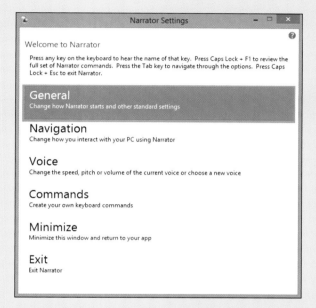

Using the On-Screen Keyboard

Follow these steps to open and use the On-Screen Keyboard feature:

1. From the Ease of Access Center, click Start On-Screen Keyboard. The On-Screen Keyboard window opens.

2. Click the keys in the keyboard window to type as needed.

3. To close the On-Screen Keyboard window, click its Close (X) button, or right-click its button in the taskbar and choose Close.

Quick Review

1. What three types of settings does a theme usually contain?

2. What is the relationship between screen resolution and icon size?

3. Where is the Ease of Access Center located and what is it for?

Changing Location-Based Settings

Location-based settings help you tell Windows where you are and what languages you read and write in while you are there. They can help you install and switch between display languages, keyboard layouts, and regional settings for how dates and times are written, what currency symbols are used, and what time it is. In the following sections, you will learn how to adjust your computer for the language and location that best fit your current situation.

Changing the Display Language

display language The language in which the commands and menus in the user interface appear.

language pack Add-on software that allows a copy of Windows originally written in one language to use a different display language.

The version of Windows 8.1 that you use has an interface in a specific language. The menus, dialog boxes, error messages, and controls are all in that language (most commonly US English). This is called the display language. If you want Windows to support more than one display language, you must install a language pack.

Step by Step

Installing a Language Pack

Follow these steps to install a language pack:

1. Right-click the Start button and click Control Panel.

2. Click the Clock, Language, and Region heading.

3. Under the Language heading, click Add a Language. The Change Your Language Preferences screen appears.

4. Click Add a language.

5. Select the desired language and click Add.

   If you just want the keyboard layout for that language, you can stop here. See "Changing the Keyboard Layout" in the next section to learn how to switch between keyboard layouts.

6. Double-click the added language to see the Language Options for that language.

7. Click the Download and install language pack hyperlink. An Internet connection is required.

8. Wait for the language pack to be downloaded and installed.

9. When a message appears that installation is complete, click Close.

Changing the Display Language

Use this procedure to change the display language, after you have installed the needed language pack:

1. Right-click the Start button and click Control Panel.

2. Click the Clock, Language, and Region heading.

3. Click the Region and Language heading. Then click the Language heading.

4. Under the Display Language heading, select the desired language and then click Move Up until the desired language is at the top of the list.

5. Restart Windows, or sign out and sign back in again, so that the new display language will take effect.

Changing the Keyboard Layout

If you create documents in different languages, you may sometimes want to use a different keyboard. You can tell Windows to use a different keyboard layout, so that when you press the keys on the keyboard, Windows displays the appropriate characters.

keyboard layout The arrangement of the keys on the keyboard.

Installing a language pack, as in the previous section, also installs the appropriate keyboard layout files for that language. However, you do not have to install a language as an alternate display language in order to use its keyboard layout.

Keyboard layouts are based on the input language you select. The input language is the language in which you input data. It is separate from the display language. Each input language has one or more keyboard layouts. You might possibly have multiple keyboard layouts for a certain input language. For example, there is an alternative English-language keyboard layout called Dvorak, named for its inventor.

input language The language on which the current keyboard layout is based.

After enabling the keyboard layouts and input languages you want, as in the previous sections, you can switch between the input languages available using keyboard shortcuts or using the Language bar. The default keyboard shortcut for switching input languages is Windows key + spacebar. A Language button appears in the notification area when multiple input languages are installed. It provides a quick pop-up menu from which you can select the desired input language, as shown in Figure A.13.

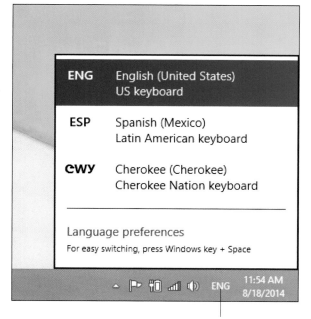

Language button

Figure A.13 Use the Language button's menu to switch between input languages.

Switching Input Languages

Use this procedure to switch input languages:

1. Hold down the left Windows key and press and release the spacebar.

   OR

   Click the Language button in the notification area. The letters on it depend on the currently selected language. For example, if English is selected, ENG appears on the button.

2. Click the desired language.

Changing Regional and Location Settings

When you are working in different parts of the world (or creating documents designed to be used in different parts of the world), dates, times, numbers, and currency may customarily be written in a different format. For example, in the United States and most countries in the Middle East, dates are written with the month first, then the day, and then the year, like this: 06/15/2015. However, in most countries in Europe, dates are written with the day and month in reverse order, like this: 15/06/2015. And in most of Asia, dates are written with the year first, like this: 2015/06/15.

When you use a certain display language, Windows automatically changes the date, time, and currency references in Windows itself to the appropriate formats. For example, on the lock screen, the current date and time is shown in the format appropriate for the display language. However, switching to a different input language or keyboard layout does not automatically change region-specific formats.

Rather than trying to memorize the appropriate format for each region, you can choose a global format in Windows for a particular country, and Windows will automatically make the appropriate settings for the chosen country the defaults. When you select a country from the list, all the regional settings are automatically set to the defaults for that country, but you can fine-tune the settings as desired. For example, you could use the date formats for the United States but the currency symbols for the United Kingdom.

Windows also has a Location setting that you can use to let Windows know where you are physically located at the moment. This setting will interact with any software that requests your location to allow it to provide you with local weather forecasts and other region-specific news.

Changing Regional and Location Settings

To change the setting for your region or location, follow these steps:

1. Right-click the Start button and click Control Panel.

2. Click the Clock, Language, and Region heading.

3. Under the Region heading, click Change the Date, Time, or Number Formats. The Region dialog box opens with the Formats tab displayed. The default setting is Match Windows display language (recommended).

4. Open the Format drop-down list and select the desired country or region. The settings in the dialog box update automatically to its defaults.

5. (Optional) Under Date and Time Formats, open any drop-down list and make a different selection, based on your preferences.

6. (Optional) Click the Additional Settings button to open the Customize Formats dialog box. Make any additional changes to the settings on the Numbers, Currency, Time, and/or Date tabs, and click OK.

7. Click the Location tab in the Region dialog box.

8. Open the Home Location drop-down list and select the country where you are.

9. Click OK to close the dialog box.

10. Close the Control Panel window.

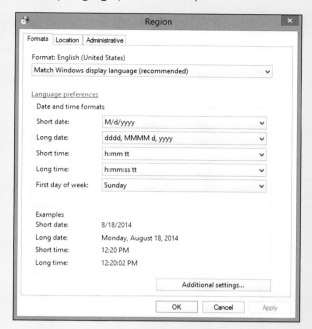

Changing the Date and Time

The current time appears in the lower-right corner of the Windows desktop, on the task-bar. You can click it to pop up a calendar that shows today's date (see Figure A.14), and you can browse this calendar to look up other dates too. The date and time are not just for your information; Windows uses the date and time to manage files. For example, Creation Date is a file property; the current date and time are automatically assigned this property for each new file you create. Some file searches are also based on dates and times assigned to the files.

Click the clock to see the calendar

Figure A.14 Click the date to pop up a small calendar.

If you set the computer's clock ahead of the current date, some Windows features that use the clock to determine when to perform certain activities may be affected. For example, you might see a message that your virus definitions are out-of-date.

CAUTION

Windows automatically updates the system date and time using Internet time servers whenever an Internet connection is available, so you should seldom have to change the clock in Windows due to it being off by a minute or two. It's possible to change the date and time manually but most people do not do it. Windows offers several choices for Internet time servers, but you can add a time server of your own choosing if you want.

However, if you travel to a location that's in a different time zone, you will need to let Windows know of your new time zone so that it can update the clock automatically for you. The Windows list of time zones includes information about Daylight Saving Time (DST) so that it can automatically set your clock forward or back as needed on the appropriate days of the year.

Time Not Updating?

Troubleshooting

If your computer's time is off in increments of exactly one hour, you probably have the time zone set incorrectly for your current location. However, if it is off by any other increment of time, the computer may be having trouble connecting to the time server. Check your Internet connection. If it seems okay, try rebooting the computer. If you are still having problems, do the following: Click the clock on the taskar and choose Change Date and Time Settings. Click the Internet Time tab and see if there is an error message. Click Change Settings to open the Internet Time Settings dialog box, and choose a different time server.

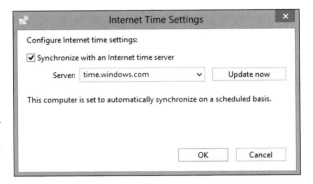

You can optionally display up to two other clocks besides the main clock. This might be useful if you frequently work with someone who lives in another time zone and you want to remember what time it is there when making phone calls or scheduling meetings. When you set up additional clocks, they appear on the pop-up panel when you click the clock, as shown in Figure A.15.

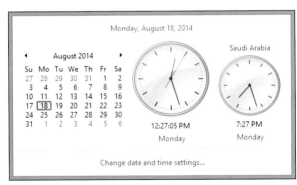

Figure A.15   Additional clocks appear when you click the time in the taskbar.

Step by Step

Changing the Date or Time

Follow these steps to change the date or time:

1. Click the time in the right corner of the taskbar to open the clock.

2. Click Change Date and Time Settings. The Date and Time dialog box appears.

3. On the Date and Time tab, click the Change Date and Time button. The Date and Time Settings dialog box opens.

4. Click a different date on the calendar if desired. Use the right and left arrows at the top of the calendar to change months.

5. Change the time in the Time text box. You can click the hour, the minutes, or the seconds and then use the arrow buttons to increment it up and down instead of typing a different number if you like.

6. Click OK to close the Date and Time Settings dialog box. The time has been changed.

7. Click OK to close the Date and Time dialog box.

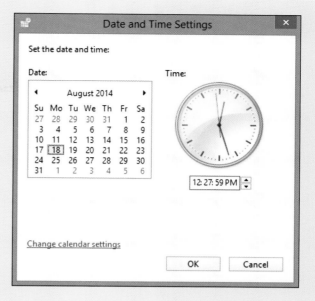

Changing the Time Zone

Use this procedure to change the time zone for your computer:

1. Click the time in the right corner of the taskbar to open the clock.

2. Click Change Date and Time Settings. The Date and Time dialog box appears.

3. Click the Change Time Zone button. The Time Zone Settings dialog box opens.

4. Open the Time Zone drop-down list and choose your current time zone.

5. Click OK to close the Time Zone Settings dialog box.

6. Click OK to close the Date and Time dialog box.

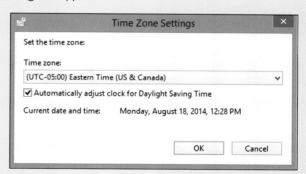

Displaying Additional Clocks

To include additional clocks in your display, follow these steps:

1. Click the time in the right corner of the taskbar to open the clock.

2. Click Change Date and Time Settings. The Date and Time dialog box appears.

3. Click the Additional Clocks tab.

4. Mark the first Show This Clock check box.

5. Open the Select Time Zone drop-down list and choose the time zone for the second clock.

6. Click OK to close the Date and Time dialog box.

Quick Review

1. What is the difference between the display language and the input language?

2. What types of information are affected by changing the Format setting in the Region and Language dialog box?

3. How does Windows automatically keep the time accurate on your system?

4. Does Windows automatically change the time zone when you travel?

Summary

Customizing the Interface

The **User Interface (UI)** can be customized in a variety of ways. You can change the keyboard's **repeat delay, repeat rate,** and **cursor** blink speed. For the mouse, you can customize button configuration, double-click speed, pointers, and movement speed.

The taskbar can be resized and locked, and can be set to auto-hide when not in use. You can change the icon size on the taskbar, pin additional shortcuts to it, and move it to another side of the screen. You can also customize the notification area's icons. You can customize the Start menu and the taskbar by right-clicking either one and choosing Properties. In the dialog box that appears, make settings changes as desired.

The **screen resolution** determines how small or large text and icons appear onscreen. Different resolutions have different **aspect ratios**. Right-click the desktop and choose Screen Resolution to access the settings.

Windows provides **themes** that customize the desktop's appearance by applying a background image, a window color, and sound setting Background, color, and **sound scheme** can also be selected separately. You can also set up a **screen saver**.

Accessibility features help people with disabilities use Windows more easily. Features are available that help with vision, hearing, and movement disabilities. The Ease of Access Center in the Control Panel provides several methods of setting them up.

Changing Location-Based Settings

The **display language** is the language in which the Windows user interface appears. You can have multiple display languages installed and switch between them if you have the right language packs and Windows edition installed.

The **input language** is the language in which you type input. An input language may have one or more **keyboard layouts** that you can switch among. You can change the display and input languages and the keyboard layouts from the Region and Language dialog box, accessed from the Control Panel. You can also choose a region from the Format list in the Region and Language dialog box to specify how Windows will handle dates, numbers, and currency symbols. The Current Location setting lets Windows know where you are physically located, which may affect certain news feeds and custom content.

Windows keeps the date and time current by connecting with **Internet time servers** automatically. You can also manually change the date and time if you like. When you travel between time zones, you must let Windows know the new time zone you want to use. If you frequently work in different time zones, you can optionally display up to two additional clocks.

Key Terms

accessibility features	input language
aspect ratio	Internet time server
brightness	jump list
cursor	keyboard layout
display language	language pack
high-contrast theme	pin
hue	repeat delay

repeat rate
saturation
screen resolution
screen saver

sound scheme
theme
user interface (UI)
window color

Test Yourself

Fact Check

1. True or false: You can change the keyboard layout in the Keyboard Properties dialog box.

   a. true

   b. false

2. True or false: The icons that appear immediately to the right of the Start button represent the Notifications area.

   a. true

   b. false

3. True or false: The Motion setting for the mouse controls how far the pointer onscreen moves in relation to the amount of mouse movement.

   a. true

   b. false

4. When the taskbar is set to _____, you can make it display by moving the mouse pointer to the bottom of the screen, where it should appear.

5. 1600 × 900 is an example of a screen _____.

6. A _____ is a preset combination of desktop formatting features, including background graphic and window color.

7. The keyboard's _____ setting determines how quickly the character repeats once it gets started doing so.

   a. display rate

   b. repeat rate

   c. aspect ratio

   d. repeat delay

8. Before you can change the display language, a _____ has to be installed.

   a. service pack

   b. keyboard layout

   c. language pack

   d. language bar

9. 16:9 is an example of a wide-screen _____.

   a. aspect ratio

   b. monitor layout

   c. color depth

   d. icon size

10. If your clock in Windows is off by exactly one hour, you probably need to change the_____

    a. internet time

    b. time

    c. time zone

    d. date

Matching

Match the accessibility feature to its function.

    a. filter keys

    b. mouse keys

    c. narrator

    d. sound sentry

    e. speech recognition

    f. sticky keys

    g. toggle keys

1. _____Provides visual notifications when system sounds play.

2. _____Ignores brief or repeated key strokes.

3. _____Plays a tone when Caps Lock is pressed.

4. _____Enables key combinations to be pressed one key at a time.

5. _____Enables the mouse pointer to be moved with the keyboard.

6. _____Enable users to control Windows with voice commands.

7. _____Reads the text in the active window aloud.

Sum It Up

1. List three ways that you can personalize the Windows desktop.

2. Explain how to set the time zone to your location.

Explore More

More Mouse Settings

There are many more mouse settings you can adjust than were covered in this appendix. Try out the following settings and then write a brief explanation of which tab of the Mouse Properties dialog box they are located on and what each of them does.

- Click Lock

- Snap To

- Pointer Trails

Many people with disabilities who use a computer have special input devices that help them issue commands and input data. Pick one of the following topics and research on the Internet what products are available and how much they cost. Write a report that details your findings. Include photos where applicable. Make sure you document your sources appropriately.

- Adaptive keyboard or other text-entry alternative to a keyboard

- Adaptive mouse or other pointer-movement alternative to a mouse

Think It Over

Screen Resolution

With a high screen resolution you can fit lots of content on the screen at once, but it may be more difficult to see because icons and text will be smaller. Windows allows you to adjust the size of the text and icons somewhat to help with this, but overall, a higher resolution results in smaller onscreen content. Try out several resolutions on your PC, and determine which one is the best for your needs. Is it the highest one, or one of the lower resolutions?

Another consideration with resolution is that on LCD monitors, the screen looks the sharpest and clearest at the highest (native) resolution. As you tried out different resolutions, did you notice that some resolutions appeared fuzzy? This doesn't happen on a CRT monitor.

Answers to Chapter Questions

Chapter 1

Fact Check

1. d
2. b
3. operating system
4. a
5. c

6. b
7. c
8. b
9. d
10. a

Matching

1. a
2. f
3. c

4. d
5. b
6. e

Chapter 2

Fact Check

1. d
2. c
3. d
4. b
5. c

6. a
7. c
8. a
9. power supply
10. a

Matching

1. e
2. c
3. b

4. f
5. a
6. d

Chapter 3

Fact Check

1. a
2. c
3. b
4. d
5. a

6. c
7. a
8. b
9. b
10. c

Matching

1. c
4. b
2. d

5. f
3. a
6. e

Chapter 4

Fact Check

1. a
2. b
3. b
4. a
5. a

6. c
7. a
8. c
9. a
10. a

Matching

1. a
2. b
3. c
4. d

5. f
6. e
7. g

Chapter 5

Fact Check

1. d
2. c
3. d
4. a
5. b

6. b
7. d
8. c
9. a
10. b

Matching

1. f
2. a
3. e
4. c

5. d
6. b
7. g

Chapter 6

Fact Check

1. c
2. b
3. a
4. b
5. b

6. a
7. b
8. d
9. b
10. a

Matching

1. b
2. f
3. a

4. d
5. e
6. c

Chapter 7

Fact Check

1. a
2. b
3. d
4. c
5. c

6. b
7. a
8. b
9. c
10. c

Matching

1. a
2. f
3. b
4. d

5. g
6. c
7. h
8. e

Chapter 8

Fact Check

1. b
2. d
3. c
4. a
5. c

6. d
7. a
8. b
9. c
10. c

Matching

1. c
2. f
3. a
4. b

5. d
6. g
7. e

Chapter 9

Fact Check

1. b
2. d
3. c
4. d
5. a

6. b
7. a
8. c
9. c
10. c

Matching

1. a
2. e
3. b

4. f
5. c
6. d

Chapter 10

Fact Check

1. a
2. d
3. c
4. a
5. c

6. d
7. b
8. c
9. b
10. a

Matching

1. g
2. e
3. b
4. c

5. d
6. f
7. a

Chapter 11

Fact Check

1. b
2. c
3. b
4. c
5. b

6. b
7. b
8. d
9. d
10. a

Matching

1. b
2. c
3. e

4. d
5. f
6. a

Chapter 12

Fact Check

1. b
2. d
3. a
4. d
5. b

6. c
7. d
8. a
9. b
10. c

Matching

1. a
2. b
3. c

4. e
5. f
6. d

Chapter 13

Fact Check

1. a
2. c
3. b
4. a
5. b

6. c
7. d
8. a
9. c
10. a

Matching

1. c	4. d
2. f	5. b
3. e	6. a

Chapter 14

Fact Check

1. c	6. b
2. d	7. b
3. b	8. a
4. a	9. b
5. b	10. d

Matching

1. e	4. b
2. c	5. f
3. d	6. a

Chapter 15

Fact Check

1. b	6. a
2. d	7. b
3. b	8. b
4. a	9. a
5. d	10. b

Matching

1. d	4. e
2. f	5. a
3. c	6. b

Chapter 16

Fact Check

1. c	6. d
2. d	7. b
3. d	8. a
4. d	9. a
5. a	10. d

Matching

1. b
2. f
3. g
4. c

5. e
6. d
7. a

Chapter 17

Fact Check

1. c
2. c
3. d
4. c
5. a

6. d
7. b
8. a
9. b
10. b

Matching

1. f
2. c
3. d

4. b
5. a
6. e

Appendix A

Fact Check

1. b
2. b
3. a
4. Auto-Hide
5. resolution

6. theme
7. b
8. c
9. a
10. c

Matching

1. d
2. a
3. g
4. f

5. b
6. e
7. c

Glossary

1000BaseT   A type of Ethernet that transfers data at up to 1000 Mbps over twisted-pair cables.

4G   Digital technology for moving data through a cell phone network at up to 100 Mbps.

3G   Digital technology for moving data through a cell phone network at up to 14 Mbps.

absolute reference   In a formula or function, a reference to another cell that does not change if that formula or function is moved or copied to another cell.

accessibility options   Features that help people with disabilities use Windows more easily.

accounting software   Software that enables a small business to manage and track its financial health and transactions.

active cell   The cell that the cell selector is on. Any content entered will appear in the active cell.

active heat sink   A heat sink that is paired with a fan.

active matrix   An LCD type in which each pixel is actively maintained by a separate transistor.

active slide   The slide that currently appears in the Slide pane in Normal view in PowerPoint.

address bar   The field above the menu bar in Windows Explorer that shows the current path.

Administrator account   A user account that has full permission to modify all aspects of Windows.

adware   A type of malware that pops up unwanted ads on the screen.

algorithm   A step-by-step procedure for performing a calculation.

Android   An open-source operating system used on a variety of portable devices, including tablets and smartphones.

animation   A movement effect of an object on a slide.

anti-spam software   Software that rejects junk email messages.

app   An application, such as for a personal computer, tablet, or smartphone.

Apps list   The list accessed from the Start screen of all installed applications.

application software   Software that helps a human perform a useful task for work or play.

archive attribute   A file attribute that indicates whether or not a file has changed since its last backup.

archive   To move items from the current location to another for backup purposes; a useful way of storing old messages while freeing up space for new ones.

argument   A variable in a function, placed in parentheses after the function name.

ascending sort   An A to Z sort, or a sort from smallest to largest.

aspect ratio   The ratio of width to height on a display screen, such as 4:3 (standard) or 16:9 (wide).

attachment   A file that travels along with a text email to a recipient.

audio adapter Also called a sound card. A component of a computer system that accepts and processes audio input and delivers audio output.

audio clip A file that stores a sound, narration, or music.

AutoCorrect A feature that automatically corrects certain spelling errors.

AutoFill The feature that enables content to be filled into adjacent cells by dragging the fill handle from the active cell.

AutoFit Automatically resizing a column width or row height to fit the largest entry.

automatic reply A feature on a mail server that automatically sends a message back to each one received when it is enabled.

AutoRecover A feature that automatically saves your work at specified intervals so you can recover it if the application terminates before you are able to save normally.

axis labels The text on the axes of the chart that shows the values.

axis titles The text on the axes of the chart that shows the meaning of the axis labels.

backbone The central connection pathways of a network, where connection speeds are high and the data pathway is wide.

Backstage view The area of an Office application where you select commands that affect the entire active document or the application itself. Access it by clicking the File tab on the ribbon.

backup appliance A specialized computer that performs backups and stores and retrieves backed up information.

backup set A set of backup files created during a single backup operation.

backup software Software that enables and automates the process of backing up files to external media.

balloon A rounded text box appearing in the space to the right of the document, containing a comment or a tracked change.

bandwidth The amount of data that can be transmitted at a sustained rate by a communication channel or device.

bar chart A chart that uses horizontal bars to represent values.

bar code reader A scanner that reads and interprets bar codes such as UPC symbols.

benchmark A consistent measurement of performance.

bibliography A list of the sources referenced in a document, commonly used in academic writing.

BIOS The software that initializes and tests the system at startup.

bit A single binary digit, with a value of either 1 (on) or 0 (off).

Bitlocker A Windows feature that encrypts the entire hard drive so that it cannot be read if it is moved to another computer.

blacklist A list of prohibited email senders.

blog A web page containing the author's personal experiences and opinions.

blog platform A web server that hosts the blogs of individuals, either free or for a small fee.

Bluetooth An inexpensive short-range networking technology used for computer-to-device connections such as computer-to-printer or phone-to-headset.

Blu-ray disc (BD)   An optical disc used for storing high-definition movies and data, holding up to 25 GB per layer.

borders   Decorative lines used to enhance the appearance of a worksheet by outlining certain cells.

bot   A type of Trojan, used to infect a zombie computer to conduct a DoS attack.

botnet   A network of zombie computers infected with bots, often numbering in the thousands. Computer criminals use botnets to conduct DoS attacks.

bridge   A connector box that enables you to connect two networks of similar types.

brightness   The degree of light or dark in a color.

broadband   A fast, always-on network connection.

bus   A conductive pathway built into a circuit board, used to move data.

byte   An 8-digit binary number, composed of 8 bits.

cable modem   A broadband modem designed to work with a cable Internet connection.

cache   A small amount of fast memory located near or within the CPU.

category 3 cable   A type of UTP cable used in telephone systems.

category 5e cable   A type of UTP cable used in 1000BaseT Ethernet networking.

cathode ray tube (CRT)   An older type of monitor technology that uses a vacuum tube and electron guns to create a display image.

cell   The intersection of a row and a column in a worksheet.

cell address   The column letter and the row number that intersect to form the cell, such as A2 or BB6.

cell cursor   The thick line around the active cell in Excel, indicating that this is where typed text will appear.

cell selector   The movable dark outline around the active cell.

censorship   The act of suppressing speech or not allowing certain communications to be made public.

central processing unit (CPU)   The main processor in a computer.

channel   An individual chat room on a chat server such as IRC.

charge-coupled device (CCD)   The light-sensitive sensor in a scanner that records the amount of light bounced back from the image.

Charms bar   A bar that appears on the right side of the screen when you swipe in from the right or move the mouse pointer to the lower-right corner of the screen, containing five charms.

charms   Icons that appear in a Charms bar when it is activated. These icons open parts of the Windows interface, such as Search or Settings.

chart   A graphic that illustrates and summarizes worksheet data. Examples include pie chart, line chart, and bar chart.

chart area   The entire chart.

chart style   A set of formatting applied to a chart as a whole.

chart title   The overall label for the chart, usually at the top of the chart area.

chat room   An online virtual room in which you can meet and talk to other people.

chipset   The controller chip on a circuit board.

Chrome OS   A thin client operating system created by Google for small notebook computers (netbooks).

circuit-switched network   A network that creates a point-to-point connection between locations that remains open for the duration of the communication.

citation   A reference to a source—that is, to the author and name of a published or unpublished work—following a quotation from said source.

client   A computer used by an individual to run applications.

client/server   A centralized network model that contains one or more servers dedicated to sharing data and resources over the network to clients.

clip art   1) A vector-based line drawing. 2) An image inserted via the Clip Art feature in Office programs.

Clipboard   A reserved area in memory for temporarily holding content that has been cut or copied from an application or from Windows Explorer.

clock cycle   One tick of the system clock.

cloud   A secure computing environment accessed via the Internet.

cloud storage   Storage that is accessed from a cloud environment.

cluster   A grouping of sectors. The number of sectors in a cluster depends on the file system and the disk size.

CMOS Setup   A built-in setup utility in the motherboard that enables users to adjust certain low-level configuration settings.

coaxial cable   Cable that consists of a solid copper core with an insulated sleeve around it.

codec   A translation file used to play back a certain audio or video format. An abbreviation of coder/decoder.

cold boot   To start up a computer from a power-off state.

color depth   The number of bits needed to describe the color of each pixel in a certain display mode, such as 16-bit or 32-bit.

color palette   A grid of color choices that opens when you click a button for a feature that is color-related.

column chart   A chart that uses vertical bars to represent values.

command-line interface   A user interface based on typing text at a command prompt.

comment   A non-printing note inserted into a document to share information or an opinion about the document with others editing it.

compact disc (CD)   An optical disc used for storing music and data, holding up to 900 MB.

compressed archive   A compressed file that contains one or more other files.

compression   The process of reducing the size of a data file by encoding information using fewer bits than the original file.

computer-aided design   The process of using computer software to produce technical drawings that include the product's precise scale, simulate its textures, and show it in full three-dimensional detail.

consumables   Printing supplies that must be replaced with use, such as paper and ink.

Contacts   The section in Outlook that stores people's contact information.

contiguous   Physically adjacent to one another.

cookie   A small file placed by a website on a computer that stores information about the user's interaction with the website.

copyright   The granting of exclusive rights to the creator of a work for a limited period of time.

core   A set of the essential processor components that work together (control unit, ALU, and registers). A CPU may have multiple cores.

cost per page   The total cost of the consumable supplies required to print a page, calculated by dividing the cost of the paper and ink/toner/ribbon by the number of pages it produces before being depleted.

crop   To cut away the unwanted parts of a picture from one or more sides.

cursor   Also called the insertion point, the blinking vertical line that appears in a text box or other area that can accept text input.

cyberbullying   Using computers and the Internet to deliberately harass or harm others by making malicious statements.

cylinder   All the tracks at a single position of the read/write heads' actuator arm.

data label   A label telling the exact value of a particular data point.

data mining   Extracting information from a database to zero in on certain facts or summarize a large amount of data.

data point   A single point of plotted data.

data series   The data representing one row or column in the data used to create the chart.

data table   An optional table that appears below the chart showing the values on which it is based.

database   A collection of data stored in a structured format, with the same facts stored about each instance. A database stores data in a way that enables you to search and locate it quickly.

database management system (DBMS)   An application that helps users create and manage databases.

Datasheet view   A view of a table in which the table's data appears in a structured grid or rows and columns.

decrypt   To reverse the encryption of a file so that the file appears in its original form again.

deduplication   The process of reducing or eliminating duplication in data backup sets.

default file location   The location where the Save As and Open dialog boxes start by default.

default gateway   The port on a router that connects to external networks.

defragment   To relocate a fragmented file on a disk so that its clusters are contiguous.

denial of service (DoS) attack   A coordinated attack in which the target website or service is flooded with requests for access, to the point that it is completely overwhelmed.

descending sort   A Z to A sort, or a sort from largest to smallest.

Design view   A viewing mode for a database object that enables you to modify the object's structure and properties.

desktop   The Windows 8.1 interface, on which windows open containing applications. Can also refer specifically to the background image.

desktop application A traditional style Windows program that runs in a window on the desktop.

desktop PC A computer designed to be set up at a desk and not often moved, with input and output devices separate from the system unit.

desktop publishing software Software that helps create page layouts with text and graphics.

detail query A query that shows all records in the dataset.

device driver A file that translates instructions and messages between the operating system and a hardware device.

Device Manager A Windows utility that provides detailed information about the hardware devices installed on the PC.

dialog box A window that appears in response to selecting a command, prompting for more information about how the user wants the command to be executed.

dialog box launcher An icon in the lower-right corner of a group on the ribbon; when clicked, it opens a dialog box or task pane.

dial-up modem A device that converts between analog and digital data so computer data can be sent over analog phone lines.

differential backup A backup operation that backs up all files that have the archive attribute set to On but does not change that attribute.

digital camera A camera that captures and stores still images in digital form.

digital projector A projector that accepts input from a computer.

digital rights management (DRM) The use of technology to control access to copyrighted material.

digital subscriber line (DSL) A broadband Internet technology provided by the telephone company.

digital versatile disc (DVD) An optical disc used for storing standard-definition movies and data, holding up to 4.17 GB per side per layer.

digital video camera A video camera that captures and stores motion video in digital form.

Digital Visual Interface (DVI) A digital port for connecting a monitor to a PC.

digital whiteboard A whiteboard that is connected to a computer, so that whatever is written on the board is saved on the computer.

digitize To convert something from hard-copy to digital (computerized) form.

direct thermal printer A printer that heats certain areas of specially coated paper so that it turns black and forms the image.

direct-attached storage (DAS) Storage that is directly connected to the computer that accesses it.

disc See *disk*.

disk One or more platters on which data is stored. Spelled *disc* when referring to the optical type (DVDs, CDs).

disaster recovery plan A written plan that explains how a company will recover its IT operations after a natural or man-made disaster that causes data or hardware loss.

disk checking program Software that finds and fixes errors in the disk storage system.

display adapter The computer component that communicates instructions from the operating system to the display.

display language   The language in which the commands and menus in the user interface appear.

display screen   A video screen that a computer uses to provide output to a human user.

distribution   A packaged collection of an open-source kernel such as Linux along with helpful add-ons and utilities. Also called *distro*.

distro   see *distribution*.

dithering   Placing different colored dots side by side in an image so that from a distance they appear to be a third color.

DNS server (domain name system)   A server on the Internet that provides DNS services, translating between domain names and IP addresses.

document feeder   A mechanical feature of some scanners that enables multiple pages to be scanned consecutively without user intervention.

domain name   A name that identifies an entity on the Internet.

Domain Name System (DNS)   The naming system employed to enable users to access websites using their domain names or URLs rather than their IP addresses.

dot matrix   A in impact printer that uses movable pins to form letters and then strikes the page through an inked ribbon with the pins.

dots per inch (dpi)   A measurement of printed image quality, the number of individually colored dots in one row (or column) of one inch of the printed file. A printout can have a different horizontal and vertical dpi, although this is not common.

double data rate SDRAM (DDR SDRAM)   SDRAM that performs two actions per clock tick.

drawing tablet   A flat rectangular touch-sensitive surface on which a user can draw with a stylus to create onscreen artwork.

drive   The mechanical components that read and write the data on a disk.

driver   A software interface between a device and the operating system.

drum   The rotating cylinder inside a laser printer, on which the page image is formed with electrical charges.

dual inline memory module (DIMM)   A small rectangular circuit board that holds DRAM, fitting into a memory slot on a motherboard.

duplexing   To print on both sides of the paper.

dynamic IP address   An IP address that is temporarily assigned to a device.

dynamic memory   Memory that does not retain its data unless it is constantly electrically refreshed.

educational software   Software that teaches or trains an individual in a particular type of knowledge or skill.

Electrically Erasable Programmable ROM (EEPROM)   ROM that can be erased and reprogrammed with electricity.

electromagnetic interference (EMI)   Distortion of electrical signals through a cable by a nearby magnetic field.

electromagnetic interference (EMI)   The corruption of data as it is passing through a cable due to the magnetic field generated by a nearby cable.

email   A computer-based system for exchanging messages through mail servers.

email application   Software that assists in sending and receiving email.

embed fonts   To save the fonts used in the document along with the document itself, so others who view the document on another computer will be sure to have access to them.

encrypt   To scramble the contents of a file so it cannot be read without the required permission to decrypt it.

End User License Agreement (EULA)   The legal agreement between the owner of an application and the user who wants to install and use it.

e-paper   A monitor technology used in book readers in which the screen retains its image but is unpowered except when the display changes.

ergonomic keyboard   A keyboard that is designed with features that help reduce stress on the user's hands and wrists.

Ethernet   The current dominant standard for local area networking devices.

expansion card   A small circuit board that fits into a slot on the motherboard to add functionality.

expansion slot   A slot in the motherboard into which an expansion card (a small circuit board) can be installed.

ExpressCard   A metal cartridge inserted into an externally accessible slot in a notebook PC that adds a capability to the system, such as wireless networking.

extranet   A special network set up by a business for its customers, staff, and business partners to access from outside the office network; may be used to share marketing assets and other non-sensitive items.

Facebook   A social network for posting interesting updates, web links, and photos, and for chatting with friends.

FaceTime   An app installed on Apple devices such as the iPhone and iPad that is used to make video calls between Apple device owners.

FAT32   A file system used in Windows 95, Windows 98, and Windows Millennium Edition. FAT stands for File Allocation Table.

Favorite   A website or page that you visit frequently, and to which you want easy access.

fiber optic cable   Cable that carries data using light pulses through a bundle of glass fibers.

field   A column in a table, storing one particular kind of information, such as Phone or Name.

file   A group of related bits stored together under a single name.

File Explorer   The file management utility in Windows 8.

file extension   A code at the end of a filename that indicates the file's type.

file system   A set of rules for storing and managing the files on a volume, such as NTFS or FAT32.

fill   A background color, such as in a cell or graphic object.

fill handle   The small dark green rectangle in the lower-right corner of the cell selector, used to extend the selection to other cells by dragging.

filter   To hide certain records according to criteria you specify.

filtering   Preventing something from getting through—in this case, content.

firewall software   Software that blocks hackers from accessing a computer by closing unnecessary services and ports.

firewall   A security barrier on your computer or network that controls what traffic is allowed to pass through.

flaming   Where Internet users interact in a hostile way with each other.

flatbed scanner   A scanner that has a large flat glass surface on which the page to be scanned is placed.

folder   A logical organizing unit for grouping related files together.

folder tree   A graphical representation of a volume's storage hierarchy, with subordinate branches for folders and subfolders.

footer   The area at the bottom of each page that contains consistent or repeated information.

footnote   Information about the source of a quote, which is marked with a number and appears at the bottom of the page.

foreign key   A field that has a relationship to the primary key field in another table.

form factor   The size and shape of a circuit board, such as a motherboard.

form   A database helper object that simplifies data entry to presenting a user-friendly form in which to enter data.

format   To create the file system on a volume.

formula   A mathematical calculation to be performed in an Excel cell. It may refer to other cells for its values.

formula bar   The bar above the worksheet where the contents of the active cell appear. If the active cell contains a formula, the formula appears in the formula bar and the result of the formula appears in the cell itself.

forum   A web-based discussion and advice-sharing site.

forum thread   A post on a forum along with all the comments to it.

Forward   A copy of a message sent on to someone other than the original sender.

fragmented   A file whose clusters are not contiguous.

frame   A still image that makes up part of a digital video clip.

full backup   A backup operation that backs up all files and sets their archive attribute to Off.

function   A named calculation that can be performed in Excel, such as AVERAGE or SUM.

fuser   The heating element in a laser printer that melts the toner, fusing it to the paper.

gateway   A connector box that enables you to connect two dissimilar networks.

General Public License (GPL)   A license used for many types of open-source software, allowing the software to be legally copied and modified.

gigahertz   One billion hertz.

global positioning system (GPS)   A device that determines your current position by communicating with an orbiting satellite and provides maps and driving directions.

graphical user interface (GUI)   A user interface based on a graphical environment, in which users interact with it using a pointing device or touch screen as the primary input device.

graphics software   Software that enables you to create and manipulate visual images.

gridlines   The lines around each cell, which may be visible or not depending on settings.

group   A named section of a ribbon tab.

groupware   Software that helps people collaborate on business projects and work together in a team environment when they are not physically together.

Guest account   A special Windows account that has very few permissions, optionally offered at start-up so users who do not have an account on the computer can sign in.

hard copy   Physically printed pages of a document or a printed photo; the opposite of soft (electronic) copy.

hard disk drive (HDD)   A mechanical drive with an integrated set of disk platters that store data in patterns of magnetic polarity.

hard drive   A sealed metal box that stores computer data using either mechanical or solid-state technology.

hard page break   A page break created by the user in order to force a page break in a certain place.

hard reset   A device reset that wipes out all custom data and settings, returning the device's software to its factory-new condition.

hardware   The physical parts of the computer system.

hashtag   See *tag*.

header   The area at the top of each page that contains consistent or repeated information.

heat sink   A copper or aluminum block that diverts heat away from a heat-generating component such as a CPU. When not paired with a fan, called a passive heat sink.

hertz   One cycle per second, a measurement of activity speed.

Hibernate mode   A power-saving mode that saves the contents of RAM to the hard drive and then shuts down all power. When the computer wakes up, it reads the saved data back into RAM so the computer does not have to restart completely.

hierarchical database   A way of organizing data from a single starting point or premise in a tree-like parent and child relationship format. All records are shown in terms of how they relate to the originating point at the top of the tree.

Hierarchical File System Plus (HFS+)   The file system used with Mac OS X.

high-contrast theme   A theme that uses starkly contrasting colors for adjacent items, such as window borders and the Windows desktop, to make them easier to see.

high-definition multimedia interface (HDMI)   A type of connector used to connect an HDTV to another device, such as a computer or a home theater system.

high-definition TV (HDTV)   A television that displays at least 1920 × 1080 resolution (also known as 1080p).

home page   The page that is displayed when you first launch your web browser.

homegroup   A small group of mutually trusted computers on a peer-to-peer network such as in a home or small office.

hotspot   A wireless network that can be used by members of the public (for free or at cost).

HTML   See *HyperText Markup Language*.

HTTP   See *HyperText Transfer Protocol*.

HTTP email account   An email account that is designed to be used with a web interface, and that uses web technology for email management.

hub   A primitive version of a switch that lacks the capability to read packet addresses and route them to the appropriate port.

hue   The color being represented, such as red, green, or blue.

hyperlink   A pointer to another point on a web page, which you access by clicking the hyperlink.

Hypertext Markup Language (HTML)   A language for encoding data and graphics for display in a web browser.

HyperText Transfer Protocol (HTTP)   The protocol used to send and receive web pages on the Internet.

icon   A small picture representing a file, folder, application, or other object.

IEEE 1394A   A connector used to connect certain types of devices to a computer that require high-speed connection, such as some external hard drives and video cameras. A competitor to USB. Also called FireWire.

IMAP account   An email account that is designed to be used with an email client and that uses IMAP protocol for receiving mail.

impact printer   A printer that makes the image on the page by striking it through an inked ribbon.

incremental backup   A backup operation that backs up all files that have the archive attribute set to On and then sets the attribute to Off.

indentation   The amount that a paragraph is offset from the document margins.

information processing cycle   The four-step process that data moves through as it is processed by a computer. Consists of input, processing, output, and storage.

information system   An interconnected environment for managing and processing data using a computer.

infrared   Older type of wireless communication that used light waves to pass simple information between nearby devices.

inkjet printer   A printer that squirts ink onto paper with small nozzles (jets) to form the page image.

input device   Hardware that enables the computer to accept commands or data from a human user.

input language   The language on which the current keyboard layout is based.

insertion point   The flashing vertical line that indicates where typed text will appear.

Instagram   A social network for posting and sharing photos.

instant messaging   Sending and receiving short text messages in real-time over the Internet.

instructions per second   A measurement of a CPU's throughput capability, taking into consideration factors such as number of cores and latency.

Intel platform   A platform that was originally based on CPUs made by Intel. The Intel platform can run Windows, UNIX, Linux, and newer versions of Mac OS X operating systems.

intellectual property (IP)   The exclusive rights to the ownership of something that has been created or produced.

Internet   A global packet-switched network created cooperatively by multiple companies, governments, and standards organizations.

Internet Mail Access Protocol (IMAP)   A protocol for receiving email through a mail client.

Internet Relay Chat (IRC)   An online system of public chat servers.

Internet service provider (ISP)   A company that maintains a direct connection to the Internet and leases access to it to individuals and companies.

Internet time server   An online server that provides the current date and time to any software that asks for it.

intranet   A special network that only staff within the company network can access. For security reasons an intranet can only be accessed onsite and not remotely.

iOS   The Apple-created operating system for Apple tablets and phones.

IP address   A numeric address by which a particular computer is known on a network.

IPv4 address   An addressing system made up of 32 binary digits, represented as four decimal numbers separated by dots like this: 131.107.23.100.

IPv6 address   An addressing system made up of 128 binary bits, represented as eight groups of hexadecimal numbers.

ISO 9660   A file system used on optical media such as CDs; also called CD File System, or CDFS.

joystick   A pointing device consisting of a vertically mounted stick that can be tilted in any direction.

jump list   A list of files that appears when you hover the mouse pointer over a program icon on the taskbar.

keyboard   An input device that allows users to type data into a computer using a standard set of typing keys.

keyboard layout   The arrangement of the keys on the keyboard.

keyboard shortcut   Two or more keys that, when pressed in combination, issue a command.

keylogger   A piece of hardware or a software program that captures every keystroke a user types.

LAN   See *local area network*.

landscape   The page orientation in which the text runs parallel to the wide edge of the paper.

language pack   Add-on software that allows a copy of Windows originally written in one language to use a different display language.

laser printer   A printer that forms the page image by transferring toner to the paper via a rotating drum with electrical charges.

latency   A period of waiting for another component to deliver data needed to proceed.

layout   A preset arrangement of placeholders on a PowerPoint slide.

layout master   The template slide that controls the appearance and repeated elements for all slides that use a certain layout in a presentation.

legal software   Software that guides the user in creating legally binding contracts and forms.

legend   The key that tells what each color or pattern represents.

libel   Putting in writing a defamatory statement that could damage a person's or organization's reputation.

library   A virtual folder that combines the contents of one or more specified folders into a single view.

line spacing   The amount of vertical space between the lines of a paragraph.

Linux   An open-source, cross-platform operating system that runs on desktops, notebooks, tablets, and smartphones.

liquid crystal display (LCD)   A flat-screen display technology that passes electricity through liquid crystals to create a display image.

local account   A user account that exists only on a specific computer and is not linked to any online identity.

local area network (LAN)   A network that connects devices housed in the same physical location.

lock   To prevent unauthorized users from using a computer by displaying a password prompt.

logical error   A hard drive error caused by an inconsistency between the drive's actual content and the Master File Table.

lookup   A menu of choices for entering data into a field.

lumens   The measurement of brightness of a digital projector's image.

Mac OS X   The graphical operating system designed for Apple's desktop and notebook computers. Newer versions now run on the Intel platform.

machine cycle   One complete cycle of the CPU's activities of fetching, decoding, executing, and storing.

magnetic card reader   A scanner that reads and deciphers the information on the magnetic strip on a credit card or other ID card.

magnetic-ink character recognition (MICR)   The scanning system used in the banking industry to read routing and account numbers on checks and deposit slips.

mail client   Software installed on a computer that is used to compose and manage email.

mail server   An online server that sends and/or receives email messages on behalf of the email addresses it supports.

mainframe   A large and powerful computer capable of serving many users and processing large amounts of data at once.

maintenance window   The time specified for Windows to perform its daily maintenance tasks.

malware   Malicious software that consists of programs designed to disrupt the normal operation of computer systems.

margins   The blank space between the edge of the paper and the document's content.

Master File Table (MFT)   The internal table of contents for a hard drive that uses the NTFS file system.

maximize   To enlarge the window to fill the entire screen.

maximum resolution   The highest display mode (the greatest number of pixels) a display can support.

mechanical mouse   A mouse that operates by rolling a rubber ball inside a chamber containing sensors.

media access control (MAC) address   A unique hardware address for a network adapter.

memory   Temporary electronic storage that holds the values of data bits using transistors.

memory address   The numeric address of a particular addressable area in memory.

menu bar   A horizontal bar near the top of a window containing the names of menus that can be opened by clicking on the names.

merge To combine two or more cells into a single cell.

metropolitan area network (MAN) A network that connects devices within the area of a city or town.

microblog A service that allows the posting of short messages.

Microsoft account A user account that is registered with Microsoft, allowing use of online features such as OneDrive and social media connections.

Microsoft Office A productivity suite of applications commonly used in businesses for word processing, spreadsheets, databases, presentation, and email.

Microsoft Windows The graphical Microsoft operating system designed for Intel-platform desktop and notebook computers.

microwave communication system A secure, point-to-point wireless networking technology that requires a line of sight between the two points.

minimize To shrink the window to a button on the taskbar.

mixed reference A reference that is partly absolute and partly relative. For example, the row number may be relative and the column letter may be absolute.

modem see *dial-up modem* or *cable modem*.

monitor A display screen on which a computer's output appears.

motherboard A large circuit board inside a computer that controls the operations of all other components.

mouse A pointing device that the user moves with his or her hand across a flat surface to move an onscreen pointer.

multi-function device (MFD) A device that combines the functions of a printer, a copier, and a scanner into one unit, and also a fax in some models.

Name box The box above cell A1 where the name of the active cell appears.

name resolution The process of translating domain names to numerical IP addresses. A DNS server is used to resolve a name to an address.

NAS appliance A specialized device that provides storage space to network users.

navigation pane (Access) The pane along the left side of the Access window that lists and organizes database objects.

navigation pane (PowerPoint) The pane on the left side of the screen in Normal view in PowerPoint, showing thumbnail images of the presentation.

netbook A small notebook PC designed primarily for accessing the Internet.

network Two or more computers connected to share data and resources.

network adapter A hardware component that enables a computer to connect to a network.

network interface card (NIC) A network adapter that is on an expansion card, rather than built into the computer's motherboard. Sometimes used informally to refer to any network adapter.

network switch See *switch*.

network-attached storage (NAS) Storage that is accessed via a network.

New Technology File System (NTFS) The proprietary Microsoft file system used in modern versions of Windows.

newsgroup An online discussion group.

newsreader Software that organizes incoming messages from newsgroups and allows users to read and respond to them.

node The point of intersection in a diagram or in a database; where several items share a node, the node itself becomes important.

non-contiguous Not adjacent.

non-impact printer A printer that makes the image on the page using a method that does not physically strike the paper.

Normal view The default PowerPoint view, in which you can edit the content of individual slides.

notebook PC A portable PC where the screen and keyboard fold up against one another for storage and transport; also known as a laptop.

Notes pane The pane in which you type speaker notes in Normal view in PowerPoint.

notification area The area to the left of the clock on the taskbar, containing icons for programs running in the background. Also called the system tray.

number format A format applied to a cell that makes the numbers in it appear in a certain way, such as currency or percentage.

object An item that is separate from the rest of the document, with its own movable and resizable frame.

Office Clipboard The enhanced version of the Windows Clipboard that appears in Office applications. It can hold up to 24 items at once.

one-to-many relationship A relationship in which the connected field is unique in one table and not unique in the other table.

open-source software Free access to a software program and the source code that produced the program.

operating system Software that maintains the computer's interface, manages file, runs applications, and communicates with hardware.

optical drive A drive that reads discs that are stored in patterns of greater and lesser reflectivity, such as a DVD or CD.

optical mark recognition A scanner that detects the presence of a pencil or ink mark on certain areas of a standardized form.

optical mouse A mouse that operates by bouncing light off a flat surface and measuring the reflection.

order of operations The order in which math operators in a formula are calculated: exponentiation, and then multiplication/division, and then addition/subtraction.

organic light-emitting diode (OLED) A flat-screen technology that uses organic matter that lights up in response to electrical current to create a display image.

orientation The direction that the text runs in relation to the paper. Can be either portrait or landscape.

out-of-office message A message that people receive when you are unable to personally answer your email for a certain time.

Outline view A view similar to Normal view in PowerPoint except it shows the text of each slide in the navigation pane.

overclock To push a CPU to run faster than the speed for which it is rated.

packet-switched network A network that transfers data by breaking it up into separately transferred packets.

paging file The area of the hard drive set aside for use as virtual memory. Also called a swap file.

pair To connect a Bluetooth input or output device to a computer.

PAN (personal area network) A network formed when several devices are all connected to the same computer.

paragraph formatting Formatting that applies to entire paragraphs, not to individual characters.

Parallel ATA (PATA) A type of connector used for older disk drives and optical drives such as CD and DVD drives.

parallel port A port used to connect some older printers to a computer. It is sometimes called an LPT port, which stands for Line Printer.

paraphrase To use different words to convey the same idea.

partition To create logical divisions of the available space on a storage medium such as an HDD; or, a logical division of space on a storage medium.

passive matrix An LCD type in which each pixel maintains its state on its own until it decays or is refreshed.

password A word, phrase, or string of characters that a user enters in order to authenticate his or her identity.

password cracking The act of attempting to identify a user's password in order to gain access to a system or program.

path The complete descriptor of a file's location, including the volume and folders.

PCI Express (PCIe) A new and updated version of the PCI motherboard slot. Different numbers of channels are used in different sized PCIe slots, such as 16, 4, or 1.

PCI Express Mini Card A small circuit board that can be installed in a notebook PC's PCI Express Mini expansion bay to add a capability to the computer, such as wireless networking.

Peer-to-peer (P2P) network A network where all computers can both share and acces resources from other computers on the same network; a decentralized network.

Peripheral Component Interface (PCI) A motherboard slot that accepts PCI expansion boards. PCI is considered a legacy interface (mostly obsolete).

personal area network (PAN) A network formed when devices are connected to an individual computer.

personal computer A computer designed to be used by only one person at a time.

personal finance software Software that enables individuals to track and manage their bank accounts and investments.

phishing The act of attempting to acquire information such as usernames, passwords, credit card information, and so forth, by pretending to be from a genuine, trustworthy source such as a bank.

physical error A hard drive error caused by a physically unreadable spot on the disk.

pie chart A chart that represents the data as slices of a pie, or parts of a whole.

pin To attach a shortcut to a program or data file to a certain menu or toolbar.

pinned Attached to a fixed feature onscreen, such as to the taskbar or the Start screen.

pixel An individual colored dot in a raster graphic or on a display screen.

pixilated   The effect of seeing the jagged edges of individual pixels that occurs when a raster image is enlarged.

plagiarism   The act of copying someone else's work and pretending that it is your own.

platform   A type of computer hardware that is compatible with certain operating systems.

platform-independent   An interaction between two computers in which the type of hardware and the operating system that each one uses is irrelevant.

plot area   The part of the chart on which the data is plotted.

plotter   A large-format printer that creates high-precision documents such as maps and engineering drawings.

Plug and Play   A standard that enables the BIOS and operating system to identify a hardware device and install a driver for it automatically if one is available.

plug-in   A piece of software added to a web browser to give it additional functionality.

point   The measurement used to describe font height; one point equals $\frac{1}{72}$ of an inch.

pointing device   An input device such as a mouse or touchpad that enables users to move an onscreen pointer to select content and issue commands.

POP account   An email account that is designed to be used with an email client and that uses POP protocol for receiving mail.

portrait   The page orientation in which the text runs parallel to the narrow edge of the paper.

POST card   An expansion board that is placed in an empty expansion slot in a motherboard; it displays a numeric code that helps in troubleshooting errors where no text appears onscreen.

post   An article published on a blog.

Post Office Protocol (POP)   A protocol for receiving email through a mail client.

posture   How a person sits or stands. When someone has good posture, the body is straight and the spine is correctly aligned.

power supply   A component that converts AC power from a wall outlet to DC power and steps down the voltage to the level needed for the computer to operate.

powered speakers   Speakers that contain their own amplification, powered by either AC current or batteries.

power-on self test (POST)   A low-level hardware test that occurs at start-up, before the operating system loads.

presentation graphics   Graphics designed to accompany a public speaking activity, a lesson, or a business presentation.

presentation graphics software   A program that combines charts, graphics, and bulleted lists of information as a series of slides that summarize a report or verbal presentation. Microsoft PowerPoint is the most widely used program.

primary key   The field that is unique for all records in the table, by which records in the table will be referenced in other tables.

primary storage   System RAM in a computer, where processed data is first stored after it exits the CPU.

processor   The chip in the computer that performs math calculations, processing data. Also called the Central Processing Unit (CPU).

productivity software   Software that helps a human perform one or more business or personal enrichment tasks.

proprietary software   Software to which the vendor retains ownership rights. Users merely have usage right.

protocol   A rule or custom that governs how something is done. In a computer context, it refers to a standard for transferring data.

protocol stack   A related group of protocols—for example, TCP/IP.

proxy server   A server that sits between the user's web browser and the Internet that intercepts all requests for web pages and processes those requests.

PS/2 port   A connector used to connect some older keyboards and mice to a computer. PS stands for Personal System. This connector was first introduced with the IBM PS/2 computer in 1987.

public switched telephone network (PSTN)   The worldwide network of circuit-switched telephone lines.

pull technology   A technology that sends information to a recipient only when the recipient requests it.

push technology   A technology that sends information to a recipient without the recipient asking for it each time.

QR code   A two-dimensional variant of a bar code, containing more information than a traditional bar code.

query   A saved set of specifications for manipulating data in one or more tables.

Quick Access Toolbar (QAT)   The small, customizable toolbar above the ribbon tabs in an Office application's interface.

QWERTY   The standard layout for English-language keyboards.

radio frequency identification (RFID) chip   A computer chip that communicates wirelessly with a device to authenticate a user.

Random Access Memory (RAM)   Memory that can have its values changed freely, an unlimited number of times.

range   A logical grouping of one or more cells that function as a single unit while selected.

ransomware   A type of Trojan that encrypts files on a user's system. It then displays a message describing how to decrypt the files—which inevitably involves sending payment over the Internet. Even after the money is sent, however, the files are not decrypted.

raster graphic   A graphic that consists of a grid of colored pixels that collectively form an image.

read/write head   A component in a disk drive that reads and writes to the disk(s).

reading pane   A pane in a mail client that previews the content of the selected message.

Read-Only Memory (ROM)   In general, memory that cannot be rewritten. However, there are exceptions to that in newer types of ROM.

record   A row in a table, storing information about a specific person, place, or thing.

Recycle Bin   A temporary holding area for deleted content.

Reddit   A social network for posting new snippets.

redundant array of independent disks (RAID)   A multi-disk storage system that optimizes performance, data safety, or both, depending on the type.

reference software   Software that provides access to established facts and information on a variety of topics.

referential integrity   A requirement that the data in related tables be matched, so that an entry in the "many" side of the relationship (the foreign key) must have a corresponding entry in the "one" side of the relationship (the primary key).

refresh   To reinstall Windows system files without disturbing existing applications and data.

refresh rate   The number of times each pixel in a display is refreshed per second.

registry   The main system configuration database for Microsoft Windows.

registry cleanup program   Software that analyzes the Windows registry and deletes unneeded entries.

relational database   A database in which data is stored in multiple, interrelated tables.

relationship   A connection between two tables based on a shared field.

relative reference   In a formula or function, a reference to another cell that changes if that formula or function is moved or copied to another cell.

render   To apply a surface texture and fill to a wireframe image to give it a solid appearance.

repeat delay   The amount of time between when a key is held down and when it starts repeating.

repeat rate   The speed at which a key repeats after the repeat delay period has passed.

repeater   A device that receives and retransmits a network signal.

Reply   A message that is sent back to the original sender.

Reply All   A message that is sent back to the original sender plus to any other recipients.

report   A saved definition of a layout for presenting database data in printed form.

reset   To return Windows to its original state, removing all applications and data installed by the user.

resolution   The number of pixels that comprise a display, horizontally and vertically.

restart   See *warm boot*.

restore   To shrink a window from its maximized state to the size it was before it was maximized.

ribbon   The main toolbar in Office applications and some other Windows applications, consisting of multiple tabbed pages of commands.

RJ-11   A connector used on one-line UTP telephone cables.

RJ-14   A connector used on two-line UTP telephone cables.

RJ-45   A connector used on UTP cables designed for Ethernet networking.

rogue Wi-Fi   A wireless network that "sniffs" traffic, making a copy of everything users type—including usernames, passwords, and credit card numbers.

roll back   To return to a previous version, as in rolling back a device driver.

root directory   The top level folder on a storage volume.

rotation handle   The arrow circle at the top of a selected picture that, when dragged, rotates the picture.

router   A connection box for Ethernet networks that physically joins the devices in the network (wired) or provides wireless connectivity (wireless), and enables a connection to an outside network such as the Internet.

satellite   A data transmitter/receiver in geosynchronous orbit with the Earth.

satellite Internet   A broadband Internet technology that uses satellites and a transmitter/receiver to provide Internet access.

saturation   The intensity of the color. A highly saturated color is vivid; a minimally saturated color looks close to gray with only a pale tint of the color.

save location   The location where files are saved when a user saves them to a library.

scatter chart   A chart that plots data in patterns of dots scattered on the plot area. Scatter charts are useful for showing the results of experiments or studies where the results may not be repeatable or absolute.

screen resolution   The number of pixels used to form the display image, expressed as width × height, like this: 1024 × 768.

screen saver   A utility that displays a moving object or changing pattern on the screen after there has been no user interaction for a specified amount of time.

ScreenTip   The information that appears about a command or button when you hover the mouse pointer over it.

scroll   To page through the document so that a different part of it becomes visible.

scroll bar   The horizontal or vertical bar to the bottom or right of the document, containing scroll arrows and a scroll box, which you can use to scroll.

scroll box   The box in the scroll bar that you can drag to scroll the display. You can also click above or below the scroll box to scroll one screenful at a time.

search engine optimization (SEO)   The process of writing web content so as to increase a page's ranking in online search results.

search engine   A software tool used to locate information on the web.

search operator   A word or symbol that has a specific function when carrying out a search.

secondary storage   Storage that retains data after the computer is turned off, such as a hard disk drive, DVD, or USB flash drive.

section break   A divider in a document that allows settings that are normally document-wide to be applied differently in parts of the document.

sector   The smallest addressable unit of storage on a disk drive, at 512 bytes.

select query   A query that selects certain fields and records from one or more tables.

selection handles   The markers on the border of an object that allow the object to be resized.

semiconductor   Material that is electricity-neutral, neither a good conductor nor a flow preventer.

Serial ATA (SATA)   A type of connector used for newer disk drives.

serial port   A port used to connect some very old external devices to a computer. It is sometimes called a COM port, which stands for Communications (although actually many types of ports operate serially, not just this one).

server   A computer that is dedicated to performing network tasks such as managing files, printers, or email for multiple users.

server farm   A group of servers located in the same physical area.

service pack   A collection of patches, released in a single package.

service set identification (SSID) The name assigned to identify a wireless access point so that other computers can find it.

Shapes The drawing feature in Office applications that enables users to create vector-based lines and shapes.

shell The user interface for an operating system. Some operating systems, like Windows, do not separate the shell from the kernel; others, like Linux, give you a choice of shells.

shielded twisted pair (STP) A type of twisted-pair cable that has an outer sheath that protects against external EMI.

Short Message Service (SMS) The text messaging technology used on cell phone networks.

shortcut menu A context-sensitive menu that appears when you right-click an object onscreen.

shortcut A pointer to a file or folder.

shut down To quit Windows and turn the computer's power off.

sign in To log into an operating system or website with a specific user account.

sign out To close a user account's session, closing all open programs and data files and unloading all of that user's personal settings.

signature Text that is automatically appended to outgoing messages.

signed drivers Drivers that are certified to work with certain versions of Windows and certain hardware models.

Simple Mail Transfer Protocol (SMTP) A protocol used for sending email for a POP3 email account.

single data rate SDRAM (SDR SDRAM) SDRAM that performs one action per clock tick.

Skype A Microsoft-owned VoIP service used to make phone calls and sometimes video calls over a broadband, Wi-Fi, or cellular mobile web connection.

slander Making a defamatory verbal statement that could damage a person's or organization's reputation.

Sleep mode A power-saving mode that keeps RAM powered but turns off everything else to save power.

sleep To place the computer in a low power consumption mode without shutting down running programs.

slide A screen of information that is displayed in a static fashion while a presenter elaborates on its contents. Often, the slide will be part of an electronic presentation file and the presenter can move through successive files on demand.

slide master The template slide that controls the appearance and repeated elements for all slides in a presentation.

Slide Master view The PowerPoint view in which you can make changes to the slide master.

Slide pane The main editing pane for a slide in Normal view in PowerPoint.

Slide Sorter view The PowerPoint view in which you can browse thumbnail images of all the slides in the presentation and easily rearrange them.

SmartArt A tool in Office applications that combines shapes with text listings to create informative and visually interesting graphics.

smartphone A cellular phone that includes computer applications and Internet access capability.

sniffing   The act of intercepting and logging traffic over a network for future analysis. A sniffer can either be a software program or a hardware device.

social engineering   The art of obtaining someone's password either by befriending her or tricking her into sharing it.

social network   An Internet-based system that enables users to interact in real-time and by using messaging programs.

soft page break   A page break made automatically by the application when the current page is full.

soft reset   A device reset that retains all the device's settings and data.

software   The programs that tell the computer what to do.

Software as a Service (SaaS)   A model of software sales that leases access to the software rather than selling a copy outright to the user.

software piracy   The unauthorized copying and distribution of software.

solid-state hard drive (SSHD)   A high-capacity solid state storage device that substitutes for an HDD as the main storage drive in a computer.

sort   To put records in a specific order according to the entry in a certain field.

sound scheme   A set of sounds that are used to indicate common events.

spam   Unsolicited "junk" mail, typically containing offers (some legitimate, some not) of products or services to buy.

speech recognition software   Software that can learn an individual's pronunciation and vocal inflection and translate it into digitized text.

spoofing   An attack in which a user pretends to be another by providing false IP address data.

spreadsheet   A program that presents rows and columns of figures and other items against which time and other variables can be plotted.

spyware   A type of malware that spies on the user's activities and reports them back to the spyware's developer.

Standard account   A user account that can only make changes to Windows that do not affect other users.

standard colors   Fixed colors that are not affected by the theme in use.

Start button   The button on the desktop taskbar that opens the Start screen.

Start screen   The tile-based interface from which you can start applications in Windows 8.1.

static IP address   An IP address that is permanently assigned to a device.

static memory   Memory that retains its data without electricity being constantly applied.

status bar   The bar at the bottom of an application's window that reports status information.

storage-area network (SAN)   A distributed storage system that appears to each individual computer as a local volume on that computer.

store-and-forward   A message delivery system in which messages are forwarded between servers and then stored on those servers until they are picked up.

striping   Spreading the data across multiple drives to improve performance or protect the data.

strong password   A password that includes a combination of uppercase letters, lowercase letters, numerals, and symbols, making it difficult to guess.

structured data Data that has a consistent pattern to it, with the same type of information in every row, as in a database.

style A named, preset combination of formatting.

style set An alternative set of style definitions for the basic built-in styles.

stylus A pen-shaped pointer used to drag across the surface of a touch-sensitive screen.

subfolder A folder within another folder.

suite A group of applications by the same manufacturer purchased as a group.

suite A group of applications designed to complement each other's capabilities and work together closely, often with a consistent interface between the applications.

summary query A field that totals or summarizes the data from the records rather than listing each record.

supercomputer The largest and most powerful type of computer, surpassing the capability of a mainframe, typically used in research and academics.

swap file See *paging file*.

switch A gathering point for the computers in a LAN to connect with to participate in the network.

synchronous dynamic RAM (SDRAM) DRAM that operates at the speed of the system clock.

system clock A crystal on the motherboard that sets the timing for data moving through the system, such as between memory and the CPU. This chip contains a crystal that oscillates at a certain frequency to produce the timing pulses.

system memory The main pool of dynamic RAM (DRAM) on the motherboard.

system requirements The minimum hardware required to install and run an application.

system software Software that starts the computer and keeps it running, performing basic system tasks such as running applications, managing files, and correcting errors.

system unit The main part of the computer, containing the essential components.

system volume The volume on which the operating system files are stored.

system-on-chip (SoC) An operating system that comes preinstalled on a chip on a portable device such as a smartphone.

tab (browser) A web browser feature that enables users to have multiple pages open at once within the same browser window.

tab (ribbon) A tabbed page of a ribbon, or the name of a particular tabbed page.

tab stop A non-printing marker in a paragraph that stops the insertion point when the Tab key is pressed.

table In Word or PowerPoint, a grid of cells into which you can place data to help organize and present it in orderly rows and columns.

table style A style that applies to an entire table, formatting it with a set of preset formatting, including borders and sharing.

tablet PC A lightweight slate-style computer with a touch screen, designed for easy portability.

tag A topic or subject assigned to a social networking post. Also called a **hashtag.**

Task Manager   A utility that shows the running applications and their processes and allows you to shut down unresponsive applications.

taskbar   The bar along the bottom of the Windows desktop, from which you can start programs and manage running programs.

tax software   Software that enables individuals and small businesses to calculate the taxes they owe and file the needed forms with the government.

TCP/IP   See *Transmission Control Protocol/Internet Protocol (TCP/IP)*

template   A file containing preset layout and formatting settings and sometimes sample content.

tether   To connect a smartphone to a computer so that the computer can use the smartphone's Internet access.

text effects   A set of special effects you can apply to text, such as outline, shadow, and glow.

texting   Sending and receiving short text messages in real-time over a cell phone network.

theme   A named set of formatting presets, governing font, color, and object effect choices.

theme colors   The colors assigned to the color placeholders in a theme.

thermal dye transfer printer   A printer that heats ribbons containing dye and then diffuses the dye onto specially coated paper.

thermal printer   A printer that transfers images to paper using heat.

thermal wax transfer printer   A printer that melts a wax-based ink onto paper in tiny dots.

thin client   A computer with minimal hardware, designed for a specific task. For example, a thin web client is designed for using the Internet.

thin-film transistor   An improved type of active matrix common in modern monitors and display screens.

tile   A square or rectangular block on the Start screen that represents an application or file.

title bar   The bar across the top of a window that shows the window's name; you can move the window by dragging it.

toner   The powdered mixture of plastic and iron used to form the image on a laser printer.

toolbar   A group of graphical buttons representing commands.

top-level domain   The code at the end of a URL that indicates the type of organization the name represents, such as COM for commercial businesses.

touch screen   A touch-sensitive display monitor that functions both as an input and an output device.

touchpad   A pointing device consisting of a touch-sensitive pad on which the user drags a finger to move the pointer.

track   One of the concentric rings in a disk's organizational system.

trackball   A pointing device in which the user moves the pointer by rolling a ball with his or her fingers.

transceiver   A unit that provides the wireless transmission for a cordless device like keyboard or mouse, usually plugged in to a USB port.

transformer block   A thick block built into a power cable for a device that handles the conversion of AC power to DC and steps down the voltage to the level needed.

transition   A movement effect between one slide and another.

Transmission Control Protocol/Internet Protocol (TCP/IP) The protocol suite (set of rules) that defines how data will move on the Internet and on most other modern networks.

trend line The straight line that runs through the data, showing the overall trend that the data represents.

triad A cluster of three phosphors: one red, one green, and one blue.

Trojan A piece of malicious software that looks harmless but has a detrimental effect on a computer when it runs.

twisted-pair cable Cable that transfers data via pairs of copper wires that are twisted around each other to reduce electromagnetic interference.

Twitter A microblogging platform used to post frequent updates and to comment on events as they happen.

uniform resource locator (URL) A string of characters that identifies the location of a resource on a website.

uninstaller utility Software that removes installed software along with its associated files and registry entries.

Universal Disc Format (UDF) An extension of the ISO 9660 file system, a file system used on optical media such as CDs and DVDs.

Universal Product Code (UPC) A bar code system used for identifying products for sale.

Universal Serial Bus (USB) A general-purpose port for connecting external devices to a PC.

UNIX A multi-user, command-line operating system for servers.

unshielded twisted pair (UTP) A type of twisted-pair cable that does not have an outer sheath that protects against external EMI.

Usenet A global distributed system of servers that host public newsgroups.

user account An account associated with an individual person, used for authenticating the user when he or she logs into Windows.

user interface (UI) The interface that a human uses to communicate with a computer.

utility software Software that performs some useful service to the operating system, such as optimizing or correcting the file storage system, backing up files, or ensuring security or privacy.

vector-based illustration A drawing that is constructed of mathematically created lines.

video chat Having an online conversation that includes both audio and video.

video clip A file that stores motion video.

Video Graphics Adapter An analog port for connecting a monitor to a PC.

videoconferencing A means of conducting a video conversation remotely using an Internet connection and the webcam or camera on your laptop, phone, or tablet.

Vine A social network for posting and sharing video clips.

virtual folder A view that resembles a folder but has no direct equivalent in the computer's file system.

virtual keyboard A replica of a keyboard on the screen that users can tap or click to simulate typing.

virtual memory Memory that is simulated by swapping data out of memory and storing it temporarily on the hard drive.

virtual private networking (VPN)   A method of creating a secure, private communication tunnel using a public communications channel such as the Internet.

virus   A type of malware that attaches itself to an executable file and spreads to other files when the program is run.

Voice over Internet Protocol (VoIP)   A means of providing web-based telephony. The best-known example is Skype.

voice recognition software   Software that recognizes spoken words that match words in its database to digitize spoken language.

volume   A physical storage device, or a portion of one, that is assigned an identifying letter. Sometimes used interchangeably with *drive*, but a physical drive may actually contain multiple volumes.

WAN (wide area network)   A network that spans at least two geographical locations; a business with two or more offices may have a LAN at each site but use a WAN to connect them all to the same network.

warm boot   To restart a computer that is already powered on.

web authoring software   Software that helps create website designs and content.

web browser   An application used to access websites and to retrieve or upload information. Often referred to as a **browser**.

web page   A file formatted for use on the World Wide Web.

web server   A server that receives requests for web page data and supplies it by sending it over the Internet.

web-based application   Software that downloads to your computer and then runs within a web browser.

webcam   A digital video camera that must remain connected to a computer as it operates.

what you see is what you get (WYSIWYG)   A feature in an application that allows users to see their work exactly as it will be when it is distributed to others, such as in print or online.

whitelist   A list of allowed email senders; also called a safe list.

wide area network (WAN)   A network that spans at least two geographical locations; a business with two or more offices may have a LAN at each site but use a WAN to connect them all to the same network.

Wi-Fi   Wireless Ethernet. A means of connecting computers and other devices wirelessly. Another name for it is IEEE 802.11, its technical standard.

Wi-Fi Protected Access (WPA)   A form of wireless encryption providing a 128-bit encryption key.

Wi-Fi Protected Setup (WPS)   A feature available on some wireless access points that enable a user to connect a device to a trusted network.

wiki   A web-based application that can be edited by anyone and that is usually informational or instructive in nature.

Wikipedia   A free, online encyclopedia. Wikipedia is an example of a wiki.

window color   The color of the window title bar and border.

window   A movable rectangular block in which content appears.

Windows 8 app   An application that is native to the Windows 8 environment, and runs only under Windows 8. Also called **Windows Store app**.

Windows Phone   The Windows version designed for smartphones.

Windows RT   The Windows version designed for SoC tablet computers.

Windows Server   The server-optimized version of Microsoft Windows.

Windows Store app   see Windows 8 app.

Windows Update   A feature in Windows that automatically downloads and installs updates to Windows and optionally to some Microsoft applications.

Wired Equivalent Privacy (WEP)   An older and less secure form of wireless encryption.

wireframe   A 3D vector drawing that consists only of drawn lines, without any surface textures applied.

wireless access point (WAP)   A wireless switch.

wireless keyboard   A keyboard that connects to the computer wirelessly rather than with a cable.

wireless mouse   A mouse that communicates wirelessly with a transceiver connected to the computer, so it does not need a cord.

word processor   A program used to create or view text-based documents.

word size   The number of bits that the CPU can accept as input simultaneously.

workbook   An Excel data file, containing one or more worksheets.

worksheet   A tabbed page of a workbook, containing a grid of rows and columns.

World Wide Web (WWW)   A network of interconnected pages of information stored on publicly accessible servers.

worm   A malicious computer program that spreads itself to other computers over a network or the Internet.

WPA2   An improved version of Wi-Fi Protected Access that provides stronger protection with a 128-bit or 256-bit encryption key.

Wrap Text   The feature in Office applications such as Word that enables you to specify how the graphic should interact with any adjacent text.

x64   The 64-bit version of the Intel platform.

x86   The 32-bit version of the Intel platform.

Yosemite   The code name for the latest version of Mac OS X (version 10.10).

YouTube   A social network for posting and sharing videos.

zombie   A computer used to conduct a DoS attack.

Zoom controls   Controls at the right end of the status bar that adjust the magnification at which the data is displayed.

Index

intranet, 450, 468, 656
iOS, 117, 132, 656
IP (intellectual property), 578, 596, 655
IP address
  about, 517–519, 539
  defined, 656
  relationship with domain names, 518–519
ipconfig command, 518
IPv4 address, 517, 539, 656
IPv6 address, 517, 539, 656
IRC (Internet Relay Chat), 480, 506, 656
IS (Information Systems) manager, 11
ISO 9660, 122, 133, 656
ISP (Internet Service Provider), 25, 27, 445, 468, 656
iTunes, 228

J

joystick, 69, 656
jump list, 606, 656
junk mail, managing, 504–505

K

KB (kilobyte), 21
Key Terms feature, 5
keyboards
  about, 98
  adjusting settings, 602–605
  defined, 21, 656
  disposing of, 595
  layout
    about, 632
    changing, 627–628
    defined, 656
  on-screen, 625
  selecting and using, 64–66
  selecting ranges with in Microsoft Excel, 331
  shortcuts
    about, 168, 271
    defined, 149, 656
    Microsoft Excel, 330
    Microsoft Office 2013, 249, 275–276
  troubleshooting, 95
keylogger, 550–551, 572, 656
kilobyte (KB), 21
knowledge base, 538

L

LAN (local area network), 448, 468, 657
land, 91
landscape, 294, 322, 656
language pack
  defined, 656
  installing, 626
Large Mouse Pointers feature, 622
laser printers, 84, 99, 656
latency, 35, 464, 656

layout master, 415, 435, 656
Layout view (Microsoft Access), 397
layouts
  about, 435
  defined, 407, 656
  keyboard, 627–628, 632, 656
  Microsoft PowerPoint, 439
  SmartArt graphics, 426
LCD (liquid crystal display), 76, 78, 79, 98, 596, 657
Learning Objectives, explained, 2
legal issues
  about, 577–578, 596
  copyright laws, 578
  digital rights management, 579–580, 596, 650
  intellectual property (IP), 578, 596, 655
  software licensing, 580–582
  software piracy, 583, 596, 666
  test answers, 643
  test questions, 597–599
legal software, 230, 237, 656
legends
  about, 366
  in charts in Microsoft Excel, 357
  defined, 352, 656
libel, 587–588, 596, 656
libraries
  about, 169
  creating, 161
  defined, 160, 656
  setting up, 161
Libraries feature, 158
licensing
  software, 580–581
  types of, 581–582
line spacing
  about, 322
  defined, 656
  setting in Microsoft Word, 288–290
Linux
  about, 113, 132
  defined, 657
  distros, 136
liquid crystal display (LCD), 76, 78, 79, 98, 596, 657
local account, 179, 657
local area network (LAN), 448, 468, 657
location-based settings
  changing
    about, 626–631, 628–629
    date and time, 629–631
    keyboard layout, 627–628
    regional and location settings, 628–629
  display language, 626–627
locations
  changing views of, 159–160
  navigating, 158–159
Lock command, 168

multi-boot, 114, 132
multi-function device (MFD), 70, 98, 658
multi-functionality, of printers, 82
multi-use computers, 13–14
music players, 228

N

Name box, 328, 658
name resolution, 519, 539, 658
named ranges, working with in Microsoft Excel, 369–370
Narrator feature
  about, 622
  using, 625
narrowing searches, 534–536
NAS (network-attached storage), 94, 99, 658
NAS appliance, 94, 99, 658
NAT (network address translation), 517
navigating
  desktop applications, 149–151
  locations, 158–159
  in Microsoft Office 2013, 252–253
  websites, 523
  worksheets in Microsoft Excel, 329–333, 365
navigation pane
  about, 169, 400, 435
  File Explorer, 157
  Microsoft Access, 379, 658
  Microsoft PowerPoint, 406, 658
Navigation Pane Method, for finding text in Microsoft Word, 311
.net domain, 516
netbook, 12, 658
network adapters, 23, 454–456, 469, 658
network address translation (NAT), 517
network cables, 458–459
network devices, checking Device Manager for, 455
network hardware
  about, 453, 469
  bridges, 457–458, 469, 647
  gateways, 457–458, 469, 653
  hubs, 456, 655
  network adapters, 23, 454–456, 469, 658
  network cables, 458–459
  repeaters, 457–458, 469, 663
  routers, 24, 25, 457, 469, 663
  switches, 24, 456, 469, 667
network installer, 454
network interface card (NIC), 454, 469, 658
Network section, 158, 169
network switch. *See* switches
network volumes, selecting and using, 94
network-attached storage (NAS), 94, 99, 658
networking and Internet. *See also* web
  about, 25, 443, 445, 468, 476, 539, 545
  blogs, 481–483, 489, 506, 646
  Bluetooth, 24–25
  chatting, 478–480
  classifying networks, 448–453, 468–469

communication systems, 444–447, 468
connections, 460–465, 462–465, 469
defined, 25, 27, 512, 655
downloading content from Internet, 528–530
email, 476–478
encrypting, 567
Ethernet, 23–24
forums, 484–485, 489, 506, 537, 653
improvement strategies, 562–571, 573
instant messaging, 232, 238, 478–480, 489, 506, 655
Internet connections, 469
microblogs, 481–483, 489, 506, 658
network hardware, 453–459, 469
newsgroups, 484, 506, 658
over cell phone networks, 464–465
privacy concerns, 557–562, 572–573
security concerns, 546–557, 572
social networking, 480, 489, 506, 510, 560, 666
speed of, 461–462, 473
structure of Internet, 460
test answers, 641–642, 642–643
test questions, 470–472, 574–576
texting, 478–480, 506, 668
troubleshooting connections, 465–467, 469
types, 476–487
uploading content to Internet, 528–530
videoconferencing, 232, 238, 486–487, 489, 506, 669
Voice over Internet Protocol (VoIP), 485–486, 489, 506, 670
wikis, 483, 506, 538, 670
networks
  about, 23, 658
  circuit-switched, 444, 468, 648
  classifying, 448–453, 468–469
  client/server, 24, 26, 449–450, 468, 648
  data, 444–445
  P2P (peer-to-peer), 24, 26, 449–450, 468, 660
  packet-switched, 444–445, 468, 660
  satellite data, 446
New Technology, explained, 3
New Technology File System (NTFS), 122, 658
newsgroups, 484, 506, 658
newsletters, 298
newsreader, 484, 506, 659
NIC (network interface card), 454, 469, 658
no response, troubleshooting, 50–51
node, 216, 659
non-contiguous, 162, 169, 659
non-impact printers, 82–83, 98, 659
Normal view (Microsoft PowerPoint), 406, 435, 659
normalization, 403
Northwind database, 403
notebook computers
  defined, 12, 659
  disposing of, 595
  Fn key, 65
  operating systems for, 112–115